A Reader's Guide to the Great Religions

A Reader's Guide to the Great Religions

EDITED BY

Charles J. Adams

Fp

THE FREE PRESS, New York

COLLIER-MACMILLAN LIMITED, London

A DIVISION OF THE MACMILLAN COMPANY

Printed in the United States of America

Collier-Macmillan Canada, Ltd., Toronto, Ontario

Library of Congress Catalog Card Number: 65–15440

Contributors

Charles J. Adams
PROFESSOR AND DIRECTOR
INSTITUTE OF ISLAMIC STUDIES
McGILL UNIVERSITY

W. A. C. H. Dobson
PROFESSOR OF CHINESE AND
HEAD OF THE DEPARTMENT OF
EAST ASIATIC STUDIES
UNIVERSITY OF TORONTO

Richard A. Gard
FORMERLY ASSISTANT PROFESSOR
DEPARTMENT OF RELIGION
YALE UNIVERSITY

Judah Goldin
PROFESSOR OF CLASSICAL
JUDAICA
YALE UNIVERSITY

Norvin J. Hein
ASSOCIATE PROFESSOR OF
COMPARATIVE RELIGION
YALE UNIVERSITY

Joseph M. Kitagawa
ASSOCIATE PROFESSOR
HISTORY OF RELIGIONS
UNIVERSITY OF CHICAGO

Charles H. Long
ASSISTANT PROFESSOR OF THE
HISTORY OF RELIGIONS
DIVINITY SCHOOL
UNIVERSITY OF CHICAGO

H. H. Walsh
PROFESSOR OF CHURCH HISTORY
FACULTY OF DIVINITY
McGILL UNIVERSITY

Contents

CONTENTS

Preface

The purpose of this volume is to give bibliographical guidance to persons who, for whatever reason, are interested in learning more of the world's great religious traditions. Its preparation was undertaken at the initiative of the Free Press, who published a somewhat similar work on the social sciences in 1959. Believing that there is a widespread need felt for a sound guide to literature about religions, the Free Press commissioned the editor to embark on the present volume. The book is presented to the public with the hope that it may prove a useful and trustworthy guide.

Among the North American public, interest in religions, especially in the religious traditions alien to the West, has experienced a tremendous upsurge in the years since World War II. Expressions of this lively new interest, to mention only two of them, may be seen in the numerous publications on religions crowding the shelves of our bookshops and in the growing trend of universities, state institutions not excepted, to include courses on religion in their curricula. In universities such as Princeton and Syracuse, where courses in religion have been offered for some time, the appeal of the subject for undergraduates is astonishingly strong and consistent. At any given time a sizeable fraction of the students in these universities follows one or another course in religion. This development is more striking for having occurred at a time when the humanities generally are on the decline in the universities and when science has achieved new and unprecedented prestige.

The situation is no different with the educated public outside the universities. If one requires evidence to support this assertion, it is amply available in the sales of books on religion to a vast group of general readers. There is today an active market for books on religion, and it shows signs of becoming stronger still. In response to the demand, publishers are offering a flood of books on religion, both new works and reprints of former ones. In paperback editions alone it is now possible to build up an extensive and respectable library on the great religious traditions. So numerous are these publications and so rich the resources they offer that one is often left in puzzled bewilderment about which among them to choose. In these circumstances it seems appropriate and useful that a volume such as this, giving bibliographical advice of trained specialists in religious studies, should be made available.

Although the purpose of this work is bibliographical, it is much more than a bare list of books. In form it is a series of essays. The authors of its various chapters have endeavored not only to state what should be read in their respective fields but have also been conscious of the need to explain why these particular recommendations have been made. Sometimes by relating a book to a general framework within which the religious tradition of their particular interest may be studied, and at other times by exhibiting the role of a work in the history of scholarly thought, or by some similar device, they have sought to show to the user of this volume why those writings recommended to him have been chosen. Where it has seemed appropriate to offer comments or criticism directed at the literature cited, this has been done. It is hoped that the result is a volume that will be of greater utility to those who employ it than would a mere list of titles.

While preparing this volume, the contributors have had in mind the needs of several classes of people. Perhaps the largest and most difficult to define group are the "general readers," members of the educated segment of the public whose interest may have been drawn to some aspect of religious studies and who may wish direction in the choice of reading materials. Another considerable group are graduate students in the history of religions, who may, by use of this volume, move toward a comprehensive overview of their field of study and the bibliographical resources requisite for a balanced grasp of it. The authors have been mindful, too, of the needs of librarians. In the smaller colleges and public libraries especially, librarians have long needed a reliable guide for the formation of an adequate collection on religion. Accordingly, the authors have attempted to list works that they consider sound and which, taken together, constitute a solid foundation for more advanced study into the life of the various religious traditions represented. Lastly, the authors have sought to provide assistance to the sizeable group of college instructors who in recent days have found themselves chosen to meet the demand upon the colleges for courses in religion. In a great number of cases these men are without professional training in the history of religions and are compelled to teach religion courses only because there is no one else to teach them. Many experience difficulty in finding out trustworthy bibliographical resources for their own and their students' purposes.

To sum up, then, this volume is intended for a broad range of people with serious interest in religion who may stand to benefit from the considered opinions of specialists on the literature of the religious field. So far as specialists are concerned, they do not require a bibliographical guide of this level within their own fields, but the volume may prove of use to the scholar who wishes a quick survey of the fields of his colleagues.

It should not be necessary to emphasize that a comprehensive bibliography on the subjects covered in this *Reader's Guide* would be all but impossible to compile. To consider in comprehensive fashion only one of the great traditions dealt with here—Christianity, for example—would be the work of a lifetime for a large group of people. Entire libraries of works on Christianity have been written through the centuries of its history, and the same is no less true of others of the religious traditions. For a student of one of the great religious traditions, the problem is not so much to discover sufficient materials for his work as it is to discriminate among the superabundance available on every hand. The purpose of this *Reader's Guide* is precisely to aid in the process of discrimination by suggesting a selection of works that appear to its authors to be the best or most useful or most typical of their kind. Doubtless in many instances there is room for disagreement with the selection made; any accomplished scholar in the fields concerned would be able to name dozens of books that might be added to the list of those recommended here or substituted for some of them. Selection, however, has been unavoidable, and it is, indeed, on the selective quality of this bibliographical guide that its value should be judged.

Some words are in order about the principles of selection employed in this volume. The general criterion that has determined whether a given title should be included or not has been one of utility. If a work has qualities that make it especially valuable for the persons whom the volume seeks to serve, it has been included, no matter whether it is published as a separate book or in the pages of a journal. Literary quality and readability are among the factors considered in judging utility. The endeavor to list useful materials has meant that the authors have sometimes passed over the most erudite and technical or the latest works in their fields to suggest reading that may be more readily understandable or more immediately relevant. It is not uncommonly the case that books which are most helpful to the sophisticated scholar are of only limited use to one who lacks a background in depth in the subject matter concerned. As this work is not intended primarily for specialists, their needs and interests have been subordinated to those of the groups mentioned above.

As a secondary criterion, the authors have also considered the availability of the reading materials they are suggesting. If a work, despite its quality and usefulness, is unlikely to be obtainable in a first-class library or purchasable in the book market, there has seemed less urgency in listing it in these pages. There are, however, many exceptions to this rule. Books are often mentioned whose sheer importance demands their inclusion apart from questions of availability. In the chapters that concern the religions of the Far East especially, a number of titles published by relatively obscure firms in various parts of the Orient are cited. The consideration reigning there has been twofold: (1) that Western readers should to some degree be aware of publications on these subjects in the non-Western world and (2) that many of these publications are still available in the book market in the Orient, though unlikely to find their way into the hands of a Western bookseller. Awareness of its existence may be an encouragement to some to exploit this body of literature.

One of the most important principles of selection used here will strike the reader immediately—namely, the heavy preference for works in English. As this *Reader's Guide* will be presented to an English-reading public, it is natural that the major part of the literature discussed should be in that language. There is no lack of works in English on the great religious traditions, but the effort to restrict the *Reader's Guide* even largely to English has imposed a considerable limitation upon its contributors. In many, if not most, fields in the study of religions, Europeans have been both the pioneers and the principal investigators, and any survey of literature on religions must take account of the enormous volume of work in European languages. Many European language works have, consequently, been included here, but there has been a conscious effort to restrict their number to those of outstanding quality or of particular influence in the history of scholarship. Where books exist both in the original language and in translation, preference has been given to the translation.

Much the same considerations apply to works in the languages of the Orient. If French and German pose difficulties for a large number of English readers, the problem is incalculably greater with such tongues as Japanese, Chinese, and Sanskrit. Works in these languages will prove of use only to specialists and a favored few others, and for this reason they have been rigorously excluded. As an implication of this policy, it follows that the citation of original materials from Oriental religions has necessarily had to be limited to those documents rendered into English.

One of the difficult problems of selection has been to decide on the proportion of secondary to primary works cited. The advantages of exposing the student of Hinduism, to take an example, to a variety of the original and formative documents of that religious tradition are too obvious to require comment. Such primary documents, however, are not always capable of being understood by the uninitiated, and for this reason a well-rounded bibliographical guide requires the inclusion of large numbers of secondary and interpretive works. It has proved impossible to formulate an adequate general rule on this point, and the proportion of primary to secondary sources has been left to the discretion of contributors.

The bibliographical information given concerning each title mentioned is sufficient in the editor's opinion to allow easy identification and location of the work. For books, place and date of publication and the publisher's name normally have been given, though there are some exceptions. In a few instances the publisher's address is included as well. The latter measure was thought necessary for Oriental books that would be impossible to procure without this information. In the case of works that are well known and that have been through numerous editions—St. Augustine's *City of God*, for example—it has not been thought necessary to give data about one particular edition unless there is special reason for preferring one above the others.

The edition of a book cited is normally the one that the contributor considers either the most useful or the most readily available. No attempt has been made to reconstruct the publishing history of the numerous works cited in the *Reader's Guide*; to have done so would have made the volume many times its length without a commensurate increase in its value. For periodicals the information given includes title of the article, title of the journal, volume number, number, date, and the page upon which the article begins.

Attached to several of the chapters of the *Reader's Guide* are appendices that list, largely without comment, the principal reference works and principal journals in the fields concerned. It was felt that this information would be particularly appreciated by librarians and more advanced students. In the chapter on Christianity similar information has been included in the text of the article rather than being confined to an appendix. The chapter on primitive religions has, as well, a special appendix, prepared by the editor, in order to extend the suggestions made there concerning the history of the study of religion in the West. For many persons the history of scholarship in an area of study offers the best way of coming to terms with the area. Furthermore, this brief appendix has afforded the opportunity to cite some of the literature bearing on the broad problems of the origin and nature of religion.

The editor's contribution to this volume, apart from the chapter which he has written, has consisted in (1) laying out the plan for the volume and attempting to maintain some unity of viewpoint in its various chapters and (2) verifying the accuracy of the bibliographical information given. The latter has been a difficult and demanding task, and if, in spite of the efforts made, errors yet remain, the editor acknowledges his responsibility for all such shortcomings. The content and method of treatment of each chapter in the volume have been solely due to the contributors. The editor would like especially to emphasize that he has not attempted to impose upon the contributors any firm conception of the nature of religion that would guide their work or orient their points of view. Each has been given perfect freedom to explore the nature of the religious tradition with which his studies are concerned. If, as appears to be the case, it is impossible to abstract from the finished volume a clear and satisfying definition of religion that covers all the traditions dealt with, this fact may be one of the volume's genuine contributions. At the least it appears to bear out the conclusions of an important recent work in the religious field where it is argued that the concept "religion" has outlived its usefulness and should be abandoned (see Wilfred C. Smith, *The Meaning and End of Religion* [N.Y., The Macmillan Co., 1963]).

The title chosen for this volume represents a compromise by the editor and was agreed upon only after the expenditure of much effort to find a more satisfactory one. Application of the terms "religion" and "religions" to such diverse phenomena as the cults of noncivilizational peoples in the more remote regions of the earth, on the one hand, and to the highly sophisticated, articulate, and self-conscious piety of the great traditions of India, China, and the Middle East, on the other, implies a closeness of connection between the two that is much too simple, if it can be accepted at all. A similar problem presents itself when one begins to consider in detail the historical manifestation of any single one of the traditions treated in the chapters of this volume. No one of them is monolithic and simple; rather each is multiform, complex, and always changing. To the thoughtful observer this state of affairs must suggest at least a question concerning the validity of a terminology that seems to imply that each tradition is a recognizable entity with a clear identity of its own. Moreover, there is reason for challenging the use of the adjective "great" in the title in view of the inclusion of a chapter on primitive religions. Objections on this point could, perhaps, be met by an argument designed to show that the so-called primitive religions are, indeed, a "great" tradition in virtue of the very extent of their spread through time and space and the numbers of persons who have been affected by them. Finally, the clarity of the title is compromised by the method of organizing the material of the volume as a whole. One of the chapters deals with a most diffuse group of phenomena that have been designated by the abstraction "primitive religions." Another group of chapters takes distinct religious traditions and treats of them separately and to some extent in relation with one another. Yet a third group of chapters, those dealing with the religions of China and Japan, have been conceived and organized in geographical terms. Although any usefulness this volume may have will not be materially affected by the felicitousness of the title chosen for it, it seems better to acknowledge these reservations about the adequacy of the title from the beginning.

Unfortunately, another acknowledgment of deficiency in this work is also called for. Within the scope of the chapters as they have been planned, there have been at least three omissions of quite major importance. No treatment is given in these pages to the Buddhist tradition in its Chinese context, to the later history of the Jewish community from the Middle Ages to the present time, to the minor religious communities of India, such as the Sikhs and the Jains. It is unnecessary to trouble the reader with the reasons for the inability to cover these important areas of study; the editor wishes only to call attention to these lacunae and to acknowledge his responsibility for them. If ever it should be possible to revise this volume, attention would be given to filling in these unfortunate gaps.

Finally, it is the editor's pleasant task to thank those who have assisted in this project. Thanks go first of all to Professor James Luther Adams of Harvard University for having suggested this piece of work to the editor and suggesting the editor's name to the Free Press. Secondly, recognition is due to Mr. John Christopher Kyle of Montreal who labored faithfully in the arduous task of confirming bibliographical details. The editor's secretaries, Mrs. Jean

Kerr, Mrs. Madeleine Widawska and Miss Eve Yuile, of Montreal, are due a large measure of gratitude for their willingness, patience and careful work in the preparation of the manuscript. Finally, the editor would like to acknowledge the assistance of the Committee on Research of the Faculty of Graduate Studies and Research, McGill University, in the form of a grant of money to employ help in confirming bibliographical details.

CHARLES J. ADAMS

Montreal, March, 1965

A Reader's Guide to the Great Religions

I

Primitive Religion

Charles H. Long

I. INTRODUCTION

The phrase "primitive religion" is usually defined within the context of the disciplines of anthropology, ethnology, and the history of religions. To a certain extent each of these disciplines has its roots in the world view of the Enlightenment. While these disciplines have added much to the meaning of the phrase in terms of method and content, they have also accepted explicitly and implicitly some of the more philosophically oriented definitions of the past in their formulations of the meaning of primitive religion. This was true especially in their understanding of the term "primitive."

Arthur O. Lovejoy and George Boas in their book, *A Documentary History of Primitivism and Related Ideas* (Baltimore, Johns Hopkins University Press, 1935) have examined some of the meanings of "primitivism" in classical antiquity. They have classified these meanings into two general categories, "chronological" and "cultural."

> Chronological primitivism is one of the many answers which may be and have been given to the question: What is the temporal distribution of good, or value, in the history of mankind, or more generally, in the entire history

> of the world? It is, in short, a kind of philosophy of history, a theory, or a customary assumption, as to the time—past or present or future—at which the most excellent condition of human life, or the best state of the world in general, must be supposed to occur (p. 1).
>
> Cultural primitivism is the discontent of the civilized with civilization or with some conspicuous characteristic feature of it. It is the belief of men living in a relatively highly involved and complex cultural condition that a life far simpler and less sophisticated in some or in all respects is a more desirable life (p. 7).

One can see the above interests reflected in the early philosophical, historical, and systematic studies of the Enlightenment. A very good description and analysis of the historical study of religion in the Enlightenment is Frank E. Manuel's *The Eighteenth Century Confronts the Gods* (Cambridge, Harvard University Press, 1959).

Though many of the Enlightenment thinkers tended to regard primitivism in either its chronological or cultural sense, they were confronted with new problems. Since most of the thinkers of this period had dissociated themselves from the Church, they were unable to regard the witness of the Bible as a norm for the study of man's history. Secondly, they were confronted with more empirical data concerning the religions and cultures of the high civilizations such as India, China, and Greece. In addition, they had to come to terms with the reports of explorers, missionaries, and traders regarding those cultures that were neither a part of the Western heritage nor members of one of the centers of high civilization, such as the cultures of the Americas, Oceania, Polynesia, Melanesia, and sub-Saharan Africa.

The immediate reaction to these new data was to apply in a modified form a variation of chronological or cultural primitivism with either "nature" or "reason" as a norm. If "reason" were the norm, the "primitives" were understood as an example of the earliest and most rudimentary instance of this human capacity. The history of man showed a development from the lowest stage to the highest and most refined exemplification of reason in its Enlightenment expression. If "nature" were the norm, the "primitives" might be seen as an example of the naturalness and innocence which originally belonged to man. The history of mankind was thus interpreted as a degeneration of man's natural freedom and innocence. The most religious form was often equated with the most primitive and vice versa.

These predominantly philosophical explanations regarding the cultures of "extracivilizational" man receded into the background as historical scholarship slowly came to terms with the reports and descriptions of primitive man. To a great extent many of the philosophical implications of Enlightenment thinking remained, but as time went on, these philosophical doctrines could not be offered as a total explanation of the historical phenomena. Ernst Cassirer has written that after David Hume's critique of deism in his *Dialogues*

Concerning Natural Religion (many editions), every conception of religion had to be based on history; see Ernst Cassirer, *The Philosophy of the Enlightenment* (Princeton, Princeton University Press, 1951), p. 182.

It was out of this developing historical consciousness that the disciplines of anthropology, ethnology, and history of religions emerged. Each one of these disciplines attempted to base its understanding as far as possible on an analysis of the empirical data, and each wished to arrive at some judgment on the meaning and nature of man as expressed in these extracivilizational cultures. Their common interest in religion resulted from the fact that this dimension of life seemed to be the most pervasive and highly elaborated form in the cultures under discussion. It was thus considered to be the most important form of human life in these cultures and the form most amenable to examination and analysis.

The subsequent discussions in these disciplines led to new evaluations regarding the nature and meaning of both "primitive" and "religion."

We shall not go into a discussion of the evolution of these terms. An excellent article by Edward P. Dozier, "The Concepts of 'Primitive' and 'Native' in Anthropology" in *Current Anthropology* (Chicago, University of Chicago Press, 1956) discusses the history and meaning of these terms in anthropology. Dozier finally summarizes what he considers to be an adequate and scientific definition of "primitive."

> By primitive we shall mean the kind of culture which has the following characteristics, (1) absence of a written language, (2) relatively simple technology, (3) social institutions which are cast in a simpler mold, (4) smaller numbers, (5) relative isolation, (6) societies whose cultures are characterized by slower rate of change (p. 188).

Joachim Wach, in his posthumous work, *The Comparative Study of Religion* (N.Y., Columbia University Press, 1958), presents some of the problems and resolutions raised by the terms "history" and "religion" in the discipline of history of religion. Wach defines religion in *Types of Religious Experience* (Chicago, University of Chicago Press, 1951), p. 32, as "a response to what is experienced as ultimate reality." If we couple Dozier's definition of a primitive culture with Wach's definition of religion, we are able to say that the experience of "ultimate reality" in societies having the characteristics given by Dozier constitutes a general definition of primitive religion which is adequate for our purposes.

II. SOURCES OF THE RELIGIOUS SENTIMENT IN PRIMITIVE SOCIETIES

Since societies demonstrating Dozier's six characteristics are prior in history to the great civilizational cultures, the expressions of their experience of "ultimate reality" were often thought to provide an insight into the meaning of man's earliest or first religion. Thus E. B. Tylor, the father of modern anthropology, in *Religion in Primitive Culture*, Vol. II of *Primitive Culture* (London, 1872; N.Y., Harper Torchbooks, 1958) set forth as a minimum definition of religion the notion of "Animism."

> It seems best to fall back at once on this essential source, and simply to claim as a minimum definition of Religion, the belief in Spiritual Beings. . . . I propose under the name of Animism to investigate the deep-lying doctrine of Spiritual Beings, which embodies the very essence of Spiritualistic as opposed to Materialistic philosophy (p. 8).

Tylor arrived at his notion of Animism from a study of the religious sentiment in the societies of early man. Tylor's general theory of cultural and religious development gained wide acceptance. Though he adhered to a form of progressivistic evolutionism in his understanding of religion, his work was characterized by a careful analysis of empirical data from the societies under discussion.

The problem raised by Tylor's definition of Animism was directly related to the problem of the origin of religion. While the empirical method of analysis of historical materials was given an impetus by Tylor's work, he was accused of being intellectualistic or too philosophical in his discussion of the origin of religion. One of Tylor's contemporary critics writes:

> The most significant point in Tylor's interpretation of religion in primitive culture is that he bases religious belief upon a psychological delusion and mistaken logical inference. Primitive man is said to confuse subjective and objective reality, ideal and real objects (David Bidney, "The Concept of Value in Modern Anthropology" in *Anthropology Today*, A. L. Kroeber, ed. [Chicago, University of Chicago Press, 1953], pp. 682–99).

Paul Radin, who wrote the introduction to the paperback edition of Tylor's *Primitive Culture* (N.Y., Harper Torchbook, 1958) defends Tylor from the charge of intellectualism by showing that intellectualism and mysticism were compatible from the point of view of Tylor's Quakerism (p. xi).

The most telling criticisms of Tylor's conception of the origin of religion came, however, from the data of field-work studies of primitives. I refer to R. H. Codrington's *The Melanesians* (Oxford, Clarendon Press, 1891), W. E. Gudgeon's "Maori Religion," *Journal of the Polynesian Society*, XIV (1905), pp. 107–30, Baldwin Spencer and F. J. Gillen, *The Native Tribes of Central Australia* (London, Macmillan & Co., Ltd., 1899), and A. W. Howitt's *The Native Tribes of South-East Australia* (London, Macmillan & Co., Ltd., 1904).

The works relating to Melanesia and Polynesia presented for the first time a description of *mana* as a basic religious concept, and the works devoted to the Australians brought to light the importance of *totemism* as a religious reality among primitives. In *The Melanesians*, Codrington describes *mana* as follows:

> The Melanesian mind is entirely possessed by the belief in a supernatural power or influence, called almost universally "mana." . . . But this power, though itself impersonal, is always connected with some person who directs it; all spirits have it, ghosts generally, some men (pp. 118–19).

Words describing the same type of religious phenomenon were subsequently discovered in other primitive societies. J. N. B. Hewitt's article, "Orenda and a Definition of Religion," *American Anthropologist*, n.s., IV, 1 (1902), pp. 33–46, is a discussion of this phenomenon among the Iroquois Indians. Paul Radin analyzes the phenomenon among various American Indians in "Religion of the North American Indians," *Journal of American Folklore*, XXVII (1914), pp. 335–73. This phenomenon—described as *mana*, *wakanda*, *orenda*, etc.—led some interpreters to see in it a new and basic source of the religious sentiment in primitive societies. Thus, before man formed a conception of Spiritual Beings (Tylor), he experienced emotionally an impersonal and dynamic power. The experience of this power was the primal religious experience. An interpretation of the religious sentiment along these lines may be seen in R. R. Marett's *The Threshold of Religion* (London, Methuen & Co., 1909); *Faith, Hope, and Charity in Primitive Religion* (Oxford, Clarendon Press, 1932); *Sacraments of Simple Folk* (Oxford, Clarendon Press, 1933); and *Head, Heart, and Hands in Human Evolution* (London, Hutchinson & Co., Ltd., 1935).

The notion of *mana* and its related terms led to the religious theory of dynamism or pre-animism. This theory sets forth the belief that the earliest and most basic religious experience came as a response on the emotional level (feeling) to the object of religion. This object of religion is defined as the power in life.

Vestiges of this theory may be seen in Rudolf Otto's nonrational interpretation of religious experience, *The Idea of the Holy* (many editions), chaps. 1–3, 15, and 16. In chapter 15, which is entitled "Its Earliest Manifestations," Otto discusses the notions of *orenda* and *mana* in relationship to his theory of religious experience. G. van der Leeuw devotes the first three chapters of his *Religion in Essence and Manifestation* (London, George Allen & Unwin, Ltd., 1938) to the notions of *mana* and analogous terms.

Totemism, which was first brought to the attention of the Western world by the investigations of Baldwin Spencer, F. J. Gillen, A. Howitt, and others, also raised the problem of the origin of the religious sentiment. Totemism describes the relationship between some human group and some natural object, such as a plant, animal, or stone. Generally speaking, the group will not marry within its totemic group or eat the animal or plant with which it is associated. The fact that members of a totem group married outside the group led Sir James Frazer to an investigation of totemism along these lines in *Totemism and Exogamy* (London, Macmillan & Co., Ltd., 1910). Earlier Andrew Lang had conceived of totemism as an early method of giving names among the primitives, *Secret of the Totem* (London, Longmans, Green & Co., Ltd., 1905). The most elaborate theoretical work on totemism is Émile Durkheim's *Elementary Forms of the Religious Life* (reprinted Chicago, Free Press, 1947). Building his views upon the investigations of the Australian aborigines by Spencer and Gillen, Durkheim understood totemism to be the basis of Australian religious life and culture. He thought also that the Australian aborigines represent the most primitive form of culture. Their religion, it would follow, represents the earliest form of religion. For Durkheim, the totemic symbol was an expression of the cohesion or integration of the social group. Religion thus consisted in the worship by the social group of a symbol of itself.

Good critical analyses of the totemistic theories of Andrew Lang, James Frazer and Émile Durkheim may be read in two writings of Alexander Goldenweiser: "Totemism: An Essay on Religion and Society," in V. F. Calverton, ed., *The Making of Man: An Outline of Anthropology* (N.Y., The Modern Library, 1931) and chap. 16 "Theories of Early Mentality" in his book *Early Civilization* (N.Y., Alfred A. Knopf, Inc., 1922).

Closely related to the notion of *mana* is *tabu* or *taboo*. This word found its way into Western language through its inclusion in a description of Captain James Cook's third voyage around the world. Cook stated (regarding the natives of Atui):

> The people of Atooi, again, inter both their common dead and human sacrifices, as at Tongataboo; but they resemble those of Otaheite in the slovenly state of their religious places, and in offering vegetables and animals to their gods. The *taboo* also prevails in Atooi in its full extent, and seemingly with more rigour than at Tongataboo. For the people here always asked, with great eagerness and signs of fear to offend, whether any particular thing, which they desired to see, or we were unwilling to shew, was *taboo*, or, as they pronounced the word *tafoo*?
>
> Part III, section xii: A voyage to the Pacific Ocean, undertaken by the Command of his Majesty, for making Discoveries in the Northern Hemisphere; to determine the Position and Extent of the West Side of North America, its Distance from Asia, and the Practicability of a Northern Passage to Europe. Performed under the Direction of Captains Cook, Clerke, and Gore in his Majesty's Ships, the Resolution and the Discovery, in the years 1776, 1777, 1778, 1779 and 1780. (Found in *A General History and Collections of Voyages and Travels*, ed. by Robert Kerr [Edinburgh, W. Blackwood & Sons, Ltd., 1811–17], Vol. 16, pp. 192–3).

"Taboo" became an important term in the interpretation of religion because of its interdictory connotation. It was thought to provide an understanding for the separation of the sacred from the profane—a separation which lies at the heart of every religion.

The history of the discussion of this term may be observed in the following literature: James G. Frazer's "Tabu," *Encyclopaedia Britannica* XXI (1957 ed.); *Taboo and Perils of the Soul* (London, Macmillan & Co., Ltd., 1911). Generally speaking, Frazer saw the origin of taboo in animistic religion. Though it later acquired moral and legal dimensions, such dimensions were due to the evil ambitions of priests and rulers. A. van Gennep in his *Tabou et totemisme à Madagascar* (Paris, Leroux, 1904) understands taboo to be primarily concerned with the passage of something in or out of the body. Taboo in this sense is concerned primarily with the orifices of the body. Rudolf Lehmann in his analysis of taboo in *Die polynesischen Tabusitten* (Leipzig, Voigtlander, 1930) divides taboos into three main types: (1) sociological taboos, (2) taboos of the body, and (3) bodily taboos. Hutton Webster's *Taboo; A Sociological Study* (London, Oxford University Press, 1942) attacks the problem from a sociological point of view. Sigmund Freud in *Totem and Taboo* (N.Y., Moffat, Yard, 1918) attempts to deal psychologically with the meaning of taboo as a method of understanding the origin of religion. Finally, the history of the interpretation of taboo in the disciplines of history of religions, psychology, and the social sciences is found in Franz Steiner's book *Taboo* (N.Y., Philosophical Library, Inc., 1956).

Another theory concerning the origin of the religious sentiment among primitives is Sir James Frazer's theory of magic. His major work is the twelve-volume edition of *The Golden Bough: A Study in Comparative Religion* (London, Macmillan & Co., Ltd., 1911–15), which probably had greater influence on the social sciences and humanities than any comparable work in the modern period. Frazer brings together a vast amount of data from a wide variety of cultures. His comparative historical method is not carefully worked out, but his twelve volumes constitute a mine of historical detail. The volumes carry the following titles: *The Magic Art*, 2 vols.; *Balder the Beautiful*, 2 vols.; *Adonis, Attis, Osiris*, 2 vols.; *The Scapegoat*, 2 vols.; *Taboo and the Perils of the Soul*, 1 vol.; *Spirit of the Corn and of the Wild*, 2 vols.; *The Dying God*, 1 vol.; and a *Bibliography and General Index*. His discussion of the origin of religion is found in *The Magic Art*. Magic, for Frazer, is a stage of human consciousness prior and inferior to religion. It may develop into religion, but it is distinct from the religious sentiment. A great deal of what is called "primitive religion" is thus classified as magic by Frazer.

A more recent discussion of the relationship between magic and religion is Bronislaw Malinowski's *Magic, Science, and Religion* (Boston, Beacon Press, Inc., 1948). Malinowski separates these as specific functions in primitive society, but he believes that they coexist in an interrelated manner in primitive cultures.

The above theories of the primitive religious sentiment emphasize either a type of mind or a kind of emotion. Lucien Lévy-Bruhl attempted to avoid the dangers of either extreme by combining the mental and emotional factors in his theory of religious origins. For Lévy-Bruhl primitives perceive reality in terms of what he calls "a law of mystical participation." This led to his theory of prelogical mentality. His theory is worked out in *Primitive Mentality* (London, George Allen & Unwin, Ltd., 1923), *Primitives and the Supernatural* (N.Y., E. P. Dutton & Co., Inc., 1935), and *How Natives Think* (London, George Allen & Unwin, Ltd., 1926). Some of his theories are modified in *Les carnets* (Paris, Presses universitaires de France, 1949), published posthumously.

By and large, all of the theories mentioned up to this point have explicitly or implicitly depended on some form of progressivistic evolutionism. This evolutionism caused them to insist on the movement from the simple to the complex and to interpret the higher form as a growth from a lower and simpler form. Andrew Lang in his *The Making of Religion* (London, Longmans, Green & Co., Ltd., 1898) offered a criticism of this trend by pointing out that many primitive peoples believed in a "high-god." He continued this same criticism in *Magic and Religion* (London, Longmans, Green & Co., Ltd., 1901). Support for Lang's general theory of primitive monotheism may be found in the work of Fr. Wilhelm Schmidt, *Der Ursprung der Gottesidee: eine historisch-kritische und positive Studie*, 12 vols. (Münster, Aschendorff, 1926–55) and *The Origin and Growth of Religion* (London, Methuen & Co., Ltd., 1931). An informative summary of the problem of primitive monotheism is given by Paul Radin in *Monotheism among Primitive Peoples*, Ethnographical Museum Publication (London, George Allen & Unwin, Ltd., 1924).

Mircea Eliade, working primarily as an historian rather than a philosopher, finds the religious sentiment arising out of man's necessity for orientation in his world. See his *The Sacred and the Profane: The Nature of Religion* (N.Y., Harcourt, Brace & Co., Inc., 1959), *The Myth of the Eternal Return* (N.Y., Pantheon Books, Inc., 1954), and *Patterns in Comparative Religion* (London and N.Y., Sheed & Ward, Ltd., 1958).

It is the religious sentiment which makes life "real" for the primitive man. For Eliade sacredness is being. Orientation in a "real world" necessarily involves a transcendent dimension. Reality for the world of man is insured because he believes in events which happened outside of history *in illo tempore*. The myth is the intense religious expression of this belief. The creative acts of man are imitations of the creative acts and models of mythic time.

Joseph Campbell, another contemporary historian of religions, interprets the origin of the religious sentiment in psychical historical and social historical terms. The history of the psychic structure reveals the manner by which the psyche has responded to the human condition—birth, death, gravity, etc. The history of man's social life reveals his discovery and adjustment to his natural environment. These two types of responses are discussed in *The Masks of God: Primitive Mythology* (N.Y., Viking Press, Inc., 1959).

III. HISTORICAL RELIGIOUS FORMS OF PRIMITIVE RELIGION

In Theodor Gaster's abridgement of James Frazer's *Golden Bough*, entitled *The New Golden Bough: A New Abridgement of Sir James Frazer's Classic Work* (N.Y., Criterion Books, Inc., 1959), the following remark is made concerning Frazer's method: "[Frazer] pays far too little regard to the necessity of a cultural stratification tending to place all 'savage' customs and beliefs on a single vague level of 'the primitive' " (p. xviii). To be sure, some investigators had recognized stages of human culture prior to the advent of the great ancient civilization. This level of cultural stratification is recognized by Tylor and Durkheim, but neither of them made it a basic ingredient in his methodology. Indeed, they could not fully appropriate their insight until the science of prehistory and archeology had developed more precise methods.

The research in these areas resulted in the recognition of the historical past of the "modern primitives." For a general orientation to prehistoric cultures the following works of V. G. Childe provide an excellent introduction: *The Dawn of European Civilization* (London, Alfred A. Knopf, Inc., 1925); *New Light on the Most Ancient East* (London, Kegan Paul, Trench, Trubner & Co., Ltd., 1934); *Man Makes Himself* (London, C. A. Watts & Co., Ltd., 1936); *What Happened in History* (Middlesex, Penguin Books, Ltd., 1943); and *Social Evolution* (London, C. A. Watts & Co., Ltd., 1951). Childe's works emphasize the role of technological development as the basic innovating element in culture. Other works in prehistory presenting a more general or eclectic point of view are Robert Braidwood's *Prehistoric Men* (Chicago, Chicago Natural History Museum, 1948) and Carleton Coon's *The Story of Man* (London, Alfred A. Knopf, Inc., 1950).

The above general works on prehistory concentrate their attention on the history of physical utilitarian artifacts. Insight into the spiritual horizon of prehistoric man was gained from a study and analysis of his artistic forms. Analysis and interpretation of prehistoric art in France and Spain may be found in H. Breuil's *Four Hundred Centuries of Cave Art* (Montignac, Centre d'études et de documentation préhistoriques, 1952), H. Breuil and H. Obermaier's *The Cave of Altamira* (Madrid, Tip. de Archivos, 1935), and H. Breuil, M. C. Burkitt, and M. Polleck's *Rock Paintings of Southern Andalusia* (Oxford, Clarendon Press, 1929). An example of the prehistoric art of a modern primitive culture is Charles Mountford's *Arnhem Land Expedition*, Vol. 1, *Art, Myth, and Symbolism* (Melbourne, Melbourne University Press, 1956).

On the basis of archeological methods we are able to classify the cultural history and religion of primitives into three periods: Paleolithic, high Paleolithic, and Neolithic. Two general books covering all of these periods are G. R. Levy's *The Gate of Horn* (London, Faber & Faber, Ltd., 1948) and Johannes Maringer's *The Gods of Prehistoric Man* (N.Y., Alfred A. Knopf, Inc., 1960); Joseph Campbell in his book cited above, *The Masks of God: Primitive Mythology*, discusses the religions of these periods in Part Two, "The Mythology of Primitive Planters"; Part Three, "The Mythology of Primitive Hunters"; and Part Four, "The Archaeology of Myth."

Mircea Eliade's article "Sources and Changes in the History of Religion," in *City Invincible* (Chicago, University of Chicago Press, 1960) pp. 351ff., presents a short and precise interpretation of the meaning of cultural stratification for the history of religion. It is the best short article available on this topic.

One may say that paleolithic culture was a culture of hunters and nomads. A thorough discussion of a religious rite of this cultural stage is presented by A. J. Hallowell's article, "Bear Ceremonialism in the Northern Hemisphere," *American Anthropologist*, XXVIII (1926), pp. 1–173. Joseph Kitagawa gives a description of this religious phenomenon in a modern primitive culture in "Ainu Bear Festival (Iyomante)," *History of Religions: An International Journal for Comparative Historical Studies*, I, 1 (Chicago, 1961). Neolithic culture came into being with the discovery of agriculture and the domestication of animals. The religious forms of this culture are intrinsically related to these dominant emphases. A. E. Jensen believes that there was a religious historical stage between the paleolithic and the neolithic. This is the religion of the cultures in which the planting and tending of plants is practiced but the cultivation of cereal grains has not been discovered. See his *Das religiöse Weltbild einer frühen Kultur* (Stuttgart, A. Schröder, 1948) and *Mythos und Kult bei Naturvölkern* (Wiesbaden, F. Steiner, 1951). This work has just been translated into English by M. Choldin and W. Weissieder as *Myth and Cult Among Primitive People* (Chicago, University of Chicago Press, 1963). Jensen develops the idea of a type of god or goddess who is sacrificed by immolation. Out of the parts of the cut-up body, the trees and cultivated plants grow. To myths and religion of such a kind Jensen gives the name *Dema* type. Both the mythical type and the historical implications arising from it are discussed in Jensen's *Hainuwele; Volkerzählungen von der Molukkeninsel Ceram* (Frankfurt-am-Main, V. Klostermann, 1939).

An over-all view of the problems involved in the historical approach to primitive religion is found in W. Koppers' *Primitive Man and his World Picture* (N.Y., Sheed & Ward, Inc., 1952).

With the coming of agriculture, a new and powerful religious force was released in human culture. The most important new religious forms developed in this period are the cult of the great mother and megalithic religion. E. O. James devotes a volume, *The Cult of the Mother-Goddess* (London, Thames & Hudson, Ltd., 1959) to this topic. A psychological interpretation of this cult along Jungian lines is Erich Newmann's *The Great Mother; An Analysis of the Archetype* (N.Y., Pantheon Books, Inc., 1955). The term "megalithic" is derived from the Greek "megas," great, and "lithos," stone. This religious form centered around ancestor worship and veneration of the dead. The dead were understood as powerful fertility symbols in the tomb of the earth. Great stone monuments were erected on the site of the grave or served as tombs for the dead. Sibylle von Cles-Reden's book, *The Realm of the Great Goddess* (New Jersey, Prentice-Hall, Inc., 1962) deals with the relationship of the great mother cult to megalithic religion. Three works, though restricted to a specific geographical interpretation of megalithic culture, are quite informative. They are G. E. Daniel's *The Megalith Builders of Western Europe* (London, F. A. Praeger, Inc., 1958–59); John Layard's *Stone Men of Melekula* (London, Chatto & Windus, Ltd., 1942); and Alphonse Riesenfeld's *The Megalithic Culture of Melanesia* (Leiden, E. J. Brill, 1950). The study of the past of modern primitives is important for those who are interested in a historical interpretation of these religions. While historical analysis is not a panacea, it does add an important element to the interpretation of primitive religion. Listed below are works dealing with the prehistory of three particular cultural areas.

Africa

The general problems of archeology, prehistory, and oral tradition are presented in R. A. Hamilton, ed., *History and Archaeology in Africa* (London, London University, 1955). Over-all problems of prehistory in Africa are treated in H. Alimen, *The Prehistory of Africa*, tr. by A. H. Broadrick (London, Hutchinson & Co., 1957); H. Breuil, "L'Afrique préhistorique," *Cahier d'Art*, No. 5 (1930); L. S. B. Leakey, *Stone Age Africa* (London, Oxford University Press, 1936); *Adam's Ancestors*, 1st ed. (London, Methuen & Co., Ltd., 1934). The works of A. J. Arkell provide a good orientation to the prehistory of the Anglo-Egyptian Sudan: *The Old Stone Age in Anglo-Egyptian Sudan* (London, Oxford University Press, 1949) and *A History of the Sudan from the Earliest Times to 1821* (London, Athlone Press, 1955). For the prehistory of South Africa see M. C. Burkitt's *South Africa's Past in Stone and Paint* (Cambridge, Cambridge University Press, 1928), G. Caton-Thompson, *The Zimbabwe Culture: Ruins and Reactions* (Oxford, Clarendon Press, 1931), John D. Clark, *The Stone Age Cultures of Northern Rhodesia*, South Africa Archaeological Society (Claremont, Cape, 1950). For East Africa see J. D. Clark, *The Prehistoric Cultures of the Horn of Africa* (Cambridge, Cambridge University Museum, 1954) and Sonia Cole, *Early Man in East Africa* (London, Macmillan & Co., Ltd., 1958). Walter B. Cline traces the history of metallurgy in Africa in *Mining and Metallurgy in Negro Africa*, General Series in Anthropology, No. 5 (Menasha, Wisconsin, G. Banta Publishing Co., 1937).

North American Indians, prehistory

The aborigines of the North American continent rank among the best-studied peoples in the world. For years they have provided the student of culture with several types of cultural situations for study and interpretation. One of the earliest general and comprehensive studies of American Indians was H. R. Schoolcraft's *Information Respecting the History, Conditions and Prospects of the Indian Tribes of the United States*, 6 vols. (Philadelphia, J. B. Lippincott Co., 1851–57). A selective bibliography in this area would include Louis A. Brennan, *No Stone Unturned* (N.Y., Random House, Inc., 1959), Samuel G. Goodrich, *History of the Indians of North and South America* (Boston, Rand, 1855), Frank C. Hibben, *Treasure in the Dust* (Philadelphia, J. B. Lippincott Co., 1951), George E. Hyde, *Indians of the High Plains from Prehistoric Period to the Coming of Europeans* (Oklahoma, University of Oklahoma Press, 1959), Diamond Jenness, *The American Aborigines, Their Origin and Antiquity* (Toronto, University of Toronto Press, 1933), Alfred L. Kroeber, *Native Culture of the South-West* (Berkeley, University of California Press, 1928), Stephen D. Peet, *Prehistoric America*, 5 vols. (Chicago, Office of the American Antiquarian, 1890–1905), *Essays in Historical Anthropology of North America*, Smithsonian Institution (Washington, 1940).

Oceania and Australia

We have already referred to the works of Layard and Riesenfeld. In addition, the prehistory of this area is dealt with in Walter Iven's *Melanesians of the Solomon Islands* (London, Kegan Paul, Trench, Trubner & Co., Ltd., 1927) and *Island Builders of the Pacific* (London, Seeley, Service & Co., Ltd., 1930). John White's *The Ancient History of the Maori*, 4 vols. (Wellington, G. Didsbury, 1887–90) is almost a classic in this field. H. G. Quaritch Wales' *Prehistory and Religion in South-east Asia* (London, B. Quaritch, Ltd., 1957) shows the historical relationship between Southeast Asia and India in prehistoric times.

IV. MYTH IN PRIMITIVE RELIGION

Many of the works in section II of this essay contain chapters on the interpretation of myths. In this section we shall present (a) additional theoretical works in the area of myth, (b) compilations of myths of many types from all parts of the world, and (c) studies which deal with a particular type or structure in the myth.

A. Theoretical works

Ernst Cassirer has probably dealt with the problem of myth from a philosophical point of view more thoroughly than any other contemporary philosopher. Within his philosophy of symbolic forms, he was able to present a very profound interpretation of myth in *Language and Myth* (N.Y. and London, Harper & Brothers, 1946); *The Philosophy of Symbolic Forms*: Vol. II, *Mythical Thought* (New Haven, Yale University Press, 1953); and *An Essay on Man* (New Haven, Yale University Press, 1944). His orientation was taken over and expanded by Susanne Langer in *Philosophy in a New Key* (Cambridge, Harvard University Press, 1942) and *Feeling and Form* (N.Y., Charles Scribner's Sons, 1953). See also the two symposia on myth: *Myth: A Symposium*, ed. by T. A. Sebeok (Philadelphia, American Folklore Society, 1955) and *Myth and Mythmaking*, ed. by Henry Murray (N.Y., George Braziller, Inc., 1960).

Psychological and psychoanalytic interpretations of myths have, since the work of Freud, opened up a whole new area of mythological interpretation. Geza Roheim interpreted Australian myths psychoanalytically in *Australian Totemism: A Psychoanalytic Study in Anthropology* (London, George Allen & Unwin, Ltd., 1925) and *The External Ones of the Dream, A Psychoanalytic Interpretation of Australian Myth and Ritual* (N.Y., International Universities Press, 1945). Malinowski applied psychology in his study of myth in *Myth in Primitive Psychology* (N.Y., W. W. Norton, Co., 1926). Carl G. Jung and Carl Kerenyi have developed a new methodological approach in terms of Jungian psychological principles in *Essays on a Science of Mythology* (N.Y., Pantheon Books, Inc., 1949).

Mircea Eliade's contribution to the field is the development of an historical approach to myth. Some comments about his interpretation have already been made above. Eliade believes the cosmogenic myth to be the basic myth in every culture. See his "The Prestige of the Cosmogenic Myth," *Diogenes*, 23 (Fall, 1958), pp. 18ff. Since all myths express some dimension of creativity, they all recall the first creation as described in the cosmogenic myth. The yearning for paradise is understood by him as the religious desire of primitive man to live again in that time before creation *in illo tempore*. This is the substance of his article "The Yearning for Paradise in Primitive Tradition," *Diogenes*, 3 (Summer, 1943), pp. 18ff., also reprinted in *Daedalus*, LXXXVIII, 2 (1959), pp. 255–66. He presents a general theory for the interpretation of myths and other religious symbols in "Remarks on Religious Symbolism" in *The History of Religions: Essays in Methodology*, ed. by M. Eliade and J. M. Kitagawa (Chicago, University of Chicago Press, 1959).

Raffaele Pettazoni, especially in his essays "Myths of Beginning and Creation Myths" and "The Truth of Myth" in his *Essays on the History of Religions* (Leiden, E. J. Brill, 1954) explicates a theory of myth which is similar in intention to Eliade. Myths are for Pettazoni true stories. They tell the story of a people and demonstrate the manner by which reality is accessible to them. Eric Dardel has analyzed the conception of myth underlying the researches of Maurice Leenhardt in "The Mythic," *Diogenes*, 7 (Summer, 1954), pp. 33–51.

B. Compilations of myths

The most ambitious effort in the compilation of mythological materials from all over the world is probably *The Mythology of All Races*, ed. by John A. MacCulloch and George Foote Moore, 13 vols. (N.Y., Archeological Institute of America, 1916–32). The volumes are as follows: Vol. 1, *Greek and Roman* by William S. Fox; Vol. 2, *Eddic* by John A. MacCulloch; Vol. 3, *Celtic, Slavic* by John A. MacCulloch and Jan Machal; Vol. 4, *Finne Ugric, Siberian* by Uno Holmberg; Vol. 5, *Semitic* by Stephen H. Langdon; Vol. 6, *Indian, Iranian* by A. Berriedale Keith; Vol. 7, *Armenian, African* by Mardires Ananikian and Alice Werner; Vol. 8, *Chinese, Japanese* by John Ferguson and Masaharu Anesaki; Vol. 9, *Oceanic* by Roland B. Dixon; Vol. 10, *North American* by H. B. Alexander; Vol. 11, *Latin American* by H. B. Alexander; Vol. 12, *Egypt, Far East* by W. Max Müller, and Vol. 13, *Index*.

Alexander Krappe's books *Mythologie universelle* (Paris, Payot, 1930) and *La genèse des mythes* (Paris, Payot, 1938) give a broad coverage of myths but in typological categories. Another compilation of myths in typological terms is *La naissance du monde*, ed. by Anne Marie Esnoul, Paul Garelli, *et al.* (Paris, Éditions du Seuil, 1959).

Regional compilations and interpretations of myth are as follows:

Africa—Hans Abrahamsson in his *The Origin of Death* (Uppsala, Studia Ethnographica Uppsaliensa 3, 1951) discusses myths of this type in Africa. Hermann Baumann deals with myths of beginning and end in Africa in *Schöpfung und Urzeit des Menschen im Mythus der Afrikanischen Völker* (Berlin, Andrews & Steiner, 1936). H. Tegnaeus interprets myths of the hero in Africa in *Le héros civilisateur* (Stockholm, Studia Ethnographica Uppsaliensa 2, 1950).

Daryll Forde, ed., *African Worlds: Studies in the Cosmological Ideas and Social Values of African Peoples* (London, Oxford University Press, 1954) is a good introduction to the mythological world view of several African societies. Geoffrey Parrinder's *West African Religion* (London, Epworth Press, 1949) describes the relationship of myth to the total religious system of West African peoples. Melville Herskovits' works do the same for the Dahomey in *Outline of Dahomean Religious Belief*, American Anthropological Association, Memoir 41 (Wisconsin, 1933) and *Dahomey: An Ancient West African Kingdom*, 2 vols. (N.Y., J. J. Augustin, Inc., 1938). Eva Meyerowitz presents an interesting study in *The Sacred State of the Akan* (London, Faber & Faber, Ltd., 1951) and *Akan Traditions of Origin* (London, Faber & Faber, Ltd., 1952). By an analysis of the myths of a West African society (the Akan), she attempts to arrive at an understanding of their historical past. Marcel Griaule relates the religious masks to the mythological forms of the Dogon people of West Africa in *Masques Dogon* (Paris, Institut d'ethnologie, 1938), and in *Dieu d'eau* (Paris, Éditions du Chêne, 1948) he presents a highly developed and systematic interpretation of Dogon mythology based on his conversations with an old Dogon seer.

North American Indians—General interpretations of North American Indian myths may be found in *Creation Myths of Primitive America* (Boston, Little, Brown & Co., 1898) by Jeremiah Curtin and *The World's Rim* by H. B. Alexander (Lincoln, Nebr., University of Nebraska Press, 1953). Ake Hultkrantz takes over a Greek mythological theme in his study of shamanistic elements in American Indian myths, *The North American Indian Orpheus Tradition* (Ethnographical Museum of Stockholm, 1957). For the New England Indians, John N. B. Hewitt's *Iroquoian Cosmology* (Washington, U.S. Bureau of American Ethnology, 1928) and John M. Cooper's *The Algonquin Supreme Being* (Washington, Catholic University of America Press, 1934) present very good examples. For a broad coverage of the myths of the Algonquin and Iroquois, Charles G. Leland's *The Algonquin Legends of New England* (N.Y., Houghton Mifflin, Co., 1884) and E. A. Smith's "Myths of the Iroquois" in *Annual Report of the American Bureau of Ethnology* (Washington, 1883) are still the best studies.

Ruth Benedict's *Zuñi Mythology* (N.Y., Columbia University Press, 1935) and Ruth Bunzel's article, "Zuñi Origin Myths" in the *47th Annual Report of the United States Bureau of American Ethnology* (Washington, 1929–30), pp. 547–609, are classics in this area. A more thorough study of Zuñi religion and mythology is Matilda Stevenson's "The Zuñi Indians: Their Mythology, Esoteric Fraternities and Ceremonies" in *United States Bureau of American Ethnology Annual Report*, Vol. XXIII (Washington, 1904). A comparable work dealing with the mythology and religion of the Pueblos is Elsie C. Parsons' *Pueblo Indian Religion*, 2 vols. (Chicago, University of Chicago Press, 1939). A. L. Kroeber has recorded the myths of the California Indians in his articles "Indian Myths of South Central California" and "The Religion of the Indians of California" in Vol. IV, No. 4 and No. 6, respectively, of the *University of California Publications in American Archaeology and Ethnology*.

Comparable research has not been done on the indigenous societies of South America. For a general orientation to the myths and religion of this area, there are the following: Paul Radin, *Indians of South America* (N.Y., Doubleday & Co., Inc., 1942), Julian Steward, ed., *Handbook of South American Indians* (Washington, U.S. Government Printing Office, 1946–59), and Alfred Métraux's *Myths of the Toba and Pilagá Indians of Gran Chaco* (Philadelphia, American Folklore Society, 1946). See also Rafael Karsten's *The Civilization of the South American Indians with Special Reference to Magic and Religion* (N.Y., Alfred A. Knopf, Inc., 1926).

Polynesia and Australia—The best introductions to Polynesian mythology are Eldson Best's "Maori Religion and Mythology" in *Dominion Museum Bulletin*, series No. 10 (1924); R. W. Williamson's *Religion and Cosmic*

Beliefs of Central Polynesia, 2 vols. (Cambridge, Cambridge University Press, 1933); Hare Hongi's "A Maori Cosmogony," *Polynesian Society Journal*, XVI (1907); John Fraser's "Folk Songs and Myths from Samoa," *Polynesian Society Journal*, VI (1897); W. W. Gill, *Myths and Songs from the South Pacific* (London, H. S. King, 1876); J. L. Young, "The Paumoto Conception of the Heavens and Creation," *Polynesian Society Journal*, XXVIII (1919); George Grey, *Polynesian Mythology and Ancient Traditional History of the New Zealand Race as furnished by their Chiefs and Priests* (Auckland, H. Brett, 1885). A very valuable study of the cultural hero in Polynesian mythology is K. Luomala, "Maui-of-a-Thousand Tricks: His Oceanic and European Biographers," *Bernice P. Bishop Museum Bulletin*, No. 198 (1949).

Very good Australian mythological accounts are given in the works cited above by F. J. Gillen and W. B. Spencer. In addition to these, two other works by Ronald Berndt describing myth and ceremonial among the Australians are valuable studies that provide especially informative descriptions of sexual symbolism in the myth and ritual: *Kunapipi* (Melbourne, F. W. Cheshire, 1951) and *Djanggawul* (N.Y., Philosophical Library, 1953). Another study pointing out the relationship between myth and art is A. P. Elkin and Catherine and Ronald Berndt, *Art in Arnhem Land* (Melbourne, F. W. Cheshire, 1950).

C. Studies of types of myth

Joseph Campbell deals with the specific mythological form of the hero in *The Hero with a Thousand Faces* (N.Y., Pantheon Books, Inc., 1949). The hero myth in specific cultural areas is discussed by D. G. Brinton in *American Hero-Myths* (Philadelphia, H. C. Watts & Co., 1882), and H. Tegnaeus deals with the hero in African myths in his *Le héros civilisateur* (Stockholm, Studia Ethnographica Uppsaliensa 2, 1950). Ugo Bianchi's *Il Dualismo Religioso* (Rome, "L'Erma" di Bretschneider, 1958) is an interpretation of dualisms in myth; Paul Radin's *The Trickster; A Study in American Indian Mythology* (London, Routledge & Kegan Paul, Ltd., 1955) is a study of the trickster-hero-twin in American Indian myths.

V. TYPES OF RELIGIOUS MAN

The best introductory discussions of this aspect of the religious life are found in chapter 8, "Types of Religious Authority" of Joachim Wach's *Sociology of Religion* (London, Kegan Paul, Trench, Trubner & Co., Ltd., 1947 and reprinted) and G. van der Leeuw's, Part II, "The Subject of Religion" in *Religion in Essence and Manifestation* (London, George Allen & Unwin, Ltd., 1938). Wach builds on and extends Max Weber's notion of *Charisma* as a basis for defining religious types. Van der Leeuw sees specific types of religious men in relationship to their apprehension or possession of power.

A. The primitive "philosopher" and the shaman

As an argument against the view that primitive man possesses an undeveloped mind, Paul Radin wrote *Primitive Man as Philosopher* (N.Y., D. Appleton & Co., 1927). A work along similar lines is A. P. Elkin's *Aboriginal Men of High Degree* (Sydney, Australasian Co., 1946). These studies show that primitive men do not have an underdeveloped intellect, but, as C. Levi-Strauss has said, the difference lies in "la nature des choses sur lesquelles portent ces opérations," *Anthropologie structurale* (Paris, Plon, 1958), p. 255. This appraisal is demonstrated by Marcel Griaule's *Dieu d'eau* (Paris, Éditions du Chêne, 1948). Here we observe the systematic working out of a mythological theology by the old Dogon, Ogotemmeli.

Closely related to these "aboriginal men of high degree" is the shaman. The shaman may function as a magician or priest, but the basic element in his make-up is his ability to have an ecstatic experience. We are here following Mircea Eliade's interpretation of shamanism. He has written a definitive book on this subject: *Le chamanisme et les techniques archaiques de l'extase* (Paris, Payot, 1951). He discusses in his article "Recent Works on Shamanism: A Review Article," *History of Religions: A Journal for Comparative Historical Studies*, I, 2 (1961), pp. 152ff., the most recent literature on this subject. In delineating the specific shamanistic religious type, he says:

> This is why we thought it useful to limit the term "shaman" to those among the various "specialists of the sacred" (Medicine men, magicians, contemplative, inspired, and possessed people, etc.) who know how to employ ecstasy for the benefit of the community. Ecstasy always involves a trance, whether "symbolic" or pretended or real, and the trance is interpreted as a temporary abandonment of the body by the soul of the shaman. During ecstasy, the soul of the shaman is thought to ascend to Heaven, to descend to the other world (to the nether world) or to travel far away in space (pp. 153–4).

Joseph Campbell in *The Masks of God: Primitive Mythology* has seen the origin of shamanism in the paleolithic stage of hunting culture (pp. 229–81). Eliade seems to confirm this belief and cites other authors in support of Campbell's position. See "Prehistory of Shamanism" in Eliade's article on shamanism (pp. 182ff.). A critical discussion of Eliade's view concerning shamanism may be found in Alois Closs' "Das Religiöse im Schamanismus," *Kairos*, II (1960), p. 29.

Eliade states that though shamanism is a specifically Siberian phenomenon, vestiges and traces of it are found throughout the world, with the possible exception of Africa (p. 153). Thus any study of the primitive religion of Oceania, the Americas, circum-polar peoples, or Asians will in some measure show signs of shamanism.

An enlarged and revised English version of Eliade's *Le chamanisme et les techniques archaiques de l'extase* was published in 1964 under the title *Shamanism: Archaic Techniques of Ecstasy*, trans. by Willard R. Trask (N.Y., Bollingen Foundation, 1964). This work is a comprehensive study from the viewpoint of an historian of religion. It also contains a complete bibliography.

B. Medicine men, kings, and priests

The shaman is a medicine man or priest, but, as Eliade states, all medicine men and priests are not shamans. As the phrase implies, the medicine man is concerned with healing. Healing is not limited to physical ailments, and even when it is, the cause of the ailment is not understood simply as an organic disorder. The medicine man may be at the same time a priest or king. If he is a priest, he has the power to act on behalf of all the people in a formalized cult. Such a role may also be combined with kingship. The king, if he is a holy man, is a symbol of an ancestral cult and may or may not have priestly powers.

Though the phenomenon represented by the term "medicine man" is almost universal among primitives, the specific term is of North American origin, and any general study of a primitive society will devote a chapter or two to its description.

The interrelatedness of healing and religion among American Indians is dealt with by John R. Swanton in his article "Religious Beliefs and Medicinal Practices of the Creek Indians," *U.S. Bureau of American Ethnology*, 42nd Annual Report (Washington, 1928). The relationship of the medicinal practices and cultural role of the medicine man is the subject of W. T. Corlett's *The Medicine-man of the American Indian and his Cultural Background* (Illinois, Charles C Thomas, 1935). Charles M. Barbeau's *Medicine-men on the North Pacific Coast* (Ottawa, Department of Northern Affairs & National Resources, 1958) demonstrates how closely medicine men are related to shamans, and Samuel Barret describes the actual practice of medicine men in his *Pomo Bear Doctors* (Berkeley, University of California Press, 1917). A sociological analysis of this same problem is undertaken by John J. Maddox in *The Medicine-man; A Sociological Study of the Character and Evolution of Shamanism* (N.Y., The Macmillan Co., 1923). The combination of the magician and medicine man may be seen in Sir Richard Winstedt's *The Malay Magician* (London, Routledge & Kegan Paul, Ltd., 1951).

Studies dealing with primitive medicine are Erwin Ackerknecht's "Psychopathology, Primitive Medicine, and Primitive Culture," *Bulletin of the History of Medicine*, XIV (1943), pp. 30–67; "Natural Diseases and Rational Treatment in Primitive Medicine," *Bulletin of the History of Medicine*, XIX (1946), pp. 467–97, and M. Bartels, *Die Medizin der Naturvölker* (Leipzig, T. Grieben, 1893). Both interpretations emphasize the magical element in medicine practices of the primitives. This mixture of magic and medicine among primitives and archaic peoples is treated by Jean Filliozat in *Magie et médecine* (Paris, Presses universitaires de France, 1943). A study of examples of the use and function of negative magic or witchcraft in primitive societies is Peter H. Buck's *Regional Diversity in the Elaboration of Sorcery in Polynesia* (New Haven, Yale University Press, 1936). For this same phenomenon in Africa the reader may consult E. E. Evans-Pritchard, *Witchcraft, Oracles, and Magic among the Azande* (Oxford, Clarendon Press, 1937); Pierre Fontaine's *La magie chez les noirs* (Paris, Dervy, 1949); and Frederick Kaigh's *Witchcraft and Magic of Africa* (London, R. Lesley & Co., Ltd., 1947).

Among modern primitives, the Africans still seem to possess the exemplary form of the priest king or divine kingship. A summary discussion of divine kingship in Africa is found in V. van Bulck's "La place du roi divin dans cercles culturels d'Afrique Noire" in *The Sacral Kingship, Contributions to the Central Theme of the VIIIth International Congress for the History of Religions* (Leiden, E. J. Brill, 1959), p. 98. Other articles relating to the religious role of kingship in this same volume are Paul Radin's "The Sacral Chief among American Indians," p. 83, and Patrick Akoi's "Divine Kingship and Its Participation in Ashanti," p. 135. The sociological and religious aspects of kingship are described by Olof Pettersson in *Chiefs and Gods: Religious and Social Elements in South Eastern Bantu Kingship* (Lund, C. W. K. Gleerup, 1953). The same aspects of the problem of kingship in Africa are the subject of Tor Irstam's *The King of Ganda; Studies in the Institutions of Sacral Kingship* (Lund, H. Ohlssons Boktr., 1944). Percival Hadfield in *Traits of Divine Kingship in Africa* (London, C. A. Watts & Co., Ltd., 1949) and Eva Meyerowitz in *Divine Kingship in Ghana and Ancient Egypt* (London, Faber & Faber, Ltd., 1960) attempt to find the origin of kingship in Africa. Luc de Heusch in *Essais sur le symbolisme de l'inceste royal en Afrique* (Brussels, Institut de sociologie Solvay, 1958) shows the social and mythological relationship of incest to the notion of kingship.

VI. RITUALS AND CULTS

The relationship of ritual and ceremonials to myth, religious symbols, and sociological forms has always posed a problem for historians and sociologists of religion. Theodor Gaster's discussion of ancient Near Eastern religion in *Thespis; Ritual, Myth, and Drama in the Ancient Near East* (N.Y., Henry Schuman, Inc., 1950) has a great deal to say concerning this problem in all archaic and primitive cultures. For Gaster all seasonal rituals express two elements: Kenosis, or emptying, and Plerosis, or filling (p. 4). The reality which is subject to this emptying and filling is denominated by Gaster as the *topocosm* (p. 4). *Topocosm* is a comprehensive term for the human community and all animate elements in a particular place. The essence of the *topocosm* is that it possesses a twofold character, at once real and punctual and ideal and durative, the former aspect being necessarily merged in the latter as a moment is merged in time (p. 5). Myth provides the necessary relation between the punctual and the durative or transcendent dimension of reality. In Gaster's interpretation myth is not an outgrowth of ritual but a parallel aspect of it.

Clyde Kluckhohn takes up this same problem in his important article "Myths and Rituals: A General Theory," *Harvard Theological Review*, XXXV (January, 1942), pp. 45ff. Kluckhohn dismisses as unfounded any general theory of the priority of myth over ritual or vice versa. He maintains that one can find either type of priority by examining the empirical evidence. Myth and ritual are for him interdependent since they refer to a common psychological basis. "Ritual is an obsessive repetitive activity—often a symbolic dramatization of the fundamental 'needs' of the society whether 'economic,' 'biological,' 'social,' or 'sexual.' Mythology is the rationalization of these same needs, whether they are all expressed in overt ceremonial or not" (p. 29).

Jean Cazeneuve in *Les rites et la condition humaine* (Paris, Presses universitaires de France, 1958) interprets rituals as arising out of the need of man to live in a sacred world. "Mais si la religion tend a sacraliner la condition humaine en la faisant dépendre d'un archetype qui la transcende, il est naturel qu'elle la transfigure tout en la conservant" (p. 439). "La religion, par ses rites, affirme à la fois cette transcendance et la possibilité pour l'homme de participer à ses archetypes sacrés" (p. 442).

It is possible to classify rituals into historical-cultural types. We could thus speak of those rituals common to paleolithic hunters and nomads, those common to the upper paleolithic period, and finally those which presuppose a neolithic background. This typology of rituals is carried out in Joseph Campbell's *The Masks of God: Primitive Mythology*. During the paleolithic period the rituals were related to the animal as a symbol of sacrality. We have referred to this type of ritual in Kitagawa's article on the Ainu Bear Festival and Hallowell's article on Bear Ceremonialism.

The upper paleolithic period is represented by the rituals of those who tend and cultivate plants but who have not discovered agriculture. A. E. Jansen's work cited above deals with these types of rituals. In addition to the sacrificial ritual which involves the killing of a person or animal, the religious meaning of cannibalism in this cultural stage was explicated by E. Volhard in *Kannibalismus* (Stuttgart, Strecker und Schröder, 1939).

With the coming of the neolithic age we find rituals which are related to seasonal changes and fertility. The model for these rituals is the sowing, tending, and reaping of cereal grains. In these rituals sacrifices are performed to insure the fertility of the soil; and the earth, symbolized as a great mother, appears as one of the dominant symbols.

We hardly, if ever, find pure types of any of these rituals. In every case new elements and survivals from the past are present. We are able to infer certain meanings from the archeological finds of paleolithic times. Johannes Maringer in his book *The Gods of Prehistoric Man* makes inferences regarding the religious rituals of paleolithic man. The Australian aborigines represent a mixture of old paleolithic and late paleolithic religious ritual. The emphasis on totemism and the sexual connotations of the *Kunapipi* and *Djanggawal* ceremonies confirm this observation.

An interpretation and historical comparative study of the corn-mother symbolism is given by G. Hatt in his article "Corn Mother in Indonesia and America," *Anthropos*, XLVI (1951), pp. 853ff. H. Baumann traces the historical and cultural meaning of the myths which have reference to androgyny and hermaphroditism in his *Das doppelte Geschlecht* (Berlin, D. Reimer, 1955). He shows that these myths and their rituals are historically related to agricultural matriarchal societies.

The early neolithic rituals developed into the great rituals and sacrifices which we associate with the ancient Near East, India, and China. The rituals of the Southwestern American Indians and the New England agricultural Indians and the great rituals of the Mayas and Aztecs are also related to this neolithic structure. The Plains Indians of North America practiced an older ritual form which probably had its origin in late paleolithic times. Examples of this ritual may be seen in Ralph Linton's account of *The Sacrifice to the Morning Star by the Skidi Pawnee* (Chicago, Field Museum of Natural History, 1922) and, by the same author, *The Thunder Ceremony of the Pawnee* (Chicago, Field Museum of Natural History, 1922). In both of these accounts three symbols are dominant: first, sky symbolism; second, the identity of human being with an animal; and, third, the sacrifice of the human for the increase of fertility.

In addition to the great rituals which are intended to insure the food supply or promote fertility in general, other rituals take place at birth, death, and initiation. We shall consider only the initiation rituals here since the rituals of birth and death are so closely related to the basic structure of the great fertility rites.

G. van Gennep's, tr. by Vizedom and Caffee, *The Rites of Passage* (Chicago, University of Chicago Press, 1960) states a position which has become a watershed for all discussions of initiation. It is his belief that initiation rites are ritual forms related to the movement from one status to another. The passage over is considered dangerous. The ritual thus protects and "carries the novice across the passage."

Mircea Eliade in *Birth and Rebirth* (N.Y., Harper & Brothers, 1958) extends van Gennep's understanding of initiation by concentrating on the process of passage itself. He sees initiation as a paradigmatic gesture which imitates the cosmogony. The novice is "reborn" in the initiation rite. To be reborn, he must return to chaos or "die" to his old mode of being. This initiatory death is the new and indispensable element in initiation (pp. xiii–xiv).

Bruno Bettelheim in *Symbolic Wounds* (Glencoe, Free Press, 1954) applies a psychological methodology to arrive at his understanding of this phenomenon. On the basis of the initiation rites of the Australian aborigines, he sees initiation rites rooted in the antagonism of the sexes. He interprets the mutilation of the penis which takes place during the course of these rites as the expression of the desire of the male to be androgynous—that is, able to bring forth a new human being.

Dominique Zahan's *Sociétés d'initiation bambara: le N'Dome, le Korè* (Paris, Mouton & Co., 1960) is the first volume of a projected study of the six initiation societies of the Bambara, a West African culture. It is interesting because of its description of initiation rites which, in addition to covering the lifespan from childhood to manhood, form a mythological-theological drama.

R. Thurnwald's "Primitive Initiations und Wiedergeburtriten," *Eranos-Jahrbuch*, VII (1940), takes up the meaning of the rebirth motif in initiation.

In addition to initiations related to the "rites of passage" are those initiatory rites by which one enters a secret society. Wach defines the secret society as a group which is open to membership on the basis of a special experience (*Sociology of Religion*, p. 114). Eliade deals with initiation rites of secret societies in chaps. III, "From Tribal Rites to Secret Cults," and IV, "Individual Initiations and Secret Societies," in his *Birth and Rebirth.*

A general discussion of the character and nature of secret societies is presented in Wach's *Sociology of Religion*, chap. V, section 2, "The Secret Society." Hutton Webster's study, *Primitive Secret Societies: A Study in Early Politics and Religion* (N.Y., The Macmillan Co., 1908) emphasizes the social and political role of secret societies in the evolution of culture. An overall view of African secret societies is found in W. D. Hambly's *Source Book for African Anthropology*, Field Museum of Natural History, Vol. XXVI (Chicago, 1937), pp. 498ff. Specific studies of African secret societies are offered in George Harley's *Notes on the Mano in Liberia* (Cambridge, Harvard University Press, 1941) and F. W. Butt-Thompson's *West African Secret-societies* (London, H. F. & G. Witherby, Ltd., 1929).

Information concerning North American Indian secret societies may be found in R. H. Lowie's *Indians of the Plains*, American Museum of Natural History, Anthropological Handbooks, No. 1 (N.Y., McGraw-Hill Book Co., 1954); Reo R. Fortune's "Omaha Secret Societies," *Columbia University Contributions to Anthropology*, No. 14 (1932), and George Boas' "The Social Organizations and Secret Societies of the Kwakiutl Indians," *U.S. National Museum Annual Report for the year 1895* (Washington, Smithsonian Institution, 1897).

Secret societies of Oceania are described in Gunnar Landtman's *The*

Kiwai Papuans of British New Guinea (London, Macmillan & Co., Ltd., 1927); D. F. Thomason, "The Hero Cult, Initiation and Totemism on Cape York," *Journal of the Royal Anthropological Institute*, LXIII (1933), pp. 453–537; and R. Piddington's "Karadjeri Initiation," *Oceania*, III (1932–33), pp. 46–86.

VII. CARGO-CULTS AND THE IMPACT OF MODERNIZATION

The term "cargo-cults" refers to a prophetic and millenaristic religious phenomenon among many modern primitives. The origin of the phrase is probably to be found in Oceania. It alludes to a myth which describes the return of a cultural hero with a cargo of useful and beautiful merchandise.

With the coming of the Westerners, the old traditional ways were seriously undermined. The cargo-cult ideology represents the longing of the primitives for a return and a renewal of their spiritual and cultural life. This longing for a return to paradise is found among all modern primitive peoples. Many of the prophetic elements among modern primitives appear within the context of this cargo-cult mentality.

Vittorio Lanternari in his article "Messianism: Its Historical Origin and Morphology," *History of Religions*, II, 1 (1962), pp. 52ff., sees in these movements the dialectical relationship between "myth" and history, a dialectic which is present in all prophetic movements. Mircea Eliade has dealt with this topic in his article "Dimensions religieuses du renouvellement cosmique," *Eranos-Jahrbuch*, XXVIII (1959), pp. 241ff. This article also appears as "Renouvellement cosmique et eschatologie" in his *Mephistopheles et L'Androgyne* (Paris, Gallimard, 1962). Eliade pays special attention to the religious symbols of return to primordial time and the paradisial elements which are present in the cargo-cult. By way of contrast, one could say that Eliade's interpretation emphasizes the mythological motifs and symbols, whereas Lanternari's essay emphasizes the historical causal elements in the cults. These two articles are highly instructive for those interested in a general religious interpretation of this phenomenon. Robert Lowie discusses the meaning of primitive messianism in "Primitive Messianism and an Ethnological Problem," *Diogenes*, 19 (1957), pp. 62–72.

Messianism appeared among the North American Indians during the latter part of the nineteenth and early twentieth centuries. A rich body of literature describes and documents this movement. A general book showing the relationship between American Indian nationalism and its religious expression in the peyote cult is *The Peyote Religion* by J. S. Slotkin (Glencoe, Free Press, 1956). Peyote is a plant containing a drug which is eaten during the cultic worship of this Indian cult. Slotkin's book is heavily documented.

Another aspect of this phenomenon among the American Indians goes by the name of "ghost dance" or "hand dance." The dances were ritualistic militant movements which looked forward to the overthrow of the dominant white culture by a Messiah who was to re-establish the old Indian way of life. Some of the representative literature dealing with this aspect of Indian cargo-cults is as follows: James Mooney, "The Ghost-Dance Religion and the Sioux Out-break in 1890," *Annual Report of U.S. Bureau of American Ethnology*, No. 14 (Washington, 1896); C. DuBois, *The 1870 Ghost Dance*, University of California Records (Berkeley, 1939); Leslie Spier's *The Prophet Dance of the Northwest and its Derivatives*, General Series in Anthropology, No. 1 (Menasha, G. Banta Publishing Co., 1935); Nat P. Phister, "The Indian Messiah," *American Anthropologist*, IV (1891), pp. 105–8.

For this phenomenon in Oceania, see Ida Lesson's *Bibliography of Cargo Cults and Other Nativistic Movements in the South Pacific* (Sydney, South Pacific Commission Technical Paper, No. 30, 1952) and Peter Worsley's *The Trumpet Shall Sound: A Study of "Cargo-Cults" in Melanesia* (London, MacGibbon & Kee, 1957).

For Africa, see G. Balandier's "Messianismes et nationalismes en Afrique Noire," *Cahiers Internationaux de Sociologie*, XIV (1953), pp. 41ff.; E. Andersson, *Messianic Popular Movements in the Lower Congo*, (Uppsala, Almquist & Wiksells, 1958); H. von Sicard, *Ngoma Lungundu* (Uppsala, Almquist & Wiksells, 1952); and Bengt Sundkler, *Bantu Prophets in South Africa* (London, Lutterworth Press, 1948).

APPENDIX I

General works on primitive religion

A section of most textbooks in the discipline of history of religion or comparative religion is almost always devoted to an interpretation of primitive religion. For example, see John Murphy, *The Origins and History of Religions* (Manchester, Manchester University Press, 1949); John B. Noss' *Man's Religions* (N.Y., The Macmillan Co., 1949); and Winston King's *Introduction to Religion* (N.Y., Harper & Brothers, 1954).

In addition to this type of text, there are other texts devoted exclusively to a study of primitive religion. Alexander Goldenweiser's *Early Civilization; An Introduction to Anthropology* (N.Y., Alfred A. Knopf, Inc., 1922) is a critical theoretical work. In it Goldenweiser examines the various theories of primitive mentality and the origin of religion. William J. Goode's *Religion among the Primitives* (Glencoe, Free Press, 1951) is a sociologically oriented study of primitive religion, as is Edward Norbeck's *Religion in Primitive Society* (N.Y., Harper & Brothers, 1961). Paul Radin's *Primitive Religion, Its Nature and Origin* (N.Y., Viking Press, 1937), Robert Lowie's *Primitive Religion* (N.Y., Boni & Liveright, 1924), and Wilson Wallis' *Religion in Primitive Society* (N.Y., F. S. Crofts & Co., 1939) combine historical, sociological, and phenomenological dimensions in their treatments. I consider them the most adequate texts.

Two other works should be mentioned: *Primitive Heritage*, ed. by Margaret Mead and Nicholas Calas (N.Y., Random House, 1953), and *Reader in Comparative Religion*, ed. by William A. Lessa and Evon Z. Vogt (Evanston, Row, Peterson & Co., 1958). Edited texts of this type enable a teacher to cover several dimensions of the topic with the aid of primary source material. Furthermore, a teacher using such an edited text is not forced to accept completely the method and point of view of a textbook or to spend a great deal of time qualifying it. The opportunity for developing his own approach is made available.

APPENDIX II

Periodicals relevant to primitive religion

American Anthropologist (AA)
Annual Reports of Smithsonian Institution (ARSI)
Anthropological Quarterly (AQ)
Anthropos (APS)
Archiv für Religionswissenschaft (ARW)
Archiv für Völkerkunde (AFV)
Bantu Studies (BS)
Bernice P. Bishop Museum Bulletin (BMB)
Bulletin de l'Institut Français d'Afrique Noire (BIFAN)
Bulletin de l'Institut Français d'Afrique Noire, Série B.
Bulletin de la Société d'Anthropologie de Paris (BSAP)
Bulletin de la Société de Géographie (BSG)
Bulletin de la Société Royale Belge de Géographie (BSRBG)
Bulletin de la Société des Recherches Congolaises (BSRC)
Carnegie Institution Publications (CIP)
Eranos-Jahrbuch (EJ)
Ethnos (ES)
Études de sociologie et d'ethnologie juridiques (ESEJ)
Field Museum of Natural History Anthropological Series (FMAS)
Folk-Lore (FL)
Folklore Fellows Communications (FFC)
General Series in Anthropology (GSA)
Harvard African Studies (HAS)
Internationales Archiv für Ethnographie (IAFE)
Journal de la Société des Africanistes (JSA)
Journal of American Folklore (JAFL)
Journal of the American Oriental Society (JAOS)
Journal of the American Society for Semitic Languages (JASS)
Journal of the Polynesian Society (JPS)
Journal of the Royal Anthropological Institute (JRAI)
Journal of the Royal Asiatic Society (JRAS)
L'année sociologique (ASoc)
Man (MN)
Mana (MA)
Mémoires de l'Institut d'Études Centrafricaines (MIEC)
Mémoires de l'Institut Français d'Afrique Noire (MIFAN)

Mémoires de l'Institut Français d'Afrique Noire, Centre du Cameroun, Série Populations (MIFCC)
Mitteilungen der Anthropologischen Gesellschaft in Wien (MAGW)
Oceania (OA)
Orientalia (ORA)
Papers of the Peabody Museum of American Archaeology and Ethnology, Harvard University (PPM)
Préhistoire (PHE)
Publications of U.S. Bureau of American Ethnology (USBAE)
Revue d'anthropologie (RAN)
Revue archéologique (RAR)
Revue d'ethnographie et de sociologie (RES)
Revue d'ethnographie et des traditions populaires (RETP)
Revue de l'histoire des religions (RHR)
Revue des études ethnographiques et sociologiques (REES)
Revue des sciences religieuses (RSR)
Rhodes-Livingstone Journal (RLJ)
Rhodes-Livingstone Papers (RLP)
Royal Anthropological Institute Occasional Papers (RAIOC)
Southwestern Journal of Anthropology (SWJA)
Studien zur Völkerkunde (SV)
University of California Publications in American Archaeology and Ethnology (UCAAE)

APPENDIX III

Bibliographies covering the geographical areas of primitive religions

Africa

W. D. Hambly, *Source Book for African Anthropology*: Field Museum of Natural History Anthropological Series, 26, part 2 (Chicago, 1937).

———, *Bibliography of African Anthropology, 1937–49*, Chicago Museum of Natural History, Fieldiana, XXXVII, 2 (1952).

Evans Levin, *Annotated Bibliography of Recent Publications on Africa South of the Sahara*, Royal Empire Society (London, 1943).

Twentieth Century Fund, *Selected Annotated Bibliography of Tropical Africa*. Compiled by the International African Institute under the Direction of Professor Daryll Forde (N.Y., 1956).

U.S. Library of Congress, European Affairs Division, *Introduction to Africa: A Selective Guide to Background Reading*. Prepared by Helen F. Conover (Washington, 1952).

U.S. Library of Congress, General Reference and Bibliographic Division, *Africa South of the Sahara, A Selected Annotated List of Writings, 1951–56*. Compiled by Helen F. Conover (Washington, 1957).

H. A. Wieschhoff, *Anthropological Bibliography of Negro Africa* (New Haven, American Oriental Society, 1948).

North American Indians

F. W. Hodge, ed., *Handbook of American Indians North of Mexico*, 2 vols., Bureau of American Ethnology Bulletin 30 (Washington, 1907–10).

Clyde Kluckhohn and Katherine Spencer, *A Bibliography of the Navaho Indians* (N.Y., J. J. Augustin, Inc., 1940).

A. L. Kroeber, *Handbook of the Indians of the Southwest*, University of California Publications in American Archaeology and Ethnology, XXIII, 9 (Berkeley, 1929).

———, *Cultural and Natural Areas of Native North America*, University of California Publications in American Archaeology and Ethnology, XXXVIII (Berkeley, 1939).

———, *Handbook of the Indians of California*, Bureau of American Ethnology Bulletin 78 (Washington, 1925).

George P. Murdock, *Ethnographic Bibliography of North America*, 1st ed. (New Haven, Yale University Press, 1941).

Oceania

A. P. Elkin, *Social Anthropology in Melanesia; A Review of Research* (London, Oxford University Press, 1953).

Léonce A. N. H. Jore, *Essai de bibliographie du Pacifique* (Paris, Éditions Duchartre, 1931).

Clyde R. H. Taylor, *A Pacific Bibliography* (Wellington, Polynesian Society, 1951).

South America

George P. Murdock, *Outline of South American Cultures* (New Haven, Human Relations Area Files, 1951).

Julian H. Steward, ed., *Handbook of South American Indians*, 6 vols. (Washington, U.S. Government Printing Office, 1946–50).

APPENDIX IV

The history of the history of religions

The original plan for this *Reader's Guide* included a chapter to be devoted to the nineteenth- and twentieth-century development of religious studies that resulted in the emergence of what is now called "history of religions," "comparative religions," or *Religionswissenschaft*. The projected chapter would have cited the important literature characterizing each stage of the development. In content it was planned that the chapter would deal with theoretical issues and with methodology—such as the controversial problems of the origin and nature of religion—rather than with the evolution of historical studies in particular religious traditions. As work on the volume progressed, however, it became evident that the chapter in question would in large part be a duplication of material already discussed in the present chapter on primitive religions. For this reason, the original intention has been abandoned, and in its place this appendix is offered as a brief guide to information on the history of religions.

From at least the time of the ancient Greeks men in the Western world have been periodically trying to understand the nature of religion and the reasons for its emergence and importance in human affairs. Their intellectual labor has produced a number of theories, some of them ingenious and all of them interesting. Many of their speculations have been the natural expression of intellectual curiosity about an important sphere of human activity, but on the whole the motives prompting their theorizing have until fairly recent times been religious. The two situations most evocative of theories on the nature of religion have been those where rival religious systems confronted one another directly and those of crisis and breakdown within an established religious community. As an example of the first, one may cite the encounter of Christianity with Hellenistic religions in the early years of its history or its struggle with Islam in medieval times. The second type is exemplified in the radical re-examination of basic Christian theological themes after the Cartesian revolution in philosophy and the rise of rationalism in Europe. Though the motives of the explanations of religion that grew out of such situations, as well as their modes of conception, were theological and polemical, nevertheless, these explanations constitute rudimentary theories of the origin and nature of religion. Theories of this type clearly are not, however, the real ancestors of the "history of religions," for they fall very far short of the ideal of disinterested scientific observation. They may rather be called prescientific theories. Properly, they belong to the history of religious apologetics within whatever tradition they may have developed and not to the history of the scientific study of religions.

The scientific study of religions can be said truly to have begun only in the early decades of the nineteenth century. It came into being as one facet of the many-sided intellectual *élan* of that remarkably creative period. Once an interest in religion had been launched, based upon the new methods of study and the greatly enlarged resources of information available to nineteenth-century scholars, schools and theories followed one another in rapid succession.

The first group worthy to be called a school were philologists whose discoveries of the relationships among the Indo-Aryan group of languages and peoples led them into comparative mythology. The greatest name among them is that of F. Max Müller whose influence and popularizing ability have earned him the title "father of the history of religions." At about the same time as the philological and comparative mythology school, there emerged also an ethnological school, soon to be succeeded by sociological and psychological schools. In the last quarter of the century a conviction began to grow that there should be a study of religions conducted for its own sake independently of all other considerations, especially of traditional theological and philosophical approaches. The interest in this newly conceived "science of religions" found concrete expression in the establishment of chairs of the history of religions in several European universities. The first was founded in Geneva in 1873, and in the next year four chairs were established in the Dutch universities. Three years later the French created a chair for the history of religions in the Collège de France. Germany, whose scholars have contributed so much to the field, was relatively late in setting up a professorship of the history of religions (1910), but interest in the Scandinavian countries developed almost simultaneously with that in Holland and France. By the turn of the century the history of religions was firmly a part of university life in Europe, and there already existed a great body of scholarly literature in the field. Details of the place of history of religions in the universities in the early twentieth century can be had by consulting the works of Louis Jordan: *Comparative Religion, Its Genesis and Growth* (Edinburgh, T. & T. Clark, 1905); *The Study of Religion in the Italian Universities* (London, Oxford University Press, 1909); "The Study of Religion in the German Universities," *Expository Times*, XXII (1911), pp. 198–201, and XXIII (1912), pp. 136–9; "The

Study of Religion in Italian Universities. A Half-century's Survey," *The American Journal of Theology*, XXIII (1919), pp. 41–60; and *Comparative Religion, A Survey of its Recent Literature*, 2nd rev. and augmented ed. (London, Oxford University Press, 1920).

Unquestionably the best treatment of the history of religious studies in the West, including the history of prescientific theories, is the first volume of H. Pinard de la Boullaye's *L'étude comparée des religions*, which bears the title *Son histoire dans le monde occidental*, (Paris, G. Beauchesne, 1922, 3rd rev. ed. 1929). With painstaking care Pinard has analyzed a host of thinkers, movements, and books, major and minor alike, in a magnificent effort to reconstruct the many currents in thinking about religion in the century and a half before his time. The range of literature considered in his survey is astonishingly broad, and the most grudging critic would have difficulty in refusing admiration to the intellectual mastery that encompasses so large a field. Pinard's principal purpose was to describe an historical development in thought, but he also indulges in a degree of criticism of the thinkers he considers. Pinard was a Catholic priest, and his commitment to orthodox Catholic theology is sometimes reflected in the objections he poses to certain thinkers and schools. He has a strong tendency, for example, to uphold the "primitive monotheism" theory of Pater Wilhelm Schmidt and to derogate its detractors. It is difficult to avoid the suspicion that his eagerness for the theory is due partially at least to the ease with which the theory can be made to fit Catholic orthodoxy. One might also cite his treatment of Rudolf Otto, to whom he does much less than justice. Pinard's opposition to Otto's views appears to have been such that he could neither appreciate the profundity of Otto's insights in *The Idea of the Holy* nor accurately estimate Otto's enormous influence on subsequent thinkers. These cavils apart, however, Pinard's book remains the standard reference work for the historical development of religious studies.

Much the same ground is covered in more cursory and less satisfactory fashion in a small work by Gustav Mensching, *Geschichte der Religionswissenschaft* (Bonn, Universitäts-Verlag, 1948). The volume is mentioned here because it may prove to be more available than Pinard's excellent work, but it does not rise to Pinard's standard.

In English the best account of the history in which we are interested is Pater Wilhelm Schmidt's *The Origin and Growth of Religion*, trans. by Herbert J. Rose (London, Methuen & Co., Ltd., 1931). Although this work itself constitutes material for a lengthy volume, it represents a condensation of the views put forward by the same author over a period of years in Schmidt's massive *Der Ursprung der Gottesidee: eine historisch-kritische und positive Studie* (Münster-in-Westphalia, Aschendorff, 1926–55), which by the time of his death had attained twelve volumes. Schmidt deals with the history of theorizing about religion by entering into critical discussion with each view he describes. His chief concern is to vindicate and uphold his own doctrine of "primitive monotheism," which he derived by application of the principles of the *Kultur-kreise* school of anthropology. Schmidt is as vigorous as German scholars are likely to be in presenting the case for his views, but his purposes have also compelled him to sketch in accurate fashion the contrary positions of those whom he opposes. There are also German and French editions of this work.

A second English book that plunges into discussion of the many theories about religion originating with ethnologists and anthropologists is Alexander Goldenweiser's *Early Civilization: An Introduction to Anthropology* (N.Y., Alfred A· Knopf, Inc., 1922). Goldenweiser's approach to the subject is not so broad as that of either Pinard or Schmidt, since he was interested only in the study of primitive peoples and kept his sight focused narrowly upon that area. Within its field Goldenweiser's volume is a useful and scholarly summary of rival views and their relationship to one another. The same field is approached by a different method in *Reader in Comparative Religion*, ed. by William A. Lessa and Evon Z. Vogt (Evanston, Row, Peterson & Co., 1958). The editors of this splendid volume have assembled excerpts from the writings of major figures in the study of religions, selecting passages carefully so that the central emphases of each scholar clearly stand out. Rather than resting content with a second-hand description of trends in the interpretation of primitive religions, the volume makes primary sources available in an easily usable form. It can be strongly recommended for the purposes of the student and the established scholar alike.

This brief appendix may be brought to a close with the mention of two further resources for the person interested in the history of the history of religions. One of them is an article, "The History of Religions in America," by Joseph Kitagawa, included in the collection of essays in methodology entitled *The History of Religions*, ed. by J. Kitagawa and Mircea Eliade (Chicago, University of Chicago Press, 1959). With the exception of the work done by that commanding figure George Foote Moore, American contributions to the history of religions in the early twentieth century were not great. Recently, however, this field of study has come to enjoy a growing popularity, and there are today a number of able people laboring in it. Kitagawa traces some of the history of the field in the United States and offers comments of a methodological nature about the role of the field in American universities. In passing, the reader's attention may be called to the remaining essays of the volume where Kitagawa's article appears. The scholars represented there are the leaders in the field at the present time, and for this reason their views on methodology have unusual interest and importance.

The final resource to be mentioned is the "Bibliographie générale" by H-Ch. Puech appearing in Volume one of the series "Mana," *Introduction a l'histoire des religions*. This volume by Jacques Vandier has the title *La religion égyptienne* (Paris, Presses universitaires de France, 1949). Puech's bibliography contains a section on the history of the history of religions that is especially good for European-language articles on the subject. Moreover, the bibliography as a whole, since it aims at giving a general introduction to the history of religions, is composed precisely of the more important works in the field from its beginnings. A student of the history of the study of religions could not do much better than to take the works listed by Puech as the materials for his inquiry.

II

The Religions of China (excepting Buddhism)

W. A. C. H. Dobson

The study of Chinese religion in any systematic and scholarly sense is in its infancy. Much of what has been written in the past has been from the hands of Christian apologists. It is rarely objective and often ill-informed. I have, in the following pages, suggested readings and sources which the student might find helpful in beginning a study of Chinese religion. Much of the basic source material, however, remains as yet untranslated.

I. INTRODUCTION: RELIGION AND RELIGIONS IN CHINA

What we call "religions" the Chinese call *chiao*, "teachings" or, more precisely, "disciplines." Confronted with proselytizing religions from outside of the Chinese tradition—for example, Buddhism (*Fo-chiao*), Islam (*Hui-hui-chiao*), or Christianity (*Chi-tu-chiao* or *T'ien-chu-chiao*)—the Chinese have apposed, as their own indigenous counterparts, Confucianism (*Ju-chiao*) and

Taoism (*Tao-chiao*).[1] In this sense, therefore, we may speak of Confucianism and Taoism as religions of China.

But to confine inquiry to the religious aspects of Confucianism and Taoism is to ignore many expressions of Chinese religious thought and feeling, whether of a "higher" or of a "lower" kind, which do not specifically relate to either of these two philosophical systems. There are, or have been, religious elements present in many facets of family and social organization, in the cults and practices of economic and other groups, in political theory and action at almost all levels from local to national government. The multiplicity and variety of temples and shrines in every city and village across the land and the presence in countless households of the domestic gods and their altars provide tangible evidence of those elements.[2]

When Buddhism came to China in the beginning of the Christian era, it brought with it the notion of religion as a formally organized institution. Taoism, in a riposte to Buddhism, evolved similar institutions, acquiring, as Buddhism already possessed, a priestly order and a hierarchy, temples and monasteries, and a sacred canon. But Confucianism, too, as the philosophy of a dominant governing class, became institutionalized in official rites and ceremonies and in the Imperial sacrifices and, in aspects such as these, served as part of the apparatus of government. Confucianism became the state cult. But both Confucianism and Taoism in their origins were simply philosophical systems followed by "schools" and individuals and were neither institutionalized nor particularly "religious."

The study of Chinese religion, by Western scholars at least, has been colored in the past by attempts to find parallels in Chinese experience for Western religious history; such as, for example, social or political dominance by a religious doctrine, struggles between Church and State or wars between States in the cause of religion, and theological disputations in which doctrinal boundaries are sharply defined. When closely comparable aspects were not found, the conclusion was rashly drawn that the Chinese were not "religious." Such studies came at a time when Chinese thought was, as it were, joining the mainstream of world thought, with its drift toward secularization. This accounts, in part at least, for the comparative thinness of modern literature in Western languages on Chinese religion written from a systematic and scientific viewpoint.

As a general introduction, C. K. Yang's *Religion in Chinese Society* (Berkeley, University of California Press, 1961) gives an excellent account of indigenous religion as it functions in Chinese society; E. R. and K. Hughes,

1. See, for example, P. A. Cohen, "The Anti-Christian Tradition in China," *Journal of Asian Studies*, XX, 2 (1961), pp. 169–80.

2. The reader might like to compare W. E. Soothill, *The Three Religions of China* (Oxford, H. Milford, 1923)—a Western missionary's view of Chinese religions—with C. K. Yang, *Religion in Chinese Society* (Berkeley, University of California Press, 1961)—a study of Chinese religion as actually encountered in contemporary Chinese society.

Religion in China (London, N.Y., Hutchinson's University Library, 1950) provides a brief history of religions both Chinese and foreign in China; and Y. C. Yang, *China's Religious Heritage* (Nashville, Abingdon-Cokesbury, 1943) is a study of Confucianism, Buddhism, Taoism, and Christianity from a Chinese Christian's viewpoint. For a more detailed bibliography, see under "Religion," chap. 13, T'ung-li Yüan, *China in Western Literature* (New Haven, Yale University Press, 1958).

II. AUGURY AND SACRIFICE, 14TH–7TH CENTURIES B.C.

In the prephilosophic age—the period of augury and sacrifice—the "old religion"—untouched by refinements of certain of its features by the philosophers and unchallenged by religious influence from beyond China—held full sway.

(a) The world of divination (Shang Dynasty, 16th–11th centuries B.C.)

Chinese recorded history begins with the Shang Dynasty. Its records are the Oracle Bones discovered at the end of the nineteenth century and, since then, our principal source for the history of the Shang. The Oracle Bones, of which some hundred thousand have been recovered, are requests engraved on bone and shell made to the spirits for guidance. They are thus essentially religious in nature. The diviner interpreted the response as either "auspicious" or "inauspicious." From our reading of these inscriptions, we gain a picture of a society regulated in almost every aspect of life by divination and governed by considerations of good or bad luck. The "powers" consulted in divination were the spirits of the deceased Kings, the *Ti*; but from requests made about the propriety of making sacrifices and performing rites, we know that, in addition to the spirits of the dead, the spirits of the hills, the streams, and other nature gods were worshipped. So, too, were the ancestors. From traces that still remain in the forms of certain graphs in the Shang writing system, and from the iconography of its ritual vessels, we know that a phallic element was present in such worship. Guidance was not only sought from the ancestors for conduct, but their aid was invoked in ensuring the fertility of man, his crops, and his beasts. Religion in the Shang Dynasty is discussed by H. G. Creel in *The Birth of China* (London, Jonathan Cape, Ltd., 1936). See also B. Karlgren, "Some Ritual Objects of Pre-historic China" in *Museum of Far Eastern Antiquities*, 14 (1942), pp. 65–9.

(b) The ancient religion

Animism (the worship of the nature deities), fertility rites and cults, and particularly ancestor worship not only are features of the earliest recorded

Chinese religious practices, but are recurring elements in a variety of different forms of the "popular religion" of subsequent times.

(c) The Royal religion (Western Chou, 11th–8th centuries B.C.)

The Shang Dynasty was superseded by that of the Chou in 1027 B.C. From this period, there have survived some archival documents and inscriptions on bronze sacrificial vessels which tell us something of the religion of the Chinese Court and its Kings. The Royal religion was concerned with the cult of the Royal ancestors, the "Former Kings." Over these deified Kings, the Supreme Ancestor, *Shang-ti*, "God most High," presided. Kingship was thought to be invested by Heaven. Heaven gave its "charge"—the Mandate of Heaven—to one appointed to be its son. The Son of Heaven (*T'ien-tzŭ*) in turn enfeoffed his vassals with "charges," which were engraved on bronze ritual vessels and used in the worship of ancestors. The priest-king, Heaven's deputy upon earth, served his royal ancestors with sacrifice, engaged in ceremonial ploughing and fishing to ensure the fertility of the earth, and sought to conserve his "virtue" (his *mana*), by means of which human society and the natural world were kept in accord. Since the whole of society, and of the state, was a projection of the extended family, the King was thus priest and paterfamilias of all mankind. His title to Kingship lay in the ritual acceptability of the King to Heaven. If he lost "virtue," he surrendered his "mandate" to govern.

The *Book of Documents*, which includes "charges" of the Kings of Western Chou, has been translated by J. Legge, *The Chinese Classics* (Oxford, 1893, reprinted Hong Kong, Hong Kong University Press, 1960), Vol. 3, *The Classic of History*, but Legge includes a number of spurious chapters. B. Karlgren, *Glosses on the Book of Documents* (Stockholm, Ostasiatiska, 1951), has translated those chapters thought to date from the pre-Han period. The "five charges" of the early Chou Kings are translated in W. A. C. H. Dobson, *Early Archaic Chinese* (Toronto, University of Toronto Press, 1962), where a selection of inscriptions, some of which describe religious ceremonials, are also translated.

(d) The Popular religion (Western Chou, 11th–8th centuries B.C.)

Some of the hymns and invocations used in the Royal worship in Western Chou are preserved in the *Book of Songs*. The *Songs*, too, preserve some folk songs. M. Granet, *Festivals and Songs of Ancient China* (N.Y., E. P. Dutton & Co., 1932), connects these songs with the fertility rites performed in spring and autumn when the country folk gathered, much as they do in parts of southeastern Asia today.

The best translation of the *Book of Songs* is that of A. Waley, *The Book of*

Songs (London, George Allen & Unwin, Ltd., 1937) which also contains useful commentary bearing on religious aspects. See too M. Granet, *Festivals and Songs of Ancient China* (N.Y., E. P. Dutton & Co., 1932).

(e) Aristocratic religion (Eastern Chou, 8th–3rd centuries B.C.)

The Kings of Western Chou gradually declined in power and influence after the shift of the capital in 771 B.C. to the east. With their decline came the rise of the city-states. Originally the feudatories of the Royal House, the city-state rulers gradually asserted their independence and, with growing independence, increasingly arrogated to themselves "kingly privileges." Among them were the priestly functions of the ancient Kings, such as presiding over the "altars of the soil and crops" and maintaining the ancestral cults in the family shrines, which became the symbols of sovereignty in the city-states. Most feudal lords attached their ancestry to the cult heroes of the past. Hou-chi, the Lord of Millet, was the putative ancestor of the Chi clan; Yü the Great, the hero of the primeval Flood, was the putative ancestor of the Szu. Since these heroes were thought of as divinities, aristocratic tenure had religious sanction. The princes of the city-states, through their possession of the local altars and their right to attend to the divinities of fertility, together with their access to the "mana" of the divine ancestors, asserted political domination over their subjects.

Studies which treat religion at this period in some detail are H. Maspero, "La religion chinoise dans son développement historique" in *Les religions chinoises* (Paris, Civilisations du Sud, S.A.E.P., 1950); *La Chine antique* (Paris, Imprimerie nationale, 1955), and M. Granet, *La religion des chinois* (Paris, Gauthier-Villars & Cie., 1922).

(f) Shamanism in the south (Eastern Chou)

The gods of the hills, the rivers, and the stars which figured little in kingly or aristocratic worship in West and North China, assumed in the South, particularly in the powerful city-state of Ch'u, an influential place. The shamans (*wu*) who could draw down these spirits or recall the spirits of the sick and dead by dancing and incantation had a more important role there than in the North. It is likely that, through their exorcism, fortune telling, and services for the sick and dead, the shamans were the witch doctors of the popular religion everywhere, but we know more about the southern shamans, because the *Nine Songs*, a shaman's liturgy, is included in the *Songs of the South* which have survived.

See A. Waley, *The Nine Songs: A Study of Shamanism in Ancient China* (London, George Allen & Unwin, Ltd., 1955), and D. Hawkes, *Ch'u Tz'u; The Songs of the South* (Oxford, UNESCO, 1959).

III. THE AGE OF PHILOSOPHY, 6TH–3RD CENTURIES B.C.

With the ritualists at the Courts of the city-states, and the shamans in the countryside, Chinese religion at the period when Chinese philosophies began to take shape had largely to do with the propitiation of ancestors, the worship of spirits, the insuring of fertility, and with the magic rites attendant upon birth, death, and marriage. It was almost totally concerned with the manipulation of powers, with engaging the sympathy of the powerful dead, with insuring good luck. It had no ethical or moral content.

These elements of primitive religion were incorporated, changed, and elevated by the philosophers into ethical and moral systems. At some time prior to the rise of the philosophers, there arose a sense of moral conscience, a concern with right and wrong, with justice and with humanity. With the passing of the premoral stage, much of primitive religion was transferred into the elements of higher religions.

Philosophy, as distinct from customary lore, began with Confucius (551–479 B.C.). From the sixth century onward, other and rival teachers arose. They were characterized, together with their followers, as the "Hundred Schools." Beginning as teachers to the sons of the city-state aristocracy, these philosophers traveled from Court to Court, attempting to persuade the princes of the virtues of their systems, and seeking preferment in state government. Thus rival systems were evolved, aired, attracted adherents, and, in the process, elevated much in the religious sphere from the "primitive" to a higher order. Of these systems those of the Confucians and of the Taoists have historically been the most influential.

For a general introduction to Chinese Philosophy, Fung Yu-lan, *History of Chinese Philosophy*, tr. by Derk Bodde (Princeton, Princeton University Press, 1952) is standard. E. R. Hughes, *Chinese Philosophy in Classical Times* (London, J. M. Dent & Sons, 1942), is a handy companion to Fung. A very useful selection of readings will be found in W. T. De Bary, ed., *Sources of Chinese Tradition* (N.Y., Columbia University Press, 1960). For further reading, consult Wing-tsit Chan, *An Outline and an Annotated Bibliography of Chinese Philosophy* (New Haven, Far Eastern Publications, Yale University, 1961).

(a) Early Confucianism

Confucius was born in 551 B.C. in the city-state of Lu and died in 479 B.C. He was a tutor to the sons of the aristocracy. He taught the "wisdom of the ancients," taking as his texts the *Book of Documents* and the *Book of Songs*, which describe mainly, though not exclusively, life under Western Chou. This period, and in particular its founder-kings Wen and Wu and the Regent, the

Duke of Chou, provide for Confucius a Golden Age and model Kings. He protested that he had "transmitted what was taught to me without making up anything of my own" (*Analects* 7.1). In reality, by using these documents as "scriptures," and by interpreting their already archaic language in contemporary senses, he created from them the design for a model kingdom. *Te*, the magical force, the *mana* of antiquity, became "virtue" in an ethical and moral sense. *Yi*, a word for custom, became "justice." *Li*, originally simply a "rite," became a code for gentlemanly behavior. *Wang*, a king, became a king in more than name, and the prince (*chün-tzŭ*), the model gentleman of the Confucian ideal. Here kings governed by virtue, exemplified justice and humanity, and gathered their subjects into one large and harmonious family, whose conduct was regulated by *Li*. Confucius withdrew attention from the spirit world, directing it toward man in society. Thus the duty to serve ancestors through sacrifice became a duty to "serve them while they are still living." *Hsiao*, "filial piety," became, not so much the duty to a dead father, but the service to parents during their lifetime. And thus was born the system of familial obligations and duties, the "five relationships," that characterize Confucian teaching. Kingship, then, becomes model parenthood, and the sovereign acts as the "father and mother" of his people. Citizenship is conceived as an extension of familial duty. There is a sense in which the genius of Confucianism was to have converted society from the domination of magic to the supremacy of morals. In the religious sphere the propitiation of ancestors became reverence for ancestors and was extended to reverence for parents, and to a rigid set of obligations among members of the family. Heaven became the God of all mankind, and not simply Shang-ti—the supreme ancestor of a kingly caste.

Mencius (*c.* 360–280 B.C.)—Confucius' next most important successor—lived nearly a century and a half after Confucius. Important developments had occurred in the teaching of the School. For Mencius the world of myth, of founder heroes and of Sages, was secularized. These figures were constructed into a secular "history." Antiquity extended further back in time, and so did Mencius' Golden Age. It was the times of "Yao and Shun." In this more ample Utopia, Confucianism became more secular still. "Any man might become a Yao or a Shun." The Gods and demigods of shaman lore became exemplary human figures who personified the moral ideals of justice and humanity—the key tenets of Confucianism. Mencius was the first Confucian to speculate on man's nature. He said that man is born innately good and that it is only through external pressure, through evil environment, that he becomes bad.

Confucius' teaching is contained in the *Analects*. An excellent translation with an admirable introduction is that of A. Waley, *The Analects of Confucius* (London, Macmillan & Co., Ltd., 1938). A critical biography of Confucius will be found in H. G. Creel, *Confucius, The Man and the Myth* (N.Y., John

Day Co., Inc., 1949), reprinted as a Harper Torchbook under the title *Confucius and the Chinese Way* (N.Y., 1960); see also Shigeki Kaizuka, *Confucius* (London, George Allen & Unwin, Ltd., 1956), tr. by G. Bownas. The works of Mencius are translated by W. A. C. H. Dobson in *Mencius* (Toronto, University of Toronto Press, 1963). Both the *Analects* and Mencius have been translated, together with a Chinese text, by J. Legge in *The Chinese Classics* (*op. cit.*).

(b) Hedonism and Utilitarianism (4th–3rd centuries B.C.)

Mencius says the prevailing philosophies of his time were the teachings of Yang Chu the Hedonist and of Mo Ti the Utilitarian. No Hedonist work has survived, and Yang Chu's philosophy must be recovered from the cautionary references to it of his rivals. *The Garden of Pleasure*, usually ascribed to him, is thought by most scholars to be a later work. Yang Chu's principal tenet, according to Mencius, was *wei ngo*, "I act in my own interests." While Confucianism was concerned with man as a social being, with his interrelationships and duties to society, Yang Chu was concerned with man as an individual. In fourth-century China great social upheavals were taking place. The city-state posed problems of an economic, political, and social kind for which the "old religion" was quite inadequate. In this turmoil was born the Hedonistic philosophy that sought, in an uncertain world, for the preservation of the integrity of the individual person.

Mo Ti (Micius *c.* 486–390 B.C.) lived a little before Mencius. He argued that the sum total of human experience attests to the existence of a Deity with a purpose and a will. That will and purpose are conceived in love and compassion, and Order is the ultimate manifestation of the Divine compassion. Since all men have the ear of Heaven, it follows that all are equal in the eyes of Heaven. Heaven rains upon the just and the unjust. Heaven manifests its love upon all regardless of person. Micius therefore argued that all men should love each other equally and without discrimination. Mencius sums up Micius' teaching in the phrase "Love all equally." To Mo Ti antiquity and its precedents were irrelevant. He sought to create an ideal society by beginning anew in the pure light of reason. He argued on the grounds of *li*, "utility." The criterion of what was right and wrong was the interests of the greatest number.

Neither Hedonism nor Utilitarianism survived the collapse of the city-states and the establishment of the Empire at the end of the third century B.C. But with the eclectic spirit that characterizes Chinese thought, something of their genius has contributed to the making of the Chinese ethos.

For Mo Ti (i.e., Motse, Mo Tzŭ, Micius), see Y. P. Mei, tr., *The Ethical and Political Works of Motse* (London, Arthur Probsthain, 1929) and *Motse, The Neglected Rival of Confucius* (London, Arthur Probsthain, 1934); W. A. C. H. Dobson, "Micius," in Douglas Grant, ed., *The Far East: China and Japan* (Toronto, University of Toronto Press, 1961), pp. 299–310; and

Hu Shih, *The Development of the Logical Method in Ancient China* (Shanghai, Oriental Book Co., 1922). For Yang Chu, see A. Forke, tr., *Yang Chu's Garden of Pleasure* (London, John Murray, Publishers, Ltd., 1912) and the comments thereon in A. C. Graham, *The Book of Lieh-tzŭ* (London, John Murray, Publishers, Ltd., 1960).

(c) Mysticism (Philosophical Taoism, 4th–3rd centuries B.C.)

There is a close parallel between the images of the flight of the soul in trance used by the shamans of the south and the descriptions of the trance state in the Taoists' philosophical classic *Chuang Tzŭ*. The early mystics were concerned with the problem of knowledge. True knowledge, they insisted, is of the transcendental kind, the mystical knowledge known only to the adept in trance. In trance, one sees the universe as a Unity, and indeed becomes identified with the One. Philosophical Taoism might be thought of as the elevation of the shamans' techniques and experiences to the level of metaphysics. To the adept in trance, all is so of itself. And this "so of itselfness" is *Tao*. Man finds his ultimate purpose in according with Tao, in refraining from "interfering" with the course of nature, and by rejecting such man-made artifices as moral systems and laws. The three main texts of Philosophical Taoism are *Chuang Tzŭ*, the *Tao Te Ching*, and *Lieh Tzŭ*.

The best introduction to Philosophical Taoism is contained in the introduction of A. Waley to *The Way and its Power*, a study of the *Tao Te Ching* (London, George Allen & Unwin, Ltd., 1934), and in *Three Ways of Thought in Ancient China* (London, George Allen & Unwin, Ltd., 1939), in which Chuang Tzŭ, Mencius, and the Realists are contrasted. The *Tao Te Ching* has also been translated by J. J. L. Duyvendak, *Tao Te Ching, Lao Tzŭ* (London, John Murray, Publishers, Ltd., 1954). The *Chuang Tzŭ* is translated in H. A. Giles, *Chuang Tzŭ, Mystic, Moralist and Social Reformer* (Shanghai, Kelly & Walsh, Ltd., 1926); seven chapters only, but preferable to Giles', are translated by Yu-lan Fung in *Chuang Tzŭ, A New Selected Translation with an Exposition of the Philosophy of Kuo Hsiang* (Shanghai, Commercial Press, 1931). *Lieh Tzŭ* has been translated by A. C. Graham, *The Book of Lieh-tzŭ* (London, John Murray, Publishers, Ltd., 1960).

(d) Late classical Confucianism (3rd–2nd centuries B.C.)

Hsün Tzŭ (*c.* 298–238 B.C.), who forms with Confucius and Mencius a trinity of classical Confucian philosophers, carries Confucian doctrine further towards naturalism. "Heaven" becomes, for Hsün Tzŭ, "nature." Hsün Tzŭ, in contrast to Mencius, argues that man's nature is evil.

For their influence in medieval Confucianism, the *Classic of Filial Piety* (*Hsiao-ching*), the *Doctrine of the Mean* (*Chung-yung*), and the *Great Learning* (*Ta Hsüeh*)—which postdate Hsün Tzŭ—are important Confucian treatises.

H. H. Dubs, *Hsüntze . . . the Moulder of Ancient Confucianism* (London, Arthur Probsthain, 1927) is a study of Hsün Tzŭ's philosophy, and *The Works of Hsüntze*, by the same author (London, Arthur Probsthain, 1928), is a translation of Hsün Tzŭ's *Works*. The *Doctrine of the Mean* and the *Great Learning* have been translated by E. R. Hughes, *The Great Learning and the Mean-in-Action* (London, J. M. Dent & Sons, Ltd., 1942).

Works on ritual and divination which were incorporated into the Confucian canon and which, because of the commentaries they accrued, are important in later philosophical development are the *Li Chi*, *Chou Li* and *Yi Li*, and the *Yi Ching*. See J. Legge, *The Lî Kî* (i.e., the *Li Chi*; The Book of Rites) in *Sacred Books of the East*, Vols. XXVII and XXVIII (Oxford, 1885); E. Biot, *Le Tcheou-li ou rites des Tcheou* (i.e., the *Chou Li*; Rites of Chou); J. Steele, *The I-Li or Book of Etiquette and Ceremonial*, 2 vols. (London, Arthur Probsthain, 1917); J. Legge, *The Yî King* (i.e., the *Yi Ching* or *Book of Changes*), *Sacred Books of the East*, Vol. XVI (Oxford, 1899).

The *Analects*, *Mencius*, the *Doctrine of the Mean*, and the *Great Learning* form the "Four Books" of medieval Confucianism.

(e) Other late classical philosophies

Confucianism, Taoism, and Mohism, the most important of the classical philosophies, emerge from a wide variety of schools, schisms, and intellectual movements that characterize the Philosophical Age. Collectively, these philosophies were known to later history as the "Hundred Schools." Certain of them are important in a study of Chinese religion.

Because of the contributions of the Logicians and Sophists to epistemology, of the Legalists to law, and of the Yin-Yang School to cosmological speculation, each has relevance to some aspects of religious thought. They are treated in the general histories of Chinese Philosophy mentioned above. More detailed studies will be found in the bibliography of Wing-tsit Chan, *op. cit.* The Legalist classic has been translated by J. J. L. Duyvendak, *The Book of Lord Shang* (London, Arthur Probsthain, 1928).

IV. RELIGION UNDER THE EMPIRE

With the unification of the city-states under the Ch'in Dynasty (221–207 B.C.) and with the Han Empire (202 B.C.–A.D. 220), which succeeded Ch'in, the "Hundred Schools," which had flourished freely and with great individuality in the city-states, were replaced by an official state orthodoxy—Confucianism. After the introduction of Buddhism in the first century A.D., with its temples and religious orders, there also arose an indigenous movement with parallel institutions, claiming to find its inspiration in the writings of Taoist authors. This was Religious Taoism.

(a) Confucianism—the State Cult

Under the Han Empire, Confucianism came under the patronage of the Court, and in the hands of its devotees became the dominant philosophy in education. Through the selective civil service examination system, Confucianism became the philosophy of the bureaucracy. Confucian rituals were observed at Court. It became, as it were, the State Cult and, as such, continued throughout much of Chinese Imperial history. Confucian rituals provided the forms under which the Emperors carried out their sacerdotal duties. This aspect of Confucianism is treated in J. K. Shryock, *The Origin and Development of the State Cult of Confucius* (N.Y., The Century Co., 1932).

Apart from the cultic aspects of Confucianism as it affected Court Ritual, the Imperial Sacrifices, and the like, Confucianism itself was subjected to progressive reinterpretations and reformulations. Under the Han—Confucianism in the hands of its apologists, and under attack from rival philosophies—a Confucianism that was characteristic of the period evolved. After the fall of Han, until the end of T'ang, Confucianism, though orthodox, was, in the hands of scholars, a sort of "classicism." Buddhism and Taoism played the major religious roles. With the Sung Dynasty (A.D. 960–1279) came the Confucian Revival; Neo-Confucianism (a very different philosophy from the classic and Han forms of Confucianism) became dominant and largely replaced Buddhism and Taoism.

(b) Religious Taoism

With the breakdown of national unity and stability at the end of Han, a period of near chaos ensued (*c.* A.D. 220–589). Confucianism as Imperial cult and as the orthodoxy of a highly organized bureaucracy lost much of its hold at this time. In this looser and freer soil, two religions were planted and flourished. The first, Buddhism, introduced from India in the first century A.D., is dealt with elsewhere in this book. The second was Religious Taoism.

Religious Taoism owes its beginnings to attempts in the first century B.C. to syncretize the classical philosophical Taoist teachings of the *Tao Te Ching* and *Chuang Tzŭ*, under the title *Huang-lao* (from Huang "yellow" in Huang-ti, "The Yellow Emperor" and *Lao*, in "Lao Tzŭ," the putative author of the *Tao Te Ching*—its cult heroes). The Huang-lao movement had a large popular following. In the second century A.D., the movement was exploited by one who set himself up as "Heavenly Teacher"—a religious title and office held hereditarily by his descendants. The Taoist "papacy" has continued into recent times. The Taoist "church" developed a canon of scriptures (the *Tao-tsang*), temples, and a priesthood—institutions paralleling those of the Buddhist Church. Religious Taoism at brief periods enjoyed Imperial patronage as the state religion, notably in the fifth and sixth centuries A.D., but after T'ang (A.D. 618–906) it survived largely as the religion of the masses. See H.

Maspero, "Le taoïsme" in his *Mélanges posthumes sur les religions et l'histoire de la Chine* (Paris, Civilisations du Sud, S.A.E.P., 1950); H. S. Levy, "Yellow Turban Religion and Rebellion at the end of Han," *Journal of the American Oriental Society*, LXXVI (1956), pp. 214–27; and H. Maspero, "Les procédés de 'nourrir le principe vital' dans la religion taoïste ancienne," *Journal Asiatique* (1937), pp. 117–430.

(c) Myth and legend

The tendency in classical philosophical writing to reduce the rich and imaginative world of myth and legend to the sober proportions of secular and human history did not extinguish the hold of myth upon the popular imagination. Rather, myth began to proliferate after the classical period, and in Han and subsequent times appeared in literature and in art in its unsecular mythological form. Or perhaps one should say "forms," for the "creation" myth, the myth of the separation of "heaven and earth," the "sun" myths, and the "flood" legend, in the complicated cosmogony of popular myth occur in a variety of forms, converge and diverge and become enriched and elaborated with elements from very disparate sources. One of the problems of scholarship is to sort this rich lore by cycle, period, and locale. The extent to which we should be justified in regarding myth as religious belief is a difficult question. As its elements occur in the iconography of temples and tombs, as its figures become objects of worship in popular cults and practices, we are presumably justified in regarding such myth as the "theology" of popular religion. But as these elements occur in the works of poets, much as the gods of Mount Olympus occur in the severely Christian Milton, or as myths are satirized in fiction (as in Wu Ch'êng-ên's *Monkey* translated by A. Waley [London, George Allen & Unwin, Ltd., 1942]), they perhaps constitute a fantasy world in which the imagination has freer play and provide for the poet and writer a world of symbols divorced from the consequences of belief.

For ancient Chinese myths, W. Eberhard, *Lokalkulturen im alten China* (Leiden, E. J. Brill, 1942) should be compared with B. Karlgren, "Legends and Cults in Ancient China," *Bulletin of the Museum of Far Eastern Antiquities*, 18 (1946), pp. 199–365, and with H. Maspero, "Légendes mythologiques dans le *Chou-king*," *Journal Asiatique* (1924), pp. 1–100. General compendia of Mythology are those of J. C. Ferguson, "Chinese Mythology," in J. A. MacCulloch, ed., *The Mythology of all Races* (Boston, Marshall Jones Co., 1930); E. T. C. Werner, *A Dictionary of Chinese Mythology* (Shanghai, Kelly & Walsh, Ltd., 1932); and H. Maspero, "Mythology of Modern China," in P. L. Couchoud, ed., *Asiatic Mythology* (London, George C. Harrap & Co., Ltd., 1932), pp. 252–384.

The above should, however, be read in conjunction with a recent study, D. Bodde, "Myths of Ancient China," in S. N. Kramer, ed., *Mythologies of the Ancient World* (N.Y., Doubleday & Co., Inc., 1961). See also D. Hawkes,

"The Supernatural in Chinese Poetry" in D. Grant, ed., *The Far East: China and Japan* (Toronto, University of Toronto Press, 1961).

(d) Neo-Taoism (3rd–4th centuries A.D.)

The writings of classical Philosophical Taoism, adopted, adapted, and augmented by the Taoist "church," provided scriptures and a canon for Religious Taoism. But a revival of interest in the classical Taoist writings themselves gave rise in the third and fourth centuries to a new philosophical movement known as Neo-Taoism, which, among other things, attempted a reinterpretation of Confucian texts in Taoist terms and injected into Philosophical Taoism itself certain social and political concepts of Confucianism, alien to its earlier beliefs.

See D. Holzman, *La vie et la pensée de Hi Kang* (Leiden, E. J. Brill, 1957), and the general histories of philosophy.

(e) Neo-Confucianism (11th–12th centuries A.D.)

From the end of Han (A.D. 200) to the beginning of Sung (A.D. 960), Buddhism and Taoism dominated religious and much of Chinese intellectual life. At times Buddhism and Taoism enjoyed Imperial patronage, threatening Confucianism as the state cult. With the rise of Sung, however, Confucianism in a new formulation (Neo-Confucianism), regained its intellectual supremacy. Part of the energies of the Neo-Confucian movement derived from its opposition to Buddhism and its determination to find, in the Confucian classics, a philosophy and faith that would replace Buddhism.

The principal figure in the new movement was Chu Hsi (1130–1200), who succeeded in synthesizing the new orthodoxy from the works of such Confucians as Chou Tun-yi (1017–73); Ch'eng Yi (1033–1107); Ch'eng Hao (1032–85) and Shao Yung (1011–67); Lu Hsiang-shan (1139–92), a contemporary of Chu Hsi, apposed to Chu Hsi's rationalism an idealist wing of Confucianism. This was developed later in Ming times by Wang Yangming (1472–1529). For a synoptic view of Neo-Confucianism, the general histories of Fung Yu-lan, etc., should be consulted, together with Carsun Chang, *The Development of Neo-Confucian Thought* (N.Y., Twayne Publishers, Inc., 1957), and L. V. L. Cady, *The Philosophy of Lu Hsiang-shan*, 2 vols. (N.Y., Union Theological Seminary, 1939), and for selected readings in Neo-Confucianism, chaps. 18–21 of De Bary, ed., *Sources of Chinese Tradition* (N.Y., Columbia University Press, 1960). Particular studies of Neo-Confucians are A. C. Graham, *Two Chinese Philosophers* (Toronto, Clarke, Irwin & Co., Ltd., 1958) (i.e. Ch'eng Yi and Ch'eng Hûo); J. P. Bruce, *Chu Hsi and his Masters* (London, Arthur Probsthain, 1923) and *The Philosophy of Human Nature* (London, Arthur Probsthain, 1922); and Siu-chi Huang, *Lu Hsiang-shan . . . a Twelfth Century Chinese Idealist Philosopher* (Philadelphia, American Oriental Series, Vol. 27, 1944).

The extent to which Confucianism (whether in its classic form or in the progressive reinterpretations and reformulations of Confucianism which occurred in the history of the Empire) influenced the religious attitudes and beliefs of the bureaucracy and the gentry is hard to define. Some studies, very miscellaneous in character (from the point of view of the reader interested in the religious aspects of Confucianism), which *en passant* may throw some light on this aspect are A. F. Wright, ed., *The Confucian Persuasion* (Stanford, Stanford University Press, 1960); D. S. Nivison and A. F. Wright, eds., *Confucianism in Action* (Stanford, Stanford University Press, 1959); A. F. Wright, ed., *Studies in Chinese Thought* (Chicago, University of Chicago Press, 1953); J. K. Fairbank, ed., *Chinese Thought and Institutions* (Chicago, University of Chicago Press, 1957); and A. F. Wright and D. Twitchett, eds., *Confucian Personalities* (Stanford, Stanford University Press, 1962). A study of state Confucianism in its twilight is J. R. Levenson, *Confucian China and Modern Fate* (Berkeley, University of California Press, 1958).

(f) Religion in recent times

An emphasis on Confucianism and Taoism, in their more philosophical formulations and as they have influenced the educated official classes, has resulted in virtual neglect of studies of the influence of Confucianism and Taoism on popular religious movements and of the popular religions themselves. "Popular Religions and Secret Societies," chap. XXII of De Bary, ed., *Sources of Chinese Tradition* (N.Y., Columbia University Press, 1960), treats this briefly. See also J. S. Burgess, *The Guilds of Peking* (N.Y., Columbia University Press, 1928); W. Eberhard, *Chinese Festivals* (N.Y., Henry Schuman, Inc., 1952); C. K. Yang, *Religion in Chinese Society* (Berkeley, University of California Press, 1961); Wing-tsit Chan, *Religious Trends in Modern China* (N.Y., Columbia University Press, 1953). Popular religion in contemporary times is referred to in Hsiao-t'ung Fei, *Peasant Life in China* (London, George Routledge & Sons, Ltd., 1939); S. D. Gamble, *Ting Hsien; A North China Rural Community* (N.Y., Institute of Pacific Relations, Inc., 1954); and F. L. K. Hsu, *Under the Ancestor's Shadow* (N.Y., Columbia University Press, 1948). In Sung times, popular religious beliefs are described in J. Gernet, tr. by H. M. Wright, *Daily Life in China, on the Eve of the Mongol Invasion, 1250–1276* (London, George Allen & Unwin, Ltd., 1962).

III

Hinduism

Norvin J. Hein

WORKS ON THE ENTIRE RELIGIOUS TRADITION

There is much to be said for beginning one's reading in Hinduism with a clear confessional presentation. Since many Hindu writers know well the idiom and feeling of the Western world, excellent books are available for such use. D. S. Sarma, *What is Hinduism?* 3rd rev. ed. (Mylapore, Madras, Madras Law Journal Press, 1945)[1] is a simple outline of the teachings and ideals of a liberal nonsectarian Hinduism which follows the monistic Vedānta[2] of Śaṅkara as interpreted by a line of modern English-educated teachers from

1. Users of this bibliography will be reminded often of the importance in the study of Hinduism of Indian books published in English. More than any other major Oriental religion, Hinduism employs English publications in its own internal communications. The local addresses of the Indian publishers mentioned hereafter can usually be learned from the *Cumulative Book Index*, from the current issue of *Indian Book Trade and Library Directory* (New Delhi, New Book Society of India), or from the "List of Publishers" which is appended to each issue of B. S. Kesavan, ed., *The Indian National Bibliography* (Calcutta, Central Reference Library, Ministry of Scientific Research and Cultural Affairs).

2. Full diacritical marks will be used only at the first occurrence in this chapter of an Indic name or term. The titles of books and the names of their authors will always be reproduced, however, with such markings as may be used on the title pages.

Vivekānanda to Rādhākṛishṇan. Satischandra Chatterjee, *The Fundamentals of Hinduism* (Calcutta, Das Gupta & Co., 1950) is a fine introductory survey of Hindu doctrinal teaching; it assumes the supremacy of Advaita Vedanta but gives due attention to the positions of other schools. The same can be said of T. M. P. Mahadevan, *Outlines of Hinduism* (Bombay, Chetana, 1956), which deals not only with doctrine but also with the scriptures, rituals, cults, and personalities of traditional Hinduism. Kenneth Morgan has edited a useful symposium, *The Religion of the Hindus* (N.Y., Ronald Press, 1953), in which the major aspects of Hindu belief and practice are explained by Hindu scholars of outstanding authority. The last chapter, an anthology of Hindu scriptures, is valuable as an indication of what is esteemed and actually used today. Produced by radical selection and radical elision, the compilation is not intended to represent the historical peculiarities of the ages and documents from which its materials are drawn.

Introductions to Hinduism written by Occidentals can and should be consulted for their characteristic attention to chronological history, for their interest in the interconnections between religion and society, and for their detached descriptions of external social fact. Sir M. Monier-Williams' *Brahmanism and Hinduism*, 4th ed. (London, J. Murray, Ltd., 1891), though it is old, remains an inclusive well-informed guide to the panorama of traditional Hinduism. Despite serious defects, Frederick Harold Smith's *Outline of Hinduism* (London, Epworth Press, 1934) is useful to the beginner in identifying typologically and chronologically the chief literatures and forms of Hinduism. Those who read French have at their disposal two up-to-date manuals of exceptional quality. Jean Herbert, *Spiritualité Hindoue* (Paris, Éditions Albin Michel, 1947) explains with great sympathy the concepts and social life of modern Hinduism. Louis Renou, *L'Hindouisme* (Paris, Presses universitaires de France, 1951) is noteworthy for its scholarly judgments regarding the historical development of the religion. Professor Renou's interpretations are available in English for more advanced students in his *Religions of Ancient India* (London, Athlone Press, N.Y., Oxford University Press, 1953), and, in sketchy form, in the introduction to his anthology *Hinduism* (N.Y., George Braziller, Inc., 1961). The body of the last-mentioned work consists of brief selections from translated Hindu religious literature of every age.

COLLECTIONS OF HINDU RELIGIOUS LITERATURE IN TRANSLATION

The most recent anthology is Renou's *Hinduism*, mentioned above. A somewhat comparable volume is *Hindu Scriptures*, ed. by Nicol Macnicol (London, Everyman's Library No. 944, 1938). Macnicol's anthology concentrates on the Ṛigveda, Upanishads, and Bhagavadgītā, omitting the more recent periods in literature; its use of translations which are not the newest and best is a common and almost necessary defect of published anthologies. *Source Book in Indian Philosophy*, ed. by S. Radhakrishnan and Charles A. Moore (Princeton, Princeton University Press, 1957), stresses the materials of the orthodox philosophical systems, but it can be used in the study of Hindu religion as well; it uses better translations from the Vedas and Upanishads than does Macnicol. Dr. Radhakrishnan's interpretive work is influenced here as everywhere by his sense of responsibility for providing modern Hindus with constructive guidance from ancient tradition. William Theodòre de Bary et al., *Sources of Indian Tradition* (N.Y., Columbia University Press, 1958) includes striking selections from Hindu scriptures with excellent introductions, but it is a compilation in support of general survey courses in Indian civilization rather than Indian religion. Its selections from Hindu religious literature are too few, too fragmentary, and too rigidly structured to satisfy the needs of a major study of Hinduism.

There have been two great continuing efforts to make available in English the outstanding Hindu scriptures as complete documents: the *Sacred Books of the East*, ed. by F. Max Müller (50 vols., Oxford, Clarendon Press, 1879–1910), and *The Sacred Books of the Hindus* (32 vols.. Allahabad, The Panini Office, 1909–37). In *S.B.E.* and *S.B.H.* together, about thirty extensive religious works have been translated and published. Many of these will be mentioned in the pages which follow.

GENERAL REFERENCE WORKS

For general reference on all aspects of Hindu thought and practice the *Encyclopaedia of Religion and Ethics*, ed. by James Hastings (N.Y., Charles Scribner's Sons, 1908–27; reprinted 1955), has not been replaced. James N. Farquhar's now old *Outline of the Religious Literature of India* (London, Oxford University Press, 1920) remains an indispensable guide to authors and documents and can be used still as a provisional encyclopedia of Hinduism. John Dowson's old *A Classical Dictionary of Hindu Mythology and Religion, Geography, History, and Literature* (London, Kegan Paul, Trench, Trubner & Co., 1878; 6th ed. 1928) continues to be useful. To locate Hindu scriptures relating to a particular concept, one may use Moriz Winternitz, *A Concise Dictionary of Eastern Religion* (Oxford, Clarendon Press, 1925), an index to the many volumes of *S.B.E.* Murray B. Emeneau, *A Union List of Printed Indic Texts* (New Haven, American Oriental Society, 1935) can be used in locating translations as well as texts in American libraries. The volumes of *The Cultural Heritage of India*, 2nd rev. ed., ed. by Haridas Bhattacharya (Calcutta, Ramakrishna Mission Institute of Culture, 1953ff.), promise to become, when completed, a comprehensive and generally reliable guide to the manifold aspects of Hinduism. Bibliographies will be discussed at the conclusion of this chapter.

THE RELIGION OF THE HARAPPĀ CULTURE

It has become apparent in the last forty years that a satisfactory account of the origins of Hinduism, when it becomes possible to write it, will give major attention to the institutions and ideas of the inhabitants of the Indus Valley in the third and early second millennia B.C. Sir Mortimer Wheeler, *The Indus Civilization* (The Cambridge History of India, Supplementary Volume, 1953) and Ernest Mackay, *Early Indus Civilizations*, 2nd rev. ed. (London, Luzac & Co., Ltd., 1948) sketch this culture with some attention to evidences of its religion. These small books perform a service of convenience in summarizing the massive original archeological reports: Sir John Marshall, ed., *Mohenjo-Daro and the Indus Civilization*, 3 vols. (London, Arthur Probsthain, 1931), the official account of excavations of 1922–27; Ernest J. H. Mackay, *Further Excavations at Mohenjo-daro*, 2 vols. (Delhi, Government of India, 1938), on the field work of 1927–31; Madho Sarup Vats, *Excavations at Harappā*, 2 vols. (Delhi, Government of India, 1940), on work of the years 1920–21 and 1933–34; and Ernest J. H. Mackay, *Excavations at Chanhu-daro* (New Haven, American Oriental Society, 1943). The small subsequent advances in knowledge are reported in Stuart Piggott, *Prehistoric India to 1000 B.C.* (Harmondsworth, Penguin Books, 1952), and in Sir Mortimer Wheeler's chapter, "Ancient India," in Stuart Piggott, ed., *The Dawn of Civilization* (N.Y., McGraw-Hill Book Co., 1961). Speculative work in the interpretation of Harappa religion has been continuous and intense, as the bibliographies of Renou and Dandekar will show. There is adequate reason for believing that the revering of animals, trees, and water, the worship of female deities, and the cult of Śiva derive from this civilization. Even more important aspects of Hindu thought and practice which cannot be revealed by artifacts, no doubt stem from this source also. But until the writing of the culture is deciphered and its seals interpreted in the light of their inscriptions, it will not be possible to say much with certainty that has not already been said by Sir John Marshall (*op. cit.*, I, pp. 48–78) in his chapter "Religion."

VEDIC RELIGION

Since the religion of the Indus Valley people remains largely unknown, substantial historical study of Hinduism must begin with their successors, the Āryas, and their earliest literature, the Vedas and Brāhmaṇas.

Ignorance of French and German is a more serious handicap in approaching the Vedas than at any other point in the study of Hinduism. A century of intensive Vedic study has been conducted in the West in the form of a trilingual interchange, and the student who lacks even one of these languages must often use materials which are less than the best. Existing English translations of the Rigveda, for instance, fall seriously short of the best scholarly insight now available. For instructional purposes A. A. Macdonell's annotated anthology, *Hymns from the Rigveda* (London, Association Press, 1922) is useful. The highly specialized selection translated in *S.B.E.*, XXXII and XLVI, is now antiquated. The only complete translation in English, Ralph T. H. Griffith, *The Hymns of the Rigveda*, 2 vols. (Banaras, E. J. Lazarus & Co., 1920–36) is unsatisfactory both because of its age and because it rests onesidedly on the interpretation of the medieval Hindu commentator Sāyanna. Those working seriously in the Rigveda must use the German translations of Karl Geldner, *Der Rigveda* (Harvard Oriental Series, Vols. XXXIIII–XXXVI, 1951–57) and Alfred Ludwig, *Der Rigveda*, 6 vols. (Prague, F. Tempsky, 1876–88). The shortcomings of Griffith's *Rigveda* pertain also to his *The Hymns of the Samaveda* (Banaras, E. J. Lazarus & Co., 1893), *The Texts of the White Yajurveda* (Banaras, E. J. Lazarus & Co., 1899), and *The Hymns of the Atharvaveda*, 2 vols. (Banaras, E. J. Lazarus & Co., 1895–96). Arthur Berriedale Keith has translated *The Veda of the Black Yajus School Entitled the Taittiriya Sanhita* (Harvard Oriental Series, Vols. XVIII and XIX, 1914). the Atharvaveda has been partially translated by Maurice Bloomfield in *Hymns of the Atharva-Veda* (*S.B.E.*, XLII, 1897) and more fully by William Dwight Whitney, with extreme literalness and extensive critical notes, in *Atharvaveda Samhitā*, ed. by C. R. Lanman (Harvard Oriental Series, Vols. VII and VIII, 1905). Maurice Bloomfield followed his translation with a secondary study, *The Atharva-veda and the Gopatha-brahmaṇa* (Strassburg, Grundriss der indo-arischen Philologie und Altertumskunde, II, 1, B, 1899).

Three important brahmanas have so far been translated into English: the Aitareya and Kaushītaki by A. B. Keith in *Rigveda Brahmanas* (Harvard Oriental Series, Vol. XXV, 1920); the Pañcaviṃśa Brāhmaṇa of the Sāma Veda (also called the Tāṇḍya Mahā-Brāhmaṇa) by W. Caland, *Pañcaviṃśa-brāhmaṇa* (Calcutta, Bibliotheca Indica, Vol. CCLV, 1931); and the Śatapatha-Brāhmaṇa of the White Yajurveda by Julius Eggeling, *The Śatapatha-Brāhmaṇa* (*S.B.E.*, XII, XXVI, XLI, XLIII, and XLIV, 1882–1900).

The most useful books in English for the interpretation of Vedic religion are Maurice Bloomfield's *The Religion of the Veda* (N.Y., G. P. Putnam's Sons, 1908) and Arthur Berriedale Keith's *The Religion and Philosophy of the Veda and Upanishads* (Harvard Oriental Series, Vols. XXXI–XXXII, 1925). Bloomfield's book is a clear judicious personal exposition, easily assimilable by beginners. Keith's larger work is valuable for its comprehensive coverage and its thorough survey and conservative criticism of earlier views.

Scholarly debates concerning Vedic religion have been particularly keen regarding two fundamental questions. The first, a methodological matter, has been the question of whether to regard the Vedas primarily as the religious literature of an Indo-European people only recently settled in India and to give priority to comparative philology and comparative mythology in interpreting them or whether to look on the Vedas as Indian scriptures and interpret them in terms of later Indian culture and with the help of Indian commentators. The tendency of the present century has been to rely more heavily on the latter approach.

The second great issue, a substantive one, has been the question of the extent to which the deities, myths, and rituals of the Vedas should be viewed as part of an attempt to conceptualize and establish relations with the conspicuous forces of nature. Professor F. Max Müller of Oxford initiated the hundred years' debate a century ago by setting forth the theory of nature worship in extreme form. It should be realized that Bloomfield, Keith, and Macdonell stand in this naturistic tradition, adhering to it in a chastened and disciplined version. The reaction against overuse of the naturistic key has been carried on by Adolph Bergaigne, Hermann Oldenberg, Alfred Hillebrandt, Georges Dumezil, and others. The myths of the Vedas have been seen as originating in efforts to explain and reinforce established rituals; as records of the struggles of ethnic groups or of human heroes raised euhemeristically to the rank of gods; as representations of the interaction of personified abstractions of good and evil or light and darkness; as reflections of the functions and interests of the divisions of a tripartite Indo-European class structure; as symbolic expressions of monistic metaphysical teaching; and as part of a priestly white magic based upon the perception of esoteric correspondences between elements of the ritual and the cosmos. Not much of this debate has been conducted in English. Fine surveys of it are available in Renou's *Religion of Ancient India* (*op. cit.*) and in R. N. Dandekar's initial chapter in *Progress of Indic Studies 1917–1942* edited by himself (Poona, Bhandarkar Oriental Research Institute, 1942). Renou's terse manual *Vedic India* (Calcutta, Susil Gupta, 1957), tr. by Philip Spratt from *L'Inde classique* (Paris, Payot, 1947), I, pp. 270–380, gives the succinct judgments of a great authority of our time on these difficult questions.

For general reference on Vedic myths and beliefs one may use A. A. Macdonell's *Vedic Mythology* (Strassburg, Grundriss der indo-arischen Philologie und Altertumskunde, III, 1, A, 1897), supplemented if possible with Alfred Hillebrandt's *Vedische Mythologie*, 2nd rev. ed. (Breslau, M. & H. Marcus, 1927–29). Macdonell and Keith's *Vedic Index of Names and Subjects*, 2 vols. (London, J. Murray, Ltd., 1912), excludes specifically religious matter but is helpful in investigations on the social and literary boundaries of Vedic religion; non-Sanskritists can locate relevant material through the indices at the end of the second volume.

With the end of the age of the Vedas and Brahmanas, we enter, in about the sixth century B.C., into the age of classical Hinduism. The essentials of this great religious culture have persisted down to the present century. During this immense sweep of time, hereditary caste occupation has given Hindu society a distinctive form. At the beginning of this period the doctrines of karma and rebirth became key concepts in the Hindu view of life, and the old Vedic conceptions of the highest blessedness became subordinated to the hope of release from rebirth. In the first centuries of this age the goals and techniques of religious activity became so profuse and so varied that a unilinear chronological account will no longer describe the developments in Hinduism adequately. Hindu tradition itself divides orthodox Hindu religious life into three streams: the Way of Action (*karma-mārga*), the Way of Mystical Knowledge (*jñāna-mārga*), and the Way of Devotion (*bhakti-mārga*). These divisions will be accepted here as a primary basis for classifying and describing the literature produced between the end of the Vedic period and the beginning of modern times.

I. THE KARMA-MARGA

The Way of Action will be dealt with first, because it is the direct continuation of the central Vedic type of religious practice, and because the ritual and moral pattern of living which it prescribes has always held a position of chronological priority in the career of all Hindus. A Hindu may resort in mature years to the path of knowledge or of devotion, but he begins the religious life as a performer of acts required by Hindu tradition. Conformity to the *karma-mārga* is an essential preparation for entry into the finally effective paths of liberation.

The Way of Action is a functional type only. The actions which it has required and sanctified have always included some element of the moral as well as the ritual, but the emphasis on moral action has varied greatly, and the rituals practiced have been diverse.

(a) The Śrauta rites

In the immediately post-Vedic age the first form of religious observance to come to prominence in literature was the Vedas' continuing cult of public sacrifice, the basic manuals of which are the Śrauta Sūtras. Of these, only the Śāṅkhāyaṇa Śrautasūtra has been translated into English—by W. Caland, *Śāṅkhāyaṇa-Śrautasūtra* (Nagpur, International Academy of Indian Culture, Saravati-Vihara Series XXXII, 1953). An impression of the nature of these elaborate rituals can be obtained from the general descriptions in Pandurang Vaman Kane's *History of Dharmaśāstra*, 5 vols. (Poona, Bhandarkar Oriental Research Institute, Government Oriental Series, Class B, No. 6, 1930–62), II, 2, pp. 976–1008; in Keith's *Religion and Philosophy of the Veda* (*op. cit.*), Part III; and in Alfred Hillebrandt's *Ritual-Literatur* (Strassburg, Grundiss der indo-arischen Philologie und Altertumskunde, III, 2, 1897), pp. 97–166.

The refining of rules and propounding of theory regarding these ancient sacrifices was continued by specialists belonging to the tradition called Karma-mīmāṃsā. Keith's *The Karma-Mīmāmsā* (Calcutta, Association Press, 1921) gives a general introduction to the history and outlook of this school. Direct reading in the Karma-mimamsa can begin advantageously with Laugākshi Bhaskara's *Arthasaṁgraha* (Banaras, Benares Sanskrit Series No. 4, 1882), tr. by G. Thibaut with an excellent introductory sketch of the essentials of the system. Āpadeva's *Mīmāṃsā-nyāya-prakāśa*, a similar work, has been translated by Franklin Edgerton (New Haven, Yale University Press, 1929). Both these manuals are of relatively recent date and show a willingness to adjust the theory of sacrifice to the outlook of the powerful contemporary theistic movement. The fundamental ancient authority of the school, the Pūrva-mīmāṃsā-sūtra, is translated by Mohan Lal Sandal, *The Mīmāmsā Sūtrās of Jaimini* (Allahabad, *S.B.H.*, XXVII–XXVIII, 1923–25); a commentary is available in Gangānātha Jhā's translation of *Śabarabhāṣya* in Gaekwad's Oriental Series, Vols. LXVI, LXX, LXXIII, CIII (Baroda, Oriental Institute, 1933–45). Jhā has translated also the *Ślokavārttika* and *Tantravārttika* of Kumārila Bhaṭṭa, an authoritative and voluminous writer on the school's epistemology and exegetical principles (Calcutta, Bibliotheca Indica, CXLVI, 1907, and CLXI, 1924).

(b) The Gṛihya rites

The traditional domestic (grihya) rituals of Hinduism were the second type of religious action to become the subject of authoritative books. These are the observances which mark the round of life in the Hindu home and solemnize the great transitions in the careers of individual members of the family. The original manuals of such rites are the Grihya Sutras, seven of the most important of which have been translated by Hermann Oldenberg, *The Grihya-sûtras* (*S.B.E.*, XXIX–XXX, 1886, 1892). W. Caland has since translated the *Jaiminigṛhyasūtra* (Lahore, Punjab Sanskrit Book Depot, 1922) and the *Vaikhánasasmārtasūtram* (Calcutta, Bibliotheca Indica, CCLI, 1929). Raj Bali Pandey in *Hindu Saṁskāras* (Banaras, Vikrama Publications, 1949) collates the ancient sources on each of the personal rituals and surveys the historical development of each. Many of these ancient family rites have fallen into disuse, and those which survive have often been mediated and modified by rehandling in dharma-śāstras, purāṇas, and tantras. The best full treatment of the domestic ceremonies as now practiced is Mrs. Sinclair Stevenson's description of the sacraments and seasonal rites of the Brahmans of Gujarāt in *The Rites of the Twice-born* (London, Oxford University Press, 1920). J. E. Padfield in his delightful *The Hindu at Home*, 2nd rev. ed. (Madras, Society for Promoting Christian Knowledge, 1908), gives a comparable account of the family rituals of Andhra. Representative liturgies for use in the individual's morning and noon *sandhyās* are given in detail in Srisa Chandra (Vasu) Vidyarnava, *The Daily Practice of the Hindus* (Allahabad, *S.B.H.*, XX, 1918). The personal rituals of members of the sect of Rāmānuja are described in detail in K. Rangachari, *The Sri Vaishnava Brahmans* (Madras, Bulletin of the Madras Government Museum, new series, general section, Vol. II, 1, 1931), pp. 44–98. Sivaprasad Bhattacharyya has written a general survey of Hindu ritual in his contribution to Morgan's *Religion of the Hindus*.

(c) Pūjā

By the turn of the Christian era, the Śrauta ceremonies had lost their dominant place in Hindu approach to the gods. The newer practice was a simpler form of ritual called "puja," involving the worship of images erected in domestic shrines or public temples. For a general account of this development see Kane's *History of Dharmaśāstra* (*op. cit.*), II, 2, pp. 705–40, 889–916. The rules for making and worshipping images were slow to appear in Sanskrit literature and have always found a significant part of their expression in obscure sectarian treatises and vernacular manuals. The most accessible sources are the iconographical and liturgical sections of the puranas, such as Agni Purana chapters 21–104 (*Agni Puranam*, tr. M. N. Dutt [Calcutta, M. N. Dutt, 1903], I, pp. 91–423) and Matsya Purana chapters 218–76 (*Matsya-Puranam*, tr. by "a Taluqdar of Oudh," [Allahabad, *S.B.H.*, XVII, 2, 1916], pp. 302–31). The *Paramasaṃhitā*, ed. and tr. by S. Krishnaswami Aiyangar (Gaekwad's Oriental Series, Vol. LXXXVI, Baroda, Oriental Institute, 1940), pp. 20–45, 114–50, gives instructions particularly for the representation and worship of Vishṇu. The Vishṇudharmottara Purana as translated by Stella Kramrisch, *The Vishṇudharmottara* (*Part III*), 2nd rev. ed. (University of Calcutta, 1938), is an inclusive manual on the images of the Hindu deities. The standard modern reference book for the identification of images is still T. A. Gopinatha Rau, *Elements of Hindu Iconography*, 2 vols. (Madras, Law Printing House, 1914–16). The history of Hindu image worship is dealt with best by Jitendra Nath Banerjea in *The Development of Hindu Iconography* (University of Calcutta, 1956).

The Hindu temple, in which Hindu religious sculpture and liturgy find their grandest expression, has so far been studied mainly by persons interested in architectural technique or general aesthetics. Frederic H. Gravely, *An Outline of Hindu Temple Architecture* (Madras, Bulletin of the Madras Government Museum, new series, general section, Vol. III, 2, 1936) gives a simple analysis of the fundamental architectural elements in temples and distinguishes their regional forms. No one has yet made a full study of the temple as a house of worship. Stella Kramrisch in *The Hindu Temple*, 2 vols. (University of Calcutta, 1946), begins this work by analyzing the symbolism of the temple as understood by Hindu writers on architecture. A. K. Coomaraswamy sets forth the view of one kind of worshipper in "The Indian Temple," *Śilpi*, II, 3 (Oct., 1941), pp. 83–90, and current theories regarding the religious meaning of temple architecture are reviewed by G. E. Monod-Herzen in "Evolution and Significance of the Hindu Temple," *Asia*, III (1953–54), pp. 246–59. Detailed descriptions of the ceremonies performed in temples are scarce. James Burgess in "The Ritual of Rameçvaram," *Indian Antiquary*, XII (1883), pp. 315–26, describes the acts and words used in the six daily pujas of a great Śaiva temple. Some information on these activities is found in Mrs. Stevenson's *Rites of the Twice-born* (*op. cit.*) and Rangachari's *Sri Vaishnava Brahmans* (*op. cit.*). Carl Gustav Diehl's *Instrument and Purpose* (Lund, C. W. K. Gleerup, 1956) is an encyclopedic compendium and analysis of Tamil rituals, including the routine and special rites of South Indian temples.

(d) Non-Brahmanical rites

Yet another level of ritual is found in rural Indian life and is commonly described in works on "popular" or "village" Hinduism. Its ceremonies are animistic in their presuppositions, subliterary in their liturgies, and non-Brahman in their priesthood. Their ends are neither liberation nor the creation of merit, but the practical purposes of aversive magic. It can be denied, therefore, that these rites are part of Hinduism, or even of religion, but since they are indigenous to the country and are usually considered religious, we shall look at the literature. For South India, where these practices were formerly especially pervasive of society, we have Henry Whitehead, *The Village Gods of South India* (London, 1916; Calcutta, Association Press, 1921) and Wilber T. Elmore, *Dravidian Gods in Modern Hinduism* (University Studies of the University of Nebraska, XV, No. 1, 1915). James Hornell surveys the subject in "The Ancient Village Gods of South India," *Antiquity*, XVIII (1944), pp. 78–88. L. S. S. O'Malley's *Popular Hinduism* (Cambridge University Press, 1935) includes North India in its scope. Contemporary anthropologists and sociologists have brought this stratum of religion to the fore again in their current village studies. Oscar Lewis, *Village Life in North India* (Urbana, University of Illinois Press, 1958), describes the festivals and religious beliefs of a village near Delhi. For a survey and criticism of current anthropological literature in this area, see Louis Dumont and D. Pocock, *Contributions to Indian Sociology*, No. III, *Religion* (Paris and the Hague, Mouton & Co., 1959).

(e) Social ethics in the dharma tradition

Behavior conforming to established ethical norms was recognized in every period of the history of Hinduism as having some degree of significance for religion. But the ritualistic religion of the Vedas and Brahmanas gave social morality a position far from the center of religious life. In the period of the kalpasutras this ritualistic imbalance in religious literature was rectified by the appearance of the dharmasutras—treatises on religious duties inclusive of ethical obligations. Of these dharmasutras, four are translated by Georg Bühler in *The Sacred Laws of the Âryas* (*S.B.E.*, II, XIV, 1879–82). Later expansions and modifications of these sutras, called dharmaśāstras, became the lasting authorities in Hindu ethics. The most famous and influential is the *Mānavadharmaśāstra*, tr. by Bühler as *The Laws of Manu* (*S.B.E.*, XXV, 1886). The names and contents of the many other works on dharma may be obtained through Kane's monumental *History of Dharmaśāstra* (*op. cit.*)

The dharmaśastras distinguish between sādhārana-dharma—norms applicable to all regardless of age and status—and varṇāśrama-dharma—prescriptions which are to be followed by persons of particular social rank (*varṇa*) and stage of life (*āśrama*). The duties of the first class, which are common to all Hindus, are described in passages which urge such ideal virtues as noninjury, truthfulness, nonstealing, purity, and forbearance. These general ideals receive only brief treatment in the ancient dharma literature. In the modern period, however, it is these abstract ideals which are being emphasized and developed, because their relevance is not limited, as in the case of most Hindu ethical writing, to a social structure which is now passing away. Some idea of the nonlegalistic ethical material which can be culled from Hindu literature may be seen in G. A. Chandavarkar, *A Manual of Hindu Ethics*, 3rd rev. ed. (Poona, Oriental Book Agency, 1925).

The duties of the aśramas—of student, householder, forest dweller, and hermit—are set forth in considerable detail in all the dharmasutras and dharmaśastras. The pattern of the four aśramas is highly theoretical; in practice only a minority of Hindus have attempted to conform to them even roughly. The fourth or *sannyāsāśrama* lies beyond the limits of the Way of Action and will be discussed under *jnana-marga*, below.

Hindu regulations regarding the varnas and their subdivisions, the *jāti's*, are highly developed both in the dharma literature and in the common law of the typical rural Hindu community. To understand the ethical discipline which has shaped the lives of almost all Hindus for 2500 years, one must study not only the prescriptions of Manu and the like on the duties and privileges of the varnas, but also the modern sociological literature on caste and intergroup relations in village life. G. S. Ghurye, *Caste and Class in India*, 2nd ed. (Bombay, Popular Book Depot, 1957), gives a responsible history of the institution of caste and a clear general description of its characteristics. For a sketch of the castes of a fairly representative modern village, with their duties and dignities, see Morris Opler and Rudra D. Singh, "The Division of Labor in an Indian Village," in Carleton S. Coon, ed., *A Reader in General Anthropology* (N.Y., Henry Holt & Co., Inc., 1948), pp. 464–96. William H.

Wiser, *The Hindu Jajmani System* (Lucknow, Lucknow Publishing House, 1936), pioneered in showing the economic and social interactions of village castes and in revealing the meaning of caste rank in terms of dignity and specific economic benefits. Subsequent studies have shown that the great power of the Brahmans in the village described by Wiser is not always matched elsewhere. Kshatriyas, or even lower castes, where they own land or predominate in numbers, sometimes reduce the Brahmans to a merely formal pre-eminence. But everywhere a hierarchical structure of wealth and honor prevails, such as Wiser found. Social studies still throw light upon the discussions of caste in the dharmaśastra, and vice versa. They support each other in revealing the outlines of the strongly ranked society which was the lasting background of traditional Hindu thought. The complementary relation between Hindu doctrine and the discriminations of this society cries out for an attention which it has not received. So far we have only a suggestive work by William Stephens Taylor, "Basic Personality in Orthodox Hindu Culture Patterns," *Journal of Abnormal and Social Psychology*, XLIII (1948), pp. 3–12, where some of the rudiments of this supportive relation between caste and dogma are identified.

Modern Hindu interpretation of caste ranges from total apologetic in Harendranath Maitra's *Hinduism: The World-Ideal* (N.Y., Dodd, Mead & Co., Inc., 1916), pp. 56–73, through Dr. Radhakrishnan's more moderate idealization in *The Hindu View of Life* (London, George Allen & Unwin, Ltd., 1927), pp. 61–130, to vehement rejection in K. M. Panikkar's *Caste and Democracy* (London, Hogarth Press, Ltd., 1933) and in B. R. Ambedkar's *Annihilation of Caste* (Bombay, B. R. Kadrekar, 1937). For an estimate of the continuing hold of caste loyalty among Hindus, see M. N. Srinivas, "Caste in Modern India," *Journal of Asian Studies*, XVI (1956–57), pp. 529–48.

II. THE WAY OF KNOWLEDGE

In the history of Hinduism the *jnana-marga*, or way of mystical knowledge, with its distinctive ends and methods, becomes explicit with the appearance of the upanishads. The cause of the rise of this nonritualistic type of religion has been found in a kshatriya revolt against Brahman religious leadership, but this analysis has not stood the test of time. Other interpreters of the relation between Vedas and upanishads have assumed an evolutionary process in which ritualistic religion gives way automatically to religion of internal experience, or in which scattered cosmological speculation matures necessarily into systematic philosophical interpretations of the universe. Franklin Edgerton foregoes these assumptions to describe from the early texts certain changes in technique which begin in the Vedic hymns and come to a revolutionary completion in the upanishads.

His writings include "The Philosophic Materials of the Atharva Veda" in *Studies in Honor of Maurice Bloomfield* (New Haven, Yale University Press, 1920), pp. 117–37; "The Upaniṣads: What Do They Seek, and Why?" *Journal of the American Oriental Society*, XLIX (1929), pp. 97–121; and a forthcoming volume of translations with interpretation, *The Beginnings of Indian Philosophy*.

Of the English translations of the upanishads, the most reliable from the point of view of historical interpretation is Robert E. Hume's *The Thirteen Principal Upanishads*, 2nd rev. ed. (London, 1931; Madras, Oxford University Press, 1949). Swami Nikhilānanda has translated eleven major upanishads into felicitous English in *The Upanishads*, 4 vols. (N.Y., Harper & Brothers, 1949–59). His translations are tendentious in the sense that they are purposely conformed to the interpretations found in Sankara's commentaries and to the outlook of Advaita Vedanta. Professor Radhakrishnan's *The Principal Upanisads* (N.Y., Harper & Brothers, 1953) offers a Sanskrit text, translation, fragments of the commentaries of Sankara and others, references to approximately parallel thoughts of Occidental writers, and an over-all interpretation in terms of his own modernization of the Vedanta. Ambiguous texts are passed over in order to explain fully certain clear passages which are important for modern doctrine.

The authoritative upanishads which are considered part of the Veda are the limit of the content of Hume's volume. Radhakrishnan includes these and five others. For translation of many minor upanishads, one must turn to Paul Deussen's *Sechzig Upanishad's des Veda* (Leipzig, F. A. Brockhaus, 1897). Deussen's *The Philosophy of the Upanishads* (Edinburgh, T. & T. Clark, 1906) is a comprehensive and well-documented secondary study. It has been subjected to telling criticism in certain matters of historical and metaphysical interpretation, but it remains the most useful survey of the thought-world of these scriptures.

THE SĀDHU

The rise of the Way of Knowledge in Indian religious literature coincided with the appearance of a new style of religious living. It involved the abandonment of the entire ritual and social pattern of brahmanism and the adoption of a life of self-denial and meditation, preferably in quiet forest retreats. These world-renouncing *religieux* came to be called *sannyāsīs* or *sādhus*. Their special meditative science was designated by the name "yoga" in one of its narrower applications.

The scriptural norms for the living of this forest life are laid out in detail in the dharmaśastras in the section on the *vānaprastha* and *sannyāsas āśramas*. Kane provides a full guide to this literature in *History of Dharmaśāstra* (*op. cit.*), II, 2, pp. 917–75. G. S. Ghurye, *Indian Sadhus* (Bombay, Popular Book

Depot, 1953) catalogues the principal divisions of Hindu ascetics and describes the peculiarities of each, mainly from literary sources. John Campbell Oman, *The Mystics, Ascetics, and Saints of India* (London, T. Fisher Unwin, 1903) has no claim to historical scholarship but is an unparalleled collection of data on the sadhu as known from observation, hearsay, and modern vernacular literature. George W. Briggs, *Gorakhnāth and the Kānphaṭa Yogīs* (Calcutta, Y.M.C.A. Publishing House, 1938) is a thorough monograph on the history, institutions, beliefs, and practices of an extremist group of Śaiva sadhus. W. M. Zumbro, "Religious Penances and Punishments Self-inflicted by the Holy Men of India," *National Geographic*, XXIV (Dec., 1913), pp. 1257–314, is valuable for sixty-nine pictorial illustrations of the aberrancy indicated by the title. The general style of life of the sādhus is described autobiographically in Shri Purohit Swami, *An Indian Monk, His Life and Adventures* (London, Macmillan & Co., Ltd., 1932) and in T. L. Pennell, *Among the Wild Tribes of the Afghan Frontier* (London, Seeley & Co., 1909), pp. 211–57. The inner spirit of Hindu renunciation is expressed classically in the *Vairāgya-śatakam* of Bhartṛihari, which has been translated freely and forcefully into verse by C. H. Tawney in *Indian Antiquary* (1876), pp. 1–3, 65–7, 285f., 305-9. Paul Brunton's *A Search in Secret India* (London, Rider & Co., 1934; N.Y., E. P. Dutton & Co., 1935) gives an account of inquiries among the leaders of the holy men and concludes with an illuminating description of the author's mystical experience in the aśrama of Śrī Ramaṇ Mahārshi.

On yoga the most comprehensive and penetrating study is Mircea Eliade, *Yoga: Immortality and Freedom* (N.Y., Pantheon Books, 1958). Persons without Indological background might begin with advantage, however, with Claude Bragdon, *An Introduction to Yoga* (N.Y., Alfred A. Knopf, Inc., 1933), a simple, very general introduction to the objectives and techniques of yoga for Occidentals. Swami Vivekânanda's *Rāja-Yoga* (London, Longmans, Green & Co., Ltd., 1896; 8th ed., Almora, Advaita Ashrama, 1947) describes and explains the eight-stage yoga of Patañjali with clarity and adds a translation of the Yoga Sutra. A standard literal translation of this work is James Haughton Woods' *Yoga-system of Patanjali* (Harvard Oriental Series, Vol. XVII, 1914), in which the traditional commentaries are included. Surendranāth Dāsgupta, *Yoga as Philosophy and Religion* (London, Kegan Paul, Trench, Trubner & Co., 1924) is an authoritative secondary work on the mystical discipline as well as on the system of metaphysics with which it was originally associated.

THE PHILOSOPHIES OF THE JNANA-MARGA

A work on Indian philosophy quite properly presents the six orthodox *darśanas* continuously and in the traditional formal order, with approximately equal attention to each system. But in this discussion the various schools will be taken up in an order determined by their place in the three *margas*, and the emphasis which each receives will be in accord with its importance in Hindu religion. The Karma-mimamsa, first in the traditional list, has been discussed in connection with the Way of Action. The Yoga system of thought has been touched on in connection with the religious life of the yogīs. The theistic varieties of Vedanta will be treated under *bhakti* religion. The others will be dealt with now.

Of prime importance for this realm of reading are the comprehensive works on Hindu philosophy. The most detailed and authoritative is Surendranath Dasgupta's monumental *A History of Indian Philosophy*, 5 vols. (Cambridge University Press, 1922–55). Out of scruple for preserving the unique character of Indian concepts Dasgupta preserves the original Sanskrit terms, not converting them into their apparent European approximations. This policy gives his work a rare trustworthiness and, at the same time, makes it almost unassimilable for the beginner. On the other hand, S. Radhakrishnan's *Indian Philosophy*, 2 vols. (N.Y., The Macmillan Co., 1923, 1927), achieves readability for the Occidental by adopting Western terminology, at the cost of a close relationship to its Indian sources. Radhakrishnan's work of historical interpretation is affected also by his responsibility as a religious leader: as he presents the traditions with which he identifies himself, he reconstructs them for modern use. On the conversion of Indian philosophical vocabulary, an advantageous middle position is taken by M. Hiriyanna, who in his succinct *Outlines of Indian Philosophy* (London, George Allen & Unwin, Ltd., 1932) and other works combines accuracy with intelligibility as successfully as could be hoped. *An Introduction to Indian Philosophy* by S. C. Chatterjee and D. M. Datta (University of Calcutta, 1939) covers the systems dependably and with clarity on an introductory level. Radhakrishnan and Moore's *Source Book in Indian Philosophy* (*op. cit.*) is the best available anthology of its kind. Its extensive bibliography (pp. 643–69) offers amends for our sketchy coverage of the systems which are of lesser importance for religion.

Thus with regard to the Nyāya and Vaiśeshika systems we shall only say that Arthur Berriedale Keith's historical and doctrinal survey in his *Indian Logic and Atomism* (Oxford, Clarendon Press, 1921) is a good first step for one who wishes to go beyond the treatment in the general works on Indian philosophy.

The concepts of the Sāṃkhya philosophy are so pervasive of wide ranges of Indian thought that the system deserves the attention of all students of Hinduism. Hiriyanna explains this darśana with special lucidity in his *Outlines of Indian Philosophy* (*op. cit.*), in his *The Essentials of Indian Philosophy* (London, George Allen & Unwin, Ltd., 1949), and in "The Samkhya System" in *The Cultural Heritage of India* (*op. cit.*), III, pp. 41–52. For the fundamental ancient authority of the system see *The Sāṅkhyakārikā of Īśvara Kṛṣṇa*, tr.

by S. S. Suryanarayana Sastri, 2nd rev. ed. (University of Madras, 1935). The rise and development of the school are traced by A. Berriedale Keith in *The Sāṁkhya System* (Calcutta, Association Press, 1918).

The nontheistic branch of Vedanta as taught by Śaṅkarācārya and his followers demands full and special study because of the dominant position it has achieved in intellectual Ḥinduism. Sankara's *magnum opus*, his commentary on the Vedanta Sutras, is available in the translation of George Thibaut, *The Vedānta-Sutras with the Commentary of Sañkarâkârya* (*S.B.E.*, XXXIV, 1890, XXXVIII, 1896), which has just been reprinted (N.Y., Dover Publications, 1962). The introduction to the first volume provides a general view of Sankara's thought. The continuous reading of the entire work can be a confusing and trying experience because Sankara writes here as a commentator on a text and is not free to develop his own thought systematically. In this situation Paul Deussen's closely documented *The System of the Vedanta* (Chicago, The Open Court Publishing Co., 1912) performs a service in pulling these commentarial fragments together in an orderly topical development. Deussen concludes (pp. 453–78) with a simple useful resumé, which has been published separately also, as *Outline of the Vedanta System of Philosophy according to Shankara* (N.Y., The Grafton Press, 1906). Agreeable systematic treatments of certain aspects of Advaita Vedanta can be obtained in several small doctrinal treatises which are attributed to Śankara. A comprehensive volume of the minor works which could reasonably have been written by him was published by G. A. Natesan & Co., Madras (n.d.) under the title *Select Works of Sri Sankaracharya.* The *Atmabodha* is available in the translation of Swami Nikhilananda, *Self-knowledge* (N.Y., Ramakrishna-Vivekananda Center, 1946). The *Vivekacudāmaṇi* has been rendered freely into English as *Crest-Jewel of Discrimination* by Swami Prabhavānanda and Christopher Isherwood (Hollywood, Vedanta Press, 1947). There is a literal translation of the same by Swami Mādhavānanda, *Vivekachudamani of Shri Shankaracharya* (Calcutta, Advaita Ashrama, 1921; 6th ed., 1957). The *Aparokshānubhūti*, tr. by Swami Vimuktānanda, is published as *Aparokshanubhuti or Self-realization* (Calcutta, Advaita Ashrama, 1938). The *Upadeśasāhasrī*, tr. by Swami Jagadānanda, is available as *A Thousand Teachings* (Mylapore, Madras, Ramakrishna Math, 1941). The study of advaita in these booklets is profitable, but one should remember that they may have been written by members of Śankara's school rather than by the master himself.

III. THE WAY OF DEVOTION

The article "Bhakti-mārga" by Sir George A. Grierson in *Encyclopedia of Religion and Ethics*, II, pp. 539–51, provides a convenient introduction to the special beliefs common to the various forms of devotional Hinduism.

For a summary of the assured findings of Western scholarship on the historical development of theistic Hinduism, see Sir Charles Eliot's *Hinduism and Buddhism*, 3 vols. (London, Edwin Arnold & Co., 1921; N.Y., Barnes & Noble, Inc., 1954), II, pp. 136–261. The rise of these monotheistic religions of salvation has not yet been subjected to comprehensive and conclusive study. The proliferation of the cults of Vishnu and Śiva is usefully treated in the secondary survey by Joseph Estlin Carpenter, *Theism in Medieval India* (London, Williams & Norgate, Ltd., 1921), which covers the ground of Eliot's work but with greater fullness. There is still value in Sir R. G. Bhandarkar's pioneer historical work *Vaiṣṇavism, Śaivism and Minor Religious Systems* (Strassburg, Grundriss der indo-arischen Philologie und Altertumskunde, III, 6, 1913). Nicol Macnicol in his *Indian Theism from the Vedic to the Muhammadan Period* (London, Humphrey Milford, Oxford University Press, 1915) deals with the vast period indicated, with attention focused primarily upon the development of the various sorts of theistic doctrine. Much of the surviving literature of early Indian theism has been preserved in the epics and puranas. The Mahābhārata, the greatest of the epics, is not the special possession of any theistic group, but it includes in its vast accumulations the myths, legends, and teachings of many kinds of theists. The new critical edition of the Mahābhārata, the last volumes of which are now appearing, has not yet been made the basis of a comprehensive translation, and old translations often differ widely from each other because of radical differences in the regional Sanskrit recensions on which they are based. The best English translation on the whole is Manmatha Nath Dutt's *A Prose English Translation of the Mahabharata*, 3 vols. (Calcutta, M. N. Dutt, 1895–1905). Dutt's renderings, here as elsewhere, are wooden and not deeply reflective, but they are redeemed by honesty and consistency. Sir M. Monier-Williams gives a useful sketch of the main plot of the Mahabharata (and of the Rāmāyaṇa as well) in *Indian Epic Poetry* (London and Edinburgh, Williams & Norgate, Ltd., 1863). The standard critical study in English is E. Washburn Hopkins, *The Great Epic of India* (N.Y. and London, 1901; New Haven, Yale University Press, 1913, 1920). Hopkins produced also an encyclopedic manual of the persons, gods, and concepts of the Mahabharata, *Epic Mythology* (Strassburg, Grundriss der indo-arischen Philologie und Altertumskunde, III, 1, B, 1915).

The bhakti-marga is a general type of religion only, without institutional unity. The social groups which produced its complex streams are often little known; in most cases we are able to follow the development of movements or cults only, rather than institutional histories. Beyond these imperfectly defined bodies, blurring the historical outlines further, lie great numbers of polytheistic Hindus who worship the same deities as do these soteriological cults, but as gods belonging to a pantheon and for ends short of salvation. The clearest lines of division within the bhakti-marga are those which differentiate the cults of Rāma, Kṛishṇa, and Śiva.

The worshippers of Rama and of Krishna are united in connecting the deity of their worship with the Vedic god Vishnu, usually through the conception that these gods are *avatāras* or descents of Vishnu, the Creator and Lord of the universe. The roots of later Vaishṇava theology in Vedic literature are described and analyzed by J. Gonda, *Aspects of Early Viṣṇuism* (Utrecht, N.V.A. Oosthoek, 1954.)

Rama worship

The worship of Rama has its earliest literary base in Vālmīki's *Rāmāyaṇa*, which has been translated into English by Ralph T. H. Griffith, *The Rāmāyana of Vālmīki* (Banaras, E. J. Lazarus & Co., 1895). In North India Rāmaism received a great impulse at the end of the sixteenth century A.D. from the appearance of Tulsī Dās' *Rāmcaritmānas*, of which we have two adequate English translations: Frederick S. Growse, *The Rāmāyana of Tulsī Dās* (Allahabad, North-Western Provinces, Government Press, 1877; 7th ed., Ram Narain Lal, Allahabad, 1937) and William Douglas P. Hill, *The Holy Lake of the Acts of Rāma* (Indian Branch, Oxford University Press, 1952), the former being a more pleasant rendering and the latter a closer translation based upon a better text. James Nelson Carpenter analyzes the teaching of this work in *The Theology of Tulasī Dās* (Madras, Christian Literature Society for India, 1918). The comparable Bengali Ramayana of Kṛittivāsa has been freely translated recently by Shudha Mazumdar, *Ramayana* (Calcutta, Orient Longmans Private Ltd., 1958). The cult of Rama has not produced a systematic theologian, nor have the Rama worshippers usually separated themselves sharply from other Hindus in their institutions.

Krishna worship

The earliest datable evidences of Krishna worship are laid out by Ramaprasad Chanda, *Archaeology and Vaishnava Tradition* (Calcutta, Memoirs of the Archaeological Survey of India, No. 5, 1920). The earliest and greatest scripture of the Krishna cult is the immortal Bhagavadgita, produced in the last centuries before Christ. The efforts of the Vaishnava author of this work to relate his religion to older non-bhakti forms of Hindu thought have made it possible for non-Vaishnavas to use the Bhagavadgita in their own way. An instance of such alien interpretation is the translation by Swami Prabhavananda and Christopher Isherwood, *The Song of God: Bhagavad-Gita* (N.Y., Mentor Books, 1954). This rendering has great literary charm, but it obscures the Vaishnava character of the book by tendentious interpretation and even deliberate interpolation, in the interest of subordinating it to advaita doctrine. Franklin Edgerton's translation, *The Bhagavad Gītā* (Harvard Oriental Series, Vols. XXXVIII and XXXIX, 1944), is not as mellifluent as some, but is unexcelled for dispassionate judgment and syllable-by-syllable accuracy. Volume XXXVIII contains romanized text and English translation on facing pages; Volume XXXIX contains Edgerton's thorough study of the teaching of the Bhagavadgita. A one-volume paperback edition omitting the Sanskrit text is available in the Harper Torchbook series. Sir Edwin Arnold's translation, *The Song Celestial*, has the virtues of the ideal opposite of Edgerton's work. Arnold was a Sanskrit scholar, mindful of the obligation of accuracy, but his highest aim was to convey the general sentiments of the book in English verse having as much charm as possible. His translation has much to offer the literary reader who is interested in general impressions only. An inexpensive current edition is that of Routledge & Kegan Paul, Ltd., London, 1961. Several other translations combine good literary qualities with good scholarship: Kashinath Trimbak Telang, *The Bhagavadgītā with the Sanatsugātīya and the Anugītā* (*S.B.E.*, VIII, 1882); William Douglas P. Hill, *The Bhagavadgītā* (London, Oxford University Press, 1928, with text; 2nd abridged ed. without text, Indian Branch, Oxford University Press, 1953); and S. Radhakrishnan, tr., *The Bhagavadgītā* (London, George Allen & Unwin, Ltd., 1948). Radhakrishnan includes an English commentary which is generally useful but which often shifts without notice from exegesis to homily.

The developing mythology of the Krishna cult is recorded primarily in three great puranas. The Harivaṃśa, dominantly but not exclusively Vaishṇava, has been translated by Manmatha Nāth Dutt, *A Prose English Translation of Harivamsha* (Calcutta, H. C. Dass, 1897). The Vishṇu Purāṇa is best used in the translation of Horace Hayman Wilson as edited by Fitzedward Hall, *The Vishṇu Purāṇa*, 5 vols. (London, Kegan Paul, Trench, Trubner & Co., Ltd., 1864–77), because of the extensive notes and ample index of that edition. The third, the Bhāgavata Purāṇa, has not been adequately translated. The best English version is M. N. Dutt, tr., *A Prose English Translation of Srimadbhagavatam* (Calcutta, 1896), but it is well to consult also the old French translation of Eugene Burnouf and his successors M. Hauvette-Besnault and Alfred Roussel, *Le Bhāgavata Purāna*, 5 vols. (Paris, Imprimerie Royal, 1840–98). The selection and interpretation of Bhagavata Puraṇa legends by later Krishna worshippers may be studied in several current booklets: Rādhākamal Mukerjee's free but fair translation from Book Ten, *The Lord of the Autumn Moons* (Bombay, Asia Publishing House, 1957); W. G. Archer, *The Loves of Krishna in Indian Painting and Poetry* (London, George Allen & Unwin, Ltd., 1957); and Hanumanprasad Poddar, *Gopi's Love for Sri Krishna* (Gorakhpur, U.P., Gita Press, 1941).

An entrée into the thought and vast literature of the ancient Vaishṇava sect known as the Pāñcarātrins is given by F. Otto Schrader, *Introduction to the Pāñcarātra and the Ahirbudhnya Saṃhitā* (Madras, Adyar Library, 1916). J. S. M. Hooper in *Hymns of the Āḷvārs* (Calcutta, Association Press, 1929) translates specimens drawn from a great body of ancient Tamil poetry claimed by the Śrī Vaishṇava sect of South India. The poetry of the Krishna-devotees of Western India of the thirteenth to seventeenth centuries is introduced by Nicol Macnicol's translations from Marathi, *Psalms of Marāṭhā Saints* (Calcutta, Association Press, 1920), and by Justin E. Abbott's *Stotramālā* (Poona, Scottish Mission Industries, 1929).

Rāmānuja, the first great Vaishnava theologian, rose among the Śri Vaishnavas of South India in the eleventh century. He remains the foundational thinker of this enduring group and has influenced the teachers of most other theistic sects as well. His greatest work, the *Śrī Bhāshya*, has been translated by George Thibaut, *The Vedānta-Sūtras with the Commentary of Rāmānuja* (*S.B.E.*, XLVIII, 1904; reprinted N.Y., Dover Publications, 1963). Ramanuja's *Gītābhāshya* is available in J. A. B. van Buitenen's summarizing translation *Rāmānuja on the Bhagavadgītā* ('s Gravenhage, the translator, 1953). Van Buitenen has translated also *Rāmānuja's Vedārthasaṃgraha* (Poona, Deccan College Monograph Series No. 16, 1956). More literal translations of this work have been made by M. R. Rajagopala Ayyangar, *Vedartha Sangraha of Sri Ramanuja* (Kumbakonam, Cauveri Colour Press, 1956) and by S. S. Raghavachar, *Vedārthasaṁgraha of Śri Rāmānujācārya* (Mysore, Sri Ramakrishna Ashrama, 1956). Rāmānuja's *Vedāntasāra*, tr. by M. B. Narasimha Ayyangar, has been published by the Adyar Library (Madras, 1953).

Secondary studies of quality on Ramanuja begin with Vasudev Anant Sukhtankar, *The Teachings of Vedānta according to Rāmānuja* (Vienna, the author, 1908), who explains the main doctrines of Ramanuja clearly from the *Śri Bhashya* and the *Vedarthasaṃgraha*. Bharatan Kumārappa in *The Hindu Conception of Deity as Culminating in Rāmānuja* (London, Luzac & Co., 1934) views Ramanuja, as did Thibaut and others, as a polemicist against Sankara. Dasgupta in his *History of Indian Philosophy* (*op. cit.*) focused upon Ramanuja's epistemology and metaphysics. Van Buitenen in the interpretive aspects of his above-mentioned works shows a new interest in Ramanuja as theologian and devotee.

We turn now to the unduly neglected Vaishnava sampradāyas, the sectarian groups which, in the time after Ramanuja, produced the fullest and most mature Vaishnava theologies. Dasgupta in *History of Indian Philosophy* (*op. cit.*), Vols. III and IV, surveys their systems of thought. Bhandarkar describes them briefly in his *Vaiṣṇavism, Śaivism and Minor Religious Systems.* Their distinctive theological positions as defined in their sectarian commentaries on the Vedanta Sutras are laid out in two good studies: V. S. Ghate, *The Vedanta* (Poona, Bhandarkar Oriental Research Institute, 1926) and S. Radhakrishnan, *The Brahma Sūtra* (N.Y., Harper & Brothers, 1960), pp. 46–102.

Ramanuja's own Śri Vaishnava Sampradaya soon bifurcated into the famous Tengalai and Vadagalai schools (cat-hold and monkey-hold). The institutional evolution of these branches is sketched by V. Rangacharya, "Historical Evolution of Śrī-Vaiṣṇavism in South India," *Cultural Heritage of India* (*op. cit.*), IV, pp. 163–85. The great themes of debate among the Śrī Vaishnavas are explained from a moderate Vadagalai point of view by P. N. Srinivasachari in *The Philosophy of Viśiṣṭādvaita*, 2nd ed. (Madras, Adyar Library, 1946), pp. 352–540. On the points of difference see also A. Govindacharya, "The Aṣṭadaśa-bhedas," *Journal of the Royal Asiatic Society* (1910), pp. 1103–12, and A. Govindacharya and George A. Grierson, "Tengalai and Vadagalai," *Journal of the Royal Asiatic Society* (1912), pp. 714–18.

Vedānta Deśika, the crowning theologian of the Vadagalai school, has become much more accessible through M. R. Rajagopala Ayyangar's translation from Tamil of his greatest work of positive theological construction, *Srimad Rahasyatrayasara* (Kumbakonam, Agnihothrum Ramanuja Thathachariar, 1956). Satyavrata Singh's *Vedānta Deśika: His Life, Works and Philosophy* (Banaras, Chowkhamba Sanskrit Series Office, 1958) is a full-scale study; and S. M. Srinivasa Chari, *Advaita and Viśiṣṭādvaita* (N.Y., Asia Publishing House, 1961) gives a substantial account of Vedānta Deśika's major polemical work against advaita, the *Śatadūshaṇī*. Knowledge of the Tengalai or Cat-hold School may be obtained through the translations of a few works of its earliest theologian, Pillai Lokācārya. Lokācārya's major metaphysical treatise, *The Vedanta Tattva-Traya*, is translated by Manmatha Nath Paul (Allahabad, The Panini Office, Vedanta Series No. 5, 1904). A. Govindacharya has translated " 'Arthapanchaka' of Pillai Lokāchārya," *Journal of the Royal Asiatic Society* (1910), pp. 565–98; and in *Indian Antiquary*, XXXIX (Nov., 1910), pp. 316–19, he has translated two minor works, "The Navaratna-mala or the Nine-Gemmed Garland of Pillai Lokāchārya" and "The Prapanna-paritrāna, or the Refuge of the Refugee." An important religious work of Lokācārya is translated anonymously in *The Visishtādavaitin*, "The *Mumukshuppadi* or *Rahasyatraya*, or the Way of the Seeker of Salvation" (Aug., 1905), pp. 1–6; (Oct., 1905), pp. 7–14; (Jan., 1906), pp. 15–18; (April–May, 1906), pp. 19–33. Dasgupta, *History of Indian Philosophy*, III, pp. 135–7, 374–81, offers brief summaries of Lokācārya's works, including his important *Śrīvacanabhushaṇa*.

As introductions to the Madhva Sampradāya we recommend Hiriyanna's sketch in his *Essentials of Indian Philosophy* (*op. cit.*), pp. 187–99, and S. Subba Rau, "The Realism of Srī Madhvāchārya," in the first edition of *The Cultural Heritage of India* (Calcutta, Sri Ramakrishna Centenary Committee, 1937ff.), I, pp. 582–96. A picture of the social and ritual life of the sect in the nineteenth century is given in *Gazetteer of the Bombay Presidency*, XXII (Bombay, Government Central Press, 1884), pp. 56–90. For its hymnology see Charles E. Gover, tr., *The Folk-songs of Southern India* (Madras, Higginbotham & Co., 1872; 2nd ed. Tirunelveli, Madras, The South India Saiva Siddhanta Works Publishing Society Publication No. 965, 1959), pp. 3–63. B. N. K. Sharma, *A History of the Dvaita School of Vedanta and Its Literature* (Bombay, Booksellers' Publishing Co., 1960) covers the developments indicated by the title to about A.D. 1400. The best comprehensive description of the Mādhva system of thought for Western students is K. Narain's *An Outline of Madhva Philosophy* (Allahabad, Udayana Publications, 1962). B. N. K. Sharma covers similar ground in two solid works: *Philosophy of Śrī Madhvācārya* (Bombay, Bharatiya Vidya Bhavan, 1962) and an anthology, *Śrī Madhva's Teachings in His Own Words* (same publisher, 1961). Helmuth von Glasenapp's *Madhva's Philosophie des Vishnu-Glaubens* (Bonn and Leipzig, Geistesströmungen des Ostens, Bd. 2, 1923) is thorough and lucidly arranged. P. Nagaraja Rao has made a specialized study, "The Epistemology of Dvaita Vedanta," *Adyar Library Bulletin*, XXII, Parts 3–4 (1958), pp. 1–120. In the field of primary writings, several of Madhva's commentaries have been translated or paraphrased by S. Subba Rau: *The Vedanta-Sutras with the Commentary by Sri Madhwacharya* (Madras, 1904) and *The Bhagavad-Gita, Translation and Commentaries in English according to Sri Madhwacharya's Bhashyas* (Madras, S. Subba Rau, 1906). Suzanne Siauve offers an important translation, *La voie vers la connaissance de Dieu* (*Brahma-Jijñāsā*) *selon l'Anuvyākhyāna de Madhva* (Pondichéry, Institut Français d'Indologie Publications No. 6, 1957). R. Naga Raja Sarma in *Reign of Realism in Indian Philosophy* (Madras, National Press, 1937) summarizes ten works of Madhva as amplified and explained by the sectarian commentator Jayatīrtha; especially valuable are pp. 235–520, a condensation of one of Madhva's most comprehensive works.

The finest introduction to the thought of the Nimbarka Sampradāya is Roma Bose Chaudhuri's "The Nimbarka School of Vedanta" in *The Cultural Heritage of India* (*op. cit.*), III, pp. 333–46. William Crooke gives modest information on the life of the sect in *The Tribes and Castes of the North-Western Provinces and Oudh* (Calcutta, Government Press, 1896), IV, pp. 88f. The most substantial publication in the entire field is the three-volume work by Roma Bose (Chaudhuri), *Vedānta-Pārijāta-Saurabha of Nimbarka and Vedānta-Kaustubha of Srīnivāsa* (Calcutta, Asiatic Society of Bengal, Bibliotheca Indica CCLIX, 1940–43), the third volume of which is a detailed study of the principal theologians of the sect. There is another comprehensive survey by Umesha Mishra, *Nimbarka School of Vedanta* (Allahabad, University of Allahabad Studies, Sanskrit Section, 1940). P. N. Srinivasachari, *The Philosophy of Bhedābheda*, 2nd rev. ed. (Madras, Adyar Library Series No. 74, 1950) pp. 155–63, explains the Nimbarkite positions in relation to those of other schools.

Reading on the Vallabha Sampradāya begins well with two articles by Govindlal Hargovind Bhatt: "The School of Vallabha," in *The Cultural Heritage of India* (*op. cit.*), III, pp. 342–59, and "The Puṣṭimārga of Vallabhāchārya" in *Indian Historical Quarterly*, IX (1933), pp. 300–6. The best-documented works in English are Helmuth von Glasenapp's *Doctrines of Vallabhacharya*, translated from German by Ishverbai L. Amin (Kapadvanj,

Dist. Khaira, Gujarat, Shuddhadvaita Samsada, 1959); and Jethalal G. Shah, *A Primer of Anu-Bhāshaya* (Nadiad, 1927; rev. ed., Kapadvanj, Shuddhadvaita Samsada, 1960). Vallabha's *Tattvārthadīpanibandha*, ed. by H. O. Śāstrī (Bombay, Trustees of Sheth Narayandas and Jethananda Asanmal Charity Trust, 1943) includes an English translation of the basic text and an informative introduction by Jethalal G. Shah. In the three works just mentioned the extensive citations in the devanagari alphabet will trouble most Western readers. Śriśa Chandra (Vasu) Vidyarnava, *Studies in the Vedanta Sutras* (Allahabad, *S.B.H.*, XXII, 1919), pp. 66–98, analyzes Vallabha's interpretation of that key work. Pierre Johanns, S.J., *A Synopsis of "To Christ Through the Vedanta." Part III, Vallabha* (Ranchi, Catholic Press, Light of the East Series No. 9, 1944) combines lucid summary in Western terms with a liberal Christian critique. Sūr Dās, a disciple of Vallabha and a poet of the first rank in Hindī, is the subject of a study by Janardan Misra, *Religious Poetry of Surdas* (Patna, 1935; 2nd ed., Kumaitha, Dist. Bhagalpur, Bihar, Rajesh Misra, 1956). There is an unfortunate scarcity of explanatory writing for outsiders by adherents of the Vallabha Sampradaya. A sensational public scandal in the life of the sect a century ago caused its members to adopt a lasting attitude of defensive seclusion. Those will understand who read Yadunāthajī Vrajaratnajī's *Report of the Maharaj Libel Case* (Bombay, 1862) and his (anonymous) *History of the Sect of Mahārājas, or Vallabhāchāryas, in Western India* (London, Kegan Paul, Trench, Trubner & Co., Ltd., 1865).

The thought of the Gauṙiyā Sampradāya, the school of Caitanya, bristles with peculiarities and scholastic complexities. The primers of Bengal Vaishnavism require of the reader more than the usual time and effort, despite the fact that the movement has produced writers unusually fluent in English. No introductory reading is more advantageous in the long run than Sushil Kumar De, *Bengal's Contribution to Sanskrit Literature and Studies in Bengal Vaisnavism* (Calcutta, Firma K. L. Mukhopadhyaya, 1960), pp. 108–53. Rādhā Govind Nāth offers an introduction in bare outlines in two articles in *The Cultural Heritage of India*, rev. ed., "The Acintya-Bhedābheda School," III, pp. 366–83, and "A Survey of the Caitanya Movement," IV, pp. 186–200. The Gaudiya Math, 16A Kali Prasad Chakravarti St., Baghbazar, Calcutta 3, publishes many promotional booklets of which the following have special value for beginners: Thakur Bhaktivinode, *Sri Chaitanya Mahaprabhu: His Life and Precepts* (1941) and *The Bhagavat: Its Philosophy, Its Ethics and Its Theology* (1936); Nisi Kanta Sanyal, *The Erotic Principle and Unalloyed Devotion*, 2nd ed. (1941). Sanyal's major work, *Sree Krishna Chaitanya* (1933), sold also by the Gaudiya Math, is prefaced (pp. 1–212) by a spirited and tenacious apologetic presentation of the theology of the sect.

A. A. Bake describes the devotional forms of the Bengal Vaishnavas, with musical scores, in "Gri Chaitanya Mahāprabhu," *Mededelingen der Koninklijke Nederlandsche Akademie Van Wetenschappen*, Afd. Letterkunde, Nieuwe Reeks, Deel 11 No. 8 (1948), pp. 279–305. On *kīrtan* see also Edward C. Dimock, "The Place of Gauracandrikā in Bengali Vaiṣṇava Lyrics," *Journal of the American Oriental Society*, LXXVIII (July–Sept., 1958), pp. 153–69. Melville T. Kennedy, *The Chaitanya Movement* (Calcutta, Association Press, 1925) is valuable for information on the Caitanyites of recent times and for general factual outlines.

Sushil Kumar De, *Early History of the Vaiṣṇava Faith and Movement in Bengal* (Calcutta, General Printers and Publishers, 1942), gives an excellent critical account of the life of Caitanya and his immediate followers. Tapankumar Raychaudhuri carries the history several generations further in his *Bengal under Akbar and Jehangir* (Calcutta, A. Mukherjee & Co., 1953), pp. 80–106. Sukumara Chakravarti, *Caitanya et sa théorie de l'amour divin (prema)* (Paris, Presses universitaires de France, 1933) is a complete historical and theological survey. A long verse biography of Caitanya, of great influence on popular sectarian theology and devotion, has just been published in a complete and improved translation: Krishnadasa Kaviraja, *Sri Sri Chaitanya Charitamrita*, 6 vols. (Puri, Chaitanyacharitamrita Karyalaya, 1940–56?). Girindra Narayan Mallik, *The Philosophy of Vaiṣṇava Religion* (Lahore, Punjab Sanskrit Book Depot, 1927), is based in great part on this poem.

Certain tangential extravagances or tantric perversions of Caitanyaism are described by Manindra Mohan Bose, *The Post-Caitanya Sahajiā Cult of Bengal* (University of Calcutta, 1930), and by Shashibhushan Dasgupta, *Obscure Religious Cults as Background of Bengal Literature* (University of Calcutta, 1946).

The Rādhāvallabha Sampradāya is all but inaccessible in English. We have only Frederick S. Growse's *Mathurá*, 2nd ed. (North-Western Provinces and Oudh Government Press, 1880), pp. 185–200, and Sir George Grierson's article "Rādhāvallabhīs" in *E.R.E.*, X, pp. 559f.

Śaivism

A general view of the forms of Śiva worship is given in the appropriate chapters in Monier-Williams' *Brahmanism and Hinduism* (*op. cit.*) and Macnicol's *Indian Theism* (*op. cit.*). Mrs. Stevenson's *Rites of the Twice-Born* (*op. cit.*), chap. 14, describes the Śiva temple and its rites generally. A good deal of Śaiva temple liturgy has been recorded by Burgess, "The Ritual of the Temple of Rameçvaram" (*op. cit.*), and by Diehl in his *Instrument and Purpose* (*op. cit.*). On Śaiva iconography see Gabriel Jouveau-Dubreuil, tr. A. C. Martin, *Iconography of Southern India* (Paris, Paul Geuthner, 1937), pp. 11–52; the plates by Auguste Rodin in "Sculptures Çivaites," *Ars Asiatica*, III (1921), Pl. I–XII, and the interpretations of Heinrich Zimmer, *Myths and Symbols in Indian Art and Civilization* (N.Y., Pantheon Books, 1946; Harper

Torchbooks, 1962), pp. 123–89, and of A. K. Coomaraswamy, *The Dance of Siva* (N.Y., 1918; rev. ed., Farrar Straus & Co., 1957), in the chapter of that title. Specimens of the Śaiva hymnology of the Tamil country, where the worship of Śiva emerges most clearly above the common polytheism, are found in F. Kingsbury and G. E. Phillips, *Hymns of the Tamil Śaivite Saints* (Calcutta, Association Press, 1921), in Māṇikka-Vāchakar, *The Tiruvāçagam*, tr. by George Uglow Pope (Oxford, Clarendon Press, 1900), and in Bishop Robert Caldwell's translations of more recent poems of the Śittar school in his *A Comparative Grammar of the Dravidian or South Indian Family of Languages*, 2nd rev. ed. only (London, Kegan Paul, Trench, Trubner & Co., 1875), pp. 146–9.

S. N. Dasgupta in the fifth volume of his *History of Indian Philosophy* (*op. cit.*) examines the history of the literature and ideas of the many branches of philosophical Śaivism, including Kashmir Śaivism and the Vīra-Śaivism of the Lingāyat sect. In such a setting of general Śaiva conceptions, S. S. Suryanarayana Sāstri, "The Philosophy of Śaivism," *Cultural Heritage of India*, rev. ed. (*op. cit.*) , III, pp. 387–99, introduces the most prominent Śaiva system, the Śaiva Siddhanta of South India. The most effective presentation of this system is still, unfortunately, H. W. Schomerus' *Der Çaiva-Siddhanta* (Leipzig, 1912). Violet Paranjoti, *Saiva Siddhānta*, 2nd rev. ed. (London, Luzac & Co., 1954), sets forth the major doctrines as the school presents them in its apologetic literature. John H. Piet, *A Logical Presentation of the Saiva Siddhanta Philosophy* (Madras, Christian Literature Society for India, Indian Research Series No. 8, 1952) translates each verse of Meykaṇḍa's *Śiva-Jñāna-Bodha* and adds the traditional argumentation by which that article of faith has been defended. Meykaṇḍa's fundamental work has been translated also by Gordon Matthews, *Siva-ñāna-bōdham* (Oxford, James G. Forlong Fund No. 24, 1948) and by J. N. Nallaswami Pillai, *Sivagnana Botham* (Dharmapuram, Gnanasambandam Press, 1945). Nallaswami Pillai has translated also a standard fourteenth-century theological work, *Thiruvarutpayan of Umapathi Sivacharya* (same publisher, 1945). A specialized epistemological study has been made by V. Ponniah, *The Saiva Siddhanta Theory of Knowledge* (Annamalainagar, Annamalai University, 1952). Study of Śaiva thought can be pushed further with the aid of D. I. Jesudoss, "The Literature of Saiva Siddhanta and Allied Schools," *Tamil Culture*, I (Sept., 1952), pp. 226–33.

IV. ŚĀKTISM

Śaktism on the popular level appears to be ordinary bhakti religion, different only in its dedication to feminine deities. But its historical roots are distinct, its ritual practices have pronounced peculiarities, and the more sophisticated reaches of its thought lead on into the unique philosophies and modes of adjustment known as tāntrism.

For preliminary classification and description of the adherents of this branch of Hinduism, see Horace Hayman Wilson, ed. Ernest R. Rost, *Religious Sects of the Hindus* (1861; 2nd ed., Calcutta, Susil Gupta, 1958), pp. 135–48. Ernest A. Payne's *The Śaktas* (Calcutta, Y.M.C.A. Publishing House, 1933) is an inclusive survey stressing the practices of modern śaktas. No reading program is complete without Sir Charles Eliot's dry discriminating factual treatment in his *Hinduism and Buddhism* (*op. cit.*), II, pp. 188–91, 274–90. *The Srimad Devi Bhagavatam*, tr. by Swami Vijnanananda, 3 vols. (Allahabad, *S.B.H.*, XXVI, 1921–22) is a compendium of śakta mythology and ritual lore. Śakta hymnology is illustrated from Sanskrit sources by Arthur Avalon, *Hymns to the Goddess* (London, Luzac & Co., 1913; 2nd ed., Hollywood, Vedanta Society of Southern California, 1953) and from vernacular literature by Edward J. Thompson and Arthur Marshman Spencer, *Bengali Religious Lyrics, Śākta* (Calcutta, Association Press, 1923). Sister Niveditā, *Kali the Mother* (London, 1900; Almora, Advaita Ashrama, 1950), though accented with Victorian sentimentalism, is helpful nevertheless in understanding śakta theology and religious feeling.

The poorly known tantras are the special theological and liturgical literature of śaktism, and the repositories of its advanced and esoteric teachings (tantrism). They are described generally by Moriz Winternitz in *A History of Indian Literature*, 3 vols. (I and II, University of Calcutta, 1927, 1933; III, Part I, Delhi, Motilal Banarsidass, 1963), I, pp. 591–606, which includes summaries of a number of popular tantras. The earliest and foremost of serious interpreters of tantrism was Sir John Woodroffe, who wrote under the pseudonym of Arthur Avalon. His most comprehensive and lucid work is *Shakti and Shākta, Essays and Addresses on the Shākta Tantrashāstra*, 3rd rev. and enl. ed. (Madras, Ganesh & Co., 1929); his other works can be seen in the listings of standard catalogues. The special Kuṇḍalinī yoga of advanced śaktism is described in detail in Woodroffe's *The Serpent Power* (London, 1919; 5th enl. ed., Madras, Ganesh & Co., 1953), which is a translation and explanation of two manuals, the Shat-cakra-nirūpana and the Pādūka-pañcakā. Mircea Eliade in *Yoga, Immortality and Freedom* (*op. cit.*), pp. 200–73, analyzes and interprets tantric yoga with great ingenuity and insight. The most satisfying general interpretive reading on tantrism is the final chapter of Heinrich Zimmer's *Philosophies of India* (N.Y., Pantheon Books, 1951; Meridian Books, 1956), which cuts its way through this dark field in bold lines of sympathetic interpretation. The reader should be grateful, but also mindful that the ramifications of tantrism are vast, complex, and little explored and that no present scheme of explanation is likely to enable us to comprehend the whole neatly.

V. MODERN FORMS OF HINDUISM

During the past century and a half, under the impact of forces and influences from abroad, teachings and movements of such novelty have arisen that they burst the banks of the ancient streams of Hinduism and defy classification under the traditional categories. The new doctrines and developments are too numerous even to mention, and the amount of attention which should be given to any one of them in a survey of the whole of Hinduism is not clear. Figures like Gāndhī, Rāmakṛishṇa, and Radhakrishnan are present influences of the greatest importance, but only time can tell whether their names will endure with those of Śankara or Ramanuja. Movements like the Brāhmo Samāj and the Ārya Samāj have passed the crest of their activity and influence but retain a claim upon our attention because of their vital place in the historical development of recent thought. Unable to make our selections by the standards of eternity, we shall attempt to divide our attention among men and movements according to their present significance. Only those names will be included which are national or international in their influence, names which one is obliged to know if he would understand the background of active Hindus of the present day.

The fundamental work for entering into the study of religious developments since 1800 is still J. N. Farquhar's *Modern Religious Movements in India* (N.Y., The Macmillan Co., 1915). Farquhar classifies the new movements according to their degree of openness to Western influence. This basis of classification is not more profound than others. It can also be said to manifest a special interest of Occidentals, but it reflects a dominant interest of Indians of the period as well. Following Farquhar, then, we shall proceed in terms of movements of (1) radical reform of Hinduism, (2) moderate defense, (3) full defense, and (4) religious nationalism. These phases were roughly chronological in their unfolding, and the passage of time requires that they be supplemented. The developments of the fifty years since Farquhar carry forward the story of religious chauvinism to its climax and disgrace in the assassination of Mahātmā Gāndhī in 1948, and bring to the forefront a new chapter, (5) Hindu cosmopolitanism. A. C. Underwood, *Contemporary Thought of India* (London, Williams & Norgate, 1930; N.Y., Alfred A. Knopf, 1931), covers these supplemental developments in survey fashion.

The most recent inclusive study of the entire modern period is D. S. Sarma's *The Renaissance of Hinduism* (Banaras, Benares Hindu University Press, 1944). It encompasses the fields covered by the two works just mentioned, omitting religious nationalism, adding major chapters on the newly emerged figures of Aurobindo, Tagore, Gandhi, and Radhakrishnan, and substituting an internal for an external point of view. Benoy Gopal Ray, *Contemporary Indian Philosophers* (Allahabad, Kitabistan, 1947) gives sketches of the religious teachings of nine prominent leaders, beginning with Rājā Rāmmohun Roy, without placing them in a frame of historical interpretation. "Chanakya" (K. M. Pannikar), *Indian Revolution* (Bombay, National Information and Publication Ltd., 1951) supplements the foregoing with a general sketch of modern Indian social history from the standpoint of the interests of a Hindu intellectual of the mid-twentieth century. Hervey Dewitt Griswold, *Insights into Modern Hinduism* (N.Y., Henry Holt & Co., 1934) has useful chapters on obscurer men and movements not treated in the preceding works. Percival Spear, *India, Pakistan and the West* (London and N.Y., Oxford University Press, 1949) is a lively history of the commingling of Indian and Western culture which could be useful to those in need of a primer of the subject.

1. The Brahmo Samaj

The list of essential readings on the Brahmo Samaj, the first great modernist movement, begins with Sophia Dobson Collet's excellent biography of the founder, *Life and Letters of Raja Rammohun Roy*, ed. by Hem Chandra Sarkar (Calcutta, Baptist Mission Press, 1913). Information on Rammohun's life in the period up to 1823 has been brought up to date in Iqbal Singh's *Rammohun Roy*, Vol. I (Bombay, Asia Publishing House, 1958). The anonymously edited *Raja Ram Mohun Roy, His Life, Writings and Speeches* (Madras, G. A. Natesan & Co., 1925) includes fair representations of Ram Mohun Roy's religious, moral, and cultural views. Prosanto Kumar Sen, *Biography of a New Faith* (Calcutta, Thacker, Spink & Co., 1950) is useful for the history of the movement from 1823 to 1866. Protap Chunder Mozoomdar, *The Life and Teachings of Keshub Chunder Sen* (Calcutta, Baptist Mission Press, 1887) gives a detailed account of the developments and schisms of the last half of the nineteenth century from the standpoint of a member of Sen's New Dispensation. The standard comprehensive history of the entire Brahmo movement, written by a moderate member of the Sādhāran Brāhmo Samāj, is Śivanāth Śāstrī's *History of the Brahmo Samaj*, 2 vols. (Calcutta, R. Chatterji, 1911–12).

2. The Arya Samaj

This society, founded by Swāmī Dayānanda Sarasvatī, occupies an intermediate position in the range of reactions to the West. It arose as a movement for radical social and doctrinal change, but its spirit is defensive. Full-scale books on the Arya Samaj in English have all been written by members of the sect. Lala Lajpat Rai's *The Arya Samaj, An Account of its Origin, Doctrines, and Activities, with a Biographical Sketch of the Founder* (London and N.Y., Longmans Green & Co., 1915) was written especially for Occidentals and is still recommendable as a first book for the outsider. Ganga Prasad Upadhyaya, *The Origin, Scope and Mission of the Arya Samaj* (Allahabad, Arya

Samaj, Chowk, 1940) is a concise booklet on the sect's history, practices, and principles. Har Bilas Sarda, *Life of Dayanand Saraswati* (Ajmer, Vedic Yantralaya, 1946) is a long anecdotal biography, eulogistic in intent but not entirely uncritical. It includes a valuable chapter on Dayananda's principles of Veda interpretation and sections on aspects of his general teaching. Dayananda's own major work, *Satyārtha-prakāśa*, has been translated from Hindi by Chīrañjīva Bhāradwāja, *Light of Truth* (Madras, Arya Samaj, 1932) and by Ganga Prasad Upadhyaya, *The Light of Truth* (Allahabad, Kala Press, 1946). This book is treated by the sect as an authoritative writing serving in many ways as scripture. It deserves reading in any serious study of Arya Samaj dogma. Satya Prakash, *A Critical Study of Philosophy of Dayananda* (Ajmir, Arya Pratinidhi Sabha of Rajasthan, 1938), attempts to systematize Dayananda's metaphysics and theology as found in his *Satyārtha-prakāśa* and his *Ṛigvedādibhāshyabhumikā*. Ganga Prasad, *The Fountainhead of Religion* (Madras, Arya Samaj, 1941, and elsewhere), adds to Hindu solutions of the problem of the relation between religions, the Arya Samaj's striking historical theory that the great world religions are decayed derivatives of the religion of the Vedas. We have a rare study of the life and condition of an Arya Samaj congregation today in P. D. Padale's *The Endowed Arya Samaj in Hinditown* (Jabalpur, Leonard Theological College, Student Research Monographs No. II, 1953).

3. The Ramakrishna movement

Farquhar estimates this movement as more negative than the Arya Samaj with regard to acceptance of Western influence. This rating is not based upon the cultural, social, and political attitudes of this group, but upon its religious complexion. It represents a return to a traditional form of Hindu mysticism. In its later phases, however, it moved in the direction of cultural nationalism under the influence of the extrapolitical patriotism of Swāmī Vivekānanda.

Romain Rolland's *Prophets of the New India* (N.Y., Albert & Charles Boni, 1930) is a good introduction to the entire Ramakrishna movement for Westerners. On the life and religion of Ramakrishna, three writings by his followers share the top position in quality and authority. *Life of Sri Ramakrishna compiled from Various Authentic Sources* (Almora, Advaita Ashrama, Mayavati, 1925; 2nd rev. ed., 1928), a collective work of the members of the Ramakrishna monastic order, is the most inclusive collection of data on Ramakrishna's life and the preferred source on questions of biographical fact. Swami Saradananda, *Sri Ramakrishna, the Great Master*, translated from Bengali by Swami Jagadananda (Mylapore, Madras, Sri Ramakrishna Math, 1952), is a voluminous work, though it stops short of the final phase of Ramakrishna's life. It is particularly good on the interpretation of Ramakrishna's teaching and of its place in Hindu thought. Mahendra Nath Gupta, *The Gospel of Sri Ramakrishna*, tr. by Swami Nikhilananda (N.Y.,

Ramakrishna-Vivekananda Center, 1942), is a remarkable transcript of conversations of Ramakrishna with disciples and visitors between the years 1882 and 1886, recorded with almost stenographic completeness.

The story of the extension of the Ramakrishna movement overseas is inseparable from the life story of Vivekananda, which is told succinctly by Swami Nikhilananda in *Vivekananda, A Biography* (N.Y., Ramakrishna-Vivekananda Center, 1953). This and other biographies have been supplemented and at points corrected by Marie Louise Burke, *Swami Vivekananada in America, New Discoveries* (Calcutta, Advaita Ashrama, 1958), a large source book combed mainly from the American press, arranged chronologically, and interpreted. Vivekananda's own writings are available not only in *The Complete Works of Swami Vivekananda*, 7 vols. (Almora, Advaita Ashrama, Mayavati, 1919–22; 6th ed., 1940–46), but also in dozens of separate booklets published by Advaita Ashrama, 5 Dehi Entally Road, Calcutta 14. The approach of the Ramakrishna missionaries in America is typified in Swami Akhilananda's *Hindu View of Christ* (N.Y., Philosophical Library, 1949). The works mentioned in this paragraph were written by firm adherents of the Ramakrishna movement. The only useful book by an outsider is Wendell Thomas' *Hinduism Invades America* (N.Y., Beacon Press, 1930), which is often faulty in understanding and is sometimes harsh.

4. Hindu religious nationalism

The union of religion with nationalism, already found to a degree in Dayananda and Vivekananda, culminated in the first decades of the twentieth century in open forms of violent religious nationalism. Valentine Chirol's *Indian Unrest* (London, Macmillan & Co., Ltd., 1910) surveys the early manifestations of such nationalism from a British point of view, using police records which were sometimes inaccurate. Lawrence J. L. D. Zetland, Earl of Ronaldshay, gives a general characterization of the movements in *The Heart of Āryāvarta; A Study of the Psychology of Indian Unrest* (London, Constable & Co., 1925), pp. 80–131. Lajpat Rai, *Young India* (N.Y., B. W. Huebsch, 1916), pp. 187–220, provides a useful analysis of the types of religious nationalism, and an essential counterbalance in viewpoint. Bankim Chandra Chatterji's popular nationalist novel *Ānanda Math* has been translated from Bengali by Basanta Koomar Roy as *Dawn over India* (N.Y., The Devin-Adair Co., 1941) with radical adaptations which make explicit a reference to the British which Chatterji had not intended but which the Hindu nationalist has always read into it. Such theological depth as revolutionary nationalism possessed arose largely out of Bal Gangadhar Tilak's activistic interpretation of the Bhagavadgītā in his *Śrīmad Bhagavadgītā Rahasya*, a commentary which has been translated by Bhalchandra Sitaram Sukthankar, 2 vols. (Poona, Tilak Brothers, 1935). In "The Philosophy of Bal Gangadhar Tilak: Karma vs. Jnāna in the Gītā Rahasya," *Journal of Asian Studies*, XVII

(Feb., 1958), pp. 197–206, D. Mackenzie Brown gives a fine analysis of this work and points out its contribution to the social ethics of the nationalist movement. Religious ultra-nationalism continues to be represented at the present day, as a minority outlook, by religiopolitical organizations like the Hindu Mahāsabhā and the Bhāratīya Jan Sangh. These groups are described in J. R. Chandran and M. M. Thomas, *Political Outlook in India Today* (Bangalore, Committee for Literature on Social Concerns, 1956), pp. 91–139, and in J. A. Curran, *Militant Hinduism in Indian Politics* (N.Y., Institute of Pacific Relations, 1952). Religious chauvinism lost its pre-eminence, however, in the second decade of the present century, with the emergence into leadership in their various spheres of Aurobindo, Gandhi, Tagore, and Radhakrishnan, representing a faith in universal human values.

5. Cosmopolitan Hinduism

(a) Aurobindo—Śrī Aurobindo Ghose illustrated in his own career the turning away from unlimited religious nationalism. His life story is sketched by A. B. Purani in the symposium, *The Integral Philosophy of Sri Aurobindo*, ed. by Haridas Chaudhuri and Frederic Spiegelberg (London, George Allen & Unwin, Ltd., 1960), pp. 332–40. Charles A. Moore in the same book (pp. 81–110, "Sri Aurobindo on East and West") shows how this man of international education and syncretistic attitudes is yet in the ultimate analysis a Hindu. The symposium terminates with "A Complete List of all the Books Published in English by Sri Aurobindo," which will guide the advanced student. The reader who is hurried, or who finds Aurobindo's massive works confusing, can find help in Sushil Kumar Maitra's simple outline of Aurobindo's ideas in *An Introduction to the Philosophy of Sri Aurobindo* (Calcutta, The Culture Publishers, 1941). Aurobindo's *The Life Divine* (Calcutta, 1939; N.Y., The Greystone Press, 1949), his *magnum opus*, is a detailed exposition of his system, stressing its metaphysics. In *Hymns to the Mystic Fire* (1952) and *On the Veda* (1956), both published by Sri Aurobindo Ashram, Pondicherry, Aurobindo uses the key of esoteric symbolism to find the seed of his mystical doctrine in the Rigveda. *The Human Cycle* (Pondicherry, Sri Aurobindo Ashram, 1949) and *The Ideal of Human Unity*, 2nd ed. (same publisher, 1950) are Aurobindo's interpretation of history and of the intellectual and spiritual evolution of man. His *Ideals and Progress* (Calcutta, Arya Publishing House, 4th ed., 1951) elaborates certain additional aspects of Aurobindo's philosophy of human social development. *Essays on the Gita* (1921–28; N.Y., E. P. Dutton & Co., 1950), a major work of Aurobindo, interprets the Bhagavadgita in line with his metaphysical and ethical teaching. He lays down the requirements of the practical religious life in the light of his system in *Synthesis of Yoga* (1948; N.Y., Shri Aurobindo Library, 1953), in *The Mind of Light* (N.Y., E. P. Dutton & Co., 1953), and in *The Mother* (Pondicherry, Sri Aurobindo Ashram, 1928).

(b) Rabindranath Tagore—In any approach to the religion of Rabindranath Tagore no reading has priority over an unhurried direct absorption of his English masterpiece, *Gitanjali* (London, The India Society, 1912; Macmillan & Co., Ltd. 1913; Boston, Bruce Humphries, 1962). The sensitive reader's immediate understanding of this classic of modern mysticism may be increased only a little by all the rest of the vast literature by and about Tagore. Edward J. Thompson, *Rabindranath Tagore, His Life and Work*, rev. ed. (Calcutta, Y.M.C.A. Publishing House, 1961), views Tagore's literary work against the background of the crises of his life, appraising his achievements with detachment and yet with affection. Tagore's literary works in English which reveal his religion significantly are contained for the most part in *Collected Poems and Plays of Rabindranath Tagore* (N.Y., The Macmillan Co., 1937); the poems *Gitanjali* (with one regrettable abridgment) and *Fruit-Gathering*, and the plays *The Post Office*, *The Cycle of Spring*, *Sanyasi*, *Malini*, and *Sacrifice*. Three works are essential which are not included in that anthology. The first is *The King of the Dark Chamber* (N.Y., The Macmillan Co., 1914), an allegorical drama. The other two are books of poetry translated from Bengali by Aurobindo Bose for the Wisdom of the East series: *A Flight of Swans—Poems from Balākā* (London, John Murray, Ltd., 1955) and *Wings of Death, The Last Poems of Rabindranath Tagore* (London, John Murray, Ltd., 1960), which carries as an appendix a striking letter in which Tagore expresses his fundamental religious convictions with rare compression.

Rabindranath himself has generalized about his world view in various prose writings and speeches. *Sādhanā* (N.Y., The Macmillan Co., 1913) was originally a series of sermons for the students at Śantiniketan. *The Religion of Man* (N.Y., 1931; Boston, Beacon Press, 1961), the Hibbert Lectures for 1930, is the fullest account of his religious experience and the most mature formulation of his beliefs. The first three chapters of both *Personality* (N.Y., The Macmillan Co., 1917; London, 1921) and *Creative Unity* (N.Y., The Macmillan Co., 1922) throw supplementary light upon his religion.

A nearly complete bibliography of Tagore's writings in Bengali and English is included in *Rabindranath Tagore, 1861–1961, A Centenary Volume* (New Delhi, Sahitya Akademi, 1961), pp. 504–19. For lists of translations into continental European languages and of books on Tagore published in the West in Occidental languages including English, see A. Aronson, *Rabindranath through Western Eyes* (Allahabad, Kitabistan, 1943), pp. 125–53.

Major secondary writing on Tagore's world view begins with S. Radhakrishnan, *The Philosophy of Rabindranath Tagore* (London, Macmillan & Co., 1918; Baroda, Good Companions, 1961), which interleaves the thought of Tagore very heavily with the thought of S. Radhakrishnan. Sushil Chandra Mitter's *La pensée de Rabindranath Tagore* (Paris, Adrien Maisonneuve, 1930) is a perceptive and detailed exposition. Sigfrid Estborn's *The Religion of Tagore* (Madras, Christian Literature Society for India, 1949) is not successful as a descriptive study because exposition is subordinated entirely to arguments on the historical and theological relation of Tagore's religion to Christianity. Benoy Gopal Ray's *The Philosophy of Rabindranath Tagore* (Bombay, Hind Kitabs, 1941) is to be valued for its faithful exploitation of Tagore's immense untranslated Bengali writings, and for its view of Rabindranath in relation to concurrent activity in Indian religious thought.

(c) MAHATMA GANDHI—Mahatma Gandhi was as original in his thought as Aurobindo, but he was by no means a metaphysician or systematizer. He was a practical moralist, working out his principles of action amid the crises of a many-sided life in which there was little time for elaboration and unification of his ideas. His thinking is best studied in conjunction with his life. Hence the special place of Gandhi's *An Autobiography; or The Story of My Experiments with Truth* (Ahmadabad, Navajivan Press, 1927; London, Phoenix Press, 1949; Boston, Beacon Press, 1959), tr. by Mahadev Desai.

The natural demand for succinct and orderly presentations of Gandhi's teachings has been met by editors who have assembled from his scattered speeches and writings the best expressions of his views on given topics. The compilations listed below are published by the Navajivan Publishing Co., Ahmadabad, and were edited—unless another name is mentioned—by Bharatan Kumarappa. *Hindu Dharma* (1950) and *My Religion* (1955) are skillful efforts to assemble the materials of Gandhi's theological and ethical creed in his own words. *Hindu Dharma* is intended for readers capable of understanding the specific historical settings in which Gandhi worked. *My Religion* omits materials which would be puzzling or not significant to outsiders and presents important statements of principle that have been extracted from their biographical matrix. It has the value of a summary in universal language, but it loses the special vitality of connection with Gandhi the man. *Truth is God*, ed. R. K. Prabhu (1955), and *Ramanama*, 2nd enl. ed. (1949), give special attention to Gandhi's worship practices. *Communal Unity* (1949) and *What Jesus Means to Me*, ed. R. K. Prabhu (1959), express his views on other religions and their adherents. *Varnashramadharma*, ed. R. K. Prabhu (1962), and *The Removal of Untouchability* (1954) present Gandhi's attitudes toward caste. *Self-restraint v. Self-indulgence*, rev. ed. (1947), deals with birth control and sexual ethics. Various aspects of social morality are covered in *How to Serve the Cow* (1954), *Non-violence in Peace and War* (1942; 3rd ed., 1948), *For Pacifists* (1949), and *Satyagraha* (1951). These collections were combed primarily from the journals which Gandhi published in India during the last thirty years of his life. The expressions of his earlier years can now be examined in *The Collected Works of Mahatma Gandhi* (Delhi, Publications Division, Ministry of Information and Broadcasting, 1958–61) which at the present moment cover the years 1884–1907 in six volumes.

Three secondary works on Gandhi's religious outlook deserve special mention. Charles F. Andrews, *Mahatma Gandhi's Ideas* (London, George

Allen & Unwin, Ltd., 1929; N.Y., The Macmillan Co., 1930), still has value. E. Stanley Jones's *Mahatma Gandhi*: *An Interpretation* (N.Y., Abingdon-Cokesbury Press, 1948) is a Christian appreciation of Gandhi's life and teachings. Dhirendra Mohan Datta's *The Philosophy of Mahatma Gandhi* (Madison, University of Wisconsin Press, 1953) is a lucid summary of Gandhi's fundamental convictions by an eminent professor of philosophy.

Further study on Mahatma Gandhi can be carried on with the help of P. G. Deshpande's *Gandhiana* (Ahmadabad, Navajivan Publishing House, 1948) and Jagdish Saran Sharma's *Mahatma Gandhi, A Descriptive Bibliography* (Delhi, S. Chand & Co., 1955).

(d) VINOBĀ BHĀVE—The background and career of Vinoba Bhave, Gandhi's great disciple, is described briefly in Hallam Tennyson's general account, *India's Walking Saint* (Garden City, N.Y., Doubleday & Co., Inc., 1955; English edition, *Saint on the March* [London, Victor Gollancz, Ltd., 1955]). Suresh Ramabhai, *Vinoba and his Mission*, 3rd rev. ed. (Banaras, Sarva Seva Sangh, 1962), chronicles Bhave's land-redistribution campaigns and adds a section on his social and political attitudes. For significant material on Bhave's religious views it is necessary to turn back to his *Talks on the Gita* (Banaras, Sarva Seva Sangh, 1958) written originally in 1932. His economic and political ethics are most fully revealed in his booklet *Swaraj Sastra* (1945; 2nd ed., Wardha, Sarva Seva Sangh, 1955). Bhave's speeches and writings have been classified and compiled by his followers in useful booklets which include *Bhoodan Yajna* (Ahmadabad, Navajivan Publishing Co., 1953), *The Principles and Philosophy of the Bhoodan Yagna* (Tanjore, Sarvodaya Prachuralaya, 1955), and *Sarvodaya and Communism* (Tanjore, Sarvodaya Prachuralaya, 1957). Fifteen interpretive articles by intimates of Bhave have been brought together by P. D. Tandon, ed., *Vinoba Bhave; The Man and his Mission* (Bombay, Vora & Co., 1952?). Study can be pushed further with the help of Jagdish Saran Sharma, *Vinoba and Bhoodan; a Selected Descriptive Bibliography of Bhoodan in Hindi, English and Other Indian Languages* (New Delhi, Indian National Congress, 1956).

(e) SARVEPALLI RADHAKRISHNAN—Radhakrishnan has written his own life story and testament of faith in "My Search for Truth," *Religion in Transition*, ed. by Vergilius Ferm (London, George Allen & Unwin, Ltd., 1937), pp. 11–59. G. E. M. Joad summarizes the message of Radhakrishnan's earlier books in *Counter Attack from the East; The Philosophy of Radhakrishnan* (London, George Allen & Unwin, Ltd., 1933). A. N. Marlow, ed., *Radhakrishnan*: *An Anthology* (London, George Allen & Unwin, Ltd., 1952), illustrates Radhakrishnan's characteristic ideas from his writings. Radhakrishnan's lectures *Fellowship of the Spirit* (Cambridge, Mass., Center for the Study of World Religions, 1961) have the value of a review of the major emphases of his lecturing and writing over many years.

The immensity of Radhakrishnan's output is displayed dramatically in

T. R. V. Murti's "Bibliography of the Writings of Sarvepalli Radhakrishnan" in Paul Arthur Schilpp, ed., *The Philosophy of Sarvepalli Radhakrishnan* (N.Y., Tudor Publishing Co., 1952), pp. 843–62. Our concern is with those writings which bear upon the study of Hinduism ancient and modern.

The first category which is relevant consists of works which are primarily historical. The more important of this class have already been mentioned: his *Indian Philosophy*, *The Brahma Sūtra*, and his translation of the major upanishads and of the Bhagavadgita. We have mentioned that Radhakrishnan is always influenced by an acknowledged intent, even in his most serious historical writing, to find edification for Hindus of the present age.

Writings of a second category review the history of Hinduism also, but without serious effort to advance knowledge of descriptive history. The tone is homiletical, and the creation of authoritative norms for a progressive Hinduism is the real end in view. Such books include *The Hindu View of Life* (London, George Allen & Unwin, Ltd.; N.Y., The Macmillan Co., 1927), *The Heart of Hindusthan* (Madras, Natesan & Co., 1932), and *Religion and Society* (London, George Allen & Unwin, Ltd., 1947). Their importance lies in their influence on the Hindu intellectuals of the present century, who often derive from them an inspiring conception of what their religion has been and should be.

A third type of writing ranges afar into the religious and cultural problems of the entire world. The universality of the themes considered and Radhakrishnan's wide reading in Occidental thought make him the first Hindu intellectual to become one of the fellowship of Western intellectuals as well. These books involve Hinduism in exhorting the world to adopt, for the cure of its ills, a mystical idealism which has its strongest roots in a renovated Advaita Vedanta. The books of this class have a characteristic progression of ideas. They begin with a sketch of the degradation, confusion, and peril of a secularized world whose faiths are shattered beyond rebuilding. The argument moves on to the healing and unification of the world through a universalistic religion not identical with any now existing but to which monistic Hinduism will make contributions of central importance. Thus *An Idealist View of Life* (London, George Allen & Unwin, Ltd., 1932; rev. ed., 1937; N.Y., The Macmillan Co., 1932) describes the philosophic disorganizations of the scientific age and presents Radhakrishnan's most ambitious philosophical construction on behalf of a religion of intuitive experience. The negative counterpart of this work is his early book *The Reign of Religion in Contemporary Philosophy* (London, 1920), a polemic against representative pluralistic thinkers of the West on behalf of an absolute idealism close to the Vedanta. *Eastern Religions and Western Thought* (Oxford, Clarendon Press, 1939; N.Y., Oxford University Press, 1940) follows the usual line of thought in urging upon a disunited and suffering world certain unifying insights of Eastern religions. In recommending them to the West, he devotes much of the book to a historical argument that the great creative periods in Western thought were ages of openness to external impulses. He hints determinedly that the flowering of Greek philosophy and the rise of the Christian gospel took place under Indian influence. Belonging to this class also are his shorter but equally eloquent books: *The Religion We Need* (London, Ernest Benn, Ltd., 1928), *Kalki, or the Future of Civilization* (London, Kegan Paul, Trench, Trubner & Co., Ltd.; N.Y., E. P. Dutton & Co., 1929), and *Recovery of Faith* (N.Y., Harper & Brothers, 1955).

Schilpp's *The Philosophy of Sarvepalli Radhakrishnan* includes some excellent analysis and criticism by academic philosophers of the U.S., Great Britain, and India. Criticism from the standpoint of various Protestant theologies is found in Hendrik Kraemer, *Religion and the Christian Faith* (London, Lutterworth Press, 1956; Philadelphia, Westminster Press, 1957) and David Gnanaprakasam Moses, *Religious Truth and the Relation between Religions* (Madras, Christian Literature Society for India, 1950), pp. 97–122.

VI. THE VITALITY OF HINDUISM TODAY

This guide to the study of Hinduism will end with an account of writings by recent observers who have described current situations and have appraised the vitality of contemporary religious life. Malcolm Pitt, "Recent Developments in Religion in India," *Journal of Bible and Religion*, XV (1947), pp. 69–74, sets forth the *dramatis personae* of the groups which are most active on the contemporary scene. Paul Devanandan in two articles marks out the areas of greatest present tension with regard to belief and discerns certain points of doctrine in which a new consensus is emerging: "Evangelism in Renascent India: The Challenge of Hinduism," *World Dominion*, XXIX (1951), pp. 340–6, and "Trends of Thought in Contemporary Hinduism," *International Review of Missions*, XXVIII (1939), pp. 465–79. H. Heras, "Problèmes religieux de l'Inde moderne," *Le bulletin des missions*, XXV (1951), pp. 196–203, is a general survey of the areas of doctrinal change and of the reconstructions which are giving new shape to Hindu beliefs. Swami Abhishikteswarananda, "L'hindouisme est-il toujours vivant?" in *Vitalité actuelle des religions non Chrétiennes* (Paris, Éditions du Cerf, 1957), describes the eroding and restoring forces which are operating in and upon Hinduism.

Raymond Panikkar, "Contemporary Hindu Spirituality," *Philosophy Today*, III (Summer, 1959), pp. 112–27, offers a useful classification of modern Hindus with regard to religious belief and analyzes the current religious opinions of the university-educated, the traditionally educated, and the illiterate. The reaction of university students against religion receives special attention in Otto Wolf's "Das religiös-geistige Gesicht des freien Indien," *Junge Kirche*, XIII (1952), pp. 596–601, 663–7. Jawaharlal Nehru, foremost among the secularized intelligentsia, makes his influential views on religion quite clear in the chapter "What is Religion?" in *Toward Freedom, The Autobiography of Jawaharlal Nehru* (London, John Lane, Ltd., 1936; Boston, Beacon Press, 1958), pp. 236–43, and in *Discovery of India* (N.Y., John Day Co., Inc., 1946; Garden City, N.Y., Doubleday & Co., Inc., 1959), pp. 9–20. The social attitudes of the traditionally religious, on which Nehru's negative feeling is based, are brought out clearly in Henry H. Pressler's survey, *Social Thought in Benares* (Lucknow, Lucknow Publishing House, 1941). Yet Edward Shils, *The Intellectual between Tradition and Modernity* (The Hague, Mouton & Co., 1961), pp. 60–7, shows that Nehru's orientation toward Hinduism is not typical of men of the educated professions, who continue for the most part not only to acquiesce in religious observance, but to engage in personal religious practices and to testify to subjective religious experience.

R. Pierce Beaver, "Centers of Vitality in Contemporary Hinduism," *Missionary Research Library Occasional Bulletin*, N.Y., IX, 5 (May 27, 1958), pp. 1–11, reports strength in the philosophical activities of religious intellectuals, in the personality cults of the middle classes, and in the folk religion. M. G. Carstairs, "The Religious Temper of Two Indian Villages," *World Dominion*, XXX (1952), pp. 48–52, finds rural religion in various kinds of flux, but not dying out. The place of non-Śrauta rituals in the life of rural India today is given a very positive evaluation by Morris Opler in "The Place of Religion in a North Indian Village," *Southwestern Journal of Anthropology*, XV (Autumn, 1959), pp. 219–26. Taya Zinkin in "Hinduism and Communism: Are They Compatible?" *Eastern World*, IX (Jan., 1955), pp. 16f. holds that only desperation could bring Hindu India to Communism.

VII. BIBLIOGRAPHIES

Excellent bibliographical help is available for the earlier periods in Louis Renou's *Bibliographie Védique* (Paris, Adrien-Maisonneuve, 1931) and in its sequel by R. N. Dandekar, *Vedic Bibliography*, Vol. I (Bombay, Karnatak Publishing House, 1949), and Vol. II (University of Poona, 1961). Both works include the Harappa or Indus Civilization in their coverage, and Dandekar in particular includes much material on periods usually classified as post-Vedic. Their chronological coverage does not approach modern Hinduism, however. The *International Bibliography for the History of Religions* (Leiden, E. J. Brill, 1954ff. for 1952ff.) deals with the new publications of each year, especially in the Western world, on all periods and aspects of Hinduism. Its coverage of current writing can be supplemented occasionally by use of bibliographies devoted to specialties which bear on religion only tangentially or incidentally —particularly the *Linguistic Bibliography* (Utrecht-Bruxelles, Spectrum, 1939ff.), the *Annual Bibliography of Indian Archaeology* of the Kern Institute

(Leyden, E. J. Brill, 1928ff. for 1926ff.), and *The Indian National Bibliography*, ed. B. S. Kesavan (Calcutta, Central Reference Library, 1958ff. for October, 1957ff.). There are no specialized guides to older writing which do not fall within the scope of the Vedic bibliographies of Dandekar and Renou. With great effort, the writings of Western indologists on a given topic from the first bloom of Oriental science to World War I can be traced through a remarkable series of comprehensive bibliographies on Oriental studies beginning with Julius Zenker, *Bibliotheca Orientalis* (1846–61), continued in the Deutsche Morgenländische Gesellschaft's *Wissenschaftlicher Jahresbericht über die morgenländischen Studien* (1859–81); Charles Friederici, *Bibliotheca Orientalis* (1876–83); Johannes Klatt and Ernst Kuhn, *Literaturblatt für orientalische Philologie* (1883–86); and *Orientalische Bibliographie* (1887–1926), compiled by A. Müller, E. Kuhn, and L. Schermann.

A number of bibliographies of writings by and about particular modern religious leaders have been mentioned in the course of our essay.

Current scholarly books on Hinduism in Western languages are commonly reviewed in the *Journal of Asian Studies*, the *Journal of the American Oriental Society*, the *Journal of the Royal Asiatic Society*, and the *Bulletin of the School of Oriental and African Studies* (University of London). *The Aryan Path* (Bombay) is worth consulting continuously for notices and reviews of general nontechnical books on Hinduism, including many published in India.

It has been necessary to limit the coverage of this chapter to religion in the narrower sense. For orientational reading in the history and culture of India, please see David Mandelbaum, "A Guide to Books on India," *American Political Science Review*, XLVI (Dec., 1952), pp. 1154–66; also the South Asia section in the American Universities Field Staff's *A Select Bibliography: Asia, Africa, Eastern Europe and Latin America* (N.Y., American Universities Field Staff, 1960).

IV

Buddhism

Richard A. Gard

Buddhism may be defined as a system of interdependent principles and practices through which man realizes experientially and existentially (1) the nature and predicament of conditioned, imperfect life, (2) the process and causes of such life, (3) the ideal of unconditioned, perfect life, and (4) the way to attain that ideal. Socially and metaphysically, Buddhists endeavor to recognize, cultivate, and actualize the human potential in a complex and changing world.

A comprehensive study of Buddhism as a world view and way of life for many peoples would include some consideration of its historical, geographical, ethnic, linguistic, doctrinal, organizational, cultural, and societal aspects. The reasons for such broad scope of treatment lie in the nature of the subject itself. Buddhist institutions, for example, have been developing for twenty-five centuries, adapting to diverse physical and social environments and interacting with various cultures in a total of some thirty Asian societies, and are now expanding elsewhere in the world. Men and women, young and old, from all strata of economic, political, and social life have become Buddhist monks, nuns, and lay leaders. Buddhist teachings have been expounded in twenty-two Asian languages and scripts and are now being described, interpreted, and translated in thirteen or more non-Asian languages. In turn, Buddhist thought and practice have been formulated and developed into numerous schools and sects. In recent years, Buddhist lay groups have been organized to complement the role of the Saṅgha (Buddhist monastic order) in society and to aid governmental and general public promotion of the Buddha Sāsana/Śāsana[1] (Buddhist principles and practices systematized and institutionalized). Thus significant lay interpretations and exemplifications of the Buddha Dhamma/Dharma (Buddhist doctrines studied and practiced) are being developed. Buddhist religious performances and aesthetic expressions have made notable contributions to Asian and world architecture, handicrafts, literature, music-drama, painting, sculpture, and folklore. In many societies Buddhist ideas, practices, and organizations have influenced, and been influenced by, those aspects of human affairs now studied under the rubrics of economics, education, jurisprudence, political thought and institutions, and social thought and customs.

Accordingly, Buddhism has developed an extensive literature of its own, to which is now being added a vast amount of published knowledge treating it as a subject for specialized study. A comprehensive collection of writings on Buddhism in all languages, particularly Asian, would be enormous—a library ideal yet to be realized anywhere. The reader may well wonder, therefore, how the more important items, even those in English, can be selected from the many publications on Buddhism and presented in an orderly and meaningful way. The method undertaken here will be to cite materials according to a topical outline in nine sections, based upon the traditional Ti-ratana/Tri-ratna components of Buddhism (the Buddha, the Dhamma/Dharma, the Saṅgha), and to indicate the expanding field of modern Buddhist scholarship. The selection of literature will be limited to items in European languages, particularly English, but it should be noted that a comparable bibliographical guide could be written for Buddhist materials in Asian languages, especially those in Japanese. If the reader wishes to have further comment on the references cited here, he may consult review notices for the desired item. Such reviews are cited in two comprehensive Buddhist bibliographies: Shinshō Hanayama, *Bibliography on Buddhism* (Tokyo, Hokweido Press, 1961) for Western-language items published until about 1930 (a few to 1936), and the *Bibliographie Bouddhique* (Paris, Imprimerie Nationale, 1930–), issued periodically, for items published since January, 1928. The latter work often includes a helpful summary or comment for its listings.

The development of modern Buddhist scholarship in Asia and Europe is briefly surveyed in P. V. Bapat, ed., *2500 Years of Buddhism* (Delhi, Govern-

1. The twofold Pāli/Sanskrit spelling of the same Buddhist name will be used in this chapter to indicate respectively the Theravāda and Mahāyāna or Vajrayāna traditional usage.

ment of India, 1956), chap. XIV, "Buddhist Studies in Recent Times," pp. 382–446. Among Asian researches, Japanese studies on Buddhism and related fields are particularly well advanced; for a bibliographical review, see Hakuju Ui, "Orientation in the Study of Japanese Buddhism" and Shinshō Hanayama, "Orientation in the Study of Japanese Buddhism" in Kokusai Bunka Shinkokai, ed., *A Guide to Japanese Studies* (Tokyo, 1937), pp. 55–86 and 87–135, respectively; A. Hirakawa and E. B. Ceadel, "Japanese Research on Buddhism since the Meiji Period," *Monumenta Nipponica*, XI, 3 (Oct., 1955), pp. 1–26 and 4 (Jan., 1956), pp. 69–96; "The Recent Activities of Indian and Buddhist Studies in Japan," *Journal of Indian and Buddhist Studies, Special Supplementary Issue* ([illegible], 19[illegible]), Part One, pp. 1–[illegible], which reviews the period 1946–57; and Hajime Nakamura, "A Brief Survey of Japanese Studies on the Philosophical Schools of the Mahāyāna," *Acta Asiatica*, I (1960), pp. 56–88. For a historical survey of Western Buddhist scholarship, the following may be used: Henri de Lubac, *La rencontre du Bouddhisme et de l'Occident* (Paris, Aubier, 1952); Marcelle Lalou, "Eleven Years of Works on Buddhism in Europe (May, 1936–May, 1947)," *The Indian Historical Quarterly*, XXV, 4 (Dec., 1949), pp. 229–62, and articles by Edward Conze in *The Middle Way* (London): "Recent Progress in Buddhist Studies," XXXIV, 1 (May, 1959), pp. 6–14; "Recent Progress in Mahayana Studies," XXXIV, 4 (Feb., 1960), pp. 144–50; and "Recent Work on Tantric and Zen Buddhism," XXXV, 3 (Nov., 1960), pp. 93–8.

A reader who carefully uses well-chosen materials may learn much about Buddhism even though he lives in a non-Buddhist environment. For the Buddhist intellectual, however, learning alone will not suffice, since he is traditionally expected to read Buddhist texts reverently (cf. *sutta/sūtra-pūjā*) as part of his learning process, to verify or reject any given exposition of Buddhist principles according to established reason, and to test those principles as practices through his own personal experience.

I. INTRODUCTORY WORKS

1. Introductions and summaries

There is an old Indian story concerning some blind men who once argued about the nature of an elephant. When they could not convince one another, they decided to touch an elephant and resolve the issue. Each man touched a different part and went away, thinking that he alone knew what an elephant was like: a piece of rope, a trunk of a tree, a huge snake, a large fan, and so on. In similar fashion, authors of introductory works on Buddhism tend to describe it each according to his own perspective. Most introductions to Buddhism are Buddhist- , Christian- , or Hindu-oriented and ethnocentric in expression. Buddhist writers often take as normative the kind of Buddhism that has been formative in the life of their own countries. Others may study or view Buddhism only in terms of a particular group interest or academic point of view, such as the comparative study of religions or philosophies. All such accounts may be relatively sound and accurate, depending upon their scholarship and lack of bias, but they are also unavoidably incomplete. It is, therefore, advisable for those who study Buddhism to read many accounts and note their different points of view.

The Western environmental background and personal views of authors should be taken into consideration when one reads popularly written works on Buddhism such as E. Conze, *Buddhism: Its Essence and Development* (Oxford, Bruno Cassirer, 1951, 1960; N.Y., Philosophical Library, Inc., 1951, 1959); Christmas Humphreys, *Buddhism*, rev. ed. (London, Cassell & Co., 1962); Maurice Percheron, *Buddha and Buddhism* (London, N.Y., Harper & Brothers, 1957); James Bissett Pratt, *The Pilgrimage of Buddhism and a Buddhist Pilgrimage* (N.Y., The Macmillan Co., 1928); August Karl Reischauer, "Buddhism," in Edward J. Jurji, ed., *The Great Religions of the World* (Princeton, Princeton University Press, 1946), pp. 90–140; and F. Harold Smith, *The Buddhist Way of Life: Its Philosophy and History* (London, Hutchinson's University Library, 1951).

With regard to modern Asian presentations of Buddhism, one might well begin by reading Kenneth W. Morgan, ed., *The Path of the Buddha* (N.Y., Ronald Press, 1956) for various Burmese, Ceylonese, Japanese, and Tibetan points of view; Gunapala Piyasena Malalasekera, "The Buddhist Point of View" in UNESCO, ed., *Humanism and Education in East and West* (Paris, UNESCO, 1953), pp. 133–48; and Buddha Prakash, "The Buddhist Methodology," *The Journal of the Bihar Research Society*, Buddha Jayanti Special Issue (1956), I, pp. 35–46. Thereafter, one may select from the following ethnocentric or nationalistic expositions of Buddhism according to his particular interest and need.

For the Burmese Theravāda view, see U Nu, *What is Buddhism?* (Rangoon, Buddha Sasana Council Press, 1956) and U Po Sa, *A Brief Outline of Buddhism* (Rangoon, Universal Printing Works, 1955).

The Ceylonese Theravāda view is expressed in numerous short introductions to Buddhism, among which three may be specially recommended: G. P. Malalasekera, *The Buddha and His Teachings* (Colombo, Lanka Bauddha Mandalaya, 1957); Nārada Thera, *A Manual of Buddhism*, 4th ed. (Colombo, Associated Newspapers of Ceylon, 1953); and Walpola Rahula, *What the Buddha Taught* (Bedford, Gordon Fraser, 1959; N.Y., Grove Press, 1962).

For the Chinese Mahāyāna view, see Miss Pitt Chin Hui (Chye Hong, comp. and tr.), *A Bilingual Graduated Course on the Fundamental Teachings of Lord Buddha*, Books 1–4 (Singapore, Buddhist Association, 2nd printing, 1950–51); T'ai Hsü, *Lectures in Buddhism* (Paris, Imprimerie Union, 1928); and Bhikkhu Yen-Kiat, *Mahayana Buddhism*, rev. ed. (Bangkok, Debsriharis, 1961).

The general Indian view of Buddhism is indicated in various studies, among which the following are representative: Bhīmrāi Rāmjī Ambedkar, *The Buddha and His Dhamma* (Bombay, People's Education Society, 1957) for popular interest and Nalinaksha Dutt, *Early Monastic Buddhism*, rev. ed. (Calcutta, Calcutta Oriental Book Agency, 1960) and Sukumar Dutt, *The Buddha and Five After-centuries* (London, Luzac & Co., 1957) for scholarship. The Hindu interpretation of Buddhism is reflected in Ananda Kentish Coomaraswamy, *Buddha and the Gospel of Buddhism* (London, George Harrap, 1916; Bombay, Asia Publishing House, 1956) and in the various philosophical-religious writings of Sarvepalli Radhakrishnan.

The Japanese Mahāyāna view is authoritatively presented by Daisetz Teitarōo Suzuki, *The Essence of Buddhism*, 2nd ed. (London, The Buddhist Society, 1947); Junjirō Takakusu, *The Essentials of Buddhist Philosophy*, 3rd ed. (Bombay, Asia Publishing House, 1956); and Entai Tomomatsu, *Le Bouddhisme* (Paris, Alcan, 1935).

For the Thai Theravāda view, see Yong Hoontrakool, *The Path of Light* (Bangkok, Charas Wanthanathavi, 1956) and Luang Suriyabongs, *Buddhism: an Introduction* (Colombo, The Lanka Buddha Mandalaya, 1957), which may be compared with an earlier statement in Henry Alabaster, tr., *The Modern Buddhist; Being the Views of a Siamese Minister of State on His Own and Other Religions* (London, Kegan Paul, Trench, Trubner & Co., Ltd., 1870), reprinted in his *The Wheel of the Law* (London, Kegan Paul, Trench, Trubner & Co., Ltd., 1871) as Part I, pp. 1–73.

My own work *Buddhism* (N.Y., George Braziller, 1961; London, Prentice-International, 1962) is an attempt to present the subject in general outline by exposition and quotation of selected passages from basic texts and Asian and Western studies.

2. Collected articles, essays, lectures

Ordinarily, a collection of articles or essays by different writers will give the reader a broader introduction to Buddhism than the views of a single writer. In this respect, the following Buddhist miscellanies are particularly useful: Bapat, ed., *2500 Years of Buddhism*; René de Berval, ed., *Présence du Bouddhisme* (Saigon, France-Asie, 1959) with chapters in English as well as French; *B.C. Law Volume*, 2 parts, ed. by D. R. Bhandarkar and others (Calcutta, 1945; Poona, 1946); *The Journal of the Bihar Research Society* (Patna) Buddha Jayanti Special Issue, 1956, Vol. 1; Gautama Buddha 25th Centenary Volume, *The Indian Historical Quarterly* (Calcutta), XXXII, 2–3 (June–Sept., 1956); Bimala Churn Law, ed., *Buddhistic Studies* (Calcutta and Simla, Thacker Spink & Co., 1931), including Haraprasād Shāstrī, "Chips from a Buddhist Workshop," pp. 818–58, which offers various historical research notes, and *Indological Studies*, Part I (Calcutta, Indian Research Institute, 1950), Part II (Calcutta, Indian Research Institute,

1952), and Part III (Allahabad, Ganganath Research Institute, 1954); Morgan, ed., *The Path of the Buddha*; and Kshitis Roy, ed., *Liebenthal Festschrift* (Santiniketan, Visvabharati, 1957).

It should also be noted that important papers on Buddhism by various writers are often contained in the conference reports, proceedings, and transactions of scholarly societies for the study of Oriental and Asian cultures, philosophies, and religions as well as in commemorative volumes for eminent Buddhist scholars and other Orientalists. For listings of such papers see the *Bibliographie Bouddhique*, section I, "Généralités."

3. Comparative studies

Comparative studies of Buddhist interactions with various cultures and philosophical or religious ways of life may help to orient the reader about Buddhism in terms of his own environmental understanding. For this purpose, however, it is desirable that such accounts embody established research principles, historiography, and acceptable comparative methods as well as reliable conceptions and statements of Buddhist views.

Among numerous studies on Buddhist relations with other systems of Indian thought, the following will serve as a brief introduction to the subject, although some of them may reflect Hindu interpretations of Buddhism. For general studies see N. Dutt, "Place of Buddhism in Indian Thought," reprinted in Gautama Buddha 25th Centenary Volume, *The Indian Historical Quarterly*, XXXII, 2–3 (June–Sept., 1956), pp. 115–40; the various writings in German by Helmuth von Glasenapp (consult the *Bibliographie Bouddhique* for listings); H. Nakamura, "Upaniṣadic Tradition and the Early School of Vedānta as Noticed in Buddhist Scripture," *Harvard Journal of Asiatic Studies*, XVIII, 1–2 (June, 1955), pp. 74–104; and A. K. Warder, "On the Relationship between Early Buddhism and Other Contemporary Systems," *Bulletin of the School of Oriental and African Studies* (University of London), XVIII (1956), pp. 43–63. Buddhist relations with Brāhmanism as the early phase of Hinduism are reviewed by Radhagovinda Basak, "The Interrelations between Brāhmanism and Buddhism," in his *Lectures on Buddha and Buddhism* (Calcutta, Sambodhi Publications, 1961), pp. 103–26; T. P. Bhattacharya, "Brahmā-cult and Buddhism," *The Journal of the Bihar Research Society*, XLII (March, 1956), pp. 91–115, (June, 1956), pp. 256–82; Y. Krishnan, "Was There Any Conflict between the Brahmins and the Buddhists?" *The Indian Historical Quarterly*, XXX, 2 (June, 1954), pp. 167–77; and Jean Przyluski and Étienne Lamotte, "Bouddhisme et Upaniṣad," *Bulletin de l'École Française d'Extrême-Orient*, XXII: 1932 (1933), 1, pp. 141–69. Comparisons of Buddhism and the Vedānta as a later phase of Hinduism are undertaken by T. R. V. Murti, "The Mādhyamika, Vijñānavāda and Vedānta Absolutism" in his *The Central Philosophy of Buddhism: A Study of the Mādhyamika System* (London, George Allen & Unwin, Ltd., 1955), pp.

311–28; P. T. Raju, "Buddhism and the Vedanta," *The Indo-Asian Culture*, VI, 1 (July, 1957), pp. 24–48; and Chandradhar Sharma, *Dialectic in Buddhism and Vedānta* (Benares, Nand Kishore, 1952) and "Buddhism and Vedānta" in his *A Critical Survey of Indian Philosophy* (London, Rider & Co., 1960; N.Y., Barnes & Noble, Inc., 1962), pp. 318–34. Two other interesting comparative studies may also be mentioned here: K. N. Jayatilleke, "Some Aspects of Gita and Buddhist Ethics," *University of Ceylon Review*, XIII, 2–3 (April–July, 1955), pp. 135–51, and P. T. Raju, "The Concept of Man in Indian Thought: 3. Man in Jainism and Buddhism" in S. Radhakrishnan and P. T. Raju, eds., *The Concept of Man* (London, George Allen & Unwin, Ltd., 1960), pp. 151–71.

Unfortunately, there are few scholarly or reliable studies in English on the nature of Buddhist relations with non-Indian systems of belief and practice. However, for Buddhist encounters with Islām, see Karl Jahn, "Kamalāshrī-Rashīd al-Dīn's 'Life and Teaching of Buddha.' A Source for the Buddhism of the Mongol Period," *Central Asiatic Journal*, II (1956), pp. 81–128, and especially S. M. Yusuf, "The Early Contacts between Islam and Buddhism," *University of Ceylon Review*, XIII, 1 (Jan., 1955), pp. 1–28. Concerning the case in Korea, note Doo Hun Kim, "The Rise of Neo-Confucianism against Buddhism in Late Koryō," *Bulletin of the Korean Research Center*, XII (May, 1960), pp. 11–29. No satisfactory historical account of the interrelations of Buddhism, Manicheanism, Nestorianism, and Zoroastrianism in Central Asia, as well as in China, can be suggested here. A reliable study of Buddhist-Bon relations in Tibet is given by Helmut Hoffmann, *The Religions of Tibet* (London, George Allen & Unwin, Ltd., 1961) and the references he cites. Elsewhere, as in southeastern Asia, anthropological field investigation of the commingling of Buddhist and animistic or shamanistic beliefs and practices is only just beginning.

Buddhist influences upon Western thought and literature is an interesting subject described in the following historical surveys: Heinrich Günter, *Buddha in der abendländischen Legende?* (Leipzig, H. Haessel, 1922); Kurt F. Leidecker "Some Buddhist Themes in Western Literature," in Horst Frenz, ed., *Asia and the Humanities* (Bloomington, University of Indiana, 1959), pp. 113–23, and "The Impact of Buddhism on the West," *The Journal of the Siam Society*, XLV, 2 (Oct., 1957), pp. 1–27; H. de Lubac, *La rencontre du Bouddhisme et de l'Occident*; A. N. Marlow, "Hinduism and Buddhism in Greek Philosophy," *Philosophy East and West*, IV, 1 (April, 1954), pp. 35–45; Raymond Schwab, "Le Bouddhisme de Wagner" in his *La renaissance orientale* (Paris, Payot, 1950), pp. 459–70; Pero Slepčević, *Buddhismus in der deutschen Literatur* (Wien, C. Gerold's Sohn, 1920).

A literary account of a Buddhist contact with Western thought is contained in the *Milinda-pañha* report of the dialogue between the Bactrian Greek king Menander (Pāli: Milinda) and the Buddhist sage Nāgasena in the second century B.C., for which see Isaline Blew Horner, tr., *King Milinda's Questions* (*Milinda-panha*), 2 vols. (London, Luzac & Co., 1963), and Caroline Augusta Foley Rhys Davids, *The Milinda-Questions* (London, Routledge & Kegan Paul, Ltd., 1930). Also of historic literary interest is the Christianized legend of the Buddha in several versions, such as the Barlaam and Josaph romance, for which see David Marshall Lang, *The Wisdom of Balahvar: A Christian Legend of the Buddha* (London, George Allen & Unwin, Ltd., 1957) and his article "Bidawhar Wa-yūdāsaf" in *The Encyclopaedia of Islam*, new ed. (Leiden, E. J. Brill, 1960–   ), pp. 1215a–17b.

Most of the attempts to compare or contrast Buddhism and Christianity are unsatisfactory because they tend to deal with doctrinal matters without sufficient reference to their historical and institutional contexts, and they usually do not employ an established comparative method of analysis or a common terminology. With regard to Christian-oriented studies, see Tucker N. Calloway, *Japanese Buddhism and Christianity* (Tokyo, Shinkyo Shuppansha Protestant Publishing Co., 1957) for the Japanese context; Winston L. King, *Buddhism and Christianity* (Philadelphia, Westminster Press, 1962) for the Burmese context; Bryan de Kretser, *Man in Buddhism and Christianity* (Calcutta, Y.M.C.A. Publishing House, 1954) for the Ceylonese context; and H. de Lubac, *Aspects of Buddhism* (London, N.Y., Sheed & Ward, Inc., 1953) for a European viewpoint. Buddhist-oriented studies are relatively few, such as Fumio Masutani, *A Comparative Study of Buddhism and Christianity* (Tokyo, Aoyoma-Shoin, 1956), and D. T. Suzuki, *Mysticism: Christian and Buddhist* (London, George Allen & Unwin, Ltd.; N.Y., Harper & Brothers, 1957). Of historical interest now is *Buddhism and Christianity*, an oral debate held at Panadura (in August, 1873) between the Rev. Migettuwatte Gunananda, a Buddhist priest, and the Rev. David De Silva, a Wesleyan clergyman, with introduction and annotations by J. M. Peebles (latest ed., Colombo, P. K. W. Siriwardhana, 1955).

Comparative Buddhist-Western philosophical studies are not yet well developed, but for general interest see Walter Liebenthal, "Existentialism and Buddhism," *Viśva-Bharati Quarterly*, XXII (Spring, 1956–57), pp. 293–313, and Murti, "The Mādhyamika and Some Western Dialectical Systems" in his *The Central Philosophy of Buddhism*, pp. 293–310.

II. HISTORIES

1. General surveys

A truly comprehensive history of Buddhism has not yet been written in any language. The task will be a difficult one, considering the diverse ethnic, cultural, and linguistic expressions, the numerous doctrinal developments, the various organizational activities, and the changing societal role of Buddhism during twenty-five centuries in a total of some thirty countries in Asia and now elsewhere in the world. When written, such a history will probably include an intellectual and institutional survey of the interrelated developments of the Buddha conceptions and veneration, the Dhamma/Dharma texts, principles, and practices, and the Saṅgha organization, schools, and activities which together comprise the traditional Ti-ratana/Tri-ratna of Buddhism as well as a cultural and social survey of the interaction of the Buddha Sāsana/Śāsana with other systems of belief and practice in various societies.

Although several Buddhist historical texts (cf. *vaṃsa/vaṃsā*, chronicles) [illegible] [illegible] developments of the Buddha conceptions, Dhamma/Dharma doctrines, Saṅgha institutions, or the Buddha Sāsana/Śāsana, they do not comprise comprehensive histories of Buddhism. Their English versions and modern accounts and studies will be cited below where more appropriate. However, two traditional Pāli narratives which survey Buddhism in India and southeast Asia in general terms should be mentioned here: the *Saddhamma-saṅgha*, attributed to the Indian Dhammakitti Mahāsāmi (fourteenth century A.D.), which has been translated by B. C. Law as *A Manual of Buddhist Historical Traditions* (*Saddhamma-Saṅgha*) (Calcutta, University of Calcutta, 1941), and the *Sāsanavaṃsa*, written by the Burmese Paññāsāmi in 1861, also translated by B. C. Law as *The History of the Buddha's Religion* (*Sāsanavaṃsa*) (London, Luzac & Co., Ltd., 1952).

In beginning his historical study of Buddhism, the student should read the following historiographical articles: Erich Frauwallner, "The Historical Data We Possess on the Person and the Doctrine of the Buddha," *East and West*, VII, 4 (Jan., 1957), pp. 309–12; Upendra Nath Ghoshal, "Early Buddhist Historiography," in his *Studies in Indian History and Culture* (Bombay, Orient Longmans, 1957), pp. 39–50; and É. Lamotte, "La critique d'authenticité dans le Bouddhisme" in Instituut Kern, ed., *India Antiqua* (Leyden, Instituut Kern, 1947), pp. 213–22.

Some of the more notable surveys of Buddhism in English are the following. Bapat, ed., *2500 Years of Buddhism*, especially chap. V, "Aśoka and the Expansion of Buddhism," pp. 60–96, provides a general sketch. E. Conze, *A Short History of Buddhism* (Bombay, Chetana, 1960) reviews the principal doctrinal and school developments. J. Deniker, "General Survey of Buddhism and its Evolution," in Alice Getty, *The Gods of Northern Buddhism*, 2nd rev. ed. (Oxford, Clarendon Press, 1928), Introduction, pp. xvii–liv, gives a useful summary of the subject. Charles Norton Edgecumbe Eliot, *Hinduism and Buddhism: An Historical Sketch*, 3 vols. (London, Routledge & Kegan Paul, Ltd., 1921; reprinted N.Y., Barnes & Noble, Inc., 1954), especially Pali Buddhism (Vol. I, Book III), The Mahayana (Vol. II, Book IV), Buddhism outside India (Vol. III, Book VI), and the sequel volume *Japanese Buddhism* (London, Edward Arnold, Ltd., 1935; reprinted N.Y., Barnes & Noble, Inc.,

1959), together form the major Buddhist history in English. René Grousset, *On the Footsteps of the Buddha* (London, George Routledge & Sons, Ltd., 1932) is a cultural survey of Buddhism in the seventh century A.D. B. C. Law, "Buddhism and its Expansion in India and Outside" in his *Indological Studies*, Part II, pp. 165–215, Balangoda Ananda Maitreya, "Buddhism in Theravada Countries" and J. Kashyap, "Origin and Expansion of Buddhism" in Morgan, ed., *The Path of the Buddha*, pp. 3–66 and 113–52, respectively, provide Asian summaries of the subject. Kenneth James Saunders, *Epochs in Buddhist History* (Chicago, University of Chicago Press, 1924) is a popularly written account. Erik Zürcher, *Buddhism: Its Origin and Spread in Words, Maps and Pictures* (London and N.Y., Routledge & Kegan Paul, Ltd., 1962) is useful as a study aid.

2. Country surveys

A comprehensive understanding of Buddhism in Asia requires a detailed knowledge and comparative study of Buddhist developments in many areas. For this purpose various country histories and descriptions of Buddhism and supplementary archeological, social science, and other data will be necessary. Such materials cannot be fully listed here, but some selected items will be cited in separate paragraphs for each major Buddhist country.

With regard to Buddhism in Bhutan, there is yet no detailed survey, but one may profitably consult the historical and anthropological descriptions in René von Nebesky-Wojkowitz, *Where the Gods are Mountains* (London, Weidenfeld & Nicolson, Ltd. 1956), and note the brief account by C. Sivaramamurti, "Buddhism in Sikkim, Ladakh and Bhutan," *The Light of Buddha*, V (1960), 1 (Jan.), pp. 34–8, and 3 (March), pp. 24–6.

For Buddhism in Burma during the traditional period to the advent of British rule, see Eliot, "Burma" in his *Hinduism and Buddhism*, Vol. III, pp. 46–77, and the valuable studies by Nihar Ranjan Ray (Roy): *An Introduction to the Study of Theravāda Buddhism in Burma* (Calcutta, University of Calcutta, 1946), "Early Traces of Buddhism in Burma," *Journal of the Greater India Society*, VI (1939), pp. 1–52, 99–123, and *Sanskrit Buddhism in Burma* (Amsterdam, H. J. Paris, 1936). The historic Pagān period (A.D. 1044–1287) is described by Pe Maung Tin, "Buddhism in the Inscriptions of Burma," *Journal of the Burma Research Society*, XXVI, 1 (April, 1936), pp. 52–70, and Than Tun, "Religion in Burma, A.D. 1000–1300," *Journal of the Burma Research Society*, XLII, 2 (Dec., 1959), pp. 47–69.

For popularly written Western accounts of Burmese Buddhist life in the late nineteenth century, see Harold Fielding-Hall, *The Inward Light* (London and N.Y., Macmillan & Co., Ltd., 1908) and *The Soul of a People* (London, 1898; 5th ed., Macmillan & Co., Ltd., 1930) and James George Scott (Shway Yoe), *The Burman: His Life and Notions* (London, Macmillan & Co., Ltd., 1892; 3rd ed., 1927). For more recent times, there are valuable descriptions in John

Frank Brohm, *Burmese Religion and the Burmese Religious Revival* (unpublished Ph.D. thesis, Cornell University, 1957) and some observations in Robert Henry Lawson Slater, *Paradox and Nirvana* (Chicago, University of Chicago Press, 1951).

The contemporary period since Independence (January 4, 1947) is officially reviewed by the Union [of Burma] Buddha Sāsana Council, *Report on Situation of Buddhism in Burma* (Rangoon, Aung Meitsat Press, 1954), *Report on the Situation of Buddhism in Burma since January 1955 C.E.* (Rangoon, Aung Meitsat Press, 1956), and *Report on Buddhism in Burma* (Rangoon, Aung Meitsat Press, 1961). Other descriptions and analyses of current trends are given by Brohm, "The Post War Government and Burma's Religious Revival" in his *Burmese Religion and the Burmese Religious Revival*, pp. 368–436; U Hla Bu, "The Nature of the Resurgence of Buddhism in Burma," *The S.E. Asia Journal of Theology*, III, 1 (July, 1961), pp. 25–31; and Hugh Tinker, "Culture and Religion" in his *The Union of Burma*, 2nd ed. (London, Oxford University Press, 1959), pp. 165–90.

Historical studies of Buddhism in Cambodia are mostly monographs about its archeological, epigraphical, or architectural-sculptural aspects, especially concerning the Khmer Empire or Angkor Monarchy, and are usually written in French. For general orientation, see Bernard Philippe Groslier, "Our Knowledge of Khmer Civilization, A Re-appraisal," *The Journal of the Siam Society*, XLVIII, 1 (June, 1960), pp. 1–28. The following works may be consulted for historical data and descriptions about Buddhism in Cambodia. Lawrence Palmer Briggs, *The Ancient Khmer Empire* (Philadelphia, Transactions of American Philosophical Society, 1951), see references to "Buddhism" and Buddhist names and concepts in the Index, and "The Syncretism of Religions in Southeast Asia, Especially in the Khmer Empire," *Journal of the American Oriental Society*, LXXI, 4 (Oct.–Dec., 1951), pp. 230–49. Pierre Dupont, "La propagation du bouddhisme indien en Indochine occidentale," *Bulletin de la Société des Études Indochinoises*, Nouvelle Série, XVIII, 1–2 (1er et 2e Trimestre, 1943), pp. 93–105. Eliot, "Camboja" in his *Hinduism and Buddhism*, Vol. III, pp. 100–36. Adhémard Leclère, *Le Bouddhisme au Cambodge* (Paris, E. Leroux, 1899). Pang Khat, "Le Bouddhisme au Cambodge" in de Berval, ed., *Présence du Bouddhisme*, pp. 841–52. B. N. Puri, "Buddhism in Ancient Kambujadesa (An Epigraphic Study)," reprinted in Gautama Buddha 25th Centenary Volume, *The Indian Historical Quarterly*, XXXII, 2–3 (June–Sept., 1956), pp. 205–10. Kalyan Sarkar, "Mahāyāna Buddhism in Fu-nan," *Sino-Indian Studies*, V, 1 (1955), pp. 69–75. Sukumar Sen Gupta, "Buddhism in Funan," *The Maha Bodhi*, LXVI (1958), pp. 344–7.

Buddhism in Central Asia, from the first century B.C. to about the tenth century A.D., is a complex subject for historical study. It requires background knowledge of the geography, trade routes, military operations, political administration, languages, and cultural arts in the area as well as study of Buddhist contacts with Chinese, Hun-Turkic-Mongol, Greek, Indian, Parthian-Iranian, Roman, Scythian, and other cultures and peoples and interactions with Chinese religious systems, Hinduism, Islām, Manicheanism, Nestorianism, and Zoroastrianism. For such information the best sources now available are the reports and studies of Chinese, English, French, German, Japanese, Russian, and other archeological expeditions to Central Asian sites, such as those of the former city-state kingdoms of Kāshgar, Khotan, Kucha, Miran, Niya, Turfan, Tun-huang, and Yarkand. For references to these accounts see Juntarō Ishihama and others, "Bibliography of the Central Asiatic Studies" in The Research Society of Central Asian Culture, ed., *Monumenta Serindica,* Vol. 1. *Chinese Buddhist Texts from Tunhuang* (Kyōto, Hozokan, 1958), pp. 53–87.

Although extensive histories of Buddhism in Central Asia are not yet available in English, the following introductions and general surveys may be helpful to the reader. Prabodh Chandra Bagchi, *India and Central Asia* (Calcutta, National Council of Education, Bengal, 1955) and *India and China: A Thousand Years of Cultural Relations*, 2nd rev. ed. (Bombay, Hind Kitabs Ltd., 1950; N.Y., Philosophical Library, 1951). Eliot, "Central Asia" in his *Hinduism and Buddhism*, Vol. III, pp. 188–222. Johannes Nobel, *Central Asia* (Nagpur, The International Academy of Indian Culture, 1952), Lecture I, "Central Asia: The Connecting Link between East and West," pp. 1–39, and Lecture II, "Spread of Buddhism," pp. 41–70. Frederick William Thomas, "Buddhism in Khotan: Its Decline according to Two Tibetan Accounts," *Sir Asutosh Mookerjee Silver Jubilee Volumes*, Vol. III, *Orientalia*, Part III, 3 (1927), pp. 30–52. Zenryū Tsukamoto, "Historical Outlines of Buddhism in Tunhuang" in *Monumenta Serindica*, Vol. 1, Introduction, pp. 1–10. Supplementary to these general accounts, four specialized studies should also be mentioned here: Annemarie von Gabain, "Buddhistische Türkenmission" in *Asiatica*, pp. 161–73, "Der Buddhismus in Zentralasien" in B. Spuler, ed., *Religionsgeschichte des Orients in der Zeit der Weltreligion* (Leiden, E. J. Brill, 1961), XVI, and "Die Frühgeschichte der Uiguren: 607–745," *Nachrichten der (Deutschen) Gesellschaft für Natur- und Völkerkunde Ostasiens*, II (1952), pp. 18–32; and Dénes Sinor, "A Közepázsiasi török Buddhismusról" (On Turkish Buddhism in Central Asia), in *Kőrösi Csoma Archivum* (Budapest, Apdel, 1939), pp. 353–96 (pp. 391–93 in English). For historic travel descriptions see those by the early Buddhist pilgrim-scholars, such as the Chinese Fa-hsien (traveled during A.D. 399–414), Sung-yün and Hui-sang (518–22), and Hsüan-tsang (or Yüan-chuang, 629–45) and the Korean Hecho (*c.* 726), whose records are listed below.

The formative period of Buddhism in Ceylon before the advent of Western rule in the sixteenth century has been traditionally recorded in several extant Pāli texts. As a general introduction to these chronicles, see B. C. Law, *On the*

Chronicles of Ceylon (Calcutta, Royal Asiatic Society of Bengal, 1947), and Garrett Champness Mendis, "The Chronology of the Early Pāli Chronicles of Ceylon," *University of Calcutta Review*, V, 1 (Jan., 1947), pp. 39–54, and "The Pāli Chronicles of Ceylon. An Examination of the Opinions Expressed about Them since 1879," *University of Calcutta Review*, IV, 2 (Jan., 1946), pp. 1–24. For the chronicles themselves, one should read Hermann Oldenberg, ed. and tr., *The Dîpavaṃsa: An Ancient Buddhist Historical Record* (London, Williams & Norgate, Ltd., 1879), which has not been entirely superseded by the later translation of B. C. Law, ed. and tr., *The Chronicle of the Island of Ceylon, or The Dipavamsa* in *The Ceylon Historical Journal*, VII, 1–4 (July, 1957 to April, 1958), and Wilhelm Geiger, tr., *The Mahāvaṃsa, or The Great Chronicle of Ceylon* (London, H. Frowde, 1912; reprinted Colombo, Ceylon Government Information Department, 1950 with *Addendum* prepared by G. C. Mendis) and W. Geiger, tr., *Cūlavaṃsa, Being the More Recent Part of the Mahāvaṃsa*, 2 vols. (London, Humphrey Milford, 1925–27; reprinted Colombo, Ceylon Government Information Department, 1953). Certain corrections and revisions of Geiger's translations are given by A. P. Buddhadatta Mahāthera, *Corrections of Geiger's Mahāvaṃsa, etc.* (Ambalangoda, The Ananda Book Co., 1957), pp. 1–39 *re* the *Mahāvaṃsa* translation, and pp. 40–93 *re* the *Cūḷavaṃsa* translation; and Heinz Bechert, ed., "Unpublished Additions and Corrections to the Translation of the Mahāvaṃsa and the Cūlavaṃsa by Geiger," in W. Geiger, *Culture of Ceylon in Mediaeval Times* (Wiesbaden, Otto Harrassowitz, 1960), pp. 228–53.

Modern, Westernized histories of Buddhism in Ceylon are still inadequate in their scope and treatment, but the reader may find the following surveys useful: Josiah Crosby, "Buddhism in Ceylon," *Journal of the Royal Asiatic Society* (*of Great Britain and Ireland*) (1947), pp. 41–52, 166–83; W. A. De Silva, "History of Buddhism in Ceylon" in B. C. Law, ed., *Buddhistic Studies*, pp. 453–528; and Eliot, "Ceylon" in his *Hinduism and Buddhism*, Vol. III, pp. 11–45. For particular periods in the development of Sinhalese Buddhism, the student may read various accounts and correlate their information into a fairly comprehensive historical survey. The following may be used for this purpose. E. W. Adikaram, *Early History of Buddhism in Ceylon* (Migoda, D. S. Puswella, 1946). P. E. E. Fernando, "An Account of the Kandyan Mission Sent to Siam in 1750 A.D.," *The Ceylon Journal of Historical and Social Studies*, II, 1 (Jan., 1959), pp. 37–83, which includes "Translation of Vilbāgedara's Account of the Mission to Siam," pp. 53–72. Geiger, "Religion and Church: III. Buddhism," in his *Culture of Ceylon in Mediaeval Times*, pp. 179–215. D. B. Jayatilaka, "Reformation of the Sangha and Revival of Buddhism in Ceylon in the Eighteenth Century," *B. C. Law Volume*, II, pp. 7–11, *Saraṇaṅkara, The Last Sangha-Rāja of Ceylon* (Colombo, Lankabhinava Vissruta Press, 1934), and "Sinhalese Embassies to Arakan," *Journal of the Ceylon Branch of the Royal Asiatic Society*, XXXV (1935), pp. 1–6. E. F. C.

Ludowyk, *The Footprint of the Buddha* (London, George Allen & Unwin, Ltd., 1958). W. Pachow, "Ancient Cultural Relations between Ceylon and China," *University of Ceylon Review*, XXI, 3 (July, 1954), pp. 182–91. Vincent Panditha, "Buddhism during the Polonnaruva Period" in S. D. Saparanade, ed., Special Number on the Polonnaruva Period, *The Ceylon Historical Journal*, IV, 1–4 (July and Oct., 1954 to Jan. and April, 1955), pp. 113–29. Senerat Paranavitana, "Ceylon and Malayasia in Medieval Times," *Journal of the Ceylon Branch of the Royal Asiatic Society*, New Series, VII, 1 (1960), pp. 1–42, his contributions in the University of Ceylon, *History of Ceylon*, Vol. I. *From the Earliest Times to 1505*, Part I (Colombo, Ceylon University Press, 1959), especially pp. 125–43, 241–68, 378–409; Part II (Colombo, Ceylon University Press, 1960), especially pp. 563–612, 745–69, his "Mahāyānism in Ceylon" in de Berval, ed., *Présence du Bouddhisme*, pp. 515–27, and his "Religious Intercourse between Ceylon and Siam in the 13th–16th Centuries," *Journal of the Ceylon Branch of the Royal Asiatic Society*, XXXII (1932), pp. 190–213. Paulus Edward Pieris, tr., *Religious Intercourse between Ceylon and Siam in the 18th Century: I. Account of King Kirti Sri's Embassy to Siam in Saka 1672 (1750 A.D.)*, translated from the Singhalese (Bangkok, Siam Observer Office, 1908); II. *Syāmūpadasampada. The Adoption of the Siamese Order of Priesthood in Ceylon, Saka Era, 1673 (A.D. 1751)*, compiled by the Rev. Siddhartha Buddharakhita Thero of Pusparamo Monastery in Kandy, Ceylon, A.D. 1776 (Bangkok, American Presbyterian Mission Press, 1914). W. Rahula, *History of Buddhism in Ceylon: The Anuradhapura Period, 3rd Century B.C.–10th Century A.D.* (Colombo, M. D. Gunasena, 1956) is a detailed study. Nanda Deva Wijesekera, "Buddhism in Practice," in his *The People of Ceylon* (Colombo, M. D. Gunasena, 1949), pp. 162–70, gives a sociological description.

The nature of the contemporary period since Independence (February 4, 1948) is indicated in William Howard Wriggins, "Religious Revival and Cultural Nationalism" in his *Ceylon: Dilemmas of a New Nation* (Princeton, Princeton University Press, 1960), pp. 169–210, and two politically influential works: *The Betrayal of Buddhism:* an abridged version of the report of the Buddhist Committee of Inquiry (of the All-Ceylon Buddhist Congress) (Balangoda, Dharmavijaya Press, 1956) and D. C. Vijayavardhana (Vijewardene), *The Revolt in the Temple* (Colombo, Sinha Publications, 1953).

Concerning Buddhism in Hong Kong, a recent report is available in English by Holmes H. Welch, "Buddhist Organizations in Hong Kong," *Journal of the Hongkong Branch of the Royal Asiatic Society* (1961), pp. 1–17.

Studies of the origin, development, decline, and recent revival of Buddhism in India—covering twenty-five centuries—are fundamental for a general history of Buddhism. Such accounts are so numerous and varied that only a very select list can be given here, arranged in four main groups for convenience.

For introductions and general surveys of Buddhism in India see the following. P. V. Bapat, "Contribution of Buddhism to Indian Culture," *Cahiers d'Histoire mondiale/Journal of World History*, IV, 2 (1958), pp. 383–401. N. Dutt, *Early Monastic Buddhism*, 2 vols. (Calcutta, Calcutta Oriental Book Agency, 1941, 1945; not the rev. ed., Calcutta Oriental Book Agency, 1960) and "Place of Buddhism in Indian Thought," Gautama Buddha 25th Centenary Volume, *The Indian Historical Quarterly*, XXXII, 2–3 (June–Sept., 1956), pp. 115–40. Eliot, *Hinduism and Buddhism*, Vol. I, Book III, Pali Buddhism, pp. 129–345, and Vol. II, Book IV, The Mahayana, pp. 3–131, and *Japanese Buddhism*, Book I, chap. III, "Buddhism in India," pp. 62–98. Jean Filliozat, "Le bouddhisme: 3. L'histoire du bouddhisme" in Louis Renou and J. Filliozat, *L'Inde classique*, tome II (Paris, Imprimerie Nationale; Hanoi, École Française d'Extrême-Orient, 1953), pp. 492–511 and "Le bouddhisme: 6. Cultes bouddhiques," pp. 605–8. Johan Hendrik Casper Kern, *Manual of Indian Buddhism* (Strassburg, Verlag von Karl S. Trübner, 1896). B. C. Law, *Geography of Early Buddhism* (London, Kegan Paul, Trench, Trubner & Co., Ltd., 1932) and *Indological Studies*, Parts I and II.

Since Sanskrit chronicles of Buddhism in India do not exist, two extant Tibetan traditional accounts are invaluable. See Bu-tön (Bu-ston, *c.* A.D. 1290–1364), *History of Buddhism* (*Chos-ḥbyung*) *by Bu-ston.* Part II. *The History of Buddhism in India and Tibet* (Heidelberg, In kommission bei Otto Harrassowitz, 1932), translated by Evgenii Evgeniewich Obermiller, and Tāranātha (A.D. 1573/75–1608), *Târanâtha's Geschichte des Buddhismus in Indien* (St. Petersburg, Kommissionare der Kaiserlichen Akademie der Wissenschaft, 1868), translated by Anton von Schiefner, and partially rendered into English by N. Dutt and U. N. Ghoshal as "Tāranātha's History of Buddhism in India," *The Indian Historical Quarterly*, IV, 3 (Sept., 1928), pp. 530–3; V, 4 (Dec., 1929), pp. 715–21; VI, 2 (June, 1930), pp. 334–44; VII, 1 (March, 1931), pp. 150–60; VIII, 2 (June, 1932), pp. 247–52. Earlier descriptions of Buddhist India are preserved in the travel accounts by Fa-hsien (during A.D. 399–414), Sung-yün and Hui-sang (518–22), Hsüan-tsang (or Yüan-chuang, 629–45), I-ching (or I-tsing, 671–95), and Hecho (*c.* 726), which are cited below.

For the rise and development of Buddhism in India, see the following accounts: Dutt, *The Buddha and Five After-centuries*; the sections entitled "Religion and Philosophy: B. Buddhism" in Ramesh Chandra Majumdar, general ed., *The History and Culture of the Indian People* (Bombay): Vol. II. *The Age of Imperial Unity* (2nd ed., Bharatiya Vidya Bhavan, 1953), pp. 365–411, by N. Dutt, J. N. Banerjea, A. D. Pusalker; Vol. III. *The Classical Age* (1954), pp. 368–403, by Dutt, Banerjea, Pusalker; Vol. IV. *The Age of Imperial Kanauj* (1955), pp. 258–87, by Dutt and Banerjea; Vol. V. *The Struggle for Empire* (1957), pp. 404–25, by N. N. Das Gupta; B. G. Gokhale, *Buddhism and Asoka* (Baroda, Padmaja Publications, 1948); É. Lamotte,

Histoire du Bouddhisme Indien: des origines à l'ère Śaka (Louvain, Institut Orientaliste, 1958), a major work which should also be consulted for bibliographical references; Kunja Govinda Goswami, "Buddhism in the Śuṅga Period," Gautama Buddha 25th Centenary Volume, *The Indian Historical Quarterly*, XXXII, 2–3 (June–Sept., 1956), pp. 103–14. The section "Religious Movements: (B) Buddhism (200 B.C.–A.D. 300)" in K. A. Nilakantha Sastri, ed., *A Comprehensive History of India*, Vol. Two. *The Mauryas & Satavahanas, 325 B.C.–A.D. 300* (Bombay, Orient Longmans, 1957), pp. 364–78, by K. A. N. Sastri and others; Govind Chandra Pande, *Studies in the Origins of Buddhism* (Allahabad, University of Allahabad, 1957); Sudha Sengupta, "Buddhism in the Classical Age (as revealed by Archaeology)," reprinted in Gautama Buddha 25th Centenary Volume, *The Indian Historical Quarterly*, XXXII, 2–3 (June–Sept., 1956), pp. 71–102.

For Buddhist developments in particular Indian regions and countries, see the following studies. Concerning Buddhism in East India: Suniti Kumar Chatterji, "Buddhist Survivals in Bengal," *B. C. Law Volume*, I, pp. 75–87; Nalini Nath Das Gupta, "Buddhism in Kāmarūpa," *The Indian Historical Quarterly*, XXVI, 4 (Dec., 1950), pp. 332–46; R. C. Majumdar, "Lāmā Tāranātha's Account of Bengal" in Narendra Nath Law, ed., *Louis de la Vallée Poussin Memorial Volume* (Calcutta, 1938), pp. 1–20; Maheswar Neog, "Buddhism in Kāmarūpa," *The Indian Historical Quarterly*, XXVII, 2 (June, 1951), pp. 144–50; P. L. Paul, "Buddhism in Ancient Bengal," *Journal of Indian History*, XVII, 1 (April, 1938), pp. 29–33; N. Sahu, *Buddhism in Orissa* (Cuttack, Utkal University, 1958); Nagendra Nath Vasu, *The Modern Buddhism and Its Followers in Orissa* (Calcutta, U.N. Bhattacharyya, Hare Press, 1911); and H. Vedāntaśāstrī, "Buddhism in Bengal and Its Decline," *The Journal of the Bihar Research Society*, Buddha Jayanti Special Issue (1956), Vol. I, pp. 66–76. Concerning Buddhism in North India: N. Dutt and Krishna Datta Bajpai, *Development of Buddhism in Uttar Pradesh* (Lucknow, Publication Bureau, Government of Uttar Pradesh, 1956), and Bhakat Prasad Mazumdar, "A Revaluation of Buddhism in Bihar and the Uttar Pradesh (*c.* 635–1197 A.D.), *The Journal of the Bihar Research Society*, Buddha Jayanti Special Issue (1956), Vol. I, pp. 173–85. Concerning Buddhism in Northeast India, see A. K. Nag, "Buddhism in Assam Tribal Areas," *Indian Review*, LIX, 6 (1958), pp. 263–5. Concerning Buddhism in Northwest India, see N. Dutt, "Buddhism in Kashmir" in his edited *Gilgit Manuscripts*, Vol. I (Srinagar, Government of Jammu and Kashmir, 1939), pp. 1–45, and J. N. Ganhar and P. N. Ganhar, *Buddhism in Kashmir & Ladakh* (New Delhi, P. N. Ganhar, 1956), which is a popularly written account. Concerning Buddhism in South India, see S. Krishnaswami Aiyangar, "The Buddhism of Maṇimēkhalai" in B. C. Law, ed., *Buddhistic Studies*, pp. 1–25; P. C. Alexander, *Buddhism in Kerala* (Annamalainagar, Registrar, Annamalai University, 1949); V. R. Ramachandra Dikshitar, "Buddhism in Tamil Literature" in

B. C. Law, ed., *Buddhistic Studies*, pp. 673–98, and "Buddhism in Āndhradeśa," *B. C. Law Volume*, I, pp. 346–53; K. A. N. Sastri, "An Episode in the History of Buddhism in South India," *B. C. Law Volume*, I, pp. 35–49; P. S. Sastri, "Some Buddhist Thinkers of Andhra," Gautama Buddha 25th Centenary Volume, *The Indian Historical Quarterly*, XXXII, 2–3 (June–Sept., 1956), pp. 55–9, and "The Rise and Growth of Buddhism in Andhra," *The Indian Historical Quarterly*, XXXI, 1 (March, 1955), pp. 68–75; and K. R. Subramanian, *Buddhist Remains in Andhra and the History of Andhra, 225–610 A.D.* (Madras, Diocesan Press, Andhra University Series, 1932).

Regarding the decline of Buddhism in India, for which various explanations have been proffered, see P. C. Bagchi, "Decline of Buddhism in India and Its Causes," *Sir Asutosh Mookerjee Silver Jubilee Volumes*, Vol. III, *Orientalia*, Part III, 2 (1925), pp. 405–21; N. Dutt, "The Rise and Fall of Buddhism in India," *The Maha Bodhi*, LXIII, 6 (1955), pp. 256–66; B. P. Mazumdar in *The Journal of the Bihar Research Society*, Buddha Jayanti Special Issue (1956), Vol. I, pp. 173–85, cited above; R. C. Mitra, *The Decline of Buddhism in India* in *Viśva-Bharati Annals*, VI (1954), pp. 1–164 and *Viśva-Bharati Studies*, XX (1954); and Arthur Waley, "New Light on Buddhism in Medieval India," *Mélanges chinois et bouddhiques*, I: 1931–32 (1932), pp. 355–76.

For Buddhism in Indonesia, there are sketches by Louis Charles Damais, "Le Bouddhisme en Indonésie" in de Berval, ed., *Présence du Bouddhisme*, pp. 813–24; Eliot, "Java and the Malay Archipelago" in his *Hinduism and Buddhism*, Vol. III, pp. 151–87; and Pieter Hendrik Pott, "Le bouddhisme de Java et l'ancienne civilisation javanaise," *Serie Orientale Roma*, V (1952), pp. 109–56. For more detailed information one must resort to archeological and textual studies of the monumental Borobuḍur stūpa in central Java (see below) and await published researches on the Buddhist Śailendra Dynasty of the Śrīvijaya Empire (seventh–thirteenth centuries A.D.), including surveys of Buddhist institutional relations with Brāhmanism-Hinduism and cultural relations with India, Ceylon, mainland southeast Asia, and China. The travel account by I-ching (or I-tsing), who visited Sumatra and India during 671–95, contains some descriptive data; it is listed below.

For Buddhism in Japan, see chapter V of the present volume.

Buddhism in Korea is a subject which awaits proper treatment by historians who will utilize the archeological reports, cultural arts studies, and scanty textual data written in Korean, Chinese, and Japanese. Meanwhile, the English reader may use the latest brief surveys by Cho Myung Gi, "Buddhism: Introduction, Development of Buddhism in Korea, Present Situation" in The Korean National Commission for UNESCO, comp., *UNESCO Korean Survey* (Seoul, Dong-a Publishing Co., 1960), pp. 37–43, and "Korean Buddhism: Introduction, Koguryo, Paekche, Silla, Unified Silla, Koryo, Yi Chosun, Present Situation" in *Korea: Its Land, People and Culture of All Ages* (Seoul, Hakwan-sa Ltd., 1960), pp. 329–37. The following sketches by Western writers are scarcely adequate but may offer the reader some points of general interest: Charles Allen Clark, "Buddhism" in his *Religions of Old Korea* (N.Y., Fleming H. Revell Co., 1929), pp. 11–90; Philipp Karl Eidmann, "An Introduction to the History of Buddhism in Korea," *The Maha Bodhi*, LXVIII, 5 (May, 1960), pp. 114–22; 6 (June), pp. 186–92. Homer B. Hulbert [rev. ed. by Clarence N. Weems] *History of Korea*, 2 vols. (N.Y., Hillary House, 1962), especially the Editor's Introduction, pp. ED 63–ED 127 and Buddhist references in the Index; Frederick Starr, *Korean Buddhism: History-Condition-Art* (Boston, Marshall Jones, 1918). Mark Napier Trollope, "Introduction to the Study of Buddhism in Corea," *Transactions of the Korea Branch of the Royal Asiatic Society*, VIII (1917), pp. 1–40.

Published accounts of the nature and history of Buddhism in Laos are meager because work has scarcely begun on the collection and study of requisite source materials. The following items therefore only sketch the subject: Thao Nhou Abhay, "Buddhism in Laos" in R. de Berval, ed., *Kingdom of Laos* (Saigon, France-Asie, 1959), pp. 237–56; Henri Deydier, "La religion" in his *Introduction à la connaissance du Laos* (Saigon, Imprimerie française d'Outremer, 1952), pp. 18–32, and *Lokapâla: Génies, totems et sorciers du Nord Laos* (Paris, Plon, 1954); Louis Finot, tr., "Establishment of Buddhism, Foundation of the Wat Keo and of the First Monasteries" in de Berval, ed., *Kingdom of Laos*, pp. 409–10, which is adapted from his French translation of the Lao Annals of Lan Xang; Pierre-Bernard Lafont, "Aperçu sur la religion" in his *Aperçus sur le Laos* (Saigon, Comité de l'Alliance française du Laos, 1959), pp. 43–50, and "Introduction du Bouddhisme au Laos" in de Berval, ed., *Présence du Bouddhisme*, pp. 889–92; and Paul Lévy, "Les traces de l'introduction du Bouddhisme à Luang Prabang," *Bulletin de l'École Française d'Extrême-Orient*, XL: 1940 (1941), 2, pp. 411–24.

A history of Buddhism in Malaya-Singapore remains to be written from the limited textual resources, inscriptions, and archeological data now being collected. In the meantime, of popular interest are Colin McDougal, *Buddhism in Malaya* (Singapore, D. Moore, 1956) which is admittedly inadequate, and Margaret Topley, "Chinese Religion and Religious Institutions in Singapore," *Journal of the Malayan Branch of the Royal Asiatic Society*, XXIX, 1 (May, 1956), pp. 70–118, and "Chinese Women's Vegetarian Houses in Singapore," *Journal of the Malayan Branch of the Royal Asiatic Society*, XXVII, 1 (May, 1954), pp. 51–67.

The historical study of Buddhism in Manchuria and how it was influenced by Chinese and Mongolian Buddhism appears to be neglected by present-day scholars. Thus two works remain from the nineteenth century for the interested reader: Charles Joseph de Harlez, *La religion nationale des Tartares orientaux; Mandchous et Mongols* (Bruxelles, Académie Royal des sciences, des lettres et des beaux-arts de Belgique, 1887) and Carl Friedrich Köppen,

"Die Mandschu und der Lamaismus" in his *Die Religion des Buddha und ihre Entstehung*, Bd. 2, *Die Lamaische Hierarchie und Kirche* (Berlin, F. Schneider, 1859; reprinted 1906), pp. 105–242.

For Buddhism in Mongolia, there are various accounts in several languages. As introductions to the subject, see Charles Bell, "Buddhism Captures Mongolia" in his *The Religion of Tibet* (Oxford, Clarendon Press, 1931), pp. 110–18; Schuyler Cammann, *The Land of the Camel* (N.Y., Ronald Press, 1951); and Robert James Miller, "The Foundations of Lamaist Inner Mongolia" in his *Monasteries and Culture Change in Inner Mongolia* (Wiesbaden, Otto Harrassowitz, 1959), pp. 1–10.

The more specialized studies and textual accounts of Mongolian Buddhism are listed as follows: A. Haneda, "Les conquérants tartares et le bouddhisme," *Cahiers d'Histoire mondiale/Journal of World History*, I, 4 (1954), pp. 922–6; Walther Heissig, "A Mongolian Source to the Lamaist Suppression of Shamanism in the 17th Century," *Anthropos*, XLVIII (1953), pp. 1–29, 493–536, and "Zur lamaistischen Beeinflussung des mongolischen Geschichtsbildes," *Serta Cantabrigiensia* (1954), pp. 37–44; Georg Huth, ed. and tr., *Geschichte des Buddhismus in der Mongolei*, . . . des ['Jigs-med Rig-p'ai rdo je; wrongly called:] Jigs-men nam-mkha, 2 vols. (Strassburg, K. G. Trübner, 1892, 1896); Köppen, "Die Mongolen und der Lamaismus" in his *Die Religion des Buddha und ihre Entstehung*, Bd. 2, pp. 85–104; A. D. Kornakowa, "Lamaica aus der Mongolei," translated from the Russian by W. A. Unkrig in *Micro-Bibliotheca Anthropos*, XXV (1958), x, 73 pp., about which see Dominik Schröder, "A. D. Kornakowa's und W. A. Unkrig's 'Lamaica aus der Mongolei,'" *Anthropos*, LIII, 3–4 (1958), pp. 585–90; M. Percheron, *Le tryptique mongol. I. Dieux et démons, lamas et sorciers de Mongolie* (Paris, Denöel, 1953); Paul Ratschnevsky, "Die mongolischen Grosskhane und die buddhistische Kirche" in *Asiatica*, pp. 489–504; Isaac Jacob Schmidt, tr., *Geschichte der Ost-Mongolen und ihres Fürstenhauses*, verfasst von Ssanang Ssetsen Chungtaidschi der Ordus (St. Petersburg, Carl Cnobloch and Leipzig, N. Gretsch, 1829; reprinted The Hague, Mouton & Co., 1962) (see references to "Buddha und Buddhaismus" and Buddhist names and concepts in the Inhalt [Index]).

Western descriptions of Buddhism in Nepal began with those by Brian Houghton Hodgson in the early nineteenth century (for listings see Hanayama, *Bibliography on Buddhism*). Recent studies, but still no historical surveys, are based on textual research, archeological exploration, and anthropological data. The more notable accounts in English are the following: John Brough, "Legends of Khotan and Nepal," *Bulletin of the School of Oriental and African Studies, University of London*, XII, 2 (1948), pp. 333–9; Jiro Kawakita, "Religion: B. The Lamaistic Highland" in H. Kihara, ed., *Peoples of Nepal Himalaya*, Vol. III (Kyoto, Kyoto University, 1957), pp. 140–227; David L. Snellgrove, "Buddhism in Nepal" in his *Buddhist Himalaya* (Oxford, Bruno

Cassirer, 1957), pp. 91–120, and *Himalayan Pilgrimage* (Oxford, Bruno Cassirer, 1961), which contains references to "Buddhism" and Buddhist names and concepts in the Index; and Giuseppe Tucci, *Preliminary Report on Two Scientific Expeditions in Nepal* (Rome, Istituto Italiano per il Medio ed Estremo Oriente, 1956) and *Nepal: The Discovery of the Malla* (N.Y., E. P. Dutton & Co., Inc., 1962).

The subject of Buddhism in Pakistan is generally viewed as an archeological-historical study of its Gandhāra-Kashmīr past in West Pakistan and Northwest India. In this respect, the following historical background and cultural materials will be interesting and useful. H. Deydier, *Contribution à l'étude de l'art du Gandhâra* (Paris, Adrien Maisonneuve, 1950) provides a descriptive and analytical bibliographical essay on writings published during 1922–49. Richard Fick, *Die buddhistische Kultur und das Erbe Alexanders des Grossen* (Leipzig, Hinrichs, 1933) is a cultural survey. Alfred Charles Auguste Foucher, *L'Art gréco-bouddhique du Gandhâra*, I (Paris, Imprimerie Nationale, 1905); II, 1 (1918), 2 (1922), 3 (1951), constitutes a major study of the subject. Harald Ingholt, "Introduction," in his and Islay Lyons' *Gandhāran Art in Pakistan* (N.Y., Pantheon Books, 1957), pp. 13–46, gives an historical summary and iconographical survey. É. Lamotte describes the contacts between Buddhists and Greeks in "Alexandre et le Bouddhisme," *Bulletin de l'École Française d'Extrême-Orient*, XLIV: 1947–50 (1951), 1, pp. 147–62, "De quelques influences grecques et scythes sur le bouddhisme," *Academie des Inscriptions et Belles-Lettres, Comptes-rendus des séances* (1956), pp. 485–504, and "Hellénisme et Bouddhisme à l'époque Śuṅga" in his *Histoire du Bouddhisme Indien*: 1. Influence du Bouddhisme sur les Grecs, pp. 457–69, 2. Influence grecque sur le Bouddhisme, pp. 469–87. Johanna Engelberta van Lohuizen-De Leeuw, *The Scythian Period* (Leiden, E. J. Brill, 1949) offers a scholarly approach to the history, art, epigraphy, and paleography of North India from the first century B.C. to the third century A.D. William Woodthorpe Tarn, *The Greeks in Bactria & India*, 2nd ed. (Cambridge, Cambridge University Press, 1951), and Mortimer Wheeler, *Rome beyond the Imperial Frontiers* (London, G. Bell & Sons, Ltd., 1954), Part III. Asia, provide general historical background information. As regards East Pakistan, archeological surveys of the Buddhist past and sociological studies of present-day Buddhist organizations have scarcely begun. *Buddhism in Pakistan* by a Pakistani Buddhist (Karachi, Government of Pakistan, Ministry of Information and Broadcasting, 1955) is a popularly written sketch.

For Buddhism in Sikkim, note the comments made above for Bhutan, and see Maharaj Kumar of Sikkim (Maharajkumar Palden Thondup Namgyal), "Tibetan Studies in Sikkim," *The Maha Bodhi*, LXVIII, 1 (Jan., 1960), pp. 2–7, and "The Namgyal Institute of Tibetology," *World Buddhism*, IX, 2 (Sept., 1960), pp. 5–6.

Buddhism in Taiwan can be generally distinguished into two related types:

the Taiwanese form (originally from the China mainland) and the Chinese form (especially since 1950 from the mainland), whereas the Japanese influences from their occupation during 1895–1945 are now scarcely perceptible. For popularly written descriptions, see Bodhedrum Publications, *Buddhism in Taiwan* (Taichung, 1961) and Kuo Huo-lieh, "Buddhism in Taiwan Today: Attitudes towards Changing Society," *The S.E. Asia Journal of Theology*, III, 2 (Oct., 1961), pp. 43–58.

The historical study of Buddhism in Thailand requires further archeological and textual research, but meanwhile several accounts have been written in English by Thai scholars: Luang Boriband Buribhand, "Buddhism in Thailand," in *In Commemoration of the Year 2500 Buddhist Era in Thailand* (Bangkok, Siva Phorn, Ltd., 1957), pp. 1–21; His Highness Prince Dhaninivat, Kromamun Bidyalabh, *A History of Buddhism in Siam* (Bangkok, The Siam Society, 1960); and the Mahamakut Educational Council of the Buddhist University of Thailand [Mahamakuta Rajavidyalaya], *Buddhism in the Kingdom of Thailand* (Bangkok, Buddhist University of Thailand, 1957). An interesting historical study of the Saṅgha has been made by Robert Lingat, "La double crise de l'église bouddhique au Siam (1767–1851)," *Cahiers d'Histoire mondiale/Journal of World History*, IV, 2 (1958), pp. 402–25. For a Westerner's description of Siamese Buddhist life in the late nineteenth century, see Ernest Young, *The Kingdom of the Yellow Robe: Being Sketches of the Domestic and Religious Rites and Ceremonies of the Siamese* (London, Westminster Press, 1898; 3rd ed., Constable & Co., Ltd., 1907).

Present-day historical knowledge of Buddhism in Tibet is considerably indebted to two traditional Tibetan chronicles which are now available in English translation: Bu-ston, *History of Buddhism* (*Chos-ḥbyung*), Part II, already mentioned above, and George N. Roerich, tr., *The Blue Annals* [Deb-ther sṅon-po], 2 vols. (Calcutta, Asiatic Society, 1949, 1953) for which one may use Turrell V. Wylie, *A Place Name Index to George N. Roerich's Translation of The Blue Annals* (Rome, Serie Orientale, ISMEO, 1957); Western accounts, such as Eliot, "Tibet" in his *Hinduism and Buddhism*, Vol. III, pp. 345–401; Köppen, "Tibet und der Lamaismus" in his *Die Religion des Buddha und ihre Entstehung*, Bd. 2, pp. 39–84; Emil Schlagintweit, *Buddhism in Tibet* (Leipzig, F. A. Brockhaus; London, 1863); and Laurence Austine Waddell, *The Buddhism of Tibet, or Lamaism* (London, W. H. Allen, 1895; reprinted Cambridge, W. Heffer & Sons, Ltd., 1934), are now being replaced by more scholarly accounts which are based on textual studies and field surveys. A select list of such works would include the following: Bell, *The Religion of Tibet;* Hoffmann, *The Religions of Tibet*; M. Lalou, *Les religions du Tibet* (Paris, Presses universitaires de France, 1957); Li An-che, "Tibetan Religion" in Vergilus Ferm, ed., *Ancient Religions*, originally published as *Forgotten Religions* (N.Y., Philosophical Library, 1950), pp. 251–69. Lobsang Phuntsok Lhalumgpa, "Buddhism in Tibet" in

Morgan, ed., *The Path of the Buddha*, pp. 237–305; Thubten Jigme Norbu (with Heinrich Harrer), *Tibet is My Country* (London, Rupert Hart-Davis, 1960), which should be read together with his brother's *My Land and My People: The Autobiography of His Holiness the Dalai Lama* (London, N.Y., Weidenfeld & Nicolson, Ltd., 1962), edited by David Howarth; Hugh E. Richardson, *Tibet and Its History* (London, Oxford University Press, 1962), also entitled *A Short History of Tibet* (N.Y., E. P. Dutton & Co. Ltd., 1962); G. N. Roerich, "Introduction of Buddhism into Tibet," *Stepping Stones* (Kalimpong), II, 5 (Sept., 1951), pp. 134–8; Louis M. J. Schram, "Introduction of Buddhism and Lamaism in Hsining (Huang-chung)," in his *The Monguors of the Kansu-Tibetan Frontier*, Part II, *Their Religious Life* (Philadelphia, American Philosophical Society, 1957), pp. 8–37; Snellgrove, *Buddhist Himalaya* and *Himalayan Pilgrimage*; and G. Tucci, "Tibetan Notes," *Harvard Journal of Asiatic Studies*, XII, 3–4 (Dec., 1949), pp. 477–96, and other scholarly writings, principally in Italian (consult the *Bibliographie Bouddhique* for listings).

Buddhism in Viêt-Nam is often studied inadequately as a part of "Vietnamese religion," which is described in such works as Léopold Cadière, *Croyances et pratiques religieuses des Viêtnamiens*, 3 vols. (I. Saigon Imprimerie Nouvelle d'Extrême Orient, 1944; 2nd ed. 1958; II. Saigon, 1955; III. Paris, École Française d'Extrême Orient, 1957); A. Coué, "Doctrines et cérémonies religieuses du pays d'Annam," *Bulletin de la Société des Études Indochinoises*, Nouvelle Série, VIII (3e Trimestre, 1933), pp. 85–193; Raymond Grivaz, *Aspects sociaux et économiques du sentiment religieux en pays Annamite* (Paris, Les Éditions Domat-Montchrestien, 1942); and Georges Lebrun, "Beliefs and Religions in Viêt-Nam," *Asia* (Saigon), I (March, 1951), pp. 75–84.

Concerning Vietnamese Buddhism itself, there are two sketches in English by Eliot: "Champa" in his *Hinduism and Buddhism*, Vol. III, pp. 137–50, and L. Finot, "Outlines of the History of Buddhism in Indo-China" in B. C. Law, ed., *Buddhistic Studies*, pp. 749–67. For more detailed information, the reader must resort to materials in French such as the following: Gustave Dumoutier, "Notes sur le Bouddhisme tonkinois," *Revue d'Ethnographie*, VII (1888), pp. 285–301; Maurice Durand, "Introduction du Bouddhisme au Viêt-Nam" in de Berval, ed., *Présence du Bouddhisme*, pp. 797–800; Lucien Escalère, "Cultes d'Annam: 1. Le Bouddhisme," in his *Le Bouddhisme & Cultes d'Annam* (Shanghai, Imprimerie de T'ou-sè-wè zi-ka-wei, 1937), Deuxième Partie, pp. 166–95; Mai-tho-Truyên, "Le Bouddhisme au Viêt-Nam" in de Berval, ed., *Présence du Bouddhisme*, pp. 801–10, and Truyên's illustrated survey *le bouddhisme au Vietnam* (Saigon, 1962) in French, English, and Vietnamese. André Migot, "Notes sur le Bouddhisme viêtnamien," *La pensée bouddhique*, V, 4 (Oct., 1954), pp. 10–13, and "Le Bouddhisme en Indochine," *Bulletin de la Société des Études Indochinoises*,

Nouvelle Série, XXI (2e Semestre, 1946), pp. 23–38; Tràn-văn-Giáp, "Le Bouddhisme en Annam. Des origines au XIIIe siècle," *Bulletin de l'École Française d'Extrême-Orient*, XXXII: 1932 (1933), 1, pp. 191–268 (reprinted Paris, 1932), and "Les deux sources du Bouddhisme annamite. Ses rapports avec l'Inde et la Chine," *Cahiers de l'École Française d'Extrême-Orient*, XXXIII (1942).

3. Councils and conferences

Buddhist councils and conferences (Saṅgīti) have been important factors in the formation of Buddhist canonical literature (authenticating the traditional oral and written texts), in the development of Buddhist schools (propounding various interpretations of the texts), and in the preservation of the Saṅgha as a monastic order (codifying the Vinaya rules of conduct).

The number and lists of such councils in Buddhist histories vary according to the particular tradition held in different Buddhist countries. For general descriptions and surveys of the subject see the following studies: André Bareau, *Les premiers conciles bouddhiques* (Paris, Presses universitaires de France, 1955), which concerns the Councils of Rājagha/Rājagṛha (cf. modern Rājgir), Vesāli/Vaiśālī (cf. Besarh), and Pāṭaliputta/Pāṭaliputra (cf. Patna); E. Frauwallner, "Die buddhistischen Konzile," *Zeitschrift der Deutschen Morgenländischen Gesellschaft*, CII (1952), pp. 240–61; B. Jinananda, "Four Buddhist Councils" in Bapat, ed., *2500 Years of Buddhism*, pp. 35–55, including three appendices concerning councils in Ceylon, Thailand (Siam), and Burma; Louis de la Vallée Poussin, "Councils (Buddhist)," in *Encyclopaedia of Religion and Ethics*, edited by James Hastings, 13 vols. (Edinburgh and N.Y.), IV, pp. 179a–85a, and "The Buddhist Councils," *The Indian Antiquary*, XXXVII (1908), pp. 1–18, 81–106; R. C. Majumdar, "Buddhist Councils," in B. C. Law, ed., *Buddhistic Studies*, pp. 26–72; and Edward Joseph Thomas, "The Councils: Early Schools," in his *The History of Buddhist Thought* (London, Kegan Paul, Trench, Trubner & Co., Ltd., N.Y., 1933; 2nd ed. N.Y., Alfred A. Knopf, Inc., 1951), pp. 27–41.

Special studies of certain Buddhist councils are also available: Kenneth Ch'en, "The Mahāparinirvānasūtra and the First Council," *Harvard Journal of Asiatic Studies*, XXI, 3–4 (Dec., 1958), pp. 128–33; Paul Demiéville, "À propos du concile de Vaiśālī," *T'oung Pao*, XL, 4–5 (1951), pp. 239–96; Jothiya Dhirasekera, "Buddhaghosa and the Tradition of the First Council," *University of Ceylon Review*, XV, 3–4 (July–Oct., 1957), pp. 167–81; N. Dutt, "The Second Buddhist Council," *The Indian Historical Quarterly*, XXXV, 1 (March, 1959), pp. 45–56; Rudolf Otto Franke, "The Buddhist Councils at Rājagāha and Vesāli as alleged in the Cullavamsa, XI, XII," *Journal of the Pali Text Society* (1908), pp. 1–80; Marcel Hofinger, *Étude sur le Concile de Vaiśālī* (Louvain, Bureaux du Muséon, 1946), and ed. and tr., *Le Congrès du Lac Anavatapta* (*Vies de Saints bouddhiques*); Extrait du Vinaya des Mūlasarvāstivādin Bhaiṣajyavastu. I. *Légendes des Anciens* (*Sthavivāvādana*) (Louvain, Publications universitaires, 1954); J. Przyluski, *Le Concile de Rājagṛha.* Introduction à l'histoire des canons et des sectes bouddhiques (Paris, Paul Geuthner, 1926–28); and Ernst Waldschmidt, "Zum ersten buddhistischen Konzil in Rājagṛha" in *Asiatica*, pp. 817–28. Chinese traditional accounts are translated in Samuel Beal, "The Buddhist Councils held at Rajagriha and Vesâlî," *Verhandlungen des fünften internationalen Orientallisten-Congresses, gehalten zu Berlin im September 1881* (Berlin, 1882), II, 2, . . . IV. *Ostasiatische Section*, pp. 13–46, reprinted in his *Abstract of Four Lectures on Buddhist Literature in China* (London, Kegan Paul, Trench, Trubner & Co., Ltd., 1882), pp. 66–94, and D. T. Suzuki, "The First Buddhist Council," *The Monist*, XIV (1904), pp. 253–82; a Tibetan account is translated in Bu-ston, "The Rehearsals of the Hīnayānistic Scripture" in his *History of Buddhism* (*Chos-ḥbyung*) *by Bu-ston*, II, pp. 73–101.

The Chaṭṭha Sangāyanā or Sixth Council, held in Burma at Kaba Aye, Rangoon, during May 17, 1954 to May 24, 1956, is described in various issues of Buddhist periodicals, such as *The Light of the Dhamma* (Rangoon) and *World Buddhism* (Colombo), and in publications by the Union Buddha Sāsana Council: *The Chaṭṭha Sangāyanā Souvenir Album* (1956), *Chattha Sangayana 2500th Buddha Jayanti Celebrations* (1956), and other materials; the editorial and publishing work of the Sixth Council is reportedly still in progress.

An historic debate held in Tibet at Lhasa in the late eighth century A.D. decided that Indian sources instead of Chinese were to be authoritative in the development of Tibetan Buddhism. It has been well studied by P. Demiéville, *Le Concile de Lhasa* (Paris, Imprimerie Nationale de France, 1952). In recent times, the World Fellowship of Buddhists has held six international conferences, with *Reports* subsequently published, at Colombo (1950), Tokyo (1952), Rangoon (1954), Kathmandu (1956), Bangkok (1958), and Phnom-Penh (1961), which report is being prepared.

4. Pilgrimages and travel accounts

From the peregrinations of the Buddha's time to the pilgrimages and foreign visits of the present day, Buddhist travels have served a variety of purposes: to demonstrate reverence for historic Buddhist objects and sites (cf. Buddha-pūjā and meritmaking acts); to seek Buddhist texts and higher instruction in the Dhamma/Dharma; to establish and maintain close relations among members of the Saṅgha and between the Saṅgha and the laity; and even to assist diplomatic and cultural missions for political and social welfare. Thus historic Buddhist travel accounts, especially those of the Chinese during the fifth to eighth centuries A.D., now provide valuable sources of information about traditional Asian political institutions, diplomatic and cultural relations, social customs and ethnic relationships, and historical geography as well as data for the writing of Buddhist histories.

For general descriptions of former Buddhist pilgrimages and travels in Asia see Herst Benz, "Hinduistische und buddhistische Missionszentren in Indien, Ceylon, Burma und Japan," *Zeitschrift für Religions- und Geitesgeschichte*, X (1958), pp. 333–63, and W. Pachow, "The Voyage of Buddhist Missions to South-East Asia & the Far East," *University of Calcutta Review*, XVIII, 3–4 (July–Oct., 1960), pp. 195–212. For studies about early Chinese Buddhist pilgrimages and travels, see Bagchi, "Ancient Chinese Pilgrims to India," in his *India and China*, 2nd ed., pp. 58–92; P. Pelliot, "Deux itinéraires de Chine en Inde à la fin du VIIIe siècle," *Bulletin de l'École Française d'Extrême-Orient*, IV (1904), pp. 131–413; Surendranath Sen, *India through Chinese Eyes* (Madras, University of Madras, 1956), and A. Waley, *The Real Tripitaka and Other Pieces* (N.Y., The Macmillan Co., 1952), Part I. The Real Tripitaka (Hsüan-tsang), pp. 9–130, and Part II. Ennin (A.D. 794–864) and Ensai, pp. 131–68. For studies of early Indian Buddhist pilgrimages and travels, see Bagchi, "Buddhist Missionaries of India to China" in his *India and China*, 2nd ed., pp. 58–92; Phanindra Nath Bose, *The Indian Teachers in China* (Madras, S. Ganesan, 1923); Mildred Cable, "The Central Asian Buddhist Road to China," *Royal Central Asian Journal*, XXX, 3–4 (Sept., 1943), pp. 275–84; Sarat Chandra Das, *Indian Pandits in the Land of Snow* (Calcutta, S. K. Lahiri, 1893); E. Müller-Hess, "The Peregrinations of Indian Buddhists in Burma and in the Sunda Islands," *The Indian Antiquary*, XLII (1913), pp. 38–41; and Bhasker Anand Saletore, "The Pilgrim Ambassadors (Seventh Century A.D. to the Eleventh Century A.D.)," in his *India's Diplomatic Relations with the East* (Bombay, Popular Book Depot, 1960), Appendix A, pp. 308–43.

Chien-chên (in Japanese: Ganjin, 688–763) and his travels to Japan, Hainan, and China during 742–54 are recorded in Junjirō Takakusu, tr., *Kanshin's (Chien-Chên's) Voyage to the East, A.D. 742–754, by Aomi-no-Mabito Genkai (A.D. 779)* (London, Arthur Probsthain, 1925).

On Ennin (Jikaku Daishi, 793–864) and his travels to China three times during 838–47, see Edwin Oldfather Reischauer, tr., *Ennin's Diary* (N.Y., Ronald Press, 1955) and his study, *Ennin's Travels in T'ang China* (N.Y., Ronald Press, 1955).

Concerning Fa-hsien and his travels to Central Asia, India, Ceylon, and Java (dvīpa) during 399–414, several translations of his *Hsi-yu-chi* should be consulted for their notes and variant renderings. S. Beal, tr., "Records of Buddhist Countries by Chi Fah Hian of the Sung Dynasty (Date 400 A.D.)" in his *Travels of Fah-Hian and Sung-yun* (London, Kegan Paul, Trench, Trubner & Co., Ltd., 1869) is reprinted without the notes in his *Si-Yu-Ki: Buddhist Records of the Western World*, translated from the Chinese of Hiuen Tsiang (A.D. 629), (London, 1884; later reprints, Kegan Paul, Trench, Trubner & Co., Ltd.), Vol. I, pp. xxiii–lxxxiii. Herbert Allen Giles, tr., *Record of the Buddhistic Kingdoms* (London, Kegan Paul, Trench, Trubner & Co., Ltd.; Shanghai, Kelly & Walsh, Ltd., 1876) was retranslated as *The Travels of*

Fa-hsien, 399-414 A.D., or Record of the Buddhistic Kingdoms (Cambridge, Cambridge University Press, 1923; reprinted London, Kegan Paul, Trench, Trubner & Co., Ltd., 1956) and largely supersedes James Legge, ed. and tr., *Record of Buddhistic Kingdoms* (Oxford, Clarendon Press, 1886). Jean Pierre Abel Rémusat, tr., *Foé Koué Ki, ou Relation des royaumes bouddhiques. . . .* Ouvrage posthume revu, complété et augmenté d'éclaircissements nouveaux par Klaproth et Landresse (Paris, Imprimerie Royale, 1836) was translated with additional notes by J. W. Laidley as *The Pilgrimage of Fa Hian* (Calcutta, Baptist Mission Press, 1848). See also D. T. Devendra, "Fa-hsien in Ceylon," *Ceylon Today*, IX, 12 (1960), pp. 22–3.

The journey of the Korean Hecho to Central Asia and Northwest India in 726 is recorded in Walter Fuchs, tr., "Huei-chao's Pilgerreise durch Nordwest-Indien und Zentral-Asien um 726," *Sitzungsberichte der preussischen Akademie der Wissenschaften, philosophisch-historische Klasse*, XXX (1938), pp. 426–62.

Hsüan-tsang (or Yüan-chuang, 602–64) and his travels to Central Asia and India during 629–45 are described in a number of varying translations and studies: Beal, tr., *Si-Yu-Ki: Buddhist Records of the Western World*, 2 vols., has been reprinted as *Travels of Hiouen-Thsang*, 4 vols. (Calcutta, Susil Gupta, Ltd., 1957–58) (see also his translation *The Life of Hiuen-Tsiang*, by the Shaman Hwui Li [London, new ed., Kegan Paul, Trench, Trubner & Co., Ltd., 1911, popular ed., 1914]); Li Yung-shi, tr., *The Life of Hsuan-tsang*, The Tripiṭaka-Master of the Great Tzu En Monastery, compiled by Monk Hui-li (Peking, Chinese Buddhist Association, 1959); Stanislas Julien, tr., *Voyages des pèlerins bouddhistes*, 3 tomes (Tome I: *Histoire de la vie de Hiouen-Thsang et des ses voyages dans l'Inde*, Tomes II–III: *Mémoires sur les contrées occidentales*) (Paris, Imprimerie Imperiale, 1853–58); Marc Aurel Stein, "La traversée du désert par Hiuan-tsang en 630 ap. J.-C.," *T'oung Pao*, XX (1921), pp. 332–54; and Thomas Watters, *On Yuan Chwang's Travels in India, 629–654 A.D.*, 2 vols. (London, Royal Asiatic Society, 1904, 1905; reprinted Peking, 1936) edited by T. W. Rhys Davids and S. W. Bushell.

On I-ching (or I-tsing, 635–713) and his travels to Sumatra and India during 671–95, see Edouard Chavannes, tr., *Voyages des pèlerins bouddhistes* (Paris, E. Leroux, 1894); V. R. Dikshitar, "I-tsing's India," *The Indian Historical Quarterly*, XXVIII, 1 (March, 1952), pp. 7–16; and J. Takakusu, tr., *A Record of the Buddhist Religion as Practised in India and the Malay Archipelago (A.D. 671–695)* (Oxford, Clarendon Press, 1896).

With regard to Sung-yün and Hui-sang and their travels to Central Asia, possibly Sogdiana, Udyāna, and Gandhāra during 518–22, see Beal, tr., "The Mission of Sung-Yun and Hwei Săng to obtain Buddhist Books in the West (518 A.D.)," in his *Travels of Fa-Hian and Sung-yun*, reprinted without the notes in his translation *Si-Yu-Ki: Buddhist Records of the Western World*, Vol. I, pp. lxxxiv-cviii; and E. Chavannes, tr., "Voyage de Song-Yun dans l'Udyāna et le Gandhāra (518–522 apr. J.C.)," *Bulletin de l'École Française d'Extrême-Orient*, III (1903), pp. 379–441, with "Note additionnelle par Paul Pelliot," p. 442. See also Sylvain Lévi and E. Chavannes, trs., "Voyage des pèlerins bouddhistes. L'itinéraire d'Ou-K'ong (751–790)," *Journal asiatique*, Série IX, Tome VI (1895), pp. 341–84.

In recent times, a number of Buddhist leaders and scholars have written accounts in Asian languages of their pilgrimages and research expeditions in Buddhist Asia. As examples of similar travels by Westerners, see John Blofeld, *The Wheel of Life* (London, Rider & Co., 1959); R. Raven-Hart, *Where the Buddha Trod* (Colombo, H. W. Cave & Co., 1956); Snellgrove, *Himalayan Pilgrimage*; and G. Tucci, *Secrets of Tibet* (London, Blackie & Son, Ltd., 1935), also entitled *Shrines of a Thousand Buddhas* (N.Y., Robert M. McBride Co., 1936).

III. THE BUDDHA: BIOGRAPHIES

1. The Buddha

The Buddha (the Enlightened One), born as Siddhattha Gotama/Siddhārtha Gautama, is traditionally remembered and venerated in Buddhist belief and practice as the first essential part of the Ti-ratana/Tri-ratna of Buddhism. His life is described in Buddhist literature and romanticized in the folklore of many peoples. The dates of the Buddha are still problematical: the Theravādins in Burma, Ceylon, and India give 624–544 B.C. and those in Cambodia, Laos, and Thailand one year later, 623–543 B.C.; whereas the Mahāyānists, especially in Japan, and most Western scholars have various opinions, such as 566–486 B.C. (the preferable date), 563–483 B.C. or 558–478 B.C.; in any case, all agree that the Buddha had a life-span of 80 years.

GENERAL STUDIES—The following scholarly biographical studies may serve the reader as modern introductions to the life of the Buddha. Dutt, "The Founder," in his *The Buddha and Five After-centuries*, Part I, pp. 3–56, and Filliozat, "Le bouddhisme: 2. La vie de Buddha" in Renou and Filliozat, *L'Inde classique*, II, pp. 463–92, are reliable introductions to the subject. A. Foucher, *La vie du Bouddha d'après les textes et les monuments de l'Inde* (Paris, Payot, 1949; abridged translation by Simone Brangier Boas, *The Life of Buddha* [Middletown, Conn., Wesleyan University Press, 1963]) is now the standard work; see the reviews by É. Lamotte, "Une nouvelle 'Vie du Buddha,'" *Muséon*, LXII (1949), pp. 251–60, and Robert Fazy, "Une nouvelle vie du Bouddha Çâkya-Mouni," *Études asiatiques/Asiatische Studien*, 1949, pp. 124–43. Lamotte, "Date et vie du Buddha Śākyamuni" in his *Histoire du Bouddhisme Indien*, pp. 13–27, offers a useful summary with references. Hermann Oldenburg, "Buddha's Life" in his *Buddha; His Life, His Doctrine, His Order* (London, Williams & Norgate, Ltd., 1882; latest reprint 1928), Part I, pp. 72–203, confirmed the historicity of the Buddha during Western doubts (and some Asian forgetfulness) in the late nineteenth century; see the postface, pp. 453–519, by H. von Glasenapp to the 13th German edition (Stuttgart, J. G. Cotta, 1958). E. J. Thomas, *The Life of Buddha as Legend and History* (London, Kegan Paul, Trench, Trubner & Co., Ltd., 1927; 3rd ed. rev. 1949; reprinted N.Y., Barnes & Noble, Inc., 1952) is still useful for the general reader.

Among numerous studies on the dates, principal events, and activities of the Buddha, which constitute exigent research problems, the following list may be helpful to the student: A. Bareau, "La date du Nirvāṇa," *Journal asiatique* (1953), pp. 27–62; Frauwallner, "The Historical Data We Possess on the Person and the Doctrine of the Buddha," *East and West*, VII, 4 (Jan., 1957), pp. 309–12. Padmanabh S. Jaini, "Buddha's Prolongation of Life," *Bulletin of the School of Oriental and African Studies, University of London*, XXI (1958), pp. 546–52; É. Lamotte, "La légende du Bouddha," *Revue de l'histoire des religions*, CXXXIV (1947–48), pp. 37–71; and B. C. Law, "Buddha's Activities at Anga Magadha," *The Journal of the Bihar Research Society*, Buddha Jayanti Special Issue, 1956, Vol. I, pp. 7–32, "The Buddha's Activities at Kasi-Kosala," *Journal of Indian History*, XXXIV (1956), pp. 139–71, and "The Buddha's Activities at Vaiśālī," *Journal of Indian History*, XXXV (1957), pp. 7–36. J. Przyluski, *Le Parinirvāṇa et les funérailles du Bouddha* (Paris, Imprimerie Nationale, P. Geuthner, 1920) is a comparison of textual accounts, reprinted from *Journal asiatique* issues (1918–20). P. C. Sengupta, "Dates and Principal Events in the Buddha's Life," Gautama Buddha 25th Centenary Volume, *The Indian Historical Quarterly*, XXXII, 2–3 (June–Sept., 1956), pp. 16–20, posits the birth on April 6, 625/624 B.C., the Renunciation on December 18, 597/596 B.C., the Enlightenment on April 10, 590/589 B.C., and the Mahā-parinibbāna/parinirvāṇa on April 22, 545/544 B.C.

Several modern, romanticized versions of the life of the Buddha may be noted here for popular interest: Marie Beuzeville Byles, *Footprints of Gautama the Buddha* (London, Rider & Co., 1957); Mrs. (C. A. F.) Rhys Davids, *Gotama the Man* (London, Luzac & Co., Ltd., 1928); Hermann Hesse, *Siddhartha* (N.Y., New Directions, 1951); Shakuntala Masani, *Gautama: The Story of Lord Buddha* (N.Y., The Macmillan Co., 1956); M. Percheron, *The Marvellous Life of Buddha* (N.Y., St. Martin's Press, 1960); S. Radhakrishnan, *Gautama the Buddha* (London, H. Milford, 1938; Bombay, Hind Kitabs, 1945); and J. Vijayatunga, *I, the Buddha* (Bombay, Hind Kitabs, 1946).

TEXTUAL ACCOUNTS—There are many Buddhist writings which traditionally depict, and revere, the Buddha's life. For general reference use E. Waldschmidt, tr., *Die Legende vom Leben des Buddha* (Berlin, Volksverband der Bücherfreunde; Wegweiser-verlag G.M.B.H., 1929), which is a selection of materials on the life of the Buddha taken from Sanskrit, Pāli, and Chinese texts.

English translations of Pāli textual accounts of the Buddha are available in the following. E. H. Brewster, comp. and tr., *The Life of Gotama the Buddha* (London, Kegan Paul, Trench, Trubner & Co., Ltd.; N.Y., E. P. Dutton & Co., Inc., 1926). J. G. Jennings, tr. and ed., "Life of the Buddha taken from the Pāli Texts" in his *The Vedantic Buddhism of the Buddha* (London, Oxford University Press, 1947), pp. 1–436 with Appendix A. Henry Clarke Warren, tr., "The Buddha" in his *Buddhism in Translations* (Cambridge, Harvard University Press, 1896), chap. I, pp. 1–110 (the 7th issue of 1922 contains only this section). Pāli accounts of the Buddha's previous existences, which prepared him for his final human life and Enlightenment, are contained in the Jātaka literature. Edward Byles Cowell, ed., *The Jātaka*, or *Stories of the Buddha's Former Births*, translated from the Pāli by various hands, 6 vols. and Index (Cambridge, Cambridge University Press, 1895–1907, 1913; reprinted in 3 vols., London, Penguin Books, 1956), is complete except for the introductory commentary *Nidānakathā*. This latter text is conveniently included in Mrs. Rhys Davids, ed., *Buddhist Birth Stories* (London, Routledge & Kegan Paul, Ltd.; N.Y., E. P. Dutton & Co., Inc., 1925). Selections from the Jātaka are available in Henry Thomas Francis and E. J. Thomas, trs., *Jātaka Tales* (Cambridge, Cambridge University Press, 1916; reprinted Bombay, Jaico Publishing House, 1957); Ethel Beswick, ed., *Jataka Tales: Birth Stories of the Buddha* (London, John Murray, Ltd., 1956); and I. B. Horner, ed. and tr., *Ten Jātaka Stories*, each illustrating one of the ten Pāramitā (London, Luzac & Co., Ltd., 1957). For other accounts of the Buddha's existential career, see B. C. Law, tr., *The Minor Anthologies of the Pāli Canon*. Part III. *Buddhavaṃsa, The Lineage of the Buddha* (London, Oxford University Press, 1938); Charles Duroiselle, ed. and tr., *Jinacarita or the Career of a Conqueror* (Rangoon, British Burma Press, 1906) from the Burmese Pāli version, and William Henry Denham Rouse, ed. and tr., "Jinacarita," *Journal of the Pali Text Society* (1904–05), pp. 1–65, from the Sinhalese Pāli version.

There are also notable Western translations of Sanskrit biographies of the Buddha: The *Buddhacarita* of Aśvaghoṣa has been translated by E. H. Johnston: Cantos I to XIV in *The Buddhacarita or Acts of the Buddha*, Part II (Lahore, Published for University of Punjab by Baptist Mission Press, 1936) and Cantos XV to XXVIII in "The Buddha's Mission and Last Journey: Buddhacarita, XV to XXVIII," *Acta Orientalia* (Leiden), XV, 1 (1936), pp. 26–62. The *Lalitavistara* has been translated into German and French but not yet English: Salomon Lefmann, tr., *Lalita Vistara, Erzählung von dem Leben und der Lehre des Çākya Simha* (Berlin, Ferd. Dümmler's Verlag, 1874), and Philippe Edouard Foucaux, tr., *Le Lalita Vistara, Devéloppement des Jeux, contenant l'histoire du Bouddha Çakya-Mouni*, 2 vols. (Paris, Ernest Leroux, 1884–92). The *Mahāvastu* is now available in English by J. J. Jones, tr., *The Mahāvastu*, 3 vols. (London, Luzac & Co., Ltd., 1949, 1952, 1956). Concerning the *Mahāparinirvāṇa-sūtra*, which describes the last days of the Buddha, see E. Waldschmidt, *Die Überlieferung vom Lebensende des Buddha*, 2 Tle. (Göttingen, Vandenhoeck & Ruprecht, 1944, 1948). The *Abhiniṣkramana-sūtra*, another traditional biography, may be extant in a Chinese version of which there is an abridged English translation by S. Beal, *The Romantic Legend of Sâkya Buddha* (London, Kegan Paul, Trench, Trubner & Co., Ltd., 1875). For Sanskrit accounts of the Buddha's previous existences, see A. Foucher, *Les vies antérieures du Bouddha d'après les textes et les monuments de l'Inde* (Paris, Presses universitaires de France, 1955); Jacob Samuel Speyer, tr., *The G̠ātakamâlâ, or Garland of Birth-stories*, by Arya S̠ûra (London, Henry Frowde [O.U.P. Warehouse], 1895); and Mark J. Dresden, ed. and tr., *The Jātakastava* or *Praise of the Buddha's Former Births* (Philadelphia, Transactions of the American Philosophical Society, 1955) which is an Indo-Scythian (Khotanese) text.

Other traditional biographies of the Buddha, both translations of Pāli and Sanskrit texts and original works, often reflect ethnocultural interpretations, beliefs, and customs. Although most of the following Western translations of such biographies need revision, they may serve as examples of "national" biographies of the Buddha. Paul Bigandet, tr., *The Life or Legend of Gaudama, the Buddha of the Burmese* (London, Kegan Paul, Trench, Trubner & Co., Ltd., 4th ed., 2 vols., 1911–12; popular ed., 1914), and Michael Edwardes, ed., *A Life of the Buddha*, from a Burmese manuscript (London, Folk Society, 1959) which is a revision of the translation by Chester Bennett in *Journal of the American Oriental Society*, III (1852), pp. 1–163. A. Leclère, tr., "La vie du Buddha" in his *Les livres sacrés du Cambodge*. Pt. I (*Annales du Musée, Bibliothèque d'Études*, Tome 20; Paris, E. Leroux, 1906), pp. 5–114, is translated from the Cambodian "Preas Pathama Samphothian" with an introduction. Léon Wieger, ed. and tr., *Bouddhisme chinois*. Tome II: *Les vies chinoises du Buddha* (Peking, 1940; reprinted Paris, Cathasia, 1951) gives "Récit de l'apparition sur terre, du Buddha des Sakya, compilé par Pao-tch'eng, moine chinois, au temps des Ming," pp. 6–278. John Laidlaw Atkinson, *Prince Siddhartha, the Japanese Buddha* (Boston, Congregational Sunday-School Society, 1893) is a free version from Japanese sources. Julius Heinrich Klaproth, tr., "Vie de Bouddha d'après les livres mongols," *Journal asiatique*, Série I, Tome IV (1824), pp. 9–23, 65–79, and in his *Mémoires relatifs à l'Asie* (Paris, Dondey Dupré, pere et fils, 1824–28), Vol. II. H. Alabaster, tr., "A Life of Buddha, Translated from the Siamese Pathomma Somphothiyan or First (Festival of) Omniscience" in his *The Wheel of the Law* (London, Kegan Paul, Trench, Trubner & Co., Ltd., 1871), Part II, pp. 76–162 and "Notes," pp. 163–241. William Woodville Rockhill, tr., *The Life of the Buddha and the Early History of His Order* (London, Kegan Paul, Trench, Trubner & Co., Ltd., 1884; reprinted 1907, and popular ed., n.d.) is derived from Tibetan sources.

PICTORIAL AND SCULPTURAL ACCOUNTS—For general reference see William Cohn, *Buddha in der Kunst des Ostens* (Leipzig, Verlag Klinkhardt & Biermann, 1925); B. C. Law, "Buddha's Life in Art" in his *Indological Studies*, Part II, pp. 113–64; and Anil de Silva-Vigier, *The Life of the Buddha* (London, Phaidon Press, 1955).

Pictorial accounts of the life of the Buddha are presented in *Buddha's Life by Modern Indian Painters* (Madras, Associated Printers, 1957); Joseph Hackin, *Les scènes figurées de la vie du Buddha d'après des peintures tibétaines* (Paris, E. Leroux, 1916); Tokan Tada, ed., *Tibetan Pictorial Life of the Buddha* (Tokyo, Tibet bunka senoykai, 1958); United States Information Service, Bangkok, *The Life of the Buddha According to Thai Temple Paintings* (Bangkok, 1957); and Wieger, "Illustrations de la vie du Bouddha, . . ." in his *Bouddhisme chinois*, Tome II, Appendix, pp. 279–424.

Sculptural accounts of the life of the Buddha are exemplified particularly in the art of Gandhāra, Borobuḍur, and Pagān. The Gandhāra account is described in Foucher, *L'Art gréco-bouddhique du Gandhâra*, Tome I (Paris, Imprimerie Nationale, 1905); H. Hargreaves, *The Buddha Story in Stone* (Calcutta, Baptist Mission Press, 1914); R. C. Kar, "The Master's Life in Stone," Gautama Buddha 25th Centenary Volume, *The Indian Historical Quarterly*, XXXII, 2–3 (June–Sept., 1956), pp. 7–15; and P. H. Pott, "Some Scenes from the Buddha's Life in Stone," *Adyar Library Bulletin*, XX, 3–4 (Dec., 1956), pp. 310–17. The Borobuḍur account is depicted in N. J. Krom, ed., *The Life of Buddha on the Stūpa of Barabudur according to the Lalitavistara-text* (The Hague, Martinus Nijhoff, 1926); C. M. Pleyte, *Die Buddha-Legende in den Skulpturen des Tempels von Bôrô-Budur* (Amsterdam, J. H. de Bussy, 1901); and Frans Carel Wilsen, *Die Buddha-Legende auf den Flachreliefs der ersten Galerie des Stûpa von Boro-Budur, Java* (Leipzig, Otto Harrassowitz, 1923). The Pagān account is presented in Karl B. Seidenstücker, *Südbuddhistische Studien*, I. *Die Buddha-Legende in den Skulpturen des Ānanda-Tempels zu Pagan* (Hamburg, Otto Meissners, 1916).

2. Eminent Buddhists

Eminent followers of the Buddha are traditionally remembered and revered in texts which contribute to national biography as well as to Buddhist literature. Nowadays, such personages may be prominent lay leaders as well as members of the Saṅgha. In the course of their historical, literary, and Buddhist researches, Asian and Western scholars have translated and written original biographical studies of famous Buddhists. A brief survey of such personages is given in "Some Great Buddhists after Asoka" in Bapat, ed., *2500 Years of Buddhism*, pp. 195–254.

For studies of Chinese monks see the references cited above; for Japanese monks, see chapter V.

Information about Kumārajīva from Kucha in Central Asia, who became famous as a translator in China, is presented by P. C. Bagchi, "Kumârajîva" in his *Le canon bouddhique en Chine*, Tome 1er (Paris, Paul Geuthner, 1927), pp. 178–200; Shinya Kasugai, "The Historical Background of Kumarajiva and His Influence on Chinese Buddhism," *Philosophical Quarterly*, XXXI (1958–59), pp. 121–5; J. Nobel, "Kumārajīva," *Sitzungsberichte der Bayerischen Akademie der Wissenschaften, philosophisch-historische Klasse*, 1927, pp. 206–33; and Z. Tsukamoto, "The Dates of Kumārajīva and Seng-chao Re-examined," *Silver Jubilee Volume of the Zinbun-Kagaku-Kenkyayo, Kyoto University* (1954), Part I, I, pp. 568–84.

Among biographical studies of Indian Saṅgha notables in general see P. S. Sastri, "Some Buddhist Thinkers of Andhra," Gautama Buddha 25th Centenary Volume, *The Indian Historical Quarterly*, XXXII, 2–3 (June–Sept., 1956), pp. 55–9, and the references cited above. The following are studies of particular Indian Buddhists: B. C. Law, *Aśvaghoṣa* (Calcutta, Royal Asiatic Society of Bengal, 1946), B. C. Law, *Buddhaghosa*, rev. ed. (Bombay, Royal Asiatic Society, 1946); Pe Maung Tin, "Buddhaghosa," *Journal of the Burma Research Society*, XII, 1 (1922), pp. 14–20; R. Subrahmanian and Nainan, "Buddhaghosa: His Place of Birth," *Journal of Oriental Research*, XIX (1956–57), pp. 278–84; Hakuju Ui, "Maitreya as an Historical Personage" in *Indian Studies in Honor of Charles Rockwell Lanman* (Cambridge, Mass., Harvard University Press, 1929), pp. 95–101, with "Note" by J. Takakusu, p. 102; É. Lamotte, "Mañjuśrī," *T'oung Pao*, XLVIII, 1–3 (1960), pp. 1–96; P. S. Sastri, "Nāgārjuna and Āryadeva," *The Indian Historical Quarterly*, XXXI, 3 (Sept., 1955), pp. 193–202; Max Walleser, "The Life of Nāgārjuna from Tibetan and Chinese Sources" in Bruno Schindler, ed., *Hirth Anniversary Volume* (London, Arthur Probsthain & Co., 1923), pp. 421–55; Gustave-Charles Toussaint, tr., *Le Dict de Padma. Padma thang yig*. Ms. de Lithang traduit du thibétain (Paris, E. Leroux, 1933); André Migot, "Un grand disciple du Buddha: Śāriputra," *Bulletin de l'École Française d'Extrême-Orient*, XLVI (1954), 2, pp. 405–554. E. Frauwallner, *On the Date of the Buddhist Master of the Law Vasubandhu* (Rome, Serie Orientale Roma, 1951), which gives a useful bibliography; and P. S. Jaini, "On the Theory of Two Vasubandhus," *Bulletin of the School of Oriental and African Studies, University of London*, XXI (1958), pp. 45–53.

With regard to Korean Buddhists, Peter H. Lee has written "The Life of the Korean Poet-Priest Kyunyŏ," *Études asiatiques/Asiatische Studien*, I–II (1957–58), pp. 42–72, and "The Importance of the Kyunyŭ Chŏn (1075) in Korean Buddhism and Literature—Bhadra-cari-praṇidhāna in Tenth Century Korea," *Journal of the American Oriental Society*, LXXXI, 4 (Sept.–Dec., 1951), pp. 409–14.

For studies of a Siamese Buddhist leader see Alexander B. Griswold, *King Mongkut of Siam* (N.Y., The Asia Society, 1961), and R. Lingat, "La vie religieuse du Roi Mongkut," *The Journal of the Siam Society*, XX, 2 (Oct.,

1926), pp. 129–48, reprinted in *The Siam Society Fiftieth Anniversary Commemorative Publication*, I (1954), pp. 18–37.

There are several notable biographical studies of eminent Tibetans: Jacques Bacot, *La vie de Marpa le "Traducteur"* (Paris, Paul Geuthner, 1937); J. Bacot, tr., *Le poète tibétain Milarepa* (Paris, Bossard, 1925); Walter Yeeling Evans-Wentz, ed., *Tibet's Great Yogī Milarepa* (London, H. Milford, 1928; 2nd ed., 1951); Toni Schmid, "The Life of Milaraspa in a Picture Series," *Ethnos* (Stockholm), 1950, 1–2, pp. 74–94, and *The Cotton-clad Mila: The Tibetan Poet-saint's Life in Pictures* (Stockholm, Statens Ethnografiska Museum, 1952); A. Grünwedel, tr., *Die Legenden des Nā·ro·pa, des Hauptvertreters des Nekromanten- und Hexentums* (Leipzig, Otto Harrassowitz, 1933). Compare G. Tucci, "À propos the Legend of Nāropā," *Journal of the Royal Asiatic Society* (*of Great Britain and Ireland*) (Oct., 1935), pp. 677–88. E. Obermiller, "Tsoṅ-kha-pa le Pandit," *Mélanges chinois et bouddhiques*, III: 1934–35 (1935), pp. 319–38.

IV. THE DHAMMA/DHARMA: TEXTS

The Dhamma/Dharma (the Buddhist Doctrine) is traditionally studied and practiced as the second essential part of the Tiratana/Tri-ratna. As source material for Buddhist teachings, it comprises both oral and written texts (in fact, the earliest written texts were based upon remembered oral accounts of what the Buddha had expounded). Canonically considered, the Dhamma/Dharma consists of three groups of texts, called Ti-piṭaka/Tripiṭaka: the Vinaya Piṭaka (Collection of Disciplinary Rules), the Sutta/Sūtra Piṭaka (Collection of the Buddha's Teachings or the Buddha Dhamma/Dharma proper), and the Abhidhamma/Abhidharma Piṭaka (Collection of the Higher Teachings or Commentaries on the Suttas/Sūtras), to which have been added various non-canonical works.

1. Histories of literature

As with many aspects of Buddhism, there is no comprehensive history of Buddhist literature in any language. When undertaken, it should review the nature and development of texts, commentaries, and translations in at least twenty-two Asian languages in various scripts as well as translations and studies in thirteen or more Western languages. It should also give some consideration to oral traditions and folklore which express or influence Buddhist beliefs.

As introduction to the nature and history of Buddhist literature, see P. C. Bagchi, "On the Original Buddhism, Its Canon and Language," *Sino-Indian Studies*, II, 3–4 (Oct., 1953; Jan., 1954), pp. 107–35. Filliozat, "Le bouddhisme: 1. Les sources" in Renou and Filliozat, *L'Inde classique*, II, pp. 315–463; E. Frauwallner, *The Earliest Vinaya and the Beginnings of Buddhist Literature* (Rome, Istituto Italiano per il Medio ed Estremo Oriente, 1956); Pande, "Studies in Early Buddhist Sources" in his *Studies in the Origins of Buddhism*, Part I, pp. 1–247; Maurice (Moritz) Winternitz, "Buddhist Literature" in his *A History of Indian Literature*, Vol. II. *Buddhist Literature and Jaina Literature* (Calcutta, University of Calcutta, 1933) as section III, pp. 1–423.

For special studies on early Buddhist languages, see the following researches: Chi Hsien-lin, "The Language Problem of Primitive Buddhism," *Journal of the Burma Research Society*, XLIII, 1 (June, 1960), pp. 1–15; Arthur Berriedale Keith, "The Home of Pāli" in B. C. Law, ed., *Buddhistic Studies*, pp. 728–48; Lamotte, "La formation des langues bouddhiques" in his *Histoire du Bouddhisme Indien*, pp. 607–57; Heinrich Lüders and E. Waldschmidt, *Beobachtungen über die Sprache des buddhistischen Urkanons* (Berlin, Akademie Verlag, Abhandlungen der deutschen Akademie der Wissenschaft zu Berlin Klasse für Sprachen, Literatur und Kunst, Jahrgang 1952, 1954), which concerns the language of the early Buddhist Canons; and M. A. Mehendale, "Some Remarks on the Language of the Original Buddhist Canon," *Bulletin of the Deccan College*, XVII, 3 (1955), pp. 157–71.

General surveys of Pāli literature are given by W. Geiger, "Pāli Literature" in his *Pāli Literature and Language* (Calcutta, University of Calcutta, 1943), Part I, pp. 9–58, and by B. C. Law, "Chronology of the Pāli Canon," *Annals of the Bhandarkar Oriental Research Institute*, XII (1931), pp. 171–201, "Non Canonical Pāli Literature," *ibid.*, pp. 97–143, and especially *A History of Pāli Literature*, 2 vols. (London, Kegan Paul, Trench, Trubner & Co., Ltd., 1933). These surveys may be supplemented by accounts of Pāli texts in particular countries, such as Shwe Zan Aung, "Abhidhamma Literature in Burma," *Journal of the Pali Text Society* (1910–12), pp. 112–32, and Mabel Haynes Bode, *The Pali Literature of Burma* (London, Royal Asiatic Society, 1909); G. P. Malalasekera, *The Pāli Literature of Ceylon* (London, Royal Asiatic Society, 1928); Phouvong Phimmasone, "La littérature bouddhique lao" in de Berval, ed., *Présence du Bouddhisme*, pp. 893–904, and "Les textes bouddhistes de la littérature laotienne," *La pensée bouddhique*, III, 10 (Avril, 1950), pp. 12–16.

Pāli texts have long been written in various scripts, there being no Pāli script itself, and have, therefore, become part of the literary heritage of Southeast Asian peoples. For information, the following articles in R. Queneau, ed., *Histoire des littératures*, Vol. 1 (Paris, Nouvelle Revue Française, 1955) may be consulted: Solange Bernard-Thierry, "Littérature birmane," pp. 1384–94, "Littérature cambodgienne," pp. 1353–61, and "Littérature laotienne," pp. 1343–52, and K. Sibunruang, "Littérature siamoise," pp. 1362–83. See also L. Finot, "Recherches sur la littérature laotienne," *Bulletin de l'École Française d'Extrême-Orient*, XVII, 5 (1917), pp. 1–[221], and C. E. Godakumbura, *Sinhalese Literature* (Colombo, Colombo Apothecaries Co., Ltd., 1955).

The nature and development of Buddhist (Hybrid) Sanskrit literature are described in various studies, notably John Brough, "The Language of Buddhist Sanskrit Texts," *Bulletin of the School of Oriental and African Studies, University of London*, XVI, 2 (1954), pp. 351–75, and Franklin Edgerton, *Buddhist Hybrid Sanskrit Language and Literature* (Banaras, Banaras Hindu University, 1954) and "The Buddha and Language," Gautama Buddha 25th Centenary Volume, *The Indian Historical Quarterly*, XXXII, 2–3 (June–Sept., 1956), pp. 21–7. G. K. Nariman, *Literary History of Sanskrit Buddhism* (from Winternitz, Sylvain Lévi, Huber) (Bombay, D. B. Taraporevada, 1920; reprinted 1923) is now inadequate. More specialized studies on the subject should also be mentioned, such as the following: A. S. Altekar, "Cultural Importance of Sanskrit Literature Preserved in Tibet," *Annals of the Bhandarkar Oriental Research Institute*, XXXV (1954), pp. 54–66, reprinted in *The Journal of the Bihar Research Society*, Buddha Jayanti Special Issue (1956), Vol. I, pp. 113–27; Sushil Kumar De, "The Buddhist Tantric Literature (Sanskrit) of Bengal," *New Indian Antiquary*, I, 1 (April, 1938), pp. 1–23; R. H. van Gulik, *Siddham. An Essay on the History of Sanskrit Studies in China and Japan* (Nagpur, International Academy of Indian Culture, 1956); Brian Houghton Hodgson, *Essays on the Languages, Literature and Religion of Nepal and Tibet* (London, Kegan Paul, Trench, Trubner & Co., Ltd., 1874), and *Illustrations of the Literature and Religion of the Buddhists* (Serampore, reprints from *Journal of the Royal Asiatic Society [of Great Britain and Ireland]*, *Journal of the [Royal] Asiatic Society of Bengal*, etc., 1841) are now of historic interest. Kashi Prasad Jayaswal, "Lost Sanskrit Works Recovered from Tibet," *Modern Review*, LXI, 2 (February, 1937), pp. 159–64. É. Lamotte, "Khuddakanikāya and kṣudrakapiṭaka," *East and West*, VII, 4 (Jan., 1957), pp. 341–8 gives a history of the formation of the collections of the minor canonical texts of various Buddhist schools; see also his "Problèmes concernant les textes canoniques 'mineurs,'" *Journal asiatique* (1956), pp. 249–64. H. Nakamura, "Historical Studies of the Coming into Existence of Mahāyāna Sūtras," *Proceedings of the Okurayama Oriental Research Institute*, II (Oct., 1956), pp. 1–22, gives a valuable summary of the subject.

The transliteration and translation of Buddhist Sanskrit texts into Central Asian, Chinese, Tibetan, Mongolian, and other languages were important phases in the development of Mahāyāna and Vajrayāna canons. Descriptions of the resultant Buddhist literatures for Central Asia are given by Georges Cuendet, "Textes sanscrits bouddhiques d'Asie centrale," *Bulletin de la Société Suisse des Amis de l'Extrême Orient/Mitteilungen der Schweizerischen Gesellschaft der Freunde Ostasiatischer Kultur*, II (1940), pp. 35–41; Louis Hambis, "Littératures indo-européenes de Haute Asie," pp. 1085–95, and "Littératures turques de Haute Asie," pp. 1096–117, in the *Encyclopédie de la Pléiade. Histoire des littératures*, Vol. I. *Littératures anciennes orientales et orales* (Paris, Raymond Queneau, 1956); and Pavel Poucha, "Indian Literature in Central Asia," *Acta Orientalia* (Prague), II (1930), pp. 27–38. For textual examples see Augustus Frederic Rudolf Hoernle, ed., *Manuscript Remains of Buddhist Literature found in Eastern Turkestan*, . . . Vol. I. *Manuscripts in Sanskrit, Khotanese, Kuchean, Tibetan, and Chinese* (London, Oxford University Press, 1916), which contains facsimiles, transcripts, translations, and notes.

Chinese translation methods and Buddhist literature are described by P. C. Bagchi, *Le canon bouddhique en Chine*, 2 vols. (Paris, Paul Geuthner, 1927, 1938); A. G. Bennett, "Chinese Translations of Sanskrit Buddhist Literature during the 5th and 6th Centuries," *The Maha Bodhi*, LXVI, 1 (Jan., 1958), pp. 2–10; Fachow, "Development of Tripiṭaka-translations in China," in *B. C. Law Volume*, I, pp. 66–74; V. Hrdličková, "The First Translations of Buddhist Sūtras in Chinese Literature and Their Place in the Development of Storytelling," *Acta Orientalia* (Prague), XXVI (1958), pp. 114–44; and Probhat Kumar Mukherji, *Indian Literature in China and the Far East* (Calcutta, Greater India Society, 1931).

Tibetan Buddhist literature is described by the following accounts, which should be collectively used in order to provide a general survey of the subject: Bell, "Sources" in his *The Religion of Tibet*, pp. 193–218; E. Frauwallner, "Zu den buddhistischen Texten in der Zeit Khri-Sron-Ide-Btsan's," *Wiener Zeitschrift für die Kunde Sud- und Ostasiens und Archiv für indische Philosophie*, I (1957), pp. 95–103; M. Lalou, "Contribution à la bibliographie du Kanǰur et du Tanǰur. Les textes bouddhiques au temps du roi Khri-sroṅ-lde-bcan," *Journal asiatique* (1953), pp. 313–53, and "Littérature tibétaine" in *Encyclopédie de la Pléiade* . . . , I, pp. 1119–39; and Prince Peter, "The Books of Tibet," *Libu, International Library Review*, V, 1 (1954), pp. 20–8. G. Tucci, "A Brief History of Tibetan Religious Literature from the XIIth to the Beginning of the XVIIIth Century" in his *Tibetan Painted Scrolls* (Rome, La Libreria dello Stato, 1949), Vol. I, Part 1, pp. 94–138, is especially valuable.

Mongolian Buddhist literature, related to the Tibetan, is described by L. Hambis, "Littérature mongole" in *Encyclopédie de la Pléiade* . . . , I, pp. 1140–57, and Berthold Laufer, "Zur buddhistischen Literatur der Uiguren," *T'oung Pao*, Série II, VIII (1907), pp. 391–409. See also J. Cuisinier, "Littérature indonésienne," pp. 1425–45, and Maurice Durand, "Littérature vietnamienne," pp. 1318–42, in Queneau, ed., *Histoire des littératures*, I; and B. Laufer, "Skizze der manjurischen Literatur" in *Keleti Szembe/Revue Orientale* (Budapest), IX (1908).

2. Collections and canons

In Buddhist studies it is customary to refer to the Pāli Tipiṭaka as the canonical literature of the Theravāda movement in slightly varying editions (in Burmese, Cambodian or Khmer, Lao, Môn, Shan, Sinhalese, Thai scripts and now also in roman letters); to the Buddhist (Hybrid) Sanskrit Tripiṭaka as the canonical literature of the Sarvāstivāda, Mahāsāṅghika, and other Schools in different collections (partly extant in Brāhmī, Kharoṣṭhī, Gupta, Devanāgarī, Siddhamātṛkā, Kavi scripts) as well as of the Mahāyāna movement (in various editions; mostly available in Chinese and Japanese translations with commentaries, and some Korean and Vietnamese translations); and to the Kanjur (Bkaḥ-ḥgyur; cf. Sūtra and Vinaya Piṭakas) and Tanjur (Bstanḥgyur; cf. commentaries and ceremonial regulations) as the canonical literature of the Vajrayāna movement in different collections (in Tibetan, Uigur, Mongolian, Manchu scripts). In general, see Lamotte, "La formation du canon des Écritures" in his *Histoire du Bouddhisme Indien*, pp. 154–210, and Thomas, "The Scriptures" in his *The History of Buddhist Thought*, Appendix I, pp. 261–87. For a survey of Prajñāpāramitā texts, which were formative in the development of Mahāyāna thought, see E. Conze, *The Prajñāpāramitā Literature* ('s Gravenhage, 1960); Ryusho Hikata, ed., "An Introductory Essay on Prajñāpāramitā" in his *Suvikrāntavikrāmi-paripṛcchā Prajñāpāramitā-sutra*, edited with "An Introductory Essay," (Fukuoka, Kyushu University, 1958), Part I, pp. ix-lxxxiii; and Tokumyo Matsumoto, *Die Prajñāpāramitā-Literatur* (Stuttgart, W. Kohlhammer, 1932).

Descriptions of the Pāli Tipiṭaka are given in the following publications. N. A. Jayawickrama, "Buddhaghosa and the Traditional Classifications of the Pali Canon," *University of Ceylon Review*, XVII, 1–2 (Jan.–April, 1959), pp. 1–17; Suzanne Karpelès, "L'édition cambodgienne du Tripiṭaka bouddhique," *Academie des Inscriptions et Belles-Lettres, Comptes-rendus des séances* (July–Sept., 1936), pp. 180–3; Arthur Charles March, "An Analysis of the Pali Canon," amended and brought up to date by Miss I. B. Horner in C. Humphreys, ed., *A Buddhist Students' Manual* (London, The Buddhist Society, 1956), pp. 193–243. Nyanatiloka, *Guide through the Abhidhamma-Pitaka*, 2nd rev. ed. (Colombo, Buddhist Sahitya Sabha, 1957); and Thomas, "The Theravada (Pāli) Canon" in his *The Life of Buddha as Legend and History*, 3rd ed., Appendix, pp. 257–77. For the titles of Pāli texts one may also usefully consult Pali Text Society, *Issues of the Pali Text Society* (London, Luzac & Co., 1961), in which Part I, Texts, pp. 2–7, lists 149 volumes printed to date, Part VI, Translation Series, pp. 9–10, lists 32 volumes to date, and Part VII, Separate Series: Sacred Books of the Buddhists Series, pp. 10–11, lists 23 volumes to date. For catalogues of Pāli manuscripts and books see those issued by or concerning libraries and museums located in Bangkok, Colombo, Leningrad, London, Luang Prabang, Paris, Phnom-Penh, Rangoon, Vientiane, and elsewhere.

For descriptions of Buddhist (Hybrid) Sanskrit texts and collections, see Anukul Chandra Banerjee, *Sarvāstivāda Literature* (Calcutta, Firma K. L. Mukhopadhyaya, 1957), and compare J. Takakusu, "On the Abhidharma

Literature of the Sarvāstivādins," *Journal of the Pali Text Society* (1904–05), pp. 67–146, and especially information about the extant works found in Nepal. In this latter respect, three analyses will be particularly useful: Eugène Burnouf, "Description de la collection des livres du Népâl" in his *Introduction à l'histoire du bouddhisme Indien*, 2nd ed. (Paris, G. P. Maisonneuve et Cie, 1876), Second Mémoire, pp. 29–524, and Table analytique, pp. 581–6; Rájendralála Mitra, *The Sanskrit Buddhist Literature of Nepal* (Calcutta, J. W. Thomas, Baptist Mission Press, 1882), which is an analytical catalogue of the manuscripts presented by B. H. Hodgson to the Asiatic Society of Bengal; and E. B. Cowell and Julius Eggeling, "Catalogue of Buddhist Sanskrit MSS. in the Possession of the Royal Asiatic Society (Hodgson Collection)," *Journal of the Royal Asiatic Society* (*of Great Britain and Ireland*) (1876), pp. 1–52. For other Buddhist Sanskrit works see the catalogues of Sanskrit manuscripts and books issued by or concerning libraries and museums located in Calcutta, Leningrad, London, Paris, and elsewhere.

Several editions of the Chinese Ta Ts'ang Ching (cf. Tripiṭaka) are described by Bagchi, *Le canon bouddhique en Chine*; K. Ch'en, "Notes on the Sung and Yüan Tripiṭaka," *Harvard Journal of Asiatic Studies*, XIV, 1–2 (June, 1951), pp. 208–14; and Luther Carrington Goodrich, "Earliest Printed Editions of the Tripiṭaka," *Viśva-Bharati Quarterly*, XIX, 3 (Winter, 1953–54), pp. 215–20.

Japanese, Korean, and Vietnamese Buddhist Collections are based upon the Chinese Ta Ts'ang Ching but have developed their own particular traditions of interpretation and commentaries. For descriptions of the Japanese Collection in various editions see Hanayama, "Orientation in the Study of Japanese Buddhism" in Kokusai Bunka Shinkokai, ed., *A Guide to Japanese Studies*, especially pp. 99–113, and Hirakawa and Ceadel, "Japanese Research on Buddhism since the Meiji Period," *Monumenta Nipponica*, XI, 3 (Oct., 1955), B. The Buddhist Canon, pp. 4–7, and 4 (Jan., 1956), G. Japanese Buddhism, pp. 69–72, followed by sections H. to R. concerning various sects and research facilities, pp. 72–96. For a description of the Korean Collection, especially the Haein-sa edition and its current reprint (16 vols. to date) by the Dong Kook University in Seoul see Nak Choon Paik (George Paik), "Tripitaka Koreana," *Transactions of the Korea Branch of the Royal Asiatic Society*, XXXII (1951), pp. 62–78, reprinted in Dong Kook University, *Tripitaka Koreana* (Seoul, Dong Kook University, 1957). Concerning the Vietnamese Collection see Trân-văn-Giáp, *Contribution à l'étude des livres bouddhiques Annamites conservés à l'École Française d'Extrême-Orient* (Tokyo, 1943), which is a descriptive catalogue of 427 items, and the lists of "Traductions de textes canoniques chinois; Traductions de textes canoniques pālis" in de Berval, ed., *Présence du Bouddhisme*, pp. 1010–12–13.

The Chinese texts found at Tun-huang, now preserved in several collections elsewhere, are described by B. Csongor, "Some Chinese Texts in Tibetan Script from Tun-Huang," *Acta Orientalia Academiae Scientiarum Hungaricae*, X (1960), pp. 97–140, and Lionel Giles, *Descriptive Catalogue of the Chinese Manuscripts from Tun-huang in the British Museum* (London, The Trustees of the British Museum, 1957), Part I. *Buddhist Texts*, pp. 1–216, and his *Six Centuries at Tun-huang*: a short account of the Stein Collection of Chinese MSS. in the British Museum (London, The China Society, 1944).

Tibetan Buddhist Collections, based mainly on Indian Sanskrit texts and consisting of canonical and noncanonical works in various editions, have been fairly well studied and catalogued. In general see J. Bacot, ed. and tr., "Titres et colophons d'ouvrages non canoniques tibétains. Textes et traduction," *Bulletin de l'École Française d'Extrême-Orient*, XLIV: 1947–50, 2 (1954), pp. 275–337; Anukul Chandra Banerjee, "The Vinayapiṭaka—Tibetan Version," *Calcutta Review*, CXVIII (Feb., 1951), pp. 162–6; Lokesh Chandra, "A Newly Discovered Urga Edition of the Tibetan Kanjur," *Indo-Iranian Journal*, III (1959), pp. 175–91, and "Transcription of the Introductory Part of the Urga Edition of the Tibetan Kanjur," *ibid.*, pp. 192–203; K. Ch'en, "The Tibetan Tripitaka," *Harvard Journal of Asiatic Studies*, IX, 2 (June, 1946), pp. 53–62, which is a translation of Mochizuki, *Bukkyō Daijiten*, IV, pp. 3618a–19a, with footnotes added; Wesley E. Needham, "The Significance of the Yale Kanjur," *The Yale University Library Gazette*, XXVII, 1 (July, 1952), pp. 48–51, and "The Tibetan Collection at Yale," *The Yale University Library Gazette*, XXXIV, 3 (Jan., 1960), pp. 127–33; P. Pelliot, "Notes à propos d'un Catalogue du Kanjur," *Journal asiatique*, IV (Juillet–Août, 1914), pp. 111–50; and G. Tucci, "The Tibetan Tripitaka," *Harvard Journal of Asiatic Studies*, XII, 3–4 (Dec., 1949), No. 1, pp. 477–81.

For the Mongolian Collection, which is based mainly on the Tibetan texts, see Walther Heissig, "Bemerkungen zum mongolischen Tandjur," *Ural-Altaische Jahrbücher*, XXIV, 1–2 (1952), and Louis Ligeti, *Catalogue du Kanǰur mongol imprimé*, Vol. I. *Catalogue* (Budapest, Société Körösi Csoma, 1942).

3. Anthologies

Numerous anthologies of selected texts and passages from Buddhist literature are available to the reader. They are often arranged to express the compiler's exposition or general conception of Buddhism or some aspect of it. Such compilations do not, however, comprise a "Buddhist Bible" because the selections must be made arbitrarily; and the spirit of Buddhist doctrinal inquiry and teaching precludes an exclusive devotion to one text (original or anthological) for all Buddhists notwithstanding the textual preferences which characterize some Mahāyāna schools. The following are some of the more notable Buddhist anthologies in English, exclusive of poetry and stories which are cited below.

For general anthologies, see E. A. Burtt, ed., *The Teachings of the Compassionate Buddha* (N.Y., Mentor Religious Classic, 1955); E. Conze, ed. and tr., *Buddhist Scriptures* (Penguin Classics, 1959), and ed., *Buddhist Texts through the Ages* (Oxford, Bruno Cassirer, 1953; N.Y., Philosophical Library, Inc., 1954); Gard, ed., *Buddhism*; Clarence Herbert Hamilton, ed., *Buddhism, a Religion of Infinite Compassion* (N.Y., Liberal Arts Press, 1952); C. Humphreys, ed., *The Wisdom of Buddhism* (London, Michael Joseph Ltd., 1960; N.Y., Random House, 1961); Buddhist Council of Ceylon, ed., *The Path of Buddhism* (Colombo, Lanka Bauddha Mandalaya, 1956); and Beatrice Lane Suzuki, comp., *Buddhist Readings*, 2 vols. (Kyoto, Hirano Shobn, 1934, 1935).

For selections from Pāli texts, see George Francis Allen (Y. Siri Nyana), *The Buddha's Philosophy* (London, Macmillan & Co., Ltd., 1959), Part II; A. K. Coomaraswamy and I. B. Horner, trs., *The Living Thoughts of Gotama the Buddha* (London, The Living Thoughts Library [Cassell & Co., Ltd.], 1948); J. G. Jennings, ed. and tr., *The Vedāntic Buddhism of the Buddha*; Nyanatiloka, tr., *The Words of the Buddha* (Colombo, Bauddha Sahitya Sabha; Santa Barbara, J. F. Rowny Press, 1950); E. J. Thomas, tr., *Buddhist Scriptures* (London, J. Murray, Wisdom of the East Series, 1913), *Early Buddhist Scriptures* (London, Kegan Paul, Trench, Trubner & Co., Ltd., 1935), and *The Road to Nirvana* (London, J. Murray, Ltd., 1950); H. C. Warren, tr., *Buddhism in Translations* (Cambridge, Mass., Harvard University Press, 1896) and Frank Lee Woodward, tr., *Some Sayings of the Buddha* (London, Oxford University Press, 1925).

For selections from Sanskrit texts, see E. J. Thomas, tr., *The Perfection of Wisdom*: the career of the predestined Buddhas (London, J. Murray, Ltd., 1952), and *The Quest of Enlightenment* (London, J. Murray, Ltd., 1950).

4. Important texts

Bibliographical information about important Buddhist texts cannot be given adequately here for lack of space. A select list of the main texts of the principal Buddhist schools in the Hīnayāna (including Theravāda), Mahāyāna, and Vajrayāna movements would contain more than 75 works. Furthermore a satisfactory bibliographical guide should mention studies as well as translations in Western languages, of which French and German (among others) would often be given preference over English. It would also require some mention of the valuable introductions in Western languages and the indices to published editions of basic texts. Therefore, a method is proposed here whereby the reader may find the necessary bibliographical information about Buddhist texts when desired.

With regard to Pāli works, their titles in roman letters are listed in "An Analysis of the Pali Canon" in Humphreys, ed., *A Buddhist Students' Manual*, pp. 193–211–27 (I. Analysis, II. Indexes), and *Issues of the Pali Text Society*,

1961, Part I. Thereupon, information about published text editions and indices, and Western translations, glossaries, and studies in books and periodicals may be obtained by consulting Hanayama, *Bibliography on Buddhism*, Index (for notices to about 1930, some to 1936); *Bibliographie Bouddhique*, VI. *Index générale des tomes I–VI* (*Janvier, 1928–Mai, 1934*), XXIIIbis. *Index générale des tomes VII–XXIII* (*Mai, 1934–Mai, 1950*), and section II. "Éditions, Traductions, Dictionnaires" in subsequent volumes until another *Index générale* is issued; Murray B. Emeneau, comp., *A Union List of Printed Indic Texts and Translations in American Libraries* (New Haven, American Oriental Society, 1935), pp. 344–66 and Index of Titles (for notices to about 1933), and *Issues of the Pāli Text Society, 1961*, Parts VI and VII. For this purpose the reader may also consult *A Critical Pāli Dictionary: Epilegomena to Vol. I* (Copenhagen, Royal Danish Society of Sciences and Letters, 1948), section B. Bibliography: a. Pāli, Sanskrit-Pāli, Buddhist Sanskrit and Jain Literature, and b. General Index: Names and Titles (pp. 70–91).

Similarly, the titles of Sanskrit, Tibetan, Chinese, and other Buddhist texts may be ascertained from the published catalogues of the various Buddhist Collections mentioned above. Thereupon, information about published text editions and indices, and Western translations, glossaries, and studies in books and periodicals may be obtained by consulting the *Bibliographie Bouddhique* and the bibliographies by Hanayama and Emeneau (pp. 359–94) as suggested above for Pāli works, as well as the various surveys and histories of Buddhist literature which were cited above. In addition to these sources of information, it should be noted that H. Nakamura, "A Brief Survey of Japanese Studies on the Philosophical Schools of the Mahāyāna," *Acta Asiatica* (Tokyo), I (1960), pp. 56–88, lists Western as well as Japanese editions, translations, and studies of important texts; and Ryūjō Yamada, *Bongo Butten no Shobunken* (Literatures of Sanskrit Buddhist Texts) (Kyōto, 1959), gives a comprehensive citation of Sanskrit text titles, editions, translations, and studies in Western as well as Japanese languages.

V. THE DHAMMA/DHARMA: PRINCIPLES AND PRACTICES

According to Buddhist custom, when the texts have been properly studied, then the Dhamma/Dharma will be understood as Buddhist principles and exemplified as Buddhist practices. Reading materials on these interdependent principles and practices will be cited here according to four main topics: general thought, special doctrines, meditative practices, ceremonies, and rituals.

1. General surveys of thought

As in the case of general introductions to Buddhism, most surveys of Buddhist thought tend to reflect some bias. They are usually Western, Theravāda, or Mahāyāna oriented, or are concerned primarily with developments in a few countries of Buddhist Asia to the exclusion of the rest. When reading such surveys one should note their biases and limitations, and whether they express Buddhist points of view or reflect non-Buddhist interpretations: Do they comprehend the Dhamma/Dharma as correlated Buddhist principles and practices?

In these circumstances, no single history or general exposition of Buddhist thought will suffice, and the reader should resort to various works, among which the following may serve as introductory surveys of the subject. E. Conze, *Buddhist Thought in India* (London, George Allen & Unwin, Ltd., 1962), expounds three major developments, called "Archaic Buddhism, the Sthaviras, the Mahāyāna," during 500 B.C. to A.D. 600. N. Dutt, *Aspects of Mahāyāna Buddhism and Its Relation to Hīnayāna* (London, Luzac & Co., Ltd., 1930) is still a useful, authoritative study on the subject. See also J. Filliozat, "Le bouddhisme: 4. Les doctrines bouddhiques," in Renou and Filliozat, *L'Inde classique*, II, pp. 511–97, and Ryukan Kimura, *A Historical Study of the Terms Hinayāna and Mahāyāna and the Origin of Mahāyāna Buddhism* (Calcutta, University of Calcutta, 1927), and *The Original and Developed Doctrine of Indian Buddhism in Charts* (Calcutta, University of Calcutta, 1920). A. B. Keith, *Buddhist Philosophy in India and Ceylon* (Oxford, Clarendon Press, 1923) is a concise and rather critical Western exposition based upon textual sources. Saṅgharakshita, *A Survey of Buddhism* (Bangalore, Indian Institute of World Culture, 1957) is a popularly written account. Th. Stcherbatsky (Fedor Īppolītovīch Shcherbatskoī), *The Conception of Buddhist Nirvāṇa* (Leningrad, Publication Office of the Academy of Science of the U.S.S.R., 1927; reprinted Shanghai, 1940) contains a summary of the main movements in Indian Buddhist thought, pp. 1–62; compare his "Die drei Richtungen in der Philosophie des Buddhismus," *Rocznik Orjentalistyczny*, X (1934), pp. 1–37, and "The Doctrine of the Buddha," *Bulletin of the School of Oriental and African Studies, University of London*, VI (1933), pp. 867–96. Thomas, *The History of Buddhist Thought* is actually a description of Buddhist doctrinal developments and not a general history of Buddhist thought. Takakusu, *The Essentials of Buddhist Philosophy* and Sôgen Yamakami, *Systems of Buddhistic Thought* (Calcutta, University of Calcutta, 1912) summarize the principles of major schools according to Japanese scholarship.

In addition, several notable surveys in French and German should be listed here: E. Frauwallner, *Die Philosophie des Buddhismus* (Berlin, Akademie Verlag, 1956); Louis de la Vallée Poussin, *Bouddhisme. Opinions sur l'histoire de la dogmatique* (Paris, G. Beauchesne, 1909), "Buddhica," *Harvard*

Journal of Asiatic Studies, III, 2 (July, 1938), pp. 137–60, and *Le dogme et la philosophie du Bouddhisme* (Paris, C. Beauchesne, 1930); Otto Rosenberg, *Die Problem der buddhistischen Philosophie* (Heidelberg, In Kommission bei Otto Harrassowitz, 1924); and Max Walleser, *Buddhistische Philosophie in ihrer geschichtlichen Entwicklung*, 4 Bde. (Heidelberg, Carl Winters Universitäts Buchhandlung, 1904–27).

With regard to reading references for the major schools in Buddhist thought, a good select list of Western-language materials is given in Constantin Regamey, *Buddhistische Philosophie*, Bibliographische Einführungen in das Studium der Philosophie, 20/21 (Bern, A. Franche, 1950), which may be supplemented by the items in the following paragraphs.

Authoritative expositions of Theravāda thought (the Teachings of the Elders or senior bhikkhus) are presented by Allen, "Buddha and Dhamma" in his *The Buddha's Philosophy*, Part One. Introduction, pp. 23–102; Beni Madhab Barua, "Some Aspects of Early Buddhism," *The Cultural Heritage of India*, 2nd ed., rev. and enl. (Calcutta, 1938), Vol. I, pp. 456–502; J. Kashyap, *The Abhi-dhamma Philosophy*, or The Psycho-Ethical Philosophy of Early Buddhism, 2 vols. (Sarnath, Benares, Maha Bodhi Society, 1942, 1943); C. L. A. de Silva, *The Four Essential Doctrines of Buddhism* (Colombo, Associated Newspapers of Ceylon, 1940; reprinted as 2nd ed., 1948); U Thittila Mahā Thera, "The Fundamental Principles of Theravada Buddhism" in Morgan, ed., *The Path of the Buddha*, pp. 67–112; and Paṭṭhān Sayadaw U Withuddha and Myanaung U Tin, *An Approach to Paṭṭhāna* (*Buddhist Philosophy of Relations*) (Rangoon, Maha Thiri Thudhamma, 1956). See also the references cited above for the Burmese, Ceylonese, and Thai Theravāda views of Buddhism. Joseph Masson, *La Religion populaire dans le canon bouddhique pâli* (Louvain, Bureaux du Muséon, 1942), gives a study of folk-beliefs in early Buddhism; compare Maung Htin Aung, *Folk Elements in Burmese Buddhism* (London, Oxford University Press, 1962).

Data on the Sarvāstivāda School (which taught that all *dharmas* [elements] exist momentarily) are provided by Banerjee, *Sarvāstivāda Literature*; N. Dutt, "The Sarvāstivāda School of Buddhism," *Sir Asutosh Mookerjee Silver Jubilee Volumes*, Vol. III, *Orientalia*, 2 (1925), pp. 589–602; A. Migot, "Un grand disciple du Buddha, Śariputra. Son rôle dans l'histoire du bouddhisme et dans le développement de l'Abhidharma," *Bulletin de l'École Française d'Extrême-Orient*, XLVI, 2 (1954), pp. 405–554; and Th. Stcherbatsky, *The Central Conception of Buddhism and the Meaning of the Word "Dharma"* (London, Royal Asiatic Society, 1923; reprinted Calcutta, Susil Gupta India, Ltd., 1956).

With regard to Mahāyāna thought (the Expansive Way, Means, Career, or the Great Method), in addition to those items cited by Regamey, *Buddhistische Philosophie*, two books by B. L. Suzuki may be particularly helpful and interesting for the reader: *Impressions of Mahayana Buddhism* (Kyōto,

Eastern Buddhist Society; London, Luzac & Co., Ltd., 1940) and *Mahayana Buddhism* (London, Buddhist Lodge, 1938; 3rd ed., N.Y., George Allen & Unwin, Ltd., 1959). For studies on the rise of the Mahāyāna see B. M. Barua (Venimadhava Baruya or Beni Madhab Barua), "Mahayana in the Making," *Sir Asutosh Mookerjee Silver Jubilee Volumes*, Vol. III, *Orientalia*, 3 (1927), pp. 163–80; E. Conze, "The Development of Prajñāpāramitā Thought" in Susumu Yamaguchi, ed., *Buddhism and Culture* (Kyōto, 1960), pp. 24–45; N. Dutt, "Emergence of Mahāyāna Buddhism," *The Cultural Heritage of India* (*op. cit.*), Vol. I, pp. 503–17; É. Lamotte, "Sur la formation du Mahāyāna" in *Asiatica*, pp. 377–96; Rāhula Sāṅkrityāyana, "I. Les origines du Mahāyāna," *Journal asiatique* (Oct.–Déc., 1934), pp. 195–208; and Susumu Yamaguchi, "Development of Mahayana Buddhist Beliefs" in Morgan, ed., *The Path of the Buddha*, pp. 153–81. See also the references cited above for India.

The Indian developments of the Mādhyamika School (which adhered to a middle or neutral epistemological and metaphysical position) are described with some comparisons to European philosophy by Murti, *The Central Philosophy of Buddhism*, but there is no comparable description in a Western language of the consequent Mādhyamika developments in Central Asia, China, Korea, Japan, and Tibet (in that historical sequence).

Recent general studies of the Yogācāra School (which emphasized ethical and meditative practices) appear to be scarce. In addition to those items cited by Regamey, *Buddhistische Philosophie*, mention may be made of a work by Ashok Kumar Chatterjee entitled *The Yogācāra Idealism*, reportedly published recently by the Banaras Hindu University (1961 ?).

There are numerous studies on Vajrayāna thought (the Way of the Vajra, exemplifying ultimate wisdom) in addition to those cited above for India, Mongolia, Nepal, and Tibet. The following is a list of specially recommended accounts: Benoytosh Bhattacharyya, "Scientific Background of the Buddhist Tantras," Gautama Buddha 25th Centenary Volume, *The Indian Historical Quarterly*, XXXII, 2–3 (June–Sept., 1956), pp. 182–8, and "The Home of Tāntric Buddhism," *B. C. Law Volume*, I (1945), pp. 354–61; Chou Yi-liang, "Tantrism in China," *Harvard Journal of Asiatic Studies*, VIII, 3–4 (March, 1945), pp. 241–332; Shashi Bhushan Dasgupta, *An Introduction to Tāntric Buddhism*, 2nd ed. (Calcutta, University of Calcutta, 1958), and its review by K. Ch'en in *Harvard Journal of Asiatic Studies*, XV, 1–2 (June, 1952), pp. 197–201; Wilhelm Filchner, *Kumbum: Lamaismus in Lehre und Leben* (Zürich, Rascher Verlag, 1954); H. von Glasenapp, *Buddhistische Mysterien* (Stuttgart, W. Spemann Verlag, 1940), tr. by Jacques Marty with some omissions as *Mystères bouddhistes* (Paris, Payot, 1944); Anagarika B. Govinda, *Foundations of Tibetan Mysticism* (London, Rider & Co., 1959); Herbert V. Guenther, *The Origin and Spirit of Vajrayāna* (San Francisco, Epicenter Press, 1959); Siegbert Hummel, *Lamaistische Studien* (Leipzig, Otto Harrassowitz, 1950);

R. Sāṅkrityāyana, "II. L'origine du Vajrayāna," *Journal asiatique* (Oct.–Déc., 1934), pp. 209–30; and Tucci, "The Religious Ideas: Vajrayāna" in his *Tibetan Painted Scrolls*, Vol. I, Part 1 (Rome, La Libreria dello Stato, 1949), pp. 209–49. J. Van Durme, 'Notes sur le Lamaïsme. La question des apports étrangers," *Mélanges chinois et bouddhiques*, I: 1931–32 (1932), pp. 263–319. For readings on the monastic institutions of the Vajrayāna, see below.

2. Special studies of doctrines

There are numerous expositions in English, as well as in other Western languages, of Buddhist concepts and doctrines. Among these the following are a few select items which supplement those studies listed in Regamey, *Buddhistische Philosophie*.

With regard to interpretations of basic Buddhist concepts see B. C. Law, *Concepts of Buddhism* (Amsterdam, for Kern Institute by H. J. Paris, 1937), and Pande, "Studies in Early Buddhist Doctrines," in his *Studies in the Origins of Buddhism*, Part III, pp. 397–566, for general treatment and the following expositions: Vidhushekhara Bhattacharya, *The Basic Conception of Buddhism* (Calcutta, University of Calcutta, 1934), and R. P. Chowdhury, "Interpretation of the 'Anatta' Doctrine of Buddhism; A New Approach," *The Indian Historical Quarterly*, XXXI, 1 (March, 1955), pp. 62–7, E. H. Brewster, "Dukkha and Sukha" in B. C. Law, ed., *Buddhistic Studies*, pp. 284–328, and W. Rahula, "Duḥkha-satya," Gautama Buddha 25th Centenary Volume, *The Indian Historical Quarterly*, XXXII, 2–3 (June–Sept., 1956), pp. 141–5; B. C. Law, "Karma," *The Cultural Heritage of India* (*op. cit.*), I, pp. 537–46; Ananta Kumar Nyaya-Tarkatirtha, "Nirodha-Satya," Gautama Buddha 25th Centenary Volume, *The Indian Historical Quarterly*, XXXII, 2–3 (June–Sept., 1956), pp. 146–52; B. C. Law, "Nirvāṇa," *The Cultural Heritage of India* (*op. cit.*), I, pp. 547–58; Shōson Miyamoto, "Freedom, Independence, and Peace in Buddhism," *Philosophy East and West*, I, 4 (Jan., 1952), pp. 30–40; II, 3 (Oct., 1952), pp. 208–25; Nārada Thera, "Nibbāna" in B. C. Law, ed., *Buddhistic Studies*, pp. 564–86; A. C. Banerjee, "Pratītyasamutpāda," Gautama Buddha 25th Centenary Volume, *The Indian Historical Quarterly*, XXXII, 2–3 (June–Sept., 1956), pp. 153–6; Nārada Thera, "Saṁsāra or Buddhist Philosophy of Birth and Death," in B. C. Law, ed., *Buddhistic Studies*, pp. 350–64; and N. Dutt, "Tathāgatagarbha," *The Indian Historical Quarterly*, XXXIII, 1 (March, 1957), pp. 26–39.

The metaphysical concepts of Buddhist thought are analyzed by A. Bareau, *L'Absolu en philosophie bouddhique*. Evolution de la notion d'asaṃskṛta (Paris, Centre de documentation universitaire, Tournier & Constans, 1951), and "The Notion of Time in Early Buddhism," *East and West*, VII, 4 (Jan., 1957), pp. 353–64; H. V. Guenther, *Philosophy and Psychology in the Abhidharma* (Lucknow, Buddha Vihara, and Calcutta, Mahabodhi Book Agency, 1957); and Jan W. de Jong, "Le problème de l'Absolu dans l'école Mādhyamika," *Revue philosophique de la France et de l'étranger*, CXL (1950), pp. 322–7.

Buddhist logic and epistemology are specially studied in the following: N. Aiyaswami Sastri, "Harivarman's Theory of Cognition," Gautama Buddha 25th Centenary Volume, *The Indian Historical Quarterly*, XXXII, 2–3 (June–Sept., 1956), pp. 211–15; H. V. Guenther, "The Levels of Understanding in Buddhism," *Journal of the American Oriental Society*, LXXVIII, 1 (Jan.–March, 1958), pp. 19–28; Gadjin M. Nagao, "An Interpretation of the Term 'Saṁvṛti' (Convention) in Buddhism," *Silver Jubilee Volume of the Zinbun-Kagaku-Kenkyayo-Kyoto University* (1954), Indo-Iranian Reprint, I, pp. 550–61; Richard H. Robinson, "Some Logical Aspects of Nāgārjuna's System," *Philosophy East and West*, VI, 4 (Jan., 1957), pp. 291–308; Th. Stcherbatsky, *Buddhist Logic*, 2 vols. (Leningrad, Akad. Nauk SSSR, 1932; reprinted 's Gravenhage, 1958; Dover Paperbacks, 1962). Alex Wayman, "Notes on the Sanskrit Term *jñāna*," *Journal of the American Oriental Society*, LXXV, 4 (Oct.–Dec., 1955), pp. 253–68.

The psychological aspects of Buddhist thought are discussed by J. Filliozat, "The Psychological Discoveries of Buddhism," *University of Ceylon Review*, XIII, 2–3 (April–July, 1955), pp. 69–82; Guenther, *Philosophy and Psychology in the Abhidharma*; Anagarika Brahmacari Govinda, *The Psychological Attitude of Early Buddhist Philosophy and Its Systematic Representation according to Abhidhamma Tradition* (London, Rider & Co., 1961); E. R. Sarathchandra, *Buddhist Psychology of Perception* (Colombo, Ceylon University Press, 1958); Bratindra Kumar Sengupta, "Buddhist Psychology," Gautama Buddha 25th Centenary Volume, *The Indian Historical Quarterly*, XXXII, 2–3 (June–Sept., 1956), pp. 157–61.

Some other interesting topics are considered in the following studies: A. Bareau, "The Concept of Responsibility in Ancient Buddhism," *East and West*, VI, 3 (Oct., 1955), pp. 216–23; B. M. Barua, "Faith in Buddhism" in B. C. Law, ed., *Buddhistic Studies*, pp. 329–49. Gokuldas De, *Significance and Importance of Jātakas* (Calcutta, Calcutta University, 1951); N. Dutt, "Place of Faith in Buddhism" in B. C. Law, ed., *Louis de la Vallée Poussin Memorial Volume*, pp. 421–8; I. B. Horner, *The Early Buddhist Theory of Man Perfected. A Study of the Arahan* (London, Williams & Norgate, Ltd., 1936); B. C. Law, *Heaven and Hell in Buddhist Perspective* (Calcutta and Simla, Thacker, Spink & Co., 1925), and *The Buddhist Conception of Spirits*, 2nd rev. ed. (London, Luzac & Co., Ltd., 1936); and Paul Mus, *La lumière sur les six voies.* Tableau de la transmigration bouddhique d'après des sources sanskrites, pali, tibétaines et chinoises en majeure partie inédites. I. *Introduction et critique des textes* (Paris, Institut d'ethnologie, 1939).

3. Meditative practices

The Buddhist method of realizing Nibbāna/Nirvāṇa (freedom of perfect existence as the ultimate goal) is customarily taught and exercised as the integration of right conduct, right thought, and right insight in man as right "becoming Enlightened." This integrative learning process is the Threefold Training, called Ti-sikkhā by the Theravāda tradition and Tri-śikṣā by the Mahāyāna and Vajrayāna traditions. It consists of (*a*) Adhisīla-sikkhā/Adhiśīla-śikṣā or training in virtuous conduct (*sīla*/*śīla*; cf. *lu*, *ritsu*) which results in higher morality, (*b*) Adhicitta-sikkhā/Adhicitta-śikṣā or training in concentrative absorption or meditation (*samādhi*; cf. *ch'an*, *zen*) which results in higher thought, and (*c*) Adhipaññā-sikkhā/Adhiprajñā-śikṣā or training in transcendent comprehension and understanding (*paññā*/*prajñā*; cf. *chih-hui*, *chi-e*) which results in higher insight. These three developments are interdependent and interactive; they are to be undertaken simultaneously or in unending succession.

It is in this context that Buddhist meditative practices should be studied and understood by the general reader and student; they are not ends in themselves but are interrelated with virtuous conduct and manifested wisdom as means for realizing and experiencing Nibbāna/Nirvāṇa. The following reading references are unavoidably inadequate because for undertaking Buddhist meditation, as in other cases of learning skills, there is no real substitute for a living master-teacher, monastic or other suitable environment, and constant practice.

The subject of Buddhist meditation is described in general terms by E. Conze, ed. and tr., *Buddhist Meditation* (London, George Allen & Unwin, Ltd., 1956), and discussed somewhat by J. Evola, *The Doctrine of Awakening. A Study on the Buddhist Ascesis* (London, Luzac & Co., Ltd., 1951). The reader should note that many schools of the Theravāda, Mahāyāna, and Vajrayāna traditions have variant, but not disparate, methods of Buddhist meditation, but a thorough comparative study of their practices has not yet been undertaken.

The Burmese meditation methods in the Theravāda tradition have recently been popularized among the laity and made known even to non-Buddhist Westerners. For instructions, see Mahāsī Sayadaw, *Buddhist Meditation and Its Forty Subjects* (Rangoon, Buddha Sāsana Council Press, 1958) and *Practical Basic Exercises in Satipaṭṭhāna Vipassanā Meditation* (Rangoon, Buddha Sāsana Council Press, 1956); Mohnyin Sayadaw, *Diṭṭha Vipassanā Cognitive Insight—Exercises* (Rangoon, Rangoon Gazette, Ltd., 1955); and U Tun Hla Oung, ed. and tr., *The Development of Mind-power. A Buddhist Method Taught at the Hanthawaddy Centre* (Rangoon, Buddha Sāsana Patipatti: Sasanapyu Aphwesyok, 1956). The experiences of Westerners about Burmese methods of Buddhist meditation are described in Marie Beuzeville Byles, *Journey into Burmese Silence* (London, George Allen & Unwin, Ltd., 1962) with Appendix: "Vipassana Meditation: The Ledi Sayadaw Method," translation by Sayalay Daw Saranawati, pp. 197–211; Winston L. King, "An Experience in Buddhist Meditation," *The Journal of Religion*, XLI, 1 (Jan.,

1961), pp. 51–61; Ernest Henry Shattock, *An Experiment in Mindfulness* (*An English Admiral's Experience in a Buddhist Monastery*) (London, 1958; N.Y., E. P. Dutton & Co., Inc., 1960); and Colin Wyatt, "Satipatthâna Meditation Centres in Burma," *The Middle Way*, XXXIII, 3 (Nov., 1958), pp. 102–5, 124.

For the Ceylonese methods of meditation in the Theravāda tradition, see G. Constant Lounsbery, *Buddhist Meditation in the Southern School* (London, Kegan Paul, Trench, Trubner & Co., 1950), and the following more authoritative accounts: Bhikkhu Ñāṇamoli, tr., *The Path of Purification* (*Visuddhimagga*) *by Bhadantācariya Buddhaghosa* (Colombo, R. Semage, 1956) particularly Part II, "Concentration," pp. 84–478; Nyanaponika Thera, *Satipaṭṭhāna. The Heart of Buddhist Meditation. A Handbook of Mental Training Based on the Buddha's 'Way of Mindfulness'* (Colombo, The Word of Buddha Publishing Co., 1954); Soma Thera, tr., *Foundations of Mindfulness.* A translation of the Satipatthana Sutta of the Majjhima Nikaya (Colombo, Henry Prelis, 1954); and F. L. Woodward, tr., *Manual of a Mystic* (London, W. Milford [for Pali Text Society], 1916; reprinted 1962).

Chinese methods of meditation in the Mahāyāna tradition are reviewed by Chang Chen-chi, "A Survey of the Practice of Buddhist Meditation" in his *The Practice of Zen* (N.Y., Rider & Co., 1960), pp. 161–76, and described by J. Prip-Møller, "Buddhist Meditation Ritual," *The Chinese Recorder*, LXVI, 12 (Dec., 1935), pp. 713–18, and his *Chinese Buddhist Monasteries* (Copenhagen, C. E. C. Gads; London, Oxford University Press, 1937), pp. 65–79, concerning meditation halls and practices. More details are promised in a forthcoming work by R. S. Y. Chi, tr., *An Introduction to Buddhist Meditation* (in press) giving a version of the instructions to his disciples by Chih I (A.D. 531–97), the founder of the T'ien-t'ai School.

There are several Japanese methods of meditation in the Mahāyāna tradition based principally upon the Chinese methods. For the Tendai (cf. T'ien-t'ai) method see Bruno Petzold, "On Buddhist Meditation," *The Transactions of the Asiatic Society of Japan*, Third Series, 1 (1948), pp. 64–100, which includes comparisons with the Theravāda and Zen methods. The Zen method has become popularized among the laity through the many writings *about* the subject. In general see B. L. Suzuki, "Meditation" in her *Mahayana Buddhism*, pp. 88–92, and D. T. Suzuki, "Life of Meditation" in his *The Training of the Zen Buddhist Monk* (Kyōto, Eastern Buddhist Society, 1934), pp. 61–91.

Meditative practices of the Vajrayāna tradition are often described in writings about Tibetan and Mongolian Buddhism (see above). The following are some of the special works on the subject: W. Y. Evans-Wentz, ed., *The Tibetan Book of the Great Liberation, or The Method of Realizing Nirvāṇa through Knowing the Mind . . .* (London, Oxford University Press, 1954), and *Tibetan Yoga and Secret Doctrines*, 2nd enl. ed. (London, H. Milford,

1958); and A. M. Pozdnejev, *Dhyāna und Samadhi im Mongolischen Lamaismus* (Hannover, Orient Buchhandlung Heinz Lafaire, 1927).

4. Ceremonies and rituals

Buddhist ceremonies and rituals serve a variety of functions: to venerate the Buddha ideal, to exemplify the Dhamma/Dharma principles and practices, to regularize and maintain the Saṅgha monastic routine, to instruct and inspire the laity, and to present and enhance the cultural role of the Buddha Sāsana/Śāsana in society. Furthermore, for the Buddhists their performance effects a desired correlation between the processes of the cosmic-natural order and the conduct of the human social order. For examples of this latter aspect of ritual, which is fundamental in traditional Asian beliefs and practices, see A. Bareau, "Les relations entre la causalité du monde physique et la causalité du monde spirituel dans le Hinayāna" in Roy, ed., *Liebenthal Festschrift*, pp. 14–20; Robert Heine-Geldern, *Conceptions of State and Kingship in Southeast Asia* (Ithaca, Cornell University Press, 1956); and C. von Korvin-Krasinski, "Der Mensch als Mikrokosmos in der symbolischen Anthropologie des tibetischen Lamaismus," *Symbolon*, I (1960), pp. 103–15. The following are some of the more notable and authoritative accounts of Buddhist monastic ceremonies.

The Pabbajjā/Pravrajya (initiation ceremony for novices following their period of probation or Parivāsa) and the subsequent Upasampadā (ordination ceremony for monks and nuns) are performed in various countries. For a note on the Burmese rite see U Tin, "The Ordination Ceremony," *The Guardian* (Rangoon), V (July, 1958), pp. 21–2. Both ceremonies in Ceylon are recorded by J. F. Dickson, ed. and tr., "The Upasampadá-Kammávācá, Being the Buddhist Manual of the Form and Manner of Ordering of Priests and Deacons" in Gard, ed., *Buddhism*, pp. 158–66. The Chinese practices are described in detail by Prip-Møller, "The Ordination Unit, Its Ceremonies and Its Development" in his *Chinese Buddhist Monasteries*, pp. 297–352. Two little-known cases in Indonesia and Viêt-Nam have been noted by H. von Glasenapp, "Ein buddhistischer Initiations-ritus des javanischen Mittelalters," *Tribus* (1953), pp. 259–74, and P. B. Lafont and Pierre Bitard, "Ordination de deux dignitaires bouddhiques 'Tay lu," *Bulletin de la Société des Études Indochinoises*, XXXII (1957), pp. 199–221. Sangharakshita, "Ordination and Initiation in the Three Yānas of Buddhism," *The Middle Way*, XXXIV, 3 (Nov., 1959), pp. 94–104, reprinted in *The Indo-Asian Culture*, VIII, 3 (Jan., 1960), pp. 246–65, is a comparative study of the subject.

The Pavāraṇā (ceremony concluding the Vassa or Vassāvāsa, monastic residence or "retreat" during the monsoon rainy season) and the related Kaṭhina (annual ceremony in which the laity dedicate cotton cloth to the monks for the making of robes) are described by Kun Chang, *A Comparative Study of the Kaṭhinavastu* ('s Gravenhage, Mouton & Co., 1957), and Phya

Anuman Rajadhon, "The End of Buddhist Lent," *The Journal of the Siam Society*, XLII, 2 (Jan., 1955), pp. 121–34.

The Uposatha (meetings at new moon and full moon to expound the Dhamma/Dharma, observe the Vinaya, and recite the *Pāṭimokkha/Prāṭimokṣa*) is studied by J. Przyluski, "Uposatha," *The Indian Historical Quarterly* XII, 3 (Sept., 1936), pp. 383–90.

Other important Buddhist rituals are described by Marguerite La Fuente, tr., *Pirit Nula. Le fil de pirit. Suttas de protection* (Paris, Adrien Maisonneuve, 1941); Otakar Pertold, "A Protective Ritual of the Southern Buddhists," *Journal of the (Royal) Asiatic Society of Bengal*, XII, 6 (1922–23), pp. 744–89, which concerns the Paritta; J. Przyluski, "Les rites d'avalambana," *Mélanges chinois et bouddhiques*, I: 1931–32 (1932), pp. 221–5; Erwin Rousselle, "Ein Abhiṣeka-Ritus im Mantra-Buddhismus," *Sinica-Sonderausgabe* (1934), pp. 58–90; and L. A. Waddell, "The 'Dhāraṇī' Cult in Buddhism. Its Origin, Deified Literature and Images," *Ostasiatische Zeitschrift*, I (1912), pp. 155–95.

Buddhist ceremonies and festivals involving the laity in Asian countries are described in the following selected studies: Maung Htin Aung, "Burmese Initiation Ceremonies," *Journal of the Burma Research Society*, XXXVI, 1 (Aug., 1953), pp. 77–87; R. J. and Beatrice Miller, "On Two Bhutanese New Year's Celebrations," *American Anthropologist*, LVIII (Feb., 1956), pp. 179–83; S. Paranavitana, "Buddhist Festivals in Ceylon" in B. C. Law, ed., *Buddhistic Studies*, pp. 529–46, reprinted in *The Buddhist*, XXXII, 2 (Aug., 1961), pp. 15–17, and 3 (Sept., 1961), pp. 32–3; Karl Ludvig Reichelt, tr., "Extracts from the Buddhist Ritual," *The Chinese Recorder*, LIX, 3 (March, 1928), pp. 160–70, being translated passages from the *Ch'ang Meng Er Sung*, and "The Origin and Development of Masses for the Dead" in his *Truth and Tradition in Chinese Buddhism*, 4th rev. enl. ed. (Shanghai, Commercial Press, 1934), pp. 67–111; D. T. Suzuki, "Gathas and Prayers" and "The Dhāranīs" translated in his *Manual of Zen Buddhism* (Kyōto, Eastern Buddhist Society, 1935; reprinted N.Y., Grove Press, 1960), pp. 1–10 and 11–43, respectively; Marinus Willem de Visser, *Ancient Buddhism in Japan. Sutras and Ceremonies in Use in the Seventh and Eighth Centuries A.D. and Their History in Later Times*, 2 vols. (Leiden, E. J. Brill, 1935); Deydier, "Cérémonies et fêtes religieuses," in his *Introduction à la connaissance du Laos*, pp. 33–47; John Brough, "Nepalese Buddhist Rituals," *Bulletin of the School of Oriental and African Studies, University of London*, XII, 3–4 (1948), pp. 668–76; Kenneth E. Wells, *Thai Buddhism: Its Rites and Activities*, rev. ed. (Bangkok, Christian Bookstore, 1960); consult Horace Geoffrey Quaritch Wales, *Siamese State Ceremonies* (London, Bernard Quaritch, 1931) for Buddhist data; Louise Alexandra David-Neel, *Initiations and Initiates in Tibet*, 2nd ed. (London, Rider & Co., 1958). Ferdinand Diederich Lessing, "Calling the Soul in a Lamaist Ritual," in Walter J. Fischel, ed., *Semitic and Oriental Studies* (Berkeley, University of California Press, 1951), pp. 263–84, "Structure and

Meaning of the Rite Called the Bath of the Buddha according to Tibetan and Chinese Sources" in *Studia serica Bernhard Karlgren dedicata* (Copenhagen, E. Munksgaard, 1959), pp. 159–71, and "Wu-liang-shou . . . A Comparative Study of Tibetan and Chinese Longevity Rites," *Bulletin of the Institute of History and Philology, Academia Sinica*, XXVIII, 2 (1957), pp. 794–824; R. Nebesky-Wojkowitz, *Oracles and Demons of Tibet:* The Cult and Iconography of the Tibetan Protective Deities ('s Gravenhage, Mouton & Co., 1956); and Schram, *The Monguors of the Kansu-Tibetan Frontier*, Part II. *Their Religious Life*.

With regard to the annual "Wesak" (Vesākha/Vaiśākha-pūjā) celebrations, held customarily on the full moon day of May, see the special Wesak issues of various Buddhist periodicals, as for example, the *Ceylon Daily News Wesak Number* (Colombo) and the *Vesakhapuja* (Bangkok) for May of each year.

The Buddha Jayanti (2500th anniversary celebration of the Buddha) was held throughout the Buddhist world in May, 1956, and May, 1957. Among the various reports of the event, see especially *Art and Letters* (London), XXX, 2 (1956), and XXXI, 1 (1957); George Coedès, "The Twenty-five-hundredth Anniversary of the Buddha," *Diogenes* (N.Y.), XV (July, 1956), pp. 95–111; *Commemoration of the 25th Buddhist Century in Pictures* (Bangkok, Buddhist Museum, 1957); Ananda W. P. Guruge and K. G. Amaradas, eds., *2500 Buddha Jayanti Souvenir* (Colombo, Lanka Bauddha Mandalaya, 1956); and The Buddhist Council of Ceylon, ed., *An Event of Dual Significance* (Colombo, Lanka Bauddha Mandalaya, 1956).

VI. THE SAṄGHA: MONASTICISM, SCHOOLS, LAITY

The Saṅgha is traditionally respected and maintained as the third essential part of the Ti-ratana/Tri-ratna. It is the Buddhist assembly, community, or collective body which institutionally follows the way of the Buddha and authoritatively studies, experiences, and expounds the Buddha Dhamma/Dharma in various Schools of the Theravāda, Mahāyāna, and Vajrayāna movements.

1. Monasticism

The Saṅgha customarily includes monks, nuns, and disciples who are male or female novices. The Buddhist laity, consisting of male and female devotees, traditionally support or assist the Saṅgha through their individual, family, community, and governmental efforts.

Canonical Buddhist literature includes detailed rules for the proper conduct of monastic life for monks and nuns. Regulations governing the Saṅgha of the Theravāda movement have been codified as the Vinaya Piṭaka in the Pāli Tipiṭaka; those for the once influential Sarvāstivāda School, which no longer exists, were codified as the Vinaya Piṭaka in a Buddhist Hybrid Sanskrit Tripiṭaka recently recovered and now being edited and studied by scholars; those for the Mahāyāna movement are codified as the Lü Ts'ang in the Chinese Ta Ts'ang Ching, as the Ritsu Zō in the Japanese San Zō Kyō, etc.; and those for the Vajrayāna movement are contained in the Ḥdul-ba (Vinaya) section of the Tibetan Kanjur. In addition to these canonical regulations, all monasteries have their own special rules for maintaining daily routine and group discipline. For references on monastic influences upon, and relations with, lay society see below. Architectural studies of some famous monasteries will be cited later.

The historical and institutional nature of the Saṅgha is described by Robert Bleichsteiner, *Die Gelbe Kirche: Mysterien der Buddhistischen Klöster in Indien, Tibet, Mongolei und China* (Wien, Belf, 1937), which has been translated into French as *L'Église jaune* (Paris, Payot, 1937), and in more general terms by Joseph M. Kitagawa, "Buddhism and the Sangha," in his *Religions of the East* (Philadelphia, Westminster Press, 1960), pp. 155–221, and Paul Lévy, *Buddhism: A 'Mystery Religion'*? (London, Athlone Press, 1957). Most studies, however, concern the Saṅgha as a national organization, influential group (Nikāya), or monastic body in a particular country.

Studies of Buddhist monastic organization and life in Burma and Cambodia are still inadequate, but in general see U Nu, "The Sangha," *The Guardian* (Rangoon), V (April, 1958), pp. 9–20, and Aung Than, "A Brief Survey of the Burmese Buddhist Samgha and its Relationship with the State and the Laity" in *Proceedings of the IXth International Congress for the History of Religion, Tokyo and Kyoto, 1958*, pp. 229–35; François Martini, "Le bonze cambodgien," *France-Asie*, IV, 37–38 (Printemps, 1949), pp. 881–8, and "Organisation du clergé bouddhique au Cambodge," *ibid.*, pp. 889–97. Ratna Chandra Agrawala, "Life of Buddhist Monks in Chinese Turkestan" in *Sarūpa Bhāratī*, pp. 173–81, refers to the early centuries A.D. Monastic organization in Ceylon is described sociologically for present times by A. Bareau, *La vie et l'organisation des communautés bouddhiques modernes de Ceylon* (Pondichery, Institut Français d'Indologie, 1957), and historically for the Anurādhapura period by Rahula, *History of Buddhism in Ceylon*, "The Monastery: Its Structure," pp. 112–34, and "The Monastery: Its Administration" pp. 135–52. For Chinese monastic life, see Prip-Møller, *Chinese Buddhist Monasteries*, especially "Monks' Offices and Daily Life in the Monasteries," pp. 353–84.

Monasticism in India and the general development of the Saṅgha are described by a number of studies: G. De, *Democracy in Early Buddhist Saṃgha* (Calcutta, University of Calcutta, 1955); N. Dutt, *Early Monastic Buddhism*, 2 vols. (Calcutta, Calcutta Oriental Series, 1941, 1945; but not the rev. ed. of 1960); S. Dutt, *Early Buddhist Monachism* (Bombay, Asia Publishing House, rev. ed., 1960) and *Buddhist Monks and Monasteries of India:*

Their History and Their Contribution to Indian Literature (London, George Allen & Unwin, Ltd., 1962); J. Filliozat, "Le bouddhisme: 5. Discipline bouddhique—Le communauté" in Renou and Filliozat, *L'Inde classique*, II, pp. 597–605; I. B. Horner, "The Almswomen" in her *Women under Primitive Buddhism* (London, Routledge & Kegan Paul, Ltd., N.Y., 1930), Part II, pp. 95–379; Lamotte, "La communauté bouddhique" in his *Histoire du Bouddhisme Indien*, pp. 58–92; B. C. Law, "Early Buddhist Brothers and Sisters," *Journal and Proceedings of the Asiatic Society of Bengal*, XI (1945), pp. 39–49, "Early Buddhist Monks and Nuns" in his *Indological Studies*, Part II, pp. 1–30, and *Early Indian Monasteries* (Bangalore, Indian Institute of World Culture, 1958), Madan Mohan Singh, "Life in the Buddhist Monastery during the 6th Century B.C. [sic]," *Journal of the Bihar Research Society*, XL (1954), pp. 131–54.

For Japanese monasticism see D. T. Suzuki, *The Training of the Zen Buddhist Monk* (Kyōto, Eastern Buddhist Society, 1934) and chapter V of the present volume. The Lao Saṅgha is described by Kruong Pathoumxad, "Organization of the Sangha" in de Berval, ed., *Kingdom of Laos*, pp. 257–67; compare the excerpts translated from the "Statut du clergé bouddhique du Royaume du Laos" in Gard, ed., *Buddhism*, pp. 169–71. William Frederick Mayers, "Mongolia and Turkestan" in his *The Chinese Government*, 3rd ed. (Shanghai, Kelly & Walsh, 1897), pp. 87–104, gives the titles of positions in the Saṅgha hierarchy; see also Miller, *Monasteries and Culture Change in Inner Mongolia*, and the Dilowa Hutukhtu, "The Narobanchin Monastery in Outer Mongolia," *Proceedings of the American Philosophical Society*, XCVI (1952), pp. 587–98. Gustave Dumoutier, "Le clergé et les temples bouddhique au Tonkin," *Revue Indochinoise*, X (1913), pp. 443–61 gives some account of monasticism in northern Viêt-Nam in the early twentieth century, but more contemporary accounts of the whole country are now needed.

Tibetan monasteries and monasticism are described in the following accounts: Robert B. Ekvall, "Three Categories of Inmates within Tibetan Monasteries: Status and Function," *Central Asiatic Journal*, V (1960), pp. 206–20; W. Filchner, *Das Kloster in Tibet: Ein Beitrag zu seiner Geschichte* (Berlin, E. S. Mittler, 1906) and *Kumbum Dschamba Ling: Das Kloster der hundert-tausend Bilder Maitreyas* (Leipzig, Brockhaus, 1933); Köppen, "Die lamaische Hierarchie und Kirche" in his *Die Religion des Buddha und ihre Entstehung*, Bd. 2, pp. 243–388; Li An-che, "A Lamasery in Outline," *Journal of the West China Border Research Society*, XIV, Series A (1942), pp. 35–68, and cited by him in his chapter "Tibetan Religion" in Vergilius Ferm, ed., *Ancient Religions . . .* (N.Y., The Philosophical Library, 1950), p. 269; Mayers, "Tibet and the Lamaist Hierarchy" in his *The Chinese Government*, 3rd ed. (1897), pp. 105–22; B. D. Miller, "The Web of Tibetan Monasticism," *The Journal of Asian Studies*, XX, 2 (Feb., 1961), pp. 197–203; and Schram, *The Monguors of the Kansu-Tibetan Frontier*, Part II. *Their Religious Life*, see

"Administration of the Lamaseries: Educational and Religious Aspects," pp. 54–73, and "Lamaseries in Huang-chung," pp. 37–54.

2. Principal schools

For many centuries in Asia innumerable Buddhist schools have developed, continued, or disappeared. Unfortunately, a comprehensive survey or even a full list of the principal schools has not yet been published in any language. Perhaps the most available sketches in English are "Principal Schools and Sects of Buddhism" in Bapat, ed., *2500 Years of Buddhism*, pp. 96–108, which includes India, Tibet and Nepal, China, Japan, Ceylon, Burma, Thailand, and Cambodia with two useful charts, and P. V. Bapat and N. Dutt, "Schools and Sects of Buddhism," *The Cultural Heritage of India* (*op. cit.*), I, pp. 456–502.

The origin and early development of Buddhist schools in India are well reviewed by Lamotte, "Les sectes bouddhiques" in his *Histoire du Bouddhisme Indien*, pp. 571–705, which includes useful lists and tables. On page 571 of his work a bibliographical note cites the most important Western-language studies on the subject, to which only N. Dutt, "The Buddhist Sects: A Survey," *B. C. Law Volume*, I, pp. 282–92, might be added. Two important items in Lamotte's list will serve the reader as fairly comprehensive outlines: A. Bareau, *Les sectes bouddhiques du Petit Véhicule* (Saigon, L'École Française d'Extrême-Orient, 1955), and "Trois traités sur les sectes bouddhiques attribués à Vasumitra, Bhavya et Vinītadeva," *Journal asiatique*, CCXLII (1954), pp. 229–66, and CCXLIV (1956), pp. 167–200.

For descriptive literature on the Buddhist schools of Japan see chapter V of the present volume. Their doctrines are summarized by Takakusu, *The Essentials of Buddhist Philosophy*, and Yamakami, *Systems of Buddhistic Thought*.

Information about Buddhist schools in Tibet is often included in studies on Tibetan Buddhism which were cited in preceding sections. For general introductory accounts see Anil Chandra Pal, "Principal Sects in Tibet," *The Maha Bodhi*, LXVII, 3 and 4 (March and April, 1959), pp. 78–81, and especially Tucci, "The Sects" in his *Tibetan Painted Scrolls*, Vol. I, Part 1, pp. 81–93. Particular studies of some of the principal Tibetan schools are listed as follows. The Ningma-pa (rñiṅ-ma-pa, "The Ancients," Old Translation or Unreformed or "Red" Sect) of Padma Sambhava (eighth century A.D.), who founded the Samye (bSam-yas) monastery, is described by Li An-che, "Rñiṅ-ma-pa: The Early Form of Lamaism," *Journal of the Royal Asiatic Society* (*of Great Britain and Ireland*) (1948), pp. 142–63, and Schram, "The Red Sect in Huang-chung" in his *The Monguors of the Kansu-Tibetan Frontier*, Part II, pp. 73–6. The Kagyu-pa (bKaḥ-(b)rgyud-pa, Oral Tradition or Semi-reformed or "White" Sect) of Marpa (Mar-pa, 1012–97; cf. Nā-ro-pa from Ti-lo-pa) and Milarepa (Mi-la-ras-pa, 1040–1123 or 1052–1135) is reviewed by Li An-che, "The Bkah-Brgyud Sect of Lamaism," *Journal of the American Oriental Society*, LXIX, 2 (April–June, 1949), pp. 51–9, and R. Nebesky-Wojkowitz, "The Tibetan Kagyupa Sect," *Stepping Stones* (Kalimpong), I, 8 (Feb., 1951), pp. 185–7; one of its subsects is specially studied by Hugh E. Richardson, "The Karma-pa Sect. A Historical Note," *Journal of the Royal Asiatic Society* (*of Great Britain and Ireland*), 3–4 (1958), pp. 139–64 and 1–2 (1959), pp. 1–18. The Sakya-pa (Sa-skya-pa, "Multiple Colored" Sect) of Konchog Gyalpo (dKon-mchog rgyal-po, 1034–1102), who founded the Sakya monastery, is described by Li An-che, "The Sakya Sect of Lamaism," *Journal of the West China Border Research Society*, XVI, Series A (1945). The remaining principal schools apparently not yet studied in monographs are the Kadam-pa (bKaḥ-gdams-pa, Advisor Sect) of Atīśa (980–1053) and 'Brom-tön (Ḥbrom-ston, 1002–58 or 1005–64), and the Geluk-pa (dGe-lugs-pa, Virtuous Way or Reformed or "Yellow" Sect) of Tsongkhapa (bTsoṅ-kha-pa, 1357–1419).

3. Lay groups and activities

For many centuries the Saṅgha was the only identifiable Buddhist organization, aided by support from households, communities, and royal courts. Within the last seventy-five years, however, Buddhist followers have established various Buddhist lay societies and associations which are supplementing the role of the Saṅgha in the twentieth century by undertaking organized educational and social welfare activities. However, in most cases, lay Buddhist leaders continue to acknowledge the authority of the Saṅgha in Buddhist matters and seek its counsel in many societal affairs.

With regard to historical studies of the Buddhist laity in India see N. Dutt, "Place of Laity in Early Buddhism," *The Indian Historical Quarterly*, XXI (1945), pp. 163–83; Horner, "The Laywomen" in her *Women under Primitive Buddhism*, Part I, pp. 1–94; É. Lamotte, "Le Bouddhisme des laïcs" in Gadjin M. Nagao and Josho Nozawa, eds., *Studies in Indology and Buddhology* (Kyōto, 1955), pp. 73–89; and Louis de la Vallée Poussin, "Les fidéles laïcs ou Upāsaka," *Bulletin de la classe des lettres et des sciences morales et politiques, Académie Royale des Sciences, des Lettres, et des Beaux Arts de Belgique* (1925), pp. 15–34.

The activities of Buddhist lay organizations in present times are frequently reported in various Buddhist journals listed below. The following are a few of the interesting studies now being made on the subject: E. Michael Mendelson, "A Messianic Buddhist Association in Upper Burma," *Bulletin of the School of Oriental and African Studies, University of London*, XXIV, 3 (1961), pp. 560–80; Rachaka, "A Short History of the Y.M.B.A., 1898–1958," *The Buddhist*, XXIX, 1 (May, 1958), pp. 43–51; M. Topley, "Chinese Women's Vegetarian Houses in Singapore," *Journal of the Malayan Branch of the Royal Asiatic Society*, XXVII, 1 (May, 1954), pp. 51–67; and H. H. Welch,

"Buddhist Organizations in Hong Kong," *Journal of the Hongkong Branch of the Royal Asiatic Society*, 1961, pp. 1–17.

VII. THE SAṄGHA: CULTURAL ARTS

For many centuries, the cultural arts have served the needs of the Buddha Sāsana/Śāsana. As Buddhist esthetics, skills, and achievements they have illustrated the Buddha, the Dhamma/Dharma, and the Saṅgha as the Ti-ratana/Tri-ratna in the daily life of many Asian peoples. Sculptures, paintings, poems, and folk-tales have portrayed conceptions and facilitated veneration of the Buddha. Paintings, architecture, texts, and popular literature have expressed principles of the Dhamma/Dharma and manifested its practices. Ceremonies, rituals, and folk-drama have guided the monastic routine of the Saṅgha and inspired the lives of the laity. Today, the Buddhist cultural arts constitute a valuable Asian heritage in a rapidly changing, Westernized world and for the reader are an important source for understanding Buddhist thought and practices.

1. General surveys and archeological studies

As already indicated, the Buddhist cultural arts encompass a wide range of activity in which the handicrafts, folklore, folk-drama, and ceremonies are as important as the fine arts for the popular expression of the Buddhist way of life. Thus, in view of the diversity of the subject and its historical span and geographical spread, the Buddhist cultural arts cannot be fully depicted in any single volume. However, the following publications may serve as literary and pictorial introductions to Buddhist art: *Catalogue: 2500th Buddha Jayanti Celebration 1956. Exhibition of Buddhist Art, New Delhi, Banaras, Patna, Calcutta, Madras, Bombay* (New Delhi, Indian Museum, 1956–57); Detroit Institute of Arts, *Buddhist Art* (Detroit, Oct., 1942); J. Hackin, *Les collections bouddhiques* (*Exposé historique et iconographique*); Inde centrale et Gandhâra, Turkestan Chine septentrionale, Tibet (Paris & Bruxelles, G. Van Dest, 1923); Shri Lad, ed., *The Way of the Buddha* (Delhi, Government of India, 1956); *Mārg* (Pathway), A Magazine of the Arts (Bombay): IX, 1 (Dec., 1955), "In Praise of Early Buddhist Art," IX, 2 (March, 1956), "In Praise of Later Buddhist Art," IX, 3 (June, 1956), "In Praise of Buddhist Art in Burma," IX, 4 (Sept., 1956), "In Praise of Buddhist Art in Cambodia, Champa, Laos, Siam and Borobudur"; Dietrich Seckel, *Buddhistische Kunst Ostasiens* (Stuttgart, W. Kohlhammer, 1957), with useful bibliography, pp. 270–80; *Twenty-five Centuries of Buddhist Art and Culture, The UNESCO Courier*, IX, 2 (Paris, Aug., 1956, Special Issue); and Jean Philippe Vogel, *Buddhist Art in India, Ceylon and Java* (Oxford, Clarendon Press, 1936).

Descriptions of the Buddhist cultural arts are often included in general studies and archeological reports about Asian art and culture, usually of a particular area or country. For references to such information, as well as for Buddhist items, the reader may consult section VII, "Art, Archéologie, Épigraphie" in the *Bibliographie Bouddhique*, the *Annual Bibliography of Indian Archaeology* (Leiden, E. J. Brill, 1926–), the publications of museums and departments of archeology in various countries, and other bibliographical sources on Asian art. The following general studies pertain to Buddhist art in several countries and omit consideration of popular literature and folk-dramas.

Buddhist art in Burma has not yet been well described, but see Reginald Le May, "The Development of Buddhist Art in Burma," *Journal of the Royal Society of Arts*, XCVII (June 17, 1949), pp. 535–55; Jane Gaston Mahler, "The Art of Medieval Burma in Pagān," *Archives of the Chinese Art Society of America*, XII (1958), pp. 30–47; and "In Praise of Buddhist Art in Burma," *Mārg*, IX, 3 (June, 1956) issue.

Buddhist art in Cambodia, Ceylon, Malaysia, and Viêt-Nam has been studied largely in terms of its architectural and sculptural achievements at certain centers or sites (e.g., Angkor, Anurādhapura and Polonnaruva, Borobuḍur, etc.) rather than historically surveyed in a comprehensive manner. Thus one must resort to monographs on some aspect of their Buddhist art which are cited below, and to the general histories of art in those countries.

Information about Buddhist art in Central Asia also tends to be studied topically (for archeological reports see above), but one may generally read J. Hackin, "Buddhist Art in Central Asia: Indian, Irānian and Chinese Influences (from Bāmiyān to Turfān)" in *Studies in Chinese Art and Some Indian Influences* (London, The India Society, 1938), and Herbert Härtel, *Turfan und Gandhara. Frühmittelalterliche Kunst Zentralasiens* (Berlin-Dahlem, Museum für Völkerkunde, Indische Abteilung, 1957).

Buddhist art in India is a large subject which continues to receive popular interest and scholarly study. For general introductory surveys, see A. Foucher, *The Beginnings of Buddhist Art, and Other Essays in Indian and Central-Asian Archaeology* (Paris, Paul Geuthner; London, H. Milford, 1917); A. Grünwedel, *Buddhist Art in India* (London, Bernard Quaritch, 1901); Walter Spink, "On the Development of Early Buddhist Art in India," *The Art Bulletin*, XL, 2 (1958), pp. 95–104; and chapters on Buddhist art in histories of Indian art.

Information about famous Buddhist sites in India is contained in a number of guide books and studies, such as A. Aiyappan and P. R. Srinivasan, *Guide to the Buddhist Antiquities* (Madras, Government Press, 1952); J. Filliozat and Louis-Frédéric, *Dans les pas du Bouddha* (Paris, Librairie Hachette, 1957), which is mostly illustrations; The Mahabodhi Society, *Buddhist Sculptures & Monuments of Orissa* (Cuttack, Mahabodhi Society, Orissa, n.d.), which is mostly illustrations; The Publications Division, Ministry of Information and Broadcasting, Government of India, *Buddhist Sculptures and Monuments* (Delhi, 1956), which is mostly illustrations, and *Places of Buddhist Interest* (Delhi, Publications Division, Government of India, 1956); and Devapriya Valisinha, *Buddhist Shrines in India* (Colombo, Mahabodhi Society of Ceylon, 1948).

The following are some descriptions of venerated places in India connected with major events of the Buddha's life. For Lumbinī (near present Rummindei in Nepal), where he was born, see B. C. Bhattacharya, "Lumbinī, the Birthplace of Buddha," *Journal of the Benares Hindu University*, V (1940), pp. 71–8, and Sailendranath Mitra, "The Lumbinī-pilgrimage Record in Two Inscriptions," *The Indian Historical Quarterly*, V (1929), pp. 726–53. For Bodh-gayā or Buddha-gayā (near present Gayā), where he attained Enlightenment, see Kuryan Abraham, *Bodh-Gaya* (Patna, Kitab Ghar, 1956); B. M. Barua, "Old Buddhist Shrines at Bodh Gaya," *The Indian Historical Quarterly*, VI, 1 (March, 1930), pp. 1–31, and *Gayā and Buddha-Gayā*, 2 vols. (Calcutta, India Research Institute, 1931, 1934); Prudence R. Myer, "The Great Temple at Bodhi-Gayā," *The Art Bulletin*, XL, 4 (1958), pp. 277–98; and D. Valisinha, *A Guide to Buddhagaya* (Calcutta, Mahabodhi Society of India, 1950). For Sarnāth (formerly Migadāya or Rishipatana, near present Vārāṇasī or Banaras), where he delivered his first sermon in the Deer Park, see V. S. Agrawala, *Sārnāth* (Delhi, Department of Archaeology, Government of India, 1956), which is a guide book. Unfortunately, there is now little archeological evidence remaining for Kapilavatthu/Kapilavastu (cf. present Padaria), the capital city of the Mallā/Malla oligarchic republic where he "renounced" his secular life, and Kusinārā/Kuṣinagarā (present Mathā Kunwār near Kasia), where he entered Mahā-parinibbāna/parinirvāṇa. In other places the remains of historic stūpas and their sculptures have been studied in considerable detail. For studies of four prominent sites see Douglas Barrett, *Sculptures from Amaravati in the British Museum* (London, British Museum, 1954), and C. Sivaramamurti, *Amarāvatī Sculptures in the Madras Government Museum* (Madras, Bulletin of the Madras Government Museum, 1942); B. M. Barua, *Barhut*, 3 vols. (Calcutta, India Research Institute, 1934–37); A. H. Longhurst, *The Buddhist Antiquities of Nāgārjunakoṇḍa, Madras Presidency* (Delhi, Manager of Publications, 1938), T. N. Ramachandran, *Nāgārjunakoṇḍa 1938* (Delhi, Manager of Publications, 1953), and P. R. Ramachandra Rao, *The Art of Nāgārjunikoṇḍa* (Madras, Rachana, 1956); and John Hubert Marshall, *A Guide to Sāñchī*, 3rd ed. (Delhi, Manager of Publications, 1955), and J. Marshall and A. Foucher, *The Monuments of Sāñchī*. With the texts of inscriptions edited, translated, and annotated by N. G. Majumdar, 3 vols. (Calcutta-London, Government of India Press, 1940).

Studies on the Buddhist art of Gandhāra and Bāmiyān are fairly extensive. For general information about Gandhāra, see those works cited above and also A. Foucher, *La vieille route de l'Inde de Bactres à Taxila*, I (Paris, Ed.

d'Art et d'Histoire, 1942); and J. Marshall, *The Buddhist Art of Gandhara. The story of the early school, its birth, growth, and decline* (Cambridge, Cambridge University Press, 1960). The Bāmiyān Caves in present Afghanistan are described in general terms by André Godard, Yvonne Godard, Joseph Hackin, *Les antiquités bouddhiques de Bâmiyân* (Paris, Bruxelles, G. Van Dest, 1928); J. Hackin, *Nouvelle recherches archéologiques à Bāmiyān* (Paris, Ed. d'Art et d'Histoire, 1933), and *Le site archéologique de Bāmiyān: Guide du visiteur* (Paris, Ed. d'Art et d'Histoire, 1934).

Buddhist art in Indonesia now largely concerns the Borobuḍur stūpa which has been studied in considerable detail as to architecture, sculpture, and symbolism. For these aspects the following works are particularly recommended. Ryusho Hikata, "Gaṇḍavyūha and the Reliefs of Barabuḍur Galleries" in *Studies in Indology and Buddhology* (Tokyo, 1959), pp. 1–50. N. J. Krom and Th. van Erp, *Beschrijving van Barabuḍur*. Deel I: *Archaeologische Beschrijving*, by N. J. Krom; Deel II: *Bouwkundige Beschrijving*, by Th. van Erp ('s Gravenhage, Martinus Nijhoff, 1920, 1931) is the basic archeological description of the site, while Krom, *Baraboedoer, Het Heiligdom van het Boeddhisme op Java* (Amsterdam, H. J. Paris, 1930) conveniently summarizes his view. Paul Mus, *Barabuḍur. Esquisse d'une histoire du bouddhisme fondée sur la critique archéologique des textes* (Paris, Paul Geuthner, 1935) is a remarkable historical and symbolic interpretation. It is formed in part from his "Barabuḍur. Les origines du stupa et la transmigration, essai d'archéologie religieuse comparée," *Bulletin de l'École Française d'Extrême-Orient*, XXXII: 1932 (1933) 1, pp. 269–439; XXXIII: 1933 (1934) 2, pp. 577–980; XXXIV: 1934 (1935) 1, pp. 175–400. The scope of the study is indicated by the following table of contents: Avant-Propos: Les sources indiennes du Bouddhisme, and Chapitres: 1. Les méthodes de la bouddhologie, 2. Le Nirvāṇa et la survie du Buddha: culte, dogme et légende, 3. Le culte royal, le Buddha cakravartin et le dharmakāya, 4. Esquisse d'une histoire du bouddhisme. The most recent notable study is C. Sivaramamurti, *Le Stupa du Barabudur* (Paris, Presses universitaires de France, 1961).

The principal work on Buddhist art in Laos is Henri Parmentier, *L'Art du Laos*, Tome I: *Texte*, Tome II: *Iconographie* (Paris, Hanoi, Imprimerie nationale, 1954).

For Buddhist art in Korea see Evelyn McCune, *The Arts of Korea*, An Illustrated History (Rutland, C. E. Tuttle, Tokyo, 1962), which contains references to Buddhist topics in the Index.

Thai Buddhist art is depicted in general terms by Theodore Robert Bowie, ed., *The Arts of Thailand* (Bloomington, Indiana University Press, 1960); the desired Buddhist subjects may be located in the Index. Otherwise, Reginald Le May, *A Concise History of Buddhist Art in Siam* (Cambridge, Cambridge University Press, 1939) is still the principal work on the subject, to which may now be added H.R.H. Prince Damrong Rajanubhab, *A*

History of Buddhist Monuments in Siam (Illustrated), tr. by S. Sivaraksa (Bangkok, The Siam Society, 1962).

The Buddhist arts of Tibet have been studied in considerable detail. Some of the more notable general surveys are the following: Antoinette K. Gordon, *Tibetan Religious Art* (N.Y., Columbia University Press, 1952); S. Hummel, *Die lamaistische Kunst in der Umwelt von Tibet* (Leipzig, Otto Harrassowitz, 1955) and *Geschichte der tibetischen Kunst* (Leipzig, Otto Harrassowitz, 1953); Lumír Jisl, Vladimír Sis, Joseph Vaniš, *Tibetan Art* (London, Spring Books, 1957); Stella Kramrisch, "The Art of Nepal and Tibet," *Philadelphia Museum of Art Bulletin*, LV (Spring, 1960), pp. 23–38; Newark Museum, *Catalogue of the Tibetan Collection and Other Lamaist Articles in the Newark Museum*, Vols.: [I] Introduction and Definition of Terms; Symbols in Tibetan Buddhist Art (Newark, Newark Museum, 1950), [II] Prayer and Objects Associated with Prayer; Music and Musical Instruments; Ritualistic Objects (1950), [III] (in preparation), [IV] Textiles-Rugs-Needlework-Costumes-Jewelry (1961); P. H. Pott, *Introduction to the Tibetan Collection of the National Museum of Ethnology, Leiden* (Leiden, E. J. Brill, 1951). G. Tucci, *Indo-Tibetica*, 4 vols. in 7 parts (Rome, Reale Accademia d'Italia, 1932–41).

2. Architecture

Buddhist architecture may be studied as symbolic structures (cf. *thūpa/stūpa-pūjā*) and as monastic buildings.

With regard to the thūpa/stūpa as a venerated tomb, see Mireille Bénisti, "Étude sur le stūpa dans l'Inde ancienne," *Bulletin de l'École Française d'Extrême-Orient*, L, 1(1960), pp. 37–116; G. Combaz, "L'évolution du stūpa en Asie, contributions nouvelles et vue d'ensemble," *Mélanges chinois et bouddhiques*, II: 1932–33 (1933), pp. 163–305; III: 1934–35 (1935), pp. 93–114; and IV: 1935–36 (1936), pp. 1–125; B. C. Law, tr., *The Legend of the Topes (Thūpavaṃsa)* (Calcutta, Baptist Mission Press, 1945); A. H. Longhurst, *The Story of the Stūpa* (Colombo, Ceylon Government Press, 1936); S. Paranavitana, *The Stupa in Ceylon* (Colombo, Ceylon Government Press, 1946–47); and the studies on Amarāvatī, Bhārhut (or Bārhut), Nāgārjunikoṇḍa, and Sāñchī cited above.

Information about Buddhist temples and pagodas in Burma is inadequate, but the following brief items may be helpful for general studies: H. G. Franz, "Pagode, Stūpa, Turmtempel; Untersuchungen zum Ursprung der Pagode," *Kunst des Orients*, III (1959), pp. 14–28; Anton K. Gebauer, *Burma, Tempel und Pagoden, Erlebnisse längs der Burma-strasse* (Wien, K. H. Bischoff, 1943); U Lu Pe Win, comp., *Historic Sites and Monuments of Mandalay and Environs* (Rangoon, Government of Burma Printing Office, 1954), and *Pictorial Guide to Pagan* (Rangoon, Government of Burma Printing Office, 1955); Henri Marchal, "Notes d'architecture birmane: 1. Zégu Est; 2. Temple à

Pagan," *Bulletin de l'École Française d'Extrême-Orient*, XL: 1940 (1941), pp. 425–37; U. Aung Than, *Shwedagon, The Sacred Shrine* (Rangoon, Government of Burma Printing Office, 1949); Than Tun, "Religious Buildings of Burma, A.D. 1000–1300," *Journal of the Burma Research Society*, XLII, 2 (Dec., 1959), pp. 71–80; Theodor Heinrich Thomann, *Pagan, ein jahrtausend buddhistischer Tempelkunst* (Stuttgart and Heilbronn, W. Seifert, 1924).

With regard to Buddhist architecture in Cambodia, there are numerous archeological and architectural studies of the Khmer Empire, especially of its capital city Angkor Thom; but in most cases one must carefully determine which temple, or even part of a building, may be characterized as Buddhist. For introductory works on Angkor in general see Jean-Yves Claeys and Michel Huet, *Angkor* (Paris, Editions Hoa-Qui, 1948), which is mostly illustrations; G. Coedès, *Pour mieux comprendre Angkor* (Paris, Adrien Maisonneuve, 1947); H. Marchal, *Les temples d'Angkor* (Paris, Albert Guillot, 1955); Bernard Philippe Groslier and Jacques Arthaud, *Angkor: Art and Civilization* (N.Y., F. A. Praeger, Inc., 1957), which is mostly illustrations; Malcolm Macdonald, *Angkor* (London, Jonathan Cape, 1958), which is mostly illustrations; and H. Parmentier, *Angkor. Guide* (Saigon, Albert Portail, 1950). John Black, "The Lofty Sanctuary of Khao Phra Vihār," *The Journal of the Siam Society*, XLIV, 1 (April, 1956), pp. 1–31, available as a reprint, describes the site which was recently the object of a border dispute between Cambodia and Thailand.

For Ceylon see especially the *Archaeological Survey of Ceylon* (Colombo, Government of Ceylon): *Annual Reports* (1890–) and *Memoirs* (1924–). Published official guides to historic Buddhist sites are useful for general orientation, as for example, D. T. Devendra, *Guide to Anuradhapura* (Colombo, Ceylon Government Press, 1952), John M. Senaveratna, *Guide to Mihintale* (Colombo, Ceylon Government Press, 1950), and S. Paranavitana, *Guide to Polannaruva* (Colombo, Ceylon Government Press, 1950).

Buddhist architecture in China is described in detail from several case studies by Prip-Møller, *Chinese Buddhist Monasteries*. An historical survey of the subject in Japan is made by Alexander Coburn Soper III, *The Evolution of Buddhist Architecture in Japan* (Princeton, Princeton University Press, 1942).

Accounts of Buddhist architecture in India are included in most histories of Indian architecture, as for example, Percy Brown, *Indian Architecture*, 3rd rev. ed., Vol. I: *Buddhist and Hindu Periods* (Bombay, D. B. Taraporevala, 1956), which also includes chapters on Kashmir, Nepal, Ceylon, Burma, Cambodia, Siam, Champa, Java, and Bali. Descriptions of famous cave temples are given by Charu Chandra Das Gupta, "Buddhist Cave Temples of India," *The Indo-Asian Culture*, VI, 4 (April, 1958), pp. 395–404; and *Cave Temples of Western India* (New Delhi, 1956) and *Temples of North India* (New Delhi, 1956), issued by The Publications Division, Ministry of Information and Broadcasting, Government of India.

Lao Buddhist architecture has been described in several studies by H. Parmentier: "Esquisse d'une étude de l'art laotien," *Bulletin des amis du Laos*, 1 (Sept., 1937), pp. 127–60, "Le Wat laotien et ses annexes," *Bulletin des amis du Laos*, 2 (June, 1938), pp. 9–64, "Éléments du Wat laotien," *Bulletin des amis du Laos*, 3 (Aug., 1939), pp. 7–49, and *L'Art du Laos* (Paris, Imprimerie Nationale, 1954).

Buddhist architecture in Thailand is receiving popular interest for which several works may be consulted. Luang Boribal Buribhand and A. B. Griswold, *The Royal Monasteries and Their Significance* (Bangkok, The Fine Arts Department, 1958) is a sketch. Helen Bruce, *Nine Temples of Bangkok* (Bangkok, Progress Book Store, 1960) is a popularly written work. Karl Siegfried Döhring, *Buddhistische Tempelanlagen in Siam*, 3 Bde. (Berlin, Asia Publishing House, 1920) largely concerns temples in Bangkok. E. W. Hutchinson, "The Seven Spires. A Sanctuary of the Sacred Fig Tree at Chiengmai," *The Journal of the Siam Society*, XXXIX, 1 (June, 1951), pp. 1–68, available as a reprint, describes the Wat Ced-Yod, formerly called Wat Mahābodharam. P. Phrombhichitr, *Buddhist Art. Architecture*, Part I (Bangkok, 1952) is an elementary study well illustrated.

For Buddhist temples in Viêt-Nam see Louis Bezacier, *L'art Viêtnamien* (Paris, Editions de l'Union Française, 1955), "Le stūpa de Trach-Lam," *Arts asiatiques*, V (1958), pp. 17–34, and "Le stūpa du Prô-minh ta, tombeau de Tran Nhan-ton à Túc-ma," *Arts asiatiques*, VII (1960), pp. 25–52; and Jean Michel de Kermadec, "Trois pagodas de Saigon-Chalon," *Indochine sud-est asiatique* (Août–Septembre, 1954), pp. 47–51.

There appear to be few, if any, detailed architectural studies of Buddhist structures in Bhutan, Ladakh, Mongolia, Nepal, Sikkim, and Tibet, which are the principal Vajrayāna areas.

3. Popular literature

In addition to the canonical and scholarly texts reviewed above in section IV, Buddhist literature also includes popular presentations of the Dhamma/Dharma in myths and legends, poems, dramas, and children's stories. These materials may be oral as well as written and are affected by non-Buddhist folklore influences. The amount of popular Buddhist literature is ever increasing. The following are a few selected examples of such Buddhist literature in English translation.

For descriptions of the so-called mythology of Buddhism see J. Hackin and others, *Asiatic Mythology* (London, G. C. Harrap, 1932); the contents may be consulted for Buddhism in India, Tibet, Indo-China and Java, Central Asia, China, and Japan. The *Larousse Encyclopedia of Mythology* (N.Y., Prometheus Press, 1959) is less detailed.

Buddhist legends and stories are related in numerous texts in the various canons and collections (described above), especially the Jātaka or birth-stories of the Buddha (cited above) as well as in Buddhist folklore. Selections from such popular literature are presented in the following anthologies. For Burmese stories see U. Kumara, "Legends of the Kyaiktiyo, Kelatha and Koktheinnayon Pagodas," *The Light of Buddha*, V, 1 (Jan., 1960), pp. 29–33, and "The Legends of Great Pagodas in Burma," *The Light of Buddha*, IV, 12 (Dec., 1959), pp. 26–36. For translations of Pāli stories see Eugene Watson Burlingam, tr., *Buddhist Parables* (New Haven, Yale University Press, 1922); Piyadassi Thera, tr., *Stories of Buddhist India*, 2nd rev. ed., Vol. I (Colombo, Sri Lankā Bauddha Samitiya, Ltd., 1953); Henry Thoṃas Rogers, tr., *Buddhaghosa's Parables* (London, Kegan Paul, Trench, Trubner & Co., Ltd., 1870) from the Burmese [illegible]; and F. L. Woodward, tr., *Buddhist Stories* (Adyar, Theosophical Publishing House, 1925). For Tibetan Buddhist stories see E. Conze, tr., *The Buddha's Law among the Birds* (Oxford, Bruno Cassirer, 1956). C. A. F. Rhys Davids, ed., *Tibetan Tales derived from Indian Sources.* Translated from the Tibetan . . . by F. Anton von Schiefner and from the German into English by W. R. S. Ralston (London, Routledge & Sons, Ltd., new ed., 1926); and A. K. Gordon, tr., *Tibetan Tales* (London, Luzac & Co., Ltd., 1953).

A representative collection of Buddhist poetry would be difficult to compile, because many Buddhist texts, scholarly as well as popular, are traditionally written in verse instead of prose. However, some appreciation of Buddhist poetry may be gained from three small anthologies: Humphrey Clarke, tr., *The Message of Milarepa* (London, John Murray, Ltd., 1958), which is compiled from the writings of the famous Tibetan scholar-poet; Mrs. (C. A. F.) Rhys Davids, tr., *Poems of Cloister and Jungle* (London, John Murray, Ltd., 1941), which is compiled from the Pāli; and R. H. Robinson, tr., *Chinese Buddhist Verse* (London, John Murray, Ltd., 1954).

Concerning Buddhist drama, three items must suffice here: J. Bacot, tr., *Three Tibetan Mysteries: Tchrimekundan, Nansal, Djroazanmo, as Performed in the Tibetan Monasteries* (London, N.Y., E. P. Dutton, 1923); Heinrich Lüders, *Bruchstücke Buddhistischer Dramen* (Berlin, Georg Reimer, 1911); and Donald H. Shively, "Buddhahood for the Non-sentient: A Theme in Nō Plays," *Harvard Journal of Asiatic Studies*, XX, 1–2 (June, 1957), pp. 135–61.

The field of Buddhist children's literature is gradually expanding with the advent of modern educational methods and practices. The following small books were prepared for the Buddhist school needs in particular countries or areas which are indicated here by their place of publication: Princess Poon Diskul, *Buddhism for the Young* (Bangkok, Sanan Bunyasiribhandhu, 1954); International Buddhist Institute of Hawaii, *Buddhist Sunday School Lessons* (Honolulu, 1945); Silācāra, *A Young People's Life of the Buddha* (Colombo, W. E. Bastian & Co., 5th impression, 1953); and Sumangalo, *Buddhist Stories for Young and Old* (Singapore, Singapore Buddhist Association, 1960), and *Buddhist Sunday School Lessons* (Penang, Penang Buddhist Association, 1958).

4. Painting

Buddhist paintings are usually murals on the walls of caves and monasteries or hanging and horizontal scrolls; they may depict historical and legendary scenes, portray the Buddhas and other eminent personages, or function symbolically as maṇḍalas (diagrammed spheres of power). Most publications on the subject refer to a particular aspect, but there is a notable introduction by Dietrich Seckel, *Grundzüge der Buddhistischen Malerei* (Tokyo, Deutsche Gesellschaft für Natur- und Völkerkunde Ostasiens, 1945).

The following items are selected to introduce the reader pictorially to some of the best surviving Buddhist paintings in Central Asia, Ceylon, India, and Tibet: Fred H. Andrews, *Wall Paintings from Ancient Shrines in Central Asia recovered by Sir Aurel Stein*, 2 vols. (London, Oxford University Press, 1948); Basil Gray, *Buddhist Cave Paintings at Tun-huang* (Chicago, University of Chicago Press, 1959) and *Ceylon: Paintings from Temple, Shrine and Rock* (Greenwich, Conn., UNESCO World Art Series, VIII, 1957); G. Yazdānī, *Ajaṇṭā*, 4 parts (Oxford, Oxford University Press, 1930, 1933, 1946, 1955); and G. Tucci, *Tibetan Painted Scrolls*, 2 vols. of text and 1 portfolio of 256 plates (Rome, La Libreria dello Stato, 1949).

5. Sculpture

In Buddhist sculpture there is a wide range of types from votive statuettes to architectural thūpas/stūpas and of compositions in stone, wood, metal, lacquer, and most recently also in ferro-concrete. The functional meaning of such Buddhist sculptures is usually studied as symbolism and iconography (see below), whereas their ceremonial use is described in works on rituals (see above).

For Buddhist sculpture in Ceylon see especially D. T. Devendra, *Classical Sinhalese Sculpture, c. 300 B.C. to A.D. 1000* (London, Alec Tiranti, 1958), and *The Buddha Image and Ceylon* (Colombo, K. V. G. de Silva & Sons, 1957).

China and Japan have made notable contributions to Buddhist sculpture; for references see the appropriate chapters of the present volume. On Korean Buddhist sculpture, see W. Watson, "The Earliest Buddhist Images of Korea," *Transactions of the Oriental Ceramic Society*, XXXI (1957/59), pp. 83–92.

Gandhāra sculpture has been fairly well investigated in its historical, cultural, and artistic aspects. For suggested references see above. One of the most recent descriptive accounts is Benjamin Rowland, Jr., *Gandhara Sculpture from Pakistan Museums* (N.Y., Asia Society, 1960).

Most studies of Indian and Khmer Buddhist sculptures are monographs about particular figures or types or are contained in general treatises or surveys of Indian and Khmer sculptural art. For references to these works consult section VII of the *Bibliographie Bouddhique*, the *Annual Bibliography of Indian Archaeology*, and similar sources of bibliographical information.

The subject of Siamese or Thai Buddhist sculpture is receiving increasing attention in publications. The following are some notable recent studies: L. B. Buribhand and A. B. Griswold, *Images of the Buddha*, 2nd rev. ed. (Bangkok, National Culture Institute, 1956); Emcee Chand and Khienh Yimsiri, *Thai Monumental Bronzes* (Bangkok, private edition, 1957); and A. B. Griswold, *Dated Buddha Images of Northern Siam* (Ascona, Artibus Asiae, 1957). Griswold has also written various articles on the subject in *Artibus Asiae*, *Arts asiatiques*, *Archives of the Chinese Art Society of America*, and *The Journal of the Siam Society*, which are listed under his name in the *Bibliographie Bouddhique*.

Buddhist sculpture in Nepal, Mongolia, and Tibet is usually studied iconographically with reference to the Vajrayāna ritualism. For references, see the next section.

6. Iconography and symbolism

The multiplicity of monographs on Buddhist iconography and symbolism has developed these subjects into a specialized field of study for increasing popular interest and further scholarly research. However, Buddhist iconography and symbolism are usually less well-known to the casual observer and non-Buddhist than to those who experience Buddhist principles, exemplify them in Buddhist practices, and are initiated in Buddhist rituals and customs. In short, the student should recognize that meaning and function are interdependent in viable Buddhist symbolism.

With regard to Buddhist iconography in Ceylon, two items will serve as introductions: Devendra, *The Buddha Image and Ceylon*, and Siri Sunasinghe, "A Sinhalese Contribution to the Development of the Buddha Image," *The Ceylon Journal of Historical and Social Studies*, III (Jan.–June, 1960), pp. 59–71.

For Buddhist symbolism in China see J. Leroy Davidson, *The Lotus Sutra in Chinese Art. A Study in Buddhist Art to the Year 1000* (New Haven, Yale University Press, 1954).

Buddhist iconography in India has been studied in a number of works such as the following: Adris Banerji, "Origins of the Buddha Image—A Study" in *Sarūpa-Bhāratī* (Hoshiarpur, Vishveshvaranand Institute Publications, 1954), pp. 197–203; Nalini Kanta Bhattasali (Bhaṭṭasāli), *Iconography of Buddhist and Brahmanical Sculptures in the Dacca Museum* (Dacca, Rai S. N. Bhadra Bhodur, 1929); A. K. Coomaraswamy, *Elements of Buddhist Iconography* (Cambridge, Harvard University Press, 1935), and

"The Origin of the Buddha Image," *The Art Bulletin*, IX, 4 (June, 1927), pp. 287–328; A Foucher, *Étude sur l'iconographie bouddhique de l'Inde* (Paris, E. Leroux, 1900–05), *L'origine grecque de l'image du Bouddha* (Challon-sur Saone, Annales du Musée Guimet, 1912), and *On the Iconography of the Buddha's Nativity* (Delhi, Manager of Publications, 1934); Raghu Vira and Chikyo Yamamoto, *The Buddha and the Bodhisattva in Indian Sculpture*, 3 vols. (Lahore, 1938–41); and B. Rowland, Jr., "A Note on the Invention of the Buddha Image," *Harvard Journal of Asiatic Studies*, XI, 1–2 (June, 1948), pp. 181–6.

For Buddhist iconography in Tibet and the Mahāyāna and Vajrayāna in general, see the following studies: B. Bhattacharyya, "Mahāyānic Pantheon," *The Cultural Heritage of India* (*op. cit.*), I, pp. 518–36, "The Buddhist Pantheon and its Classification" in *Commemorative Essays Presented to Professor Kashinath Bapuji Pathak* . . . (Poona, Bhandarkar Oriental Research Institute, 1934), pp. 80–93, and *The Indian Buddhist Iconography*, 2nd rev. ed. (Calcutta, K. L. Mukhopadhyay, 1958), which is mainly based on the Sādhanamālā and cognate Tāntric texts of rituals; Walter Eugene Clark, ed., *Two Lamaistic Pantheons*, 2 vols. (Cambridge, Harvard-Yenching Institute, 1937); A. Getty, *The Gods of Northern Buddhism* reviews their history, iconography, and subsequent development; and A. K. Gordon, *The Iconography of Tibetan Lamaism*, rev. ed. (Tokyo, Rutland, C. E. Tuttle, 1959). S. Hummel, "Ikonographische Notizen zum Lamaismus," *Jahrbuch des Museums für Völkerkunde zu Leipzig*, XII (1954), pp. 63–81. M. Lalou, . . . *Iconographie des étoffes peintes* (*paṭa*) *dans le Mañjuçrīmūlakalpa* (Paris, Paul Geuthner, 1931). F. D. Lessing, . . . *Yung-Ho-Kung. An Iconography of the Lamaist Cathedral in Peking*, Vol. I (Stockholm, Sino-Swedish Expedition Publication No. 18, 1942) includes notes on Lamaist mythology and cult. R. de Nebesky-Wojkowitz, *Oracles and Demons of Tibet* ('s Gravenhage, Mouton & Co., 1956) describes the cult and iconography of Tibetan protective deities. Toni Schmid, *The Eighty-five Siddhas* (Stockholm, Statens Ethnografiska Museum, 1958). G. Tucci, "Tibetan Classification of Buddhist Images according to Their Style," *Artibus Asiae*, XXII (1959), pp. 179–87.

For Buddhist expressions in Japan see Masaharu Anesaki, *Buddhist Art in Its Relation to Buddhist Ideals*, with special reference to Buddhism in Japan (Boston and N.Y., Houghton & Mifflin, 1915), and chapter V of the present volume.

Regarding Thailand note J. J. Boeles, "Two Aspects of Buddhist Iconography in Thailand," *The Journal of the Siam Society*, XLVIII, 1 (June, 1960), pp. 69–79, and the studies on Siamese or Thai sculpture cited above.

The Buddhist pantheon in Viêt-Nam is partly described by L. Bezacier, "Le panthéon des pagodes bouddhiques du Tonkin," *Bulletin de la Société des Études Indochinoises*, Nouvelle Série, XVIII, 3 (3e Trimestre, 1943), pp. 29–68, and sketchily in *Review Horizons*, *The Disposition of Buddhist Temples in Vietnam. The Composition of the Buddhist Pantheon* (Saigon, special ed., 1956).

Other studies on Buddhist symbolism should be mentioned here: B. Bhattacharyya, *An Introduction to Buddhist Esoterism* (London, Oxford University Press, 1932), and "Buddhist Worship and Idolatry" in B. C. Law, ed., *Buddhistic Studies*, pp. 657–68, which refutes the view that Buddhism practices idolatry; E. Conze, "The Iconography of the Prajñāpāramitā," *Oriental Art*, II, 2 (Autumn, 1949), pp. 47–52 and III, 3 (1951), pp. 104–9; C. Feroci, "The Aesthetics of Buddhist Sculpture," *The Journal of the Siam Society*, XXXVII, 1 (Oct., 1948), pp. 39–46; A. B. Govinda, *Foundations of Tibetan Mysticism* (London, Rider & Co., 1959; N.Y., E. P. Dutton, 1960), and *Some Aspects of Stupa Symbolism* (Allahabad and London, Kitabistan, 1940); Erik Haarch, "Contributions to the Study of Maṇḍala and Mudrā. Analysis of Two Tibetan Manuscripts in the Royal Library in Copenhagen," *Acta Orientalia* (Leiden), XXIII, 1–2 (1958), pp. 57–91. Willibald Kirfel, *Symbolik des Buddhismus* (Stuttgart, Hiersemann, 1959); Tyra de Kleen, *Mudras: The Ritual Handposes of the Buddha Priests and the Shiva Priests of Bali* (London, Kegan Paul, Trench, Trubner & Co., Ltd.; N.Y., E. P. Dutton & Co., Inc., 1924); Lamotte, "La religion bouddhique" in his *Histoire du Bouddhisme*, pp. 707–88; Gustav Mensching, *Buddhistische Symbolik* (Gotha, Klotz, 1929); P. Mus, "Le Buddha paré. Son origine indienne. Çākyamuni dans le Mahāyānisme moyen," *Bulletin de l'École Française d'Extrême-Orient*, XXVIII: 1928 (1929), pp. 153–280; E. Dale Saunders, "A Note on Śakti and Dhyānibuddha," *History of Religions*, I, 2 (Winter, 1961), pp. 300–6, "Symbolic Gestures in Buddhism," *Artibus Asiae*, XXI (1958), pp. 47–63, and *Mudrā. A Study of Symbolic Gestures in Japanese Buddhist Sculpture* (N.Y., Pantheon Books, 1960); G. Tucci, *The Theory and Practice of the Mandala* (London, Rider & Co., 1961).

VIII. THE SAṄGHA: BUDDHISM AND SOCIETY

In contrast to the traditional, monastic learning of the Saṅgha, present-day academic Buddhist studies are attempting to analyze, determine, and describe the changing role of the Buddha Sāsana/Śāsana in Asian societies and its potential elsewhere in the world. These studies customarily employ the methods and data of the social sciences which, in turn, are influencing the nature and direction of Buddhist thought and activity. Thus, leaders of Saṅgha monastic centers and Buddhist lay organizations, who are engaged in educational and social welfare work, are beginning to think in terms of the needs and problems now commonly dealt with by the Westernized fields of economics, education, jurisprudence, political thought, and social thought. Consequently, a new kind of Buddhist literature is developing which will be reviewed here under the title of "Buddhism and Society."

1. Economics

Modern views of the economic role of Buddhism are often presented in studies of Buddhist monasticism (see above), and indicated in the more detailed histories of Buddhism (see above).

Some economic aspects of contemporary Theravāda Buddhism are noted by David E. Pfanner and Jaspar Ingersoll, "Theravāda Buddhism and Village Economic Behavior. A Burmese and Thai Comparison," *The Journal of Asian Studies*, XXI, 3 (May, 1962), pp. 341–61.

The historic economic role of Chinese Mahāyāna Buddhism has been described in part by a number of studies: K. Ch'en, "The Economic Background of the Hui-ch'ang Suppression of Buddhism," *Harvard Journal of Asiatic Studies*, XIX, 1–2 (June, 1956), pp. 67–105; Jacques Gernet, *Les aspects économiques du Bouddhisme dans la société chinoise du Ve au Xe siècle* (Saigon, L'École Française d'Extrême-Orient, 1956); D. C. Twitchett, "The Monasteries and China's Economy in Medieval Times," *Bulletin of the School of Oriental and African Studies, University of London*, XIX (1957), pp. 526–49; Arthur Frederick Wright, "The Economic Role of Buddhism in China," *The Journal of Asian Studies*, XVI, 3 (May, 1957), pp. 408–14, which refers particularly to the work by Gernet cited above; and Lien-shen Yang, "Buddhist Monasteries and Four Money-raising Institutions in Chinese History," *Harvard Journal of Asiatic Studies*, XIII, 1–2 (June, 1950), pp. 174–91.

With regard to Buddhist economic institutions in Tibet and Mongolia see Pedro Carrasco, *Land and Polity in Tibet* (Seattle, University of Washington Press, 1959); R. J. Miller, "Buddhist Monastic Economy: The Jisa Mechanism," *Comparative Studies in Society and History*, III, 4 (July, 1961), pp. 427–38, concerning Mongolia, with a "Comment" by George Murphy, pp. 439–42; see also A. Bareau, "Indian and Ancient Chinese Buddhism: Institutions Analogous to the Jisa," *ibid.*, pp. 443–51.

2. Education

The pedagogy of the Buddha is summarized by N. Dutt, "Method of Preaching and Teaching" in his *Early Monastic Buddhism*, Vol. I (Calcutta, Calcutta Oriental Press, 1941), pp. 124–34, reprinted in Gard, ed., *Buddhism*, pp. 63–8. Descriptions of traditional Buddhist monastic education in India are given by S. Dutt, "Buddhist Education" in Bapat, ed., *2500 Years of Buddhism*, pp. 176–94, and the following studies: Radha Kumud Mookerji, "Buddhist Education" in his *Ancient Indian Education* (*Brahmanical and Buddhist*) (London, Macmillan & Co., Ltd., 1947), Part II, pp. 374–610, which incorporates his paper "Ancient Indian Education from the Jātakas" in B. C. Law, ed., *Buddhistic Studies*, pp. 236–56, and "The University of Nālandā," *The Journal of the Bihar Research Society*, XXX, 2 (June, 1944), pp. 126–59;

H. D. Sankalia, *The University of Nālandā* (Madras, B. G. Paul & Co., 1934); K. A. N. Sastri, "Nālandā," *Journal of Madras University*, XIII (1941), pp. 147–202; E. J. Thomas, "Buddhist Education in Pāli and Sanskrit Schools" in B. C. Law, ed., *Buddhistic Studies*, pp. 220–35. For examples of traditional Buddhist textual criticism, see É. Lamotte, "La critique d'authenticité dans le bouddhisme" in *India Antiqua*, pp. 213–22, "La critique d'interprétation dans le bouddhisme," *Actes du XVIIIe Congrès international des Orientalistes, Leiden, 7–12 Septembre 1931* (Leiden, 1932), pp. 191–2, and "La critique d'interprétation dans le bouddhisme," *Annuaire de l'Institut de philologie et d'histoire orientales et slaves*, IX (1949), pp. 341–61.

Information about modern Buddhist education in Burma is contained in the *Report of the Committee appointed to Consider and Report upon Buddhist Religious Instruction for Buddhist Pupils in Vernacular Lay Schools under Buddhist Management, 1928–29* (Rangoon, Superintendent, Government Printing & Stationery, 1931); *Report of the Committee to Consider the Syllabus in Buddhist Religious Instruction for Vernacular and Anglo-Vernacular Schools, 1934* (Rangoon, Superintendent, Government Printing & Stationery, 1934); and official reports of the Union [of Burma] Buddha Sāsana Council (Rangoon, 1954, 1956, 1961), cited above.

Some historical aspects of Buddhist education in Ceylon are described by M. B. Ariyapala, "Education" in his *Society in Mediaeval Ceylon* (Colombo, K. V. G. De Silva, 1956), pp. 269–80; G. P. Malalasekera, "The Influence of Buddhism on Education in Ceylon" in William Loftus Hare, ed., *Religions of the Empire* (London, G. Duckworth & Co., Ltd., 1925), pp. 160–75; Rahula, "Education" in his *History of Buddhism in Ceylon*, pp. 287–302, and "L'éducation bouddhiste à Ceylon dans le temps anciens," *La pensée bouddhique*, VI, 12 (Octobre, 1959), pp. 4–6; and *The Betrayal of Buddhism* (Colombo, All Ceylon Buddhist Congress, 1956).

For modern Buddhist education in Cambodia and Laos, see the following reports: Institute Bouddhique/Buddhist Institute, *Un centre d'études bouddhiques au Cambodge/A Center of Buddhist Studies in Cambodia* (Phnom-Penh, 1961); Suzanne Karpelès, "Le développement des études bouddhiques au Laos et au Cambodge," *Actes du XXe Congrès international des Orientalistes, Bruxelles, 5–10 Septembre 1938* (Louvain, 1940), pp. 141–2, and "L'effort de l'Institut Bouddhique au Cambodge et au Laos," *Bulletin de l'École Française d'Extrême-Orient*, 20–21 [1942]; Phouvong Phimmasone, "L'École Supérieure de Pâli au Laos," *France-Asie*, IX, 87 (Août, 1953), pp. 723–5, and "The Buddhist Institute and Religious Teaching" in de Berval, ed., *Kingdom of Laos*, pp. 441–3. Service d'inspection et de contrôle des établissements d'enseignement du Bouddhisme, ed., *Aperçu sur l'enseignement du Bouddhisme au Cambodge* (Phnom-Penh, 1961); and *The Preah Sihanouk Raj Buddhist University Souvenir on the Occasion of the Sixth Conference of the World Fellowship of Buddhists* (Phnom-Penh, 1961).

Some aspects of Tibetan monastic education are noted by Li An-che, "The Lamasery as an Educational Institution," *Asiatic Review*, XLVI (Jan., 1950), pp. 915–22, and Margaret Evelyn Miller, "Educational Practices of Tibetan Lama Training," *Folklore Studies*, XVI (1957), pp. 187–267. Authoritative descriptions are also given by the present Dalai Lama in his *My Land and My People*, by his brother Thubten Jigme Norbu, *Tibet is My Country*, and by Chang Chen-chi, "Life in a Tibetan Vajaryāna Monastery" in Gard, ed., *Buddhism*, pp. 196–202.

3. Jurisprudence

The subject of Buddhist jurisprudence may be studied in several respects: as the principle of universal righteousness or justice expressed in various texts, as the codified monastic regulations stated in the Vinaya Piṭaka, and as Buddhist doctrinal-ethical and monastic-organizational influences upon the development of traditional concepts of law in Buddhist Asia.

As an example of the first approach, see U. N. Ghoshal, *A History of Indian Political Ideas* (Bombay, Oxford University Press, 1959) especially pp. 69–73, 263–5, 342–7, 535, and "Principle of the King's Righteousness (In the Pali Canon and the Jātaka Commentary)," Gautama Buddha 25th Centenary Volume 1956, *The Indian Historical Quarterly*, XXXII, 2–3 (June–Sept., 1956), pp. 196–204; and Ratilal N. Mehta, "Crime and Punishment in the Jātakas," *The Indian Historical Quarterly*, XII, 3 (Sept., 1936), pp. 432–42. See also the references cited below.

The second approach is based upon textual study of the Vinaya in various Buddhist canons. For example, regarding the Pāli Vinaya Piṭaka, see Ananda Thero, "Some Features of Early Buddhist Ecclesiastical Law," *The Buddhist*, XXXII, 2 (June, July, August, 1961), pp. 20–21, 24; Durga N. Bhagvat, *Early Buddhist Jurisprudence* (*Theravāda Vinaya-Laws*) (Poona, Oriental Book Agency, 1939); and especially I. B. Horner, tr., *The Book of the Discipline* (*Vinaya-Piṭaka*), 5 vols. (London, Oxford University Press, 1938, 1940, 1942, 1951, 1952).

Studies and descriptions of Buddhist influences upon Asian systems of law have also been made. In general see the following accounts: Frederic Austin Hayley, *A Treatise on the Laws and Customs of the Sinhalese*, including the portions still surviving under the name Kandyan law (Colombo, H. W. Cave & Co., 1923). R. Lingat, "Evolution of the Conception of Law in Burma and Siam," *The Journal of the Siam Society*, XXXVIII, 1 (Jan., 1950), pp. 9–31, "La conception du droit dans l'Indochine Hînayâniste," *Bulletin de l'École Française d'Extrême-Orient*, XLIV: 1947–50 (1951), 1, pp. 163–87, "The Buddhist Manu or the Propagation of Hindu Law in Hinayanist Indochina," *Annals of the Bhandarkar Oriental Research Institute*, XXX, 3–4 (1950), pp. 281–97, and "Vinaya et droit laïque. Études sur les conflits de la loi religieuse et de loi laïque dans l'Indochine hinayaniste," *Bulletin de l'École*

Française d'Extrême-Orient, XXXVII: 1937 (1938) 2, pp. 416–77. John Henry Wigmore, "The Buddhist Branch" in his *A Panorama of the World's Legal Systems* (Washington, Washington Law Book Co., 1928, reprinted 1936), pp. 224–42.

There is an extensive literature on so-called Burmese Buddhist law, of which the following items may be used as introductions to the subject. Maung Htin Aung, "Customary Law in Burma" in Philip W. Thayer, ed., *Southeast Asia in the Coming World* (Baltimore, Johns Hopkins, 1953), pp. 203–16; Émile Forchhammer, *The Jardine Prize: An Essay on the Sources and Development of Burmese Law from the Era of the First Introduction of the Indian Law to the Time of the British Occupation of Pegu. With Text and Translation of King Wagaru's Manu Dhammasattham* (Rangoon, Government Press, 1885). John Sydenham Furnivall, "Man in Burma: Some Burmese Dhammathats," *Journal of the Burma Research Society*, XXX (1940), pp. 351–70, is an essay on early Burmese Buddhist law. John Jardine, *Notes on Buddhist Law* (Rangoon, Government Press, 1882–83) consists of 8 parts: I–III. Marriage, IV. Marriage and Divorce, V–VII. Inheritance and Partition, VIII. Marriage and Divorce. As textbooks, see Sisir Chandra Lahiri, *Principles of Modern Burmese Buddhist Law*, 5th ed. (Calcutta, Eastern Law House, Ltd., 1951) and Orby Howell Mootham, *Burmese Buddhist Law* (London, Oxford University Press, 1939).

4. Political thought

Although Buddhist doctrinal principles and Saṅgha relations with political authority have been traditionally operative in many Asian societies, and are undergoing reinterpretation and revaluation today, the subject of Buddhist political thought is only beginning to receive due attention from political scientists and Buddhist historians. For a general statement of the subject see my "Buddhist and Political Authority" in Harold D. Lasswell and Harlan Cleveland, eds., *The Ethic of Power* (N.Y., Harper & Brothers, 1962), pp. 39–70, and J. M. Kitagawa, "Buddhism and Asian Politics," *Asian Survey*, II, 5 (July, 1962), pp. 1–11. The following is a select list of materials on Buddhist political thought according to countries.

For Burma, John F. Cady, *Political Institutions of Old Burma* (Ithaca, South East Asia Program, Cornell University [mimeographed], 1954), and "Religion and Politics in Modern Burma," *The Far Eastern Quarterly*, XII, 2 (Feb., 1953), pp. 149–62; Cecil Hobbs, "The Influence of Political Change on the Buddhist Priesthood in Burma," *Asia* (Saigon), I, 3 (1951), pp. 360–71, reprinted as "The Political Importance of the Buddhist Priesthood in Burma," *Far Eastern Economic Review*, XXI, 19 (November 8, 1956), pp. 586–90; Fred von der Mehden, "The Changing Pattern of Religion and Politics in Burma," in Robert K. Sakai, ed., *Studies on Asia, 1961* (Lincoln, University of Nebraska Press, 1961), pp. 63–73; E. M. Mendelson, "Religion and

Authority in Modern Burma," *The World Today*, XVI, 3 (March, 1960), pp. 110–18; [E]manuel Sarkisyanz, "On the Place of U Nu's Buddhist Socialism in Burma's History of Ideas," in Sakai, ed., *Studies on Asia, 1961*, pp. 53–62, and *Russland und der Messianismus des Orients*; Sendungsbewusstsein und politischer Chiliasmus des Ostens (Tübingen, J. C. B. Mohr, 1955): XXV. "Das buddhistische Staatsideal in der Geschichte Burmas," pp. 327–38, XXVI. "Vom Zusammenbruch des burmanischen Weltbildes zu messianischer Reaktion," pp. 339–49, and XXVII. "Über buddhistischen Messianismus als Hintergrund der burmanischen Revolution. Buddhismus als Sozialismus?" pp. 350–68; and U Thaung, "Burmese Kingship in Theory and in Practice during the Reign of Mindon," *Journal of the Burma Research Society*, XLII, 2 (Dec., 1959), pp. 171–85.

For Cambodia, G. Coedès, "Le culte de la royauté divinisée, source d'inspiration des grands monuments du Cambodge ancien," *Serie Orientale Roma*, V (1952), pp. 1–23; Solange Thierry, "La personne sacrée du roi dans la littérature populaire cambodgienne" in *The Sacral Kingship/La Regalià Sacra* (Leiden, E. J. Brill, 1959), pp. 219–30; and *Speech by Prince Norodom Sihanouk, Head of State of Cambodia, at the Opening of the Sixth Conference of the World Fellowship of Buddhists* (Phnom-Penh, Nov. 14, 1961). See also various institutional studies of the Khmer Empire.

For Ceylon, *History of the Connection of the British Government with Buddhism* (Colombo, 1889); Rahula, "Buddhism as State Religion," in his *History of Buddhism in Ceylon*, pp. 62–77; *The Betrayal of Buddhism*; and Vijayavardhana, *The Revolt in the Temple*; Wriggins, "Religious Revival and Cultural Nationalism" in his *Ceylon: Dilemmas of a New Nation*, pp. 169–210.

For China, there is an abundance of source materials in Chinese Buddhist texts, monastery records, dynastic histories, and related data. The following studies may serve as introductory points of view about Buddhist relations with, and conceptions of, political authority before the Communist period. K. Ch'en, "Anti-Buddhist Propaganda during the Nan-ch'ao," *Harvard Journal of Asiatic Studies*, XV, 1–2 (June, 1952), pp. 166–92, and "On Some Factors Responsible for the Anti-Buddhist Persecution under the Pei-ch'ao," *Harvard Journal of Asiatic Studies*, XVII, 1–2 (June, 1954), pp. 261–73; Wolfram Eberhard, *A History of China*, rev. ed. (London, Routledge & Kegan Paul, Ltd., 1960); the references to "Buddhism" and "Buddhists and Toba empire" in the Index, *Conquerors and Rulers*, Social forces in medieval China (Leiden, E. J. Brill, 1952); the references to "Buddhism" in the Index, *Das Toba-Reich Nord Chinas*. Eine soziologische Untersuchung (Leiden, E. J. Brill, 1949); the references to "Buddhismus" in the Index, and "Die buddhistische Kirche in der Tobazeit," *Dil ve Tarih-Coğrafya Fakültesi Dergisi* (Ankara), IV, 3 (1946), pp. 297–311; Jan Jakob Maria de Groot, "Militant Spirit of the Buddhist Clergy in China," *T'oung Pao*, Série I, II, 2 (Juin, 1891), pp. 127–39, also in *Journal of the North China Branch of the Royal Asiatic*

Society, New Series, XXVI (1894), pp. 108–20. Leon Hurvitz, tr., " 'Render unto Caesar' in Early Chinese Buddhism. Hui-Yüan's Treatise on the Exemption of the Buddhist Clergy from the Requirements of Civil Etiquette" in Roy (ed.), *Liebenthal Festschrift*, pp. 80–114; Richard B. Mather, "Buddhism with Native Chinese Ideologies," *The Review of Religion*, XX (1955–56), pp. 25–37; Karl A. Wittfogel and Feng Chia-shêng, *History of Chinese Society: Liao, 907–1125* (Philadelphia, American Philosophical Society, 1949) consult Buddhist topics in the Index, and their "Religion under the Liao Dynasty," *The Review of Religion*, XII, 4 (May, 1948), pp. 355–74; A. F. Wright, *Buddhism in Chinese History* (Stanford, Stanford University Press, 1959), see *passim*, "Fu I and the Rejection of Buddhism," *Journal of the History of Ideas*, XII, 1 (Jan., 1951), pp. 33–47, and "The Formation of Sui Ideology, 581–604" in John K. Fairbank, ed., *Chinese Thought and Institutions* (Chicago, University of Chicago Press, 1957), pp. 71–(esp. 93–)104; E. Zürcher, "Zum Verhältnis von Kirche und Staat in China während der Frühzeit des Buddhismus," *Saeculum*, X, 1 (1959), pp. 73–81.

For India, the doctrinal basis of the Theravāda political thought will be found in various Pāli texts, such as the *Aggañña-sutta*, *Cakkavatti-Sīhanāda-sutta*, *Mahā-parinibbāna-sutta*, and *Mahā-sudassana-sutta* of the Dīgha-Nikāya, the *Vajji-vagga* of the Aṅguttara-Nikāya, and passages in the Majjhima-Nikāya, Samyutta-Nikāya, the Jātaka, the *Visuddhimagga* of Buddhaghosa, and other noncanonical works. The doctrinal basis of the Mahāyāna, and relatedly the Vajrayāna, political thought will be found in various Buddhist Hybrid Sanskrit texts and their translations into Central Asian, Chinese, Tibetan, and other languages, such as the *Mahāvastu* of the Mahāsāṅghika School, the *Suhrllekha* attributed to Nāgārjuna, the *Suvarnaprabhāsa-(uttamarāja-)sūtra*, the *Catuḥśataka* by Āryadeva, the *Rāṣṭrapāla-paripṛcchā(pāla-sūtra)*, the *Buddhacarita* and *Saundarānanda-kāvya* by Aśvaghoṣa, the *Śikṣasamuccaya* (which quotes other relevant texts now lost) and *Bodhicaryāvatāra* by Śāntideva, the *Jātakamālā* by Āryaśura, and the *Kāruṇikarāja-Prajñāpāramitā-sūtra* (available now in the Chinese translation *Jên-wang hu-kuo pan-chê po-lo-mi ching*). For general, modern accounts of Indian Buddhist political thought see the following descriptions: A. L. Basham, "Society and the State in Theravāda Buddhism," in William Theodore de Bary and others, comps., *Sources of Indian Tradition* (N.Y., Columbia University Press, 1958), pp. 127–53, "The Blessings of Peace" in *ibid.*, pp. 184–5, and "The Divine Right (and Duty) of Kings" in *ibid.*, pp. 185–9; D. Mackenzie Brown, "Didactic Themes of Buddhist Political Thought in the Jatakas," *Journal of Oriental Literature*, VI, 2 (April, 1955), pp. 3–7; De, *Democracy in Early Buddhist Saṃgha*; Ghoshal, *A History of Indian Political Ideas*, especially pp. 62–79, 258–69, 337–49, and "The Ancient Indian Republic and Mixed Constitutions from the Sixth Century B.C. to the Third Century A.D." in his *Studies in Indian History and Culture* (Bombay, Orient Longmans,

Ltd., 1957), pp. 360–405; Kashi Prasad Jayaswal, "Republican Origin of Buddhist Saṃgha and Republics in Buddhist Literature (500–400 B.C.)," in his *Hindu Polity*, 3rd enl. ed. (Bangalore, Bangalore Printing & Publishing Co., Ltd., 1955), pp. 40–8; R. C. Majumdar, "The Constitution of the Licchavīs and the Sākyas," *The Indian Historical Quarterly*, XXVII, 2 (June, 1951), pp. 327–33; Vishwanath Prasad Varma, *Studies in Hindu Political Thought and Its Metaphysical Foundations*, 2nd rev. ed. (Delhi, Motilal Banarsidass, 1959), especially "The Buddhistic Metaphysics of Dharma," pp. 114–19, and "Psychological Foundations of the Buddhist Theory of Kingship," pp. 174–85.

In Japan, Buddhism has been so interdependent with political authority that the subject can be viewed generally in terms of Japanese political history and particularly in studies of Buddhist personages and monastic power from Shōtoku Taishi (A.D. 572–622) to the anti-Buddhist policy (*haibutsu kishaku*) in the Meiji period (1868–1912) and the recent political activities of the Sōka Gakkai branch of the patriotic Nichiren-shū. For references, see my chapter "Buddhism and Political Authority," cited above, to which may be added the following notable items: Seiichiro Ono, "Buddhism and the State," *The Young East*, New Series, V, 19 (Autumn, 1956), pp. 2–5; Gaston Renondeau, "Histoire des moines guerriers du Japon," *Mélanges publiés par l'Institut des Hautes Études Chinoises*, I (1957), pp. 159–344, which has been well reviewed by P. Demiéville, "Le Bouddhisme et la guerre," *ibid.*, pp. 347–85. See also de Visser, *Ancient Buddhism in Japan.*

For Thailand, there is an interesting, authoritative statement of 1916: *The Buddhist Attitude Towards National Defence and Administration.* A special Allocution by His Holiness Prince Vajirañâna, Supreme Patriarch of the Kingdom of Siam (Bangkok, 1916).

The nature of Buddhist political thought and institutions in Tibet is generally studied with reference to the history and functions of the Dalai and Panchen Lamas, about whom there is a sizable literature. In this respect, see William Woodville Rockhill, "The Dalai Lamas of Lhasa and Their Relations with the Manchu Emperors of China, 1644–1908," *T'oung Pao*, Série II, XI (1910), pp. 1–104, and Guenther Schulemann, *Die Geschichte der Dalai-Lamas* (Heidelberg, Carl Winter, 1911; reprinted Leipzig, 1958), as well as other works cited above. For general introductions to Tibetan Buddhist political institutions, see Carrasco, *Land and Polity in Tibet*; Tsung-lien Shen and Shen-chi Liu, "A Government of the God, by the God, and for the God" in their *Tibet and the Tibetans* (Stanford, Stanford University Press, 1953), pp. 89–116; and D. L. Snellgrove, "The Notion of Divine Kingship in Tantric Buddhism" in *The Sacral Kingship*, pp. 204–18.

Since 1950 the subject of Buddhist political thought has also been studied with regard to the situation of Buddhism in Communist countries, for which selected references are given in the bibliographical footnotes to pp. 64–6 of my

"Buddhism and Political Authority," cited above. Descriptions of Buddhist conditions and trends in Communist areas have been made by Walter Kolarz, "Buddhism" in his *Religion in the Soviet Union* (N.Y., St. Martin's Press, 1961), pp. 448–69; E. Sarkisyanz, "Communism and Utopianism in Central Asia," *The Review of Politics*, XX, 4 (Oct., 1958), pp. 623–33, and *Russland und der Messianismus des Orients*, XXVIII. "Lamaistischer Messianismus und seine politischen Wirkungen," pp. 369–77, and XXIX. "Russland und der lamaistische Messianismus," pp. 378–91; and H. H. Welch, "Buddhism under the Communists," *The China Quarterly*, 6 (April–June, 1961), pp. 1–14, which refers to the Chinese situation.

5. Social thought

According to the traditional Buddhist point of view, Buddhist ethical and social thought are inherent in the Dhamma/Dharma and exemplified in the Buddha Sāsana/Śāsana. For examples of Buddhist guidances to the laity on daily conduct see the *Sigālovāda-sutta*, *Uggaka-sutta*, and *Mahā-maṅgala-sutta* of the Pāli Theravāda tradition as quoted in translation in Gard, ed., *Buddhism*, pp. 222–6 with references noted to the *Vimalakīrti-nirdeśa-sūtra* of the Mahāyāna tradition.

The following are some modern studies and expositions of Buddhist social thought and conditions: E. Frauwallner, "Die Anthropologie des Buddhismus," *Anthropologie religieuse*, *Numen* (Supplement II, 1955), pp. 120–32; B. G. Gokhale, "The Buddhist Social Ideals," Gautama Buddha 25th Centenary Volume, *The Indian Historical Quarterly*, XXXII, 2–3 (June–Sept., 1956), pp. 33–9; L. Krader, "Buryat Religion and Society," *Southwestern Journal of Anthropology*, X (1954), pp. 322–51; G. P. Malalasekera and K. N. Jayatilleke, *Buddhism and the Race Question* (Paris, UNESCO, 1958); A. W. Macdonald, "Bouddhisme et sociologie," *Archives de sociologie des religions* (Juillet-Décembre, 1956), pp. 88–97; Kiyomi Morioka, "Buddhist Orders & the Japanese Family System," *Orient/West*, VII, 1 (Jan., 1962), pp. 55–9; Buddha Prakash, "Buddhist Sociology," *Bhāratiya Vidyā*, XVII, 3–4 (1957), pp. 27–40; Frank N. Trager, "Reflections on Buddhism and the Social Order in Southern Asia," *Burma Research Society, Fiftieth Anniversary Publication*, I (1961), pp. 529–43; Varma, "The Sociology of Early Buddhist Ethics," in his *Studies in Hindu Political Thought and Its Metaphysical Foundations*, pp. 258–92; S. J. de S. Weerasinghe, "Changing Social Ideals and Buddhism in Ceylon," *The S. E. Asia Journal of Theology*, III, 2 (Oct., 1961), pp. 34–42; and O. H. de A. Wijesekera, *Buddhism and Society* (Colombo, M. D. Gunasena & Co., Ltd., 1951).

IX. REFERENCE WORKS

1. Guides and manuals

Buddhist Library Association, *The Common Classification Scheme of Buddhist Books* (Tokyo, 1959) 50 pp. in Japanese and English headings is intended for incorporation into the Nippon Decimal Classification, 180 to 189 inclusive, and otherwise serves as a topical outline of Buddhism according to Japanese scholarship.

George Francis Allen (Y. Siri Nyana), *The Buddha's Philosophy* (London, N.Y., Macmillan & Co., 1959) constitutes a handbook with exposition, anthology from the Pāli Canon, appendices, maps, and charts.

Radha S. Burnier, "Decimal Classification for a Library of Oriental Studies, Part II. Buddhism," *Adyar Library Bulletin*, XVIII, 3–4 (Dec., 1954), pp. 229–40 serves as a topical outline of Buddhism according to Indian scholarship.

Clarence Herbert Hamilton, *Buddhism in India, Ceylon, China and Japan. A Reading Guide* (Chicago, University of Chicago Press, 1931).

Christmas Humphreys, ed., *A Buddhist Students' Manual* (London, The Buddhist Society, 1956).

Erik Zürcher, *Buddhism: Its Origin and Spread in Words, Maps and Pictures* (London, N.Y., Routledge & Kegan Paul, Ltd., 1962).

2. Bibliographies

Bibliographie Bouddhique, I–XXXI (Paris, Librairie Orientaliste, Paul Geuthner, 1930–61) to date.

Shinshō Hanayama, *Bibliography on Buddhism* (Tokyo, The Hokuseido Press, 1961).

Constantin Regamey, *Buddhistische Philosophie*, Bibliographische Einführungen in das Studium der Philosophie, 20/21 (Bern, A. Franche, 1950).

3. Encyclopedias, dictionaries, concordances

A Critical Pāli Dictionary. Begun by V. Trenckner, revised, continued, and edited by Dines Andersen and Helmer Smith, Vol. I, Part 1 (Copenhagen, Royal Danish Academy, 1924–26–) and *Epilegomena to Vol. I* (Copenhagen, Royal Danish Society of Sciences and Letters, 1948).

Thomas William Rhys Davids and William Stede, eds., *The Pali Text Society's Pali-English Dictionary* (Chipstead, Surrey, Pali Text Society, 1921–25).

Paul Demiéville, ed., *Hôbôgirin*. Dictionnaire encyclopédique du Bouddhisme d'après les sources chinois et japonaises. 3 Fascicules: *A-Chi* (Tokyo, Maison Fr.-Jap., 1929, 1930; Paris, Adrien Maisonneuve, 1937) and Fascicule Annexe: *Tables du Taishô Issaikyô* (Tokyo, Maison Fr.-Jap., 1937) to date.

Franklin Edgerton, *Buddhist Hybrid Sanskrit Grammar and Dictionary*, Vol. 2: *Dictionary* (New Haven, Yale University Press, 1953).

Heinrich Hackmann, *Erklärendes Wörterbuch zum Chinesischen Buddhismus*. Chinesisch-Sanskrit-Deutsch. Lfg. I-VI: *A-Ni* (Leiden, E. J. Brill, 1951–54) to date.

Gunapala Piyasena Malalasekera, *Dictionary of Pāli Proper Names*, 2 vols. (London, John Murray, Ltd., 1938; reprinted 1960).

Gunapala Piyasena Malalasekera, ed., *Encyclopaedia of Buddhism*, Fascicule *A-Aca* (Colombo, Government of Ceylon Press, 1961) to date.

Nyanatiloka, *Buddhist Dictionary*. Manual of Buddhist Terms and Doctrines, 2nd rev. ed. (Colombo, Frewin & Co., Ltd., 1956).

William Edward Soothill and Lewis Hodous, comps., *A Dictionary of Chinese Buddhist Terms*. With Sanskrit and English equivalents and a Sanskrit-Pali Index (London, Kegan Paul, Trench, Trubner & Co., Ltd., 1937).

Frank Lee Woodward and others, E. M. Hare, ed., *Pāli Tipiṭakaṃ Concordance*, 10 parts *a-ñātī* (London, published for Pali Text Society by Luzac & Co., Ltd., 1952–57) to date.

4. Collected works and series

Bibliotheca Buddhica (St. Petersburg/Leningrad, l'Academie Impériale des Sciences, 1898/1902–).

Buddhica. Documents et travaux pour l'étude du bouddhisme:
Première Série: *Mémoires* (Paris, Paul Geuthner, 1928–), Deuxième Série: *Documents* (Paris, Paul Geuthner, 1928–).

Indo-Iranian Reprints ('s Gravenhage, 1957–) see the Buddhist volumes.

Materialien zur Kunde des Buddhismus (Heidelberg, 1923–31).

Pali Text Society Translation Series (London, Luzac & Co., Ltd., 1909–).

Sacred Books of the Buddhists (London, 1895–).

Serie Orientale Roma (Rome, 1950–) see the Buddhist volumes.

The Wheel. A Series of Buddhist Publications (Kandy, 1958–).

Untersuchungen zur Geschichte des Buddhismus und verwandter Gebiete, I–XXIII (Hannover, 1920–27).

5. Periodicals

Ceylon Daily News Vesak Annual (Colombo, May).

La pensée bouddhique (Paris, 1939–).

Mélanges chinois et bouddhiques (Bruxelles, 1932–).

The American Buddhist (San Francisco, 1957–).

The Buddhist (Colombo, 1888–?; new series 1930–).

The Eastern Buddhist (Kyoto, 1921–).

The Golden Light (Penang, 1958–).

The International Buddhist News Forum (Rangoon, 1961–).

The Light of Buddha (Mandalay, 1956–).

BUDDHISM

The Light of the Dhamma (Rangoon, 1952–).
The Maha Bodhi (Calcutta, 1892–1904, 1920–; Colombo, 1906–19).
The Middle Way (London, 1943; succeeded *Buddhism in England*, 1926–43).
The Young East (Tokyo, 1925–41; new series 1952–).
Visakhapuja (Bangkok, annual, May).
World Buddhism (Colombo, 1952–).
Zeitschrift für Buddhismus und verwandte Gebiete, Jahrgang I–IX (München-Neubiberg, 1913–31).
Zen Notes (N.Y., 1954–).

V

The Religions of Japan

J. M. Kitagawa

INTRODUCTION

Anyone who attempts to study the religions of Japan will soon discover the ambiguities involved in the subject matter. Some people interpret the designation "religions of Japan" in a narrow sense, referring to the religions that developed on Japanese soil without including Buddhism and other religions introduced from abroad. In this article we have permitted ourselves a more inclusive categorization and have dealt with religions of non-Japanese origin that exerted significant influences within Japan, even though we have made no attempt to deal with their origins, doctrines, and development prior to their introduction to the Japanese homeland.

We have also had to face another ambiguity in regard to the term "religion" itself. We have found, for example, that some people do not classify Confucianism as a religion and that even Shinto is often regarded as a "national cult"—that is, as something other than a religion, properly speaking. We have, however, included Shinto, Japanese Confucianism, and various other systems and movements in our discussion of the religions of Japan because we feel them to constitute important elements in the religious life and history of the Japanese people. On the other hand, we have excluded militarism, nationalism, and communism from this discussion even though they have semireligious or pseudoreligious features.

Some readers may ask why the Ainu religion is included in our discussion. Although the Ainus are not "Japanese" in their ethnic affiliation, the largest concentration of them has lived in the northern section of Japan for over two millennia; hence, if for no other reason, some knowledge of Ainu religion is pertinent to one's understanding of the religious situation in the prehistoric period in Japan.

Another problem we must clarify is that of perspective, since the religions of Japan may be, and have been, studied from a number of different viewpoints. For example, Japanologists consider that the Japanese religions provide important data for their study of Japanese history and culture. Buddhologists tend to look at religious developments in Japan from within the framework of the history of Buddhism, while Sinologists approach Japanese religious history as a whole from the perspective of the expansion of Chinese culture and civilization. Likewise, students of world history, archeology, prehistory, folklore, and anthropology utilize their own perfectly valid perspectives in analyzing Japanese religions. We, however, prefer to approach our subject from the perspective of *Religionswissenschaft*, commonly known as the "history of religions" or the "comparative study of religions." Thus, our concern will be to reach an understanding of these religious phenomena *qua* religious rather than to arrive at any philosophical, theological, anthropological, or socioeconomic rationalizations of them.

A few words may be said at this point about Japanese study in the West as it affects our materials. During the period of roughly thirty years between the 1880's and World War I, a number of Western teachers, missionaries, and diplomats in Japan were engaged in serious scholarly investigations of Japanese language, history, culture, and religions. Among them were Sir Ernest M. Satow, Basil Hall Chamberlain, William George Aston, Ernest F. Fenollosa, Hans Haas, Michel Revon, Sir Charles Eliot, Karl Florenz, August Karl Reischauer, and John Batchelor, to name only the best known. Their books and articles contributed a great deal toward the West's understanding of various aspects of Japan and the Japanese people.

The initiative taken by Western scholars in Japanology also stimulated the study of able Japanese scholars, notably Bunyiu Nanjio (Buddhology), Masaharu Anesaki (Science of Religions), Genchi Kato (Shinto Study), D. T. Suzuki (Zen Buddhist Study), Nobuhiro Matsumoto (Mythology), and Kunio Yanagida (Folklore). The period between the two world wars was marked by an impressive growth in Japanese scholarship and also by a concomitant general decline of Western scholarship in the field. Unfortunately, most Japanese scholars published their works only in the Japanese language, and thus the Japanese contribution to the study of Japanese religions, for example, was virtually inaccessible to Western scholars during this period. To be sure, there were some able Westerners, such as Sir George B. Sansom, Wilhelm Gundert, and Daniel C. Holtom, who continued their research, but for the most part Western understanding of Japanese religions and culture depended upon works by earlier Western scholars or upon those by a very limited number of Japanese scholars who wrote in Western languages.

This observation does not imply that there is a scarcity of Western books on matters Japanese. However, many of those in use, if not dated, are either too technical or too popular. Moreover, while some aspects of religion in Japan, such as Zen, have attracted the attention of many people, other important dimensions of Japanese religion have not even begun to be touched as yet. Happily, in recent years a number of younger Western scholars have become interested in Japanese religions, and an increasing number of younger Japanese scholars in the field have begun to write in Western languages. It is to be hoped that cooperation between Japanese and Western scholars will provide for greater "understanding" of the complex but fascinating religious phenomena that Japan offers for serious consideration.

I. GENERAL SURVEY

Information on Japan

Religions in Japan, as in any other part of the world, are more than systems of beliefs and practices. Their religions do not exist in isolation from the social and cultural life, as well as the historic experience, of the Japanese people. Therefore, those who study the religions of Japan are advised to acquaint themselves with the general characteristics of Japanese culture and the historical development of Japan.

Probably the most comprehensive (1077 pages in all) and up-to-date single volume on Japan in general is *Japan: Its Land, People and Culture*, compiled by the Japanese National Commission for UNESCO (Tokyo, Bureau of Ministry of Finance, 1958); the religious development of Japan is briefly sketched in chapter XIX, "The Formation of the Thoughts of the Japanese and Their Spiritual Characteristics," pp. 491–528. *The Encyclopaedia Britannica*, Vol. XII (1961 ed.) has a comprehensive article, "Japan," pp. 893–954G. For geographical information concerning Japan, one might consult G. T. Trewartha, *Japan: A Physical, Cultural and Regional Geography* (Madison, University of Wisconsin Press, 1945) or George B. Cressey, *Asia's Lands and Peoples*, 2nd ed. (N.Y., McGraw-Hill Book Co., Inc., 1951).

Some of the older books, though naturally dated, still provide helpful insights regarding various aspects of the Japanese tradition. For example, the popularity of B. H. Chamberlain, *Things Japanese* (London, John Murray, Ltd., 1902) was such that its sixth edition (1940) is still used by some people.

Likewise, Edmond Papinot, *Dictionnaire d'histoire et de géographie du Japon* (Tokyo, 1906) and its English translation, *Historical and Geographical Dictionary of Japan* (Yokohama, 1909; Ann Arbor, University of Michigan Press, 1948) have been widely circulated. Some of the books written by Japanese authors soon after the turn of the century, such as Kakuzo Okakura, *The Awakening of Japan* (N.Y., Century Co., 1904) and Inazo Nitobe, *The Japanese Nation* (N.Y., G. P. Putnam's Sons, 1912), both of which are still read in some quarters, reflect the attitude of Japanese intellectuals of that period. Also in this connection, mention should be made of works by Lafcadio Hearn, an eccentric, romantic, and very gifted interpreter of Japan. Born in the Ionian islands of an Anglo-Irish father and Maltese mother, he was educated in Ireland, England, and France and became a newspaper reporter in America. He went to Japan in 1890, married a Japanese woman, and eventually renounced his British citizenship in order to become a naturalized Japanese with the name Yakumo Koizumi. Hearn died in 1904, leaving behind him numerous articles, short stories, and sixteen books, the most important being *Japan: An Attempt at Interpretation* (N.Y., The Macmillan Co., 1904). His critics are no doubt right in characterizing him as a conservative romanticist who loved those aspects of Japanese life that were passing away even during his time. Nevertheless, his poignant description of his adopted land should be read by those who try to understand Japanese religions and culture. There are two recent anthologies of his works: Henry Goodman, ed., *The Selected Writings of Lafcadio Hearn* (N.Y., Citadel Press, 1949) and Edwin McClellan, ed., *Tales and Essays from Old Japan* (Chicago, Regnery Gateway Editions, 1956).

Some of the publications of the Society for International Cultural Relations (*Kokusai Bunka Shinkokai*), Tokyo, have been very useful in introducing Japan to Westerners. For example, their production, "The Japanese Arts through Lantern Slides" with companion handbooks, has been profitably used in some circles. Among the handbooks, *Japanese Architecture* (Tokyo, 1938) contains fairly good factual materials concerning Shinto shrines and Buddhist temples. Some of the travel books, such as Atsushi Sakai, *Japan in a Nutshell —Religion, Culture, Popular Practices* (Yokohama, 1949) and Japan Travel Bureau, *Japan: the Official Guide*, rev. ed. (Tokyo, 1952), are goldmines of factual information. The Japan Travel Bureau also publishes handy topical booklets in a series called the *Tourist Library*; among them, *What is Shinto?* by Genchi Kato (No. 8), *Japanese Buddhism* by D. T. Suzuki (No. 21), and *Ainu Life and Legend* by Kyosuke Kindaichi or Kindaiti (No. 36) are important for students of religions.

During World War II a number of books and articles on Japan appeared in the West. The wartime slant of many of these works is well illustrated in *Fortune*, XXIX, 4 (April, 1944), the issue dedicated to "Japan and the Japanese." While many wartime publications on Japan are no longer taken seriously, some of them have continued to be read as good introductory materials. For example, John F. Embree, an anthropologist well-known for his study of a peasant village, *Suye Mura* (Chicago, University of Chicago Press, 1939), published *The Japanese Nation, A Social Survey* (N.Y., Farrar & Rinehart, Inc., 1945) which is a well-balanced account of Japanese culture and society. Ruth Benedict, *The Chrysanthemum and the Sword—Patterns of Japanese Culture* (Boston, Houghton Mifflin Co., 1946) has some good insights into certain cultural features of Japan, although her work is more controversial than Embree's book. One only wishes that Embree and Benedict had lived a little longer, so that they could have revised certain sections of their books through the incorporation of the criticisms and suggestions of others!

Space does not permit us even to list the titles of numerous general works on Japan that have appeared since the end of the war. We can safely recommend, however, "Perspective of Japan" (an Atlantic Supplement), *The Atlantic* (January, 1955); Donald Keene, *Living Japan* (London, Doubleday & Co., Inc., 1959); and Fosco Maraini, *Meeting with Japan*, tr. by Eric Moshacher (N.Y., Viking Press, 1959), as helpful introductory works on various aspects of Japanese culture.

Turning to the materials dealing with the general historical orientation of Japan, no one will go wrong by starting with *Japan—Past and Present* (N.Y., Alfred A. Knopf, Inc., 1946; rev. ed., 1953) by Edwin O. Reischauer, the United States ambassador to Japan, who is the son of August Karl Reischauer and brother of Robert Karl Reischauer. This small book, unlike his other more technical works, presents Japanese history in general and broadly interpretive terms with a significant degree of success and clarity. Another merit of the revised edition is its inclusion of a sober analysis of the postwar period of Japanese history. Slightly more detailed than Reischauer's book, but an equally readable one-volume survey of Japanese history up to 1863, is Sir George B. Sansom, *Japan: A Short Cultural History* (N.Y., Appleton-Century-Crofts, Inc., 1931; rev. ed., 1943; London, Cresset Press, 1946). It is a mature production, reflecting the many years of Sansom's research and thought on his subject. His own perspective is succinctly discussed in his *Japan in World History* (N.Y., American Institute of Pacific Relations, 1951). Having the two foci of world history and Japanese history, and using the comparative method in the broad sense of the term, Sansom tries to differentiate what is general and what is characteristically Japanese in historical phenomena. In recent years, Sansom has been busy writing a three-volume history of Japan. Judging from its first volume, *A History of Japan to 1334* (Stanford, Stanford University Press, 1958), the forthcoming work can be expected to reflect the thoroughness and lucidity that are characteristic of Sansom's writing. In addition to Reischauer's and Sansom's books, some people have found Arthur L. Sadler, *Short History of Japan* (Sydney, Angus &

Robertson, Ltd., 1946) useful. For classroom purposes, *A History of East Asian Civilization*, by E. O. Reischauer and John K. Fairbank (Boston, Houghton Mifflin Co., 1960) and *Sources of Japanese Tradition*, comp. by Ryusaku Tsunoda, William Theodore de Bary, and Donald Keene (N.Y., Columbia University Press, 1958) are to be highly recommended.

We do not imply, however, that the earlier works dealing with Japanese history should be discarded altogether. For example, Captain F. Brinkley, *Japan: Its History, Arts and Literature*, 8 vols. (Boston, J. B. Millet, 1901–02) uncritical though they are, have some good descriptions of certain periods, and *History of Japan*, 3 vols., by James Murdoch and Isoh Yamagata (London, Kegan Paul, Trench, Trubner & Co., Ltd., 1910), which are just as dated as Brinkley's *magnum opus*, are still to be consulted regarding some political events. Similarly, E. Honjo, *The Social and Economic History of Japan* (Kyoto, Institute for Research in Economic History of Japan, 1935) and Yosaburo Takekoshi, *The Economic Aspects of the History of the Civilization of Japan*, 3 vols. (N.Y., The Macmillan Co., 1930) are invaluable in the study of the socioeconomic factors involved in the religious development of Japan. For the most part, historical works written in Japanese during the same period share the virtues and failings of the books mentioned here. All these authors lived in a period when the task of the historian was regarded as the amassing of data without much effort in interpretation.

The modern period of Japanese history has attracted the attention of many able scholars, both Western and Japanese, such as Chitoshi Yanaga, *Japan Since Perry* (N.Y., McGraw-Hill Book Co., Inc., 1949); G. B. Sansom, *The Western World and Japan* (N.Y., Alfred A. Knopf, Inc., 1950); Jintaro Fujii, ed., *Outline of Japanese History in the Meiji Era*, tr. by H. K. Colton and Kenneth Colton (Tokyo, Obunsha, 1958); and Hugh Borton, *Japan's Modern Century* (N.Y., Ronald Press, 1955). Works that lean heavily on the political and economic aspects of modern Japan include Walter W. McLaren, *A Political History of Japan during the Meiji Era, 1867–1912* (London, George Allen & Unwin, Ltd., 1916); G. C. Allen's two books, *A Short Economic History of Modern Japan, 1867–1937* (London, George Allen & Unwin, Ltd., 1946) and *Japan's Economic Recovery* (London, Oxford University Press, 1958); W. W. Lockwood, *The Economic Development of Japan: Growth and Structural Change, 1868–1938* (Princeton, Princeton University Press, 1954); E. H. Norman, *Japan's Emergence as a Modern State* (N.Y., American Institute of Pacific Relations, 1940); H. Feis, *The Road to Pearl Harbor* (Princeton, Princeton University Press, 1950); F. C. Jones, *Japan's New Order in East Asia: Its Rise and Fall, 1937–1945* (London, Oxford University Press, 1954); E. J. Lewe, Baron van Aduard, *Japan from Surrender to Peace* (Hague, M. Nijhoff, 1953); Edwin M. Martin, *Allied Occupation of Japan* (Stanford, Stanford University Press, 1948); R. A. Fearey, *The Occupation of Japan—Second Phase, 1948–1950* (N.Y., The Macmillan Co., 1950); T. A. Bisson,

Prospects of Democracy in Japan (N.Y., The Macmillan Co., 1949); and C. Yanaga, *Japanese People and Politics* (N.Y., John Wiley & Sons, Inc., 1956).

While many of these publications do not make direct reference to religions as such, they provide us with that general framework of Japanese culture and history that is essential for our understanding of the religious development of Japan.

Works on Japanese religions

It is almost impossible to mention and evaluate all the books that deal directly or indirectly with the religions of the Japanese nation. Some indication must be given, however, of the different approaches used by writers on the subject.

First, let us look briefly at books that may be classified as reading materials for the general history of religions or the comparative study of religions. In North America, be it noted, the interest in this field developed gradually from the end of the last century. The popularity of comparative religion reached its peak in the 1920's, and then it steadily declined in the 1930's and early 1940's. Since the end of World War II, study of world religions has again become a favorite subject. Publications in this field reflect the rise, decline, and the renewed popularity of the discipline. For the most part, scholars in the history of religions or comparative religion are more concerned with "major world religions," such as Buddhism, Hinduism, Islām, Judaism, Christianity, and Chinese religions, at the expense of the so-called "minor religions," including Shinto. However, even those books that have no section on Shinto or Japanese religions usually discuss some aspects of Japanese religions per se in connection with the development of Buddhism.

Among the earlier American works, both George Foote Moore, *History of Religions*, Vol. I (N.Y., Charles Scribner's Sons, 1913) and George A. Barton, *The Religions of the World* (Chicago, University of Chicago Press, 1929) have special chapters on Japanese religions. In fact, Moore has one chapter on Shinto and another chapter on Japanese Buddhism but makes little effort to relate the two. Others that include sections on Japanese religions are John Clark Archer, *Faiths Men Live By* (N.Y., Thomas Nelson & Sons, 1934), chaps. VI, "Japan and Religion," and VII, "Shinto"; Selwyn G. Champion, *The Eleven Religions and Their Proverbial Lore* (N.Y., E. P. Dutton & Co., Inc., 1945), section on "Shinto," pp. 223–41; Horace L. Friess and Herbert W. Schneider, *Religion in Various Cultures* (N.Y., Henry Holt & Co., Inc., 1932), chap. III, "Shinto," and a section on Japanese Buddhism in chap. V, "Buddhism"; A. Eustace Haydon, *Biography of the Gods* (N.Y., The Macmillan Co., 1941), chap. VIII, "Amaterasu-Ōmikami"; E. Washburn Hopkins, *The History of Religions* (N.Y., The Macmillan Co., 1918), chap. XVI, "Religions of Japan, Shintoism and Buddhism"; Robert E. Hume, *The World's Living Religions* (N.Y., Charles Scribner's Sons, 1924; rev. ed., 1959), chap. VIII, "Shinto"; and Edmund D. Soper, *The Religions of Mankind* (N.Y., Abingdon Press, 1921), chap. IX, "The Religions of Japan." The chief merit of these discussions of Japanese religions is their brevity, but as far as their quality is concerned none of them comes close to, say, A. Bertholet and E. Lehmann, *Lehrbuch der Religionsgeschichte*, 4th ed., ed. by P. D. Chantepie de la Saussaye (Tübingen, J. C. B. Mohr, 1925), Vol. I, section on "Die Japaner" by Karl Florenz, pp. 262–422.

Some postwar publications also include brief descriptions of Japanese religions; see, for example, Charles S. Braden, *The Scriptures of Mankind: An Introduction* (N.Y., The Macmillan Co., 1952), chap. X, "The Sacred Literature of the Japanese"; Vergilius Ferm, ed., *Religion in the Twentieth Century* (N.Y., Philosophical Library, 1948), chap. IX, "Shinto" by D. C. Holtom; Jack Finegan, *The Archeology of World Religions* (Princeton, Princeton University Press, 1952), chap. VIII, "Shinto"; Edward J. Jurji, ed., *The Great Religions of the Modern World* (Princeton, Princeton University Press, 1946), article on "Shintoism" by D. C. Holtom, pp. 141–77, and also a part of the article on "Buddhism" in the same volume by A. K. Reischauer, pp. 90–140; Quinter M. Lyon, *The Great Religions* (N.Y., Odyssey Press, 1957), chaps. XXIII, "Shinto, the Japanese Religion," and XXIV, "Religion and Nationalism in Modern Japan"; John B. Noss, *Man's Religions* (N.Y., The Macmillan Co., 1949; rev. ed., 1956), chap. XI, "Shinto"; and R. C. Zaehner, ed., *The Concise Encyclopedia of Living Faiths* (N.Y., Hawthorn Books, 1959), chap. VII-C, "Buddhism in China and Japan," by R. H. Robinson, and chap. VIII, "Shinto," by G. Bownas. In the main, the quality of the postwar publications is superior to the older works in regard to Japanese religions. Those who have access to *Proceedings of the IXth International Congress for the History of Religions, Tokyo and Kyoto, 1958* (Tokyo, Shinto Committee Report, 1960) will find many excellent papers by Western and Japanese scholars on various aspects of Japanese religions.

Secondly, there are many works that are concerned primarily with one of the religions of Japan. While some of them are fairly adequate treatises on the respective religions, they do not always help readers in relating the specific religion under discussion to the total historical development of Japanese religions.

On Shinto, one of the oldest works, and yet still helpful in some ways, is W. G. Aston, *Shinto, The Way of the Gods* (London, Longmans, Green & Co., Ltd., 1905), even though his classification of Shinto deities and his naturalistic interpretation of religion have been rightly questioned by many. K. Florenz, *Die historischen Quellen der Shinto-religion* (Leipzig, J. C. Hinrichs, 1919) and H. Haas, "Shintoismus," *Religion in Geschichte und Gegenwart*, V, pp. 466–70, though naturally dated, are still read with profit. On the other hand, recent works are not always reliable or well balanced. Even D. C. Holtom's careful study, *Modern Japan and Shinto Nationalism*

(Chicago, University of Chicago Press, 1943), to say nothing of R. O. Ballou, *Shinto: The Unconquered Enemy* (N.Y., Viking Press, 1945), betray the wartime psychology, and Chikao Fujisawa's *Zen and Shinto* (N.Y., Philosophical Library, 1959) and *Concrete Universality of the Japanese Way of Thinking* (Tokyo, Hokuseido, 1958) are but part of the sad legacy of a chauvinistic ethnocentricism. The two most frequently cited works on Shinto are Genchi Kato, *A Study of Shinto: The Religion of the Japanese Nation* (Tokyo, Meiji Japan Society, 1926) and Daniel C. Holtom, *The National Faith of Japan* (N.Y., Kegan Paul, Trench, Trubner & Co., Ltd., 1938). Readers must be aware, however, that Kato, using a now dated evolutionary theory, tries too hard to show the development of Shinto from its earliest stage of nature religion to that of an ethical and intellectual religion, while at the same time he tries to maintain a lofty place for the divine emperor. Nevertheless, Kato's confusing work is a landmark in the recent development of Japanese scholarship in Shinto studies. Holtom's *The National Faith of Japan*, together with his "The Political Philosophy of Modern Shinto: A Study of the State Religion of Japan," *Transactions of the Asiatic Society of Japan*," XLIX (1922), Part 2, pp. 1–325, and other articles, are the best sources in the English language concerning the general characteristics and history of Shinto, even though readers may not agree with Holtom's own ethical liberalism and evolutionary conception of religion. A. C. Underwood, *Shintoism* (London, Epworth Press, 1934), depends heavily on the works of Anesaki, Aston, W. E. Griffis, Kato, and Michel Revon. Although it has no particular originality, this small book is a handy introduction to the study of Shinto. It is interesting to note that Shinto intrigued Raffaele Pettazzoni, the well-known Italian historian of religion, as evidenced by his *La mitologia giapponese* (Bologna, N. Zanichelli, 1929) and *Religione e politica religiosa del Giappone moderno* (Rome, Istituto Italiano per il Medio ed Estremo Oriente, 1934).

Books on Japanese Buddhism are many and varied. Bunyiu Nanjio (also spelled Bunyu Nanjo), *A Short History of the Twelve Japanese Buddhist Sects* (Tokyo, Meiji, 1886) and Arthur Lloyd, "Development of Japanese Buddhism," *Transactions of the Asiatic Society of Japan*, XXII (1894), Part 3, pp. 361–405, are important pioneering works. Lloyd's later work, *Creed of Half Japan* (N.Y., E. P. Dutton & Co., Inc., 1912) suffers from his too lively imagination. Robert C. Armstrong's *Buddhism and Buddhists in Japan* (N.Y., The Macmillan Co., 1927) and *Introduction to Japanese Buddhist Sects* (a posthumous publication, privately printed somewhere in Canada, 1950) are good as introductory materials. E. Steinilber-Oberlin and K. Matsuo, *The Buddhist Sects of Japan*, tr. by Marc Loge (London, George Allen & Unwin, Ltd., 1938) may be characterized as a sensitive religious travelogue. Two important scholarly works on the subject are A. K. Reischauer, *Studies in Japanese Buddhism* (N.Y., The Macmillan Co., 1917) and Sir Charles Eliot's posthumous publication, *Japanese Buddhism* (London, 1935; reprinted, N.Y., Edward Arnold, Ltd., 1959). Both are dull reading, and both undoubtedly need revision in the light of current research; yet they are substantial works to be reckoned with by serious students of Japanese religions.

In addition to works on Japanese Buddhism, most books on Buddhism in general, especially those on Mahayana Buddhism, make reference to Japanese Buddhism. Among them, James B. Pratt, *The Pilgrimage of Buddhism and a Buddhist Pilgrimage* (N.Y., The Macmillan Co., 1928) devotes chapters XXI–XXXI to Buddhism in Japan, and Kenneth W. Morgan, ed., *The Path of the Buddha* (N.Y., Ronald Press, 1956) includes an important section on Buddhism in Japan, pp. 307–63. Junjiro Takakusu, *The Essentials of Buddhist Philosophy*, ed. by C. A. Moore and W. T. Chan (Honolulu, University of Hawaii, 1947) is in fact a book on the doctrines of eleven Japanese Buddhist schools.

Some of the Japanese Buddhist schools have been studied by specialists; these will be mentioned later in their proper context. The abundance of books on Zen, however, calls for some comment at this time. Briefly stated, Zen Buddhism in Japan should not be linked solely with the name of D. T. Suzuki. To be sure, some of his writings, especially *The Training of the Zen Buddhist Monk* (Kyoto, Eastern Buddhist Society, 1934) and *Zen and Japanese Culture* (N.Y., Pantheon Books, 1959) deal directly with Zen Buddhism in Japan, but most of his books are interpretations of Zen Buddhism in general. It must also be noted that there are other books on Zen Buddhism in Japan, such as Kaiten Nukariya, *Religion of the Samurai, A Study of Zen* (London, Luzac & Co., Ltd., 1913) and Reiho Masunaga, *The Soto Approach to Zen* (Tokyo, Layman Buddhist Society Press, 1958). In our discussion, only those works that deal directly with Zen in Japan—or with other Japanese Buddhist schools, for that matter—will be treated.

In sharp contrast to the abundance of works on Japanese Buddhism, those on Japanese Confucianism are very meager, to say the least. This is all the more surprising and distressing because of the significant role that the Confucian tradition has played in Japanese history. Those who want to study Japanese Confucianism must either learn to read books written in Japanese or go through such works as A. Lloyd, "Historical Development of the Shushi (Chu Hsi) Philosophy in Japan," *Transactions of the Asiatic Society in Japan*, XXXIV (1906), Part 4, p. 80, or R. C. Armstrong, *Light from the East: Studies in Japanese Confucianism* (Toronto, University of Toronto Press, 1914), both of which are quite dated. Its modern development is studied in Warren Smith, *Confucianism in Modern Japan* (Tokyo, Hokuseido Press, 1959). There is a brief historical study of Japanese Confucianism in Joseph J. Spae, *Ito Jinsai, A Philosopher, Educator and Sinologist of the Tokugawa Period* (Peking, The Catholic University of Peking, 1948; *Monumenta Serica* No. 12). Some of the studies of Japanese Confucianist leaders include

Olaf Graf, *Kaibara Ekken* (Leiden, E. J. Brill, 1942), Galen M. Fisher's "Kumazawa Banzan, His Life and Ideas," *Transactions of the Asiatic Society of Japan*, Second Series, XVI (1938), pp. 221–58; Ken Hoshino, *The Way of Contentment*, translations of selections from Kaibara Ekken (London, Orient Press, 1904); and T. Yoshimote, *A Peasant Sage of Japan* (London, Longmans, Green & Co., Ltd., 1912). Also D. S. Nivison and A. F. Wright, eds., *Confucianism in Action* (Stanford, Stanford University Press, 1959) makes reference to Japanese Confucianism.

Many of the Christian publications dealing with Japanese religions are apologetic or evangelical in character. There are some historical studies of Christianity in Japan, however. The two earliest works that are still consulted are Hans Haas, *Geschichte des Christentums in Japan* (Tokyo, Der Rikkyo Gakuin Press, 1902–04) and Otis Cary, *A History of Christianity in Japan*, 2 vols. (N.Y., F. H. Revell Co., 1909). On the Catholic development, one might read Johannes Laures, *The Catholic Church in Japan* (Rutland, Charles E. Tuttle Co., 1954) and Joseph Jennes, *History of the Catholic Church in Japan—From its Beginnings to the Early Meiji Period: 1549–1873* (Tokyo, Committee of the Apostolate, 1959). On the Protestant development, Winburn T. Thomas, *Protestant Beginnings in Japan—The First Three Decades: 1859–89* (Rutland, Charles E. Tuttle Co., 1959) and Charles W. Iglehart, *A Century of Protestant Christianity in Japan* (Rutland, Charles E. Tuttle Co., 1959) will provide basic information.

Thirdly, some scholars have undertaken the very difficult task of studying, not the individual religions and their schools, but the ethos and development of the multidimensional religious history of Japan. The older works, such as William E. Griffis, *The Religions of Japan: From the Dawn of History to the Era of Meiji* (N.Y., Charles Scribner's Sons, 1895 and 1901) and George W. Knox, *The Development of Religion in Japan* (N.Y., G. P. Putnam's Sons, 1907), remind us of a quickly moving kaleidoscope without any central theme. The standard works in this area are Masaharu Anesaki, *History of Japanese Religion, with Special Reference to the Social and Moral Life of the Nation* (London, Kegan Paul, Trench, Trubner & Co., Ltd., 1930) and Wilhelm Gundert, *Japanische Religionsgeschichte* (Stuttgart, D. Gundert, 1943). In our historical survey, we will assume that readers will follow Anesaki's *History of Japanese Religion* and Tsunoda *et al.*, *Sources of Japanese Tradition*, which were cited before, as basic reading and source materials.

In addition, mention should be made of *Religious Studies in Japan*, ed. by the Japanese Association for Religious Studies (Tokyo, Maruzen Co., 1959), which is a collection of papers by leading Japanese scholars on Shinto, Japanese Buddhism, etc. Some Buddhist materials are also to be found in philosophical works. For example, *Philosophical Studies of Japan*, compiled by the Japanese National Commission for UNESCO (Tokyo, 1959), has an excellent article on Japanese Tendai Buddhism by H. Ui; and H. Nakamura,

The Ways of Thinking of Eastern Peoples (Tokyo, Japanese Government Printing Bureau, 1960), Part IV, "The Ways of Thinking of the Japanese," is important for the study of Japanese religions. T. Harada, *The Faith of Japan* (N.Y., The Macmillan Co., 1914) is still useful as an introductory study, and T. Kishinami, *The Development of Philosophy in Japan* (Princeton, Princeton University Press, 1915) and K. Tsuchida, *Contemporary Thought of Japan and China* (N.Y., Alfred A. Knopf, Inc., 1927) deal with modern philosophical trends in Japan.

It has been the experience of many who have tried to "understand" Japanese religions that some knowledge of Japanese art is extremely helpful. In fact, some go so far as to say that "religion is art" and "art is religion" in Japan. One of the pioneers in this field was Ernest F. Fenollosa, whose *Epochs of Chinese and Japanese Art*, 2 vols., (London, William Heinemann, Ltd., 1912) were important contributions of his time. More up to date and comprehensive are *Pageant of Japanese Art*, 6 vols., published by the Tokyo National Museum (Tokyo, 1952), Yukio Yashiro and P. C. Swann, *Two Thousand Years of Japanese Art* (N.Y., H. N. Abrams, Inc., 1958), and Hugo Munsterberg, *The Arts of Japan: An Illustrated History* (Rutland, Charles E. Tuttle Co., 1957). There are also several excellent interpretations of Japanese art, such as Laurence Binyon, *The Spirit of Man in Asian Art* (Cambridge, Harvard University Press, 1935); Rene Grousset, *The Civilization of the East*, tr. C. A. Philipps (N.Y., Alfred A. Knopf, Inc., 1941); Robert T. Paine, Jr., and Alexander Soper, *The Art and Architecture of Japan* (Middlesex, Penguin Books, 1955); P. C. Swann, *An Introduction to the Arts of Japan* (Oxford, Bruno Cassirer, Ltd., 1958); and Langdon Warner, *The Enduring Art of Japan* (Cambridge, Harvard University Press, 1952). If one of them should be recommended particularly—and this would indeed afford a difficult choice—we would point to Warner's book.

Among books on the arts of Japan, those that deal with music, especially religious music, are extremely rare. Sir Francis Piggott, *Music and Musical Instruments of Japan* (London, Kelly & Walsh, Ltd., 1909), Katsumi Sunaga, *Japanese Music*, Tourist Library No. 15, (Tokyo, Maruzen Co., Ltd., 1936), and H. Tanabe, *Japanese Music* (Tokyo, 1959) provide some information concerning this difficult subject. Students of religions are also strongly advised to listen to recordings, such as the seven volumes of Gagaku classical court music, transcribed by Sukehiro Shiba into Western notation (Tokyo, 1956?) and the record accompanying Douglas G. Haring, *Japanese Buddhist Ritual* (N.Y., 1954; record No. P449, Ethnic Folkways Library). On traditional dance, one should consult *Introduction to the Classic Dances of Japan*, by R. Umemoto and Y. Ishikawa (Tokyo, Sanseido Co., 1935).

II. HISTORICAL SURVEY

Japanese religion in the prehistoric and early periods

In spite of many years of research and speculation by devoted scholars, we are not at all certain about the religious development in the Japanese islands during the early period. The expression "primitive Shinto" is often used in referring to early Japanese religion, but the term "Shinto" arose only in the sixth century to distinguish Buddhism from traditional Japanese religious beliefs and practices that were not in themselves united within a single religious entity. The earliest chronicles of Japan are the *Kojiki* and the *Nihongi* (or *Nihon-shoki*), both of which are considered to be semisacred scriptures of Shinto. See B. H. Chamberlain's translation of Ko-ji-ki: "Records of Ancient Matters," Supplement to *Transactions of the Asiatic Society of Japan*, X (Tokyo, 1906), and W. G. Aston's translation of *Nihongi; Chronicles of Japan from the Earliest Times to A.D. 697* (London, George Allen & Unwin, Ltd., 1956; originally published by the Japan Society of London, 1896). We must bear in mind, however, that both the *Kojiki*, which appeared in 712, and the *Nihongi*, which appeared in 720, were colored by Chinese influence, although they were both supposed to be faithful collections and compilations of ancient oral traditions. Thus, we cannot reconstruct the early history of Japan by basing it solely on these chronicles. There are references to Japan in the Chinese sources which are conveniently collected in Ryusaku Tsunoda and L. C. Goodrich, eds., *Japan in the Chinese Dynastic Histories* (South Pasadena, P. D. & I. Perkins, 1951). But, again, we cannot depend on the Chinese records alone to reconstruct the prehistory of Japan.

Fortunately, thanks to the untiring efforts of many scholars, we know considerably more today than, say, fifty years ago, about Japanese origins. Three excellent recent publications on the subject are G. J. Groot, *The Prehistory of Japan*, ed. by B. S. Kraus (N.Y., Columbia University Press, 1951), Charles Haguenauer, *Origines de la civilisation Japonaise*, Part I (Paris, Imprimerie Nationale, 1956), and Jonathan E. Kidder, *Japan before Buddhism* (N.Y., F. A. Praeger, Inc., 1959). In the main, scholars agree that the Japanese islands were inhabited as early as two or three millennia B.C. and that the earliest dwellers there were in part of northern Asiatic origin and in part from southern Asia. But there seems to be a variety of opinions among scholars as to which group migrated to which section of Japan at which age and by what route. Also, while most scholars accept the fact that there were two stages in prehistoric Japanese cultural development—namely, the Jōmon ("The rope-pattern") and the Yayoi (so named because of certain characteristic pottery found in a Neolithic site at a place called Yayoi in present-day Tokyo)—their opinions differ widely as to how to trace specific cultural influences to Ural-Altaic or South Sea origins.

To complicate the matter further, scholars are also confronted with the question of the Ainu, one of the Paleo-Asiatic groups that originated in the arctic or subarctic zones of Asia. That the Ainus dwelt in the northern part of Honshu (the main island of Japan) in the prehistoric period is clear. But how and when they migrated from Asia to Sakhalin, Kurile, and Hokkaido, and their relation to non-Ainu peoples on Honshu, cannot be ascertained accurately. Understandably, many pioneers in Japanology, such as W. G. Aston, B. H. Chamberlain, E. O. E. von Baelz, Hans Haas, and Frederick Starr, were intrigued by the Ainus. The best-known Ainu scholar was John Batchelor, an Anglican missionary who worked among the Hokkaido Ainus for fifty years; he wrote numerous articles and books, such as *The Ainu of Japan* (London, Religious Tract Society, 1892), *The Ainu and Their Folk-lore* (London, Religious Tract Society, 1901), *Ainu Life and Lore* (Tokyo, Kyobun Kwan, 1927), and "The Ainu Bear Festival," *Transactions of the Asiatic Society of Japan*, Second Series, IX (1932), pp. 37–44.

The Ainus offer a number of interesting questions to us. Having no written language of their own, they have preserved an impressive quantity of their oral tradition. And, although they lived in close geographical proximity to the Japanese for centuries, they maintained intact their own social and cultural patterns until quite recently. One of the main questions arising in this situation is the relation of the Ainus to other peoples of arctic or subarctic origins who also practice the bear festival and other similar rites. This problem is dealt with in A. Irving Hallowell, *Bear Ceremonialism in the Northern Hemisphere* (Philadelphia, 1926; published Ph.D. thesis). It must be mentioned, however, that R. Torii and other scholars hold that the bear festival was not a fundamental feature of the Ainu tradition but that it was probably borrowed from neighboring peoples. Some of these issues are discussed in J. M. Kitagawa, "Ainu Bear Festival (Iyomante)," *History of Religions*, I, 1 (Chicago, 1961), pp. 95–151.

Another question presented by the Ainus is their relation to the Japanese people, especially in regard to their religious beliefs. The Batchelor-Chamberlain controversy—Batchelor, "On the Ainu Term 'Kamui,' " *Transactions of the Asiatic Society of Japan*, XVI (1888), pp. 17–32, vs. Chamberlain, "Reply to Mr. Batchelor on the Words 'Kamui' and 'Aino,' " *ibid.*, pp. 33–8—aroused great interest among scholars concerned with possible connections between the Ainu religion and primitive Shinto, but this problem is far from being solved. Meanwhile, a number of Japanese scholars have taken up Ainu study. The most prominent and productive is Kyōsuke Kindaichi (also spelled Kindaiti); unfortunately, his only work available in English is *Ainu Life and Legends*, Tourist Library, No. 36 (Tokyo, Board of Tourist Industry, 1941). Also lamentable is the fact that none of the writings of Mashio Chiri, himself an Ainu and an eminent professor of linguistics at Hokkaido University, is available in Western languages. John A. Harrison deserves our gratitude for translating and annotating S. Takakura's difficult work "The Ainu of Northern Japan: A Study in Conquest and Acculturation," *Transactions of the American Philosophical Society*, New Series, L, Part 4 (1960), although it does not have much to say about the prehistoric aspects of the Ainu. The only recent book on the Ainu in English is Carl Etter, *Ainu Folklore* (Chicago, Wilcox & Follett, 1949) which is spotty and misleading. But there have been some articles on the Ainus appearing from time to time in such places as the *Journal of the Royal Anthropological Institute*, LXXIX (1949), *Contemporary Japan*, XVIII (1949), the *Journal of American Folklore*, LXIV (1951) and LXV (1952), and the *Southwest Journal of Anthropology*, X (1954). All the writers on the Ainu question realize that it is a risky undertaking to reconstruct the prehistoric religion and culture of the Ainus and their relation to the Japanese solely on the basis of a study of their descendants in our own period.

In recent years scholars have not been as optimistic as Chamberlain once was in depending on Ainu studies for a clarification of the prehistoric culture of Japan. Cf. B. H. Chamberlain, "The Language, Mythology, and Geographical Nomenclature of Japan viewed in the Light of Aino Studies," *Memoirs of the Literature College*, No. 1 (Tokyo, Imperial University, 1887). Rather, they are turning toward archeology, folklore, and mythology for possible clues. The most detailed historical study of early Japan is Robert K. Reischauer, *Early Japanese History*, 2 vols. (Princeton, Princeton University Press, 1937). For a very good brief discussion of Japanese mythology, see E. Dale Saunders, "Japanese Mythology," *Mythologies of the Ancient World*, ed. by S. N. Kramer (N.Y., Doubleday Anchor Books, 1961), pp. 409–40. On this subject, Post Wheeler's attempt to reconstruct a coherent story of the origin of the cosmos to the seventh century A.D. out of various Shinto myths in *The Sacred Scriptures of the Japanese* (N.Y., Henry Schuman, Inc., 1952) is neither successful nor reliable. The difficulty lies in learning how to correlate the analysis of the myths with archeological, historical, and other types of evidence, even though the main lines of development of the prehistoric peoples in Japan are fairly well established.

It is more or less taken for granted among scholars that various tribes both from the northern and southern parts of Asia infiltrated the Japanese islands during the Neolithic and Eolithic ages, and that they intermarried among the people there. Another question is not settled so easily, however, in respect to how and when the so-called Tennō clan (the dominant group among the Japanese) arrived. This tribe is believed to have brought with it the horseback-riding culture and the "uji" or clan social organization. Many scholars hold that the Tennō clan, originally one of the Altaic peoples, moved southward to the Korean peninsula about the beginning of the Christian era and migrated from there to Kyūshū island around the third century A.D. Eventually, this group established the so-called Yamato kingdom in the present Nara prefecture around the fourth century A.D. On the other hand, many scholars argue that the myths of the Tennō clan, especially those of the Sun-Goddess (Amaterasu-Ōmikami), share similarities with South Asian myths. The standard work on Japanese mythology is Nobuhiro Matsumoto, *Essai sur la mythologie japonaise: Austro-Asiatics*, Vol. II (Paris, P. Geuthner, 1928), and the best-known ethnological work, though not published, is Masao Oka's dissertation, *Kulturschichten in Alt-Japan* (Wien, 1934?). Oka's influence is clearly evident in Alexander Slawik, "Kultische Geheimbünde der Japaner und Germanen," *Wiener Beiträge zur Kulturgeschichte und Linguistik*, IV (Salzburg-Leipzig, 1936), pp. 675–764, and his "Zur Etymologie des japanischen Terminus marebito 'sakraler Besucher,' " *Wiener volkundliche Mitteilungen*, II, 1 (1954), pp. 44–58.

What, then, were the main features of primitive Shinto? This is a difficult question, indeed; for the term Shinto probably referred to a loosely organized religious cult that developed with the growth of the Yamato kingdom, which was *de facto* a confederation of semiautonomous clans with the imperial clan as the center. All we are certain of is that the early Japanese accepted the whole of life and the cosmos as sacred because the *kami* nature pervaded everything, and that the Shinto religion developed as a manifestation of the tribal and communal cult with simple ceremonies. On the term *kami*, see D. C. Holtom, "The Meaning of Kami," *Monumenta Nipponica*, III, 1 (1940), pp. 1–27. Judging from the Chinese records concerning early Japanese myths, female shamanic-diviners played significant roles both in the religious and the sociopolitical domains, but their relation to the tradition of Korean shamanism, for example, is not clear at all. While Satow, Chamberlain, and Griffis held that ancestor worship was an original feature of Shinto, Aston and Florenz believed that primitive Shinto presented no conception of ancestor worship. Michel Revon, in his *Le Shinntoïsme* (Paris, E. Leroux, 1907) and "Ancestor-worship and the Cult of the Dead (Japan)," *Encyclopaedia of Religion and Ethics*, I, pp. 455–7, characterized primitive Shinto primarily as nature worship, containing the seed for veneration of the ancestors, the full growth of which occurred only after Chinese influence penetrated Japan. Edmund Buckley, on the other hand, sought the meaning of Shinto in terms of a combination of ancestor worship, nature worship, and phallicism; cf. his *Phallicism in Japan* (Chicago, University of Chicago Press, 1895; published doctoral thesis). Franz Kiichi Numazawa, an ethnologist and a leading Japanese Roman Catholic, contributed an article on the subject, "Die Religionen Japans," to F. König, ed., *Christus und die Religionen der Erde*, III (Freiburg, 1951), pp. 393–436. Controversy on this subject will undoubtedly continue for many years to come. Meanwhile, for a Japanese Shinto scholar's evaluation of the views of Western scholars, see Motokiko Anzu, *Shinto as Seen by Foreign Scholars* (Los Angeles, Perkins Oriental Books, 1938).

Penetration of Chinese civilization and Buddhism

During the fifth and sixth centuries, Sino-Korean civilization began to penetrate Japan, introducing the ethical teachings of Confucianism, the magico-mystical system of Taoism, and the gospel of Buddhism. The administration of Prince Shōtoku (d. 621), the regent under the Empress Suiko (reigned 592–628), was an important landmark in Japanese history, for it was he who envisaged the establishment of a unified empire, patterned after the Chinese political structure. The underlying principles of Shōtoku's "Seventeen-article Constitution," assigning national and communal cults to Shinto, public and private morality to Confucianism, and the spiritual and metaphysical domains to Buddhism, exerted significant influence on the subsequent religious and social development. After the overthrow of the Soga clan, which resisted Shōtoku's policies, the court depended heavily on Sinified aristocrats and scholars who enhanced the introduction of Chinese thought and institutions into Japan. For the religious development of this period, see Clarence H. Hamilton, *Buddhism in India, Ceylon, China and Japan: A Reading Guide* (Chicago, University of Chicago Press, 1931), Part IV; M. Anesaki, *Prince Shotoku, the Sage Statesman* (Rutland, Charles E. Tuttle Co., 1949); and K. Asakawa, *The Early Institutional Life of Japan, A Study in the Reform of 645 A.D.* (Tokyo, Shueisha, 1903).

The eighth century was an important period for the religious, cultural, and artistic development of Japan. In the metaphor of L. Warner, "the T'ang dynasty of China was hanging like a brilliant brocaded background, against which we must look at Japan and its capital city of Nara to watch the eighth century, while the Japanese were at work weaving their own brocade on patterns similar but not the same" (Warner, *op. cit.*). One finds brief expositions of the doctrines of the so-called Nara Buddhist schools—The Kusha ("Abhidharmakosa"), Jōjitsu ("Satyasiddhi"), Hossō ("Yogacara"), Sanron ("Madhyamika"), Kegon ("Avatamsaka"), and Ritsu ("Vinaya")—in most of the general works on Japanese Buddhism. The Buddhist scriptures and rites used in the seventh and eighth centuries in Japan are discussed in M. W. de Visser, *Ancient Buddhism in Japan*, 2 vols. (Leiden, E. J. Brill, 1935), while the religious arts of this period are discussed in International Buddhist Society, ed., *History of Buddhist Art in Japan* (Tokyo, International Buddhist Society, 1940).

The Nara period produced not only the *Kojiki* ("Records of Ancient Matters") and the *Nihongi* ("Chronicles of Japan,") which have been mentioned earlier, but also a number of provincial historical records known as "Fūdoki." The *Kogoshūi*, which is an historical account of early Japan according to the Imbe clan, an hereditary Shinto priestly family and the traditional rival of another priestly family called the Nakatomi, was translated by G. Kato and Hikoshiro Hoshino under the title *Kogoshūi: Gleanings from*

Ancient Stories, 2nd rev. ed. (Tokyo, Meiji Japan Society, 1925). J. S. Snellen translated another historical work, "Shoku-Nihongi: Chronicles of Japan, Continued, from 697–791 A.D.", *Transactions of the Asiatic Society of Japan*, Second Series, XI (1934), pp. 151–239; XIV (1937), pp. 209–79. Unfortunately, the *Shinsen Shojiroku* ("The New Compilation of the Register of Families"), a very important document, dating from 815, has not been translated into Western languages. The importance of the *Manyōshu*, which is a collection of ancient poems, for the understanding of Japanese religions cannot be exaggerated. Among several translations, we recommend the Japanese Classics Translation Committee's edition, *The Manyōshu: One Thousand Poems* (Tokyo, Iwanami shoten, 1940). Ichiro Hori discusses religious beliefs that can be traced to the pre-Nara and Nara periods in "Japanese Folk-beliefs," *American Anthropologist*, LXI (June, 1959), pp. 405–24. The precarious relationship between Shinto and Buddhism during the eighth century is briefly discussed in J. M. Kitagawa, "Kaiser und Schamane in Japan," *Antaios*, II, 6 (1961), pp. 552–66.

In the transition from the Nara period (710–94) to the Heian period (794–1192), as a result of the transfer of the capital from Nara to Kyoto, there was a general decline in the Nara Buddhist schools together with the growth of two new Buddhist movements—the Tendai and the Shingon schools—that were introduced from China by Saichō (Dengyō-daishi) and Kūkai (Kōbō-daishi), respectively. Both schools gave doctrinal justification to the pattern of coexistence between Shinto and Buddhism. The Tendai scheme, known as "Sannō-ichijitsu Shinto," is discussed in T. Ishibashi and H. Dumoulin, "Yuitsu-Shinto-Myōbō-Yōshū: Lehrsbriss der Yuitsu-Shinto," *Monumenta Nipponica*, III, 1 (1940), pp. 187–239. The scheme of Buddhist-Shinto coexistence that lasted until the nineteenth century came to be known under the Shingon title "Ryōbu ('Two Aspects') Shinto." The Shingon school, being of the "Esoteric" variety, stressed elaborate rituals and the use of art objects. These aspects of Shingon are discussed in M. Anesaki, *Buddhist Art in its Relation to Buddhist Ideals, with Special Reference to Buddhism in Japan* (Boston, Houghton Mifflin Co., 1915) and E. Dale Saunders, *Mūdra: A Study of Symbolic Gestures in Japanese Buddhist Sculpture* (N.Y., Pantheon Books, Inc., 1960). The most concise description of Shingon Buddhism is R. Tajima, *Les deux grands mandalas et la doctrine de l'ésotérisme Shingon* (Paris, Presses universitaires de France, 1959), and the best summary of Tendai doctrine is H. Ui, "A Study of Japanese Tendai Buddhism," *Philosophical Studies of Japan*, *op. cit.*, pp. 33–74. E. O. Reischauer, *Ennin's Travels in T'ang China* (N.Y., Ronald Press, 1955) and his translation of *Ennin's Diary* (N.Y., Ronald Press, 1955) are important documents concerning the contacts between Japanese and Chinese Buddhism in the ninth century.

In spite of the prosperity of the Tendai and the Shingon schools, during the

Heian period Buddhism did not exterminate the cults of Onmyō-dō (Taoist-Shinto exorcism) or of Shugen-dō (the Shinto-Buddhist order of mountain priests). Percival Lowell studied some of these practices in his "Esoteric Shinto," *Transactions of the Asiatic Society of Japan*, XXI (1893), pp. 106–35; XXI, pp. 152–97; XXI, pp. 241–70, XXII (1894), pp. 1–26. See also I. Hori, "On the Concept of Hijiri (Holy-Man)," *Numen*, V (1958), Fasc. 2, pp. 128–60; Fasc. 3, pp. 199–232. The Heian period also produced the *Engi-shiki*, a compilation of laws and ritual regulations from A.D. 927, which includes many ancient Shinto prayers (*Norito*) and other material important for Shinto studies. There are two old but useful articles on these subjects: Sir Ernest M. Satow, "Ancient Japanese Rituals (Norito)," *Transactions of the Asiatic Society of Japan*, VII (1879), Part 2, pp. 97–132; VII, Part 3, pp. 409–55; IX (1881), Part 2, pp. 183–211; and Karl Florenz, "Ancient Japanese Rituals," *Transactions of the Asiatic Society of Japan*, XXVII (1900), pp. 1–112. Also, there is a recent booklet, *Norito: A New Translation of the Ancient Japanese Ritual Prayer* by Donald L. Philippi (Tokyo, Institute for Japanese Culture and Classics, 1959).

The peaceful atmosphere of Kyoto helped to create an elegant culture centering around the court during the Heian period. Among other literary works available in English are "Kagero Nikki (Journal of a 10th Century Nobleman)," tr. by Edward Seidensticker, *Transactions of the Asiatic Society of Japan*, Third Series, IV (1955), pp. 1–243; *Konjaku Monogatari* (Ages Ago: Thirty-seven Tales from the Konjaku Monogatari Collection), tr. by S. W. Jones (Cambridge, Harvard University Press, 1959); and the *Tosa Diary*, tr. by W. N. Porter (London, 1912; see Donald Keene, *Anthology of Japanese Literature*, N.Y., Grove Press, 1955, p. 443). By far the most famous available work from this period is Arthur Waley's translation of *The Tale of Genji*, 2 vols. (London, George Allen & Unwin, Ltd., 1935). One may also consult *Translations from Early Japanese Literature* by E. O. Reischauer and J. Yanagiwa (Cambridge, Harvard University Press, 1951) and the Kokusai Bunka Shinkokai, *Introduction to Classical Japanese Literature* (Tokyo, 1948). These poetical and literary works are invaluable resources for our understanding of the religious and cultural atmosphere of the Heian period.

Indigenous religious movements

The refined, aristocratic, and somewhat artificial culture of the Heian period gave way to the austere atmosphere of the Kamakura period (1192–1336) under the military rule of the Minamoto and the Hōjō families, followed by the eventful and chaotic "Warring States" period (1338–1568) under the nominal rule of the Ashikaga Shogunate. With the establishment of the military regime (*Bakufu*) in 1192, the imperial court became a powerless institution and, with the exception of a short-lived restoration of direct imperial rule (1333–36), remained in obscurity until the latter half of the nineteenth century. For the general historical background of this period, one might consult Minoru Shinoda, *The Founding of the Kamakura Shogunate, 1180–1185, with Selected Translations from the Azuma Kagami* (N.Y., Columbia University Press, 1960) and Helen C. McCullough, tr., *The Taiheiki: A Chronicle of Medieval Japan* (N.Y., Columbia University Press, 1959).

The Kamakura period is noted for the vigorous spiritual awakening of Japan. The return from China of Eisai (d. 1215), founder of the Rinzai sect of Zen Buddhism, in 1191 ushered in an all but new religious age. Another branch of Zen, called the Sōtō, was established in Japan by Dōgen (d. 1253), and a third, the order of homeless mendicancy, known as the Fuke, was founded by Kakushin in 1255. Among the numerous works on Zen, the most concise historical account of its development in Japan is given in Heinrich Dumoulin, *Zen: Geschichte und Gestalt* (Bern, Francke Press, 1959). One might also consult Nukariya's *Religion of the Samurai*, which was mentioned earlier. Undoubtedly, Bushido ("The Code of the Samurai or Warrior") was greatly influenced by Zen Buddhism. On this subject, see Inazo Nitobe, *Bushido: The Soul of Japan* (N.Y., G. P. Putnam's Sons, Inc., 1905), and D. T. Suzuki's *Zen and Japanese Culture* (*op. cit.*).

The most colorful religious leader during the Kamakura period was Nichiren (d. 1282), a patriotic prophet who became the founder of the Nichiren sect. His warning of a foreign invasion and bitter denunciation of other Buddhist schools brought a death sentence upon him, which he skillfully avoided. His prestige soared when his prophecy was fulfilled in the Mongol invasions (of 1274 and 1281). Nichiren's life and his teaching, based on the Lotus Sutra, are succinctly portrayed in M. Anesaki, *Nichiren, the Buddhist Prophet* (Cambridge, Harvard University Press, 1916) and G. B. Sansom's article, "Nichiren," in Eliot's *Japanese Buddhism* (*op. cit.*). The most dogmatic view of the Nichiren school is found in K. Satomi, *Japanese Civilization: Its Significance and Realization, Nichirenism, and the Japanese National Principles* (London, Kegan Paul, Trench, Trubner & Co., Ltd., 1923). One should also consult N. R. M. Ehara, tr., *The Awakening to the Truth or Kaimokushō, by Nichiren* (Kyoto, Perkins Oriental Books, 1941).

The Kamakura period also witnessed the growth of the Amida Pietist sects. Amida Pietism, it should be noted, had its roots in the popular "Nenbutsu" movement ("Recitation of prayers offered to the Buddha Amitabha who reigns over the 'Jōdo' or the Western Pure Land") that was widely spread among the masses in the tenth and eleventh centuries. In the thirteenth century Hōnen (d. 1212), inspired by the writings of a Chinese Pure Land Buddhist, reformed the "Nenbutsu" movement and established the Jōdo sect. His disciple, Shinran (d. 1262), founded the Jōdo Shin ("The True Pure Land") sect, which, incidentally, is the largest Buddhist group in Japan today. The third branch of Amida Pietism, known as the Ji ("the Perpetual Invocation") sect, was founded by Ippen (d. 1289). The most detailed study of Hōnen is H. H. Coates and R. Ishizuka, *Hōnen the Buddhist Saint, His Life and Teaching* (Kyoto, Kyon, 1925). For Shinran, see A. Lloyd, *Shinran and His Work* (Tokyo, Kyōbun Kwan, 1910), G. Nakai, *Shinran and His Religion of Pure Faith* (Kyoto, 1946), D. T. Suzuki, *A Miscellany on the Shin Teaching of Buddhism* (Kyoto, Perkins Oriental Books, 1949), Ryosetsu Fujiwara, tr., *Tannishō; Notes Lamenting Differences* (Kyoto, Ryukoku Translation Centre, Ryukoku University, 1962), and G. Sasaki, *A Study of Shin Buddhism* (Kyoto, Eastern Buddhist Society, 1925).

The spiritual revival of the Kamakura period encompassed Shintoists as well. Under the leadership of the hereditary priests of the Watarai family of the Ise shrine, Shintoists, adding a new element to the interreligious exchange, asserted that the Buddhas and Bodhisattvas of India were manifestations of the great *kami* of Shinto. The decline of the Kamakura feudal regime in 1333 and the restoration of imperial rule, even though it lasted as it did for only three years, nevertheless helped to encourage Shinto resurgence. A famous loyalist, Kitabatake Chikafusa (d. 1354), wrote the Jinnō Shōtōki ("Records of the Valid Succession of the Divine Emperor"); excerpts from this important document are included in Tsunoda *et al.*, *Sources of Japanese Tradition* (*op. cit.*), pp. 273–82. We might add that G. B. Sansom, tr., "The *Tsurezure Gusa* of Yoshida no Kaneyoshi, Being the meditations of a recluse in the fourteenth century," *Transactions of the Asiatic Society of Japan*, XXXIX (1911), pp. 1–141, enables us to appreciate the original author's sharp criticisms of the social conditions of his time and to share in his inner spiritual struggle.

The "Warring States" period (1338–1568) is also known as the Ashikaga period because of the nominal rule of the nation at that time by the Ashikaga Shogunate. It is also called the Muromachi period, from the city of Muromachi not far from the imperial court in Kyoto. This troublesome time was marked by social and political chaos on the one hand and by the growth of various arts on the other. Cultural contacts with China were resumed, which accounts for some of the new artistic inspiration. During this period Zen Buddhist priests were the social and cultural elite whose influence was felt in education, foreign trade, the establishment of the tea cult, and various other cultural activities. In this period also a unique synthesis of the spirit of Zen and the ethos of Shinto was achieved, as exemplified in the so-called Nō play. Beside Zen and Shinto, the Tendai, Shingon, Nichiren and the Jōdo Shin Buddhist sects were active; and they were often involved in bloody battles resulting from jurisdictional disputes. All in all, the religious mood of this period can be appreciated through examining studies of general history and of the arts, particularly K. Okakura, *The Book of Tea* (N.Y., Fox, Duffield, 1906), B. L. Suzuki, *Nogaku: Japanese Nô-plays* (London, John Murray, Ltd., 1932), A. Waley, *The Nō Play of Japan*, new ed. (London, George Allen & Unwin, Ltd., 1950), and Wilhelm Gundert's excellent study, "Der Shintoismus im Japanischen No-drama," *Nachrichten der (Deutschen) Gesellschaft für Natur- und Völkerkunde Ostasiens*, XIX (Tokyo, 1925).

"Kirishitan" and national seclusion

One of the by-products of foreign trade in the sixteenth century was the arrival of merchants and Roman Catholic missionaries from Europe. The famous Jesuit, Francis Xavier, reached Japan in 1549 and initiated the missionary activities of Catholicism, then known as "Kirishitan" in Japan. Oda Nobunaga (d. 1582), the "strong man" of that time, favored Catholicism, partly to counteract the power of uncooperative Buddhist groups. The guiding principle of the later Tokugawa feudal regime (1603–1867), which did not favor Catholicism, was the Neo-Confucianism of the Chu Hsi tradition. The Kirishitan movement was virtually wiped out after the revolt of Japanese Catholics (1637–38), and every Japanese family was required to belong to some Buddhist temple. Furthermore, the Tokugawa regime took the drastic step of declaring national seclusion, cutting off all contacts with foreign nations with the exception of China and the Netherlands. For the historical background of this period, see Walter Dening, *The Life of Toyotomi Hideyoshi, 1536–1598* (Tokyo, Hokuseido Press, 1955), A. L. Sadler, *The Maker of Modern Japan: The Life of Tokugawa Ieyasu* (London, George Allen & Unwin, Ltd., 1937), M. Takizawa, *The Penetration of Money Economy in Japan and Its Effect upon Social and Political Institutions* (N.Y., Columbia University Press, 1927), T. C. Smith, *Agrarian Origins of Modern Japan* (Stanford, Stanford University Press, 1959), Charles D. Sheldon, *The Rise of the Merchant Class in Tokugawa Japan* (Locust Valley, J. J. Augustin, Inc., 1958), John W. Hall, *Tanuma Okitsugu, 1719–1788: Forerunner of Modern Japan* (Cambridge, Harvard University Press, 1955), and Donald Keene, *The Japanese Discovery of Europe: Honda Toshiaki and other Discoverers, 1720–1798* (London, Routledge & Kegan Paul, Ltd., 1952).

During the Tokugawa period the populace was sharply divided into the four distinct social classes of the warrior, farmer, artisan, and merchant in that descending order. The warriors were expected to live by Bushido (the "Code of the Samurai"), as exemplified by the famous 47 retainers who sacrificed their lives in order to maintain the honor of their master. For this incident, see F. V. Dickins, tr., *Chūshingura, or the Loyal League* (London, 1880). The lot of women then was anything but enviable, judging from S. Takaishi, *Women and Wisdom of Japan* (London, John Murray, Ltd., 1905). Yet strange as it may seem, under "permanent martial law" the Tokugawa period produced all kinds of poetry (*waka* and *haiku*) and other literature. The theatrical arts (*kabuki* and *bunraku*) flourished, and schools of painters from the great Koyetsu tradition to that of popular *ukiyo-e* were prominent. For the cultural development of this period, see R. H. Blyth, *Haiku*, 4 vols. (Tokyo, Kamakura Bunko, 1949–52), and his translation of *Senryū: Japanese*

Satirical Verses (Tokyo, Hokuseido Press, 1949), H. H. Honda, tr., *A Hundred Poems from a Hundred Poets: Ogura-Hyakunin-Isshu* (Tokyo, Hokuseido Press, 1948), A. Miyamori, *An Anthology of Haiku, Ancient and Modern* (Tokyo, Maruzen Co., Ltd., 1932), H. G. Henderson, *An Introduction to Haiku* (N.Y., Doubleday & Co., Inc., 1958), *Basho's Oku no Hosomichi*, tr. by Y. Isobe (Tokyo, 1933), Max Bickerton, "Issa's Life and Poetry," *Transactions of the Asiatic Society of Japan*, Second Series, IX (1932), pp. 111–54, A. L. Sadler, *Japanese Plays: No, Kyogen, Kabuki* (Sydney, Angus & Robertson, 1934), Earle Ernst, *The Kabuki Theatre* (London, Oxford University Press, 1956), Earle Ernst, ed., *Three Japanese Plays from the Traditional Theatre* (London, Oxford University Press, 1959), F. Bowers, *Japanese Theatre* (N.Y., Hermitage House, Inc., 1952), A. C. Scott, *The Kabuki Theatre of Japan* (London, George Allen & Unwin, Ltd., 1955), A. Miyamori, *Masterpieces of Chikamatsu, the Japanese Shakespeare* (N.Y., E. P. Dutton & Co., Inc., 1926), Donald Keene, *The Battle of Coxinga: Chikamatsu's Puppet Play* (London, Taylor's Foreign Press, 1951), Howard Hibbett, *The Floating World in Japanese Fiction* (London, Oxford University Press, 1959), Jippensha Ikku, *Hizakurigé*, tr. by T. Satchell (Japan, Kobe Chronicle, 1929), L. Binyon, *Japanese Colour Prints* (N.Y., Charles Scribner's Sons, 1923), J. Hillier, *Japanese Masters of the Cloud Print* (London, Phaidon Press, Ltd., 1954), and J. A. Michener, *The Floating World* (N.Y., Random House, 1954).

The standard work on the Kirishitan movement is C. R. Boxer, *The Christian Century in Japan, 1549–1650* (Berkeley, University of California Press, 1951), while *Monumenta Nipponica* published by Sophia University, Tokyo also has good materials such as *Kirishito-ki und Sayo-yoroku* by G. Voss and H. Cieslik (1940), *Nobunaga und das Christentum* by J. Laures (1950), and *Kirishitan Bunko* by J. Laures (1957). Also useful is F. V. Williams, *The Martyrs of Nagasaki* (Fresno, Academy Library Guild, 1956). The general features and the role of Japanese Confucianism during the Tokugawa period are discussed in R. C. Armstrong, *Light from the East*, which was mentioned earlier, Joseph J. Spae, *Ito Jinsai, a Philosopher, Educator and Sinologist of the Tokugawa Period* (*op. cit.*), and John W. Hall, "The Confucian Teacher in Tokugawa Japan," *Confucianism in Action*, ed. by D. S. Nivison and A. F. Wright (Stanford, Stanford University Press, 1959).

In the main, Buddhism lost its spiritual vitality during the Tokugawa period, and was content to uphold the *status quo*. Shinto, on the other hand, received the cooperation and support of Neo-Confucian scholars. Toward the latter part of the Tokugawa period, able Shinto leaders, such as Kamo Mabuchi (d. 1769), Moto-ori Norinaga (d. 1801), and Hirata Atsutane (d. 1843) greatly expedited the Shinto revival. For Shinto development during the Tokugawa period, see Horst Hammitzsch, *Die Mito Schule* (Tokyo, Tokugawa-Zeit, 1940), H. Dumoulin, *Kamo Mabuchi* (Tokyo, Sophia University Press, 1943: *Monumenta Nipponica* Monograph), Tsunoda *et al.*, *Sources of*

Japanese Tradition (*op. cit*), pp. 506–51, and Naofusa Hirai, *The Concept of Man in Shinto* (unpublished M.A. thesis, University of Chicago, 1954). In the meantime, the folk elements in Shinto began to break through the traditional framework, especially among the oppressed peasantry; and several messianic movements sprang up under charismatic leaders; among them were Tenri-kyo and Kurozumi-kyo, who were destined to play important roles in the modern period. There were also semireligious movements, such as that of Ninomiya Sontoku, "Hōtoku" ("Repay the Indebtedness"), and Ishida Baigan's "Shingaku" ("Mind Learning") movement. For information on these movements, see R. C. Armstrong, *Just before the Dawn, The Life and Work of Ninomiya Sontoku* (N.Y., The Macmillan Co., 1912); Robert N. Bellah's excellent sociological analysis, *Tokugawa Religion: The Values of Pre-Industrial Japan* (Glencoe, Free Press, 1957), makes special reference to Ishida Baigan and the "Shingaku" movement.

Modern period

The decline of the Tokugawa regime was accelerated by the Perry expedition (1853–54), and the last Tokugawa *shogun* resigned in 1867. Thus began the Meiji era (1868–1912), followed by the Taisho era (1912–26) and the Shōwa era (1926 to the present). The architects of the Meiji regime attempted to establish a modern nation state without losing Japan's traditional religious and cultural foundation. The best single volume on the religious development of this period is H. Kishimoto, ed., *Japanese Religion in the Meiji Era*, tr. and adapted by J. F. Howes (Tokyo, Obunsha, 1956), which has separate chapters on Shinto, Buddhism, and Christianity. Among numerous other works, especially useful for our purposes are M. Kōsaka, *Japanese Thought in the Meiji Era*, tr. by D. Abosch (Tokyo, Pan-Pacific Press, 1958), Inazo Nitobe *et al.*, *Western Influence in Modern Japan* (Chicago, University of Chicago Press, 1931), Shigenobu Ōkuma, ed., *Fifty Years of New Japan*, 2 vols. (London, Smith, Elder & Co., 1909–10), K. Shibusawa, ed., *Japanese Life and Culture in the Meiji Era*, tr. by A. H. Culbertson and M. Kimura (Tokyo, Obunsha, 1958), and some of the biographical and autobiographical studies, such as M. E. Cosenza, ed., *The Complete Journal of Townsend Harris* (N.Y., 1930; rev. ed. Rutland, Charles E. Tuttle Co., 1959), Y. Fukuzawa, *The Autobiography of Fukuzawa Yukichi, 1834–1901*, tr. by E. Kiyooka (Tokyo, Hokuseido Press, 1934), H. van Straelen, *Yoshida Shōin: Forerunner of the Meiji Restoration* (Leiden, E. J. Brill, 1952), K. Obata, *An Interpretation of the Life of Viscount Shibusawa* (Tokyo, Bijutsu insatsusho, 1937), K. Hamada, *Prince Ito* (Tokyo, Sanseido Press, 1936), and J. Ijichi, *The Life of Marquis Shigenobu Ōkuma* (Tokyo, Hokuseido Press, 1940).

The Meiji regime lifted the edict banning Christianity, and religious freedom was guaranteed, at least officially, in the 1889 constitution. Encouraged by this action of the government, Protestant, Eastern Orthodox, and Roman Catholic missionaries engaged in evangelistic activities. The Meiji regime also issued a separation edict in an attempt to abolish the age-old pattern of Shinto-Buddhist cooperation. Some of the messianic movements were separated from Shinto proper and were classified as Sect (*Kyōha*) Shinto; thirteen of them were recognized by the government as "churches" (kyōha or kyōkai) between 1882 and 1908. These measures were taken by the regime in order to restore the ancient Japanese pattern of Saisei-itchi ("unity of religion and state"). Thus Shinto was proclaimed the national cult for all subjects of the emperor who was revered as the living manifestation of the *kami*. In addition, the imperial edict on education was promulgated as the guiding principle for universal education. For Christian development in modern Japan, see, in addition to the above-mentioned books, J. Natori, *Historical Stories of Christianity in Japan* (Tokyo, Hokuseido Press, 1957), Part III, "Modern Times"; Kanzo Uchimura, *How I became a Christian* (Tokyo, Keiseisha, 1913), and R. P. Jennings, *Jesus, Japan, and Kanzo Uchimura* (Tokyo, Kyo Bun Kwan, 1958). For Sect Shinto, the best description in English is found in Holtom's previously mentioned *National Faith of Japan*. One of the Sect Shinto denominations, the Kurozumi-kyo, is portrayed in C. W. Hepner, *The Kurozumi Sect of Shinto* (Tokyo, Meiji Japan Society, 1935), while another school, called Tenri-kyo, is portrayed in The Headquarters of Tenrikyo Church, *A Short History of Tenrikyo* (Tenri, Nara Prefecture, 1958). For the Confucian influence in the Meiji era, see Warren W. Smith, *Confucianism in Modern Japan* (Tokyo, Hokuseido Press, 1959) and D. H. Shively, "Motoda Eifu: Confucian Lecturer to the Meiji Emperor," *Confucianism in Action* (*op. cit.*), pp. 302–33. For the guiding principles of the Meiji regime, see R. K. Hall, *Kokutai no Hongi* (Cambridge, Harvard University Press, 1949) and his *Shūshin: The Ethics of a Defeated Nation* (N.Y., Columbia University Press, 1949).

No one has yet attempted a systematic study of religious developments during the period between 1912 (the beginning of the Taisho era) and World War II. In this era two of Japan's neighbors, China and Russia, underwent political revolutions, while Japan itself took part in World War I, the Siberian expedition, and engaged in an undeclared war with China. Internally, she suffered from the tensions existing between liberal democratic tendencies and chauvinistic militarism. There is a brief description of the relation between government and various religions during this eventful period in William K. Bunce, *Religions in Japan—Buddhism, Shinto, Christianity* (Rutland, Charles E. Tuttle Co., 1955). Christian activities were minutely reported in various denominational publications, as well as in *Monumenta Nipponica*, the *Japan Christian Quarterly*, and the *Japan Christian Year Book*. There are a number of books and articles about Toyohiko Kagawa, but probably the best way to understand him and his life is to read his own writing, *Christ and Japan* (N.Y., Friendship Press, 1934). Michi Kawai, a leading Christian woman educator, also wrote an interesting book, *My Lantern*, 3rd ed. (Tokyo, Kyo Bun Kwan, 1949). Buddhist activities were reported in the *Young East*, the *Eastern Buddhist*, and other journals. There were a number of articles written in English by eminent Japanese Buddhists, such as M. Anesaki, Junjiro Takakusu, and D. T. Suzuki. One book that reflects a popular Buddhist view of this period is Haya Akegarasu, ed., *Selections from the Nippon Seishin Library* (Kōsōsha, Kitayasuda, Ishikawaken, Nippon, 1936). The Shinto activities of this period are succinctly presented in D. C. Holtom, *The National Faith of Japan* and in his *Modern Japan and Shinto Nationalism*, both of which have been cited earlier.

Memoirs and biographical accounts are also helpful for an understanding of this period. See, for example, B. Omura, *The Last Genro: Prince Saionji* (Philadelphia, J. B. Lippincott Co., 1938), Joseph Grew, *Ten Years in Japan* (N.Y., Simon & Schuster, Inc., 1944), C. Hull, *The Memoirs of Cordell Hull*, 2 vols. (N.Y., The Macmillan Co., 1948), Shigenori Togo, *The Cause of Japan*, tr. by F. Togo and B. B. Blakeney (N.Y., Simon & Schuster, Inc., 1956), Mamoru Shigemitsu, *Japan and Her Destiny*, tr. by Oswald White (N.Y., E. P. Dutton & Co., Inc., 1958), and Toshikazu Kase, *Journey to the Missouri* (New Haven, Yale University Press, 1950). The life of women in this transitional period is portrayed in Etsu I. Sugimoto, *A Daughter of the Samurai* (Garden City, Doubleday & Co., Inc., 1925), as well as in her *A Daughter of the Narikin* (Garden City, Doubleday & Co., Inc., 1932) and *A Daughter of the Nohfu* (Garden City, Doubleday & Co., Inc., 1935); see also Shidzue Ishimoto, *Facing Two Ways* (N.Y., Farrar Rinehart, 1935), Katherine Sansom, *Living in Tokyo* (N.Y., Harcourt, Brace & Co., 1937), and S. Akimoto, *Family Life in Japan* (Tokyo, Japanese Government Railways, 1937).

One of the interesting features of the postwar (1945 to the present) period is the quantity of feverish activity on the part of various religious groups. Two good introductory works on the postwar religious situation are Bunce's *Religions in Japan*, which was mentioned previously, and Niels C. Nielsen, Jr., *Religion and Philosophy in Contemporary Japan* (Houston, 1957; The Rice Institute, Pamphlet XLIII, No. 4, Monograph in Philosophy). On the two thorny issues of the emperor system and the religious juridical persons law, see G. Okubo, "Problems of the Emperor System in Postwar Japan" (Tokyo, 1948; Institute for Pacific Relations, Pacific Studies Series) and William P. Woodard, "The Religious Juridical Persons Law," *Contemporary Japan* (Tokyo, The Foreign Affairs Association of Japan, 1960), pp. 1–84. As a result of the initiative of the occupation authorities, technically referred to as General Headquarters (GHQ) of the Supreme Commander for the Allied Powers (SCAP), State Shinto was disestablished; but Shinto as a religion (Shrine Shinto) continues to attract adherents. Of about 110,000 shrines governed before the war by the Home Ministry, over two-thirds now belong to the Association of Shinto Shrines (*Jinja Honcho*). Sect (*Kyōha*) Shinto denominations are enjoying their freedom and independence; and two of them, Tenri-kyo and Konko-kyo, are not only expanding rapidly in Japan but are also attempting missionary work abroad. Buddhist denominations, while suffering from internal ecclesiastical divisions, are holding their strength both among the intelligentsia and with the rural populations. Among the Christian groups, the Roman Catholics and the so-called fundamentalist wings of Protestantism have made rapid advances, while older Protestant denominations are also making some progress. By far the most significant development in the postwar religious scene in Japan is the emergence of new religions (*Shinkō Shūkyō*). Some of these are more properly splinter sects that were identified either with Shinto or Buddhism before the war. About 100 of them belong to the Union of New Religions (*Shin-shū-ren*).

The most useful and up-to-date information regarding the contemporary Japanese religious situation can be secured from the publications of the International Institute for the Study of Religions (*Kokusai Shukyo Kenkyu Sho*), Tokyo. This Institute not only publishes an English quarterly, *Contemporary Religions in Japan*, but also produces a number of informative bulletins on such topical subjects as *Religion and Modern Life* (1958), *Religion and State in Japan* (1959), *The Kami Way: An Introduction to Shrine Shinto* by S. Ono (1960), and *Living Buddhism in Japan*, by Y. Tamura and W. P. Woodard (1959). The Christian Center for the Study of Japanese Religions, Kyoto, publishes a bilingual quarterly, *Japanese Religions*, which has good articles on new religions. Another group called the Institute for Research in Religious Problems (*Shukyo Mondai Kenkyu Sho*), Tokyo, occasionally publishes reports in English called *Religions in Japan—At Present*.

On Shinto and related subjects, the Institute for Japanese Culture and Classics (*Nihonbunka Kenkyusho*) at Kokugakuin University, Tokyo, has been actively engaged in scholarly research. While most of its publications are in Japanese, it has published, in conjunction with the Association of Shinto Shrines, various informative booklets, such as *An Outline of Shinto Teachings* (1958) and *Basic Terms of Shinto* (1958). The postwar publications on Japanese Buddhism provide a true panoply, ranging from scholarly works to popular apologetics, and including as well quarterlies and bulletins such as *Young East* and *Zen Culture*. *The Journal of Indian and Buddhist Studies* and books published in honor of prominent scholars (D. T. Suzuki and S. Yamaguchi, for example) include articles in Western languages. In 1959 the Association of the Buddha Jayanti printed *Japan and Buddhism* and many short pieces in English. Articles by some of the Japanese Buddhist scholars have appeared in international academic journals, too. Somewhat unique is the account of Shinsho Hanayama, a Buddhist chaplain who spent three years with the condemned Japanese war criminals in the Sugamo prison, *The Way of Deliverance* (London, Victor Gollancz Ltd., 1955). On the Christian side, both Roman Catholic and Protestant books and articles in Western languages have appeared in large quantity, including such works as Everett F. Briggs, *New Dawn in Japan* (Toronto and N.Y., Longmans, Green & Co., Inc., 1948), R. T. Baker, *Darkness of the Sun* (Nashville, Abingdon-Cokesbury Press, 1947), W. C. Kerr, *Japan Begins Again* (N.Y., Friendship Press, 1949), C. W. Iglehart, *Cross and Crisis in Japan* (N.Y., Friedburg Press, 1957), N. Ebizawa, *Japanese Witness for Christ* (London, Association Press, 1957), Masao Takenaka, *Reconciliation and Renewal in Japan* (N.Y., Friendship Press and Student Volunteer Movement for Christian Missions, 1957), T. Ariga, "Christian Mission in Japan as a Theological Problem," *Religion in Life*, XXVII, 3 (Summer, 1958), pp. 372–80, and Carl Michalson, *Japanese Contributions to Christian Theology* (Philadelphia, Westminster Press, 1960).

Some of the Sect (*Kyōha*) Shinto denominations have been actively engaged in presenting their histories and doctrines in Western languages. This is especially true of Tenri-kyo, Konko-kyo, as well as of the semireligious movement called Itto-en. On the so-called new religions (Shinkō Shūkyō), there is only one book, M. A. Bairy, *Japans neue Religionen in der Nachkriegszeit* (Bonn, Ludwig Röhrscheid Verlag, 1959), but there are informative articles in some issues of *Japanese Religions* and *Contemporary Religions in Japan*, both of which have been cited before. One might also read W. Schiffer, "New Religions in Postwar Japan," *Monumenta Nipponica*, XI (1955), pp. 1–14; B. Watanabe, "Modern Japanese Religions: Their Success Explained," *ibid.*, XIII, 1–2 (1957), pp. 153–62; H. Neill McFarland, "The New Religions of Japan," *The Perkins School of Theology Journal*, XII, 1 (Fall, 1958), pp. 1–21; Bunce, *Religions in Japan* (*op. cit.*); pp. 160–5, and Nielsen, *Religion and Philosophy in Contemporary Japan* (*op. cit.*), pp. 82–109.

APPENDIX I

The reference works relevant to religions of Japan

Religion in Geschichte und Gegenwart, Gunkel, H. and Zscharnack, L., eds.

Encyclopaedia of Religion and Ethics, Hastings, James, ed. (N.Y., Charles Scribner's Sons, 1908–26).

Encyclopaedia Britannica, 1961 edition.

Religionswissenschaftliches Wörterbuch, König, Franz, ed. (Freiburg, Herder, 1956).

An Encyclopedia of Religion, Ferm, Vergilius, ed. (N.Y., The Philosophical Library, 1943).

Sources of Japanese Tradition, comp. by Tsunoda, Ryusaku, de Bary, William Theodore, and Keene, Donald (N.Y., Columbia University Press, 1958).

Japan Christian Year Book (Tokyo: Kyo Bun Kwan).

Bibliotheca Japonica, by Cordier, Henri (Paris, Imprimerie nationale, 1912).

Encyclopaedia of Buddhism, Japan Compilation Office, ed. (Tokyo, 1957).

Hôbôgirin: Dictionnaire encyclopédique du bouddhisme d'après les sources chinoises et japonaises, Demiéville, Paul, ed. (Tokyo, 1929–37).

A Catalogue of the Chinese Translation of the Buddhist Tripitaka, by Nanjio, Bunyiu (Oxford, Clarendon Press, 1883); reprint with additions, Tokiwa, Daijo *et al.*, eds. (Tokyo, 1929).

Japan—Its Land, People and Culture, by the Japanese National Commission for UNESCO (Tokyo, Printing Bureau, Ministry of Finance, 1958).

Proceedings of the IXth International Congress for the History of Religions, Tokyo and Kyoto, 1958 (Tokyo, Maruzen Co., 1960).

Religious Studies in Japan, Japanese Association for Religious Studies, ed. (Tokyo, Maruzen Co., 1959).

APPENDIX II

Published bibliographies

1. General bibliographies on Japan

Borton, Hugh, Elisseef, Serge, Lockwood, William W., and Pelzel, John C., *A Selected List of Books and Articles on Japan*, rev. ed. (Cambridge, Harvard University Press, 1954).

Wenckstern, Friedrich von, *A Bibliography of the Japanese Empire*, Vol. 1 (Leiden, E. J. Brill, 1895), Vol. 2 (Tokyo, Z. P. Maruya & Co., Ltd., 1907).

Nachod, Oskar, *Bibliography of the Japanese Empire*, Vols. 1 and 2 (London, E. Goldston, 1928), Vols. 3 and 4 (Leipzig, K. W. Hiersemann, 1931–35).

Kokusai Bunka Shinkokai, *A Short Bibliography on Japan* (English Books) (Tokyo, 1936).

———, *Kurze Bibliographie der Bücher über Japan, in Deutsch, Hollandisch, Danisch, Schwedisch und Norwegisch* (Tokyo, 1938).

Hall, John W., *Japanese History: A Guide to Japanese Reference and Research Materials* (Ann Arbor, University of Michigan Press, 1954).

Haring, D. G., *Books and Articles on Japan: A Reference List* (mimeo) (Syracuse, Syracuse University Book Store, 1960).

Japan—Economic Development and Foreign Policy: A Selected List of References (Washington, Library of Congress, 1940).

Kublin, Hyman, *What Shall I Read on Japan? An Introductory Guide* (N.Y., Japan Society, 1956).

Ward, Robert E., *A Guide to Japanese Reference and Research Materials in the Field of Political Science* (Ann Arbor, University of Michigan Press, 1950).

See also in the annual bibliography of the *Journal of Asian Studies* (formerly the *Far Eastern Quarterly*), the section on Japan.

2. Shinto

Kato, Genchi *et al.*, *A Bibliography of Shinto in Western Languages from the Oldest till 1952* (Tokyo, 1953).

3. Japanese Buddhism

Bando, Shōjun *et al.*, *A Bibliography on Japanese Buddhism* (Tokyo, C.I.I.B. Press, 1958). (This bibliography, pp. 1–7, lists other bibliographies that contain references to Japanese Buddhism.)

4. New religions

The Christian Center for the Study of Japanese Religions, *Bibliography on the New Religions* (Kyoto, 1960).

5. Religions in general

International Association for the History of Religions, *International Bibliography of the History of Religions* (Leiden, E. J. Brill, 1954ff.)

APPENDIX III

Periodicals relevant to religions of Japan

Bulletin de l'École Française d'Extrême-Orient (BEFEO)
Bulletin de la Maison Franco-Japonaise (BMFJ)
Contemporary Religions in Japan (CRJ)
Eastern Buddhist (EB)
East and West (EW)
France-Asie (FA)
Harvard Journal of Asiatic Studies (HJAS)
History of Religions, An International Journal for Comparative Historical Studies (HR)
Japan Quarterly (JQ)
Japanese Religions (JR)
Journal asiatique (JA)
Journal of the American Oriental Society (JAOS)
Journal of Asian Studies (JAS) formerly *Far Eastern Quarterly* (FEQ)
Journal of the Royal Asiatic Society of Great Britain and Ireland (JRAS)
Monumenta Nipponica (MN)
Nachrichten der Deutschen Gesellschaft für Natur- und Völkerkunde Ostasiens (NDGNVO)
Numen, International Review for the History of Religions (NMN)
Ostasiatische Zeitschrift (OAZ)
Philosophy East and West (PEW)
Proceedings of the Imperial Academy of Japan (PIAJ)
The Middle Way (TMW)
The Young East (TYE)
Transactions of the Asiatic Society of Japan (TASJ)
Wiener völkerkundliche Mitteilungen (WVM)
Zeitschrift für Missionskunde und Religionswissenschaft (ZMKR)

VI

Judaism

On a Selective Bibliography in English for the Study of Judaism

Judah Goldin

I. INTRODUCTION[1]

Drawing up a select bibliography on the Jewish religion presents something of a serious problem, particularly if the works to be included are to be limited essentially to the English language. To take but one example, no study of Judaism may ignore the investigation of the use and interpretation of Scripture in the Synagogue, for this was central to Jewish worship as well as intellectual development; but there is nothing in English to replace, or even correspond to, L. Zunz's classic *Die gottesdienstlichen Vorträge der Juden*, which appeared in 1832—and, incidentally, inaugurated the modern critical-historical study of Judaism—and was amplified in its second edition in 1892.

1. I want to thank Doctor Leon Nemoy for a number of valuable suggestions which I have incorporated in the following pages. Since the invitation to draw up this essay came to me in 1959–60, I decided to list works that appeared only up to 1960 and those items which appeared in 1961 that I had had an opportunity to read with some attentiveness. Inevitably, then, by the time this essay appears it will already be guilty of a number of omissions. I would, therefore, like to call attention to an excellent collection of short notices on books that have appeared since early 1961: The Society for Old Testament Study, *Book List, 1962.*

Since the modern critical study of Judaism, its history and literature, began in Germany, German was the language in which many pioneering and important works were written, and the earnest student must refer to them again and again.

Zunz's volume is today available in Hebrew translation, *Ha-Derashot be-Yisrael* (Jerusalem, Mosad Bialik, 5707–1946), and by adding his notes to this edition, Ch. Albeck has enriched the work and brought it up to date. But even more serious is the problem created by the fact that quite a number of works such as this, which are fundamental requirements for the understanding of major aspects of Judaism, are written in Hebrew. Without a knowledge of Hebrew it is almost hopeless to gain insight into this complex religion and its traditions: despite its limitations and its being out of date, there is no counterpart either in English or in any European language to I. H. Weiss's *Dor Dor ve-Doreshav* (several times reprinted; I have before me the Wilna, Verlag der Buchhandlung L. Goldenberg in Elisawetgrad, 1911 edition), which attempted to trace the development of the tradition that became normative for Judaism through the authoritative role of the Oral Torah and the Talmud. (On this work, see at least S. Schechter's essay, "The History of Jewish Tradition," in *Studies in Judaism*, First Series [N.Y., The Macmillan Co., 1896; Philadelphia, Jewish Publication Society, 1938], pp. 182–212.) Or, again, for critical study of the development and character of the Mishnah, that "code" which is the cornerstone of the whole talmudic structure, one must still turn and return to the literature from Z. Frankel's *Darke ha-Mishnah* (Warsaw, M. L. Cailingold, 1923) to J. N. Epstein's *Mabo le-Nusah ha-Mishnah* (Jerusalem, the author, 5708–1947)—there is no substitute for such works.

It is tempting to give illustration after illustration to make adequately vivid how dependent one is on Hebrew, not only for the study of the religion's primary sources (which goes without saying), but also for access to responsible and illuminating secondary ones. But, to avoid belaboring the point, only one more example will be given. Without G. Scholem's two-volume work on Sabbatai Zevi, *Shabtai Zvi* (Tel Aviv, Am Obed, 1956–57), the first and extremely important stages of a revolutionary seventeenth-century messianic movement cannot be adequately understood. (In his *Major Trends*, on which see below, Scholem deals briefly with this subject.)

The language problem is serious enough, but there are two further problems which cannot be solved by a simple formula (that is, to learn the languages) and to which attention must be directed even in a bibliographical essay, although they are of more than bibliographical consequence. The first is that when a work describes the religion as it is reflected in the primary literary source—the Bible, let us say—to what extent is the description a description of the actual religious mentality and practice of the moment and to what extent is it a description of the idealized formulation? Are the collections of laws incorporated in the Pentateuch, for example, a record of generally accepted norms of conduct (when? right after the conquest of the Holy Land? during the period of the kings? in post-exilic times?) or merely idealized constructions of priestly or prophetic demands while the current religious practice, sincerely followed and faithfully obeyed and conventionally approved, was something different? When in postbiblical times a particular ceremony is described in the Mishnah—say, the ordeal for the suspected wife (Numbers 5 : 11–31)—how much, if any, of the description is an actual account of the proceedings, and how much is merely the result of academic imagining and exegetical exercise?

This is a serious problem for the historian; but it is no less a problem for the bibliographer who wishes to select a partial but properly representative list of works which describe the Jewish religion *as it was*. This kind of problem, however, faces the student of other religions too. Special complications arise for Judaism because there is an indivisible connection between the people called Jews and the religion called Judaism. Often the very character of the religion can be understood only in terms of the history of the Jews. Had it not been for the destruction of the Jerusalem Temple in the first century, presumably Jewish worship would still include institutions now of archeological interest only—or of eschatological yearning. The specific texture or flavor of Jewish cultural life was often determined by conditions governing the particular country where one of the diaspora communities was located (for example, the intellectual idiom of eleventh-century Spanish Jewry was quite different from that of Franco-German Jewries of the same century), and proper appreciation of the religious life of the Jews involves frequently not only the study of purely religious expression but also attention to the history of the people. Furthermore, since so much *cultural* activity was related to the religious sources and the religious life—poetry being the poetry of the synagogue, philosophy being a rational defense of the faith, grammar being an attempt to explain holy scriptures, and so on—the study of Judaism always becomes more profound and more revealing as more and more attention is paid to the study of Jewish literature as a whole—at least so long as we deal with Judaism and Jewish life up to the beginnings of modern times (let us say, up to the latter part of the eighteenth century). And even in modern times, by way of one final word, much of so-called secular Jewish literature can be properly understood only against the background of—as in response to or reaction against—the religious life and ideal.

II. JUDAISM AND THE JEWS

The relationship between Judaism and the Jews, the extraordinary vitality of the religion and the people under various and frequently disastrous circumstances, the continuity of a recognizable tradition despite varieties of adaptation, the role of the religion not only in the history of the Jews but in the history and context of the world, the future direction of Judaism as well as the future of the Jews—in short, the meaning of the total Jewish experience—have been subjects for reflection on the part of practically every serious Jewish thinker and historian. It would be most naive to imagine that such reflection began with modern times; in one form or another, the meaning of Jewish existence and experience is already contemplated by the prophets, is reflected upon by Philo and by the talmudic rabbis in many Midrashim, is a compelling theme for post-talmudic homilists and compilers of chronicles, and so on down through the centuries. On the other hand, it is very probably true that the modern formulation of questions about the meaning of Jewish experience is characterized by its nontheological idiom; even if the answer given in the end is not entirely dependent on exclusively rational categories, the modern man attempts to ask his question and to make answer in the vocabulary and framework which are independent of dogmatic considerations and credal imperatives. A great many essays have been written on the meaning of Judaism and the Jews, some in English. (Since below we shall be speaking of H. Graetz, let me mention his fine essay *Die Konstruktion der jüdischen Geschichte* [Berlin, Schocken Verlag, 1936], with an epilogue and useful bibliography.) We shall refer to four (but see by the way the essay by M. R. Cohen, "Philosophies of Jewish History," in the first volume of *Jewish Social Studies* [1939], pp. 39–72).

In S. M. Dubnow's *Jewish History* (Philadelphia, Jewish Publication Society of America, 1903) (a short book which appeared originally in 1893 as an essay in Russian) the distinguished historian and author of the *Weltgeschichte* does not yet make the sociological emphasis which characterized so much of his subsequent thinking and writing—that is, the emphasis on Jews and Judaism as a national minority culture and their autonomy within a larger majority political framework. But he does attempt to answer the question, "What is the essential meaning, what the spirit, of Jewish History?" After a compact review of Jewish history from its beginnings through the nineteenth century, Dubnow presents briefly what are to him the lessons of that long experience (his language is characteristically nineteenth-centuryish spiritual-idealistic): Jewry is a spiritual nation at all times permeated by a creative principle which is itself the product of religious, moral, and philosophical ideals; of historic memories; and of a consciousness that it has yet great deeds to accomplish in the future, as it accomplished them in the past. In the light of the events of the past three decades, there is even a kind of pathos to the last sentence of Dubnow's essay: "Jewish history in its entirety is the pledge of the spiritual union between the Jews and the rest of the nations."

Views much more characteristic of Dubnow's reflections on Jews and Jewish history are available in *Nationalism and History. Essays on Old and*

New Judaism by Simon Dubnow, by K. S. Pinson (Philadelphia, Jewish Publication Society of America, 1958) (in which, by the way, his essay *Jewish History* is reprinted). In his introductory essay Pinson also discusses Dubnow's theories of nationalism.

More philosophical, and possibly more profound, is the essay *Galut*, by Y. F. Baer (N.Y., Schocken Books, Inc., 1947), originally written in German. This work by the leading authority on the Jews in Christian Spain (Vol. I of his history has now been translated into English by L. Schoffman and issued by the Jewish Publication Society of America, Philadelphia, 1961, under the title *The History of the Jews in Christian Spain*) begins with the proposition that "because of the Jews' exalted consciousness of religious superiority and of their mission among the nations, a consciousness all the more infuriating because it exists in a nation totally without power," the Jew is inseparably bound up with Galut—that is, not only exile but all the outrages of being an exile, an alien. For Baer the principles historians employ when they attempt to understand and explain all other nations are inadequate for the understanding of Jewish history and experiences. That is not to say that economic and social and political and international forces do not operate within Jewish history, but that these "natural" laws fail to explain the Jewish character, the persistence of this tiny people that has been without the basic material equipment the successful nations have enjoyed. ". . . The history of the Jewish people remains distinct from the astrologically determined history of the nations (i.e., a history determined by causes operating within the finished framework of nature), for the Jewish people in its special relationship to God is removed from the context of natural law." Jewish history, therefore, follows its own laws. One may put it this way perhaps: whereas in his essay Dubnow's categories were spiritual and hopeful, Baer's are more forthrightly religious, growing particularly out of the cataclysm in German-Jewish life. This will explain why so much of the essay concentrates on aspects of redemption and messianism.

One Jewish thinker and writer very well-known among intellectuals of the Western world (his impact on some contemporary Protestant expression has been profound) is M. Buber. Much of his writing has been devoted to an exploration of the meaning of the Jewish spirit and the Jewish word and Jewish living, but for our immediate purpose the volume of essays called *Israel and the World. Essays in a Time of Crisis* (N.Y., Schocken Books, Inc., 1948) is probably most relevant. The essays were not all written at one time or for one particular audience; nevertheless, taken together, they "combine into a theory," as Buber says, "representing the teachings of Israel." For Buber the most essential fact of the Jewish faith is that history, of all nations and of every individual, is a dialogue with God; not dogma but encounter is of primary importance in Judaism. Under the headings "Jewish Religiosity," "Biblical Life," "Learning and Education" (in connection with the essays in this section it would be profitable to see Franz Rosenzweig, *On Jewish Learning*, ed. by N. N. Glatzer [N.Y., Schocken Books, Inc., 1955]), "Israel and the World," "Nationalism and Zion," Buber undertakes not only to "clarify the relation of certain aspects of Jewish thinking and Jewish living to contemporary intellectual movements," but also to "analyze and refute" whatever current ideologies within Jewish life lead to the weakening and defeat of the internal authentic Jewish teaching. Since the whole world of humanity is intended to achieve a genuine unity, that one nation (Israel) which once heard the charge and assented to it must so live, not merely as masses of individuals but entirely as a nation, as to bring true humanity into fulfillment. It is in terms like these that Buber finds the meaning of Judaism and the Jews; but in nothing less than terms like these does he see the meaning of Zionism too (see further below).

On the relationship of Jews and Judaism, it will be wise to consult also the opening chapter of S. W. Baron's multivolume history, *A Social and Religious History of the Jews* (N.Y., Columbia University Press, 1952–58; on this work, see further below). The essay in a sense serves to make prominent what are, to the author, the distinctive features of Jewish society and religion: the interdependence of Jews and Judaism, the historical-ethical direction given by the religion to what may have been in remote origins nature festivals, the ethical dimension of the chosen-people concept, the independence, ultimately, of the religion from the fate of any particular state or territory, simultaneous affirmation by Judaism of nationalism and universalism. It is the presence of these features within Judaism that gives both the people and the religion their particular insights into reality, their historical preoccupations, and the impulse toward achievement in certain directions.

Reflections more or less along the lines of the four works we have referred to occur in many other writings to which reference will be made under other rubrics. One work, written in Hebrew, Yehezkel Kaufmann's *Gola Ve-Nekar* (*In Exile and among Aliens*; 1929–32, Tel Aviv, Debir; 2nd ed., 1954), would especially have to be consulted by the serious student concerned with the philosophy of history, for Kaufmann's two-volume work is one of the most serious and thoroughgoing historical-sociological investigations of Jewish history and fate in any language, and by any thinker. To attempt to summarize this work in a sentence or two would be almost caricaturing it, for it is a detailed review of basic issues and movements from biblical days to the present time. Only against Kaufmann's full discussion can justice be done to his emphasis on the ideals of national redemption, of which not even independent statehood is the realization, let alone fulfillment. To Kaufmann what national redemption involves is a completely radical reorientation on the part of the people as it recognizes in itself the *need* for redemption from the political and cultural servitude of generations of dependence on others and the yearning to lose its individuality.

At all events, whatever the direction taken by any particular thinker on the theme of Jews and Judaism, one point is clear (and perhaps this is the most significant fact about such works): none of them is able to assume that this relationship, and the destiny that may be in store for it, is only accidental, and that, therefore, no special meanings are to be sought. On the contrary, even when the reflection is carried on in purely secular discourse, all of these thinkers try to clarify the organic nature of that relationship and to evaluate its significance in terms not only of the past but also of the future. The relation of Jews and Judaism, in short, is for them not only a datum of past history or current events but also a condition for the future vitality of the religion and achievement of the people, whatever that may be. Thus this very relationship between Jews and Judaism brings the student of Judaism to a study of the history of the Jews.

III. HISTORIES AND THE STANDARD WORKS

As for full-scale histories, one inevitably begins with H. Graetz's six-volume *History of the Jews* (Philadelphia, Jewish Publication Society of America, 1891, but frequently reprinted), and again I must apologize for not being able to refer to the original German work (*Geschichte der Juden*, 11 vols. in 13, 1897–1911) with its copious notes, or to the Hebrew translation, which is also rich in notes of its own (although because of the Russian censor, some of the German notes had to be omitted). The English version is a condensation of the original German volumes but has no notes at all; however, while in the original the account went from the beginnings to 1848, in the English version the history is continued (not too fully) to 1870. A companion volume on Jewish life from the middle of the nineteenth century to Hitler's war against the Jews was published in 1944 by the Jewish Publication Society of America, Philadelphia, I. Elbogen, *A Century of Jewish Life*.

Of course, in many ways Graetz's work is outdated; major sources of Jewish history which were discovered at the end of the last and beginning of the present century were unknown to him, let alone momentous discoveries of recent decades and the results of archeological work. Moreover, on some subjects Graetz disqualified himself: he was totally impatient with mysticism in any of its manifestations, and he was insensitive to the color of life in the eastern European centers. Even more serious is the charge by the critical historians that Graetz saw Jewish history principally as response to persecution, as suffering on the one hand and spiritual and literary creation on the other.

The fact remains that Graetz's performance is still overwhelming. His single-handed attempt at a *complete* critical accounting of Jewish history from the beginnings to the mid-nineteenth century, not only using the results of research by other men but himself furnishing the material he would require in synthesis, is one of the principal achievements of nineteenth-century Jewish scholarship. Especially because he wrote with fervor, his work is still eminently readable, and for a coherent account (even if sometimes we would prefer a different scheme or organization), his work is still where one begins. Even when one disagrees, he does not pass Graetz by.

More sociological, and much more understanding of the eastern European milieu and its movements and personalities, is S. Dubnow's ten-volume work, to which we have already referred, *Die Weltgeschichte des jüdischen Volkes* (1925–29). A Hebrew translation of this work exists, but unfortunately no English one (his three-volume *History of the Jews in Russia and Poland*, tr. by I. Friedlaender [Philadelphia, Jewish Publication Society of America, 1916–20] is an excellent counterbalance to Graetz). Dubnow's history takes much more into account social and economic influences than does Graetz, his attention to purely secular manifestations is much more lively than is Graetz's, and the organization of his subject matter along the lines of development within different geographical centers makes his chapters more immediately comprehensible than does a purely chronological scheme.

An ambitious and impressive undertaking, still in the course of appearing, is S. W. Baron's *A Social and Religious History of the Jews*. An earlier and shorter version in three volumes first appeared in 1937 (N.Y., Columbia University Press), but in 1952 the longer version began to appear. To date eight volumes plus an index volume have been published (N.Y. and Philadelphia), covering the history from the beginnings to 1200. Baron's work is particularly noteworthy on three scores. First, it provides one of the most comprehensive bibliographies on Jews and Judaism one is likely to find anywhere; the references in the notes especially are a rich source of assistance not only to a beginner but often to specialists as well. Second, the organization of themes and problems offers a fresh approach for students of Jewish history. Baron is concerned with principal motifs of the history rather than aspects of chronicling, either by way of centuries or geographical centers: one may say that Baron is eager to describe not events, even major ones, but major patterns of development. Thus the *History* is not a narrative but a commentary on the narrative one has learned in other and earlier works. Third—and this obviously is related to the second point—Baron has approached Jewish history with the skills and perspective of the modern general social scientist. His approach is familiar to the modern student of general history. By exploring, for example, demographic factors, by paying especially close attention to economic and sociological influences in the milieu at large, Baron has often provided explanations for the dynamics of Jewish life which were not anticipated, inevitably, by earlier historians. The *Social and Religious History* is thus a characteristic *modern* work; that is to say, it is the product of the advances made by the social science disciplines in modern times and an awareness of modern historiographical tendencies.

As a companion to Baron's *History*, it is often instructive to examine his three-volume study of *The Jewish Community* (Philadelphia, Jewish Publication Society of America, 1942) from the biblical Palestinian municipality down to the period of the American revolution. The principal focus of the work is on the structure of the European community of the Middle Ages and early modern times. Here too we see Baron preoccupied with the social institution, the features of and the forces operative in a complex societal reality. And while he is expressly aware of the ambiguities of the term "community" in relation to diverse Jewish communities in the Diaspora, his analysis helps create coherence in what might otherwise be a confused picture with a host of disjointed facts—and this in a universe of discourse especially congenial to the modern social scientist and historian.

There is today no longer any dearth of shorter, one-volume histories of the Jews, though unfortunately not many are either reliable or particularly illuminating. The three works we shall refer to have at least the merit of trustworthiness and competence in understanding the original sources, despite their other limitations. *A History of the Jewish People* by M. L. Margolis and A. Marx (Philadelphia, Jewish Publication Society of America, 1927 and frequently reprinted), is, strictly speaking, a chronicle of events, persons, and achievements, with hardly any attempt at interpretation or explanation. As a handbook of "facts," it is still perhaps the most convenient and accurate single-volume collection.

A History of the Jews by S. Grayzel (Philadelphia, Jewish Publication Society of America, 1947) begins its account, not with the biblical period, but with the Babylonian exile and goes down to the end of World War II. Grayzel's volume is essentially a textbook, the kind of work one would use for classroom instruction, and while it suffers from a homiletical tone of voice and point of view, it is by and large a dependable account of Jewish experience and achievement. Furthermore, the author's attitude can at least suggest which aspects of Jewish history have taken on special value for Jews devoted to their tradition and settled in Western countries.

The third one-volume work is a collaborative enterprise by a number of scholars, *Great Ages and Ideas of the Jewish People*, ed. by L. W. Schwarz (Toronto, Random House of Canada, Ltd., 1956). As the title itself reveals, the various chapters are essentially essays attempting to present principal intellectual and cultural developments during key periods of Jewish history, from biblical days to modern times. Perhaps the aim of the work may best be suggested by the following sentence from the editor's introduction: "We do not hesitate to say that four thousand years of experience have evolved a cluster of ideas and values that are uniquely Jewish and that remain significant for modern men and women." In other words, the individual chapters seek, each for its own period, to find the principal ideas growing out of the Jewish experience and governing Jewish expression and expectation.

There are, even in English, a number of historical studies of particular Jewries in particular countries, and of particular periods, to which the student with special interests will turn (and to some of which reference will be made below in relevant sections). But if it is true that a knowledge of what was happening to the Jews will often make the emphases of their religion intelligible, it is even more true that a knowledge of Jewish culture, especially literature, will introduce one to the intellectual and articulate form—to the very vocabulary, one might say—of the religious substance.

Here, too, we are not dealing with an altogether simple phenomenon. Despite the strong attachment of Jewish intellectual activity to religious living and conduct, one is often hard put to it to classify certain Jewish writings even before modern times—even before, that is, Jewish society, like Western society in general, was secularized. First of all, one might say that the abundance of secular medieval Hebrew poetry, for example, is *not* relevant to the religion. But, secondly and more importantly, a historian of literature might well and justly classify certain works as studies (let us say) in lexicography and grammar—categories which to a modern Westerner hardly suggest religious exercise. (And possibly for the original grammarian too *as he worked*, the purely technical and substantive problems of his work proved so entirely engaging that for the time being he too thought more in terms of his immediate problems than in terms of the religious background to which his work belonged.) Nevertheless, these works may constitute an active expression of religious concern—an undertaking, for instance, to explain the language or the teaching of a sacred text. Especially since for Judaism the study and interpretation of sacred texts became a paramount activity in *piety*, and the range of study and interpretation was as extensive as the resources and the age provided, a considerable amount of Jewish literature has direct bearing on Jewish religious thought and the very life of the religion. That is why some study of Jewish literature is germane to the study of Judaism as a religion. And a convenient survey of this literature from the close of the Bible down to almost the present is available in the five volumes by M. Waxman, *A History of Jewish Literature* (N.Y., Thomas Yoseloff, Inc., latest edition, 1960): the discussions do attempt to be comprehensive and incorporate the results of much modern research.

Finally, among such general accounts might be mentioned several useful standard works of reference, most prominent of which (though in many ways outdated) is *The Jewish Encyclopedia* in twelve volumes (N.Y., Funk & Wagnalls, Co., 1901–06). Leading scholars and authorities were among the contributors of articles, and, especially in the first few volumes, there are a number of studies that are still of prime significance. The discussions of classical literature and subjects uppermost in the minds of nineteenth-century western European Jewish scholars are especially valuable. In German and not completed because of the Hitler disaster (only ten volumes appeared through "Lyra," Berlin, 1928–34) is the *Encyclopedia Judaica*; like the *Jewish Encyclopedia* in English, this is a very serious work on the highest possible standards, with many articles by very distinguished scholars who incorporated the results of their own (and others') major research. *The Universal Jewish Encyclopedia*, 10 vols. (N.Y., Universal Jewish Encyclopedia Inc., 1939–43), is largely a popular work, particularly for the historical subjects covered more fully in the older *Jewish Encyclopedia*; but on certain subjects related to modern times—above all, events and developments in the twentieth century—it is not only more up to date but at times truly extensive in treatment.

In addition to the encyclopedias, there are available two excellent works which present not only surveys of Jewish history but also studies of the wide range of Jewish thought and expression and experiences in both the past and the present. They are both popular in that they deliberately avoid the speech of the technical monograph and the specialist's tone of voice, but the serious and responsible presentations are admirable as introductions to the study of numerous aspects of Judaism. One is *The Jewish People: Past and Present* (N.Y., Central Yiddish Culture Organization, 1946–52) in four volumes (based principally on an earlier version in Yiddish); the other is *The Jews: Their History, Culture and Religion*, ed. by L. Finkelstein, 3rd ed. (N.Y., Harper & Brothers, 1960), which is more extensive than the two earlier editions. Both works are handsomely published. Especially valuable are the bibliographies they provide in connection with each subject discussed. Above all, they convey a genuine sense of the dynamic character of Jewish life—its manifoldness, its tensions and resolutions, its response to external and internal pressures in the different periods of its existence. And in both a concern for continued Jewish existence and achievement is evident. (For an earlier collection of essays on what might be called aspects of the Hebrew and Jewish genius, still both readable and instructive, see E. R. Bevan and C. Singer, *The Legacy of Israel* [Oxford, Clarendon Press, 1927]).

It is probably true to say that such works are themselves illustrative of a ferment or restlessness or vitality within Jewish society, especially since the third decade of the present century. As a result of critical and historical research of the previous hundred years, the beginnings of summary formulation and synthesis could finally be contemplated. Moreover, as a result of the shift of center of gravity, particularly from eastern Europe to America, and the rise of a generation whose language was English, whose sense of relationship to a Jewish past was fading, and whose identity as Jews might to them be meaningless except on terms of ethnic liability, it was inevitable that Jewish scholars should once again (as in previous ages) undertake to explore the origins and direction of Jewish existence in an idiom which would be comprehensible to contemporaries. Furthermore, the extent of the disasters which overtook Jews in Europe and various parts of Asia and Africa unavoidably stirred up a renewed self-consciousness among Jews, one of whose phases was bound to be a re-examination of what they were and what they could expect of and for themselves. It is a safe guess that just as in recent general fiction Jewish themes and characters have begun to appear with a frequency unanticipated early in the century, so in the next two to three decades there will be increasing attention to Judaism by Jewish and non-Jewish students of religion and culture and social science (compare, for example, the essay by Edmund Wilson, "The Need for Judaic Studies" in his *A Piece of My Mind* [N.Y., Farrar, Straus & Cudahy, Inc., 1956] pp. 151–8). And the existence of the independent State of Israel will add to the liveliness of curiosity and speculation and argument.

IV. A FEW REMARKS ON PRIMARY SOURCES IN TRANSLATION

The very circumstances which have led to the creation of a growing body of literature in English *on* Judaism have, at the same time, led to the translation into English of primary literary sources, hitherto either not translated at all or translated into one of the other European languages (most often in the past century into German). Although it may not seem to be immediately germane to our discussion of books in English, something of the vigorous efforts being made in the present to revive preoccupation with the roots of the classical intellectual and religious tradition may be conveyed by the fact that in the State of Israel basic works of research composed in the past century in German (the work of Zunz and Geiger and Goldziher, for example) are now being translated into Hebrew and brought up to date through the addition of notes. These include not only secondary sources, but primary ones as well: a Hebrew translation of the Babylonian Talmud (from the original Aramaic) is being prepared, and substantial portions of the Kabbalistic classic, the *Zohar*, have been translated into Hebrew (and also rearranged in organization to help study particular motifs.)

Of course, there is more than one reason for such developments. Evidently, even with a knowledge of Hebrew one may be far removed from the basic texts and sentiments of the classical religious tradition. The point is that in order properly to appreciate why increased activity of translation into English is taking place, it is necessary to look upon that activity not as some accidental and local phenomenon, but against the larger background of contemporary Jewish life as a whole. That the primary sources require translation everywhere is a sign not only of the results of alienation, but also of the resolution to recover for a new generation a sense of immediate kinship with the past. And the translations into Hebrew as well as English must be understood as an expression of that same resolution. But obviously the problem is much more serious where there is no knowledge of Hebrew at all.

Rather than list each and every work now available in English translation, we will refer only to some general series of publications; and only in the appropriate sections will specific reference be made to the relevant individual items. At this point it will be sufficient therefore if we call attention to the following: the Schiff Classics of the Jewish Publication Society of America; the translations by the scholars associated with the Soncino Press in England: *The Babylonian Talmud*, under the editorship of I. Epstein (London, Soncino Press, 1936), *Midrash Rabbah*, under the editorship of H. Friedman and M. Simon (1939), and *The Zohar*, by H. Sperling and M. Simon, the various Jewish texts published in translation by scholars for the Society for Promoting Christian Knowledge; the translations published by the East and West Library in England (Phaidon Press, Ltd.); and the Yale University Judaica Series. For apocrypha and pseudepigrapha there is not only the well-known collection in two volumes under the editorship of R. H. Charles, *The Apocrypha and Pseudepigrapha of the Old Testament in English* (Oxford, Clarendon Press, 1913), but a series of text and translation, in the Dropsie College Jewish Apocryphal Literature Series, of which five volumes have thus far appeared.

V. ON THE RELIGION OF ISRAEL AND THE HEBREW SCRIPTURES

Even if one limits himself to works in the English language, there is such a fantastic volume of studies on the history, literature, and religion of Israel and the Hebrew Scriptures (what Christians call the Old Testament), that if we were to do no more than list a long bibliography, even incomplete, the titles themselves would run on, seemingly endlessly. But this would achieve only a hypnotic effect. We shall deliberately choose only a few works—naturally such choice does reflect a personal value judgment—and content ourselves with the following additional observation: in several of the works referred to there are excellent bibliographical lists, which will lead the student to further discussion of the particular subject he decides to explore.

So closely related to the problems of the *literature* of the Hebrew Scriptures are the problems of the *religion*, that some orientation toward the literature is required before one can properly appreciate the discussions and presentations of the religion. For an approach characteristic of what is called the "higher critical school," associated especially with the epochal work of J. Wellhausen (for the English reader there is available, now in paperback, his *Prolegomena to the History of Ancient Israel* [Toronto, Longmans, Green & Co., Inc., 1957])—the different documentary sources it distinguishes, the dates it attaches to these respective sources, its view of the line of development of Israelite thought and faith—and for detailed discussion in defense of that approach, plus a very full bibliography and documentation, R. H. Pfeiffer's *Introduction to the Old Testament* (N.Y., Harper & Brothers, 1941) is about as thorough and painstaking a one-volume work on the subject as is available. On the basis of conclusions arrived at by such literary analysis, there are many histories of Israelite religion, and we shall mention three: H. P. Smith, *The Religion of Israel* (N.Y., Charles Scribner's Sons, 1914), W. O. E. Oesterley and T. H. Robinson, *Hebrew Religion, Its Origin and Development* (N.Y., The Macmillan Co., 1930), and, most recently, R. H. Pfeiffer's own posthumous *Religion in the Old Testament* (N.Y., Harper & Brothers, 1961), edited by C. C. Forman. It would be preposterous to say that these three works, and others that are close to them in outlook and spirit, agree in every detail or present the same outline of the religion from beginning to end. Nor are they necessarily the best of their kind. But they are representative and essentially united by the following: a robust dismissal of the possibility that a number of traditions ascribed to the Age of Moses is credible; a conviction that most of the narratives about the periods before the Conquest of the Promised Land are later legends pure and simple; an evolutionary hypothesis that explains the development of the religion of Israel from primitive conceptions and institutions, in the beginnings regarded as legitimate and proper, to an exalted monotheism of profound spiritual and ethical content arrived at gradually and only in the course of the prophetic period; and a strong feeling that notions and practices and expressions recorded by Scripture, if they can be compared with parallels in other cultures, almost certainly have the same meaning in Scripture as they have in the other contexts. (For a strong protest against this last presumption see N. H. Snaith, *The Distinctive Ideas of the Old Testament* [Philadelphia, Westminster Press, 1946].)

Altogether opposed to these conclusions, and indeed to all the more or less current accounts of Israelite religion, is Y. Kaufmann, whose great work *The Religion of Israel* has finally been superbly abridged and translated from the original eight volumes in Hebrew by M. Greenberg (Chicago, University of Chicago Press, 1960: strictly speaking, the translation and abridgement are of the first seven volumes). Kaufmann accepts the idea that different documentary sources were combined to form the present Pentateuch no less than do the critics generally, but, by attentive study of these very sources, and especially by close analysis of the critical argumentation in defense of the chronological scheme imposed on those sources, he is led to fundamental revisions of dating and a presentation of the religion of Israel radically and most profoundly different from that at which the critics arrive. In the first place, Kaufmann derives from the biblical sources themselves the concept that Israel's monotheism was not an idea gradually attained (after many centuries) and then only by an intellectual, prophetic, or priestly elite, but, on the contrary, was an original, primary intuitive conception held by the folk at large, governing all Israelite thinking from the Mosaic period on (to such a degree that no longer can one find in the biblical record an adequate or just understanding of the pagan religions of Israel's neighbors; these religions to Israel are mere fetishism). Second, the added knowledge today of the high civilizations in the ancient Near East makes unwarranted many of the critics' assumptions about the necessary late dates for some forms of biblical speculation. In the third place, although Israelite life and thought were rooted in the high civilizations of the ancient Near East, a comparative study of religious forms (cult, mythology, magic, morality, notions of sin) underscores the *essential* differences that separate pagan religions from the religion of Israel. The distinguishing mark of pagan thought is "the idea that there exists a realm of being prior to the gods and above them, upon which the gods depend, and whose decrees they must obey," while "the biblical religious idea, visible in the earliest strata, permeating even the 'magical' legends, is of a supernal God, above every cosmic law, fate, and compulsion; unborn, unbegetting. . . . An unfettered divine will transcends all being—this is the mark of biblical religion and that which sets it apart from all the religions of the earth." Biblical religion is thus *absolutely* different from the religion of the pagan world. (In this connection see also the important essay by M. Greenberg, "Some Postulates of Biblical Criminal Law" in *Yehezkel Kaufmann Jubilee Volume* [Jerusalem, 1960], pp. 5–28.)

Whatever else Kaufmann's biblical studies may accomplish (and their influence was felt among those scholars who were reading his volumes as they appeared in Hebrew from 1937 on), it is clear that they have made much more tentative a number of propositions which had been regarded as basic and almost beyond dispute by European and American biblical criticism. This is particularly true as regards the relationship between Pentateuch and Former Prophets literature and the writings of the literary prophets.

Kaufmann's history of the religion of Israel does represent a milestone in biblical studies (see in this connection N. M. Sarna, "From Wellhausen to Kaufmann," *Midstream* [N.Y., Summer, 1961], pp. 64–74 and, even earlier [Sept., 1950], H. L. Ginsberg's essay, "New Trends in Biblical Criticism," in *Commentary*, pp. 276–84). But it would be inaccurate to leave the impression that, except for his challenge, studies of Israelite religion have otherwise been uniformly written along the lines suggested by the classical *literary* criticism. Archeology and the advances made in the knowledge of ancient Near Eastern languages have also had a strong effect on biblical studies (and yet in this connection see the remarks by J. J. Finkelstein, "The Bible, Archaeology and History," in *Commentary* [April, 1959], pp. 341–9); inevitably this has led to reconsideration of the character of the religion. Especially noteworthy of the new trends in biblical research has been the distinguished work of A. Alt, whose investigations of what he calls "territorial history" have related the problems of Palestinian events and records to the larger Near Eastern framework as a whole and thus made intelligible the information provided in biblical data by the data available in extra biblical sources or resulting from fastidious topographical and inscriptional studies. Alt writes in German (see his 3 vols., *Kleine Schriften zur Geschichte des Volkes Israel* [München, C. H. Beck, 1953–59]), but the English reader may get some notion of the point of view of Alt and his school from M. Noth, *The History of Israel*, tr. by S. Godman (London, Adam & Charles Black, Ltd., 1958).

The many writings of W. F. Albright have also been influential in this respect, and in particular his two volumes *From the Stone Age to Christianity* (first published in 1940 but it is important to consult the latest edition, [Baltimore, Johns Hopkins Press, 1957] because of the considerable revisions) and *Archaeology and the Religion of Israel* (Baltimore, Johns Hopkins Press, 1942; latest edition, 1959), which is both a complement and amplification of the former volume. Albright has insisted that biblical history can become a scientific discipline only through archeological research, and that research, he declares, "has confirmed the substantial historicity of Old Testament tradition"; though divergences from historical fact are present in the biblical record, he feels these are explicable as due to oral tradition, but they do not seriously affect the historical picture. And his emphasis is perhaps best conveyed in his own words, for they reveal at the same time the direction of concern and interpretation adopted by a number of Albright's students (such as G. E. Wright and F. M. Cross, Jr.) in their writings (see, for example, G. E. Wright, *God Who Acts* [Chicago, Henry Regnery Co., 1952]; or, even earlier, *The Challenge of Israel's Faith* [Chicago, University of Chicago Press, 1944]) as they contemplate the nature of biblical religion: "The tradition of Israel represents Moses as a monotheist; the evidence of ancient Oriental religious history, combined with the most rigorous critical treatment of Israelite literary sources, points in exactly the same direction. The tradition of Israel represents the Prophets as preachers and reformers, not as religious innovators; rigid historical and philological exegesis of our sources agrees with tradition." For the student of biblical literature and religion, the very tenor of such statements has constituted a challenge to re-examine the religion of Israel in the light of newly acquired data and the alternative perspective and development they suggest.

Special mention must be made of R. de Vaux's *Ancient Israel: Its Life and Institutions*, tr. by J. McHugh (N.Y., McGraw-Hill Book Co., Inc., 1961), which has just appeared, for it incorporates the latest results of literary and archeological research. Its detailed descriptions of the family and the civil and political, military, and religious institutions are a model of compactness and careful statement; it is no less valuable for its critical appraisal of current theories about the origins, and meaning, of some of Israel's institutions.

For histories of Israel, T. H. Robinson and W. O. E. Oesterley, *History of Israel* (Oxford, Oxford University Press, 1st ed., 1932, and reprinted several times), while in some respects outdated, is still an excellent historical summary; but now the student should also consult J. Bright, *A History of Israel* (Philadelphia, Westminster Press, 1959). For introductions to the Old Testament, in addition to Pfeiffer's *Introduction* referred to earlier, the little book by M. L. Margolis, *The Hebrew Scriptures in the Making* (Philadelphia, Jewish Publication Society of America, 1922) might be used with profit. G. E. Wright and F. V. Filson, *The Westminster Historical Atlas to the Bible*, rev. ed. (Philadelphia, Westminster Press, 1956) is an excellent volume. In the field of comparative studies of texts and rituals in the ancient Near East, the texts and pictures assembled by J. B. Pritchard in *Ancient Near Eastern Texts Relating to the Old Testament*, 2nd ed. (Princeton, Princeton University Press, 1955) and *The Ancient Near East in Pictures Relating to the Old Testament* (Princeton, Princeton University Press, 1954) are indispensable; a stimulating discussion of ritual and myth in the ancient Near East is presented by T. H. Gaster, *Thespis* (N.Y., Henry Schuman Inc., 1950). On "Authority and Law in the Ancient Orient," consult the symposium prepared as a *Supplement to the Journal of the American Oriental Society*, Supp. 10–17, No. 17 (July-Sept., 1954).

New translations of the Bible, commentaries on individual books of the Bible, and biblical encyclopedias all help in various ways to arrive at a better understanding of the religion. In recent years a number of textbooks for school use have attempted a synthesis of technical discussion of the individual books of the Hebrew Bible, history of the people of Israel, and theological discussion of principal religious teachings of the Hebrew Scriptures, particularly as compared with the ideas to be found in important ancient Near Eastern literary sources; such works may serve the general reader, as well as the student in the classroom. See for example B. W. Anderson, *Understanding the Old Testament* (Englewood Cliffs, N.J., Prentice-Hall, Inc., 1957) and N. K. Gottwald, *A Light to the Nations* (N.Y., Harper & Brothers, 1959); in the latter, there are thumbnail characterizations of many works in English recommended for further reading.

A final word about one more work, J. Pedersen's *Israel, Its Life and Culture* (Oxford, Oxford University Press, Vols. 1–2, 1926, Vols. 3–4, 1946), which explores patiently and in detail social institutions and, above all, the psychology behind and within key biblical concepts. By penetrating into the thinking process that inheres in the terms for these key concepts, this instructive study of biblical anthropology is able to suggest the ideas that governed Israelite mentality, the thoughts associated with various forms of conduct and acts and expressions, and the auxiliary notions that cluster about a word as it is employed in a specific statement. As the richness of these terms is uncovered and their movement is traced, something of the depth of biblical religion is apprehended. At the same time, it is likely that through such analysis and interpretation one can discern those elements, or categories, which lie at the base of all the biblical literary sources, the late ones no less than the earliest ones, and thus examine the literature as a unit and not merely as an assembly, fortuitous or tendentious, of independent documents. Nevertheless, see the strong protest by J. Barr, *The Semantics of Biblical Language* (Oxford, Oxford University Press, 1961).

VI. IN CONTACT WITH THE GREEKS

Products of Greek, and especially Athenian, industry apparently made their way to Palestine, as to other western parts of the Persian empire, even prior to the time of Alexander the Great; and while in the middle of the fourth century B.C. a decline in trade with Athens set in, both archeological and literary sources reveal that Jewish life in Palestine not merely could not escape Hellenistic influence but in a sense received such influence without hostility, particularly from the late fourth century and mid-third century B.C. on. The encounter of Judaism with Hellenism was to have major consequences, not only in political and materialistic, but also in intellectual and religious, spheres; and, fortunately, there are available in English several good studies to make this encounter and its consequences vivid. M. I. Rostovtzeff's monumental *Social and Economic History of the Hellenistic World* (Oxford, Clarendon Press, 1941)—and for the later period see his *Social and Economic History of the Roman Empire* (Oxford, Clarendon Press, 1957)—is obviously devoted to the Hellenistic world at large, not merely to Palestine. But precisely this extensive treatment helps put events and developments within Palestine into proper perspective by making it possible for the student of Judaism to appreciate why some aspects of Hellenism could almost imperceptibly penetrate Jewish thought and conduct, with hardly a murmur of protest; why other aspects would produce a spirit of outright rejection; and, above all, why still others—though at times passively accepted—would become subjects for strong feelings and debate in the course of strained relations between Jews and Gentiles. Even this is hardly a just summary of the effects of the encounter of Hellenism and Judaism: a not unknown phenomenon of the millennium from about the fourth century B.C. to the fifth century A.D. is this at times severe general criticism of the ways of the Gentiles, on the one hand, and the innocent (and deliberate too!) adoption of particular notions and customs and even turns of speech which are not part of the earlier biblical tradition, on the other. This should hardly surprise us, for the truism that realities are subtler than rules had best be recalled to mind again and again in the study of Judaism from the time Greek ideas and artifacts came to the attention of Jews until the classical forms of the Jewish religion were crystallized.

A brief and still useful account of Jewish history from the Babylonian captivity in the sixth century B.C. to the fourth century A.D. is available in M. Radin's *The Jews among the Greeks and Romans* (Philadelphia, Jewish Publication Society of America, 1915). Unlike writers like Willrich, for example, Radin does attempt to understand the sentiments of the Jews in their response to and reaction against the political and intellectual milieu in which they found themselves. The volume is by now too elementary, however. Much more instructive is *Hellenistic Civilization and the Jews by* V. Tcherikover, tr. from the Hebrew by S. Applebaum (Philadelphia, Jewish Publication Society of America, 1959), which investigates "the material foundation of Jewish life in the Hellenistic period, and the political, economic and public bases of Jewish life in the Greek world" and discusses religious and literary questions only insofar as these bear on the material aspects. Tcherikover does not limit himself to a study of Hellenism in Palestine but studies also the effects of this civilization in the Diaspora. In effect, this means principally (but definitely not exclusively) Alexandria; and in this connection, the student will find it profitable to read the introductory essay, "Prolegomena," in V. A. Tcherikover and A. Fuks, *Corpus Papyrorum Judaicorum*, Vol. I (Cambridge, Mass., Harvard University Press, 1957), pp. 1–111, which gives an account of Egyptian Jewry down to the seventh century in the Byzantine Period.

Since we are dealing with the over-all theme of Hellenism and Judaism, it is important to call attention to the many-volumed and major work by E. R. Goodenough, *Jewish Symbols in the Greco-Roman Period* (the first three volumes appeared in 1953 in the Bollingen Series, N.Y., Pantheon Books, Inc.; to date eight volumes have been published, and at least three more are to be included). This extremely impressive, pioneering, and challenging collection, description, and discussion of artistic representations in Jewish tombs, homes, and synagogues, on household and ornamental objects, buildings, and sarcophagi furnishes us with the very realia one needs to supplement the picture that emerges otherwise from purely literary sources. The data assembled are not only material for the filling in of historical outlines but raise the fundamental question of the conception of Judaism held by the Jews themselves in Hellenistic-Roman times (note, for example, C. H. Kraeling's discussion in his volume *The Synagogue of Dura* [New Haven, Yale University Press, 1956], pp. 340ff.). Granted that even within a particular tradition there are dissenting groups and points of view (and on sectarians see further below); what in the last analysis was the *normative* conception? Or are we still in a time of flux, and, strictly speaking, has no one particular view triumphed as normative? This need not necessarily suggest that the Judaism reflected by midrashic-talmudic sources is unrepresentative of Judaism of the time, nor that the artifacts demonstrate the existence of a different kind of Judaism; but perhaps current interpretations of rabbinic sources are still too narrowly, too partially formed. Even the literary texts may reveal hitherto only partially understood details when the realities this art reflects are taken into account.

The meaning of Judaism's contact with Hellenism is nowhere so beautifully and fastidiously analyzed as in the writings of E. J. Bickerman. His studies are primary not only for a proper chart of the historical course of events but also for the appreciation of religious consequences. It would be wise, indeed, for the student to begin with Bickerman's essay on "The Historical Foundations of Postbiblical Judaism" in L. Finkelstein's first volume of *The Jews* (N.Y., Harper & Brothers, 1949), pp. 70–114 (cited above), for here the orientation provided toward the whole period of the Second Commonwealth applies to subsequent periods of Judaism no less. Because he never loses sight of "the polarity of Jerusalem and the Dispersion," Bickerman escapes many superficialities which unfortunately are still current (for example, the idea that what distinguishes Diaspora Judaism from Palestinian Judaism is that the former adapted itself happily to Hellenistic civilization while the latter utterly rejected it). But, more positive and important is that Bickerman is sensitive to the richness and complexity of Jewish civilization in Hellenistic times, and, once again, reference must be made to a work not in English: his brilliant German volume, *Der Gott der Makkabäer* (Berlin, Schocken Verlag, 1937). It is the best discussion of the events which led to the Maccabean revolt and the *religious* crisis of the age, of the conflict *within Jewry* as a result of the resistance to attempts on the part of Hellenized Jews in Palestine to "modernize" an ancestral faith. Since preservation and change are like two opposing forces pressing simultaneously on a living tradition, Bickerman's study makes understandable not only the specific chapter of Jewish history to which his study is devoted but suggests as well an approach to the understanding of developments in subsequent periods. For example, Bickerman demonstrates beautifully in his little book *The Maccabees* (N.Y., Schocken Books, Inc., 1947) how the triumphant Maccabees themselves assimilated Hellenistic notions: "With the Maccabees . . . the internal Jewish reconcilement with Hellenism begins." By strengthening their people, and by appropriating from Hellenism what they could use to enrich Torah teachings, the Maccabees saved Judaism "from the mummification that overtook the religion of the Egyptians, for example, which shut itself off from Hellenism completely."

Along entirely independent lines, a kind of "chapter and verse" confirmation of this thesis is superbly furnished for the English reader in two volumes by S. Lieberman: *Greek in Jewish Palestine* (N.Y., Jewish Theological Seminary of America, 1942) and *Hellenism in Jewish Palestine* (N.Y., Jewish Theological Seminary of America, 1950). Although his individual essays are devoted to somewhat technical and textual problems, the lucidity of Lieberman's expositions makes the material accessible even to the non-specialist. And, again, we have here the kind of discussion absolutely essential for the proper understanding of the vocabulary, the institutions, and the attitudes of the religious tradition. What Palestinian talmudic Judaism was trying to teach, what were some of its preoccupations, and what is the character of its discourse—insofar as these are the products of a particular time and place—become intelligible to the historian and student of Judaism through studies like these. Lieberman makes us see that not merely Jews in general but the talmudic Rabbis themselves were influenced by the Hellenistic world. It should be added that our understanding of Judaism during Hellenistic-Roman times has been immensely deepened by Lieberman's many publications, particularly his commentaries, and at present especially his commentary in the Tosefta which is appearing: to date, on the first part of the Tosefta, three volumes have appeared (N.Y., Jewish Theological Seminary of America, 1955), and on the second part four more volumes (N.Y., Jewish Theological Seminary of America, 1961)—but these are in Hebrew.

Even at the risk of some repetition, let us consider the significance of these recent studies to which we have referred. Judaism's meeting with Hellenism we now know did not inevitably mean clash and antagonism. And obviously it did not mean submerging Judaism in the waves of a conquering civilization. A truly complex interrelationship began, aspects of the biblical religion being modified, forms and substance of speculation making their appearance now for which no background is provided in the biblical *literature* at least. For example, a religion rooted in this-worldly conceptions, so firmly expressed by Scripture (except for the late sections in Daniel), is gradually superseded by a religion whose yearning and goal become other-worldly; specific cultic features have such close counterparts in Hellenistic religious practice that the impression is inescapable that more or less direct influence is here at work; echoes of exegetical methods familiar in Alexandrian schools reverberate in the rabbinic academy.

Additional details the student will accumulate from his careful attention to the works to which we have already referred, and it will reward him greatly if he will follow the bibliographical leads suggested by the footnotes in these volumes. I am thinking specifically of such studies as E. J. Bickerman, "The Maxim of Antigonus of Socho" in the *Harvard Theological Review*, XLIV (1951), pp. 153–65, which in the course of analyzing social institutions illuminates at the same time religious conceptions. (See also M. Smith, "The Image of God," in the *Bulletin of the John Rylands Library* [March, 1958], pp. 473–512.) In short, what is to be kept in mind is that contact with the "Greeks" did not produce a Judaism insulated from Hellenism, but in fact the very reverse: a complex of revised and enriched traditions which added vitality to the religion, affecting by the way the character of Christianity and later Islām too.

The immediately recognizable Hellenistic influence is, of course, to be located in those Jewish writers who wrote in Greek. As for Josephus, the most sober and instructive study is still that by H. St. John Thackeray, *Josephus*, *the Man and the Historian* (N.Y., Hebrew Union College Press, 1929). Thackeray began the translation of Josephus' works for the Loeb Classics, which was continued by R. Marcus, though the *Antiquities* in that series is still not completed. Very useful too is a little volume done by Thackeray in 1919 for the Society for Promoting Christian Knowledge, *Selections from Josephus* (London). In addition to introductory comments, the passages translated are accompanied by fine brief notes, but, to return to Thackeray's biography of Josephus, its real value lies in the author's disciplined assessment of that writer against the actualities and literary fashions of Josephus' own time. More recently N. N. Glatzer's selection of Josephus' writings, *Rome and Jerusalem: The Writings of Josephus* (N.Y., Meridian Books, Inc., 1960), has a neat introduction.

Fragments from the works of Hellenistic Jewish writers are conveniently assembled in W. N. Stearns, *Fragments from Graeco-Jewish Writers* (Chicago, University of Chicago Press, 1908). We have already referred to the collections of apocrypha and pseudepigrapha by Charles and the editors of the Dropsie College Series (see above); and the bibliographies listed in those works will serve well for deeper study of specific texts and the religious thought expressed therein. Of some interest in this connection is the volume by R. H. Charles, *Religious Developments between the Two Testaments* (N.Y., Henry Holt & Co., Inc., 1914); see also R. T. Herford, *Talmud and Apocrypha* (London, The Soncino Press, Ltd., 1933). For consideration of some specific aspects of religion related to apocryphal literature, one may want to consult R. Marcus, *Law in the Apocrypha* (N.Y., Columbia University Press, 1927), H. J. Wicks, *The Doctrine of God* (London, Hunter & Longhurst, 1915), N. B. Johnson, *Prayer in the Apocrypha and Pseudepigrapha* (Philadelphia, Society of Biblical Literature & Exegesis, 1948). For additional literature on this subject and related matters discussed in this and the following section R. H. Pfeiffer's discussion and bibliography in his *History of New Testament Times* (N.Y., Harper & Brothers, 1949) are very useful.

We come finally to Philo, in whose work interest has grown considerably during the last four to five decades. Fortunately for the English reader, there is an excellent translation of Philo's works in the Loeb Classics (thus far nine volumes, begun by F. H. Colson and G. H. Whitaker, then continued by the former alone) and the two volumes of *Philo Supplement* by R. Marcus (N.Y., G. P. Putnam's Sons, Inc., 1929–53). For Philo's *Legatio ad Gaium*, not yet translated in the Loeb Series, see now the learned edition with commentary by E. M. Smallwood (Leiden, E. J. Brill, 1961). A little book of *Philo* selections with a learned and sensitive introduction and some comments was prepared by H. Lewy for the East and West Library Series (Oxford, 1946). (This fine scholar's studies deserve careful reading and should be translated into English and presented like the superior studies in Jewish Hellenism brought together in his posthumous Hebrew volume *Olamot Nifgashim*

[Jerusalem, Mosad Bialik, 1960].) Still another anthology worth reading is that drawn up by C. G. Montefiore, "Florilegium Philonis," in the old series of the *Jewish Quarterly Review*, VII (London, 1894–95), pp. 481–545.

What Philo represents, and the significance of his writings for an understanding of Judaism, is a subject still stirring discussion. To get two distinct points of view on this subject, one should examine E. R. Goodenough's *By Light, Light* (New Haven, Yale University Press, 1935) and H. A. Wolfson's two-volume *Philo* (Cambridge, Mass., Harvard University Press, 1947). (Goodenough's short *Introduction to Philo Judaeus* [New Haven, Yale University Press, 1940] is also relevant in this connection.) The former sees in Philo the great articulation of a mystic conception of Judaism distinctive of Alexandrian intellectual-religious Jewry: "The fact is, it seems to me," says Goodenough, "that by Philo's time, and long before, Judaism in the Greek-speaking world, especially in Egypt, had been transformed into a Mystery."

For Wolfson, on the other hand—for whom the work on Philo, incidentally, is a kind of "prolegomenon to the major problems of religious philosophy for the seventeen centuries following Philo"—the Alexandrian Jewish philosopher no doubt represents a Judaism being brought into intimate contact with the thought patterns of Hellenistic culture, but his distinctive Jewish heritage and idiom are in no way radically different from what one could find in Palestine and even in rabbinic teaching. Not only is this true of Philo himself but of Hellenistic Judaism in general. If, says Wolfson, the Alexandrian Jewish writers "happen to use the terminology of the mysteries in their presentation of Jewish rites, it is either for the purpose of emphasizing the contrast between the religion of the Jews and the mysteries of the heathen, or because the terms derived from the mysteries have become part of the common speech and are used in a sense completely divorced from their original meaning." And Philo himself, Wolfson reaffirms (in the prefatory statement of his *Religious Philosophy* [Cambridge, Mass., Belknap Press of Harvard University Press, 1961]), "is the interpreter of Greek philosophy in terms of certain fundamental teachings of his Hebrew Scripture, whereby he revolutionized philosophy and remade it into what became the common philosophy of the three religions with cognate Scriptures, Judaism, Christianity, and Islam. This triple scriptural religious philosophy, which was built up by Philo, reigned supreme as a homogeneous, if not a thoroughly unified, system of thought until the seventeenth century, when it was pulled down by Spinoza."

The data at our disposal demonstrate that the effect of Hellenism on the Jewish mind and thought was a profound and highly complicated phenomenon. Any attempt to simplify it is almost sure to become *over*simplification, and to that extent misleading.

VII. THE FORMATION OF CLASSICAL JUDAISM

There is bound to be a certain overlapping in our discussion, for several works referred to in the previous section (such as those by Lieberman and Bickerman) are relevant to this section, and, contrariwise, a number of volumes referred to here are no less relevant to the preceding section. And perhaps it would be helpful to come to an understanding of what is meant by the expression "classical Judaism" before we proceed to bibliographical statement. What, then, is classical Judaism?

"Classical" Judaism, with the biblical books and emphases as its heritage, appropriated what it found in the world congenial to the passion of the law and prophetic ideal and by intellectual exercise found sanction for its adaptations and innovations in those books that had become authoritative, while anticipating an otherworldly destination for man (to which "this world is an antechamber") it is rooted firmly in the historical affiliation with the Holy Land and the indestructibility of the folk Israel, and so convinced of God's ultimate triumph that it demanded an immediate practice and acting out of His commands and regulations, the behavior patterns of the Messianic age. Some of the clauses in this long sentence might not have been subscribed to by the Sadducees, for example (who are reported to have rejected the belief in Resurrection, for instance, and the authority of the Oral Torah); but it is likely that not only Pharisees but philosophical Jews like Philo, the different sectarians of whom Josephus speaks, the groups represented by material from the Dead Sea region, and the early Jewish Christians too (until they removed to Pella)—indeed, all the varieties of Jews until almost a millennium after Alexander the Great—were engaged in a life which was sometimes more and sometimes less an expression of this Judaism I have called "classical." The tensions and controversies and animosities between these groups—and even within Pharisaism, which ultimately triumphed through talmudism—were the result of conflicts over whether this or that particular interpretation or institution contributed to or detracted from the strengthening of this Judaism. If our description of classical Judaism does not do justice to the Sadducees and those in sympathy with them, it may indeed be because even before they disappeared, the Sadducees had already lost that interior confidence in the capacity of Judaism to appropriate and transform without losing contact with its past—in other words, had already then confused the archaic with the classical. But a word of caution is in order: what little we know of the Sadducees we know only from their critics and antagonists. If groups like the Essenes did not in the end survive, it may be that they cut themselves off so radically from what the larger surrounding civilization could offer them that they starved to death on a limited diet.

In the actual mêlée of Hellenistic-Roman times, then, classical Judaism was in the process of being formed. As it developed, the talmudic approach eventually succeeded, for reasons that can to some extent be suggested by a number of works to which we must now turn. (A very helpful bibliographical tool for what follows is H. L. Strack, *Introduction to the Talmud and Midrash* [Philadelphia, Jewish Publication Society of America, 1931].)

For primary sources, there is the English translation of the Talmud and the Midrash Rabbah to which reference has already been made. The English translation of the *Mishnah* by H. Danby (Oxford, Clarendon Press, 1933) is fine but is to be used with care, for a number of passages are not properly translated (or understood). In recent years a translation with useful commentary and notes (and a printed Hebrew text) has been prepared by P. Blackman (London, Mishna Press, Ltd., 1951–56). For a first-rate pointed Hebrew text of the Mishnah, there is nothing even to compare with the edition by Ch. Albeck and Ch. Yalon, *Shishah Sidre Mishnah* (The Six Orders of the Mishnah) (Tel Aviv, Mosad Bialik, 1952–59). An excellent translation of the Mishnah treatise on relations with idol-worshippers, *Abodah Zarah*, with important philological and historical notes, was done by W. A. L. Elmslie (Cambridge, Cambridge University Press, 1911); in 1945 the first three treatises of the *Mishnah* were issued by the H. Fischel Institute scholars (Jerusalem) in Danby's translation (with corrections) and a good commentary. This may be a bit too technical for the general reader, but one can learn a lot from it. There is also an edition by P. R. Weis with translation by E. Robertson of the treatise *Horayoth* (Manchester, Manchester University Press, 1952) and of *Mishnah Megillah* by J. Rabbinowitz (London, Oxford University Press, 1931). Several other treatises, with corresponding sections of the Tosefta, were prepared by different scholars under the auspices of the Society for Promoting Christian Knowledge (see above), and these are of a more popular character.

A particularly important treatise of the Mishnah for the understanding of classical Judaism is *Pirke Aboth*. The most valuable edition (with translation and commentary in English) is that by C. Taylor, *Sayings of the Jewish Fathers*, 2nd ed. (Cambridge, Cambridge University Press, Vol. I, 1897; Vol. II, 1900); although out of print, it will richly reward the specialist, and the general reader can acquire solid instruction by concentrating on Volume I. Every traditional Jewish prayerbook which is accompanied by a translation will provide also a translation of *Pirke Aboth*, for it was incorporated into the prayerbook as "liturgical" reading and study at an early time. The translation with commentary by R. T. Herford, *Pirke Aboth, the Tractate "Fathers,"* 3rd rev. ed. (N.Y., Jewish Institute of Religion, 1945, recently reissued in paperback), although not always correct, is marked by a sympathetic approach to Pharisaism in reaction against the antipharisaic prejudice current generally among Christian scholars. J. Goldin's *The Living Talmud: The Wisdom of the Fathers* (N.Y., 1957, Chicago, University of Chicago Press, 1958) is an attempt to transmit the literary quality of the text with strict attention to philological detail, and to provide for the first time in English selections from the great early-medieval commentators on this treatise. And in connection with *Pirke Aboth*, there is available the talmudic companion volume, *The Fathers According to Rabbi Nathan*, also by J. Goldin (New Haven, Yale University Press, 1955).

A reliable translation of the *Mekilta de Rabbi Ishmael* accompanies the splendid edition by J. Z. Lauterbach (Philadelphia, Jewish Publication Society of America, 1933). Parts of the *Sifre* on Numbers were translated by P. P. Levertoff, *Midrash Sifre on Numbers* (London and N.Y., Macmillan & Co., 1926). Of later Midrashim there is in English the careful two-volume work by W. G. Braude, *The Midrash on Psalms* (New Haven, Yale University Press, 1959); G. Friedlander's learned *Pirkê de Rabbi Eliezer* (London, Kegan Paul, Trench, Trubner & Co., Ltd., 1916); and a beautiful little book of selections by N. N. Glatzer, *Hammer on the Rock: A Short Midrash Reader*, tr. by J. Sloan (N.Y., Schocken Books, Inc., 1948).

Probably one of the most useful anthologies of talmudic passages is still that by C. G. Montefiore and H. Loewe, *A Rabbinic Anthology* (reprinted in Philadelphia, Jewish Publication Society of America, 1960), for it has some fine notes on a number of passages. But the apologetics and tone of the introductory essays are acutely irritating.

Finally (though doubtless some texts have been omitted inadvertently), there has recently been reprinted the French translation of the Palestinian Talmud, M. Schwab, *Le Talmude de Jérusalem* (Paris, Maisonneuve, 1871–89). This should be used with much caution; I mention it since there is no English translation of this important source.

Relevant chapters and sections on the history of this period, which for our present purpose might be delimited as 200 B.C.–A.D. 500, the reader will find in the histories referred to earlier. Here we shall refer to only one work, despite its very serious limitation, E. Schürer's *History of the Jewish People in the Time of Jesus Christ*, which appeared in Edinburgh, 1886–90, and apparently eleven issues of this English translation of the original German, in its second edition, came out until 1924 (N.Y., Charles Scribner's Sons). Since this work is a deservedly standard presentation and discussion of what is generally called Judaism in New Testament Times, a few comments on its nature are in order. The time scope it sets for itself is from about 175 B.C. to about A.D. 200, although the political history it outlines goes only to the end of the Bar Kochba revolt in A.D. 135.

The English translation is excellent, although in a few places (in Division II) the translators misunderstood the original German, and their version is misleading. This is not the most serious limitation of the translation—which to repeat, lest a wrong impression be left, is an excellent one. Schürer was a very exacting scholar, and his *Geschichte* appeared in four constantly revised editions. If a student is eager to learn Schürer's final conclusions, it is essential that he check with the German volume in either its third or fourth edition (ed. 1901, 1907, 1909, 1911).

As a summary of political history, a compilation of data on some institutions or literary sources, or a synthesis of what the primary sources preserve regarding specific problems of the period (for example, the three principal groups, Sadducees, Pharisees, Essenes, or what the daily service in the Jerusalem temple was like, according to the Mishnah), Schürer's is still the best work to consult. About some matters we are of course better informed today than Schürer could be: discoveries relating to the Dead Sea sectarians have furnished us with data Schürer did not have, and we can listen, for instance, to Essene or Essene-like groups as they expressed themselves rather than as they were paraphrased. Our knowledge of the state of postbiblical Hebrew is better grounded than Schürer's could be because of these finds. Thanks especially to the researches of Bickerman and Lieberman, our understanding of the penetration of Hellenism into Jewish Palestine is more profound and richer than Schürer's.

But it is noteworthy that so painstaking was Schürer in his work that the basic outline he drew up of events (in large part following Josephus) is still the basic outline of our picture of the period. And Schürer's disciplined gathering of literary sources, epigraphic material, coinage, and results of archeological expeditions is a model for every historian. Schürer's work is therefore strongly recommended to the student; and in the recent paperback abridgement (the volume is confined to political history) prepared by N. N. Glatzer, *A History of the Jewish People in the Time of Jesus* by Emil Schürer (N.Y., Schocken Books, Inc., 1961), one will find not only a very useful selected bibliography to cover results of scholarship in the years 1900–60, but a sensitive evaluation of Schürer's work and outlook.

The serious limitation of this work, alluded to above, is that it is absolutely tone-deaf to the spirit of talmudism and the mood of rabbinic preoccupation with the Law (see his discussion "Life under the Law" in Division II, Volume II). Moreover, Schürer persists in presenting Judaism as no more than a preparation for Christianity, and hence as something that had to be outgrown. Schürer reads like an accurate reporter of all the finger exercises a concert pianist has prepared for himself who then says: "From this catalogue, judge the concert performance." Inevitably such an outlook was bound to stir up opposing reactions, from Jews and non-Jews (and, alas, the reactions have sometimes involved all sorts of unnecessary special pleadings).

One specific aspect of the problems of this period has to do with the Pharisees. A sympathetic presentation of what the Pharisees were and stood for is available in R. T. Herford's *Pharisaism* (N.Y., G. P. Putnam's Sons, Inc., 1912)—see also his *The Pharisees* (London, George Allen & Unwin, Ltd., 1924)—which argues against the group being judged by Christian standards and attempts to see Pharisaism's merits even in the conflict between the Pharisees and Jesus (as well as Paul): "The conflict," Herford feels, "was one between two fundamentally different conceptions of religion, viz. that in which the supreme authority was Torah, and that in which the supreme authority was the immediate intuition of God in the individual soul and conscience. The Pharisees stood for the one; Jesus stood for the other."

Somewhat of the same tenor, though disagreeing in details, and certainly more learned, and exploring Pharisaic teaching more fully, is J. Z. Lauterbach's essay "The Pharisees and Their Teachings," reprinted in his posthumous volume *Rabbinic Essays* (Cincinnati, Hebrew Union College Press, 1951). This volume incidentally has several studies of importance for the understanding of talmudic Judaism.

An ambitious undertaking, attempting to explain Pharisaic and rabbinic law and thought and institutions by reference to economic and sociological forces in Palestine, is the two-volume work by L. Finkelstein, *The Pharisees* (Philadelphia, Jewish Publication Society of America, 1938; but one should consult the latest edition which is announced for publication, since Finkelstein has been trying to refine his original presentation in the light of severe criticism). The approach has the merit of being a fresh one, of attempting to see the "sect" against the larger social background rather than against the purely doctrinal one—even if serious reservations are retained against specific interpretations. The cue for his approach Finkelstein found in L. Ginzberg's essay—originally in Hebrew (Jerusalem, 5691–1931) and now reprinted in English translation, by A. Hertzberg, as "The Significance of the Halachah for Jewish History," in the volume of essays *On Jewish Law and Lore* (Philadelphia, Jewish Publication Society of America, 1955)—which was, if I am not mistaken, the first attempt to view aspects of rabbinic law (specifically as reflected by the controversies of the famous schools of Shammaites and Hillelites) against economic conditions.

Recent attempts at presenting the Pharisees must undertake to establish some correlation between the teachings of the group and the milieu to which the group belongs. In this connection, but with different results from Finkelstein's, see M. Smith's essay "Palestinian Judaism in the First Century" in *Israel: Its Role in Civilization*, ed. by M. Davis (N.Y., Jewish Theological Seminary of America, 1956), pp. 67–81. The student especially interested in the Pharisees will find a useful essay by R. Marcus in Vol. XXXII of the *Journal of Religion* (Chicago, 1952), pp. 153–64, "The Pharisees in the Light of Modern Scholarship"; and since Marcus not only discusses a number of important works on this subject, but also lists a selected bibliography at the end of his paper, we shall leave the Pharisees as such, and move on to more comprehensive themes.

There is, first, S. Schechter's *Some Aspects of Rabbinic Theology*, chapters of which began to appear toward the end of the nineteenth century in the

Jewish Quarterly Review (old series), and later (1909) appeared as a volume (the edition before me is N.Y., 1936; the original volume has been out of print for some time, and now a paperback edition [N.Y., Schocken Books Inc., 1961] has appeared, with an Introduction by L. Finkelstein). The presentation is still instructive, vigorous, and relevant, because Schechter wrote with a keen sense of the fervor of original sources and was not averse to engaging in polemic, where he felt that less than justice had been done to the life reflected by midrashic-talmudic texts. Without passion, but excellently written (with a refreshing cleanliness in the prose) is the more extensive and systematic three-volume work of G. F. Moore, *Judaism in the First Centuries of the Christian Era, the Age of the Tannaim* (Cambridge, Mass., Harvard University Press, 1927; Vol. III appeared in 1940). It has become fashionable recently to take issue with this work, and some of the criticism is certainly justified. But Moore's remains one of the best introductions to and presentations of basic features of classical Judaism, for he tried most earnestly to listen to the rabbinic texts he studied and was attentive to critical problems raised by this literature. "The aim of these volumes," wrote Moore at the beginning of his Preface, "is to represent Judaism in the centuries in which it assumed definitive forms as it presents itself in the tradition which it has always regarded as authentic." This aim the writer realized to a remarkable degree.

But one can no longer assume that the teachings of the tradition—which Moore said characterized Judaism in the age of the Tannaim—but in actuality treated as though they characterized the later Amoraic age too—were quite as uniform, as stable, as unaffected by reinterpretation and change as Moore assumed them to be. And even within the first two centuries, the age of the Tannaim—more especially, within the period from Sirach to the compilation of the Mishnah, from roughly 200 B.C. to A.D. 200—there is good reason to see gradual developments, so that emphases of one period give way to other emphases entirely, even if the vocabulary seems to be the same for both periods.

What is more, a basic assumption made by Moore is just the assumption which today calls for re-examination and demonstration. In reaction against those scholars who had largely adopted the idea that the sentiments and thoughts derived from the apocrypha, the pseudepigrapha, and even the New Testament were essentially normative of Judaism, and that talmudism was an unfortunate deviation which, however, finally conquered the main expressions and institutions of the religion, Moore assumed that the very reverse was true (see also Schechter's volume already referred to)—namely, that what was normative *in those early centuries* was the Judaism reflected by the midrashic-talmudic sources. But this is the very issue which confronts the historian, particularly today, because of many realia to which archeology especially has alerted us, and because of forms of speculation and expression, gnostic and otherwise, which research has underscored in recent years and talmudists were prone to underestimate.

It is not that Moore has been proven wrong, but the question, simply, of what *was* normative in the Judaism of Greco-Roman times remains. No answer to this question can be given yet, for very much painstaking research is required along new lines, and this will very likely be one of the primary items on the agenda of Judaica scholars in the coming decades.

But a brief comment is in order, for it is pertinent to the way we read not only the primary sources but also the major secondary ones which attempt to represent Judaism. When we seek to discover what is normative for these centuries, we must recognize that *all* the sources are a record of particular teachings striving to become normative, all represent the ambition of particular groups to have the whole of Israel adopt their particular emphases. And so long as they were still vigorously arguing *with each other*, Judaism was *in process toward final formulation*, one might say it was feeling its way toward definitiveness (and in some respects finality was never attained). What made the teachings of some one or other group *not* normative was the withdrawal of the particular group from the common argument, from this resolution to press its point of view on the folk as a whole, where the folk as a whole was located. Issuing polemical statements from a reservation to which one has retired, and where one has adopted a particular routine for privileged initiates, is already an expression of giving up and disengagement, and a sign of having become tangential. Whatever else talmudism was, it was the determination of its exponents, the Rabbis, to engage themselves with what was daily happening in society as a whole and to engage that society with the terms of their, the Rabbis', debates and values. This does not mean that therefore their word was "everywhere" law; but it does mean that there was widespread consciousness of their law, considerable contact with its demands and the value structure these exhibited. By being aggressively present within Palestinian Jewish society at all times, talmudic Judaism asserted itself on that society as a kind of norm, to which gradually more and more of the religious life related (and later still, accommodated) itself. I am tempted to say that early talmudism was the one form of the inchoate classical Judaism which won a dominant position even in these early Tannaite and Amoraic centuries because, on the one hand, it was relatively open to many influences and points of view crisscrossing that society and, on the other hand, its leading representatives stayed on the scene, never allowing their own preoccupations to get too far removed from the concerns of the folk at large and not giving the folk at large the impression that *its* common practices and predilections were exempt from rabbinic judgment.

What happened later, when classical Judaism came to be defined virtually in terms of talmudism, we shall see below. But the marginal comment introduced above was essential if we are properly to appreciate what the studies we go on to list have to cope with.

A number of aspects of rabbinic Judaism, which are treated by Moore as chapters of his full presentation, receive more elaborate treatment in several special studies. Much information is offered and carefully analyzed in the works of A. Büchler; specifically, *Types of Jewish-Palestinian Piety from 70 B.C.E. to 70 C.E.* (London, Oxford University Press, 1922) and *Studies in Sin and Atonement in the Rabbinic Literature of the First Century* (London, Oxford University Press, 1928). Several essays in his posthumously published *Studies in Jewish History*, ed. J. Brodie and J. Rabbinowitz (London, Oxford University Press, 1956) may also be mentioned. Büchler is learned and exact, though his wandering in discussion and pedestrian style sometimes discourage the general reader—legitimately, for Büchler supplies a healthy corrective to a number of seemingly plausible generalizations.

Even more closely related to purely "theological" themes are J. Abelson, *The Immanence of God in Rabbinical Literature* (London, Macmillan & Co., Ltd., 1912) and A. Marmorstein, *The Doctrine of Merits in Old Rabbinical Literature* (London, Oxford University Press, 1920); the two volumes, *The Old Rabbinic Doctrine of God* (London, Oxford University Press, 1927 and 1937; the second volume, "Essays in Anthropomorphism," is relevant also to the study of Philo); and finally, his volume of essays, *Studies in Jewish Theology*, ed. J. Rabbinowitz and M. S. Lew (London, Oxford University Press, 1950). For serious studies of what might be called the way of rabbinic thinking, and a thoroughly original approach to basic concepts indigenous to midrashic-talmudic discourse, there are three volumes by M. Kadushin: *The Theology of Seder Eliahu* (N.Y., Bloch Publishing Co., Inc., 1932), *Organic Thinking* (N.Y., Jewish Theological Seminary of America, 1938), and *The Rabbinic Mind* (N.Y., Jewish Theological Seminary of America, 1952).

Without commenting in detail on the following works, I shall call attention to them as valuable and sometimes sensitive analyses of the problems they treat: N. N. Glatzer's essay "A Study of the Talmudic Interpretation of Prophecy," *Review of Religion* (N.Y., 1946), pp. 115–37; B. J. Bamberger, *Proselytism in the Talmudic Period* (Cincinnati, Hebrew Union College Press, 1939)—a careful and fresh dissertation on a theme which had been discussed by a number of leading scholars and not always with as close study of the texts as Bamberger brought to them (conclusions fairly similar to the ones arrived at by Bamberger, that the dominant rabbinic attitude towards proselytism remained favorable, were reached also by W. G. Braude in his doctoral dissertation, *Jewish Proselytizing in the First Five Centuries of the Common Era* [Providence, Brown University Press, 1940]); and, also by Bamberger, *Fallen Angels* (Philadelphia, Jewish Publication Society of America, 1952), which has two sections (Parts Two and Five) relevant to the period we are discussing and other sections treating the themes of the fallen or rebel angels in Christianity and in post-talmudic Judaism.

For studies of the Messianic theme as it is treated in the literature of

Hellenistic-Roman times, see J. Klausner, *The Messianic Idea in Israel* (N.Y., The Macmillan Co., 1955) and W. D. Davies, *Torah in the Messianic Age and/or the Age to Come* (Philadelphia, Society of Biblical Literature and Exegesis, 1952). In this connection it is also illuminating to consult R. Wischnitzer, *The Messianic Theme in the Paintings of the Dura Synagogue* (Chicago, University of Chicago Press, 1948).

What Jewish imagination did with its biblical heritage—especially biblical narratives and personalities—is nowhere better presented than in L. Ginzberg's *Legends of the Jews* (Philadelphia, Jewish Publication Society of America, 1909–38; the first four volumes consisting of the text; Vols. 5 and 6 of the notes, nothing short of a treasury of learning; Vol. 7, the index volume, was drawn up by B. Cohen). For the folklorist and the student of religion this work is indispensable: the material assembled and the critical discussion in the notes reveal not only what interpretation and reinterpretation can do to an inherited corpus of writings when they are endowed with canonical authority, but also how speculative themes of universal range are naturalized and are given a specific Jewish character and idiom. For Judaism this is not only of literary and purely cultural importance; it is consequential for the religion. This is the haggadic substance and vocabulary which the pietists will invoke and with which the homilists especially will fill the minds of the folk. An abridged one-volume edition of this monumental work, omitting the notes, was published under the title *Legends of the Bible* (Philadelphia, Jewish Publication Society of America, 1956), with an introductory essay by S. Spiegel which is one of the most beautiful and illuminating statements of the nature of haggadah and Jewish legend in any language. (Students of folklore who do not read Hebrew are unfortunately deprived of Spiegel's outstanding study of the Binding of Isaac legends and theme, *Me-Agadot Ha-Akedah*, which appears in the *Alexander Marx Jubilee Volume*, Hebrew section, pp. 471–547 [N.Y., Jewish Theological Seminary, 5710–1950]. It is a pity that this work has not yet been translated into English.) Ginzberg also has a suggestive essay on "Jewish Folklore: East and West," originally prepared as a lecture at the Harvard Tercentenary in 1936, included in the volume *On Jewish Law and Lore*, to which we have referred previously. All the essays in the volume are relevant to this period (even the one on the "Cabala," to which we shall refer later).

The way haggadic material was molded into sermonic form is painstakingly studied and presented by J. Mann in *The Bible as Read and Preached in the Old Synagogue*, Vol. I (Cincinnati, the author, 1940)—a technical study to be sure, but a very important one.

On the nature of the mystical teachings, particularly of an esoteric kind, in these early centuries, there is now the important and exciting volume by G. G. Scholem, *Jewish Gnosticism, Merkabah Mysticism, and Talmudic Tradition* (N.Y., Jewish Theological Seminary of America, 1960), which has established the existence of a Jewish gnosis ("That is to say," to quote him, "knowledge of an esoteric and at the same time soteric . . . character") in rabbinic circles in the very period when the classical tradition as a whole was being shaped. Not only does this open up new vistas for students of Judaism on the varieties of expression of the Jewish religion, but for students of Gnosticism too certain roots and origins are uncovered. For the charting of the inner religious development of Judaism, studies along such lines as Scholem's are a prime requirement.

On the subject of synagogue worship there is in English a passable volume by A. Z. Idelsohn, *Jewish Liturgy and its Development* (N.Y., Henry Holt & Co., Inc., 1932); but the standard work is still that by I. Elbogen in German, *Der jüdische Gottesdienst in seiner geschichtlichen Entwicklung* (Leipzig, G. Fock, 1913)—although, perhaps needless to say, specific phases of the liturgy continue to be studied and discussed by scholars, and specific views of Elbogen are modified. Useful explanatory notes to the Jewish prayerbook are provided by I. Abrahams, *A Companion to the Authorized Daily Prayer Book* (London, Eyre & Spottiswoode, Ltd., 1922); for a translation of the prayerbook, see *The Authorized Daily Prayer Book*, tr. by S. Singer (London, Eyre & Spottiswoode, Ltd., 1944, but frequently reprinted before and after that date) or, more recently, *Daily Prayer Book, Ha-Siddur Ha-Shalem*, tr. by P. Birnbaum (N.Y., Hebrew Publishing Co., 1949).

There are several so-called biographies in English of rabbinic personalities, such as N. N. Glatzer, *Hillel the Elder: The Emergence of Classical Judaism* (N.Y., B'nai B'rith Hillel Foundations, 1956), B. Z. Bokser, *Pharisaic Judaism in Transition: R. Eliezer the Great and Jewish Reconstruction after the War with Rome* (N.Y., Bloch Publishing Co., 1935) and L. Finkelstein, *Akiba* (N.Y., Covici, Friede Inc., 1936)—(the bibliographies and notes in these volumes will lead the reader further on). These are to some extent useful, but such works are hardly biographies in the serious sense of the word (though the studies are undertaken seriously), for not only do the primary sources disappoint us deeply in the amount of reliable *historical* detail they provide, but even as regards the opinions and teachings of the Sages, one is left to guess what is early and what is late. In short, there is practically no way to get at *development*, surely and desperately necessary for the historian and biographer. These books therefore are filled with speculation, sometimes plausible, sometimes not. As reflections of the author's own imagination and interpretation, however, and as *collections* of data about the specific sage, they are informative exercises.

Though the following are in Hebrew, mention must be made of them: G. Allon's two-volume history, *Toledot ha-Yehudim be-Erez Yisrael bi-Tekufat ha-Mishnah veha-Talmud*—the History of the Jews in Palestine in Mishnaic and Talmudic Times (Tel Aviv, Ha-Kibbuz Ha-Meuhad, 1952–55)—and two volumes of collected essays, *Mehkarim be-Toledot Yisrael*—Studies in Jewish History (Tel Aviv, Ha-Kibbuz Ha-Meuhad, 1957–58), particularly the latter and the first volume of the former, are very important for the serious student. Allon brings to the exegesis of the talmudic and Hellenistic sources the acute sensibilities and skills of the social historian: in his hands texts which seemed dry as dust and problems that for many general historians were too technical or recherché have been made to release fundamental information on religious thought and practice of this period. See at least his essay on "The Attitude of the Pharisees to the Roman Government and the House of Herod," in *Scripta Hierosolymitana*, Vol. VII (Jerusalem, 1961), pp. 53–78.

The Hellenistic-Roman age, as has been suggested, was the age when the biblical traditions were assembled and given both a refreshed and fresh consistency and a new momentum by the native wit and whatever techniques could be safely appropriated from the larger civilization surrounding the Jews. It took almost a millennium to achieve this. But once it was achieved, and particularly after the Palestinian and Babylonian Talmuds were redacted (*c.* 400 and 500 respectively), the *groundwork* of the classical tradition had been laid. Thereafter, the post-talmudic scholarly and religious authorities, the Geonim, did everything in their power to establish this Judaism as standard. This, in turn, required almost another half-millennium to accomplish fully. Of course, all variety did not henceforth disappear, and all the tensions of further development were not painlessly resolved; but from this time, whatever developments were recommended or elaborated or accepted (cheerfully or reluctantly) had to be in accommodation with talmudic law and the main lines of talmudic teaching. The climax of classical Judaism was reached with the establishment of the Babylonian Talmud as authoritative by the Geonim. On this theme, see L. Ginzberg's essay "An Introduction to the Palestinian Talmud," reprinted in his volume *On Jewish Law and Lore*, and the first volume of his *Geonica* (N.Y., Jewish Theological Seminary of America, 1909).

VIII. THAT WHICH IS SECTARIAN

What is a sect? For the purpose of our discussion, it is sufficient, I believe, if we classify as a sect any group within the larger communion which insists on persisting as a distinct association even after its terms have been essentially adopted by society, or—more particularly our concern in this section—which in the course of time fails to impose its terms—its articulated principal doctrines and its "heroes" and its institutional forms—on that establishment it is battling against and wishes to replace. Some sects are longer-lived than others, and within sects further fission is possible. Often sects have a profound influence on the development and even revitalization of their strongest opposition (and, of course, never have been officially recognized for or credited with their influence); many an establishment, speaking historically, began originally as a sectarian push and demand. But the fact remains that that group within any large complex which fails to impose its terms, as we have said, and therefore to be acknowledged as *representative* of the society, is a sect.

Sects fail—in other words, remain sects—for different reasons in different circumstances and for different sects; and from the bibliography listed below the student may try to form some idea of what prevented the various sects from successfully making Judaism in their image. I would like to suggest that, whatever else is responsible for the sects' failures, within Jewish history at least it has always been the sects' confusing prevalent forms of real discontent on the part of the folk with the folk's capacity totally to reject the past, or even the irritations of the present.

On the earliest Jewish sect that we have any knowledge of the best work is still J. A. Montgomery, *The Samaritans* (Philadelphia, John C. Winston, Co., 1907); M. Gaster's *The Samaritans* (London, Oxford University Press, 1925) does not replace it. Some very pertinent remarks are made by Y. Kaufmann in the last volume (especially pp. 185ff.) of his history of the religion of Israel (see above), not yet translated from the Hebrew, to suggest that the Samaritans were *not* of Israelite stock: "they adopted (their) new God not as the God of *Israel*, but as the God of the Land of Israel" (p. 190, author's italics). For an outline and summary of the kind of defense of the Samaritan position which would be drawn up in later times to bolster Samaritan morale, see A. S. Halkin's monograph, "Samaritan Polemics against the Jews," in Vol. VII of *Proceedings of the American Academy for Jewish Research* (Philadelphia, 1936), pp. 13–59.

That the Jewish colony at Elephantine ought to be included in our section here seems to me far from certain. Pockets of Jewish settlement in different places doubtless, and at all times, came under local influences and therefore reflect variations of expression and custom, but they were not necessarily attempting to impose their customs or emphases on Catholic Israel, to use S. Schechter's famous expression. But those interested in following up some discussion of this subject might consult the Introduction in A. E. Cowley, *Aramaic Papyri of the Fifth Century B.C.* (Oxford, Clarendon Press, 1923) and E. G. Kraeling's discussion, especially pp. 83–99, in his *The Brooklyn Museum Aramaic Papyri* (New Haven, Yale University Press, 1953).

Of the famous sects in the period of the Second Commonwealth we know chiefly through Josephus, talmudic sources, and Philo, and now through discoveries in the neighborhood of the Dead Sea. Literature on the Pharisees has already been cited above; Pharisaism ceased to be a sectarian phenomenon once it triumphed, and in this connection I would like to call attention to a lecture delivered in 1960 by H. L. Ginsberg, "New Light on Tannaite Jewry and on the State of Israel of the Years 132–135 C.E.," published in Vol. XXV of the *Proceedings of the Rabbinical Assembly of America* (N.Y., 1961), pp. 132–42. In the works listed the reader will again and again find discussion of the Sadducees. L. Finkelstein's *Pharisees* (Philadelphia, Jewish Publication Society of America, 1938) provides an extensive bibliography which is most useful, and a number of specific items (though not in English) concentrate more specifically on the Sadducees. Many works devoted to a study of the Pharisees inevitably deal also with the Essenes; but of the older literature on this group, I should like to mention C. D. Ginsburg, *The Essenes* (London, Longmans, Green & Co., Ltd., 1861); in addition to his own discussion and a review of leading "modern" opinions, Ginsburg reproduces also the descriptions of this sect as these are furnished by the ancient sources, from Philo to Epiphanius.

The Essenes have once again become a subject of considerable interest because of the discoveries in the caves of the Dead Sea region. It would serve little purpose, even in a bibliographical essay, to try to list all the works which deal with the Dead Sea literature: one can hardly improve on the *Revue de Qumran* appearing in Paris since 1958, and the reader keenly concerned with this material ought to keep consulting that periodical. For the general student, I believe the following works are not only easily accessible but dependable and fair—that is, avoiding excessive speculation and polemic—in treatment: M. Burrows, *The Dead Sea Scrolls* (N.Y., The Viking Press, Inc., 1955) and *More Light on the Dead Sea Scrolls* (N.Y., The Viking Press, Inc., 1958); F. M. Cross, Jr., *The Ancient Library of Qumrân and Modern Biblical Studies* (N.Y., Doubleday & Co., Inc., 1958). Writings of the Dead Sea sectarians are available in translation not only in M. Burrows' volumes (where, by the way, there are excellent bibliographies too), but also in T. H. Gaster's *The Dead Sea Scriptures in English Translation* (N.Y., Doubleday & Co., Inc., 1956) which is accompanied by notes; there is a translation by S. S. Nardi of *A Genesis Apocryphon*, ed. N. Avigad and Y. Yadin (Jerusalem, Hebrew University Magnes Press, 1956), and of the much talked about copper scroll by J. M. Allegro, *The Treasure of the Copper Scroll* (N.Y., Doubleday & Co., Inc., 1960).

Regarding some phases of sectarian practice, particularly as it may be related to practices recorded in the Talmud, there is a most illuminating study by S. Lieberman, "Light on the Cave Scrolls from Rabbinic Sources" in Vol. XV, pp. 395–404, of *Proceedings of the American Academy for Jewish Research* (N.Y., 1951); see also his paper "The Discipline in the So-Called Dead Sea Manual of Discipline" in *Journal of Biblical Literature*, LXXI (1952), pp. 199–206. Finally, H. L. Ginsberg's essay, "The Dead Sea Manuscript Finds" in *Israel: Its Role in Civilization* (N.Y., Harper & Brothers, 1956), pp. 39–57, discusses problems significant not only for biblical *textual* study but also for the understanding of early biblical interpretation (and *its* relation to crisis in the religious life) and the idiom of liturgy.

Literature on the early Christians, when they were still a sect within the framework of Jewish society, the reader will find in the essay on Christianity in this volume.

During Second Commonwealth times there were very likely still other sects than the ones we have referred to: the Mishnah, for example, refers to certain forms of liturgical recitation which must have characterized some Jews deviating from Rabbinic practice—and who exactly these people were, we still cannot say; their specific identity has not yet been established.

For the period after the redaction of the Talmud and its adoption by the academies as the authoritative source for Jewish orthodoxy, a good deal (but not all) of the difficulty in deciding what is sectarian is removed. The post-talmudic authorities regarded as a sectarian one who rejected talmudic authority. This of course did not mean that henceforth absolute uniformity of thought or practice or expression prevailed, but, whatever the varieties or vagaries endorsed or urged, precedent and sanction for them had to be found in the Talmud. There were those, alongside the Judaism governed by the Talmud, who refused to acknowledge the Talmud's authority. On this famous antitalmudic sect, itself the culmination of several inchoate dissident movements, see J. Mann, "An Early Theologico-Polemical Work" in Vols. XII–XIII of the *Hebrew Union College Annual* (1937–38), pp. 411–59; and on the affinities of such sectarianisms with heterodoxies in the Islāmic world, see the important study by I. Friedlaender, "Jewish-Arabic Studies" in the *Jewish Quarterly Review*, I–III (1910–12). Ultimately—the early Rabbanite authorities still wondered at times how according to talmudic law these new dissenters were to be regarded—this sect became a branch *severed* from the main stock, the Karaites.

An excellent anthology of Karaite writings up to 1500 (including, however, extracts from the Karaite prayerbook after that date) is available in L. Nemoy, *Karaite Anthology* (New Haven, Yale University Press, 1952). The histories and encyclopedias listed earlier obviously discuss the Karaite movement as part of Jewish history, but, as Nemoy writes in his Introduction, "Modern critical study of Karaite history and theology is as yet in its infancy." One of the best general presentations of the movement is still that by S. Poznanski in his article, "Karaites," written for Vol. VII of Hastings' *Encyclopedia of Religion and Ethics*, pp. 662–72; see, in addition, J. Mann, "New Studies in Karaism" in Vol. XLIV of the *Yearbook of the Central Conference of American Rabbis* (1939), pp. 220–41, and *Texts and Studies in Jewish History and Literature*, Vol. II (Philadelphia, 1953) for essential source material.

An important contribution to this field of study is Z. Ankori's *Karaites in Byzantium* (N.Y., Columbia University Press, 1959). In addition to its discussion of the specific region upon which it concentrates, the volume is a sophisticated assessment of the character of dissent from Babylonian talmudism and the relation of such nonconformity to messianic frustrations. There is a rich bibliography at the end of the book—most of it, alas, not in English.

The subject of the Karaites brings us at last into the period when, as we have said, the dominant cultural-religious reality is represented by the concentrated activity to establish Babylonian talmudic teaching as authoritative.

VII

Christianity

H. H. Walsh

INTRODUCTION

Christians have always regarded themselves as belonging to a worshipping community, perpetuating the work of Christ in history. Since this community, generally known as the Church, constructs its faith on what it alleges are historical facts and has been supremely concerned with the shaping of history, every era of its existence is a part of the story of the Christian faith. It follows, then, that an understanding of the Christian view of history is a necessary preliminary to a critical examination of the relevant material upon which the Christian faith is based—namely, the New Testament. The New Testament, however, is not comprehensible without some acquaintance with the Old Testament and with Jewish literature produced between the two Testaments (which is generally referred to as intertestamental literature). Some overlapping of this chapter with the one on Judaism is therefore necessary, but only to the extent of indicating how Christians interpret Jewish literature in the light of New Testament insights.

More germane to an understanding of Christianity is the literature concerned with Christian beliefs about the central figure of the New Testament,

Jesus Christ; it is also important to know how Christians have responded to the demands that Christ has made upon them. The first of these concerns is usually classified under "Christian doctrine," which often shades off into a philosophy of Christianity; the second may be considered under the general heading of "Christian sociology." As is the case with all institutions with high moral goals, the ideal and reality are often in conflict. The failure of the Christian Church to achieve its chief goal, to be "perfected into one" (St. John 17:23) has produced a large body of literature which is usually classified under the term "Irenics." Irenics, in turn, has given rise to an ecumenical movement which has produced a peculiar literature of its own.

All the material so far suggested would fail to give a true reflection of Christianity as a way of life if it did not include some reference to the struggles and temptations of Christians trying to do the work of Christ and to keep themselves "unspotted from the world" (St. James 1:8). No doubt such literature comes under the over-all heading of Christian sociology, but in this case sociology must include such specifically Christian disciplines as liturgy, pastoralia, moral theology, ethics, and social welfare. Nor are the inner recesses of the Christian life exhausted under these more activist disciplines; for fundamentally the Christian life is one of worship, in which personal devotion, meditation, and mysticism play most significant roles. It is from this inner life of devotion that Christianity has found its mood and the creativity to develop its own specific culture.

It is in the cultural sphere that we will be introduced to the most lively writings on Christianity today, for this is an age of meeting and crossing of different cultures. Consequently this chapter will appropriately conclude on the theme of Christianity and other religions.

THE CHRISTIAN VIEW OF HISTORY

It goes without saying that the Christian view of history has been molded by the Christian faith. This fact creates the suspicion that those who composed the earliest Christian documents were under the restraint of maintaining a thesis that the prophecies of the Old Testament were fulfilled by Jesus, the Messiah. There was also an inclination on the part of early Christians to disparage past history because of their expectation of the immediate culmination of the historical process. But, as R. L. P. Milburn observes in *Early Christian Interpretations of History* (London, Adam & Charles Black, Ltd., 1954), Christians inherited much of their conception of history from the Jews, and this gave them a vision of history with a definite plan; this plan is for both Jews and Christians in the hands of God, but for the Christians it has its center in Jesus and his redemptive work. Thus the Christian historian sets forth a series of historic events in which God Himself acts, but the full meaning of these events is beyond history. Such a view of history has been called by German writers *Heilsgeschichte*, "salvation-history," or perhaps a better English translation is "sacred-history." The relation of sacred history to the complex phenomena of world history has been explained in some detail by E. C. Rust in *The Christian Understanding of History* (London, Lutterworth Press, 1947). A thorny problem for sacred history is the ambiguity of the primitive Christian conception of time and history. The first Christians believed that Christ had won in their day an eschatological victory, but there is also evident in their writings a future expectation of a coming kingdom. The relation between what has been called the "realized eschatology" of the New Testament and its future reality is a subject much debated among Christian writers today, particularly since the publication of C. H. Dodd's *History and Gospel* (N.Y., Charles Scribner's Sons, 1938). It has also been the subject of an interesting monograph by O. Cullman, *Christ and Time*, tr. by F. V. Filson (Philadelphia, Westminster Press, 1950; Original German, Switzerland, 1945), in which he attempts to set forth a consistent interpretation of the Christian view of *salvation.*

Christian historiography

The role played by sacred history in historiography is an interesting story in itself and has brought about many modifications and reinterpretations of the Christian view of history. The story begins with the Acts of the Apostles, the author of which, as M. Dibelius has pointed out in *Studies in the Acts of the Apostles*, tr. by Mary Ling (N.Y., Charles Scribner's Sons, 1956) not only produced a consecutive narrative but also endeavored to interpret events in the light of divine rather than human activity. After this first tentative approach in Acts, there is no formal attempt to write church history until we come to Eusebius (*c.* 260–*c.* 340), who wrote a monumental *Ecclesiastical History*, tr. by K. Lake (N.Y., G. P. Putnam's Sons, Inc., 1926–32) in seven books, covering the history of the church from apostolic times down to 303. Eusebius is extremely important in that he was not only the first systematic historian of the origin and expansion of the Christian Church, but he also embodied in his history the earliest Christian theme, carried over from Jewish history, the vindication of God's justice, emphasizing God as the controller of history.

It remained for Augustine of Hippo (354–430) to set forth this theme in philosophical form. The great challenge that Augustine had to face in his day was the obvious disintegration of the Roman Empire during the opening phases of the Christian era. He met the challenge by pointing out that the calamities under which society was then reeling were not so great as those which had overtaken earlier empires and at the same time emphasizing that there was still a reasonable sequence running through history in accordance with the divine plan. This was set forth in the *City of God*, 8th ed. (Edinburgh, T. & T. Clark, 1934), an outline of a theology of history in which all human events are seen as carrying out a plan foreordained by God. The book is a first example of a Christian philosophy of history in which oriental conceptions of eternally recurring phases of history are abandoned and time becomes linear, not cyclical.

The work of Augustine is a landmark in Christian thought and has had a permanent influence on the Christian interpretation of history. It was carried on by Orosius (*c.* 380–*c.* 420), who was directed by Augustine to set out in greater detail the providential acts of God even in the midst of calamities. This he did in *The Seven Books of History against the Pagans*, ed. by G. Bolsuinge (N.Y., Columbia University Press, 1936), in which he deals with four world empires and comments on their rise and fall. He enlarges upon their calamities in order to minimize the calamities of his own day. Despite even greater calamities than those faced by Augustine and Orosius besetting the tottering Roman Empire, Salvian (*c.* 400), a priest of Marseilles, in a treatise entitled *De gubernatione Dei*, tr. by J. F. O'Sullivan (N.Y., Cima Publishing Co., 1947) still held that these events indicate the providential purposes of God. He wrote in the manner of the Old Testament prophets, denouncing the Romans and the lukewarm Christians of his day, and concluded that the barbarian invaders were a scourge of sinners, a proof that God controls history. This theme was continued in the sixth and seventh centuries by Gregory, Bishop of Tours (538–594), and Venerable Bede (672–723), the former in *The History of the Franks*, tr. by M. Guizot (Paris, Didier, 1874) and the latter in *The Ecclesiastical History of the English Nation*, tr. by E. Thomson (Boston, Directors of Old South Work, 1902). But these writers were very credulous, and they saw in miracles and marvels the hand of God. They are more important as recorders of contemporary events than as examples of Christian interpreters of history. Their influence is evident throughout the medieval period, during which annals and chronicles rather than interpretive history were the vogue.

There are some exceptions to this generalization, of which Bishop Otto Freising (*c.* 1114–*c.* 1158) is an illustrious example. His *The Two Cities*, tr. by C. C. Mierow (N.Y., Columbia University Press, 1928), may be regarded as a philosophy of history rather than a chronicle but borrows its ideas chiefly from Augustine. Other exceptional medieval historians are Jean Froissart (1337–1410), whose *Chronicles of England, France, Spain and adjoining Countries* (N.Y., E. P. Dutton & Co., 1906) is concerned with the manners and customs of these countries, and Philip de Comines (1445–1509), whose *Memoirs* (London, Joseph Whitaker & Sons, Ltd., 1823) are a commentary on contemporary events. This concern reflects the displacement of the providential view of history. Both these writers dwell strongly on the underlying motives behind the trend of events, and they mark a transition to the Renaissance mood, in which the emphasis upon divine providence in history begins to recede before the revived classical interest in human events.

The rise of humanism in western Europe brought about a gradual secularization of history, first discernible perhaps in Petrarch's (1304–74) *History of Rome*, but even more so in the writings of Machiavelli (1469–1527), and of Guicciardini, both of whom pioneered in modern political and national historical writing. Thus was brought about a close association of history with political science, as set forth by Jean Bodin (1530–96) in *Method for the Easy Comprehension of History*, tr. by B. Reynolds (N.Y., Columbia University Press, 1945), in which he also laid great emphasis upon the geographical factors in history. Both these ideas were taken up in the age of Enlightenment and helped to bring about the complete secularization of historical writing in Europe.

The age of Enlightenment contributes little to the development of Christian historiography except for the problems it created for the Christian view of history. It was the remarkable development of science that most influenced historical writers, both secular and Christian, during this era and was evidenced in a more critical analysis of all historical documents, biblical as well as nonbiblical, thus abolishing the distinction between sacred and profane history. Perhaps the most influential historian of the Enlightenment was Giovanni Battista Vico who in *Principî di una scienza nuova* (2nd ed., 1730; Mexico, El Colegio de México, 1941) put forth a theory of cycles in history through which all nations pass: heroic, classical, and a new barbarism. In his analysis he found that each cycle is differentiated from the preceding one and that there is a spiral movement of progress. Thus arose the general idea of an inevitable progress forward based upon the idea of the perfectibility of human nature. Through all this development ran a constant emphasis upon the capability of human reason to discover the true causes of events and thus to improve human relations. Historians entered upon a campaign to free men from bigotry and superstition, and especially from the dominance of the church. All this led to the composition of nationalistic histories in which the providential purpose of God was abandoned as a principle of explanation and replaced by geographic, commercial, and fiscal interpretations of events. From the point of view of Christianity, the most significant history of the era was Edward Gibbon's *The History of the Decline and Fall of the Roman Empire* (1776–88) with its famous fifteenth and sixteenth chapters dealing with the rise of Christianity in a completely objective manner, coloured by "grave and temperate irony." The "clamour" following the publication of the first volume created "what might almost be called a library of controversy."

But even during the age of Enlightenment there was a reaction against a purely rationalist approach to historical phenomena, of which Rousseau was the outstanding voice. Rousseau's influence on historiography is to be found among the romanticists of the nineteenth century rather than in the eighteenth, particularly in François René Chateaubriand, who in 1802 published the *Génie du Christianisme*, 7th ed., (Philadelphia, J. B. Lippincott Co., 1868), an elaborate defence of Christianity based upon the emotional side of life. The summary of his argument in proof of Christianity may be put in this way: the works of Christianity indicate its perfection; a perfect consequence cannot spring from an imperfect principle; the logical conclusion is, therefore, that Christianity is not the work of men, but of God.

Romantic church history, which became allied with nationalistic and liberalistic trends, proved to be a weak defense for the Christian faith. As was inevitable, a gradual reaction set in against highly colored church history. The reaction is evidenced in the works of Leopold Von Ranke, who is generally regarded as the father of scientific history. During 1834–36, there appeared three volumes of his *Die römischen Päpste, ihre Kirche und ihr Staat im 16 und 17 Jahrhundert*, which were translated into English by W. K. Kelly in 1844 (Philadelphia, Lea & Febiger) and with new editions in 1845 and 1847. He based his work on the most careful and detailed research and set a vogue for church historians to adhere vigorously to the rules of scientific method. One of the most brilliant of Ranke's school was Johann Döllinger, whose *Church History*, tr. by E. Cox (London, 1840) was a revolution in the interpretation of Christian documents, particularly in its stress upon evidence and the testing of facts. Döllinger's ideas were carried to England by his pupil, Lord Acton, who was to have a decisive influence upon the writing of church history in England, particularly upon Mandell Creighton, whose *History of the Papacy during the Period of the Reformation* (1887–94) is a landmark in balanced historical writing on a very controversial subject.

Scientific history, however, did not solve the problem of history, for with its attempt to be purely objective it showed a bias toward contemporary liberal ideas and failed to answer the question of the ultimate force or forces which determine historical developments. Such doubts arose out of W. Hegel's *Lectures on the Philosophy of History*, which appeared in Germany in 1837 and were made available to English readers by J. Sibree's translation in 1852. In this first direct approach to a philosophy of history Hegel attempted to show that mankind has developed through a dialectical process, culminating in the ultimate self-realization of the idea of freedom. Hegel's philosophy of history was to have a stimulating effect upon Christian historians, but this enthusiasm was somewhat dampened by Karl Marx, who adopted Hegel's dialectical conception but, in place of Hegel's idealism, proclaimed that material conditions rather than spiritual forces underlie historical development, from thesis through antithesis to synthesis. These steps in the dialectic of development he held were open to scientific study. Not dissimilar to Marx's view was Auguste Comte's, who in *Cours de philosophie positive* (Paris, Hachette Co., 1927) outlined a three-stage historical development—

the theological, the metaphysical, and the scientific or positive eras—and foresaw in the final positivistic era a world ruled by a sociological priesthood. In this same general mood were the social evolutionists, such as Herbert Spencer in his *The Principles of Sociology*, 3rd ed. (N.Y., Appleton-Century-Crofts, Inc., 1895), who assumed that historical development is an evolutionary process governed by unrelenting forces that cannot be changed by human action and that this inevitable development is in the direction of perfection and ultimate happiness for the human race.

Historism

It is against this background of utopian ideas and a concern with simple or scientific explanations of history, often called "historism," that modern Christian historians have attempted to reassert a specifically Christian interpretation of history. An early approach to the problem raised by "historism" was made by W. E. Collins in *The Study of Ecclesiastical History* (N.Y., Longmans, Green & Co., Inc., 1903). He undertook to distinguish church history from other historical disciplines by pointing out that it is not subject to the deductive method because the history of the church is not finished. More recently, Herbert Butterfield, in *Christianity and History* (London, G. Bell & Sons, Ltd., 1949) issued a similar warning against the pitfalls into which the scientific approach to history may lead the church historian and made a strong plea for a reassertion of the providential view of history. Shirley Jackson Case, in *The Christian Philosophy of History* (Chicago, University of Chicago Press, 1943), attempted to meet the problem raised by secular historians as to the purpose and meaning of history by freeing the study of history from the perversions of metaphysical theories apart from historical data. He insisted that history can serve as a tonic against threatening evils and again vigorously reasserted the providential view of history.

Moving somewhat away from this defensive position was R. W. McLaughlin, who in *The Spiritual Element in History* (N.Y., Abingdon Press, 1926) found an agreement among Hegel, Marx, and Augustine on the "why" or meaning of history and arrived at the conclusion "that in Christianity is found the most convincing proof of the continuity of history." With even more confidence M. C. D'Arcy, S.J., in *The Sense of History: Secular and Sacred* (London, Faber & Faber, Ltd., 1959), taking Christian truths for granted, attempted to see what light they throw on the human scene. In a similar vein Christopher Dawson in *The Dynamics of World History*, ed. by J. Mulloy (London, Sheed & Ward, Ltd., 1957), contends that "Christianity laid the foundations for a new view of history, which is both universalist and progressive." He sees history moving toward an ultimate goal; so also does Nicholas Berdyaev, who in *The Meaning of History* (London, Geoffrey Bles, Ltd., 1936) accepted much of the Marxian dialectic and used it for a dynamic interpretation of Christianity. He found an interior dialogue underlying

European literature from Augustine to Dostoievsky, Proust, Joyce, and even some of the Soviet writers which has helped to shape Christianity. A novel exposition of the dynamics of history is to be found in Karl Löwith's *Meaning in History* (Chicago, University of Chicago Press, 1949), in which he puts forth the idea that the historical consciousness of Europe has been "determined by an eschatological motivation from Isaiah to Marx, from Augustine to Hegel and from Joachim to Schelling." His conclusion is that "cyclic motion and eschatological direction have exhausted the basic approaches." It follows that Christians must repudiate both these approaches and fall back on the radical Christian faith that "the Christian times are Christian only in so far as they are the last time," which makes a "Christian history" nonsense. Despite this pessimistic view of Christian history, there are a number of what may be called theological historians working within the framework of the dialectical theology of Karl Barth and Emil Brunner, who still find the eschatological view of history to be the Christian answer to the historical relativism of secular historians. Among them is Paul Tillich, who in his *Interpretation of History* (London, Charles Scribner's Sons, Ltd., 1936) accepts the existentialist approach to history and provides it with several categories, such as philosophical, political, and theological. Erich Frank, who is also among the existentialists, suggests in chapter five of his *Philosophical Understanding and Religious Truth* (London, Oxford University Press, 1945) that "the Christian is a contemporary of Christ, and time and the world's history are overcome." For Reinhold Niebuhr in *Faith and History* (London, James Nisbet & Co., Ltd., 1949) none of the problems of history can be solved in time, since the end of history lies outside time; the Christian can only overcome history within the community of grace. The Neo-Thomist Jacques Maritain accepts much of the existentialist insight, but he also relies on many axiomatic or functional laws for the study of history. His views have been set forth in a volume edited by J. W. Evans, entitled *Jacques Maritain on the Philosophy of History* (N.Y., Charles Scribner's Sons, 1957).

The most drastic attempt to deal with the problems that historism has posed for the modern students of Christianity, and particularly for New Testament scholars, has been made by K. Rudolph Bultmann in *Kerygma and Myth*, tr. by R. H. Fuller (London, Society for Promoting Christian Knowledge, 1953) and in *History and Eschatology* (Edinburgh, Edinburgh University Press, 1957), both of which serve as good introductions to the literature on the problem of the interpretation of Scripture. Not all Christian scholars are in agreement with his radical ideas of interpretation of Christian documents, but many theologians welcome his approach to the Scriptures as a way through the maze of modern historical criticism of the Bible and as an escape from historical nihilism. The story of this controversy has been well told by Friedrich Gogarten in *Demythologizing and History* (Stuttgart, 1953), tr. by N. H. Smith (London, Student Christian Movement Press, 1955). The reason for the controversy, Gogarten explains, is that Bultmann insists upon a fundamentally different understanding of reality than that assumed in the classical form of Christian dogma. The change has come about because modern man does not, as medieval man did, try to adapt himself to a pre-established order. History for modern man can only be envisaged from the point of view of his own responsibility for it; thus history cannot be a subject-object pattern, in that man cannot take himself out of it. Consequently, he must approach history within the historical character of human existence. The essence of history, then, is that man tries to understand himself by participating in it; so Bultmann believes that one must try to understand the essential character of the New Testament revelation in accordance with the essential nature of history. To give an objective history of the so-called redemptive facts of the New Testament, he feels, would be a rationalization which would cause it to lose its own historical character. For Bultmann, Jesus is not perceptible from the standpoint of historical investigation, so we must take seriously that "reality which discloses itself in faith," faith in the *kerygma* as the proclamation of the work of God. This, however, according to Bultmann, does not exclude applying to the study of Scripture all the principles of historical and literary criticism, which are the common tools of both sacred and profane historians.

THE HOLY SCRIPTURES

Christianity, like several other of the higher religions, has a sacred literature—the written record of God's communication to his people. The core of that communication for Christians is what the New Testament calls the *kerygma*, or the proclamation of good news that is the fulfillment of a promise that God has made to his people. Thus, as C. H. Dodd has emphasized in *According to the Scriptures* (N.Y., Charles Scribner's Sons, 1953), the church was committed by the terms of its proclamation "to a formidable task of biblical research," both for its own understanding of the Gospel and to make its message intelligible to the outside world. The earliest fathers of the church found the ultimate source and authority for the *kerygma* in the person and work of Jesus Christ, but they explained this in the context of the Old Testament, which was for them, as also for the writers of the New Testament, "The Scriptures." The significance of the Old Testament for the early Christians is briefly told by W. F. Lofthouse in chapter X of a volume edited by H. W. Robinson, *Record and Revelation* (Oxford, Clarendon Press, 1938), in which he undertakes to help his readers to understand the profound meaning of Augustine's dictum "the Old Testament is patent, lies open in the New" and "the New Testament is latent, lies hidden in the Old." Nevertheless, for the first hundred years of the church's history, the term "Scriptures" meant the Old Testament alone.

The Old Testament

Since the Old Testament was the doctrinal norm for the primitive church, it is evident that it cannot be overlooked in any study of Christianity. In order to bring the Old Testament into accord with the Gospel message, Christians early began to make use of two methods of exegesis: typology and allegory. The first took as its premise that the events and personages of the Old Testament were types which anticipated the events and personages of the new dispensation. That this is still an acceptable form of exegesis is the contention of G. W. H. Lampe and K. J. Woolcombe in *Essays on Typology* (London, Student Christian Movement Press, 1957). This book provides an interesting analysis of the difference between allegorism and typology, with the balance in favor of typology. In allegorical exegesis the text was treated more as a symbol of deeper spiritual truths, but this inevitably led to a disregard of the content and the original meaning of the text. Nevertheless, these two methods of interpretation became almost universal for Christian exegetes, particularly during the medieval period, and were also used by the reformation scholars, along with hermeneutics, the science of the interpretation of the Scriptures in the original languages in which they were written. Thus the continuity of the two Testaments was accepted; all the writers were regarded as inspired by the selfsame divine spirit, and little interest was shown by the exegetes in dating the books of the Old Testament or analyzing the conditions under which they were written. From them could be drawn a continuing theme or a divine epic in which all the parts fitted together, as was brilliantly done by J. B. Bossuet in *Discours sur l'histoire universelle* (Paris, Lefèvre, 1836). But with the rise of the scientific spirit during the century in which Bossuet was writing, all the comfortable acceptance of a divine epic began to fade away. The new spirit of the time, with its quest for sources and origins and with its greater knowledge of the evolution of the universe, could no longer accept the simple biblical explanation. This change of outlook is briefly told by G. W. Anderson in an introductory chapter to his *A Critical Introduction to the Old Testament* (London, Gerald Duckworth & Co., Ltd., 1959). Linguistic and literary methods of criticism were used with startling effect in an analysis of Old Testament writings by a German scholar, J. G. Eichhorn, in his *Einleitung in das Alte Testament*, 3 vols. (Leipzig, Weidmann, 1803).

It was not, however, until the latter part of the nineteenth century that J. Wellhausen and other German scholars began to apply in a systematic way all the critical apparatus that was being used upon classical literature. Their results were made known to English students by S. R. Driver in 1891, in his justly famous *An Introduction to the Literature of the Old Testament* (N.Y., Charles Scribner's Sons, 1891), of which a ninth edition appeared in 1913.

Under the impact of literary criticism, the Old Testament was broken up into its constituent elements, and this development has caused Christian scholars to revise their earlier conceptions of revelation in the Old Testament. Still a very readable book on this subject is A. Loisy's *The Religion of Israel*, first written for *Revue du clergé français* in 1900 and translated into English by A. Galton (London, George Allen & Unwin, Ltd., 1910). Loisy bluntly asserted that the old theory of an inspired book dictated by God from cover to cover must be abandoned and that the legendary character of many Old Testament stories must frankly be recognized. At the same time, he held that the study of the evolution of prophecy and messianism are still valuable for an understanding of Christianity. We must, as it were, see the Old Testament as pioneering in ideas that were finally taken over by the Christian Church. This is a theme that occupies a great many Christian writers on the Old Testament today and has been dealt with in some detail by R. H. Pfeiffer in his *Introduction to the Old Testament* (N.Y., Harper & Brothers, 1941).

Today, however, a new school of Old Testament scholars, the tradition-historical school, is compelling a revision of much of the work of the literary-critical school. The new school was preceded by a development associated with the name of Herman Gunkel, who made a rather drastic criticism of the "Wellhausen fabric of learning." The tradition-historical school led by Professor Engnell accepts Gunkel's view that it is impossible to carry through an exact chronological treatment of Israelite literature by the old literary methods, that there must be a recognition of conventional forms of literature appropriate to particular occasions. It is the function of literary history to recognize and classify these forms, to relate each to its setting in life (*Sitz im Leben*) and thus to trace their development with an exactitude impossible to the older literary-critical school. Following this suggestion, the tradition-historical school centered at Uppsala, Sweden, is applying this new approach vigorously to the books of the Old Testament. A good summary of the accomplishments of these Scandinavian scholars has been made by E. Nielsen in two articles published in *Dansk Teologisk Tidsskrift*, XIII (1950) and XV (1952). Both have been translated into English under the title *Oral Tradition, A Modern Problem in Old Testament Introduction* (Illinois, A. R. Allenson, Inc., 1954).

For those desirous to keep up with the latest developments in the field of Old Testament interpretation there are available two excellent quarterlies: *Vetus Testamentum* (1951–) published by the International Organization for the Study of the Old Testament, at Leiden, Netherlands, and *Interpretation, A Journal of Bible and Theology* (1947–) published at Richmond, Virginia.

Biblical archeology

All these new approaches to an understanding of the Old Testament are inspired by the modern desire to have as authentic documents as possible in order to gain a clearer comprehension of the origin of fundamental Christian beliefs. Naturally the findings of biblical archeologists are of great importance in this quest, particularly in establishing the age and authenticity of many key documents. Although biblical archeology is concerned with stratigraphy and typology, its underlying motive is to understand and expound the Scriptures. A brief introduction to this fascinating study is provided by G. E. Wright, assisted by R. Tomes, in *An Introduction to Biblical Archeology* (N.Y., Doubleday & Co., Inc., 1960). Professor Wright has also given a more detailed account of the subject in his *Biblical Archeology* (Philadelphia, Westminster Press, 1957). The introductory chapter enlarges upon the connection between archeology and biblical theology. Both books carry the story of archeological research down to New Testament times.

A good summary of the work of biblical scholars in recent years and their contribution to an understanding of the Christian background, particularly through archeological research, is provided in a volume entitled *The Old Testament and Modern Study: A Generation of Discovery and Research* (Oxford, Clarendon Press, 1951). This book, edited by R. H. Rowley, consists of essays by members of the Society for Old Testament Study.

Intertestamental literature

Almost equal in importance to the Old Testament for understanding the underlying doctrines of the New Testament is the literature produced by Jewish writers after the Old Testament period and before the New Testament had become a canonical book. As is now well known, Judaism had been in great ferment during those years and had divided into many parties, particularly on the question of the messianic hope. It was from this dream of the ultimate triumph of the Jewish nation through a messianic deliverer that Christianity issued. The subsidiary doctrines that arose around it, such as an apocalyptic judgment, separatism, asceticism, the nature of the Messiah, the resurrection of the dead, are all of significant importance for the origins of Christian beliefs. They are pre-eminently the subject of intertestamental literature. An excellent introduction to these intertestamental speculations is S. B. Frost's *Old Testament Apocalyptic, Its Origin and Growth* (London, The Epworth Press, 1952), a book which deals with the whole field of apocalyptic both in the Old Testament and in noncanonical Jewish literature. The latter literature as well as the Apocrypha, composed, roughly between 200 B.C. and A.D. 100, has been collected by R. H. Charles in two large volumes under the title, *The Apocrypha and Pseudepigrapha of the Old Testament in English* (Oxford, Clarendon Press, 1913). In this work he had the aid of many scholars, and each of the books is provided with an introduction and critical explanatory notes. These are formidable volumes for the layman but are indispensable for the serious student of the background of Christian beliefs. Less formidable is C. C. Torrey's *The Apocryphal Literature, A Brief Introduc-*

tion (New Haven, Yale University Press, 1945), which defines the term "apocrypha" as applying to all Jewish religious writings not found in the canon of sacred scripture. An even simpler approach than Professor Torrey's is R. C. Dentan's *The Apocrypha, Bridge of the Testaments* (Greenwich, The Seabury Press, 1954), which attempts to explain in nontechnical language how to understand this literature as a key to much New Testament writing. Nor should one overlook a popular manual by the great scholar of this literature, R. H. Charles, whose *Religious Development between the Old and New Testament* (N.Y., Holt, Rinehart & Winston, Inc., 1914) is an interesting analysis of the development of both Jewish and Christian ideas on the ultimate destiny of mankind.

The Dead Sea Scrolls

The Dead Sea Scrolls have become an exciting addition to intertestamental literature as well as an aid to textual criticism of the Old Testament. Eleven caves in the area of Qumran have yielded to the archeologists very important material for the critical study of both Old and New Testaments. Every book of the Old Testament is represented in fragments, but there are also fragmentary remains of the library of the Essenes, a Jewish sect that lived in the area, probably during the second century B.C. Other fragments are of a later date, but all are earlier than A.D. 68.

The most ambitious work in connection with the scrolls, so far, is Millar Burrows, *The Dead Sea Scrolls* (N.Y., The Viking Press, 1955), in which he discussed the problem of dates, identification, and significance and also included six translations. It has been supplemented with a second volume, *More Light on the Dead Sea Scrolls* (N.Y., The Viking Press, 1958), in which Professor Burrows discusses new scrolls and new interpretations and also includes new translations. A good part of the second book is devoted to the question whether the "Essene" teacher of righteousness anticipated Christian beliefs, a suggestion made by J. M. Allegro in a series of lectures delivered over the B.B.C. in the spring of 1956 and since enlarged upon in his work, *The Dead Sea Scrolls* (N.Y., Penguin Books, 1956). In this book he gives many parallels between documents from Qumran and New Testament writings, particularly on messianic and eschatological concerns. This so-called challenge to Christian faith has been accepted by twelve New Testament scholars whose opinions have been collected in a book edited by Krister Stendahl, *The Scrolls and the New Testament* (N.Y., Harper & Brothers, 1957). All but three of the chapters had been previously published in German, English, or Latin periodicals of a scholarly nature and are but a preliminary approach to a re-evaluation of the documentary study of the New Testament. Since the discovery of the scrolls is a very contemporary event, there will undoubtedly be new evaluations of their significance; these may be followed in such learned journals as *Bulletin of American Schools of Oriental Research* (1919–),

Bulletin of John Rylands Library, (1903–), *Catholic Biblical Quarterly*, (1939–), *Journal of Biblical Literature* (1881–), *Revue d'histoire des religions*, and *Zeitschrift für die alttestamentliche Wissenschaft* (1881–).

TEXT AND CANON OF THE NEW TESTAMENT

The ordinary reader of the New Testament probably gives little thought to its original composition, or to the long history behind the collection of the books that make up either authorized or revised versions. Nevertheless, this is important information for any student of Christianity, since the collection of Christian books was part of the evolution of Christian doctrine; and it is through textual criticism that the original reading of Christian documents has been preserved down through the centuries.

Textual criticism

Textual criticism is necessary because the twenty-seven documents which constitute the New Testament have not been preserved in their original form. As new copies of the originals are discovered, they often show variant readings from the texts in use. The object of the textual critic is to recover as nearly as possible the original text. A good introduction to the whole field of textual criticism is G. F. Kenyon's *Handbook to the Textual Criticism of the New Testament* (London, Macmillan & Co., Ltd., 1st ed., 1901; 2nd ed., 1912). The opening chapter deals with the function of textual criticism and is followed by an illuminating description of manuscripts and ancient versions of the New Testament, including a delineation of periods marked by the style of the writing employed—uncial, minuscule, or cursive—with comments on the material used, such as papyrus, vellum, and paper.

The history of the discovery of manuscripts and the significance of each discovery add to the interest of any book in textual criticism, and Kenyon tells very well the story of such important manuscripts as *Codex Sinaiticus*, ed. by C. Tischendorf (London, 1862), discovered by Constantin Tischendorf in the Monastery of St. Catherine at Mount Sinai in 1844 and now preserved in the British Museum. As a matter of fact, all the important manuscripts like the *Codex Vaticanus*, ed. by H. Fabiani (London, 1859) preserved in the Vatican Library and the *Codex Alexandrinus*, ed. by E. M. Thompson (London, 1881–83), now after many hazardous adventures safely housed in the British Museum, have romantic stories attached to them. It is beyond the compass of this chapter to detail the various manuscripts of the New Testament, but very few of them are omitted from Kenyon's book, which also includes ancient versions in languages other than Greek that are often relied upon in the search for the original text. Nor does the search rely wholly upon manuscripts and ancient versions. Quotations of New Testament writings found in the works of early ecclesiastical writers are also extremely valuable in the quest for the proper reading, since these quotations often come from manuscripts long since lost. A book highly recommended for the inquiring student in this field of research is *The Text and Canon of the New Testament* by A. Souter, first published in 1912 and recently revised by C. S. C. Williams, 2nd rev. ed. (London, Gerald Duckworth & Co., Ltd., 1954).

It was to A. Souter that the editors of the Oxford series of Greek and Latin classics entrusted the task of preparing a critical edition of the New Testament in Greek with a selected critical apparatus of variant readings. His *Novum Testamentum Graece* (Oxford, Oxford University Press, 1910; 2nd ed., 1947) gives the text which by inference lies behind the English Revised Version (1881), to some extent behind the American Standard Revised Version (1946) and the New Testament of the New English Bible (1961).

A much valued text based upon meticulous research is E. Nestles' convenient pocket edition of the *Greek Testament* first published in 1898 and now in its twenty-first edition (N.Y., Prentice-Hall, Inc., 1952).

Canon

Closely allied with textual criticism is the problem of the canon of the New Testament. "Canon" used in this sense may be defined as the rule whereby some of the writings of early Christians were recognized as divinely inspired, while others were not. The history of the collection and official approval of New Testament Scriptures is very involved and begins with a consideration of the writings of the earliest fathers of the church, includes heretical writers as well, and continues on into the fourth century and even beyond. Indeed, B. F. Westcott, who wrote *A General Survey of the History of the Canon of the New Testament* (London, Macmillan & Co., Ltd., 1881) carries his story through eight centuries. This book has long been a standard authority on the subject.

It is interesting to note that the first known person to draw up a list of New Testament books was the heretic Marcion. He had rejected the Old Testament and sought for an alternative set of scriptures for his heretical following. This occurred around A.D. 144, and there seems little doubt that he was revising a list of books currently in use in the church; and so it would appear that there was a fixed list or canon around the middle of the second century.

Excluded books

A study of the canon raises the question, Why were some Christian writings of the first two centuries admitted and others rejected? Obviously the canon was drawn up to prevent heretical books from masquerading as Christian, but there were Christian books in circulation to which no doctrinal objection could be made but which failed to be recognized as canonical. It would seem that the church in its contest with heretics laid down a criterion which prevented the acceptance as canonical of many books that could still be read with profit. One such criterion was apostolicity: a canonical book must have been written by an apostle or at least have apostolic authority behind it.

Besides those rejected because of lack of apostolic authority, other books in circulation in the primitive church were referred to as apocryphal. For the most part they are imaginative works, written either to edify or to commend a peculiar doctrinal view. This apocryphal literature has been gathered together and translated into English by M. R. James in a volume entitled *The Apocryphal New Testament* (Oxford, Clarendon Press, 1924). To it may be added a supplementary volume entitled *Excluded Books of the New Testament* (London, Nash & Grayson, 1927), translated by J. B. Lightfoot, M. R. James, H. B. Sweet, and others, with an Introduction by J. A. Robinson. The latter includes not only apocryphal literature, but also books that may have some genuine historical value.

Interest in this literature has been greatly stimulated in recent years by the discovery of Gnostic documents unearthed in Egypt in 1945, near a village called Nag Hummadi, far up the Nile. Only a few fragments of this discovery have been published, the most interesting being the *Gospel according to Thomas*, a Coptic text, established and translated by A. Guillaumont and others (N.Y., Harper & Brothers, 1959). The significance of this discovery for New Testament students has been commented on by R. M. Grant in collaboration with D. N. Freedman in a book entitled *The Secret Sayings of Jesus* (N.Y., Doubleday & Co., Inc., 1960).

Spurious or rejected Christian literature has a long and checkered history. Even today there are in circulation writings professing to be genuine documents of Christian antiquity. Since many people have been misled by them, it has become the task of Christian scholars to apply to them the same tests applied to early apocryphal literature. Some of these modern forgeries have been analyzed by E. Goodspeed in *Strange New Gospels* (Chicago, University of Chicago Press, 1931), to which he has added a supplement, *Modern Apocrypha* (Boston, Beacon Press, Inc., 1956).

NEW TESTAMENT INTERPRETATION

The critical study of the New Testament is a fairly modern discipline. A century ago the Christian student would have relied upon typology and allegory for interpreting the Christian Scriptures. The new method of interpretation has created, as it were, a serious breach between the modern student and his reformation and medieval predecessors. To Richard Simon (1688–

1712), a French Oratorian priest, goes the distinction of pioneering in the application of literary criticism to New Testament writings. His essay on the New Testament was translated into German in 1750 and started a series of critical works on Christianity, which became forerunners of the Tübingen school of research. An outstanding member of this school was F. C. Baur (1792–1860), whose *The Church History of the First Three Centuries*, tr. by Rev. A. Menzies, 3rd ed. (London, Williams & Norgate, 1878–79), stimulated a revolutionary interpretation of early Christian documents. The story of this development has been briefly told by J. Moffat in a prolegomena to his *Introduction to the Literature of the New Testament* (N.Y., Charles Scribner's Sons, 1911).

Synoptic problem

Any study of the nature and quality of Christianity must give pre-eminence to the first three gospels. In recent years there has been great concentration on what has been called the synoptic problem—that is, how to harmonize the variations of the gospels when they relate similar events. Another problem is presented by the fact that similarity of the gospels is so great that when a good deal of the material from all three is placed in three parallel columns striking resemblances in phrasing and wording can be perceived. In 1907 A. Huck made such a harmony, which was translated into English by R. L. Finney, with the title *Huck's Synopsis of the First Three Gospels* (N.Y., The Methodist Book Concern, 1929). The similarities thus revealed strengthened an hypothesis put forward by G. E. Lessing as early as 1778, and developed by J. G. Eichhorn in 1794, that the authors of these gospels drew much of their material from an older, primitive gospel, perhaps in Aramaic. This was still a respectable theory when B. F. Westcott wrote his *Introduction to the Study of the Gospels* in 1862 (Boston, Gould & Lincoln) but now seems no longer tenable. As A. H. McNeile has expressed it in his very useful *Introduction to the Study of the New Testament* (1927), 2nd ed., revised by C. S. C. Williams (Oxford, Clarendon Press, 1953), there is considerable agreement that oral tradition played a role in the formation of the gospels, but "the idea of a primary stereo-typed *corpus* of preaching has been abandoned." The balance of opinion is that written gospels appeared only after the church had entered the Greek-speaking world.

Scholarship today regards Mark as the foundation document used by both Matthew and Luke. They used other sources as well, one of which they had in common, designated as "Q" (from *Quelle*, the German word for source). Pioneer works supporting this theory are Hund's *Commentar zum Neuen Testament*, 4 vols. (Freiburg, Mohr, 1889–91), and B. Weiss's *Die Quellen der synoptischen Überlieferung* (Leipzig, J. C. Hinrichs, 1908). Two scholars who brought the problem of sources forcibly to the attention of English scholars were J. C. Hawkins, with his *Horae synopticae* (Oxford,

Clarendon Press, 1909), and W. Sanday, with his *Studies in the Synoptic Problem* (Oxford, Clarendon Press, 1911). B. H. Streeter's *The Four Gospels, A Study of Origins* (London, Macmillan & Co., Ltd., 1924) was also a notable advance in New Testament criticism. He along with V. Taylor in *Behind the Third Gospel* (Oxford, Clarendon Press, 1926) suggested a Proto-Luke theory —namely, that someone, perhaps Luke, gathered into one document, "L," previously unwritten stories and teachings. Then Luke combined L with Q to form Proto-Luke; later Luke inserted large sections of Mark into Proto-Luke to form the Third Gospel. Streeter also suggested that behind the First Gospel lies a Jewish-Christian document, "M," which makes Matthew's sources: Mark, Q, M, and L. This four-document theory has been vigorously challenged by M. S. Enslin in *Christian Beginnings* (N.Y., Harper & Brothers, 1938). On the other hand, F. C. Grant in *The Gospels: Their Origin and Their Growth* (London, Faber & Faber, Ltd., 1959) advocates a "multiple source" theory somewhat similar to Streeter's four-document theory. Involved in all these speculations are questions relating to the origin, place of writing, and dating of the gospels. Exact dating is impossible, and authorities vary in their conjectures from A.D. 40 to the opening of the second century. The suggestion of W. L. Knox in *The Sources of the Synoptic Gospels*, II: *St. Luke and St. Matthew* (Cambridge, Cambridge University Press, 1957) that Luke was written somewhere in the middle of the second century is not generally accepted by New Testament scholars. A rather clear exposition on the problem of dating the gospels is to be found in A. H. McNeile (*op. cit.*), pp. 25–31.

Form criticism

Form criticism came into prominence in the early 1920's as a method in the interpretation of the New Testament. This method, as explained by M. Dibelius in *From Tradition to Gospel*, tr. by B. Woolf from the revised 2nd ed. of *Die Formgeschichte des Evangeliums* in collaboration with the author (London, Nicholson & Watson, Ltd., 1934) is to put into their original purity the forms which the gospel material assumed during the shaping of the tradition—that is, to explain the origin of these forms and their development before they were committed to writing. To some extent it is the application to the New Testament, of the categories which H. Gunkel (*op. cit.*) applied to the Old Testament in looking for the formative influence of a people's life pattern (*Sitz im Leben*) upon literary composition. One of the pioneers of this school of research, R. Bultmann, in *Die Geschichte der synoptischen Tradition* (Göttingen, 1921; 2nd ed., Vandenhoeck & Ruprecht, 1931) has used the method with great skill to show that the gospels are primarily witnesses to the life and teaching of the early church. A smaller book by Bultmann, *Die Erforschung der synoptischen Evangelien* (1929; 4th ed., Berlin, 1961), on the same subject has been translated into English by F. C. Grant and is included in a book entitled *Form Criticism: A New Method of New Testament Research* (Chicago, Willett, Clark & Co., 1934). In the same volume is also included a translation of Karl Kundsin's *Primitive Christianity in the Light of Gospel Research.*

In their attempt to classify the forms of gospel material form critics are not always in agreement, but there appears to be a fairly unanimous opinion that the Passion Story took form first and that it is the one exception to the claim that each event as a teaching story was originally a separate unit. V. Taylor in *The Formation of the Gospel Tradition* (London, Macmillan & Co., Ltd., 1933) has laid special emphasis upon the typical forms he finds in the gospels; particularly upon what he has designated the Pronouncement Story, which is preceded by either a problem, a controversy, or a miracle and reaches its climax in a pronouncement of Jesus. It has also been observed by P. Carrington in *The Primitive Christian Catechism* (Cambridge, Cambridge University Press, 1940) that stories about Jesus were preserved by those who were in constant touch with the worship and teaching of the church, and who would emphasize their points by saying, "Hear what our Lord Jesus Christ says!" A good summary of the achievements as well as the limitations of form criticism is to be found in E. B. Redlich's *Form Criticism: Its Values and Limitations* (London, Gerald Duckworth & Co., Ltd., 1939).

The Fourth Gospel

Form criticism as a method of New Testament interpretation is useful only to a limited degree beyond the Synoptic Gospels. This is particularly true in the case of the Fourth Gospel, which is obviously the work of an outstanding personality rather than the product of popular tradition. Much has been written on the purpose of John's Gospel. Among the early church fathers there was general agreement that the author's purpose was to supplement the Synoptics; in the nineteenth century the idea was put forth that the author shaped his material with the purpose of giving depth to the picture of Jesus conveyed in the other gospels, the so-called improvement theory. At the beginning of the twentieth century there emerged the displacement theory—namely, that the author wrote with the intention of displacing or replacing the other gospels. R. Bultmann, for example, in *Das Evangelium des Johannes* (Göttingen, Vandenhoeck & Ruprecht, 1941) sees signs of Hellenistic and even Gnostic strains of thought influencing the doctrinal outlook of the Gospel. B. W. Bacon is in accord with this interpretation and entitled his work on John's Gospel, *The Gospel of the Hellenists* (N.Y., Henry Holt & Co., Inc., 1933). Moving in the opposite direction, C. F. Burney, impressed with the Semitic mind of the author, entitled his work *The Aramaic Origin of the Fourth Gospel* (Oxford, Clarendon Press, 1922). An excellent summary of the critical debate that has raged around John's Gospel during the first quarter of the twentieth century is W. F. Howard's *The Fourth Gospel in*

Recent Criticism; first published in 1931, it has gone through four revisions, the last in 1955 (London, The Epworth Press). Critical debate is by no means over, but recent books on this gospel such as C. H. Dodd's *The Interpretation of the Fourth Gospel* (Cambridge, Cambridge University Press, 1953) leave critical questions to one side and concentrate on the background and the dominant concepts within which the author wrote. Thus Aileen Guilding's *The Fourth Gospel and Jewish Worship* (Oxford, Clarendon Press, 1960) attempts to assess "the relation of the Fourth Gospel to the ancient Palestinian synagogue lectionary system."

Pauline literature

The Pauline epistles are very much an aspect of New Testament criticism, since the question of date and authorship (whether written by St. Paul or not) reflects upon other books of the New Testament. These are important questions to solve, in that they are vital for establishing the earliest forms of Christianity. A classic work on the whole Pauline problem is A. Deissmann's *St. Paul; A Study in Social and Religious History* (London, Hodder & Stoughton, Ltd., 1912). A brief but very useful book is A. D. Nock's *St. Paul* (London, Butterworth & Co., 1938), which provides the reader with an extensive bibliography.

Chronology is always an important factor in any study of St. Paul. Most scholars attempt to synchronize the Acts and Paul's epistles with Jewish and Roman history, so that archeological discoveries in either of these fields usually revive interest in Pauline studies. A recent discovery helps to fix the date of Gallio's proconsulship, leading to reconstructions of chronology, such as John Knox's *Chapters in a Life of Paul* (N.Y., Abingdon Press, 1950), in which the historical accuracies of Paul's letters are emphasized over against the inaccuracies of Acts. Each of Paul's epistles has come in for exhaustive treatment; all of them are dealt with adequately in *The Interpreters Bible*, 12 vols. (N.Y., Abingdon-Cokesbury, 1951–57), an excellent guidebook to all the books of the Bible. There are, however, some monographs on many of Paul's epistles that the inquiring reader should not overlook. E. J. Goodspeed in *The Meaning of Ephesians* (Chicago, University of Chicago Press, 1933) emphasized the encyclical character of this epistle, and C. L. Mitton's *The Epistle to the Ephesians* (Oxford, Clarendon Press, 1951) has revived considerable interest in the very thorny problem of Paulinism, to which this letter is a vital key.

The so-called pastoral epistles, I and II Timothy and Titus, because of their second-century vocabulary and style, are difficult to ascribe to Paul. P. N. Harrison in *The Problem of the Pastoral Epistles* (Oxford, Oxford University Press, 1921) thinks he finds five genuine Pauline fragments embedded in the letters but does not indicate how these fragments might occasion a letter. C. Spicq in *Les Épitres Pastorales* (Paris, J. Gabalda & Cie, 1947) maintains the traditional view of Pauline authorship, asserting that there is counseling in all Pauline epistles and that all vary in style.

Many Pauline terms—justification by faith, being in Christ, grace, etc.—call for close definition. For a definition of such terms as well as for specialized words used throughout the New Testament, G. Kittel's *Theologisches Wörterbuch zum Neuen Testament*, tr. and ed. by J. R. Coates (N.Y., Harper & Brothers, 1949–61), is indispensable.

Homilies and pastorals

With the exception of Acts, the rest of the canonical literature may be classified under the caption "homilies" and "pastorals," as does Moffat in his *Introduction* (*op. cit.*). In chapter III he points out that none of these writings contain any narrative as they are mainly intended for edification. The Revelation of John belongs to a different category from the others and must be studied in close association with Jewish eschatology. The suggestion of R. B. Y. Scott in *The Original Language of the Apocalypse* (Toronto, University of Toronto Press, 1928) that our present book is a Greek translation of a Hebrew original has not been generally accepted by scholars, nor has C. C. Torrey's suggestion in *Documents of the Primitive Church* (N.Y., Harper & Brothers, 1941) that the author wrote in Aramaic. What the author was trying to achieve has been interestingly set forth by C. H. Allen in *The Message of the Book of Revelation* (Nashville, Cokesbury Press, 1939).

The Epistles of Peter and Jude, though they may be regarded as homilies or tracts, belong to some extent to the realm of eschatology. They are generally linked together in commentaries, particularly Jude and II Peter, as J. W. Wand does in *The General Epistles of St. Peter and St. Jude*, prepared for the *Westminster Commentaries* (London, Methuen & Co., Ltd., 1917). Recently there has arisen a considerable interest over the date of I Peter. F. W. Beare in *The First Epistle of Peter* (Oxford, B. H. Blackwell, Ltd., 1947; 2nd ed., 1958) dates it about A.D. 112, whereas E. G. Selwyn in *The First Epistle of St. Peter* (London, A. R. Mowbray & Co., Ltd., 1940) suggests that it was sent out about Easter A.D. 64.

Because of the fluency and grammatical niceties of the Greek in the Epistle of James, it is very doubtful that it could have been written by James the Apostle. It is considered probable by A. T. Cadoux in *The Thought of St. James* (London, James Clarke & Co., Ltd., 1944) and by other commentators that James may have secured the services of a Hellenist to write the epistle for him. There are many theories about the authorship and date of Hebrews, fully dealt with by T. W. Manson in *The Epistle to the Hebrews, an Historical and Theological Reconstruction* (London, Hodder & Stoughton, Ltd., 1951).

It is fairly well accepted that an eminent church leader in Asia Minor, who called himself the "Elder," wrote the First, Second, and Third Epistles ascribed to John. He may also have been the author of John's Gospel. But

C. H. Dodd in an article, "The First Epistle of John and the Fourth Gospel" in the *Bulletin of John Ryland's Library*, XXI (1937), pp. 129–56, cannot agree that they were written by the same person, because of the differences of style and thought between I John and the Fourth Gospel. W. F. Howard in an article in *The Journal of Theological Studies*, XLVIII (1947), does not concur with Dodd and makes out a good case for his opinion.

The Acts of the Apostles, which belongs to the topic of church history, also plays an important role in New Testament interpretation, being, as H. J. Cadbury notes in his *The Making of Luke and Acts* (N.Y., The Macmillan Co., 1927), an independent history of the apostolic age; but it is also a sequel to Luke's Gospel and completes a chronological story that opens with the birth of John the Baptist and continues down to the anticipated departure of Paul from Rome to Spain.

It is evident from this brief review of literature relating to New Testament interpretation that there remain many open questions in the field of biblical criticism. These are being constantly debated in theological journals; besides those mentioned above, the following are particularly devoted to New Testament criticism: *Novum Testamentum: An International Quarterly for New Testament and Related Studies, Based on International Cooperation* (Leiden, 1956–) and *New Testament Studies* (N.Y., 1954–), an international journal published quarterly under the auspices of Studiorum Novum Testamenti Societas.

PATRISTICS AND PATROLOGY

From New Testament literature the student of Christianity normally proceeds to a study of patristic literature, the writings of those who have been designated fathers of the church. The logic behind this is the recognition that Christianity cannot be fully understood apart from the contemporary literature reflecting the environment in which it arose, developed, and defined its faith. H. B. Swete in a brief outline of *Patristic Study*, 3rd ed. (London, Longmans, Green & Co., Inc., 1904) felt so strongly the need of some acquaintance with the fathers of the church for an understanding of Christianity that he provided in his book a suggested minimum reading course. J. Quasten in *Patrology, I, The Beginnings of Patristic Literature* (Westminster, Newman Press, 1950) calls for an even broader course of reading after the New Testament and includes within patrology not only orthodox writers of Christian antiquity but heretical writers as well—as, indeed, did many collectors of the patristic writings. Quasten defines patrology "as the science of the fathers of the church" and "includes in the West all Christian writers up to Gregory the Great (d. 604) . . . and in the East it usually extends to John Damascene (d. 749)."

Special importance has always been attached to the apostolic fathers, so designated first by J. B. Cotelier in his *Apostolic Fathers* (Paris, 1672), in which he described Barnabas, Clement of Rome, Hermos, Ignatius, and Polycarp as "The Fathers who flourished in the times of the Apostles." Since then the list has been extended and J. B. Lightfoot in his *The Apostolic Fathers*, ed. and completed by J. R. Harmer (N.Y., The Macmillan Co., 1907) includes also as apostolic literature *The Epistle to Diognetus, The Teaching of the Apostles, The Fragments of Papius, The Reliques of the Elders Preserved in Irenaeus.*

Origins of patrology

In an introductory chapter to *Patrology* (*op. cit.*) Quasten provides an interesting commentary on the development of the idea of a history of Christian literature in which the theological point of view predominated. Eusebius pioneered in this field, and his *Ecclesiastical History* (*op. cit.*) remains one of the most important sources for patrology. The first writer, however, to compose a history of theological literatures was Jerome in *De viris illustribus* (392) (Leipzig, 1896), which covered the period from the apostles to his own time. Around 480 Gennadius, a priest of Marseilles, made an addition to Jerome's work; a further continuation was made by Isidore of Seville between 615 and 618. Another contributor was Isidore's disciple Ildephonsus (d. 667).

After Ildephonsus there was a pause in the development of patrology until the end of the eleventh century, when Sigebert of Gembloux (d. 1112) again took up the task of bringing the history of Christian literature up to date. In his *De viris illustribus* he closely followed Jerome and Gennadius and then added some biographical notes on the Latin theologians of the early medieval period. There were a few other compilations around this time, but nothing significant until the appearance of Johannes Trithemius, who composed *De scriptoribus ecclesiasticis* (*c.* 1494) which includes biographical and bibliographical details of about 693 writers.

Great collections

In the sixteenth and seventeenth centuries an era of great collections of patristic works was inaugurated. Cardinal Bellarmine's *De scriptoribus ecclesiasticis liber unus* appeared in 1613, followed by the L. S. Nain de Tillemont's *Mémoires pour servir à l'histoire ecclésiastique des six premiers siècles*, 16 vols. (Paris, C. Robustel, 1693–1712), and R. Ceillier, *Histoire générale des auteurs sacrés et ecclésiastiques*, 23 vols. (Paris, 1729–63). Such collections were much enriched in the nineteenth century by new discoveries of patristic writings, and so the need arose for new critical editions. The Academies of Vienna and Berlin responded to the challenge and began to put forth critical editions of the Latin and Greek series of the fathers, while French scholars began critical editions of Oriental Christian literature.

The most famous of these collections is J. P. Migne's *Patrologiae cursus completus* (Paris, Garnier, 1912) containing 388 volumes: 222 Latin fathers, and 166 Greek, the latter accompanied with Latin translations. Other famous collections are *Corpus scriptorum ecclesiaticorum latinorum*, ed. by the Academy of Vienna since 1866 (70 vols. complete), *Die griechischen christlichen Schriftsteller der ersten drei Jahrhunderte*, ed. by the Academy of Berlin since 1897 (41 vols. complete), *Corpus scriptorum christianorum orientialium*, ed. by J. B. Chabot and others, published in Paris, since 1903. Since 1948 the Benedictine monks of St. Peter's Abbeye, Steenbrugge, Belgium, have been publishing an enormous *Corpus Christianorum*. Along with patristic texts are included conciliar and legal documents and inscriptions. It is also intended to include non-Christian writers in this huge collection.

Translations

Along with the collection of texts in their original languages has proceeded the work of translation into vernacular languages. A famous Oxford series in English is the *Library of the Fathers*, 45 vols. (1838–88), ed. by Pusey, Keble, and Newman. At Edinburgh was produced *The Ante-Nicene Christian Library*, 25 vols. (Edinburgh University Library, 1867–97), edited by A. Roberts and J. Donaldson. An American reprint of the Edinburgh edition was made under the title *The Ante-Nicene Fathers*, 8 vols. (1884–86), with a supplement by A. Menzies (Vol. 9); a tenth volume has been added containing a bibliographical synopsis and a general index (N.Y., Charles Scribner's Sons, 1925). Between 1886 and 1900 P. Schaff and H. Wace have issued *A Select Library of Nicene and Post Nicene Fathers of the Christian Church*, 28 vols., 2 series (N.Y., Christian Literature Co.). More recent ambitious works are *Ancient Christian Writers* (Westminster, Newman Press, 1946–) edited by J. Quasten and J. C. Plumpe, and *The Library of Christian Classics* (Philadelphia, Westminster Press, 1953–) under the general editorship of J. Baillie, J. T. McNeill, and H. P. Van Dusen. This series when completed will present in the English language 26 volumes of the most indispensable Christian treatises written before the end of the sixteenth century.

It has been recognized that the general reader of Christian literature is not going to be able to read extensively in the fathers, and so smaller collections of selected portions of this literature have been made for such readers. An older collection of selections was made by H. M. Gwatkins. His *Selections from Early Writers Illustrative of Church History to the Time of Constantine*, rev. ed. (London, Macmillan & Co., Ltd., 1897) has long been a popular textbook. Equally popular is B. J. Kidd's *Documents Illustrative of the History of the Church*, 2 vols. (N.Y., The Macmillan Co., 1920). F. L. Cross has made a useful set of extracts for the purpose of illustrating church doctrine, *The*

Early Christian Fathers (London, Gerald Duckworth & Co., Ltd., 1956). Professor Cross is now engaged in making an analytical survey of Christian literature from the apostolic fathers to the beginning of the fourth century. The first volume, *The Early Christian Fathers*, appeared in 1960 and is to be followed by *The Later Greek Fathers* and *The Later Latin Fathers*.

Background studies

Obviously, patristic literature was not produced in a vacuum; so it is part of the discipline of patrology to become acquainted with the contemporary literature with which early Christian writers would be familiar as well as with the conditions of the society in which they formulated their ideas. It is particularly important that the student in this field should know something of the rhetorical devices and the topics of the popular philosophies of the first few centuries of Christianity. Also, though in the analysis of Christian texts the basic method is philological, the style and literary methods of Christian writers must be investigated against the background of Greek and Roman rhetoric. An excellent little book for patristic background is M. L. W. Laistner's *Christianity and Pagan Culture in the Later Roman Empire* (Ithaca, N.Y., Cornell University Press, 1951). The author deals with the interesting phenomenon of the decline of ancient science at the time of the emergence of Christianity. C. N. Cochrane's *Christianity and Classical Culture* (Oxford, Clarendon Press, 1940) is also a helpful background study but is somewhat less useful for patrology, as its emphasis is heavily on the side of economics. G. B. Caird's *The Apostolic Age* (London, Gerald Duckworth & Co., Ltd., 1955), though primarily concerned with the Christian community, provides in an appendix a painstaking chronology of the apostolic age, a very important element in patristic studies.

CHRISTIAN DOCTRINES

The work of scholars in the field of patristics has for its object a clearer understanding of Christian doctrine. It is also intended as an aid to the systematic theologian who has the perilous task of discriminating between orthodoxy and heterodoxy. The task begins logically enough with an analysis of the *kerygma*; but as the *kerygma* was proclaimed against the background of Old Testament and intertestamental thought, it can only be understood in relation to Old Testament theology.

Old Testament theology

In recent years there has been much interest displayed in this subject. Prominent students in the field are M. Burrows, who in *An Outline of Biblical Theology* (Philadelphia, Westminster Press, 1946) stresses the Old Testament view of God as the Lord of history and nature, and H. W. Robinson, who in *Inspiration and Revelation in the Old Testament* (Oxford, Clarendon Press, 1946) gives special attention to the concept that man, as God's chief creation, has a special relation to God, expressed in the Old Testament term "covenant." Both these writers are in agreement that the dominant concepts in the Old Testament which are carried over into the New are the creative and redemptive acts of God in history. The redemptive aspect arises out of the covenant relationship which it was righteous for God's people to observe and sinful to disregard.

It is probably the concept of a compact between God and his people that accounts for the legalistic character of Jewish religion, but, as G. E. Wright takes pains to illustrate in an article "The Faith of Israel" in *The Interpreters Bible* (*op. cit.*), I, pp. 348–89, the legal aspect was often overcome by the introduction of the term "grace" which bound the people to God with an attachment stronger than legal bonds. Nevertheless, these writers agree that there are many frustrations and unresolved problems in Old Testament theology, particularly in the realm of prophetic eschatology with its messianic overtones; and it was the unfulfilled hopes of Israel that New Testament theology was challenged to explain.

New Testament theology

Although the New Testament writers make Jesus of Nazareth their central theme, he always appears as the climax to the unfinished work of the Old Testament. This aspect of New Testament theology has been clearly outlined by C. H. Dodd in *According to the Scriptures: The Substructure of New Testament Theology* (*op. cit.*). Dodd finds "according to the scriptures" to be the key phrase which gives a unity of outlook to the whole of the New Testament. All the writers, he says, are concerned to show how the evangelical facts took place "according to the scriptures"; thus arose "the fundamental and regulative ideas of Christian Theology"—namely, "that the Church according to the *testimonia* from the Old Testament is the true and ultimate people of God" and its "operative centre was the passion and death and resurrection of Jesus Christ." From this conviction emerged the problem of Christology, a problem not fully faced by the early fathers until after they had defined Jesus' relation to God by a Trinitarian formula.

Trinitarianism

The transition of New Testament Christianity to early catholicism is the basic problem in the study of the doctrines of the early church. Long the best book in English on this problem was H. F. Bethune-Baker's *An Introduction to the Early History of Christian Doctrine* (1903; 6th ed., London, Methuen & Co., Ltd., 1938), but it has been somewhat displaced by J. N. D. Kelly's *Early Christian Doctrines* (London, Adam & Charles Black, Ltd.,

1958). Both these writers find the implications of a divine triad among the subapostolic fathers, defined in the spirit of Judaism, but no discernible doctrine of a Trinity. It is not until they come to the apologists that they see the emergence of a Trinitarian formula. The problem arose, as G. L. Prestige so succinctly phrased it in *God in Patristic Thought* (London, Society for Promoting Christian Knowledge, 1956), because "The overwhelming sense of divine redemption in Christ led Christians to ascribe absolute deity to their Redeemer." Consequently, *logos* theories were adopted by the apologists to try to frame an intellectually satisfying explanation of the relation of Christ to God. But, as Prestige says, "the doctrine of the Logos, great as was its importance for theology, harbored deadly perils in its bosom." Dr. Prestige is an excellent guide through the many perils Christian theism had to survive (adoptionism, Christ deified only after his ascension; subordinationism, the Son an impersonal function of the Father; etc.) until the church resolved at the Council of Nicea (325) that there was an identity of substance of Father and Son. A good analysis of the evolution of this doctrine is to be found in *Essays on the Trinity and the Incarnation*, ed. A. E. J. Rawlinson (N.Y., Longmans, Green & Co., Inc., 1928). This book is particularly helpful for understanding later developments of the doctrine as formulated at the Council of Constantinople (381), where the Holy Spirit was also declared consubstantial with the Father and the Son.

Christology

The problem of Christology—how could full and perfect divinity and full and perfect humanity be united in one person, and what are the relations existing between them when united in one person?—was not resolved in the first two ecumenical councils of the church. Two further councils, Ephesus (431) and Chalcedon (451), battled with this problem. At both councils two schools of thought were in conflict: the Alexandrine, emphasizing the reality of the Godhead, and the Antiochene, emphasizing the reality of the manhood of Jesus. An excellent study of these two points of view has been made by R. V. Sellars in *Two Ancient Christologies* (London, Society for Promoting Christian Knowledge, 1940), in which he points out that the extremes of both schools were condemned at the Council of Chalcedon (451).

But even after Chalcedon the problem of Christology was not solved, nor is it even yet a closed subject for Christian theologians. In the latter half of the nineteenth century it was eclipsed by the search for the Jesus of history, a search stimulated by Sir John Seeley's *Ecce Homo* (Toronto, J. M. Dent & Sons [Canada], Ltd., 1865), in which the emphasis was upon the human personality of the historical Jesus of Nazareth. Thus arose kenotic (self-emptying of the divine) theories regarding the human knowledge of Jesus. This new approach was adopted by A. Harnack in *What is Christianity?* (N.Y., Harper & Brothers, 1957; first published in 1900 under the title *The*

Essence of Christianity) in which he drew a distinction between the gospel about Jesus and the gospel of Jesus.

The assumption that it was possible to gain an historical portrait of Jesus apart from Christology was challenged by A. Schweitzer in *Von Reimarus zu Wrede* (1906), translated into English by W. Montgomery under the title *The Quest of the Historical Jesus* (London, Adam & Charles Black, Ltd., 1910). Form critics also arrived at the conclusion, as D. M. Baillie points out in *God Was in Christ* (N.Y., Charles Scribner's Sons, 1948) that the New Testament story of Jesus is Christological from beginning to end.

Both Emil Brunner in *The Mediator*, 2nd impression (N.Y., The Macmillan Co., 1934) and Karl Barth in *Dogmatics in Outline* (N.Y., Philosophical Library, Inc., 1949) affirm a strong orthodox Christology, but Brunner has reservations on the Chalcedonian formula and hesitates to define the relations between the divinity and humanity of Christ in two-nature terms.

There have been attempts to abandon Greek philosophical terms to explain Christ's person and to replace them with either modern philosophical or psychological expressions. A pioneer attempt is L. Thornton's *The Incarnate Lord* (N.Y., Longmans, Green & Co., Inc., 1928) based upon the organic philosophy of A. N. Whitehead. Even earlier W. Sanday in *Christologies, Ancient and Modern* (N.Y., Oxford University Press, 1910), had sought a solution of Chalcedonian dualism by placing the divinity of Christ in the subliminal consciousness. More recently W. R. Matthews has suggested in *The Problem of Christ in the Twentieth Century* (N.Y., Oxford University Press, 1950) that Jung's theory of the racial unconscious may help us to understand the corporate significance of Christ's redemptive work. An excellent criticism of these modern Christologies is to be found in W. N. Pittenger's *The Word Incarnate* (N.Y., Harper & Brothers, 1959). He also offers a restatement of his own based upon an existentialist philosophy.

Human destiny

Christological speculation, which is so often concerned with fallen human nature, inevitably raises the problem of human destiny. A classic on this subject is F. R. Tennant's *The Sources of the Doctrines of the Fall and Original Sin* (Cambridge, Cambridge University Press, 1903). This book deals with the Fall story in Genesis II, and follows its development through the intertestamental literature down to the fathers before Augustine. During this period there was a division between East and West, the former being more optimistic than the latter as to the nature of man. Though both agreed that man was a composite of body and soul, they did not always agree on where the soul came from. Many held a traducianist view—that each soul is somehow generated from the parent's soul—while others held a creationist view—that each soul was created by God at the moment of its infusion into the body.

H. W. Robinson in *The Christian Doctrine of Man* (Edinburgh, T. & T.

Clark, 1911) supplements Tennant's book by continuing the story through the medieval and Reformation periods; the latter period introduces a new division in the West, since the Reformation theologians have been far less optimistic about the nature of man than the Counter-Reformation theologians. Robinson's book also deals with current views.

N. P. Williams in *The Ideas of the Fall and Original Sin* (London, Longmans, Green & Co., Ltd., 1927) justifies his rather large volume, covering the same ground as Tennant, on the fact that the "new psychology" and the revival of the theory of a cosmic fall call for a new constructive view of the whole subject of the nature of man.

A massive study of human nature and human destiny has been made by Reinhold Niebuhr in *The Nature and Destiny of Man*, 2 vols. (N.Y., Charles Scribner's Sons, 1941–43) based upon the belief that "there are resources in Christian faith for an understanding of human nature that have been lost in modern culture." A less ambitious but more optimistic book on the subject is E. L. Mascall's *The Importance of Being Human* (N.Y., Columbia University Press, 1958).

Soteriology

Implicit in all Christian discussion of human nature is the belief that man through self-determined rebellion has become enmeshed in evil and is in need of redemption or restoration to his original righteousness. The Christian solution to this aspect of evil is that the image of God in man is restored through the Incarnation and the Atonement; but the latter is a doctrine that has never been clearly adumbrated in Christian theology. Nor was attention particularly directed toward it until Anselm in his famous book *Cur Deus Homo* (1098) proclaimed that Christ on behalf of men through His death made the satisfaction for sin which God's justice demands. It is often contended that this emphasis on the death of Christ as an isolated event stands in sharp contrast to the patristic view in which the death of Christ is the climax of a long conflict and constitutes a victory. The patristic view, however, as H. E. W. Turner makes evident in *The Patristic Doctrine of Redemption* (London, A. R. Mowbray & Co., Ltd., 1952), was never consistent. It consists of a variety of theories; a mystical theory (human nature sanctified by Christ becoming man), a ransom theory (Christ's death regarded as a ransom paid to the devil), and a realist theory (Christ took upon Himself the penalty which justice demanded). Associated with all these is a theory derived from Paul, which sees Christ as the representative of the whole human race, the recapitulation theory. All these theories were brought together by Augustinus in his *Enchiridion* (421), tr. and ed. by M. Dods (Edinburgh, T. & T. Clark, 1872–1934, 8 eds.), and passed on to the Middle Ages, where they provided Anselm with the material upon which he based his satisfaction theory. No sooner was it put forth than it was challenged by Peter Abelard (1079–1142), with his doctrine that Christ's example had a subjective effect upon mankind, the so-called subjective view of the Atonement, set forth in his *Expositio* to the Epistle to the Romans and referred to in his *Christian Theology.* The latter work has been translated into English by J. R. McCallum (Oxford, B. H. Blackwell Ltd., 1948).

It was the Anselmian view that prevailed in the Middle Ages and on into the Reformation period, but, as G. Aulén in *Christus Victor* (N.Y., The Macmillan Co., 1951) has pointed out, with some very significant modifications. Aulén's book is a useful study of the changes that came about in the interpretation of the doctrine of the Atonement through the Later Middle Ages, the Reformation, and the Enlightenment.

In recent days a strong attack has been launched against the satisfaction theory. It began with McLeod Campbell's controversial book *The Nature of the Atonement* (London, Macmillan & Co., Ltd., 1886) and was continued by R. C. Moberley's *Atonement and Personality* (N.Y., Longmans, Green & Co., Inc., 1901). Both these writers repudiated penal satisfaction and stressed Christ as representative man, not merely a substitute. P. T. Forsyth in *The Cruciality of the Cross*, 2nd ed. (London, Independent Press, Ltd., 1948), concurs with this view.

But the penal concept still has some important supporters such as E. Brunner in *The Mediator* (*op. cit.*) and L. Hodgson in *The Doctrine of the Atonement* (N.Y., Charles Scribner's Sons, 1951). On the other hand, there has been considerable criticism of the use of individual categories in relation to the Atonement. The objection was raised by R. Neibuhr in *Moral Man and Immoral Society* (N.Y., Charles Scribner's Sons, 1932); also by J. G. Bennett in *Social Salvation; A Religious Approach to the Problems of Social Change* (N.Y., Charles Scribner's Sons, 1935); Nels F. S. Ferré in *The Christian Understanding of God* (N.Y., Harper & Brothers, 1951); and Karl Heim in *Jesus the World's Perfecter* (Edinburgh, Oliver & Boyd, Ltd., 1937; 2nd ed., 1959). A fair summary of these modern views of redemption, including those who regard the "Fall" as a step upward, based upon the idea of evolution, is to be found in T. H. Hughes' *The Atonement—Modern Theories of the Doctrine* (London, George Allen & Unwin, Ltd., 1949).

Ecclesiology

An emphasis upon the corporate aspect of redemption through Christ leads, as K. Heim (*op. cit.*) stresses, to a recognition of the importance of the church as the body which "carries on His Life's work with supra-spatial and supra-temporal power." The doctrine of the church has always been closely associated with the doctrine of the Holy Spirit. Consequently, when Charles Gore came to write the third volume of his famous trilogy *The Reconstruction of Belief*, he entitled it *The Holy Spirit and the Church* (London, John Murray Publishers, Ltd., 1924). The reason, he said, was that Jesus "gave few directions to His Church but left it to organize itself under the guidance of the Holy Spirit."

Unfortunately, the doctrine of the church has been subject to much controversy. Roman Catholics, Eastern Orthodox, Anglicans, and Protestants, all hold varying views about its constitutional structure, its source of authority, and the relative prestige of its ancient sees. But the subject is even more complicated, for in almost all the major churches there is a high and low view on the nature of the church. C. Gore, for example, represents a high church view within Anglicanism, while J. B. Lightfoot in a very notable study, *The Christian Ministry* (London, Macmillan & Co., Ltd., 1903), presents a radical departure from Anglicanism on the historic status of the episcopate.

The primacy of the papacy has long been a controversial subject, for which Karl Adam makes a very convincing case in *The Spirit of Catholicism* (London, Sheed & Ward, Ltd., 1929). Eastern churches, on the other hand, have never regarded Rome as a constitutional center, much less an oracle of faith. The point of view of the orthodox churches has been carefully set forth by B. J. Kidd in *The Roman Primacy to A.D. 461* (N.Y., The Macmillan Co., 1936). An excellent historical examination of the reformed tradition is Geddes MacGregor's *Corpus Christi: The Nature of the Church according to the Reformed Tradition* (Philadelphia, Westminster Press, 1958). All the traditional concepts of the church have been gathered together in a volume prepared by the Theological Commission on the Church, set up by the World Conference on Faith and Order, entitled *The Nature of the Church*, ed. by R. N. Flew (London, Student Christian Movement Press, 1952).

Sacraments

Vital to the doctrine of the church and its ministry is the place of the sacraments. All the books referred to in the previous section give a prominent position to the sacramental aspect of church life. In the earliest Christian literature there is the implicit assumption that the sacraments are the outward and visible signs of invisible but genuine grace, but it was a long time before their number was fixed.

A very learned treatise on the sacraments is B. Leeming's *Principles of Sacramental Theology* (Westminster, Maryland, The Newman Press, 1956), covering the general principle upon which sacraments are based and their origin and development in the Christian Church as well as the attitudes of the various branches of Christianity. Such matters as validity, objective efficacy, causality, and intention are minutely discussed. The book also contains a bibliography, in which all points of view are represented. A good cross-section of denominational views is set forth in a volume prepared by the Theological Commission appointed by the Continuation Committee of Faith and Order, entitled *The Ministry and the Sacraments*, ed. R. Dunkerley (1937).

Pre-eminent among the sacraments are Baptism and the Eucharist, and much has been written on both. A recent book on Baptism which has received favorable comment from many quarters is G. W. Lampe's *The Seal of the Spirit* (London, Longmans, Green & Co., Ltd., 1951), which deals with the confusing question of the relation of Baptism to Confirmation. The controversial aspect of the Eucharist is the problem of the "real presence." An historical examination of this doctrine has been made by E. Masure in *The Christian Sacrifice* (N.Y., P. J. Kenedy & Sons, 1943).

During the Middle Ages the number of the sacraments was fixed at seven, with penance taking a far more prominent position than it ever held in the early church. This was due to medieval concentration on grace and merit as an aspect of personal religion. Thus arose an insistence on private confession to a priest. The origin of this practice has been the subject of careful research by R. C. Mortimer in *The Origins of Private Penance in the Western Church* (Oxford, Clarendon Press, 1939). It was the reformers' attack upon the system of merits and indulgences that constituted the first step toward creating the great difference between medieval and modern society in the West. The differences between Roman Catholic and Protestant sacramental views have been candidly discussed by O. C. Quick in *The Christian Sacraments* (N.Y., Harper & Brothers, 1928). The occasional sacraments such as Holy Orders, Matrimony, and Unction are all discussed in great detail by B. Leeming (*op. cit.*).

Eschatology

Systematic Christian theology always closes on the theme of eschatology—the doctrine of the last things. Although Christian history is supposed to have reached its climax in the coming, death, and resurrection of Jesus Christ, yet there is a final denouement. Four chief moments are prominent in the denouement: (1) the return of Christ, the parousia; (2) the resurrection; (3) the judgment; (4) the catastrophic end of the present world order. There has been a tendency to regard these moments as symbols rather than literal facts, but how to interpret these symbols is a matter of some controversy. A theory gaining much approval, set forth by C. H. Dodd in *The Apostolic Preaching* (N.Y., Willett, Clark & Co., 1937), is that the final age is here ("realized eschatology")—that is, the final phase of God's dealing with men has already arrived—and yet "there remains a residue of eschatology" which is implied in the second coming of the Lord and the last judgment, which can only be expressed in mythological terms. J. Baillie in *The Belief in Progress* (N.Y., Charles Scribner's Sons, 1951) speaks of this final phase as "years of Grace" and regards the second coming, the last judgment and the resurrection as "symbols of a reality unimaginable by us except in symbolic form"; but they are necessary defenses against "secular progressiveness." R. Niebuhr in *The Nature and Destiny of Man* (*op. cit.*), II, X sees the significance of eschatology as a symbol of the fact that the final consummation of history is beyond time; but O. Cullman in *Christ and Time* (*op. cit.*) returns to the Hebraic idea that eternity is a simple extension of time and suggests abandoning the Greek idea of a qualitative difference between time and eternity. He sees the Christian drama as a continuous redemptive line, "unlimited in one direction." W. C. Robinson in *Christ the Hope of Glory* (Michigan, Wm. B. Eerdmans Publishing Co., 1945) reasserts the position of historic Protestantism that Christ will return, but objects to the Premillennialist's programming the future. The latter base their views on the promise in *The Revelation of John* (20:6) that "they, the saints, shall reign with him [Christ] a thousand years." Various interpretations of this hope have been set forth by E. T. Clark in *The Small Sects in America*, rev. ed. (N.Y., Abingdon Press, 1949). Eschatological timetables have occupied groups of Christians from earliest days down to the present time. These have been the subject of careful research by S. J. Case in *The Millennial Hope* (Chicago, University of Chicago Press, 1918), who begins his book with an analysis of pre-Christian Millennarianism and concludes with a modern estimate of millennial hopes.

CHRISTIAN PHILOSOPHY

In the background of all discussion of Christian doctrines lurks the question: How do Christians know that God revealed Himself in Jesus Christ, or how do they know God exists? It is the task of Christian philosophy to answer these and allied questions. A good introduction to the subject is Geddes MacGregor's *Introduction to Religious Philosophy* (Boston, Houghton Mifflin Co., 1959), which opens with the preliminary question: What is religion? The book also provides simple definitions of the many technical terms that occur in philosophical discussions of Christianity.

J. S. Whale in *Christian Doctrine* (N.Y., The Macmillan Co., 1941; reissued, 1957) frankly regards Christian doctrine as a philosophical problem and reviews the traditional arguments for the existence of God as a preface to his presentation of the Christian faith.

Reason and revelation

There are, however, many theologians vigorously opposed to the term "Christian philosophy." Conflicting views on the subject have been collected together in a volume edited by J. Baillie and H. Martin entitled *Revelation* (London, Faber & Faber, Ltd., 1937). In this book representatives of various Christian traditions—Roman Catholic, Lutheran, Reformed, Orthodox, Anglican, and Baptist—discuss the antithesis of reason and revelation and also raise the question whether God has revealed himself in non-Christian religions. One contributor, K. Barth, considers that Christian philosophy is a contradiction in terms and asserts that the Christian faith is based solely on revelation; the theologian's task is to provide scientific conceptions of this revelation. M. C. D'Arcy, representing the Roman Catholic point of view, defends a long-standing distinction between natural and revealed religion, but partly agrees with Barth in asserting that there is only a limited revelation outside Jesus Christ. S. Bulgakoff, speaking for the Orthodox, finds a glimmer of revelation in all pagan religions. A difficulty associated with this book is that the representatives of the various traditions do not necessarily speak for a consensus within their respective traditions. E. Brunner, who is often aligned with the neo-orthodox school of K. Barth, has in *The Philosophy of Religion from the Standpoint of Protestant Theology* (London, Nicholson & Watson, Ltd., 1937) conceded a legitimate relation between revelation and rational knowledge. An Anglican, L. Hodgson, is hardly in agreement with the Anglican representative in *Revelation* (*op. cit.*) when in *Towards a Christian Philosophy* (London, James Nisbet & Co., Ltd., 1942) he questions whether revelation and philosophical inquiry can still be united as they were in former eras, since philosophy is now bogged down in analyzing its own procedures. On the other hand, John Wilson in *Language and Christian Belief* (N.Y., St. Martin's Press, Inc., 1958) suggests that Christian theologians, by using the new methods of analytical philosophy, could greatly improve the language of religion. Be that as it may, Christian philosophy has had a long and honorable career which no student of Christianity can overlook.

Early Christian philosophy

The history of Christian philosophy began, as A. Harnack says in *What is Christianity?* (*op. cit.*), when Christian apologists laid down the equation, "The Logos is Jesus Christ"—perhaps even earlier, when the writer of the Fourth Gospel said, "In the beginning was the Word . . . " (John 1:1) or when Paul spoke of Christ as the wisdom (*sophia*) of God.

With Justin Martyr's *Apologies* (*c.* 155), ed. by A. W. F. Blunt (Cambridge, Cambridge University Press, 1911), the claim was made that all good philosophies are "the property of the church." A little later Athenagoras in his *Plea* (*c.* 176) attempted to show that Christianity is a respectable philosophy. Closely associated with this interest in a philosophical statement of Christianity is the problem that the Gnostics were creating for the church fathers in trying to use Christianity for their own purposes. A good study of this problem is R. McL. Wilson's *The Gnostic Problem* (London, A. R. Mowbray & Co., Ltd., 1958), in which he stresses the fact that Gnosticism was a problem for Hellenistic Judaism before it became a problem for the church. In combating Gnosticism, both were compelled to use contemporary philosophical terms.

Some Jews, such as Philo (born about 25 B.C.), frankly sought to justify Judaism by the use of Hellenistic philosophical language and thus paved the way for a similar use by Christian theologians. Hans Lewy in *Philo: Philosophical Writings* (Oxford, East & West Library, 1956) has made brief selections from Philo's works which are good background introduction to the philosophy of the early church fathers, as is also H. A. Wolfson's *Philo* (Cambridge, Harvard University Press, 1947). The latter is a study of Philonic problems as they relate to patristic problems and is continued in Wolfson's *The Philosophy of the Church Fathers*, Vol. I (Cambridge, Harvard University Press, 1956). An important book in this field is C. Bigg's *The Christian Platonists of Alexandria* (1886; reprinted Oxford, Clarendon Press, 1913), particularly good for its comments on the writings of Clement of Alexandria, such as *Stromateis* (*c*. 202), and the *De Principiis* (*c*. 230) of Origen. Both these writers imported a great deal of Platonism into Christian theology, a tradition carried on by the Cappadocian fathers, whose contribution to Christian philosophy is clearly outlined in G. L. Prestige's *Fathers and Heretics* (N.Y., The Macmillan Co., 1940).

Augustinian Platonism

It was, however, in the writings of Augustine of Hippo that philosophical speculation was to reach its highest peak in Christian theology. His monumental contribution to Christian thought and culture has been well documented by seventeen contributors to *A Companion to the Study of Saint Augustine*, ed. R. W. Battenhouse (N.Y., Oxford University Press, 1955).

It was early recognized by the church fathers that there were serious difficulties with a Platonic or a Neo-Platonic interpretation of Christian doctrine, but no alternative was considered possible until the scholastics of the Middle Ages discovered Aristotle. In the meantime the Platonic tradition was preserved in a mystical garb by the Pseudo-Dionysius in his *The Celestial Hierarchy* and *Concerning the Divine Names*, first appearing about 532, and by Joannes Scotus Erigena (*c*. 800–*c*. 877) in a great work entitled *De divisione naturae*, tr. C. Schwartz (Annapolis, St. John's, 1940). This work was condemned by the church, which was becoming alarmed with the "illumination" approach to understanding, but it survived underground and came to the surface in the speculative mysticism of Bernard of Clairvaux (1090–1153).

Scholasticism

After Erigena the hierarchical church was opposed for some time to any speculation on the data of faith, but with the revival of learning in the eleventh century there was a distinct change of attitude. This is evidenced in the *Monologion* and *Prosologium* of Anselm (1033–1109). In the first he made his famous utterance *credo ut intelligam*, and in the second he developed his famous ontological proof of God's existence. This so-called "father of scholasticism" raised a subject which was to be much debated throughout the Middle Ages, the nature of universals (whether they exist in reality or whether they are merely names). Those who asserted the former were known as realists, the latter as nominalists. Such speculation had been formulated by Porphyry (233–*c.* 304) in an *Introduction to Aristotle*, translated into Latin by Boethius (480–524) and used in the Middle Ages as a compendium of Aristotelian logic.

The questions raised by Porphyry were taken up by Roscellin (*c.* 1050–1122), who accepted the nominalist point of view, and by William of Champeaux (1070–1121), who held a realist view; and so the great medieval debate began. Its opening phases are told by Abelard in his *History of Calamities*, in which he himself took a mediating view known as conceptualism. The story of medieval philosophy from the beginning to its denouement in William of Ockham is told by G. Leff in a very readable book, *Medieval Thought: St. Augustine to Ockham* (Middlesex, Penguin Books, Ltd., 1958).

After Abelard the story of medieval Christian philosophy takes on a new dimension because of the acquisition of a greater knowledge of both Plato and Aristotle through the mediation of Islamic scholars. This phase is satisfactorily dealt with by Leff, but a more detailed account can be obtained in J. W. Sweetman's *Islam and Christian Theology*, 2 vols. (London, Lutterworth Press, 1945–47).

The new era was characterized by the making of "summaries," such as the *Summa Theologica* of Alexander of Hales (d. 1245) (London, 1924), of Albert the Great (*c.* 1206–80), and of Bonaventura (1221–74). The latter is also famous for his commentary on the *Sentences of Peter Lombard*, a much-used theological textbook written between 1145 and 1150. From it the medieval masters raised many questions (*quaestio disputa*); hence the remarkable number of questions asked and answered in the medieval summaries of theology.

The greatest of the summaries was from the pen of Thomas Aquinas (*c.* 1227–74), whose *Summa Theologica* (English ed. pub. by J. Rickaby, London, 1872) is still accepted as the basis of the theological position of the Roman Catholic Church. Thomas Gilby's *St. Thomas Aquinas' Philosophical Texts* (London, Oxford University Press, 1952) is a selection of translations with notes from the many works of the great Catholic doctor and is useful for those who cannot hope to read all of his works. This may be supplemented by a very excellent collection by A. C. Pegis: *Basic Writings of St. Thomas Aquinas*, 2 vols. (N.Y., Modern Library, Inc., 1948). Shortly after Aquinas' death a doctrinal storm broke out in Europe, heralded by Duns Scotus (*c.* 1266–1308), who in his *Commentaries on the Sentences of Peter Lombard* began a retreat of reason from faith. With the advent of William of Ockham (*c.* 1300–49) and his *Sentences* and *Quodlibeta*, the collaboration of faith and reason as it had prevailed in high scholasticism came to an end. For both the Reformation and the Counter-Reformation philosophy no longer appeared to be a buttress of faith; the former relied upon justification by faith alone, the latter upon the authority of the church and mysticism. In Anglican circles, however, a rational approach to faith was not wholly abandoned as evidenced in R. Hooker's (1553–1600) *Laws of Ecclesiastical Polity* (Oxford, Clarendon Press, 1905, and many other editions).

Cartesianism

In the seventeenth century Christian philosophy received a new lease on life when René Descartes (1596–1650) published his *Discourse on Method* with its famous *cogito ergo sum*, and thus laid the foundations of modern philosophical rationalism. Both Blaise Pascal in his *Pensées* (1670, English translation, *Thoughts on Religion and Evidences of Christianity* [London, 1850]), and J. B. Bossuet in *De la connaissance de Dieu* (1732; rev. ed., 1741; also Paris, Garnier, 1937) attempted to use the Cartesian method in defense of faith; the former held, however, that actual faith is a gift of divine grace, while the latter added Thomism to Cartesianism.

The story of the attempt to re-establish faith on a rationalistic foundation can be followed in a volume edited by A. Caldecott and H. R. Mackintosh, *Selections from the Literature of Theism*, 3rd ed. (Edinburgh, T. & T. Clark, 1931); it opens with the ontological argument of Anselm and includes some reference to scholastic philosophy, but it is particularly useful for its selections from the outstanding philosophers of modern rationalism, including Descartes, Spinoza, the Cambridge Platonists, Berkeley, Kant, Schleiermacher, Comte, Lotze, Sorley, and Ritschl. Two notable omissions are Joseph Butler's *Analogy* (1736), and William Paley's *View of the Evidences of Christianity* (Philadelphia, 1795).

Liberalism

The above writings to a large extent belong to the age of the Enlightenment, but even during this era it became evident to most serious Christians that the Cartesian philosophy and its subsequent development were leading nowhere. But there was a revived hope for an alliance of philosophy and religion with the publication of Immanuel Kant's *Critique of Practical Reason* (1788), in which Kant attempted to base religious faith on the categorical imperative. G. W. F. Hegel sought to buttress this approach with an emphasis upon the universe as a constant development of the Absolute. An interesting collection of the theological writings of Hegel, who played an unusually significant role in the development of liberal Christianity, has been made by T. M. Knox and Richard Kroner in a volume entitled *Early Theological Writings* (Chicago, University of Chicago Press, 1948). Prominent among the liberal theologians are Schleiermacher, Ritschl, and A. Harnack, whose *What is Christianity?* (*op. cit.*) is the classical statement of liberal theology.

Crisis or dialectical theology

Liberalism, however, was constantly challenged for its use of a relativist interpretation of Christian faith. As early as the middle of the nineteenth century Sören Kierkegaard (1813–55) denounced the spectator-like attitude of the Hegelian philosopher indulging in speculative theories apart from existential experience. Stimulated by Kierkegaard's works, particularly *Training in Christianity* and the *Concept of Dread* (which have been made available to English-speaking readers by the translations of W. Lowrie, the former in 1941 [Oxford University Press, N.Y.] and the latter in 1944 [Princeton University Press, New Jersey]), there has arisen a theology of crisis in which theological analysis is based upon a dialectical method of thinking as one way of overcoming the contradictions of human existence—or, as it has otherwise been expressed, that actual relations between God and man can only be described in paradoxical terms (hence, the alternative title "dialectical theology").

Several books have been written on this modern approach to theological problems; among them W. Lowrie's *Our Concern with the Theology of Crisis* (Boston, Meador Publishing Co., 1932), J. McConnachie's *The Barthian Theology and the Man of Today* (N.Y., Harper & Brothers, 1933), and F. W. Camfield's *Reformation, Old and New* (London, Lutterworth Press, 1947).

Distinctive philosophies

It is perhaps necessary to add that liberal theology has not yet wholly abandoned the scene, or at least there are still many supporters of a modified liberalism, such as H. H. Farmer, who in *God and Men* (Nashville, Abingdon-Cokesbury, 1947) adheres to the Bible as the supreme authority of faith. There is a continuation of the humanist tradition, represented by H. N. Wieman in *The Growth of Religion* (Chicago, Willett, Clark & Co., 1938); Neo-Thomism has been attractively expounded by E. H. Gilson in *Elements of Christian Philosophy* (N.Y., Doubleday & Co., Inc., 1960). Philosophical theology on the basis of believing in order to understand was stoutly maintained by W. Temple in *Nature, Man and God*, 2 vols. (London, Macmillan & Co., Ltd., 1932–35); Nels F. S. Ferré in *The Christian Understanding of God* (N.Y., Harper & Brothers, 1951) combines evangelical insight with the metaphysics of Whitehead. Still appearing is P. Tillich's *Systematic Theology* (Chicago, University of Chicago Press, 1951–), with its stress on the *Logos* as the center of a new life. There is, therefore, little evidence that the philosophical debate on Christian doctrines is in decline; its future development may be followed in such magazines as *The Hibbert Journal* (London, 1902–), *Revue d'histoire et de philosophie religieuses* (Strasbourg, 1921–), *Journal for the Scientific Study of Religion* (1961–), and *The Modern Churchman* (1911–).

CHRISTIAN SOCIOLOGY

Not all Christians are in agreement that there is a sociological approach to Christianity; those dissenting hold that what is primarily a proclamation of good news cannot be subject to a scientific analysis, such as the term "sociology" implies. Nevertheless, there does seem to be need for some designation of a study concerned not only with the collective behavior of Christians, but also with the functional relation of Christianity to society in general. Since Ernst Troeltsch wrote *The Social Teaching of the Christian Churches* (1912; English translation, N.Y., The Macmillan Co., 1931), a brilliant analysis of the influence of the Christian spirit upon the ancient, medieval, and modern world and of the influence of the natural and political structure of these worlds upon the church, there has arisen a deep interest in the sociological approach to religion. J. Wach in *Sociology of Religion* (Chicago, University of Chicago Press, 1944), a study of the sociology of all religions, concedes the influence of Troeltsch upon his own work. But he gives Max Weber the credit for conceiving a systematic sociology of religion. The latter in a very controversial essay, *Die protestantische Ethik und der Geist des Kapitalismus*, tr. by T. Parsons (London, George Allen & Unwin, Ltd., 1930), identified business acumen with Calvinism. There have been many refinements upon this theme, the best known being R. H. Tawney's *Religion and the Rise of Capitalism* (London, John Murray Publishers, Ltd., 1926). A more recent discussion of the same theme is V. A. Demant's *Religion and the Decline of Capitalism* (N.Y., Charles Scribner's Sons, 1952).

Weber's and Troeltsch's researches stimulated R. H. Niebuhr to make a similar analysis of American denominational religion; his *The Social Sources of Denominationalism* (N.Y., Holt, Rinehart & Winston, Inc., 1929) is an outstanding contribution to the sociology of religious sects.

The social gospel

A variant approach to the sociological problem, known as the social gospel, emphasizes what ought to be the collective behavior of Christians. V. A. Demant in *Theology of Society* (London, Faber & Faber, Ltd., 1947) defends this approach on the basis that since "the Christian religion is a religion of redemption" and "redemption is always a restoration," the essential nature of the Christian approach to the social problem is therefore to restore things to their true nature.

At the opening of the nineteenth century it became the hope of many Christians that the application of Christian principles to the ordering of society would pave the way for the establishment of a better world order. In Europe this new interest was manifested by H. R. de Lamennais in France, G. Mazzini in Italy, H. Kutter in Switzerland, and A. Harnack in

Germany. The theology of the movement, particularly among Roman Catholics, is set forth by A. R. Vidler in *Prophecy and Papacy: A Study of Lamennais, the Church and the Revolution* (N.Y., Charles Scribner's Sons, 1954). Although the movement initiated by Lamennais and other liberal Roman Catholics was condemned by the papacy, the concern for a better social order was nevertheless clearly manifest in the papal encyclical *Rerum Novarum* (May 15, 1891) and in the many epochal documents issued by Pope Leo XIII, which have been arranged and annotated by J. Husslein in a volume entitled *Christian Social Manifesto* (N.Y., Bruce Publishing Co., 1939).

A pioneer historical study of the influence of the social gospel in the early days of the church is A. Harnack's *The Expansion of Christianity in the First Three Centuries*, 2 vols. (N.Y., G. P. Putnam's Sons, Inc., 1904–05) in which he illustrates from early Christian literature the growing popularity of the church in the first three centuries because of its warmth and kindliness to those in distress. A similar study is S. J. Case's *The Social Origins of Christianity* (Chicago, University of Chicago Press, 1923).

The study of the social gospel has been greatly intensified by the impact of the industrial revolution upon social life. It was seen by many churchmen that the individualistic social philosophy that had been accepted by Christians generally was inadequate in a world of large-scale production with a concentration of economic power in few hands. This was particularly the stimulus behind the Christian socialist movement initiated in England by J. F. D. Maurice and Charles Kingsley, and kept alive in the writings of such prominent Anglicans as A. C. Headlam, B. F. Westcott, H. Scott Holland, C. Gore, and W. Temple; the latter while Archbishop of York wrote his justly famous *Christianity and Social Order* (N.Y., Penguin Books, Inc., 1942). The origin and early history of the movement has been well told by C. E. Raven in *Christian Socialism 1848–1854* (London, Macmillan & Co., Ltd., 1920); its later development may be followed in M. B. Reckitt's *Maurice to Temple: A Century of Social Movement in the Church of England* (London, Faber & Faber, Ltd., 1947).

The most startling evidences of the change that had been taking place in the social outlook of the churches in England were the reports issued by a Conference on Christian Politics, Economics and Citizenship (C.O.P.E.C.), held at Birmingham in 1924. From this conference emerged twelve volumes of reports dealing with every aspect of social life, with recommendations based upon the conference's interpretation of the social gospel. The series concludes with *Historical Illustrations of the Social Effects of Christianity* (Birmingham, 1924). In the United States the social gospel made little headway until the closing years of the nineteenth century, when Washington Gladden began to urge a more humane approach to social problems on the part of Christians, a theme which he set forth in *Social Salvation* (N.Y., Houghton Mifflin Co., 1902); he was followed by Walter Rauschenbusch, who made considerable advance towards a Christian socialism in *Christianity and the Social Crisis* (N.Y., The Macmillan Co., 1920). The story of the movement initiated by these two men has been told by C. H. Hopkins in *The Rise of the Social Gospel in American Protestantism 1865–1915* (New Haven, Yale University Press, 1940), which may be supplemented with H. M. May's *Protestant Churches and Industrial America* (N.Y., Harper & Brothers, 1949).

Orthodox churches until recent times seem to have remained somewhat remote from these social movements, but there were some stirrings within the Russian Church which have been touched upon by N. Berdyaev in *The Origin of Russian Communism* (London, Geoffrey Bles, Ltd., 1937).

Pastoralia

The social gospel, as set forth by its more radical advocates, met with considerable opposition from many clergy concerned with the cure of souls. These clergy saw Christian vocation as the guidance of individuals in moral development; they held that the unique contribution of the Christian pastor to human welfare is his shepherding function. This point of view has been set forth by F. Greeves in *Theology and the Cure of Souls* (London, The Epworth Press, 1960). It is generally recognized by most writers on pastoralia, however, that pastoral care is not a unique Christian activity but that all religions have provided guides to the good life here on earth. John T. McNeill in *A History of the Cure of Souls* (N.Y., Harper & Brothers, 1951) has made a study of these guides in the antique world, in Israel, and in the Hellenic world, with a special emphasis upon the rise of the confessional in medieval Christianity; he also includes the specialized functions of the Protestant pastors in the contemporary scene.

Pastoral theology is heavily weighted on the side of methodology, as is the case in A. Curran's *Counseling in Catholic Life and Education* (N.Y., The Macmillan Co., 1953), a book designed for "sure guidance" in every conceivable eventuality in Christian counseling. C. A. Wise, however, in *Pastoral Counseling: Its Theory and Practice* (N.Y., Harper & Brothers, 1951) emphasizes the decisive factor that the pastor's religious interpretation of man must play in all counseling. This is also the emphasis of A. T. Boisen in *The Exploration of the Inner World* (Chicago, Willett, Clark & Co., 1936), in which he urges the importance of relating pastoral training to the theology and philosophy of religion.

Moral theology and Christian ethics

An association of theology with counseling raises the problem of the foundations of moral consciousness. A good introduction to this problem is E. Westermarck's *Christianity and Morals* (London, Kegan Paul, Trench, Trubner & Co., Ltd., 1939), which views the subject from a very broad perspective.

Christian moral theology begins with the assumption that Christian conduct is guided by the revelation of God's own character as depicted in both the Old and New Testaments; thus Christian morals have been greatly affected by the prophetic insights of the Old Testament as has been pointed out in R. B. Y. Scott's *The Relevance of the Prophets* (N.Y., The Macmillan Co., 1944). From the prophets Christianity inherited the basic idea that religion and morals are inextricably bound together, but the eschatological setting of Jesus' teaching obscured any long-term specifically Christian ethic and has complicated the task of Christian moral theology. The difficult struggle of early Christian thinkers to apply the ethical principles of Jesus to society in general has been well told by C. J. Cadoux in *The Early Christian Church and the World* (Edinburgh, T. & T. Clark, 1925). As has been pointed out by A. Nygren in *Agape and Eros*, 2 vols. (London, 1932–39; republished in one volume, Philadelphia, Westminster Press, 1953), Christians like Paul and Augustine fell back upon the freedom of love to decide moral issues. An outstanding exponent of Christian morals during the medieval period was Thomas Aquinas, who worked out a natural moral law as a basis for the church to provide moral guidance. A diligent student of Aquinas, E. Gilsòn in *Moral Values and Moral Life* (London, B. Herder Book Co., 1931) has used Thomist insights to answer some of the more pressing moral issues of contemporary life. Concern with natural law and the opposition raised against it by the passions of men led the fathers of the church to evolve a system of casuistry for solving doubtful cases of conscience. This system has a long history. A very readable book on the subject is K. E. Kirk's *Conscience and Its Problems* (N.Y., Longmans, Green & Co., Inc., 1931).

Casuistry to a large extent is confined to individual cases, as is also moral theology, and so is distinguished, as it were, from Christian ethics. The latter tries to answer the question, What does it mean to be a Christian, a Christian with civic responsibilities? An excellent study from this point of view is P. Ramsey's *Basic Christian Ethics* (N.Y., Charles Scribner's Sons, 1950). W. Beach and H. R. Niebuhr have collected into one volume, *Christian Ethics: Sources of the Living Tradition* (N.Y., The Ronald Press Co., 1955), representative selections on ethics from the writings of leading Christian thinkers down through the ages. It is the opinion of the editors that these selections indicate that Christian ethics inevitably lead on to a Christian sociology.

Welfare work

Because of the New Testament imperative to go about doing good, Christians have always been engaged in some kind of welfare work. Very early in Christian history there emerged orders of both men and women dedicated in some specific way to the service of the Master. Although there were many motives behind the rise of monasticism, the most prominent, as H. B. Workman has pointed out in *The Evolution of the Monastic Ideal*

(London, C. H. Kelly, 1913), was the opportunity to do good works unhampered by selfish distractions. With the repudiation of monasticism by the reformed churches, Protestants for a time lacked the techniques for relieving human distress. In more recent days this lack has been overcome by trained Christian social workers. A good account of this modern development is to be found in an article by B. M. Boyd, "Protestant Social Work" in the *Social Work Year Book* (N.Y., American Association of Social Workers, 1951). Social service activity, carried on not only by Protestants but also by Roman Catholics and Jews, has been outlined by L. A. Stidley in *Sectarian Welfare among Protestants: A Comparative Study of Protestant, Jewish and Roman Catholic Welfare Federations* (N.Y., Association Press, 1944). Within the present century there has been a considerable revival of monasticism within both the Anglican and the reformed churches of Europe that has spread to the North American continent. This revival has been sympathetically discussed by J. D. Benoit in *Liturgical Renewal Studies in Catholic and Protestant Developments on the Continent* (London, Student Christian Movement Press, 1958). The prominent part played by women in Christian social service is obvious from the large number of female religious communities. Their role has been set forth by Kathleen Bliss in *The Service and Status of Women in the Churches* (London, Student Christian Movement Press, 1952).

There are several journals concerned with the pastoral work of the church, among them the *Journal of Religion and Health* (1961–), published by the Academy of Religion and Mental Health; *The Journal of Pastoral Care* (1947–49), published by the Council for Clinical Training, Kutztown, Penn.; *Religion in Life* (N.Y., Abingdon Press, 1932–). *The Student World* (N.Y., 1908–), a quarterly published by the World Student Christian Federation, devotes a great deal of space to the social aspects of Christianity.

CHRISTIAN WORSHIP

An appreciation of the inner life of Christianity can only be achieved by an intimate knowledge of its worship from which so much of its moral practice arises. As Charles Gore has pointed out in his *Body of Christ: An Inquiry into the Institution and Doctrine of the Holy Communion* (London, John Murray Publishers, Ltd., 1907), if an observer were able to return to any period of the Christian era, he would find Christians at some time or other gathering together for a service of worship in which bread and wine would be a prominent feature. This service of Holy Communion has from apostolic days to the present time remained a permanent feature of Christian worship.

It is well known, however, that Christian public worship began in the Jewish temples and synagogues, and, therefore, no historical introduction to Christian worship is complete without some reference to Jewish piety.

Although Christians and Jews early drifted apart, yet, as Eric Werner has phrased it, "a sacred bridge still spans the abyss and allows for an exchange of views and moral concepts." His *Sacred Bridge* (N.Y., Columbia University Press, 1959) is an excellent study of the origins of Christian worship, as is W. O. E. Oesterley's *Jewish Background of the Christian Liturgy* (Oxford, Clarendon Press, 1925). The latter must be read with some caution as not all Oesterley's conclusions are acceptable to modern scholarship.

Liturgy

"Liturgy" is an over-all term for fixed forms of service in public worship. It is agreed that in the early church, apart from Jewish models, there were no rigid forms but rather a fluid rite based upon accounts of the last supper of Christ with his disciples. Gradually there grew up collections of prescribed forms of public worship; interest in the origin and form of these early liturgies has recently been greatly stimulated by Gregory Dix's *Shape of the Liturgy* (London, The Dacre Press, 1945); J. H. Srawley in *The Early History of Liturgy* (Cambridge, Cambridge University Press, 1947) covers much the same ground as Dix but is more cautious in his conclusions.

Along with the development of the liturgy, there emerged the Christian year. The association of the Christian year with liturgical practices has been set forth by A. A. McArthur in *The Evolution of the Christian Year* (London, Student Christian Movement Press, 1953).

Liturgical study divides into periods and areas. The books recommended above cover fairly adequately the early church both East and West; H. De Lubac's *Corpus Mysticum: L'Eucharistie et l'Église au moyen âge* (Paris, Aubier, 1944) provides an illuminating analysis of the medieval period; it is also an interesting commentary on the decline in frequency of communion and in congregational participation in worship from late antiquity through the Middle Ages.

E. E. Yelverton's *The Manual of Olavus Petri* (London, Society for Promoting Christian Knowledge, 1953) is a study of the first vernacular prayer book to appear in a modern language. The first two prayer books of the Church of England (1549 and 1552) were also in the vernacular but were mainly translations and revisions of medieval service books. The liturgy as received by the Church of Scotland in 1564, commonly called *John Knox's Liturgy* (rep. 1886), is a good illustration of a reformed church liturgy. A full bibliography of Roman Catholic reformed liturgies may be found in H. Jedin's "Das Konzil von Trient und die Reform des Romish Messbuches," *Ephemerides Liturgicae*, LIX (1945).

The liturgical revival

The modern period has been marked by a great revival of interest in the history and meaning of Christian worship. Books on the subject are many;

only a few can be mentioned here. E. B. Koenker's *The Liturgical Renaissance in the Roman Catholic Church* (Chicago, University of Chicago Press, 1954) provides a good outline of the modern liturgical movement within the Roman communion. A. G. Herbert's *Liturgy and Society, The Function of the Church in the Modern World* (London, Faber & Faber, Ltd., 1935), though an Anglican work, has been deeply influenced by modern Roman Catholic development.

It is inappropriate to speak of a liturgical revival within the Orthodox churches, since they have never experienced a decrease in liturgical practices; but there has been on the part of both Protestants and Catholics a desire to become better acquainted with Eastern liturgical worship, a desire that has been partially met by F. E. Brightman's *Liturgies Eastern and Western*, Vol. I, "Eastern Liturgies" (Oxford, 1896).

A study of liturgy is incomplete without some acquaintance with Christian music and hymnody. A detailed study of the subject is to be found in Winfred Douglas' *Church Music in History and Practice* (N.Y., Charles Scribner's Sons, 1937). A brief book covering the whole field of church music and its relation to theology and morals which can be highly recommended is E. Routley's *Church Music and Theology* (London, Student Christian Movement Press, 1959). The latter is particularly valuable for its comments on Christian hymnody and for a section dealing with Bach and pietism.

There are several periodicals that concentrate on liturgical subjects; one of the best of these, published in Paris, is *La Maison de Dieu* (1946–); frequently it has numbers devoted to one aspect of liturgical thought and practice. Another valuable periodical is *Worship* (1926–), published by the Liturgical Press, Collegeville, Minnesota. *Jahrbuch für Liturgik und Hymnologie* (1955–) is a Protestant publication from Kassel, Germany, with an international contributing staff.

Art and symbolism

The close association of art and religion has long been recognized, and the claim is well founded that religion has been the fountainhead of art. Art and symbolism are also closely associated with the subject of worship, since art and architecture provide the aesthetic framework in which public worship is conducted; but it is important to remember that this aesthetic framework is the outcome of the inner spirit of Christianity. Consequently, to gain an intimate understanding of Christian art it is necessary to have some knowledge of the inner meaning of the sacramental life of the church; a helpful book for this purpose is N. Clark's *An Approach to the Theology of the Sacraments* (London, Student Christian Movement Press, 1956); also useful is F. W. Dillstone's *Christianity and Symbolism* (Philadelphia, Westminster Press, 1955), in which the author discusses the signs, symbols, and sacraments of the church and relates them to the poetic image. *Signs and Symbols in Christian Art* (N.Y., Oxford University Press, 1954) by G. Ferguson is a well-arranged book with beautiful illustrations of paintings from the Renaissance period. It also provides explanations of all the symbols connected with Christian art.

Christian architecture is a study in itself. E. Short's *A History of Religious Architecture*, 3rd rev. ed. (N.Y., W. W. Norton & Co., Inc., 1951) provides a broad perspective of the subject; it begins with the first God's house of ancient Egypt and concludes with two modern cathedrals, a Roman Catholic and an Anglican, at Liverpool, England. A very practical book is P. Hammond's *Liturgy and Architecture* (London, Barrie & Rockliff, 1960), which relates past developments in church symbolism to the contemporary setting.

Mysticism

Imperceptibly one moves from the aesthetic aspect of religion to mysticism, so much dependent upon symbolism. Mystic contemplation is sometimes spoken of as the highest form of Christian worship, a thought carried over from the classical world, where contemplation, following the lead of Aristotle, was regarded as the most significant activity of which human nature is capable. It was in the thought of Plato, however, that contemplation assumed the character of religious aspiration. Mediated to western Europe by the Pseudo-Dionysius in his *The Celestial Hierarchy* (*op. cit.*), in a Neo-Platonic form based upon the philosophy of Plotinus, contemplation gave to Christianity a goal of union with God through a state of ecstasy in which discursive reasoning has been transcended. The classic work on this subject in modern times is W. R. Inge's *The Philosophy of Plotinus* (N.Y., Longmans, Green & Co., Inc., 1918), and *Personal Religion and the Life of Devotion* (N.Y., Longmans, Green & Co., Inc., 1924). The latter is an outstanding apologetic for the retention of the mystical element of religion.

Not all Christian mysticism has followed Plotinus and Dionysius in what has been called the "way of negation." In contrast to this anti-intellectualism was the school of St. Victor, which emphasized intellectual travail as well as renunciation. Thomas Aquinas also insisted on a study of the works of God as well as a quest for an intuitive vision. Two books which discuss these contrasting methods are K. E. Kirk's *The Vision of God* (London, Longmans, Green & Co., Ltd., 1931) and E. C. Butler's *Western Mysticism* (London, Constable & Co., Ltd., 1922).

Many Protestants have turned to the devotional writings of Catholic mystics for consolation and inspiration. Among these was Evelyn Underhill, who, in *Mysticism, A Study in the Nature and Development of Man's Spiritual Consciousness* (1911; 12th rev. ed., N.Y., E. P. Dutton & Co., Inc., 1930) has in her own right made a remarkable contribution to the literature of mysticism. In an appendix she gives an historical sketch of European mysticism from the earliest times to the death of Blake; she also provides a bibliography that covers almost everything written on mysticism up to 1930.

Priest and prophet

Integral to the liturgical life of the church is the ministry of word and sacrament, a subject already dealt with under the headings of pastoralia and ecclesiology; but, apart from a social ministry, there is the concern of the church over safeguards for the proper administration of the sacraments and an equal concern for the freedom of preaching as fundamental to the inspirational life of the body of believers. On this whole subject the church has been seriously divided, since in it is involved the question of the validity of the ministry. The question has been frankly discussed by Anglican contributors to *The Apostolic Ministry* (London, Hodder & Stoughton, Ltd., 1946), ed. by K. E. Kirk. A reply to this volume has been written by T. W. Manson in *The Church's Ministry* (London, Hodder & Stoughton, Ltd., 1948).

Prophecy, which had been much valued by Christians in apostolic and subapostolic times, came under suspicion during the church's contest with the Montanists, who were extravagant in their reliance upon an "inner light." The story of this contest and its influence upon the church has been brilliantly told by John De Soyres in *Montanism and the Primitive Church* (London, G. Bell & Sons, Ltd., 1878). One result of this episode in church history was that for a thousand years Christian faith was largely mediated by priest and ritual. Nevertheless, there were throughout this period sporadic outbursts of the Montanist spirit which became particularly pronounced during the Reformation era. These have been set forth by E. B. Box in *Rise and Fall of the Anabaptists* (London, Macmillan & Co., Ltd., 1903). R. M. Jones in *Spiritual Reformers of the Sixteenth Century* (London, Macmillan & Co., Ltd., 1914) deals with the radical concepts of the ministry that arose during the Reformation era, particularly the emphasis upon prophecy.

Recently there has arisen a new interest in prophecy from an historical point of view, as well as a revised concept of the function of a priest in the Old Testament era. Two important books that have created this interest are A. C. Welch's *Prophet and Priest in Old Israel* (London, Student Christian Movement Press, 1936) and J. Hoschander's *Priests and Prophets* (N.Y., Jewish Theological Seminary of America, 1938). Various signs now indicate that the pulpit is more and more guided by prophetic preaching, as has been advocated by K. M. Yates in *Preaching from the Prophets* (N.Y., Harper & Brothers, 1942). At the same time, there has been a decline in Protestant churches of a bias against liturgical forms of worship and priestly guidance of an individual's moral development.

Christian education

Part of the Christian ministry is the guiding of children, youths, and adults into a mature discipleship. As in so many instances in Christian origins, such educational activity is a Jewish inheritance from the synagogue schools. Very early, church schools rivaled the synagogue schools, particularly the Catechetical school at Alexandria founded about 185. The story of the development of Christian education from Hebrew foundations on to the medieval schools has been briefly told by L. J. Sherrill in *The Rise of Christian Education* (N.Y., The Macmillan Co., 1950).

Before Constantine, when the church lived in a pagan world, Christian education consisted mainly in teaching converts the morals, creed, and discipline of the church; after Constantine all education gradually came under the control of the church with the attempt, as can be seen in A. C. Pegis' *The Wisdom of Catholicism* (N.Y., Random House, Inc., 1949), to make Christian faith the basis of knowledge.

Modern secular education was born during the Renaissance, and the churches were compelled to find new means to impart biblical knowledge. The Roman Catholic Church as well as many Protestant churches fell back upon catechisms as a method of inculcating fundamental doctrines and morals. The substance of the Roman teaching as set forth by the catechism of the Council of Trent can be found in *The Catholic Catechism* (N.Y., P. J. Kenedy & Sons, 1936) drawn up by Peter Cardinal Gasparri. The catechisms of the reformed churches are too numerous to be mentioned here, except perhaps a very famous one, the Westminster shorter catechism, of whose uses and abuses S. W. Carruthers has recently given an historical account in *Three Centuries of the Westminster Shorter Catechism* (Fredericton, University of New Brunswick Press, 1957). This book also contains a facsimile reproduction of the original manuscript presented to the English Parliament, November 25, 1647.

In Protestant circles there has been much debate on the content and method of Christian education. Horace Bushnell in his epoch-making book, *Christian Nurture* (N.Y., Charles Scribner's Sons, 1847) opposed the individualistic revivalism of his day as a means of conversion and sought to establish a biblical basis for teaching within the home and the church. Most denominations have attempted to carry on Christian education with a complex set of agencies: the Sunday school, vacation school, and released time from day schools, but with somewhat frustrating results. For this reason there has arisen a large collection of literature devoted to ways and means of Christian education. G. A. Coe in *What is Christian Education?* (N.Y., Charles Scribner's Sons, 1929) attempts to make Christian education relevant to contemporary life. Some penetrating questions on the subject have been posed by H. S. Elliott in *Can Religious Education be Christian?* (N.Y., The Macmillan Co., 1940) and by R. C. Miller in *The Clue to Christian Education* (N.Y., Charles Scribner's Sons, 1950).

CHRISTIANITY AND CIVILIZATION

A tension between civilization, which is a human achievement, and an organization which belongs primarily to the eternal and the absolute would appear to be inevitable. Nevertheless, the church which arose within an advanced civilization could not fail to be affected by its surrounding environment and attempt to make some accommodation to it. As W. F. Albright has pointed out in *From the Stone Age to Christianity* (1940; 2nd ed., Baltimore, The Johns Hopkins Press, 1946), even if Hellenism had little influence on Jesus' idea of God, it did have some effect "in the formation of Jesus' other religious ideas." Nor does he think it possible to deny that the religious emotions and impulses that had swayed the Near East for three millennia were "part of the divine preparation for Christianity." This is a subject to which a great deal of attention has been given in recent years by A. J. Toynbee, who in *Civilization on Trial* (N.Y., Columbia University Press, 1948) takes issue with Sir James Frazer's theory set forth in *The Golden Bough*, 3rd ed. (London, Macmillan & Co., Ltd., 1915), that Christianity has been a destroyer of civilization; on the contrary, he holds that it has been the reproducer of civilizations. Toynbee has somewhat modified this view by seeing civilizations as the handmaids of religion.

Be that as it may, Christianity, as Christopher Dawson in *Understanding Europe* (London, Sheed & Ward, Ltd., 1952) says, has from the beginning been a missionary and, hence, a world-transforming movement. Because of its proclamation of a coming new order, it has been essentially a dynamic force in society and, consequently, has never been at peace with the world around it. This has led to continuous conflict, usually dealt with by historians under the over-all heading "church and state."

Church and state

The church's approach to the state has been historically one of cooperation when possible, but also of judgment. It is in the act of judgment that it has come into conflict with the state. This conflict has produced an immense library of literature, part of which has been critically analyzed by F. Gavin in *Seven Centuries of the Problem of Church and State* (Oxford, Oxford University Press, 1938).

A good introduction to what has been called the struggle between "Christ and Caesar" is H. B. Workman's *Persecution in the Early Church*, 3rd ed. (London, C. H. Kelly, 1911). Hans Lietzmann's *From Constantine to Julian*, Vol. III of *A History of the Early Church*, tr. by B. Lee Woolf (London, Lutterworth Press, 1950), gives a good insight into the relations of church and state immediately following upon the recognition of the church as a favored religion of the Roman Empire.

During the medieval period there was much discussion about the division of authority between secular and spiritual powers. This may be followed in G. Tellenbach's *Church, State and Christian Society at the Time of the Investiture Contest*, English translation (Oxford, B. H. Blackwell, Ltd., 1940); also in J. Bryce's *The Holy Roman Empire*, 8th ed. (N.Y., The Macmillan Co., 1889). A parallel contest in the Eastern Church, centering around the veneration of icons, is described by G. Every in *The Byzantine Patriarchate 451–1204* (N.Y., The Macmillan Co., 1947).

The relations of church and state during the Reformation era were much complicated by an internal quarrel within the Christian community. This struggle had considerable influence on the attitudes of both churchmen and statesmen toward political matters, as can be seen in J. W. Allen's *A History of Political Thought in the Sixteenth Century* (N.Y., Dial Press, Inc., 1928) and also in R. H. Bainton's *The Travail of Religious Liberty* (Philadelphia, Westminster Press, 1951).

With the rise of modern nationalism and new conflicting ideologies, the problem of the relations of church and state has taken on a new complexity. Two books dealing with this new phase in Europe are A. Keller's *Church and State on the European Continent* (London, The Epworth Press, 1937), and L. Pfeffer's *Church, State and Freedom* (Boston, Beacon Press, Inc., 1953). A. L. Drummond's *German Protestantism since Luther* (London, The Epworth Press, 1951) is concerned with some peculiarly German problems, particularly in Part II, which deals primarily with the relations of church and state.

W. K. Jordan's *The Development of Religious Toleration in England*, 4 vols. (London, George Allen & Unwin, Ltd., 1932–40) is a detailed study of many phases of church and state development in England. A work on the same scale, dealing with the intricacies of church–state relations in the United States is A. P. Stokes' *Church and State in the United States*, 3 vols. (N.Y., Harper & Brothers, 1950). A one-volume study, *Religious Liberty: An Inquiry* (N.Y., International Missionary Council, 1945) by M. Searle Bates, carried on under the auspices of a Joint Committee appointed by the Foreign Missions Conference of North America and the Federal Council of Churches of Christ in America, covers the whole field of the relations of church and state down to the present time. It is particularly good concerning Latin America and also the present situation of the churches in non-Christian lands.

Christian missions

The Christian imperative to go into all the world to preach the gospel has, down through the ages, created novel problems in the relations of church and state. The missionary imperative has compelled the church to assume civilizing activities—that is, to attempt to enlighten and refine newly converted people. Such activities have often aroused the suspicion of the state into which the church has expanded. The story of this expansion is practically a history of Christianity itself, and it is in this sense that K. S. Latourette wrote his monumental *A History of the Expansion of Christianity*, 7 vols. (N.Y., Harper & Brothers, 1937–45). A less formidable work is W. O. Carver's *The Course of Christian Missions*, rev. ed. (N.Y., Fleming H. Revell, Co., 1939).

With the collapse of the Roman Empire, Europe became a great field for Christian expansion, posing a challenge for a systematic form of missionary work; the challenge was met by religious orders dedicated to the spread of the gospel. A good account of the work and method of these orders can be found in C. H. Robinson's *The Conversion of Europe* (N.Y., Longmans, Green & Co., Inc., 1917); a brief but painstaking study which supplements Robinson's book is J. T. Addison's *The Medieval Missionary* (N.Y., International Missionary Council, 1936).

The age of exploration and the discovery of a new world in the fifteenth century provided a new challenge to the missionary imperative. It was the Roman Catholic Church that first accepted this challenge through the instrumentality of its older orders; also new orders emerged to meet the new conditions. The complexity of the work in non-Catholic lands led to the establishment in the seventeenth century of the Sacred Congregation *de Propaganda Fide* to coordinate the work of evangelization. Its history has been told by Otto Meier in *Die Propaganda ihre Prorinzer und ihre Recht* (Göttingen, Dietrich, 1852).

Although the Protestant churches were rather slow in taking up missionary work, they did finally help to make the nineteenth century, as Latourette has emphasized (*op. cit.*), one of the most expansive centuries in all Christian history. For the origins of Protestant missions both G. Warneck's *History of Protestant Missions* (N.Y., Fleming H. Revell, Co., 1904) and R. H. Glover's *The Progress of World-wide Missions*, rev. and enl. by J. H. Kane (N.Y., Harper & Brothers, 1960), are useful books. To some extent the Orthodox Church shared in this expansive mood, as is indicated in S. Bolshakoff's *The Foreign Missions of the Russian Orthodox Church* (London, Society for Promoting Christian Knowledge, 1943).

Because of the rapid expansion of the church during the nineteenth century, there has developed a science of missions such as has been set forth in J. H. Bavinck's *An Introduction to the Science of Missions*, tr. by D. H. Freeman (Philadelphia, Presbyterian & Reformed Pub. Co., 1960). This book seeks to ascertain the scriptural basis of missions and their status in the life of the church. A Roman Catholic definition of this science has been propounded by J. Schmidlin in *Katholische Missionslehre in Grundriss*, tr. by M. Braun (Techny, Ill., Mission Press, 1923). This new interest has led to the establishment of chairs of missions in theological colleges and the founding of societies to engage in missionary research and publication; the fruits of such investigation are reported in such journals as *The International Review of Missions* (Edinburgh, 1912–) and the *Allgemeine-Missions Zeitschrift* (Berlin, 1874–).

THE ECUMENICAL MOVEMENT

While the nineteenth century was an era of expansion for the Christian Church, it now appears that the twentieth may well be an era of integration. Such integration is best exemplified in the ecumenical movement, the history of which has been carefully compiled by R. Rouse and S. C. Neil in *A History of the Ecumenical Movement 1517–1948* (London, Society for Promoting Christian Knowledge, 1954).

Faith and Order

As R. S. Bilheimer has emphasized in his *The Quest for Christian Unity* (N.Y., Association Press, 1952), the origins of ecumenicity reach back to the sixteenth century and even beyond; yet he, along with other writers such as H. P. Van Dusen in *World Christianity: Yesterday-Today-Tomorrow* (Nashville, Abingdon-Cokesbury, 1947), gives great credit to the gathering together of missionary societies in world conferences for stimulating efforts toward organic church unions, the most successful to date being the church of South India, whose exciting story has been told by B. Sundkler in *Church of South India: The Movement towards Union 1900–1947* (London, Lutterworth Press, 1954). Preceding this historic event had been many international gatherings of churchmen, the most notable being a meeting of a World Missionary Conference at Edinburgh (1910), which formed a continuation committee known as the International Missionary Council. A brief but adequate account of the purpose of this council as well as the significance of Edinburgh is given by N. Goodall in *The Ecumenical Movement* (London, Oxford University Press, 1961). He points out that, although matters of faith and doctrine were excluded from the Edinburgh Conference, yet this conference was responsible for the origin of the Faith and Order Movement.

To find a satisfactory doctrinal and disciplinary basis for the reunion of Christendom has been the avowed task of the world conference on Faith and Order. Descriptions and interpretations of these conferences are contained in E. S. Wood's *Lausanne* (1927), H. Martin's *Edinburgh* (1937), and E. H. Robertson's *Lund* (1952).

Life and Work

Parallel with the search for doctrinal unity was an attempt to bring the mind of Christ to bear on the great social, industrial, and international questions so urgent in twentieth-century civilization. The leaders of this movement were Nathan Söderblom and the Ecumenical Patriarch of Constantinople, who simultaneously issued appeals for the churches to cooperate in social and moral action. These appeals led to the formation of a Universal Christian Conference on Life and Work at Stockholm in 1925, to be followed by several similar conferences. Official reports of these conferences are *Report of the Stockholm Conference, 1925*, ed. by G. K. Bell (1926), and *The Churches Survey Their Task, The Report of the Conference at Oxford, July 1937, on Church, Community and State* (London, George Allen & Unwin, Ltd., 1937).

World Council of Churches

It soon became evident that there was much overlapping in the aims and activities of the Faith and Order and Life and Work committees, and this led to their integration into the World Council of Churches. The First Assembly met at Amsterdam, Holland, in 1948 and adopted a constitution which proclaimed, "The World Council of Churches is a fellowship which accepts our Lord Jesus Christ as God and Saviour." Official reports of the *First and Second Assemblies of the World Council of Churches* were published in 1948 (London) and 1955 (N.Y.), ed. by W. A. Visser't Hooft. A most comprehensive collection of documents on all phases of the ecumenical movement leading up to and beyond the formation of the World Council has been made by G. K. Bell in *Documents on Christian Unity*, 3 series (London, Oxford University Press, 1920–48). More recent developments as well as reports on the progress of negotiations for unity may be followed in *The Ecumenical Review* (Geneva, 1948–), a quarterly published by the World Council of Churches.

Christian dialogue

Until recently the Roman Catholic Church has remained somewhat aloof from the ecumenical movement, but with the establishment by John XXIII of a secretariat for Christian unity, there has arisen a keen "dialogue" between Roman and non-Roman churches, with a preliminary attempt to understand one another's point of view. Such an attempt was foreshadowed in G. H. Tavard's *The Catholic Approach to Protestantism* (N.Y., Harper & Brothers, 1955), which outlines steps that have been taken by Roman Catholic authorities for the promotion of ecumenism. Another interesting book on the same theme is Y. M. Congar's *After Nine Hundred Years* (N.Y., Fordham University Press, 1959).

As has been observed by Jacques Madaule in a preface to a most relevant book on this subject, *The Catholic Protestant Dialogue* (Baltimore, Helicon Press, 1960) by J. Bosc, J. Guitton, and J. Danileau, "In a certain sense it could be said the dialogue between Catholics and Protestants has never been wholly interrupted since Martin Luther posted his famous theses at Wittenberg." Nevertheless, it has taken on a new intensity since the establishment of a secretariat for Christian unity and produced a large amount of literature in a very brief time, much of which is listed in *The Catholic Protestant Dialogue* (*op. cit.*).

TRADITION AND TRADITIONS

Christianity has expressed itself in variant forms in different ages and in different places. These distinctive developments are loosely termed "traditions"; the acceptance of these traditions as part of the ongoing life of the church is based upon faith in the uninterrupted and abiding presence of the Lord in his church. Also implicit in this faith is the belief that behind divergent expressions of Christianity is a common tradition or history from which these separated traditions derive their true existence.

This frank recognition of a living tradition which expresses itself in different ecclesiastical forms associated with certain ways of thinking or molded by certain temporal circumstances has permitted church historians to divide church history into distinct fields of research—early, medieval, orthodox, reformed, modern—all of which represent different expressions of the original apostolic tradition. Modern church history is also subdivided into European, Eastern, Oriental, American, African, etc. No one historian can hope to deal adequately with all these traditions but must, for the most part, confine himself to one or two fields of research.

A common tradition

Nevertheless, there have been serious attempts to find one common tradition to which all the various traditions might be related or by which they may be tested. One such attempt is A. C. Outler's *The Christian Tradition and the Unity We Seek* (N.Y., Oxford University Press, 1957). Also there have been many attempts to write an over-all history of the church. Reference has already been made to K. S. Latourette's monumental work on the expansion of Christianity, but the same author has also written in one volume *A History of Christianity* (N.Y., Harper & Brothers, 1953) in which he essays "to place the story of Christianity in the setting of universal history." A similar and more concise account of the onward march of the Christian faith is *Twenty Centuries of Christianity* (N.Y., Harcourt, Brace & Co., 1959) by P. Hutchinson and W. E. Garrison. Earlier A. H. Newman produced a notable compendium of Christianity entitled *A Manual of Church History*, 2 vols. (Philadelphia, American Baptist Publication Society, 1900).

A similar kind of manual, extremely condensed, is Williston Walker's *History of the Christian Church* (N.Y., Charles Scribner's Sons, 1918), which has been revised and brought up to date by Richardson, Pauck, and Handy (1959). All these histories suffer seriously from compression, which necessitates arbitrary selection, and also from the fact that one author or even several cannot be proficient in all the various church traditions. An obvious method of overcoming this deficiency is to ask experts in the various fields of theological research to write articles on those aspects of Christianity with which they are most familiar and bring such articles together in Christian dictionaries or encyclopedias. *The Oxford Dictionary of the Christian Church* (London, Oxford University Press, 1957), ed. by F. L. Cross, is one recent attempt to provide an authoritative account of Christianity. *The New Schaff Herzog Encyclopedia of Religious Knowledge*, 13 vols. (N.Y., Funk & Wagnalls Co., 1908–14), is an earlier attempt to cover the same field; it has recently been extended by *Twentieth Century Encyclopedia of Religious Knowledge*, 2 vols. (Michigan, Baker Book House, 1955), ed. by L. A. Loetscher. *The Catholic Encyclopaedia*, 17 vols. (N.Y., Encyclopaedia Press, 1907–22), as its preface indicates, is intended to provide "full and authoritative information on the entire cycle of Catholic interests." *The Encyclopedia of Religion and Ethics*, 13 vols. (N.Y., Charles Scribner's Sons, 1908–27), ed. by J. Hastings, is probably the most comprehensive of all these encyclopedias.

Early church history

Early church history has long been a most intensive field of research for church historians, so that it is extremely difficult to give any fair or adequate selection from the mass of literature on the subject. B. J. Kidd's *A History of the Church to 461*, 3 vols. (Oxford, Clarendon Press, 1922), is a carefully documented piece of work and a mine of information. A much-valued study of the early church is H. Lietzmann's 4-volume series, tr. by B. L. Woolf, *The Beginnings of the Christian Church* (London, Nicholson & Watson, Ltd., 1937), *The Founding of the Universal Church* (London, Nicholson & Watson, Ltd., 1938), *From Constantine to Julian* (London, Lutterworth Press, 1950), and *The Era of the Church Fathers* (N.Y., Charles Scribner's Sons, 1952). L. Duchesne's *The Early History of the Christian Church*, tr. from the 4th French rev. ed. by Claude Jenkins, 3 vols. (London, John Murray Publishers, Ltd., 1909–24), is a classic history of the ancient church. An extended bibliography on the period is furnished in *A Bibliographical Guide to the History of Christianity*, ed. by S. J. Case (Mass., Peter Smith, 1952).

The medieval period

It is impossible to extricate medieval church history from general medieval history; consequently, the justly famous *The Cambridge Medieval History*, 8 vols. (N.Y., The Macmillan Co., 1911–36) is indispensable for the student of Christianity. A good over-all survey of the period is H. Pirenne's *A History of Europe from the Invasions to the XVI Century*, tr. by B. Miall (London, George Allen & Unwin, Ltd., 1939).

CRUSADES

One of the most dramatic episodes of the medieval period was the long-drawn-out contest between Christendom and the Islamic world generally designated as the "crusades". The crusades have given rise to a voluminous literature, of which the most recent contribution is S. Runciman's *A History of the Crusades*, 3 vols. (Cambridge, Cambridge University Press, 1951–54). A series of interesting historical essays on the crusades is to be found in *The Crusades and other Historical Essays* presented to Dana C. Munro by his former students, ed. by L. J. Paetow (Conn., Arthur C. Croft Publications, 1928).

Reformation

It is difficult to separate the period known as the Reformation from the Renaissance and the Counter-Reformation, as they are inextricably bound together but antipathetic to one another. All of them are part and parcel of the decline of the medieval synthesis. This is clearly brought out in J. Huizinga's *The Waning of the Middle Ages*, tr. by F. Hopman (1924; rev. ed. N.Y., Doubleday & Co., Inc., 1954). There is again an embarrassment of literature on the period, but all the significant aspects are encompassed in E. M. Hulme's *The Renaissance, the Protestant Reformation, and the Catholic Reformation*, 2 vols. (N.Y., Century House, 1914).

Additional material for Reformation

Reformation literature, while patristic, has long been subject to minute analysis by specialized scholars. For this reason, much interest has been manifested in great collections of the works of the leading reformers, such as the *Corpus Reformatorum*, ed. by K. G. Bretschneider and H. E. Bindseit (Halle, Hallis Saxonum, 1834–) and the *Schriften des Vereins für Reformationsgeschichte*, Vols. 1–93 (1883–). The latter covers all phases of the history of the Reformation and is almost complete. There are also large collections of the works of the leading figures, such as the famous Weimar edition of Martin Luther's *Werke* (*Kritische Gesamtausgabe*) (Böhlau, 1883–). This edition, which is almost indispensable for the student of Luther, is now being translated, though not in full and with some departures from its readings and findings, by a group of American scholars under the over-all title *Luther's Works*, ed. by J. Pelikan and H. T. Lehman (St. Louis, Concordia Publishing House, 1955–). Of almost equal interest to Luther's are the works of John Calvin, particularly his *Institutes of the Christian Religion*, which have been translated from the Latin and collated with the author's last edition in French by John Allen (London, James Clarke & Co., Ltd., 1949).

A very useful bibliography of the Reformation is now being published under the auspices of La commission internationale d'histoire ecclésiastique comparée au sein du comité internationale des sciences historiques, entitled *Bibliographie de la Réforme 1450–1648* (Leiden, E. J. Brill, 1960–). Small collections of documents containing important creeds have been made by H. S. Bettenson, entitled *Documents of the Christian Church* (N.Y., Oxford

University Press, 1956); also B. J. Kidd has made a useful collection in *Documents Illustrative of the Continental Reformation* (Oxford, Clarendon Press, 1911).

The Counter-Reformation is now beginning to receive from Roman Catholic scholars equally as close a scrutiny as that given to the Reformation by Protestant scholars. This renewed interest centres around the Council of Trent and has been greatly aided by H. Jedin, *A History of the Council of Trent* (N.Y., Thomas Nelson & Sons, 1957–), tr. by Dom Ernest Graf, O.B.S. Four volumes are planned.

Modern Christendom

With the break up of Western Christendom and the rise of nationalism, traditions become so multiple that it would encumber this chapter far beyond its allotted space to attempt to list denominational and church histories of the ongoing church of our times. It must suffice to refer the reader to *A Bibliographical Guide to the History of Christianity* (*op. cit.*). There are, however, some excellent journals which specialize in the field of historical research and contain reviews of all significant publications; among them may be singled out three semiannuals: *Revue de l'histoire des religions* (Paris, 1880–), published at the Collège de France; *Archiv für Reformationsgeschichte* (Berlin, 1903–), published under the auspices of the Verein für Reformationsgeschichte and the American Society for Reformation Research; and *The Journal of Ecclesiastical History* (1950–), published at the University of London.

Two important quarterlies are *The Catholic Historical Review* (Washington, 1915–), the official organ of the American Catholic Association, and *Church History* (Pennsylvania, 1932–), published by the American Society of Church History.

CHRISTIANITY AND OTHER RELIGIONS

With the clash of Occidental and Oriental cultures in our modern world, Christianity has become acutely conscious of rival non-Christian religious traditions. The question of what the church's attitude towards these other higher religions should be has produced a large library of lively literature both of a philosophic and polemical nature. F. S. C. Northrop in *The Meeting of East and West* (N.Y., The Macmillan Co., 1946) speculates about a possible synthesis of Occidental and Oriental cultures and sees in the rich culture of Mexico the beginnings of such a synthesis. In *Civilization on Trial* (*op. cit.*) A. J. Toynbee makes the prediction that the impact of Western civilization on its contemporary civilizations in the second half of the twentieth century "was the first step towards the unification of mankind." In *Christianity among the Religions of the World* (N.Y., Charles Scribner's Sons, 1957) he is less the prophet and more the analyst and feels that if Christianity is to play its part in reconciling the diverse cultures of the world, it must be purged both of its exclusiveness and of its Western accretions.

Toynbee's critical attitude towards Western culture has not gone unchallenged. D. Jerrold in *The Lie about the West* (London, J. M. Dent & Sons, Ltd., 1954) asserts that Toynbee (particularly in *The World and the West* [London, Oxford University Press, 1953]) has made Christianity a false religion; for, if it is true, it must be unique.

Another of Toynbee's critics is H. Kraemer, who in *World Cultures and World Religions* (Philadelphia, Westminster Press, 1960) takes "issue with almost every aspect" of the former's idea of religion; nevertheless, he agrees that "the religious is the deepest in the total meeting of the Orient and the Occident." Furthermore, he gives Toynbee the credit for hammering home the undeniable fact that "Late modern Western technology has brought all the living higher religions over the world into closer contact with one another than ever before." His objection to Toynbee's analysis and to the syncretists is that they write from a humanist rather than a Christian viewpoint. W. E. Hocking's *The Coming World Civilization* (N.Y., Harper & Brothers, 1956) probably comes under Kraemer's rebuke, but Hocking maintains that if we take some lessons from the East we will only be moving nearer "to the spirit of an earlier Christianity."

Besides the problem involved in the meeting of Eastern and Western cultures, Christianity faces the challenge of living in a Western secularized society which can no longer be regarded as motivated by Christian ideals. John Baillie has pointed out in *What is Christian Civilization?* (*op. cit.*) that "the Christian can never offer more than a qualified loyalty or attachment to an earthly civilization"; nevertheless, he feels that Christians must strive for a Christian community and to retain a "conception of a Christian civilization" which "it is still our duty to export"—a theme dealt with in greater detail by E. Brunner in *Christianity and Civilization*, 2 vols. (London, James Nisbet & Co., Ltd., 1948–49). Brunner deals with the problem raised by the secularization of all aspects of life and asks the question, "What are the chances of a Christian civilization in our age?" to which he gives no certain answer. He has, however, intensified a debate about two cities, the spiritual and the secular, that reaches back to Augustine, if not to the beginnings of Christianity itself.

VIII

Islām

Charles J. Adams

I. THE NAME

Approximately one-seventh of the world's population profess a faith and a religious involvement to which they give the name "Islām." Unlike the names of the other major religions, most of which came into common use in response to the need of outsiders for a convenient term to designate people different from themselves, the name "Islām" has an integral relation to the religious experience of those who claim it. Its origins are to be found in the very beginning of the Islamic adventure in history in the mouth of the Prophet, Muḥammad, who employed this word both to signify his own response to the Almighty Being who had called him and to describe that to which he was summoning his fellow Arabs. The word continues today, as it has through 1300 years, to be used by members of the community tracing their spiritual ancestry to Muḥammad as a name for their faith. It is evident, therefore, that the name expresses something fundamental in the religious experience of Muslims (Arabic for those who make or do Islām).

From the standpoint of grammar "Islām" is a verbal noun, the infinitive of a verb meaning "to accept," "to submit," or even "to surrender." It might be translated as "acceptance" or "surrender" but better as "submission"; in modern theological language the word coming closest to rendering its sense is probably "commitment." To be emphasized is the verbal quality of the word; by its very form it conveys a feeling of action and ongoingness, not of something which is static and finished, once and for all, but of an inward state which is always repeated and renewed. In its most basic meaning, "Islām" is the name of a relationship between a man or a group of men and their Sovereign Lord, the type of relationship in which men self-consciously and reverently commit, submit, or surrender themselves anew with each moment to the highest reality they are capable of apprehending. One who thoughtfully and with awareness of the sense of the words declares "I am a Muslim" has done much more than affirm his membership in a community or social group. Though it has obvious sociological connotations, the declaration is above all religious, profoundly so. This fact is perhaps easier to appreciate if one speaks Arabic rather than English, since so rich a word as "Muslim" or "Islām" is certain to be denuded of much of its meaning when carried over into another language. But were the Arabic word to be translated so that the sentence read "I am one who commits himself to God," its essential religious import would at least be adumbrated.

The foregoing comments refer to the original, Qur'ānic or prophetic meaning of "Islām" as this author understands it, but, like every other important word, "Islām" has undergone changes in meaning in the centuries during which it has been used. The word was common in pre-Islamic Arabia, being employed in commercial dealings, especially among the rich traders of Makkah; one of the achievements of Muḥammad was to have invested it with profound new meanings, to have transformed it from an expression signifying acceptance of the conditions of a contract to one that sums up humankind's place in the scheme of things. There is a discussion of this early history and an examination of the word generally in H. Ringgren, *Islam, 'aslama, and Muslim* (Uppsala, C. W. K. Gleerup, 1949).

By far the most thoughtful and provocative consideration of the changes rung on this key term may be read in chapter IV of Wilfred Cantwell Smith's *The Meaning and End of Religion* (N.Y., The Macmillan Co., 1963). In footnotes 105 and 107 to this chapter, pp. 298–9, may be found a brief bibliography of other writings on the subject. Smith's specific treatment of "Islām" and its meaning is part of a broad analysis of some methodological problems in the study of religion and should be commended to the reader in its entirety. Apart from the fact that the argument of the chapter on Islām will be only partially understandable taken from its context, the book as a whole presents a powerfully reasoned thesis of great importance for students of religion. Smith holds that the conceptual tools used by most modern scholars are inadequate, even obstructive, for understanding man's religiousness. In the specific case of Islām he illustrates the process by which this originally religious word was transmuted and debased into becoming the name of an abstraction, a system of thought and practice—in short, how it came to be considered the name of a "religion." The result is that for most moderns, including Muslims, the word has lost its implications of a personal act of faith and is used as though "Islam" were an entity in its own right, having an independent reality separable from the inner state of the men of faith who call themselves Muslims. Not the least of the merits of Smith's analysis is the light it sheds on important aspects of contemporary Muslim thinking, where Islām as a perfect ideal of thought and action is often contrasted sharply with the actual mundane conduct and achievement of Muslims. Smith's work offers rich documentation in support of his general thesis (that the concept "religion" is inadequate and no longer useful), and much that is said in this *Reader's Guide* concerning the complexity and diversity of what we commonly call the "religion" of the Buddhist, Jews, Muslims, etc. will serve to buttress his case.

II. THE PRE-ISLAMIC BACKGROUND

Like every other major historical phenomenon, the Islamic community must be seen against the background from which it emerged if we are to understand it. The Prophet Muḥammad lived, preached, and established his community among the Arabs of the Arabian Peninsula in the early years of the seventh century A.D. For centuries the inhabitants of the interior of the peninsula had been in contact with the higher civilizations bordering the desert areas, and around the fringes of the peninsula itself, notably in the south, several higher civilizations had risen and fallen. Though in these circumstances one might expect to be able to reconstruct the history of pre-Islamic Arabia in some detail, very little is in fact known of that history. One important reason for the poverty of our knowledge is the unwillingness of governments in the Arabian peninsula to allow foreign scholars or archeological expeditions within their borders to carry out the necessary research. If ever the restrictive policies of governments in the peninsula should be relaxed, or if they should develop a tradition of scholarship in this field for themselves, the result might well be a major breakthrough in our knowledge of the ancient world. The material waiting to be exploited, judged even from the slender evidence available, is of vast extent. For the time being, however, we must content ourselves with the insights afforded by literary sources and the meager reports of travelers and scholars clever and hardy enough to have penetrated the forbidding interior of Arabia.

The substance of modern knowledge of pre-Islamic Arabian history is presented in readable and succinct fashion in Part I of Philip K. Hitti, *History of the Arabs*, 5th rev. ed. (London, Macmillan & Co., Ltd., 1953). As the title indicates, the book surveys the whole of Arab history and not merely the pre-Islamic period. Hitti's is the best known and certainly the most usable of the one-volume histories of the Arabs available in the market. Its chief virtues lie in Hitti's command of the sources, the felicitousness of his presentation, the meticulous accuracy of detail, and an excellent index. The writer's love for his own people shines through on every page; the volume is an extended effort to present the beauty, achievements, and glory of Arab civilization to the English reader by the man who, as much as any single individual, is responsible for the firm place that Arab and Islamic studies now enjoy in North American universities. The work has, however, been subjected to serious criticism for its sometimes too close dependence upon its sources and for its preference of detailed factual treatment above broad interpretations. Of quite a different type is the small but incisive volume by Bernard Lewis, *The Arabs in History* (London, N.Y., Hutchinson's University Library, 1950). Far more than a chronicle of significant events or of kings, rulers, thinkers, etc., *The Arabs in History* sets out to analyze the great trends of Arab development and to interpret the role of the Arabs in the region where they have lived and flourished and in the development of world history as a whole. Consequently, there is less concern with factual material or description and more with analyses, judgments, and interpretations. Pre-Islamic Arab history is, of course, considered with emphasis upon the relationship between the "days of ignorance" and the cultural flowering that followed. If the reader should require a more thoroughgoing and comprehensive presentation of early Arabian history, there is none better than the three volumes of A. P. Caussin de Perceval: *Essai sur l'histoire des arabes avant l'Islamisme* (Paris, Didot, 1847–48), though these are now more than 100 years old. There may be added the introductory work by DeLacy O'Leary, *Arabia before Muhammad* (London, Kegan Paul, Trench, Trubner & Co., Ltd., 1927), but of it, as of the others, the judgment must be sustained that no satisfactory history of pre-Islamic Arabia has yet been written.

Specifically, Islām arose in the western coastal region of Arabia known as the Ḥijāz, in the city of Makkah. In an effort to establish in depth the background of the rise of Islām, the Belgian scholar Henri Lammens has devoted several careful studies to this region. His *Le berceau de l'Islam*, Vol. I (Rome, Sumptibus Pontificii Instituti Biblici, 1914) discusses its geography and climate, something of its history, and the religious and social customs of its inhabitants. The treatment extends into the Islamic period and illuminates some of the activities of the Prophet. A companion article describes life in the city of Makkah at a slightly later period: "La Mecque à la veille de l'Hégire," in *Mélanges de la faculté orientale de l'Université St. Joseph de Beyrouth*, IX (1924), pp. 240–54. For this writer personally the most helpful reconstruction of life in Makkah and the changes effected through Muḥammad has been the insightful article of Eric R. Wolf: "The Social Organization of Mecca and the

Origins of Islam," *Southwestern Journal of Anthropology*, VII (1951), pp. 329–56. Having first shown the dislocations in Makkan life consequent upon the development of a mercantile economy in the city and the disparity between the theories of social organization on the one hand and the realities of power and social control on the other, Wolf is able to demonstrate the significance of Muḥammad's innovations with great precision and clarity. Though it is short and has been superseded by the fuller studies of other scholars, such as Montgomery Watt, working along similar lines, Wolf's article is important for every student of Islām.

The success of Muḥammad was dependent in large part upon his ability to build upon while at the same time modifying the traditional ways of life of his people. Many of the customs of pre-Islamic Arabia, often in changed form, continued to be observed among the members of Muḥammad's community. *Kinship and Marriage in Early Arabia* by W. Robertson Smith (Cambridge, Cambridge University Press, 1885) and the same author's *Religion of the Semites* (Cambridge, 1889; republished N.Y., Meridian Books, Inc., 1956) are perhaps the best introductions to the time-honored mores of Arabian life, including its religious aspect. The fundamental values of the Arabs of Jāhilīyah times, as the pre-Islamic period is called, are studied sociologically by Bichr Farès in *L'honneur chez les Arabes avant l'Islam* (Paris, Adrien-Maisonneuve, 1932). Farès traces many elements of what to modern eyes appears to be excess in the behavior of the Arabs to a central concern for reputation or the image that a man and his tribe project to the surrounding world. Relying, as does Farès, on information gleaned from pre-Islamic poetry, Toshihiko Izutsu carries the study a step further by analyzing the relation of pre-Islamic values and concepts of the end of man to the great themes of Muḥammad's preaching in his *The Structure of the Ethical Terms in the Koran* (Tokyo, Keio Institute of Philological Studies, 1959). The result is a work that causes the impact of Muḥammad's proclamations upon his hearers to be brought home to the modern reader as perhaps no other work has done. A substantial part of the first volume of Ignaz Goldziher's famous *Muhammedanische Studien* (Halle, 1888; Hildesheim, Georg Olms, 1961) is also given to discussion of pre-Islamic Arabia; the first two chapters and the first two notes at the end of the volume have been influential in Western scholarship and are of importance.

Specifically on the subject of religion, W. Robertson Smith's *Religion of the Semites* is the classic study. Its central thesis, that sacrifice among the ancient Semites was a type of communion with the deity, has long since been rejected, but in other respects it is a masterly survey and analysis of the evidence on Semitic religion. The student of Islamics will find particularly interesting the discussion of certain pagan practices, such as the cult of the Ka'bah, that were carried over into Islām, albeit reformed and infused with a new meaning by the Prophet. Among the elder books that discuss the religion of the pagan Arabs with authority and detail mention should be made of Julius Wellhausen, *Reste Arabischen Heidenthums*, 2nd ed. (Berlin and Leipzig, Walter de Gruyter, 1927). The results of more recent studies are brought together in G. E. Ryckman, *Les religions arabes préislamique* (Louvain, Bibliothèque du Museon, 1951), Vol. XXVI. Fortunately, one of the literary sources on pre-Islamic religion dating from early Islamic times is now also available in English translation. It is the *Kitāb al-aṣnām* of ibn al-Kalbī, translated by Nabīh Amīn Fāris as *The Book of Idols* (Princeton, Princeton University Press, 1952).

The principal cultural monument of pre-Islamic Arabia and the best source of information about it is a body of poetry originally preserved in an oral tradition before being committed to writing in Islamic times. Eloquence of expression was among the most respected accomplishments of the ancient Arabs, and one of the factors in the success of Muḥammad no doubt lay in the impact of the sonorous phrases of the *Qur'ān* upon the ears of a people accustomed to revere force and felicity of verbal expression. Even today the poetry of pre-Islamic Arabia for Arabic-speaking people has the status of "a model of unapproachable excellence" (R. A. Nicholson); its influence upon literary standards throughout Islamic history is incalculable. The best English book on this ancient literature is Sir Charles Lyall, *Translations of Ancient Arabian Poetry* (London and Edinburgh, 1885; republished London, Williams & Norgate, Ltd., 1930). The most famous poems of all, the seven *Mu'allaqāt* or "Suspended Ones" have recently been translated and studied by A. J. Arberry in *The Seven Odes* (London, George Allen & Unwin, Ltd., 1957). Another collection of ancient poetry known as *The Mufaḍḍaliyāt* was edited, translated, and annotated by Sir Charles Lyall in three volumes (Oxford, Clarendon Press, 1918–21; Vol. III, Leiden, 1924). The ancient poetry is set within its historical context and related to the evolution of Arabic literature by Reynold A. Nicholson in chapters I to III of *A Literary History of the Arabs* (London, 1907; republished Cambridge, Cambridge University Press, 1953). Special attention should be called to Nicholson's book as one of the classics in the Islamics field; it is a treasurehouse of careful and appreciative scholarship whose treatment of pre-Islamic literature and history is only one of the many merits it may claim. No serious student of Arab life can be content to neglect as fundamental a cultural expression as Arabic literature. Nicholson's magnificent volume is not only an excellent introduction to the field but a sensitive historical study of the connection between literature and other aspects of Arab development in their always changing interrelationships.

III. THE PROPHET

The central figure of Islamic history is Muḥammad ibn 'Abdullāh who was born into a prominent Makkan family about A.D. 570 (the precise date is unknown). According to Muslim historians, when he was 40 years old—some say 43—a divine commission to serve as prophet to his people was laid upon him. Thereupon, the series of revelations collected in the *Qur'ān* began to come to him, and he assumed the at first highly unpopular role of religious teacher, reformer, and preacher. In a little more than twenty years, by the time of his death in 632, not only had he won a large following for himself and established in Madīnah a state based on commitment to God and His chosen Prophet, but had done what no man in previous history had ever been able to accomplish, by uniting virtually the whole of Arabia under his rule.

Not unnaturally, Muslim piety has lavished generous attention upon the Prophet. His contemporaries fastened upon his sayings and actions, remembered them, and passed them on to their descendants in a living oral tradition, later to become a written one. As the number of stories about the Prophet increased and reflection upon his character become more intense, Muḥammad rapidly began to assume the characteristics of a superhuman creature, sinless and capable of performing miracles. The tendency throughout Muslim history has been toward an always greater idealization, even romanticization, of the Prophet. The trend has culminated in the modernist biographies of Muḥammad that portray him as the great hero of all history, the most profound thinker ever to have lived, and the perfect exemplar of all the virtues. This development testifies to the effect and continuing significance of Muḥammad for Islamic faith; and for a comprehension of the meaning of the Prophet to Muslims, it is of little significance that the claims he made for himself are much more modest than those of his biographers.

In contrast to his Muslim biographers, Western students of the Prophet have often been unsympathetic in their portrayals. Some scholars have gone to the extreme of explaining Muḥammad's strange trancelike states while receiving revelations as due to epilepsy, and no less a scholar than Sprenger (see below) has diagnosed him as an hysteric. Others have outspokenly condemned Muḥammad on moral grounds for certain of his actions. Virtually all Western scholarship, almost without thinking, considers Muḥammad and his teaching to be the results of historical and personality factors rather than of divine activity. Such elements in Western writings about the Prophet shock and offend Muslim sensibilities and are in no small part responsible for the defensive and apologetic tone of so much contemporary Muslim literature. In support of the Westerners, it may be said that their motives in studying the Prophet necessarily differ from those of Muslims and that they can hardly be expected to view the Prophet in the light in which the eyes of faith look upon him. Although much that they write may seem disrespectful and antagonistic to a reverent Muslim, its purpose is often the laudable one of applying critical methods to the study of Muḥammad's life.

One of the knottiest of all problems in connection with Muḥammad from a methodological point of view arises in relation to the use of the *Qur'ān* as a source for the Prophet's biography. There is no serious doubt among even the most skeptically inclined of Western scholars—and it goes without need for emphasis that Muslims concur—that the *Qur'ān* is genuinely Muḥammadan. The weight of critical study supports the conclusion that the *Qur'ān*'s pages offer a reliable record of the proclamations which the Prophet attributed to a divine source. When seen against the background of the untrustworthiness of so much of the material bearing on Muḥammad's life, the *Qur'ān* would seem to offer especially valuable resources to the biographer. Almost universally, non-Muslim writers have recognized and employed these resources; and though the usefulness of the *Qur'ān* as biographical material is dependent on prior solution of the sticky problem of establishing its chronology, it has seemed to such writers to offer the one uncorrupted fountainhead of information about Muḥammad. The methodological problem to which we refer becomes apparent when it is seen that use of the *Qur'ān* for biographical information on Muḥammad involves the assumption that the book is in some sense the product and outcome of Muḥammad's personality in interaction with the factors of his environment. The view of history and historical causation held by most modern scholars demands such an assumption of them; in fact, any other stand regarding the *Qur'ān* would be unintelligible to many if not all.

To the pious Muslim mind this assumption is wholly unacceptable. In the eyes of Muslim faith the *Qur'ān* is an eternal book whose author is God, not Muḥammad, and which is, therefore, in no respect subject to forces of historical conditioning. Since the personality of Muḥammad played no part in the formation of the *Qur'ān*, the Holy Book cannot provide a key to that personality or its development.

Furthermore—and this is the vital issue—it is often impious and wounding to the religious sensibilities of a Muslim to suggest that the *Qur'ān* can or should be a source for the study of Muḥammad's life. We encounter here again the fact that many facets of a Muslim's faith look different to observers who are themselves Muslims and to observers who view that faith from outside the community. The outside observer, especially, must be aware of this fact and take measures to come to terms with it if his understanding of Muslim religiousness is to be a faithful reflection of the experience in the hearts of Muslims. Though from a limited perspective the determination of the events of Muḥammad's life and the analysis of their underlying causes and relationships may appear to be purely "objective" and "scientific" questions, any attempt to deal with them brings one inevitably into confrontation with the content of Muslim faith and with Muslims as persons. Ultimately, all religious studies probably have this extra dimension of personal involvement, and such involvement makes extraordinary and peculiarly sharp demands of the student of religion. The difference between Muslims and others about the possibility of employing the *Qur'ān* as a biographical source may never be resolved, but it is important that the difference should be recorded and that its implications should be cause for reflection.

A. Muslim biographies of the Prophet

The earliest sources for the life of the Prophet go back to the oral tradition of his sayings and doings that sprang from the circle of his immediate companions. Among the pagan Arabs there was an established and much enjoyed custom of reciting the exploits of the past, especially the valorous deeds of great heroes. Gradually, as the Prophet gained more esteem and the influence of his community spread, the tales of dead and living heroes were replaced by tales of the Prophet. At first the stories with greatest appeal seem to have been those of his *maghāzī* or military campaigns. In the first generations after Muḥammad's death these stories began to be collected, and there arose what is known as the *maghāzī* literature. As the earliest material concerning the Prophet outside the *Qur'ān*, it is one of the most promising sources of information about him. Very little of this literature has survived, however, and only two small portions of it are available in Western languages. One of them, a fragment of a lost book by Mūsā ibn 'Uqbah of the third generation after Muḥammad, is translated by Alfred Guillaume in his *The Life of Muhammad* (London, Oxford University Press, 1955), pp. xliii–xlvii. The other example is an abridged translation of al-Wāqidī's *maghāzī* book by Julius Wellhausen: *Muhammad in Medina* (Berlin, G. Reimer, 1882). Al-Wāqidī, who lived between 797 and 874, is one of the two basic sources for the life of Muḥammad, both in respect of his own book and in respect of his influence on a prominent disciple, Ibn Sa'd, who also set down the (untranslated) life of the Prophet, his companions, and successors in a famous book, *Kitābu-l-Ṭabaqāt*, whose Arabic text was edited and published by Ed. Sachau (Leiden, E. J. Brill, 1904–28).

The first systematic effort to compile a biography of Muḥammad is attributed to Ibn Ishāq, who was born (85 A.H.) and grew up in Madīnah, where he had ample opportunity to collect the stories of the Prophet current among its populace. These stories he set down as he received them, with a barest minimum of editorial comment, to form a connected narrative in three parts. Although Ibn Ishāq's biography is the fundamental source on Muḥammad's life for the early Muslim historians, it has come down to us independently only in a shortened and radically edited form. One, Ibn Hishām, of the generation after Ibn Ishāq, edited the latter's text in accord with certain principles which he explains in his Preface. Ibn Hishām's work has been translated by Alfred Guillaume in the volume cited just above, and it is by all odds the most important single early source for Muḥammad's life. Something of Ibn Ishāq has also been preserved in the writings of historians who employed his book as source material, notably by al-Ṭabarī, the foremost historian of the early Islamic era. Al-Ṭabarī's version of the Prophet's life in a translation from the Persian by M. Herman Zotenberg is available in *Chronique de Tabari* (Paris, G. P. Maisonneuve & Cie, 1958), Vols. I–III. A much later biography, which was for a long time the only one known in the West, is that by Abū'l-Fidā', translated by Noël Desvergers along with other texts in *Classiques de l'Islamologie* (Algiers, La Maison des Livres, 1950).

After the initial burst of interest in the biography of Muḥammad, the subject was neglected for many centuries. This is not to say that there were no biographies written or that the role of the Prophet in Muslim thought or piety became any the less, but only that the explicit concern to ferret out the story of his life lost its momentum. The exception to this generalization belongs rather to the history of piety and dogma than to the tradition of biographies of the Prophet; it is the Ṣūfī or mystical versions of Muḥammad's life. When mysticism began to develop among Muslims, its exponents were quick to find sanction for both their practice and belief in the example of Muḥammad. In course of time the mystical trend of piety created a veritable cult of the Prophet that has been of enormous importance among all levels of Muslims. The only English example of a Ṣūfī approach to Muḥammad known to this writer is the poem *Mevlid Sharif* of Sulayman Chelebi, translated by F. Lyman MacCallum (London, John Murray, Publishers, Ltd., 1943). This, however, is a particularly excellent example and, even in translation, a moving one.

In quite recent times, since about 1875, Muslim interest in the biography of Muḥammad has reawakened, and there have been more biographies of the Prophet in the past seventy-five years than in perhaps the entire previous span of Islamic history. The causes of this effusion are clearly bound up with the deep stirrings of self-consciousness and vitality affecting the Muslim world in our day. Most of these new biographies are reactions against what Muslims consider to be calumnies of the Prophet by orientalists, missionaries, and others. They have been written to rectify the so often unfavorable image of the Prophet in Western literature. Because their purpose and tone are avowedly apologetic and argumentative, the majority have little worth as sober historical work; their value lies rather in what they tell us of the contemporary meaning of Muḥammad in Muslim hearts and minds. Probably the best-known work of this kind is *The Spirit of Islam* by Sayyid Amīr 'Alī (London, Christopher's, Ltd., rev. ed., 1922, and many others). Also representative of the great number of such books available are al-Hajj Qassim Ali Jairazbhoy, *Muhammad "A Mercy to all the Nations"* (London, Luzac & Co., Ltd., 1937) and Hafiz Ghulam Sarwar, *Muhammad the Holy Prophet*, 3rd imp. (Lahore, Ashraf, 1949).

B. Western biographies

The lives of Muḥammad written in the early nineteenth century, in spite of some reservations about particular points, tended on the whole to accept as authentic the version of the Prophet's biography presented in the source materials available. About the middle of the century the works of Ibn Sa'd, al-Ṭabarī, and, above all, Ibn Hishām became known in Europe, and the new biographies based on examinations of this variety of sources rapidly displaced the older ones which had drawn their information from Abū'l-Fidā', who in his turn depended upon the relatively late historian Ibnu-l-Athīr. The new state of knowledge of the sources is reflected in Sir William Muir, *The Life of Mohammad* (1861; rev. ed., Edinburgh, John Grant, Ltd., 1912), which has introductory chapters discussing sources and the early history of Arabia. Unfortunately, these chapters have been omitted from the second and subsequent editions. There is a similar focus on sources in A. Sprenger's *Das Leben und die Lehre des Mohammad*, 3 vols. (Berlin, Verlagsbuchhandlung, 1861–65). The appearance of these two writings marks the birth of serious biographical work on Muḥammad.

As in so many other aspects of Islamic studies, the publication of Ignaz Goldziher's *Muhammadanische Studien* and other studies on early Muslim traditional material wrought a revolution in thought about the biography of Muḥammad. Goldziher demonstrated that a large part of the early traditional sayings attributed to the Prophet or stories about him are the product of contending sects and viewpoints within the Muslim community, each one eager to claim the authority of Muḥammad for its own peculiar stand. During the early years there was such a wholesale fabrication of traditions, particularly of spurious prophetic sayings, for this purpose, as Muslim collectors of tradition themselves recognize and deplore, that the entire body of traditional material falls under the shadow of doubt as regards its historical reliability. Since the attainment of Goldziher's insight, biographers of Muḥammad have been compelled to subject their source materials to a critical sifting. One group of Western scholars has drawn from Goldziher's work the radical conclusion that the tradition is not to be used at all. These men hold that the *Qur'ān* alone is reliable as a biographical source on Muḥammad. This trend of thinking is most strongly expressed by Henri Lammens. See his "Qoran et tradition, comment fut composée la vie de Mahomet," *Recherches de Sciences Religieuse*, I (1910), pp. 26–51, and "L'age de Mahomet et la chronologie de la Sīrā," *Journal asiatique*, Tenth Series, XVII (1911), pp. 209–50.

The best of more recent work on Muḥammad is typified by the books of W. Montgomery Watt, who, while duly aware of the pitfalls awaiting the incautious, is more inclined than many to rely upon traditional materials. His chief works are *Muhammad at Mecca* (Oxford, Clarendon Press, 1953) and *Muhammad at Medina* (Oxford, Clarendon Press, 1956). These two are abridged in a short and quite useful volume, *Muhammad Prophet and Statesman* (London, Oxford University Press, 1961). Watt's writings on the Prophet are notable for the meticulous care with which he has traced the alliances and tribal relationships that account for the Prophet's success in consummating his control over Arabia, the broadly sympathetic treatment of Muḥammad's personality, and the author's conviction that religious developments are accompanied by, related to, and in part determined by economic developments. The third of these—which, in fact, constitutes his method—he has thought of enough importance to devote an entire volume to explaining, defining, and illustrating; *Islam and the Integration of Society* (London, Routledge & Kegan Paul, Ltd., 1961).

The work of the Swedish scholar Tor Andrae (one of the leading students of Muḥammad's life) must be mentioned. His *Mohamed the Man and His Faith*, tr. by Theophil Menzil (N.Y., Barnes & Noble, Inc., 1935; latest ed., Harper Torchbooks, 1960) is the most readable and sympathetic biography available in English. Andrae emphasizes the similarity of much in Muḥammad to Monophysite Christianity and stresses especially the eschatological side of the Prophet's teaching. A second book, *Die Person Muhammeds in Lehre und Glauben seiner Gemeinde*, Archives d'Études Orientales, Vol. XVI (Stockholm, J. A. Lundell, 1918 and reprinted) is the fundamental work of its kind. Strictly speaking, it does not belong among biographies of the Prophet, since it is rather a study of the changing roles of the Prophet in Muslim piety and the growth of legends about his figure. The development is presented from the perspective of a comparative method that gives full range to Andrae's superb knowledge of the history of religions as well as his interest in religious psychology.

One of the sanest and best-balanced works on Muḥammad is Frants Buhl's full treatment in *Das Leben Muhammeds*, tr. by H. H. Schaeder, 2nd ed. (Heidelberg, Quelle & Meyer, 1955). The essential views of this Danish scholar are presented in shorter form in English in his article "Muḥammad" in *Shorter Encyclopaedia of Islam.*

Many special problems in connection with Muḥammad have intrigued scholarly interest, one of the most important being the sources of his ideas and teachings. Much of nineteenth-century scholarship was preoccupied with tracing out the historical antecedents of movements, ideas, institutions, etc., and Muḥammad did not escape attention from this perspective. At first the tendency was to emphasize the Prophet's dependence on Judaism. The case for the Jewish background of Islām is best stated by C. C. Torrey in *The Jewish Foundation of Islam* (N.Y., Jewish Institute of Religion Press, 1933). Abraham I. Katch also has written a volume *Judaism in Islam* (N.Y., Bloch Publishing Co., 1954) to show the "Biblical and Talmudic Backgrounds of the Koran and its Commentaries" (sub-title). Since the work of Tor Andrae, mentioned above, and his *Der Ursprung des Islams und das Christentum*

(Uppsala, Kyrohist, Söreningen, 1926), the majority of students have come to believe the major influence upon the Prophet to have been Syrian Christianity rather than Judaism. In addition, Richard Bell's *The Origin of Islam in its Christian Environment* (London, Macmillan & Co., Ltd., 1926) examines the relations of Muḥammad's thought to Christianity.

For a final reference on Muḥammad, the reader's attention may be called to the short, incisive study by Régis Blachère, *Le problème de Mahomet* (Paris, Presses universitaires de France, 1952). Surveying the present state of our knowledge of Muḥammad in masterly fashion, the volume demonstrates that Muḥammad is not the well-known figure he is often thought to be. On the contrary, at many crucial points our sources are entirely silent, and at many others their reliability and the method of their use are so much in doubt that little can be said with certainty. There is no better sketch of the critical problems arising in the study of Muḥammad than this.

IV. THE *QUR'ĀN*

As central as the Prophet's person has become for Muslims, there is another factor in the Islamic scheme of things with which he is indissolubly linked and to which in an important sense he is subordinate. This other factor is the *Qur'ān*, the divine book containing God's message of mercy, guidance, and warning for mankind that came through the Prophet's agency. When Muslims affirm that Muḥammad is the Prophet of God, the meaning is that he, like others in the past, was chosen as the human means for the delivery of a divine message to the people of his time and, through them, to all succeeding generations everywhere. There is little doubt that in Muḥammad's own eyes his message was of more importance than his person, though he insisted upon a close relationship between the two (as, for example, in the dictum that obedience to God implies obedience to His Prophet). The basis and explanation of the Prophet's claim on the loyalty of believers had to do with his acting in the name of God and not with his peculiar personal characteristics. The fact of massive significance was that God had spoken through His Prophet, renewing the guidance already offered through former prophets but corrupted and spurned by the contumacy of men. In renewing His revelation through Muḥammad, God also undertook to preserve it against loss or distortion for all time to come. The *Qur'ān* is thus a final and definitive expression of the divine will for the guidance of men and, as such, the foundation upon which the entire Islamic structure rests, even its view of the Prophet.

Muslims consider the *Qur'ān* to be the very words of God Himself, delivered to Muḥammad piecemeal by an angelic messenger, usually said to be Gabriel, at intervals after the prophetic call. The developed Muslim theology of classical times holds the *Qur'ān* to be eternal and uncreated, always to have existed alongside God as an eternal manifestation of the divine will. The book that men possess, bound between covers and written on paper, is a partial reproduction of that eternal original known to Islamic thought as the "Well Preserved Tablet" or the "Mother of the Book."

Many features of Islamic faith and practice have their explanation in the conviction that the *Qur'ān* contains the very speech of God. For instance, that conviction lies at the basis of the resistance to translating the *Qur'ān* that until recently was all but universal among Muslims. A. L. Tibawi has reviewed the variety of Muslim opinion in history about translation of the *Qur'ān* in an article in the *Muslim World*, LII, 1 (1962), pp. 4ff., "Is the Qur'ān Translatable?" The conviction is also the motivation for the great reverence and affection shown the *Qur'ān*. Millions of Muslims have committed the entire book to memory, including many who do not understand the sense of the Arabic but who cherish the divine words for their very sound. Most important of all, the conviction supplies the justification for the *Qur'ān's* place as supreme and undisputed authority in both Muslim law and theology.

A. Translations

The *Qur'ān* is expressed in Arabic that is strikingly forceful, epigrammatic, and vivid. Though it does not exemplify the canons of formal Arabic poetry, it has many of the qualities of poetry, including a strong rhythm and elements of rhyme. The style of its expression so affected the Arabs—who, it must be remembered, revere beauty of expression as a cardinal accomplishment—that the classical Islamic proof for the divine origin of the *Qur'ān* has been its inimitability as literature. To translate such a book is obviously a monumental and somewhat daring undertaking, and it should come as no surprise that the attempt has often been less than successful. In the Prefaces to two renderings of the *Qur'ān* by A. J. Arberry, his complete *The Koran Interpreted*, 2 vols. (London, George Allen & Unwin, Ltd., 1955), and his selection *The Holy Koran* (London, George Allen & Unwin, Ltd., 1953, Ethical and Religious Classics East and West, No. 9), there are excellent discussions of both the history of *Qur'ān* translations into English and of the problems encountered in translating.

The older translators of the *Qur'ān*, recognizing its significance as a scripture, tended to render it into language resembling that of the English Bible. Such a style of expression sacrifices the force of the Arabic original, and these translations often seem heavy and dull. Otherwise, some of the older translations are excellent, notably that by E. H. Palmer for the *Sacred Books of the East*, Vols. VI and IX, which is still widely admired and used. J. M. Rodwell's translation, *The Koran* (London, J. M. Dent & Sons, Ltd., 1909), Everyman's Series, is perhaps as widely used, though its chapters have been rearranged in sequence to reflect the translator's views of Qur'ānic chronology.

The translation by George Sale, *The Koran* (Philadelphia, 1855, and several reprints), the earliest to be widely used in the English-speaking world, can also be recommended.

The best of recent translations is that by A. J. Arberry, mentioned above. Arberry has made a detailed study of the rhythm patterns of the *Qur'ān* along lines that no previous scholar has pursued, seeking in this way to discover the secret of the *Qur'ān's* unique drawing power and force. He has been boldly experimental in devising verse forms to express these patterns. The result is a translation that has great variety and that makes the *Qur'ān* come to life for the English reader with something of the freshness and power of the original. Arberry's literary gifts are matched by great erudition so that his translation will likely remain the foremost work of its kind for many years to come.

Two other recent translations are worth mentioning since they are readily available and often seen. One, by an English convert to Islām, Marmaduke Pickthall, *The Meaning of the Glorious Koran* (Hyderabad, 1938; N.Y., Mentor, 1953), was prepared after consultation with eminent Muslim scholars and reference to the standard commentaries on the Holy Book. Pickthall renders the verses in a fashion that always gives a clear sense, but many of his interpretations and explanatory comments are questionable. The other, *The Koran*, tr. by N. J. Dawood (Middlesex, Penguin Books, Ltd., rev. ed., 1959) has been prepared to exhibit the literary quality of the *Qur'ān*. Dawood has also rearranged the chapters, in this case to create a literary effect. His translation is pleasing and readable and has some notes based on classical authorities.

B. Commentaries on the *Qur'ān*

In a sense the entire body of Islamic religious writing might be considered as an extended commentary on the *Qur'ān*. There is also, however, a specific literature that aims at expounding and elucidating the Holy Book, a literature that is extensive and that has been of great historical importance in the development of Muslim religious thought. For all its importance, however, there is real difficulty in making use of the *tafsīr* literature, as it is called (from the verb, *fassara*, meaning to explain, expound or to comment upon), for one who does not know the Muslim languages. Very little of *tafsīr* has been translated, because these works are often long and technical, and but little of it was originally written in Western languages. Among the *tafsīrs* most respected and used by Sunnī Muslims is that by al-Bayḍāwī, a thirteenth-century scholar and controversialist. Parts of it exist in translation in Eric F. F. Bishop, *Chrestomathia Baidawiana* (Glasgow, Jackson, Son & Co., Ltd., 1957) and D. S. Margoliouth, *Chrestomathia Baidawiana* (London, Luzac & Co., Ltd., 1894). Each of these volumes translates the commentary on one chapter of the *Qur'ān*; and though they were prepared primarily as aids for students of Arabic, they may and should be studied for their substance as well.

There are also several modern works of commentary on the *Qur'ān* in English written by Indian Muslims. The one that most deserves to be called a *tafsīr* in the traditional sense is that by Muḥammad 'Alī, *The Holy Qur'ān* 4th rev. ed. (Lahore, Ahmadiyyah Anjuman Ishā'at Islām, 1951). Quite similar in character is A. Yusuf 'Ali's three-volume *The Holy Quran, Text, Translation and Commentary*, 3rd ed. (Lahore, Ashraf, 1938). Either of these works will serve to introduce the reader to the nature of *tafsīr*, though they are hardly substitutes for the classical works of the type.

Not only has *tafsīr* failed to attract translators; it seems to have inspired but little attention from historians and analysts. The paucity of literature may perhaps be attributed to the difficulty of the subject and the voluminousness of the source materials. There is but one major work on *tafsīr* in Western languages, and that in German. It is the monumental study by Ignaz Goldziher, *Die Richtungen der Islamischen Koranauslegung*, 2nd ed. (Leiden, E. J. Brill, 1952). A Dutch scholar has attempted with indifferent success to supplement this history by a study of several contemporary *tafsīr* writers: J. M. S. Baljon, *Modern Muslim Koran Interpretation 1880–1960* (Leiden, E. J. Brill, 1961). Baron Carra de Vaux surveys the development of commentaries on the *Qur'ān* in Vol. III of his *Les penseurs de l'Islām*, chap. XI (Paris, Geuthner, 1923), but his sketch is both more rapid and less profound than Goldziher's masterly work.

Readers interested in modern expressions of *Qur'ān* exegesis will find a detailed analysis of tendencies in early twentieth-century Egypt in J. Jomier, *Le commentaire coranique du Manâr* (Paris, G. P. Maisonneuve & Cie, 1954). Jomier is concerned with the group of Muslim modernists surrounding Rashīd Riḍā who founded the periodical *al Manār* as the vehicle for spreading their ideas. This book might also be read as a study of one important phase of modern Muslim development among the Arabs, the trend toward reappropriation of the fundamental sources of Muslim piety.

Finally, we should like to call attention to a study of al-Ṭabarī, mentioned above as a basic source for the life of the Prophet, whose *tafsīr* is the best known and most important of all the classical commentaries. His work is discussed in a long article in Vol. XXXV of *Zeitschrift der Deutschen Morgenländischen Gesellschaft* (1881) "Ṭabarī's Korankommentar" by O. Loth.

C. Critical works on the *Qur'ān*

The issues that have preoccupied Western students of the *Qur'ān* are principally four: (1) its origin and chronology, (2) the process by which it attained its present form, (3) the history of the standard *Qur'ān* text, and (4) the historical sources of its teaching. From the standpoint of Western scholarship—though by no means is it so for Muslims—the latter is equivalent to the problem of the sources of Muḥammad's ideas. We have already called attention above to the fundamental difference of point of view separating those who stand within the Muslim faith from those outside it. The implications of this difference should be borne in mind as one reads critical studies of the *Qur'ān*.

The foundation stone of Western Qur'ānic studies was laid in the nineteenth century in the epoch-making work of Theodor Nöldeke: *Geschichte des Qorans*, 2 vols., best known in its 2nd revised edition prepared by Friedrich Schwally (Leipzig, Dieterich, 1909). In the 1930's a third volume dealing with the history of the *Qur'ān* text was added to the work by G. Bergsträsser and O. Pretzl, and the whole has now been reprinted in a readily available single-volume edition (Hildesheim, Georg Olms, 1961).

Nöldeke's first volume, entitled *Concerning the Origin of the Qu'rān*, is largely an attempt to establish the chronological sequence of the materials collected in the *Qur'ān*. He has distinguished four periods in Muḥammad's life, during each one of which the revelations to the Prophet show identifying marks, and classified the chapters of the *Qur'ān* accordingly. The Scottish scholar Richard Bell has taken up this problem in his work and devoted a major effort to a "higher criticism" of the *Qur'ān*. Bell advances beyond Nöldeke by dividing the individual chapters of the *Qur'ān* into what he considers to be their component parts and then rearranging the whole in chronological order. The results, worked out in meticulous detail, may be seen in his *The Qur'ān*, translated with a critical rearrangement of the Surahs, 2 vols. (Edinburgh, T. & T. Clark, 1937–39) and the short companion work *Introduction to the Qur'ān* (Edinburgh, Edinburgh University Press, 1953). The latter, though it is short, is the best full-length introduction to the *Qur'ān* in English, and its treatment touches upon all the major problems. Virtually all Western scholars have accepted Nöldeke's basic sketch of *Qur'ān* chronology, but many are unwilling to press the detailed application of the scheme to the extent that Bell has.

By far the most readable and usable summary of the state of scholarship respecting the *Qur'ān* as well as the best introduction to the problems arising from it is Régis Blachère, ed. and tr., *Le Coran*, 3 vols. (Paris, G. P. Maisonneuve & Cie, 1947–51) Vol. I. Blachère is capable of clarity and great simplicity in his writing without sacrificing a sound treatment of the subject matter, and he is nowhere better than here. This volume also accompanies a translation of the *Qur'ān* in which a critical rearrangement of the chapters has been essayed. The state of *Qur'ān* scholarship is brought more up to date and treated in more technical fashion in Arthur Jeffrey's "The Present Status of Qur'anic Studies" in *Report on Current Research on the Middle East* (Washington, Spring, 1957), pp. 1ff. Jeffrey before his recent death was perhaps the leading student of textual problems in the *Qur'ān*, and his grasp of the work already done as well as that remaining to be done will satisfy the most exacting specialist. In passing, attention should be called to the value of the publication in which Jeffrey's article appears; it supplies one of the better and more accessible tools for keeping oneself abreast of work in progress.

Those who require a brief introduction to the *Qur'ān* should consult the article "al-Kur'ān" in *Shorter Encyclopaedia of Islām.*

D. Analyses of the contents of the *Qur'ān*

The *Qur'ān's* teachings have been studied from a number of different points of view. As we have said, one of the foremost among Western scholars has been a type of historicism that led to intensive investigation of the historical origins of its ideas and concepts. Recently a fruitful new line has been opened up by the application of techniques of linguistic analysis to the text of the *Qur'ān.* A Japanese Arabist, Toshihiko Izutsu, has employed these methods to produce one of the most illuminating studies of fundamental Qur'ānic concepts ever made. The outcome of his work is a revelation of the peculiarly Qur'ānic force and meaning of such common but important terms as "faith," "unbelief," "good," and "evil." His book is called *The Structure of the Ethical Terms in the Koran* (Tokyo, Keio Institute of Philological Studies, 1959). A second book which employs a similar approach, but with less self-consciousness about its methodology, is Daud Rahbar's *God of Justice* (Leiden, E. J. Brill, 1960). Rahbar believes the original sense of much that the *Qur'ān* says about God to have been lost and obscured through being layered over by later thinkers who read their own interpretations, often influenced by Greek thought, into the text. By grouping together and studying the contexts in which some of the basic epithets applied to God occur, he has sought to penetrate through the historical accumulation of pious interpretations to lay bare the significance of the *Qur'ān* for Muḥammad's contemporaries. The conclusion to which he comes is evidenced in the title of the volume. This work has an even greater interest and significance than it might otherwise have for the reason that at the time of writing its author was a Muslim. His work represented a boldly radical new step for Muslim thought about the *Qur'ān* in modern times, and it has earned him the distrust of many who are unwilling to follow his rapid lead.

The late American scholar, Arthur Jeffrey, mentioned above, has written a small volume expounding the concept of "Scripture" as it is used in connection with the *Qur'ān.* Several of the major religious communities of the world possess scriptures which they revere as sacrosanct, but the significance of these sacred writings differs, often sharply, from community to community. Jeffrey's effort has been to make clear the unique features of the Muslim concept of Scripture, and this has led him inevitably into a broad consideration of many aspects of *Qur'ān* teaching. The work to which we refer is *The Qur'ān as Scripture* (N.Y., Moore Publishing Co., Inc., 1952). Another of Jeffrey's works, *The Foreign Vocabulary of the Qur'ān* (Baroda, Oriental Institute, 1938) should also be called to the reader's attention, even though it is a rather specialized philological study. It offers many insights into the thought of the *Qur'ān* as well as showing the relationship of its contents to preceding and surrounding cultures. Sections I and II of Jeffrey's article "The Present Status of Qur'ānic Studies" have a critical bibliography of works analyzing the content and teaching of the *Qur'ān*; advanced students will wish to profit from the guidance it offers.

The final book on the *Qur'ān* we shall mention is Robert Roberts, *The Social Laws of the Qoran* (London, Williams & Norgate, Ltd., 1925), where one will find a convenient summary of the Qur'ānic teachings on such matters as marriage and divorce, inheritance, the treatment of slaves, and commercial relations. This work is valuable, therefore, as a discussion of the *Qur'ān* bases of some important aspects of Islamic law.

V. *ḤADĪTH*

Among the sciences traditionally studied by Muslims one of the foremost in importance is the science of *ḥadīth*, or of the sayings of Muḥammad. We have spoken before of the interest manifested among the early Muslims in every action and word of the Prophet and of the fact that zealous efforts were made to collect and preserve the enormous body of material relative to him. This material has been the building blocks not only of the prophetic biography but, as well, of the greater part of *Qur'ān* commentary and Islamic law and even of theology. Considered from the standpoint of its function, as opposed to the theological theory about it, the tradition of the Prophet has perhaps played an even greater role in Islamic history than the *Qur'ān* itself, since it is principally in the light of the tradition that the *Qur'ān* is viewed and understood. Some in the earliest generations explicitly acknowledged the primacy of the tradition as a religious authority although later Muslim thought tended to subordinate it, at least in theory, to the Book of God. The great Indian thinker of the eighteenth century, Shāh Walīyullāh of Delhi, estimates the significance of knowing the prophetic tradition as follows:

> The base and crown of the assured sciences, the basis and foundation of the religious arts is the science of Tradition, which tells of the sayings, doings and approbations of the best of the apostles (may God grant His favour to him and to his family and to all his companions). It is a lamp in the darkness, the sign-post of guidance and is as a shining full-moon. He who submits to it and understands it fully is surely sound and rightly guided and is brought to great good.

A. Collections

In the third Islamic century earnest efforts began to be made to collect the corpus of prophetic tradition in systematic fashion and to develop a critical machinery for distinguishing its genuine elements from spurious ones. The work of the collectors was spurred on the one hand by the great reverence for the Prophet's precept and example and on the other by revulsion against a wholesale tendency to fabricate prophetic sayings in justification of novel ideas and practices or partisan views. The more important of the collections of prophetic sayings that resulted are known as *as-Sittah aṣ-Ṣaḥīḥ* or the Six Sound Books of Traditions. By far the best known are the collections of al-Bukhārī and Muslim, though the others are widely used. It is these books upon which Muslims rely when they endeavor to discover the guidance offered by prophetic example on any point of belief or practice.

The only one of the *Ṣaḥīḥ* books readily available to Westerners is that of al-Bukhārī. It has been partially translated into English by Muḥammad Asad, whose ambition was to make the whole available to English readers. He was successful, however, in producing only one of eight projected volumes, and that one (No. 5 in the series) deals with the life of the Prophet and his companions: *Ṣaḥîḥ al-Bukhârî* (Lahore, Arafat Publications, 1938). In French there is a complete translation with notes and index prepared by O. Houdas and W. Marçais, published under the title *Les traditions islamiques*, 3 vols. (Paris, Imprimerie Nationale, 1903–14). Probably the most useful gateway to the literature of tradition for most readers will be one of the collections of selected sayings of Muḥammad; for example, *Selections from Muḥammadan Traditions*, tr. by William Goldsack (Madras, Christian Literature Society for India, 1923), which is based on a well-known Arabic book combining the six sound books with some other minor authorities. The traditions in Goldsack's selection are arranged under subject headings that make it easy for a reader to locate the materials relevant to any particular area of interest. Reading is made easier by elimination of the long chains of transmission that occupy so much of the space in traditional Muslim collections of *ḥadīth*. The original work from which Goldsack's selection was drawn, *Mishkāt-ul-maṣābīḥ*, is in process of being published in a complete English translation by James Robson. When finished, it will comprise four volumes of which one and some fascicules of the second have appeared (Lahore, 1960). Robson's introduction to the translation, though concise and learned, serves to set the background of the development of *ḥadīth* generally as well as to give information about the work concerned. Another broadly based anthology is Mīrzā Abu'l-Fadl's *Sayings of the Prophet Muhammad* (Allahabad, Reform Society, 1924). A compendium of al-Bukhārī's *ḥadīth* book is available in Muhammad Ali: *A Manual of Hadith*, 2nd ed. (Lahore, Ahmadiyyah Anjuman Isha'at Islām, n.d.). None of these books constitutes easy reading, but in view of the fundamental importance of *ḥadīth* in Muslim thought, their perusal will amply repay the reader.

B. Critical works

The fundamental critical study of the *ḥadīth* literature is Vol. II of Ignaz Goldziher's *Muhammedanische Studien* (Halle, Max Niemeyer, 1890) which bears the volume title *Ueber die Entwickelung des Ḥadîth*. With an erudition and critical acumen that have seldom been matched in any field, Goldziher lays bare the fundamental concepts, the historical development, and the significance of the *ḥadīth* in early Islamic history. While he concludes that much of *ḥadīth* is not what it claims to be and cannot be relied upon for the information it purports to offer concerning Muḥammad, he demonstrates at the same time the unique and invaluable merits of the *ḥadīth*, even spurious *ḥadīth*, as a key to intellectual, religious, and political tendencies in the first two Islamic centuries. Unfortunately, this epoch-making book has not been translated into English. There does exist a shortened French version prepared and translated by Léon Bercher under the title *Études sur la tradition Islamique* (Paris, Adrien-Maisonneuve, 1952). In spite of the barriers which languages may pose, the serious student will find Goldziher's work indispensable.

For English readers there is available a short but excellent volume, based on Goldziher, by the British Arabist Alfred Guillaume: *The Traditions of Islam* (Oxford, Clarendon Press, 1924). In his Preface Guillaume expresses wonder that there should not already have been in English a book on this important subject, and it is a cause for still greater surprise—and perhaps distress—that even now there is no full-scale study other than his. For additional material in English the reader may turn to periodical literature. An article by D. S. Margoliouth, "On Moslem Tradition," *Moslem World*, II (1912), pp. 113–21, may be recommended, as also a series of three articles by J. Robson in *Muslim World*, XLI (1951), entitled "Tradition, the Second Foundation of Islam" (pp. 22–33), "Tradition: Investigation and Classification" (pp. 98–112), and "The Material of Tradition" (pp. 166–80). To this list may be added the article of J. Schacht, "A Revaluation of Islamic Traditions" in *Journal of the Royal Asiatic Society* (1949), pp. 143–54. Schacht has made significant use of the critical study of *ḥadīth* to throw light on the origins of Muslim jurisprudence. One of the foremost names in the study of *ḥadīth* is that of A. J. Wensinck who in cooperation with a number of other European students has been in the process of publishing (in fascicule form since 1933) a comprehensive *Concordance de la tradition Musulmane* (Leiden), a kind of concordance of the *ḥadīth* literature that will make its content readily available to the research scholar. Wensinck has explained the fundamental place of tradition in the study of Islām in an article in *Moslem World*, XI (1921), pp. 239–45, entitled "The Importance of Tradition for the Study of Islam."

C. Works by Muslims

Just as in the case of the primary foundation of Islām, the *Qur'ān*, the *ḥadīth* have brought into being an enormous literature. There is, in fact, an entire group of sciences related to the study of *ḥadīth* that concern themselves with such matters as the classification of tradition according to reliability and the investigation of the chains of transmission through which individual *ḥadīth* have come. Very little of this literature has been translated, since it is the concern for the most part of specialists. It may be sampled, however, in such works as J. Robson's translation, *An Introduction to the Science of Tradition* (London, Royal Asiatic Society of Great Britain and Ireland, 1953), and in Raimund Köbert's edition and translation of a work by Ibn Fūrak under the title *Bayān Muškil al-Aḥādīt des ibn Fūrak* (Rome, Pontificium Institutum Biblicum, 1941). The latter is an attempt to offer acceptable explanations of *ḥadīth* that appear to pose difficulties for the theological views cherished in the Ash'arīyah school of Sunnī Muslims.

VI. *KALĀM*

There is in common use among the Muslims no word that corresponds strictly to the English term "theology," although the Arabic word *kalām* is often so translated. From a strict etymological point of view this word signifies discussion or speech; but in its technical use as the name of one of the traditional Islamic religious sciences, it refers to the systematic statement of a religious belief or the reasoned argument supporting it. A detailed discussion of the term and its historical development is available in the article "Kalām" in *Shorter Encyclopaedia of Islām.*

Throughout the greater part of their history Muslims have shown little interest in the systematic intellectual expression of their faith. *Kalām* was one of the sciences that developed and flowered in the third Islamic century, after the early conquests had been consolidated and the great 'Abbāsī empire had reached its creative peak. It was, thus, not one of the earliest concerns of the community, which is hardly surprising since the Arabs had no tradition of refined intellectual inquiry in pre-Islamic days. Nor, once it had developed, did *kalām* long continue to occupy the minds and hearts of Muslims. For a variety of reasons that we cannot sketch here, the religious commitment of the community rapidly led it away from the somewhat arid doctrinal expositions of the learned into a preoccupation on the one hand with practical matters of the religious law and on the other with mysticism. This long-range development of the Muslim religious drive is studied and analyzed by H. A. R. Gibb in a brilliant essay entitled "The Structure of Religious Thought in Islam" most readily accessible in the recent volume of Gibb's writings edited by S. J.

Shaw and W. R. Polk: *Studies on the Civilization of Islam* (Boston, Beacon Press, Inc., 1962). In our own day it is extremely difficult, often impossible, to elicit from Muslims a serious response to theological questions; and this indifference poses a most bewildering puzzle for Westerners, who have been taught by their own religious tradition to put theology at the center of religious concern. Clearly to understand the fact, however, that the Muslim's faith does not center in theology, and, beyond this, to understand the reasons therefor, is to make a major advance toward penetrating the Islamic view of the world.

The factors stimulating the growth of *kalām* when it did make its appearance were in the main two: internal tensions within the community, particularly over political issues, and the confrontation in such centers as Damascus and Baṣrah with sophisticated and articulate polemicists of different religious persuasions, possessed of the resources of Hellenistic thought, and eager to attack the ill-formulated doctrines of the young Islamic community. Partly for reasons of piety and partly for reasons of self-defense, the Muslims found themselves compelled to give a precise statement of the major tenets of their faith. The earliest development along these lines is treated in considerable detail by W. Montgomery Watt in *Free Will and Predestination in Early Islam* (London, Luzac & Co., Ltd., 1948). The book carries the treatment of its theme—the first major subject of theological dispute among Muslims—well into the period when *kalām* had achieved its major development and is, thus, important for the whole history of *kalām*. The most useful English sketch of the history continues to be the volume by Duncan B. MacDonald, *Development of Muslim Theology, Jurisprudence, and Constitutional Theory* (N.Y., Charles Scribner's Sons, 1903). The fundamental study of *kalām* is the massively erudite *Introduction à la théologie musulmane*, by Louis Gardet and M. M. Anawati (Paris, J. Vrin, 1948). The volume bears the sub-title "Essai de théologie comparée" and represents the efforts of its authors to come to terms with the great issues of Muslim theological thought through comparisons with Christian thought, as a precondition for a "dialogue" between Muslims and Christians. The authors are both Catholic priests, thoroughly trained in scholastic thought, and their approach to *kalām* reflects their scholastic orientation. Among the basic works on the subject also must be listed A. J. Wensinck, *The Muslim Creed* (Cambridge, Cambridge University Press, 1932), a very careful work of great erudition that, in addition to its delineation and discussion of the principal themes of Muslim religious thought, offers translations, analyses, and comparisons of several of the basic documents from the early Islamic period. The serious reader will wish also to use the work of A. S. Tritton, *Muslim Theology* (London, Luzac & Co., Ltd., 1947), which is a mine of careful scholarship, but somewhat difficult to read because of its author's style of writing. The most recent survey of *kalām* is W. Montgomery Watt's *Islamic Philosophy and Theology*, Islamic Surveys I

(Edinburgh, Edinburgh University Press, 1962). Watt sketches the development of religious thought in accord with his usual methodological principle, by relating the history of thought to social and political change in the society at large. Despite its title, the volume has little to say concerning philosophy among the Muslims. The last general history of *kalām* to be cited, though one of the oldest works on the subject, is among the most lucid and valuable: the chapter "Dogmatische Entwicklung" in Ignaz Goldziher's *Vorlesungen über den Islam*, 2nd rev. ed. (Heidelberg, Carl Winter, 1910), which will perhaps be more accessible to some readers in its French translation by Félix Arin: *Le dogme et la loi de l'Islam* (Paris, P. Geuthner, 1920).

There are several specialized works having to do with *kalām* that may be commended to the reader. J. W. Sweetman has embarked upon the major undertaking of effecting period-by-period comparisons of Islamic and Christian thought with an effort to show the historical interrelationships between their respective developments. Vols. I and II of Part I and Vol. I of Part II of this massive projected work, entitled *Islam and Christian Theology* (London, Lutterworth Press, 1945), have appeared in print. There is an informative and sympathetic study of Aḥmad ibn Ḥanbal, one of the great men of Islamic history and a central figure of the religious ferment and controversy of early 'Abbāsī times, in Walter M. Patton: *Aḥmad ibn Ḥanbal and the Mihna* (Leyden, E. J. Brill, 1897). Aḥmad ibn Ḥanbal was perhaps the finest representative of pious traditionalism in his day, and his influence has been perpetuated among earnest followers who stretch in an unbroken chain down to the Wahhābīs of Arabia in our own time. The later history of his school was studied by Ignaz Goldziher in another of his masterly books, *Die Ẓâhiriten, ihr Lehrsystem und ihre Geschichte* (Leipzig, Otto Schulze, 1884).

The group in Islamic history probably most responsible for the emergence of *kalām* and for the direction which its development eventually took is known as the Mu'tazilah. For a short time the Mu'tazilah enjoyed the patronage of the 'Abbāsī rulers in Baghdād, during which their views became the official creed of the 'Abbāsī state. In due course, however, they were rejected by the majority of the community and disappeared, to be known only from the works of their opponents; but the vigor of their intellectual probing had served to provoke other thinkers to work out the position that the great majority of Sunnī Muslims have since held. In spite of their historical importance, there is no full-length work on this group that may be unqualifiedly recommended. The basic writings about them in English are H. S. Nyberg's two articles in *Shorter Encyclopaedia of Islam*, "al-Mu'tazilah" and "al-Naẓẓām." There is also available a work studying the philosophical foundations of Mu'tazilah thought by Albert N. Nader: *Le système philosophique des Mu'tazila* (Beirut, Éditions les lettres orientales, 1956). The same scholar is responsible for the translation of the first authentic Mu'tazilah treatise describing the group to be known to scholarship (published in Arabic in Cairo, 1925), *Kitāb al-Intiṣār*, by al-Khayyāṭ (Beirut, Éditions les lettres orientales, 1957). Al-Khayyāṭ wrote his book to defend the Mu'tazilah against allegations of a deserter from the sect. Recently there have been discovered in the Yemen, where Mu'tazilah views have survived, other heretofore unknown materials about the group. As a result, scholarship will doubtless profit by an increase in its knowledge of these important thinkers in the near future.

Among the English works devoted to Muslim theological themes one stands alone in a class by itself for its ability to evoke sympathetic insight into the Muslim religious mind. *The Call of the Minaret* (N.Y., Oxford University Press, 1956) by Kenneth Cragg aims at presenting the religious appeal of Muslim faith to Christians. Though Cragg in the final analysis believes the faith of Muslims to be inadequate and to be transcended in the Christian revelation, he has penned a compelling and persuasive, even poetic, exposition of the fundamental Islamic religious views. Part II of the volume is the section particularly relevant for the present purpose.

The task of introducing material on *kalām* would be incomplete without pointing the reader to some of the original writings of Muslim thinkers. We are fortunate to possess a full translation by Walter Klein of the basic work of Abū Ḥasan al-Ash'arī, *al-Ibānah 'an Usūl ad-Diyānah* (New Haven, American Oriental Society, 1940). Al-Ash'arī, who was a Mu'tazilah in his youth, in later age underwent a conversion that transformed him into a spokesman for the traditional position of the community—with the difference, however, that he began to employ a highly developed *kalām* to support and expound his views. Ash'arism, as his position is often called, has affected most subsequent creedal statements of Sunnī Muslims and is the variety of theological position usually referred to when people speak (wrongly) of "orthodox" Islām. A theological treatise in the same tradition which is widely studied in traditional Muslim schools even today is al-Taftazānī's *Commentary on the Creed of Islam* (N.Y., Columbia University Press, 1950), tr. by E. E. Elder. This work is doubly interesting since Taftazānī, who lived in the fourteenth century, belonged to a theological school different from that of the man upon whose creed he was commenting. Both this volume and the preceding one cited have introductions of great value for reconstructing the history of religious thought among the Muslims. Some additional works by al-Ash'arī as well as biographical information about him from other Arabic sources, have been translated by Richard J. MacCarthy in *The Theology of al-Ash'ari* (Beirut, Imprimerie Catholique, 1953). Mention should also be made of the translation of the *Kitab nihāyat ul-iqdām fi 'ilm ul-kalām* of the twelfth-century thinker al-Shahrastānī done by Alfred Guillaume (London, Oxford University Press, 1934). This volume does not have the general interest of some of the preceding ones, as it concentrates discussion on one single problem confronting the practitioners of *kalām*—that of the "eternity of the world"—but it does illustrate the refinement and subtlety of the scholastic method employed by these thinkers. Finally, the reader may be pointed to the translations of works in the *kalām* tradition included in Arthur Jeffrey's *Reader on Islam* ('s Gravenhage, Mouton & Co., 1962).

VII. *FALSAFAH*

During the same era when the Mu'tazilah, using the tools of Hellenistic thought, began to forge their religious system and to compel the traditionists of the community to adopt the same tools for the defense of their views, another group, even more thoroughly Hellenistic, made its appearance among the Muslims. They came to be known as philosophers, or *falāsifah* in Arabic, the very name indicating their close dependence upon the heritage of Hellenistic philosophy (*falsafah*) with which they became widely acquainted through the efforts of a number of translators. The men concerned occupied themselves with the speculative problems of Greek philosophy as presented in the Neo-Platonic commentators on Aristotle and Plato, but they were, in spite of the predominantly Greek mode of their thought, at the same time Muslims, living in a Muslim society as inheritors of the Islamic tradition. It was the necessity of accommodating these two elements in their intellectual constitution, the Greek and the Islamic, which posed the characteristic problem of the Muslim philosophers.

The task of wedding Hellenistic thought and traditional Muslim faith proved far from easy, and the philosophers soon were in conflict with the traditionalists of the community. In their own eyes the *falāsifah* were keeping faith with the religion of their ancestors when they endeavored to grasp and express its insights by the use of Greek concepts. Even when the rigor of their thought led them flatly to reject convictions held in the community at large, such as creation *ex nihilo* or the resurrection of the body, they believed their stand to be a truer appropriation of the revelation given through the Prophet than the traditional one. For the majority of the community, however, things appeared otherwise. Tradition-minded Muslims could see no clear benefit to be gained from following or encouraging the activities of the philosophers and much to make them suspicious. The philosophers, who were perhaps never more than a small intellectual élite, were subject to harsh attacks and bitter calumny. In the end they were repudiated by the community; their philosophizing never became an integral part of the developing common Muslim religious mind but remained always something apart, alien and suspect. Serious philosophical speculation among the Muslims ceased in early medieval times, and for centuries thereafter the philosophers' works were ignored in traditional schools of religious learning, except as instances of deviation from the way of the "people of tradition and of the community."

The last truly great name among them was that of Ibn Rushd (Averroës), the Spanish thinker, who died in 1198.

Only in very recent times have the *falāsifah* enjoyed a revival of their fame. Modern Muslims recognize in the philosophers' towering intellects a resource of mental strength and energy which they wish to appropriate for themselves. At the same time, the philosophers stand as concrete evidence of the Muslim mentality's ability to comprehend, digest, and contribute to the most subtle intellectual discussions while remaining consciously fixed upon its Islamic roots. Much of modern writing about the *falāsifah* ignores the traditional rejection of them, but it has served to remind Muslims of the work of these great men of the past.

Although the *falāsifah* have not played an important role in traditional Muslim religious thought, they are nevertheless of importance for the student of the Islamic tradition. The methods and concepts of their speculative philosophy, if not its content, were an important element in molding the *kalām*, and their transmission of Neo-Platonic ideas doubtless affected mystical theology and theory among the Muslims. Furthermore, they constitute a basic link in the transmission of the philosophic thought of antiquity to later times; the medieval philosophers of Europe gained their knowledge of Aristotle through the Arabic language works and translations of the Muslims and shaped much of their thought against the anvil of the massive Muslim philosophical erudition. Most important of all, the philosophers demonstrate the tenacity of the Islamic ideal for life in the world and its capacity for meeting the challenges posed to it. Properly understood, the philosophers should be seen as defenders and advocates of the Islamic ideal, not as deviators from it. Their historical function was to turn to the service of the Muslims a weapon (Greek thought) that might have destroyed the very bases of classical and medieval Islamic society.

A. Introductions

The best single sketch of the progress of Muslim philosophy, including the phase of translation of Hellenistic works from Syriac and Greek into Arabic, may be read in T. J. deBoer's *The History of Philosophy in Islam*, tr. by E. R. Jones (London, Luzac & Co., Ltd., 1903; republished 1961). This is not to say that it is a good, or even an adequate, treatment of the subject; it has gained the recommendation given it here by the default of any serious rival. The same ground is covered in briefer fashion by R. Walzer in chapter XXXII, "Islamic Philosophy," in Vol. II of *History of Philosophy Eastern and Western* (London, George Allen & Unwin, Ltd., 1953). This essay has been reprinted in a recent volume of Walzer's works that includes other and more detailed writings on the Muslim philosophical heritage: *Greek into Arabic*, Oriental Studies, Vol. I (Oxford, Bruno Cassirer, Ltd., 1962). Perhaps the most extensive study of Islamic thought, considered from the standpoint of its contribution to the growth of scientific ideas, is in the pages of George Sarton's *Introduction to the History of Science*, 4 vols. (Baltimore, Williams & Wilkins Co., 1927–48). There is also a short survey of the subject with emphasis on the contribution of Muslims to European philosophy in Alfred Guillaume's chapter, "Philosophy and Theology" in *The Legacy of Islam* (Oxford, Clarendon Press, 1931). Although all these introductions have the undoubted merit of providing orientation for the reader who is willing to pursue his inquiries into more specialized works, none, regrettably, constitutes an adequate English-language survey of the development of philosophy among Muslims.

Two noteworthy works set out to study the crucial problem of the entire Muslim philosophical tradition, that of bringing together traditional Islām with speculative Greek philosophy. All of the philosophers were compelled by their own thought as well as the pressures of society about them to consider the relation of revealed religion to their speculative systems. The necessity under which they found themselves constitutes what A. J. Arberry calls the "scholastic problem" in his study *Revelation and Reason in Islam* (London, Forwood Lectures delivered in University of Liverpool, 1957). This book ranges far beyond the narrow circle of the philosophers to offer a survey of the "scholastic problem" in many aspects of Islamic thought, including the mystical and the theological. Faẓlu-r-Raḥmān, one of the ablest of living students of Muslim philosophy, has wrestled with the same problem by inquiring into the philosophers' doctrine of prophecy in his *Prophecy in Islam*, Ethical and Religious Classics of East and West, No. 21 (London, George Allen & Unwin, Ltd., 1958). As the work of a professional philosopher steeped in both the Greek and the Muslim traditions, it is more sharply focused than Arberry's wide-ranging volume.

B. Specialized works and translations

The most productive approach to *falsafah* lies in resort to specialized studies of individual thinkers and the translations of their work. Many such are available in a variety of languages, and we shall cite here only some of the more useful. DeLacy O'Leary's *Arabic Thought and its Place in History* (London, Routledge & Kegan Paul, Ltd., 1922) is especially good for its survey of the transmission of Hellenistic philosophical thought to the Arabs. Soheil M. Afnān has devoted a volume to the greatest of all the Muslim philosophers, Ibn Sīnā, which he calls *Avicenna: His Life and Works* (London, George Allen & Unwin, Ltd., 1958). Along with discussion of problems in Ibn Sīnā's thought, this work is particularly effective in setting the great thinker in his historical context of both political events and prevailing intellectual atmosphere. Afnān's information on the life of Ibn Sīnā may be supplemented by the philosopher's autobiography and the biography written by one of his students, both translated with other excerpts from Ibn

Sīnā's writings by A. J. Arberry in *Avicenna on Theology* (London, John Murray, Ltd., 1951), Wisdom of the East Series. An important chapter from *The Book of Salvation*, one of Ibn Sīnā's more famous works, has been translated with notes by Fazlu-r-Raḥmān as *Avicenna's Psychology* (London, Oxford University Press, 1952). Finally, attention may be called to the slim volume of lectures on this thinker by A. M. Goichon, *La philosophie d'Avicenne et son influence en Europe médiévale*, 2nd rev. ed. (Paris, Adrien-Maisonneuve, 1951). Mme Goichon has produced other more extensive studies of Ibn Sīnā, but this book presents his thought and influence with conciseness and insight that make it particularly valuable to the non-specialist.

The Muslim philosopher who has drawn the greatest attention in the West is doubtless al-Ghazālī (d. 1111), though it is the mystical rather than the philosophical facet of his personality that has been the most attractive. The autobiography of this remarkable man, a source as valuable for the insight into his times as it is interesting for the revelation of his inner life, is readily available in a translation by W. Montgomery Watt, *The Faith and Practice of al Ghazali* (London, George Allen & Unwin, Ltd., 1953). A great part of al-Ghazālī's *chef d'œuvre, The Revivification of the Religious Sciences*, has been translated into European languages at various times, but since the work is encyclopaedic, we shall here call attention only to Nabīh Amīn Fāris' translation of a section entitled *The Book of Knowledge* (Lahore, Ashraf, 1962). Al-Ghazālī's chief claim to be considered in the philosophic tradition of Islām rests upon his famous *Incoherence of the Philosophers*, where he mounts a scathing attack upon these "heretics" of the community, specifically in the persons of Ibn Sīnā and al-Fārābī, in regard to their teachings that the world is eternal, that God cannot know particulars, and that there is no resurrection from the dead. The entire treatise is available in an excellent translation by Ṣabīḥ Aḥmad Kamālī: *al-Ghazali's Tahafut al-Falasifah* (Lahore, Pakistan Philosophical Congress, 1958). The text of al-Ghazālī's polemic is also reproduced by Ibn Rushd (Averroës), the Andalusian thinker, in the course of his vigorous defense of the tradition that had produced him; Ibn Rushd penned a reply to al-Ghazālī's formidable assault which he called *The Incoherence of the Incoherence*. It is translated by Simon Van den Bergh: *Averroes' Tahāfut al-Tahāfut* (London, Luzac & Co., Ltd., 1954).

One of the greatest of Muslim minds who stands in close relation with, if not in the direct line of, the *falāsifah*, is the North African, Ibn Khaldūn (d. 1406). Ibn Khaldūn's peculiar concern, sparked by his frustration in active political life, was the application of the principles of philosophy to history in such a way that the meanings of history might become clear. In a book so far surpassing previous writings on the subject as to be on a plane by itself, Muḥsin Mahdī reconstructs the life and circumstances and analyzes the thought of Ibn Khaldūn: *Ibn Khaldūn's Philosophy of History* (London,

George Allen & Unwin, Ltd., 1957). Dr. Mahdī's purpose has been to present Ibn Khaldūn according to his own intentions and, thus, to rescue him from the obscurantist effects of contemporary writing that would make him a precursor of modern sociology. Part of the original work upon which Mahdī's analysis largely depends, the introduction to Ibn Khaldūn's universal history, has been translated into English by Franz Rosenthal as *The Muqaddimah*, 3 vols. (London, Routledge & Kegan Paul, Ltd., 1958).

Readers who may wish to carry their study into works that lack of space does not allow us to mention here will find a short bibliography featuring translations of Muslim philosophical works into European languages at the conclusion of R. Walzer's article "Islamic Philosophy," mentioned above. A more extensive bibliography that takes into account secondary works, analyses, and periodical materials as well may be had in P. J. de Menasce, *Arabische Philosophie*, Bibliographische Einführungen in das Studium der Philosophie, No. 6 (Bern, 1948).

VIII. ISLAMIC INSTITUTIONS

A. *Sharī'ah*

There is no subject more important for the student of Islām than what is usually called Islamic "law." It is universally agreed that the heart of the Islamic commitment lies in a practical concern to live according to a divinely ordained pattern made known in the guidance given through the Prophet. Accordingly, Muslims have been vitally interested to work out and systematize rules of conduct that reflect the divine guidance. Historically this concern produced a class of jurists whose particular business it was to elucidate the implications of the revelation of the *Qur'ān*, the example of Muḥammad, and the practice of the earliest community for the everyday lives of Muslims. In time their labors resulted not only in systematic compilations of legal rules touching many different spheres of life but in the emergence of an elaborate structure of jurisprudential theory as well. Islamic "law" is the creation of the jurists; it is also an expression of the most deeply held religious instincts of the community and the characteristic Islamic activity.

Even so, there are few facets of Muslim religiosity more difficult to comprehend than the "law." Its study is confused on the one hand by the persistence and reiteration of a time-hallowed theory about the origin of the "law" that obscures its historical development and on the other by the failure to evolve, except in a few noteworthy cases, a satisfactory methodology. The use of the word "law" itself contributes to the confusion by creating in the mind the concept of a principle laid down and enforced by sovereign authority, usually the state. In the Islamic instance such a concept does not pertain, for Islamic "law" implies no institution, either governmental or ecclesiastical, that may be said to have sovereignty or that is clearly charged with the sanctions of enforcement. With but few exceptions, the rules in Muslim "law" books refer to persons, conceived as individually responsible to God. Furthermore, Islamic "law" contains rules bearing upon spheres of life that are elsewhere considered to fall outside the province of law (such as, for example, religious belief and religious practice and even personal hygiene and dress). An adequate grasp of Islamic "law" therefore makes extraordinary demands on the student.

There are a number of introductory works offering discussions of the basic concepts, problems, and history of Islamic "law." Two books already mentioned, D. B. MacDonald's *Development of Muslim Theology, Jurisprudence and Constitutional Theory* and Ignaz Goldziher's *Le dogme et la loi de l'Islam*, may serve as beginning points. Reuben Levy also treats aspects of the law in various parts of his wide-ranging effort to construct a sociology of the Islamic community: *The Social Structure of Islam*, 2nd rev. ed. (Cambridge, Cambridge University Press, 1957), especially chaps. IV and VI. Goldziher discusses "Principles of Law in Islam" in Vol. VIII of *Historian's History of the World*, ed. by H. S. Williams (London, History Association, 1907) pp. 294–304. One of the better introductory articles is D. de Santillana's "Law and Society" in *The Legacy of Islam*, pp. 284–310. Several articles by the leading living student of law, Joseph Schacht, should also be read—notably "Islamic Law" in Vol. VIII of *Encyclopaedia of the Social Sciences*, pp. 344–9 and "Sharī'a" in *Shorter Encyclopaedia of Islam*, pp. 524–9. Of basic importance also is Goldziher's article "Fiḳh" in *Shorter Encyclopaedia of Islam*, pp. 102–7.

The special concern of Joseph Schacht has been to uncover the processes leading to the view of "law" held by the schools that appeared in the third Islamic century. Once these schools had consolidated their position and articulated a systematic theory of jurisprudence that traced the specific rules of "law" back to certain *uṣūl*, or sources, the tendency among Muslims was to accept the jurisprudential theory as an accurate description of the actual historical formation of the "law." In medieval times these schools and their founders were invested with such a degree of authority that Muslims believed all further investigation of matters of "law" to be strictly forbidden. In his *Origins of Muhammedan Jurisprudence* (Oxford, Clarendon Press, 1950), Professor Schacht demonstrates that the theory of the "sources of law" is itself the product of historical evolution, especially of the influence of the great jurist, al-Shāfi'ī (d. 820). The new directions pointed out in this book are of such importance that it must necessarily be the beginning point of studies in the history of Muslim "law" for many years to come. Attention may also be called to Schacht's articles in the large volume edited by M. Khadduri and H. Liebesny, *Law in the Middle East* (Washington, Middle East Institute, 1955). One entitled "Pre-Islamic Background and Early Development of

Jurisprudence" is found on pp. 28–56, and the other, "The Schools of Law and Later Developments of Jurisprudence," on pp. 57–84. This volume is a symposium that assembles essays from several prominent students of Muslim "law" and is worth perusal in its entirety. On the origins of "law" one should certainly read S. Vesey-Fitzgerald "Nature and Sources of the Sharī'a," pp. 85–112.

One of the treatises of al-Shāfi'ī upon which Schacht's analysis relies heavily has recently been translated by Majid Khadduri in *Islamic Jurisprudence, Shāfi'ī's Risāla* (Baltimore, Johns Hopkins Press, 1961). It offers to the person not reading Arabic one of the few basic works in the history of Islamic "law" that have found their way into European languages.

For achieving insight into the substantive concerns of Islamic "law" and the methods adopted by jurists in approaching them, there is obviously no substitute for first-hand acquaintance with books that Muslims consider authoritative in this area. Fortunately, a variety of manuals of "law" in European languages faithfully reproduce in systematic fashion the normative teachings of the Muslim "law" schools. These books endeavor to present the "law" from a lawyer's point of view, as it were, giving the detailed rules, with exceptions and special applications, that serve to govern matters such as marriage, inheritance, and divorce. Asaf A. A. Fyzee has prepared such a manual to cover "that portion of the Islamic Civil Law which is applied in India to Muslims as a personal law" in *Outlines of Muhammadan Law*, 2nd ed. (London, Oxford University Press, 1955). Fyzee's special virtue is his concern with "law" among the Shī'ah sect, to which he himself belongs: several other of his writings are devoted specifically to Shī'ah "law." One of the oldest manuals of "law" and one that has been widely used by scholars in the field is Th. W. Juynboll's *Handbuch des Islāmischen Gesetzes* (Leiden, E. J. Brill, 1910); its purpose is to present the teachings of the school of al-Shāfi'ī. Skillful use and comparison of manuals presenting the teachings of the other three schools that, along with al-Shāfi'ī's, have been recognized as authoritative since medieval times will enable one to judge the basic agreement but also to discern the detailed differences among them. A study of "law" according to the school of Mālik ibn Anas which is followed by most Muslims in North Africa is offered by G. H. Bousquet in his *Précis de droit musulman*, 2 vols., 2nd rev. ed. (Algiers, Maison des Livres, 1950). Henri Laoust, who has done so much otherwise to illuminate the influence of Aḥmad ibn Ḥanbal, has devoted a volume to his school of "law": *Le précis de droit d'Ibn Qudāma* (Beirut, Institut Français de Damas, 1950). Finally, a comprehensive compendium of the "law" as it is interpreted in the school of Abū Ḥanīfah is available in Sir Charles Hamilton's translation of the *Hedaya* of al-Marghinānī, 2nd rev. ed. (Lahore, New Book Co., 1957). Abdul Rahim has attempted to achieve a comparison of these four schools in reasonably brief compass in *The Principles of Muhammadan Jurisprudence* (London, Luzac & Co., Ltd., 1911).

Like every other legal system in history, Islamic "law" has given birth to certain characteristic judicial institutions. There have been several different types of courts in the Muslim world, each with distinctive functions and each presided over by a distinctive type of judge having special qualifications for office. The nature of these judicial institutions is treated at length in the masterly work of Émile Tyan, *Histoire de l'organization judiciaire en pays d'Islam*, 2 vols., 2nd rev. ed. (Leiden, E. J. Brill, 1960), which must be considered the basic writing on the subject. The same ground is covered in English in chapter VII of Reuben Levy's *The Social Structure of Islam*, cited above. For the nature of judicial institutions in the Ottoman Empire on the eve of modern times, there is the analysis of H. A. R. Gibb and Harold Bowen in Part II of Vol. I of their *Islamic Society and the West* (London, Oxford University Press, 1957). A larger-scale work on the judicial institutions of the Mughal Empire of India may be found in M. B. Ahmad, *The Administration of Justice in Medieval India* (Karachi, The Manager of Publications, 1951).

With the advent of strong European influence in the Muslim world, there began a tendency to modify the rules and, particularly, the institutions of traditional Islamic "law". In a number of countries the trend has led to outright replacement of Islamic "law" by systems of jurisprudence based on European models, while in others the traditional "law" was relegated to the status of personal law. The most important student of this new development is J. N. D. Anderson, who offers a general survey of the contemporary situation in *Islamic Law in the Modern World* (N.Y., New York University Press, 1959). We cannot list all of Anderson's writings on this subject, but note should be taken of *Islamic Law in Africa* (London, Her Majesty's Stationery Office, 1954); the series "Recent Developments in Shari'a Law," *Muslim World*, XL, 4 (1950) to XLII, 4 (1952); and "Law Reform in the Middle East," *International Affairs*, XXXII, 1 (1956), pp. 43–51. For the reaction of Muslim minds to the situation of traditional "law" in the modern world, the *Report of the Marriage and Family Law Commission* appointed by the Government of Pakistan with the dissenting note by a conservative *'ālim* (Karachi, 1956) offers an interesting practical example. The theoretical issues of adapting the traditional "law" to new situations as they appeared to one of the most acute Muslim intellects of our age are set out in chapter VI of Sir Muhammad Iqbal's *The Reconstruction of Religious Thought in Islam* (Lahore, Ashraf; reprinted 1954).

B. The state

Although the primary sources of Islamic "law," the *Qur'ān* and the tradition of the Prophet, do not explicitly detail the constitution of a state, Muslims believe these sources to have teachings relevant for the organization and conduct of society in general. In this field, as in others, they have attempted to work out the implications of basic teachings and so to form a political theory. Characteristically, the discussions in this area center upon the caliphate, the institution evolved by the community for its own government after the death of the Prophet.

The best brief presentation of the basic concepts in traditional Islamic political thinking known to this writer is Sir Hamilton Gibb's article "Constitutional Organization" in *Law in the Middle East*, pp. 3–27. Louis Gardet has essayed a full-scale treatment of Islamic political philosophy as it is implied in some of the fundamental attitudes of Islamic "law" and in the historical practice of the Muslim community. Taking his cue from St. Augustine's *City of God*, he entitles his description of the Islamic ideal *La cité musulmane, vie sociale et politique* (Paris, J. Vrin, 1954). Though this book is not easily read or understood, it is indispensable for the serious student. Majid Khadduri's scholarly investigation of *War and Peace in the Law of Islam* (Baltimore, Johns Hopkins Press, 1955) pushes far beyond the narrow realm set for itself to expound the broad view of the ideal society, its nature and purpose and its relation with other societies, that underlies Muslim thinking about the holy war. Khadduri's book makes wide use of original source materials and has the rare virtue of being written with great clarity of organization and expression. The classic English work on the institution of the caliphate is the book of Sir Thomas Arnold, *The Caliphate* (Oxford, Clarendon Press, 1924). From a Muslim pen comes the lengthy volume of A. Sanhoury, *Le Califat* (Paris, Geuthner, 1926), in which he discusses the central political institution of the early Islamic world as it has been in both theory and practice. Émile Tyan also deals with the caliphate in Vol. I of his *Institutions du droit public Musulman*, 2 vols. (Paris, Recueil Sirey, 1954 and 1956).

Perhaps the most important—at all events, the best known—exposition of the caliphate in a classical Islamic source is the book of al-Māwardī (d. 1058), *al-Aḥkām as-Sulṭānīyah*, tr. by E. Fagnan as *Les statuts gouvernementaux* (Algiers, Adolphe Jourdan, 1915). In twenty chapters a great variety of questions, ranging from the necessity of there being a leader for the community to the administration of pious bequests and the conduct of the holy war, have been treated in the light of Qur'ānic teaching, prophetic example, and the prior practice of pious men. Al-Māwardī's book was, thus, an attempt to describe a norm for the state sanctioned by religion, and his views are important material for the analyses of scholars such as Arnold, Sanhoury, and Tyan. H. A. R. Gibb has supplied some of the historical background for al-Māwardī's book as well as an analysis of it in an essay "al'Mawardi's Theory of the Caliphate" in *Studies on the Civilization of Islam*.

In addition to theoretical work of the type of al-Māwardī's, the Muslims have also produced practical manuals of statecraft that reflect the actual problems and conditions of rule rather than the ideal. The most valuable of its kind was prepared by the famous Saljūq wazīr, Niẓāmu-l-Mulk, for his master, the Sulṭān Malikshāh, and translated by Hubert Darke as *The Book of Government, or, Rules for Kings* (London, Routledge & Kegan Paul, Ltd., 1960). This book may be read both to ascertain the approach to practical problems of one of the most astute and powerful men of his time and as a source of information for the disturbed conditions of life in the 'Abbāsī empire in the years after its flowering.

Muslims have also given a certain amount of attention to the state from a purely philosophical point of view. Among the early philosophers in the East al-Fārābī is most notable for his concern with the state and may be considered the real originator of philosophical interest in the subject among the Arabs. He was strongly influenced by Plato's *Republic* and devoted several of his writings to the elaboration of very similar views. These may be sampled in English in D. M. Dunlop's translation, *Fuṣūl al-Madanī or Aphorisms of the Statesman* (Cambridge, Cambridge University Press, 1961) and in French in the translation of R. P. Jaussen, Y. Karam, and J. Chlala, *Idées des habitants de la Cité Vertueuse* (Cairo, L'Institut Français d'Archéologie Orientale, 1949). In the Western Islamic regions the principal thinker in this area was unquestionably Ibn Khaldūn, some guide to whose works we have already offered.

We may conclude this section on the state by recommending to the reader an ambitious volume by Erwin I. J. Rosenthal in which the effort is made to survey both the history of "constitutional" thought among Muslims and the progression of philosophical speculation in respect of the state. It is the first conspectus of Muslim political thought on such a large scale and, while less successful than it might be, constitutes an important addition to the literature. The volume is called *Political Thought in Medieval Islam* (Cambridge, Cambridge University Press, 1958).

C. Cultus and worship

The overt practices and observances made obligatory upon all Muslims are commonly spoken of as the "Pillars of Islām." They are five in number: confession of faith, prayer, alms giving, fasting in the month of Ramadhān, and pilgrimage to the holy shrine at Makkah. Some authorities add a sixth duty to this list, that of participating in the holy war. The detailed rules for performance of these obligations may be read in any standard compendium of Islamic "law." For Western readers there are brief discussions of them in such volumes as Reuben Levy, *The Social Structure of Islam* (Cambridge, Cambridge University Press, 1957) and Henri Lammens, *Islam, Beliefs and Institutions*, tr. by E. Denison Ross (London, Methuen & Co., Ltd., 1929). E. E. Calverly describes the daily prayers of Muslims in meticulous detail in his book *Worship in Islam* (London, Luzac & Co., Ltd., 1945; rev. ed., 1957), which consists for the most part in a translation of the "Book of Worship" from al-Ghazālī's *magnum opus*, *The Revivification of the Religious Sciences.*

On the pilgrimage there is a full-length volume in French by Gaudefroy-Demombynes, *Le pèlerinage à la Mekke* (Paris, Geuthner, 1923), that offers an abundance of historical material about the holy shrine, the Ka'bah, as well as minute consideration of the varied rites performed by the pilgrim. As for many other things, the most useful source on the pillars is probably the *Shorter Encyclopaedia of Islam* where the following articles should be consulted: "Ṣalāt," "Zakāt," "Ḥadjdj," "Ṣawm," and "Masdjid."

The overt expressions of religious life in the Muslim community are by no means comprehended in these five pillars, however; Muslims also cherish a variety of other practices, festivals, and the like that are esteemed as having great religious value. The devotional formulas and prayers, other than the prescribed ritual prayers, in use in different countries have been collected and presented with great sensitivity by Constance Padwick in her *Muslim Devotions* (London, Society for Promoting Christian Knowledge, 1961). The material in Miss Padwick's book is a convincing refutation of the polemical opinions of the many, often Christian missionaries, who hold that ordinary Muslims lack either a sense of their own sinfulness and creaturehood or an appreciation of the warmth, love, and nearness of God. The more important festivals celebrated by Muslims are described in the slim volume by G. E. von Grunebaum, *Muhammadan Festivals* (N.Y., Henry Schuman Inc., 1951). One work in this general area surpasses all others for its range and brilliance, Duncan Black MacDonald's *The Religious Attitude and Life in Islam* (Chicago, University of Chicago Press, 1909). MacDonald set himself to lay bare the real content of the religious perceptions of the greater mass of Muslims, and he succeeds in showing the inner nature of their religion as no treatise on theology or description of theology, including his own, can do. This book is one of the fundamental works in the entire field of Islamic studies and should be read in conjunction with the perusal of the more systematic expressions of Islamic faith in the *kalām* tradition. As a kind of bonus, the last three chapters of the masterly book offer one of the finest studies of al-Ghazālī ever penned in the English language.

IX. THE *SHĪ'AH*

The Muslims of the world may be divided into two great groups, usually called the *Sunnīs* and the *Shī'ah*, each with a number of subgroups. The term "*Sunnī*" may be translated as "followers of the traditional way or *sunnah* of the community" and clearly has a normative import for those who claim its implication. *Shī'ah* on the other hand means "partisan," having its origin as a name for the supporters of the claims of 'Alī, the cousin and son-in-law of the Prophet, to the leadership of the community after Muḥammad's death. In attempts to explain the differences between the two groups, the analogy of relations between the Catholic and Protestant branches of Christianity has often been suggested, with the Catholics representing the *Sunnīs* and the Protestants the *Shī'ah*. Such an analogy is misleading for a number of reasons, not least because it suggests that the *Shī'ah* were a relatively late offshoot from an already firmly established tradition and because it encourages the conception, implicit in the terms themselves, that the *Shī'ah* are heterodox. The fact is that the *Shī'ah* as a religious group developed out of the same complex and many-faceted situation in the early days of the Muslim community from which the crystallization of beliefs and institutions we call *Sunnī* Islām also emerged. The roots of the *Shī'ah* go as far back into Muslim history as do those of persons who appropriate the title "the people of tradition and the community," as *Sunnīs* like to style themselves. Furthermore, in a number of respects the *Shī'ah* have influenced and contributed to *Sunnī* Islam profoundly so that historically the gap between the two is by no means so great as most treatments of the subject would suggest.

One result of considering the *Shī'ah* heterodox has been a relative neglect of their contribution to Islamic history by Western scholars, who for the most part look upon the *Sunnīs* as the main line of Islamic development. Students of Muslim faith, therefore, experience some difficulty in regard to materials bearing on the *Shī'ah*, and in many areas there is nothing available but the original sources in Persian and Arabic. The situation is in process of being remedied by the efforts of such scholars as A. A. Fyzee, M. G. S. Hodgson, W. Ivanow, and Henri Corbin, who have taken *Shī'ah* studies as their particular concern; but much remains to be done.

The best general introduction to the history, thought, institutions, literature, etc. of the *Shī'ah* is the book of the long-time missionary to Persia, Dwight M. Donaldson, *The Shi'ite Religion* (London, Luzac & Co., Ltd., 1933). Donaldson reproduces considerable portions of the traditional material about the lives of the *Imāms* and quotes liberally from accepted *Shī'ah* authorities in his expression of the central doctrines; the strength of his book lies in the abundance of material rather than in his interpretive efforts. He also gives attention to the great shrines of the *Shī'ah* in Irāq and Persia and describes the rites associated with pilgrimages to them. Donaldson's treatment is limited to Persia and Irāq, however, and requires supplementing by works on the *Shī'ah* elsewhere. Another missionary, John N. Hollister, has written concerning: *The Shi'a of India* (London, Luzac & Co., Ltd., 1953); he gives a history of the group in India and describes the several unique communities of *Shī'ah* origin that have grown up in the subcontinent. In order to set his treatment of the Indian *Shī'ah* into proper context, Hollister had first of all to sketch the origins, history, and characteristics of this important group of Muslims. His book is, therefore, also a good introduction to the study of the *Shī'ah* and relative to Donaldson's work has the advantage of treating the more radical *Shī'ah* sects as well as the moderate ones. The books of both men have excellent and extensive bibliographies. As an introduction to the religious system of the *Shī'ah*, mention may also be made of E. G. Browne's *A Literary History of Persia*, Vol. IV (Cambridge, Cambridge University Press, 1951–53), pp. 354ff. This volume and its three companions are to Persian history and literature what Reynold Nicholson's literary history is to the Arabs. Browne was among the greatest of British orientalists, and these indispensable volumes amply exhibit the sensitivity, critical acumen, grace of style, and learning which have made him great.

For original statements of *Shī'ah* theology from authoritative writers, there are two short treatises available in English translations. One is the well-known book with the curious title *The Eleventh Chapter*, tr. by William Miller, *al-Bābu 'l-Ḥādī 'Ashar* (London, 1928, The Royal Asiatic Society of Great Britain and Ireland, reprinted 1958). The author of this treatise was 'Allāmah al-Ḥillī, a prominent theologian who lived during the period of Mongol supremacy. The original short statement, almost creedal in form, is accompanied by a commentary that offers fuller explication of the principles set forth. The other writing of this type is a treatise on religious doctrine by one of the most highly respected of all *Shī'ah* doctors, Ibn Bābawayhī (d. 991). It has been translated by Asaf A. A. Fyzee as No. 9 of the Islamic Research Association Series: *A Shi'ite Creed* (London, Oxford University Press, 1942). The works of both Ibn Bābawayhī and al-Ḥillī reflect the religious position of the moderate branch of the *Shī'ah*, the so-called Twelvers. A similar writing exhibiting the convictions of the radical wing has been translated by W. Ivanow as *Kalami Pir* (Bombay, Islamic Research Association Series, No. 4, 1935). Although the date of *Kalami Pir* is quite late and its authorship impossible to ascertain exactly, it is nevertheless judged an accurate statement of Ismā'īlī theology belonging to the same genre as Ivanow's translation of *A Fatimi Creed* (Bombay, 1936). Quite a different type of expression of *Shī'ah* faith may be read in James Merrick's translation of Vol. II of al-Majlisī's *Ḥayātu-l-Qulūb* published as *The Life and Religion of Mohammed* (Boston, Phillips, Samson, 1850). One of the bitter charges *Shī'ah* Muslims level against the *Sunnīs* is that of having suppressed or distorted information about the Prophet's preference for 'Alī, his son-in-law, and, especially, about the specific appointment of 'Alī as the Prophet's successor. Al-Majlisī gives the story of the Prophet's life as it is recounted in *Shī'ah* sources and avails himself of every opportunity to put forward the *Shī'ah* case, in many instances citing and refuting recognized *Sunnī* authorities.

The cause of the radical *Shī'ah* has been much better served by recent scholarship than that of the moderates. No small part of the credit for the advancing state of knowledge in this field goes to the efforts of a single man, the Russian scholar, W. Ivanow. Ivanow has worked diligently to make translations of important Ismā'īlī writings available and to unravel the incredibly complex and often distorted history of various *Shī'ah* groups. His publications are too numerous to list completely, but we may take note of the following in addition to those already mentioned: *Studies in Early Persian Ismailism* (Bombay, Ismaili Society, 1955); *Brief Survey of the Evolution of Ismailism* (Leiden, E. J. Brill, 1952); *On the Recognition of the Imam* (Bombay, Ismaili Society, 1947); and *Ibn ul-Quddah* (*The Alleged Founder of Ismailism*), 2nd rev. ed. (Bombay, Ismaili Society, 1957). More recently a younger American scholar, Marshall G. S. Hodgson, has also begun to contribute to studies on the radical *Shī'ah*. His published doctoral dissertation *The Order of Assassins* ('s Gravenhage, Mouton & Co., 1955) is in a class by itself for mastery of the sources and critical sifting of them. The very weight of Hodgson's erudition often makes his writing difficult to read, but his views must be taken into account by any serious student. His is also the most authoritative piece on the early history of the Druze, another group having its origin in radical Shī'ism: "Al-Darazī and Ḥamza in the Origin of the Druze Religion," *Journal of the American Oriental Society*, LXXXII, 1 (1962), pp. 5–20. In a very condensed work that was also originally a doctor's thesis, *The Origins of Ismā'ilism* (Cambridge, W. Heffer & Sons, Ltd., 1940), Bernard Lewis has endeavored to distinguish the many strands in the historical background of the Ismā'īlīs. True to the tradition of British Orientalism, Lewis enumerates his original sources and assesses their value. His work is as useful, therefore, for the orientation to Ismā'īlī studies it provides as for the conclusions it reaches.

As a parallel development to their tendency to differ from *Sunnī* Islam in theological matters, in authoritative collections of traditions, etc., the *Shī'ah* have also evolved a jurisprudence and system of "law" peculiarly their own. In basic principle the chief point of difference lies in the authority which the *Shī'ah* ascribe to the *Imāms* or divinely appointed successors to 'Alī as leaders of the community. In detail the differences are not nearly so great as one might expect, it being very readily apparent that *Shī'ah* and *Sunnī* "law" share a common Islamic origin and point of view. For the person who requires details, there is a manual of *Shī'ah* "law" available in English in translation by Neil B. E. Baillie: *A Digest of Moohummudan Law*, Vol. 2, *Imameea* (Lahore, Premier Book House, 1957). Asaf A. A. Fyzee, because of his own background as both a lawyer and a *Shī'ah*, has evinced particular interest in this subject. Among his articles the following may be noted: "Isma'ili Law and its Founder," *Islamic Culture*, IX (1935), pp. 107–12, and "Qadi an-Nu'man, the Fatimid Jurist and Author," *Journal of the Royal Asiatic Society* (1934), pp. 1–32. In a longer work he has studied *The Isma'ili Law of Wills* (Bombay, 1933).

X. ṢŪFISM

In the experience of the Prophet and in the *Qur'ān* are to be found elements of a distinctly mystical nature. The presence of these elements provided both the ground and much of the material for the early development of a mystical tradition within the Muslim community. In the Islamic context mysticism is usually called Ṣūfism, or *taṣawwuf*, the etymology of the word being traceable to the rough robes of wool (*ṣūf* in Arabic) that were the identifying badges of the mystics. As the name suggests, the first stage of development was marked by ascetic practices, but there soon emerged an active quest for the experiences of intimate closeness to God that are the climax of genuine mysticism. Eventually an elaborate system of mystical thought and theory came to be articulated.

Within four hundred years of the death of Muḥammad the principal features of the Ṣūfī approach to life were clearly established, and from at least the fifth Islamic century, if not earlier, Ṣūfism tended increasingly to occupy the central place in the religious life of the great majority of Muslims. Its hold on the religious consciousness was strengthened precisely in the degree that other expressions of Islamic faith lost vitality. During medieval times there grew up organized mystical brotherhoods or orders, each with a hierarchy of saints who formed its spiritual ancestry and each with a peculiar discipline and ritual form. In many cases these brotherhoods came into close association with craft guilds and thus served among the fundamentally important formative forces in medieval Islamic society. In the premodern era, however, Ṣūfism began to evidence serious corruption and degeneration that have caused modernist reform movements to adopt a negative attitude toward the mystical aspect of the Islamic heritage.

For something more than five centuries Ṣūfism dominated Muslim religious life, and any effort to trace the many lines in the historical development of Muslim faith must, therefore, give it a major place. Although for the first time since its origins Ṣūfism is on the wane among some classes of Muslims, in thousands of hearts in many different parts of the world the great *Ṣūfī* concerns are yet alive. Particularly among those classes not strongly affected by education of a Western type, religion is suffused with *Ṣūfī* ideas, stories of the *Ṣūfī* saints, pilgrimages to the tombs of saints, and the like. Of such areas as Sindh or the Northwest Frontier of Pākistān it is no exaggeration to say that Ṣūfism continues to be, as it has been for centuries, their true religious commitment.

For all of its importance, the history of Ṣūfism was relatively late in being written and still lacks the definitive treatment for which one would hope. Among the early students in the field was the incomparable Goldziher, whose chapter "Asketismus und Ṣūfismus" in his *Vorlesungen über den Islam* established the historical progression from asceticism to mysticism among the early Muslims. The best English history of the *Ṣūfīs* is *Sufism* by A. J. Arberry (London, George Allen & Unwin, Ltd., 1950). Like his teacher, Reynold Nicholson, before him, Arberry has devoted a major portion of his scholarly career to *Ṣūfī* studies. The small volume in question reflects his wide acquaintance with the *Ṣūfī* texts and with the principal trends of scholarship in the field. Its approach is simple enough and its manner of expression felicitous enough that it may serve as an orientation for the beginning student while at the same time attracting the advanced scholar repeatedly to taste its richness of learning. More recently, M. M. Anawati and Louis Gardet have published a major study of Ṣūfism offering a sketch of the historical development in its first part, supplemented by close analysis of *Ṣūfī* experiences and methods in the remaining three: *Mystique musulmane* (Paris, J. Vrin, 1961). One feature of the book that increases its usefulness is the generous citation and translation of texts in support of its analyses.

The two greatest names in the study of Muslim mysticism are probably those of Reynold Nicholson and Louis Massignon. Both have been unusually productive scholars, and both have responded to the loftier reaches of the Muslim spirit in a fashion to make them personally involved with the objects of their study. Massignon's principal contribution consists of two works. One is a study of the great personality, al-Ḥusayn ibn Manṣūr al-Ḥallāj, *La passion d'al-Ḥallāj* (Paris, Geuthner, 1922), carried out on a grand scale; it not only illuminates the spirituality of this commanding figure but touches upon virtually every other aspect of Ṣūfism and, indeed, of the entire religious life of the early Muslim community. Its bibliography is comprehensive. The second, *Essai sur les origines du lexique technique de la mystique musulmane* (Paris, Geuthner, 1922), is a study of the technical vocabulary of the *Ṣūfīs*, which Massignon holds to be the essential foundation for all scientific work in the field. From this analysis, which traces the basic terms back to purely Muslim sources, Massignon gained support for his conviction that the origins of Ṣūfism are to be found within the dynamics of Islām itself; he has urged this point of view strongly against Nicholson, among others, who has argued for the Christian and Neo-Platonic roots of the *Ṣūfī* tradition.

Reynold Nicholson is distinguished both for his analytical studies on the *Ṣūfīs* and for his superb translations of some of their most compelling writings. It is very rare that the mastery of technical scholarship and literary ability are wedded in one man as they were in Nicholson. His principal analytical works are *Studies in Islamic Mysticism* (Cambridge, Cambridge University Press, 1921), *The Mystics of Islam* (London, G. Bell & Sons, Ltd., 1914), and *The Idea of Personality in Ṣūfism* (Cambridge, Cambridge University Press, 1923). The pinnacle of his ability as a translator was attained in his rendering of the *Mathnawī* (London, Luzac & Co., Ltd., 1925–40) of Jalālu-d-Dīn al-Rūmī, who perhaps deserves to be ranked as the greatest mystical poet of all times. There is a selection of translations of Rūmī's poetry from the Mathnawī and other sources in the little volume *Rūmī, Poet and Mystic* (London, George Allen & Unwin, Ltd., 1950). Of a different nature but quite important as material for the history of Ṣūfism is his translation of the *Kashf al-Maḥjūb of al-Hujwīrī* (d. A.D. 1064) (London, Luzac & Co., Ltd., 1911). Al-Hujwīrī's Persian treatise, which belongs to the period when Ṣūfism had just reached its full development, traces out the spiritual ancestry of various *Ṣūfī* schools and expounds many of the principal *Ṣūfī* doctrines.

There are also, of course, a number of lesser writings on this attractive subject. John Clark Archer has endeavored to uncover the prophetic roots of mysticism in his little book *Mystical Elements in Muhammad* (New Haven, Yale University Press, 1924). Margaret Smith has added to the literature both a book of selections, *Readings from the Mystics of Islam* (London, Luzac & Co., Ltd., 1950), and a full-scale study of an early woman mystic, *Rabi'a, Poet and Mystic* (Cambridge, Cambridge University Press, 1928). Her *Studies in Early Mysticism in the Near and Middle East* (N.Y., The Macmillan Co., 1931) is an extended argument for the Christian backgrounds of Ṣūfism. In his *Sufism* (Lucknow, Lucknow Publishing House, 1938) Bishop John Subhan gives a veritable catalogue of the mystic orders in India, where this phenomenon took a deep hold, flourished, and continues to be a significant moment in Indian Muslim life. The foremost study of the *Ṣūfī* brotherhoods is the French volume *Les confréries religieuses musulmanes* by O. Depont and X. Coppolani (Algiers, Adolphe Jourdan, 1897), which concentrates its attention on the orders of North Africa. One of the brotherhoods prominent in Turkey has been subjected to searching probing in John K. Birge's *The Bektashi Order of Dervishes* (London, Luzac & Co., Ltd., 1937); this order is particularly interesting for its relationship with the Ottoman government, many of whose servants were Bektashis, and the clear dependence upon *Shī'ah* concepts and practices that it exhibits. The thought of the single most important monistic thinker among the *Ṣūfīs* and one of the intellectually most subtle and difficult mystics of all times is analyzed by A. E. Affifi in *The Mystical Philosophy of Muḥyid Dīn-Ibnul 'Arabī* (Cambridge, Cambridge University Press, 1939).

The great Muslim mystics, like similarly minded men of other traditions, have held that true knowledge of the mystic verity may be gained only by him who joins in the quest for union with God, who oversteps mere intellectual contemplation to a direct experience or taste (*dhawq*) of the divine nature. Those who view the mystics from the outside can, perhaps, hope for no more than a distant and indistinct hint of the ineffable experience which is the goal of the *Ṣūfīs'* quest. It is surely the case, however, that the best source for the earnest student who would understand what he can is to be found in the *Ṣūfīs'* own descriptions of the way and its climax. There are many translations of *Ṣūfī* writings available, some already mentioned above, and the number grows each year. For example, in addition to already cited translations of Persian mystical poetry, there are *Selected Poems from the Divānī Shamsi Tabrīz* (Cambridge, Cambridge University Press, 1952) and *Tales of Mystic Meaning* (N.Y., Frederick A. Stokes Co., 1931), both rendered by Reynold Nicholson and both presenting the works of Jalālu-d-Dīn Rūmī. A. J. Arberry has added to the literature of Rūmī in English with his *Tales from the Masnavi* (London, George Allen & Unwin, Ltd., 1961) and *Discourses of Rūmī* (London, John Murray, Ltd., 1961); the latter constitutes the only prose work of the poet to have been given an English version. This same team of scholars, teacher and student, who are responsible for English leadership in *Ṣūfī* studies and upon whose foundational work of text edition and translation later generations will build, have given similar service for other greats of the *Ṣūfī* tradition. Nicholson has translated a collection of mystical odes with commentary from the most difficult of *Ṣūfī* masters, Muḥīyu-d-Dīn ibnu-l-'Arabī, *The Tarjumān al-Ashwāq* (London, Royal Asiatic Society, 1911). From Arberry's pen comes *The Poem of the Way* (London, Emery Walker, 1952) of Ibnu-l-Fāriḍ, whose mystical longings, in company with those of many others, centered on the figure of the Prophet. His translations of a book by Abū Bakr al-Kalābadhī, *The Doctrine of the Ṣūfīs* (Cambridge, Cambridge University Press, 1935), and of works by al-Niffarī, *The Mawāqif and Mukhāṭabāt of Muḥammad ibn 'Abdi 'l-Jabbār al-Niffarī* (London, Luzac & Co., Ltd., 1935), are important contributions to the knowledge of *Ṣūfī* theology.

The Muslim saint who is usually given credit for having reconciled the concerns of the mystics with the tenets of *Sunnī* Islām and for having won acceptance of Ṣūfism by the community at large is the great al-Ghazālī. The flavor of his mystical thought may be experienced in a little book taking its title from a famous verse in the *Qur'ān*: *Mishkāt al-Anwār* tr. by W. H. T. Gairdner (London, Royal Asiatic Society, 1924). Al-Ghazālī's autobiography in the translation by W. Montgomery Watt, mentioned above, is also an important source of information about his mysticism.

As a final source on Ṣūfism, the small book by Margaret Smith, *The Ṣūfī Path of Love* (London, Luzac & Co., Ltd., 1954), may be strongly recommended. This anthology draws its materials both from the *Ṣūfīs* themselves and from their many interpreters. In six chapters, made up of an elaborate fabric of quotations, it traces the nature of Ṣūfism and the principal doctrines of its devotees. The bibliography and acknowledgments are a guide to the treasurehouse of *Ṣūfī* materials in English.

XI. THE MODERN PERIOD

As demanding as the study of the historical development of a religious community may be, the task of assessing what is happening to it in the living present is infinitely more difficult. The student must attempt to understand forces and actions whose consequences have not yet been fully worked out and to come to terms with situations constantly changing. Men are too much involved in the historical stream of their own times to be able easily to view that stream from a sufficiently detached and comprehensive perspective. It should not be surprising, therefore, that, in spite of the many volumes now appearing, there are but few whose discussions contribute substantially and profoundly to an understanding of the Muslim mind of the twentieth century. Yet there is no more vital aspect of Islamic studies than the effort to uncover what is occurring in the spiritual life of our Muslim contemporaries; the effort is as important for the Western peoples, whose lives daily become more closely linked with those of Muslims, as for the Muslims themselves. If the often repeated dictum that the future of the human race is dependent upon the ability of men of different cultures, faiths, and nations to learn to live in accord has any truth at all, the study of the spiritual travail of the one-seventh of the human race that constitutes the Muslim community is one of the urgent enterprises of our time.

The place to begin one's reading on the modern Islamic period is undoubtedly H. A. R. Gibb's *Modern Trends in Islam* (Chicago, University of Chicago Press, 1947). This volume, which constituted the Haskell Lectures in the University of Chicago for 1945, is small but a gem of its kind. In tribute, one writer professes himself to consider all subsequent studies of the subject as mere "footnotes" to Gibb's masterly analysis. The great virtue of the book is exhibited in the author's ability to set the central concerns of modernism against the background of the entire historical tradition of Islamic thought and experience. Gibb knows as much, perhaps, as any man living about the history of the Muslims, and he employs his vast range of knowledge to elucidate the tensions of Muslim religious thought in the modern age, the ways that Muslim modernism has tried to resolve these tensions, and the successes and failures it has attained.

For a second general study of modern Islamic developments, the reader may be pointed to the work of Wilfred Cantwell Smith, *Islam in Modern History* (Princeton, Princeton University Press, 1957). The distinguishing element in all Smith's later work is his keen sense of personal involvement with Muslims and his awareness of the moral obligation to speak of Islām in a fashion that is at the same time scrupulously scholarly but also acceptable to the sensitive Muslim mind. His book is, therefore, as much an effort to enter into discussion with Muslims about their situation in the modern world as it is an attempt to inform outsiders of the nature of the situation. Smith's thesis has to do with the nature of history; he argues that Islām even now, as always, is becoming what it shall be and that Muslims, as the principal actors in the always unfolding drama of the Islamic adventure, have the opportunity, privilege, and responsibility of directing the drama in accord with their deepest spiritual perceptions. *Islam in Modern History* has chapters on the Arabs, the Turks, the Muslims of post-partition India, and the Pakistānīs. It is thus somewhat broader and also more precise in its analyses than Gibb's compact work, which deals largely with Arab and Indian developments.

One of the most fruitful ways of approaching modern Islamic developments lies in turning one's attention to studies of specific Muslim countries or groups. The cause of scholarship has been better served with respect to these more specialized works than in the case of general ones. On Turkey, for example, there is the two-part study of H. A. R. Gibb and Harold Bowen, *Islamic Society and the West*, Vol. I (London, Oxford University Press, Part I, 1950; Part II, 1957), which endeavors systematically to describe Turkish society (including the Arab provinces) in the eighteenth century as a foundation for demonstrating the effects of Western impact on the society. It is obvious that no accurate estimate of the degree and importance of social change in a given period is possible if there is no solid grasp of the state of the society at the beginning of the period. Gibb and Bowen have taken seriously the need to sketch the background against which modern developments have occurred, and it is unfortunate for all that their work was abandoned with the appearance of only one volume of the several projected. Among the best work now available on Turkey in the modern period is *The Emergence of Modern Turkey* by Bernard Lewis (London, Oxford University Press, 1961). Written from the perspective of one personally involved with the events he describes is the fine study of Niyāzī Berkes, *The Development of Secularism in Turkey* (Montreal, McGill University Press, 1964). It is the most ambitious study of modern Turkish trends yet attempted and, in view of the author's scholarly ability and knowledge of things Turkish, will undoubtedly come to be considered a classic in its field.

For the background to the modern period in the Arab countries, there is the remarkable memoir of Edward Lane, *Manners and Customs of the Modern Egyptians* (in many editions), a book as much to be recommended for its charm and sheer interest as for its usefulness to the scholar. Lane was an engineer who lived in Egypt during the early part of the nineteenth century and who possessed both an abundant curiosity about the people among whom he sojourned as well as an acute faculty of perception. To the lucid and always fascinating verbal descriptions of Arab society at the time he added his considerable ability as a draftsman, using it to illustrate in drawing much of what he saw. Working on a broader scale and in respect to a later period, George Antonius has described *The Arab Awakening* (London, Hamish Hamilton, Ltd., 1938, and several reprintings), a book that is now famous. Antonius is much preoccupied with the political struggle of the Arabs to free themselves from the Turks and later from the encroachments of European imperialism, but his discussion also takes into account the growing Arab intellectual ferment and the many new forces released in Arab society from the latter part of the nineteenth century onward. On the religious side, the most profound and best-informed study of Muslim modernism among the Arabs is Charles C. Adams, *Islam and Modernism in Egypt* (London, Oxford University Press, 1933). Adams devotes the major portion of his attention to the work of two men, Jamālu-d-Dīn al-Afghānī and Muḥammad 'Abduh, and the movements which they inspired. Both men are looked upon throughout the Muslim world as heroes of recent history, and their influence, especially that of 'Abduh, has been enormous. There is a detailed study of the religious opinions held among the disciples of 'Abduh in J. Jomier's *Le commentaire coranique du Manār* (already mentioned). As a final work on the Arabs, attention should be directed to *Arabic Thought in the Liberal Age, 1798–1939* by Albert Hourani (London, Oxford University Press, 1962). Hourani takes the Arabs as the focus of his study, including the Christians as well as the Muslims among them, but his treatment has at many points to deal with the modern Arab's understanding of Islām. The book is learned and perceptive, presents its material in a lively, engaging style, and is altogether the best summation of the process of Arab thought in the past century and a half to be had.

For the recent religious history of Muslims in India, one book stands alone for its excellence: Wilfred Cantwell Smith's *Modern Islam in India* (London, Victor Gollancz, Ltd., 1946), a vigorous and uncompromising Marxist analysis of movements and trends in the subcontinent from the latter third of the nineteenth century until the eve of partition. Although the author's youthful enthusiasm for Marxism led him to judgments that now seem sweeping and tendentious, he assembled a body of information on modern Indian Islām that is unequalled. Until recently it constituted the only serious connected account of modern developments in India in the English language. Lately Indian Muslims have turned to writing the history of their own community. A book by Ishtiaq Husayn Qurayshi, *The Muslim Community of the Indo-Pakistan Subcontinent (610–1947)* ('s Gravenhage, Mouton & Co., 1962), has already appeared, and two others are promised for the near future from the pens of Muḥammad Mujīb and 'Azīz Aḥmad, both scholars of exceptional sensitivity and ability. The older work by Murray Titus, *Indian Islam* (London, Oxford University Press, 1930), continues to be useful though it is outdated.

Although Indonesia is the largest Muslim country of the world in terms of population, there is a poverty of English literature dealing with Islām in the island republic. In Dutch, by contrast, there is an abundance of good scholarship having to do both with past history and with more recent trends, but very few of these writings have found their way into more accessible languages. At present there is no alternative to knowledge of Dutch for the serious student of Islām in Indonesia. There are three works, however, that will introduce the reader to modern currents among Indonesia's Muslims. One, by an anthropologist, Clifford Geertz, called *The Religion of Java* (Glencoe, Free Press,

1960), offers a detailed study of religion in a village in Java in all its facets, those that are clearly Muslim as well as those that are not. The book makes no effort to survey Islamic movements in the country as a whole but, in accord with its purpose, gives a picture of the meaning of their Islamic faith to one group of villagers. The second work, by Harry J. Benda, is called *The Crescent and the Rising Sun* (The Hague, van Hoeve, 1958). The author's primary purpose is to sketch the policy of the Japanese toward Indonesian Muslims during the occupation of the islands, but the development of his argument has required that he also trace tendencies among Indonesian Muslims in the previous period of Dutch colonial rule. The treatment breaks off with the end of the occupation and the beginnings of the Indonesian struggle for independence. The third book, C. A. O. van Nieuwenhuijze's *Aspects of Islam in Post-Colonial Indonesia* (The Hague, van Hoeve, 1958), returns to the theme of Japanese policy toward the Muslims and also adds essays on the background of Indonesian Islām and on some of the more important movements and concepts in the contemporary situation.

The best source for knowledge of contemporary Muslim thought is undoubtedly, as in all other fields, the writings of Muslims themselves. Several influential works are readily available, and their perusal will give the reader a glimpse into the working of the modern Muslim mind. The most important of Muhammad 'Abduh's treatises, in which all the major emphases of his thought emerge, has been translated into French by B. Michel and Moustapha Abdel Razik, *Rissalat al Tawhid, Exposé de la religion musulmane* (Paris, Geuthner, 1925). This small book is one of the formative documents for the Arab mentality of the twentieth century and deserves the closest study. A collection of essays from the pen of the Turkish sociologist, Ziya Gökalp, whose ideas played an important role in the emergence of modern Turkey and the accommodation of "Turkish culture, Islam and contemporary civilization" worked out there has been translated by Niyāzī Berkes as *Turkish Nationalism and Western Civilization* (London, George Allen & Unwin, Ltd., 1959). The most engaging and able exposition of the modernist understanding of Islamic faith is a lengthy book by Muḥammad 'Alī called *The Religion of Islam* (Lahore, Ahmadiyyah Anjuman Ishā'at Islām, 1950). Muḥammad 'Alī himself was a member of the Aḥmadīyah sect, but the interpretation of Islamic faith he presents is all but universal among the educated and Westernized classes of Muslims both in his native India and elsewhere. The book is a veritable bible of Muslim modernism. The best-known and most widely read expression of modernism in English is probably Sayyid Amīr Ali's *The Spirit of Islām*, to which we have referred in connection with the Prophet.

Among the many attempts to study the meaning of Islamic faith in the light of the twentieth-century revolution in thought, the most impressive intellectually is Sir Muḥammad Iqbāl, *The Reconstruction of Religious*

Thought in Islam (Lahore, Ashraf, 1951). Iqbāl was foremost among Muslims in his grasp of the significance of recent developments in philosophy and scientific thought; he is alone in having appreciated the radical necessity these developments pose for rethinking the very foundations of religious knowledge. These famous six lectures are thus essays in philosophy of religion, a field of thought that, for all its importance, has produced little of value in the Muslim community of the twentieth century.

FOR TEACHERS

It remains now only to make some suggestion about materials that may be given to students who wish to study something of Islām.

By far the most successful single-volume introduction to the Muslim tradition yet achieved is that by H. A. R. Gibb: *Mohammedanism* (N.Y. and London, 1949; reprinted 1950); it is superior to all its competitors in virtually every respect; in the material it comprehends, in the skillfully woven interpretation of Islamic development it offers, and in the clear but elegant style that makes it a joy to peruse. By emphasizing historical development, the book avoids mere narrative or description and thus has something not only for the beginner but also for the advanced student, who will perceive more of depth and insight with each rereading of its pages. In 1955 this splendid volume was reprinted by the New American Library of New York in an inexpensive paperback edition. Henri Lammens, *Islam, Beliefs and Institutions*, tr. by E. D. Ross (London, Methuen & Co., Ltd., 1929) is a lengthy and substantial introductory work that at many points offers more detail than Gibb's volume; yet it is sufficiently nontechnical in its approach to be appropriate for students. There is a serious criticism to be made of it, however, for the author's attitude is often less than sympathetic toward the Muslims. Students who have passed beyond the need for introductory materials may be given G. E. von Grunebaum's *Mediaeval Islam* (Chicago, University of Chicago Press, 1953). This is a superb work of scholarship, erudite and profound but beautifully and clearly written. No finer or more skillful portrayal of medieval Muslim society exists in any European language.

One of the best types of literature for student use is the anthology that endeavors to allow the Islamic tradition to speak for itself. Several good books of this kind bring together representative pieces of Muslim religious writing, ranging from the *Qur'ān*, classical creeds, and dogmatic writings to mystical and legal treatises. The carefully chosen cross-section of readings with short introductions to the selections by John A. Williams, ed., *Islam* (N.Y., George Braziller, Inc., 1961) can be especially recommended. The late Arthur Jeffrey, ed., did two works of this kind: *Islam, Muhammad and his Religion* (N.Y., The Liberal Arts Press, 1958) and *A Reader on Islam* ('s Gravenhage,

Mouton & Co., 1962). The latter is the most ambitious effort of its kind in English. Somewhat different in purpose and broader in scope is the uniquely beautiful and excellent anthology of Eric Schroeder, ed., *Muhammad's People* (Portland, Bond Wheelwright Co., 1955), in which are translated and combined, mosaic-fashion, a wide range of extracts from the Arabic literature of the first five Islamic centuries. The editor's work has been done with consummate literary taste and a most extraordinary sensitivity to the emotional values of beliefs, institutions, and events for the Muslim mind itself. Religious writings are included, but the collection ranges beyond them to comprehend history, poetry, literature, even finance, and so on to give a picture of Islamic life that is at once authentic and captivating.

The last book we shall recommend is one prepared especially with the needs of students in mind. It is Kenneth Morgan, ed., *Islam—The Straight Path* (N.Y., Ronald Press, 1958). The essays in this volume were all written by eminent Muslim scholars under Professor Morgan's able guidance. Unfortunately, the book is not as successful as the similar ones on the Buddhists and Hindus in the same series; it has often been commented that most Muslim attempts to interpret their tradition to the Western mind lack real effectiveness and appeal. Nevertheless, the work in question represents an earnest effort by men thoroughly versed in things Islamic to lay bare for the Western student the spiritual tradition that has nourished them.

APPENDIX I

Reference books

The indispensable reference source for the student of Islām is *The Encyclopaedia of Islām*, ed. by M. Th. Houtsma *et al.* (Leyden, E. J. Brill, 1913–38), four volumes and a Supplement. The *Encyclopaedia* has articles on a wide variety of subjects, all pitched at the highest of scholarly standards, and all written by specialists with particular qualifications for the work undertaken. At the time of its publication the *Encyclopaedia* was, in effect, a compendium of the state of Western knowledge about the Islamic world. Among its numerous virtues is the inclusion of a bibliography of the most significant literature on the subject concerned at the end of each article. These bibliographies not only survey the European literature of relevance but give, as well, the principal primary and secondary works in Oriental languages. Their value to a serious student can scarcely be overstated.

The *Encyclopaedia* is currently in process of revision and republication under the title *The Encyclopaedia of Islām New Edition*, ed. by H. A. R. Gibb and J. H. Kramers *et al.* (Leiden, E. J. Brill, 1960–). To date Vol. I and several fascicules of Vol. II have appeared; new fascicules continue to appear at the rate of four to six per year. When completed, the *New Edition* will not only have been revised to make it reflect the current state of knowledge more truly but will be considerably expanded to include a number of subjects not treated in the original edition.

During the preparations for launching the *New Edition* its editors brought out a shorter work that includes only articles having to do with religion, many of which have been revised and enlarged in relation to the original edition. This volume is called *Shorter Encyclopaedia of Islam*, ed. by H. A. R. Gibb and J. H. Kramers *et al.* (Leiden, E. J. Brill, 1953). Persons without a knowledge of Arabic may sometimes find this work and the other editions of the *Encyclopaedia* somewhat difficult to use in pursuing a particular topic because the titles of articles are often given in the appropriate Arabic word. The article on the mosque, for example, will be found in the alphabetical order under the Arabic term *Masdjid*. The difficulty encountered is very minor, however, when measured against the enormous usefulness of these various versions of the *Encyclopaedia*.

Older in date and on a much smaller scale, but still useful, is Thomas Patrick Hughes, *A Dictionary of Islam* (London, W. H. Allen & Co., Ltd., 1895). Like *The Encyclopaedia of Islām*, this volume has articles on a variety of subjects that concern the Muslim's faith, but the articles are much shorter and far fewer subjects are covered.

APPENDIX II

Periodicals

The following is a select list of periodicals devoted in whole or in part to articles on aspects of Islām.

Arabica
Ars Islamica
IBLA, Institute des belles lettres arabes
Islamic Culture (IC)
Islamic Quarterly (IQ)
Journal of the American Oriental Society (JAOS)
Journal of Near Eastern Studies (JNES) Formerly *American Journal of Semitic Languages and Literatures.*
Journal of the Royal Asiatic Society (JRAS)
Middle Eastern Affairs (MEA)
Middle East Journal (MEJ) This journal has a monthly survey of periodical literature that is particularly useful for keeping abreast of current work.
Muslim World (MW) Formerly *Moslem World.* The pages of this journal from its inception to date constitute the best single source for modern developments in all of the Muslim world.
Numen
Oriente Moderno (OM) One of the useful features of this Italian journal is its full chronology of events in the Near and Middle East. It is often a convenient way for following a development through its various stages day by day.
Revue des études islamiques (REI)
Revue de l'histoire des religions (RHR)
Rivista degli studi orientali (RSO)
Studia Islamica (SI)
Die Welt des Islams (IW)

Islamicists enjoy a considerable advantage over their colleagues in other fields in the possession of a tool that opens the rich periodical literature on their subject to them: *Index Islamicus 1906–1955* compiled by J. D. Pearson and Julia F. Ashton

(Cambridge, W. Heffer & Sons, Ltd., 1958; reprinted, 1961) and *Index Islamicus Supplement 1956–1960* by J. D. Pearson (Cambridge, W. Heffer & Sons, Ltd., 1962). This magnificent piece of work, directed by the Librarian of the School of Oriental and African Studies in London, catalogues periodical articles and some other materials under subject headings. *Index Islamicus 1906–1955* gives a complete cataloguing of articles pertaining to Islām in 510 European-language periodicals, 120 Festschriften, and 70 proceedings of congresses and other bodies. The *Supplement* enlarges its scope to take in some things omitted from the first volume in addition to bringing the catalogue up to 1960. There are doubtless omissions in the list of periodicals surveyed, but the student with these volumes at his disposal may survey the vast bulk of periodical literature on a given subject at a glance. It is the compiler's intention to continue to issue the *Index Islamicus* from time to time.

Index of Authors, Editors, Translators and Compilers[1]

1. Oriental names appearing in this index have been treated as Western names for the purpose of alphabetization; i.e. the last element in the name has been considered to be a surname, and the alphabetical position of the name has been determined by the spelling of its last element.

Bushell, S. W., ed., 108
Bushnell, Horace, 276
Bu-ston, 103, 106
Butler, E. C., 274
Butler, Joseph, 265
Bu-tön, 97
Butt-Thompson, F. W., 22
Butterfield, Herbert, 235
Byles, Marie Beuzeville, 100, 129

Cable, Mildred, 107
Cadbury, H. J., 250
Cadière, Léopold, 104
Cadoux, A. T., 249
Cadoux, C. J., 270
Cady, John F., 153
Cady, L. V. L., 43
Caffee, tr., 21
Caird, G. B., 253
Caland, W., tr., 49, 51, 52
Calas, Nicholas, 25
Caldecott, A., ed., 265
Caldwell, Bishop Robert, tr., 69
Calloway, Tucker, N., 90
Calverly, E. E., 321
Calverton, V. F., ed., 6
Calvin, John, 284
Camfield, F. W., 266
Cammann, Schuyler, 101
Campbell, Joseph, 8, 10, 16, 17, 20
Campbell, McLeod, 258
Carpenter, Joseph Estlin, 61
Carpenter, James Nelson, 62
Carrasco, Pedro, 150, 156
Carrington, P., 247
Carruthers, S. W., 276
Carstairs, M. G., 81
Carsun, Chang, 43
Carver, W. O., 279
Cary, Otis, 171
Case, Shirley Jackson, 235, 261, 268; ed., 283
Cassirer, Ernst, 3, 12, 13
Caton-Thompson, G., 11
Cazeneuve, Jean, 20
Ceadel, E. B., 85, 120
Ceillier, R., 251
Chabot, J. B., ed., 252
Chakravarti, Sukumara, 68
Chamberlain, B. H., 163, 175; tr., 173
Champion, Selwyn G., 167
Chan, Wing-tsit, 36, 40, 44; ed., 170
"Chanakya," 72
Chand, Emcee, 147
Chanda, Ramaprasad, 62
Chandavarkar, G. A., 55
Chandra, Lokeśh, 121
Chandran, J. R., 75
Chang, Kun, 131
Chari, S. M., Śrinivasa, 65
Charles, R. H., 212, 240, 241: ed., 203
Chateaubriand, François René, 239
Chatterjee, Ashok Kumar, 126
Chatterjee, Satischandra, 46
Chatterjee, S. C., 59
Chatterji, Bankim Chandra, 74
Chatterji, Suniti Kumar, 98
Chaudhuri, Haridas, ed., 75
Chaudhuri, Roma Bose, 66
Chavannes, Edouard, tr., 108, 109
Chelebi, Sulayman, 296
Ch'en, Kenneth, 105, 120, 126, 150, 154; tr., 121
Chen-chi, Chang, 130, 152
Chi, R. S. Y., tr., 130
Chia-shêng, Feng, 155
Chien-chên (Ganjin), 107
Chikafusa, Kitabatake, 181
Childe, V. G., 9
Chirol, Valentine, 74
Chlala, J., tr., 321
Choldin, M., tr., 10
Chowdhury, R. P., 127
Christian Center for the Study of Japanese Religions, The, 187, 190
Chuang-Tzŭ, 39
Cieslik, H., 183
Claeys, Jean Yves, 143
Clark, Charles Allen, 100
Clark, E. T., 261
Clark, John D., 11
Clark, N., 273
Clark, Walter Eugene, ed., 148
Clarke, Humphrey, tr., 145
Clement of Alexandria, 263
Cles-Reden, Sibylle von, 11
Cleveland, Harlan, ed., 153
Cline, Walter B., 11
Closs, Alois, 17
Coates, H. H., 181
Coates, J. R., tr. and ed., 249
Cochrane, C. N., 253
Codrington, R. H., 4, 5
Coe, G. A., 276
Coedès, George, 133, 143, 154
Cohen, B., 222
Cohen, M. R., 194
Cohen, P. A., 32
Cohn, William, 113
Cole, Sonia, 11
Collet, Sophia Dobson, 72
Collins, W. E., 235
Colson, F. H., tr., 212
Colton, H. K., tr., 166
Colton, Kenneth, tr., 166
Combaz, G., 142
Comines, Philip de, 232
Comte, Auguste, 234
Conference on Christian Politics, Economics, and Citizenship (C.O.R.E.C.), 268
Confucius, 37, 38
Congar, Y. M., 281
Conover, Helen F., comp., 26
Conze, Edward, 85, 86, 91, 119, 124, 126, 149; ed. and tr., 122, 129, 145
Cook, Captain James, 6
Coomaraswamy, Ananda Kentish, 54, 69, 87, 147; tr., 122
Coon, Carleton, 9; ed., 55
Cooper, John M., 15
Coppolani, X., 328
Cordier, Henri, 188
Corlett, W. T., 18
Cosenza, M. E., ed., 184
Cotelier, J. B., 251
Couchard, P. L., ed., 42
Coué, A., 104
Cowell, Edward Byles, 120; ed., 111
Cowley, A. E., 225
Cox, E., tr., 234
Cragg, Kenneth, 311
Creel, H. G., 33, 37
Creighton, Mandell, 234
Cressey, George B., 163
Crooke, William, 66
Crosby, Josiah, 95
Cross, F. L., 252, 253; ed., 283
Cross, F. M., Jr., [illegible]
Csongor, B., 121
Cuendet, Georges, 117
Cuisinier, J., 118
Culbertson, A. H., tr., 184
Cullman, O., 231, 261
Curran, A., 269
Curran, J. A., 75
Curtin, Jeremiah, 15

Dalai Lama, His Holiness, 104, 152
Damais, Louis Charles, 99
Danby, H., tr., 215
Dandekar, R. N., 48, 50, 81
Daniel, G. E., 11
Danileau, J., 281
D'Arcy, M. C. (S.J.), 235, 262
Dardel, Eric, 13
Darke, Hubert, tr., 321
Das, Sarat Chandra, 107
Das Gupta, Choru Chandra, 143
Das Gupta, Naline Nath, 97, 98
Dasgupta, Shashibhushan, 68
Dasgupta, Shashi Bhushan, 126
Dāsgupta, Surendranāth N., 58, 59, 64, 65, 69
Datta, D. M., 59
Datta, Dhirendra Mohan, 78
David-Neel, Louise Alexandra, 132
Davids, C. A. F. R., 90, 110; ed. 108, 111, 145; tr. 145
Davids, T. W. Rhys, ed., 158
Davidson, J. Leroy, 147
Davies, W. D., 222
Davis, M., ed., 218
Dawood, N. J., tr., 301
Dawson, Christopher, 235, 277
Dayananda, 73
De, Gokuldas, 128, 134, 155
De, Sushil Kuman, 67, 68, 117
de Bary, William Theòdore, ed., 36, 43, 44, 47, 155, 166, 188
de Groot, Jan Jacob Maria, 154
de Harlez, Charles Joseph, 100
Deissmann, A., 248
de Jong, Jan W., 127
Demant, A. V., 267
Demiéville, Paul, 105, 106, 156; ed., 158, 188
Deniker, J., 91

Index of Subjects

Haas, Hans, 162
Ḥadīth, 305
  classification, 307
  collections, 305
  critical works on, 307
  historical development, 307
  selective collections, 306
Ḥadjdj, 322
Haibutsu kishaku, 156
Haiku, 182
Halachah, 218
al-Hallāj, al-Ḥusayn ibn Manṣūr, 327
Han Empire, 40
Hanayama, Shinsho, 187
"Hand dance," 24
Hao, Ch'eng, 43
Harappā culture, religion, 48
Harivaṃśa Purāṇa, 63
Harnack, A., 265, 267
Ḥbrom-ston sect, 137
Ḥdul-ba, 134
Headlam, A. C., 268
"Heaven," China, 39
"Heavenly Teacher," 41
Hearn, Lafcadio, 164
Hebrew language, 192
  post-biblical, 217
Hebrews, book of, 249
Hecho, 94, 97
  travels, 108
Hedonism, China, 38
Hegel, G. W. F., 235, 236, 265
Heian period, 178
Heilsgeschichte, 231
Heim, K., 258
Hellenism, 208, 211, 217, 277
Hermeneutics, 238
Hermos, 251
Herod, 224
"High-god," 8
High Paleolithic, religion and culture, 9ff.
Higher criticism, 203
Ḥijāz, 290
Hillebrandt, Alfred, 50
Hillel, 223
Hillelites, 218
Hīnayāna, 122, 124, 131
Hindu
  image-worship, history, 53
  Mahāsabhā, 75
  religious nationalism, 74
Hinduism
  anthology, 46
  bibliographies, 81ff.
  classical, 51
  confessional views, 45
  contemporary trends, 80ff.
  cosmopolitan, 75
  current book reviews, 82
  devotional, 60
  introductions, 46
  literature, anthology, 46
  manuals, 46
  modern, 71
  philosophy, 59: anthology, 59
  philosophical systems, 47
  popular, 54
  reference works, 47
  scripture, 47
  theistic, 61
  village, 54: South India, 54
  vitality, today, 80ff.
  Western writings on, bibliography, 82
Historiography, Christian, 231ff.
Historism, 235ff., 236
History
  Christian, 236: concept of, 231; view of, 229, 230ff.
  Church, 235: romantic, 234
  concept of, 3
  cyclical view of, 233
  dynamics of, 236
  early Arabian, 290
  eschatological view of, 236
  evolutionary process, 235
  existentialist, approach to, 236
  geographical factors in, 233
  Israel, 206
  Israelite religion, 203
  Japan, 165: early, 175; political and economic aspects, 166; modern, 166
  Jewish, 194, 195, 196, 197, 223: Byzantine, 209; Hellenistic, 208, 210; medieval, 199; one-volume surveys, 199ff.; popular, 201; sociological, 198; social and religious, 198.
  Karaite, 227
  nationalistic, 233
  philosophy, 234
  positivism, 235
  progress in, 233
  providential view of, 232, 235
  rationalist approach, 233
  scientific, 234
History of Calamities, 264
History of religions, 24, 25, 27, 162, 167
  in America, 30
  discipline, 3
  history of, 24, 27
  methodology, 30
  in the universities, 28
Hodgson, B. H., 120
Hodgson, M. G. S., 323
Holland, H. Scott, 268
Holtom, Daniel C., 163
Holy Communion, 271
Holy Land, 214
Holy men, 58
  India, 58
Holy Orders, 260
Holy Spirit, 258
Holy War, Islamic, 320
Homilies and pastorals, 249
Hōnen, 180
Hong Kong, Buddhism, 96
Horayoth, translation, 215
Hossō (Yogacara), 177
Hōtoku, 184
Hou-chi, the Lord of Millet, 35
Hsi, Chu, 43, 182
Hsiang-shan, Lu, 43
Hsiao, 37
Hsiao-ching, 39
Hsi-yu-chi, 107
Hsüan-tsang, 94, 97
  travels, 108
Hsün Tzu, 39
Huang-lao, 41
Hui-ch'ang suppression, 150
Hui-hui-chiao, 31
Hui-sang, 94, 97
  travels, 108
Hui-Yän, 155
al-Hujwīrī, 328
Human destiny, Christian, 256
Humanism, 233, 266
Hundred schools, 36, 40
Hûo, Ch'eng, 43
Hymnody, Christian, 273
Hymnology
  Madhva Sampradāya, 65
  Śaiva, 69
  Śākta, 70

Ibn Bābawayhī, 324
Ibn Hishām, 295, 297
Ibn Isḥāq, 295
Ibn Khaldūn, 315, 321
  translation, 316
Ibn Rushd, 313, 315
Ibn Sa'd, 295, 297
Ibn Sīnā, 314
  al-Ghazālī on, 315
  biography and autobiography, 314
  The Book of Salvation, 314
Ibnu-l-'Arabī, 328, 329
Ibnu-l-Athīr, 297
Ibnu-l-Fāriḍ, 329
I-ching, 97, 99
  travels, 108
Iconography, 444
  Buddhist, 147ff.: Ceylon, 147; Indian, 147; Thailand, 148; Ṭibet, 148
  Śaiva, 68
Icons, 278
Idea of the Holy, The, 29
Ignatius, 251
Ildephonsus, 251
In illo tempore, 8, 13
Image worship, 53
Images, Hindu, 53
Imāms, 323, 325
Imperial edict on education, Japan, 185
Improvement theory, 247
Incarnation, 257
Incoherence of the Incoherence, The, 315
Incoherence of the Philosophers, 315
India
  bibliography, 82
  Buddhism, 91, 96ff.: surveys, 97; decline of, 99
  East, Buddhism, 98
  North, Buddhism, 98, 102